The Oxford Book of
LETTERS

THE
OXFORD Book of
LETTERS

Edited by

Frank Kermode and Anita Kermode

Oxford   New York
OXFORD UNIVERSITY PRESS
1995

Oxford University Press, Walton Street, Oxford OX2 6DP

Oxford New York
Athens Auckland Bangkok Bombay
Calcutta Cape Town Dar es Salaam Delhi
Florence Hong Kong Istanbul Karachi
Kuala Lumpur Madras Madrid Melbourne
Mexico City Nairobi Paris Singapore
Taipei Tokyo Toronto
and associated companies in
Berlin Ibadan

Oxford is a trade mark of Oxford University Press

Introduction, selection, and editorial matter
© Frank Kermode and Anita Kermode 1995
Additional copyright information appears on pp. 543–53

First published 1995

British Library Cataloguing Publication Data
Data available

Library of Congress Cataloging in Publication Data
The Oxford book of letters / edited by Frank and Anita Kermode.
p.   cm.
1. English letters.   2. American letters.
3. Great Britain—Social life and customs.
4. United States—Social life and customs.
5. Commonwealth countries—Social life and customs.
I. Kermode, Frank, 1919–   . II. Kermode, Anita.
PR1343.O94 1995 826.008—dc20 94-36412
ISBN 0–19–214188–0

1 3 5 7 9 10 8 6 4 2

Typeset by Graphicraft Typesetters Ltd., Hong Kong
Printed in Great Britain
on acid-free paper by
Bookcraft (Bath) Ltd.
Midsomer Norton, Avon

Acknowledgements

We gratefully acknowledge the kindness of Mrs Valerie Eliot and Sir Stephen Spender in allowing us to print the exchange of verse-letters between T. S. Eliot and Spender. Lord Norwich generously permits us to use his mother's letter about the 1953 Coronation, which was conveyed to us from Natasha Spender, in a transcription by Patrick Leigh Fermor.

Many libraries have provided indispensable assistance: they include the Cambridge University Library; the London Library; the Huntington Library at San Marino, California; the Australian National Library at Canberra; and the Rhodes University Library at Grahamstown, South Africa.

Over several years we have talked of this project with many friends, and this list of those who have helped us in one way or another is almost certainly incomplete: Bernard Bergonzi, Guy Butler, Natalie Charcow, Stephen Fender, John Kelly, Jim Kweskin, Richard Poirier, Lorelei Slater, John Stokes. To the patience and skill of Judith Luna of Oxford University Press this book owes its very existence.

CONTENTS

INTRODUCTION

'MONTAIGNE says that if he could have excelled in any kind of writing, it would have been in Letters . . .' So Swift reports, but he seems to doubt the wisdom of the remark; such letters, written with a view to publication, would not be natural letters. Pope, to whom this remark was pointedly addressed, replied in a joint letter with Lord Bolingbroke that he had no wish for 'Epistolary Fame', and Bolingbroke added that the pleasure of reading other people's letters arises in part at least from the fact that 'we pry into a Secret which was intended to be kept from us'.[1]

Most of the letters in this collection are of the private and more or less spontaneous kind favoured by Swift. This does not mean that writers stop writing like writers when they are writing letters, and their skills, which they have no reason to repress, make theirs on the whole the most interesting letters to pry into. But there is no shortage of other contenders, of letters written by people who write only letters. The archives of the world are crammed with letters. Even when, around the beginning of the present century, the telegram and then the telephone took over much of the quotidian correspondence, the old epistolary habit persisted; huge numbers of letters continued as usual to be written, most, as usual, dashed off with little premeditation, some, as before, carefully composed, polished perhaps from an original draft; and if the writers were at all famous many scribbles were preserved along with the weightier and more considered effusions. According to Dan H. Laurence, the editor of a four-volume selection, there are 'tens of thousands' of G. B. Shaw letters extant, and of these his very large book includes only about a couple of thousand. Of a far less busy writer, E. M. Forster, about 11,000 letters survive. The correspondence of Virginia Woolf occupies six big volumes, and that of D. H. Lawrence, who died at 44, requires seven. These people were not, so to speak, professional letter writers like Horace Walpole, whose correspondence fills almost fifty volumes in the Yale edition; their letters were incidental to their main business in life, though one could say they had the scribbling habit.

Perhaps these totals are less extraordinary than they look; they will seem less amazing if one reflects that most of us write at least half a dozen letters of one sort or another every week, so that in the fifty or sixty years of a normal writing life many people must dispatch about 18,000 letters. If the

[1] 26 Feb. 1729; 9 Apr. 1730. *The Correspondence of Jonathan Swift*, ed. Harold Williams, 5 vols. (Oxford: Clarendon Press, 1963), iii. 373, 388.

writers are ordinarily obscure people very few of these will be intentionally preserved—a bundle of love-letters, perhaps, or records of some important family business; but some will survive and come to light by sheer accident, or as a reward to persistent frequenters of attics and the basements of libraries.

It will be obvious, and, it is to be hoped, welcome, that this book makes no attempt to provide a 'canon' of English letters. Such an enterprise would from one point of view be heroically foolish, and from another tediously constricting: above all, it would involve the insupportable and presumptuous claim that the editors had the authority to bind and loose, to decide between the canonical and the apocryphal. Consequently we have been compelled only to do as we please. Certain letters that would demand inclusion in any conceivable canon find no place in this collection. For instance, Dr Johnson's devastating letter to Lord Chesterfield (a good example, incidentally, of a composition based on careful drafting) would be among the first to demand entrance; it is a very good letter, but since it is so well known already it has yielded its place to others from the same hand, including that remarkable late letter which provides an account of the author's stroke and his reaction to it. We have dealt respectfully and admiringly with the great, but have tried to leave room for the less illustrious, whose performances as writers may well be confined to epistolary correspondence undertaken for reasons of business, friendship, or love—the reasons, after all, for which the vast majority of us exchange letters—and written quite without regard for qualities that might win the admiration of an uninvited posterity.

On the other hand letters have not been excluded simply because their authors happen to be famous, or known to be good writers. So the reader will find plenty of Lady Mary Wortley Montagu, a fair amount of Horace Walpole, and rather large quantities of George Bernard Shaw, who, as we believe, has some claim, though it is rarely made on his behalf, to join the other two in any short list of the best letter writers in the language.

Clearly the interest of letters by quite unknown people will often arise from qualities other than the stylistic. For example, some included here were written home by emigrants to America, Australia, and South Africa; there seems to have been a general tendency for such letters to be withheld until the writers were, if not settled, at least in a position to make a moderately cheerful report. There are some understandable complaints and lamentations, but on the whole the letters of emigrants testify to the spirit with which they faced homesickness, hardship, and sometimes danger in dismayingly strange new worlds, their only links to friends and families being the slow, fickle post and the English language, which they had perhaps not often written before this necessity required them to do so or remain silent for ever.

Other letters by unknown persons are included for a variety of reasons: some are amusing, some curious, like the letter of Mr A. T. Harris to the Superintendent of the Atlantic City Railroad, which E. M. Forster somehow got hold of and copied into his Commonplace Book; or the one sent by some sprightly Birmingham schoolmistresses to Sir Edward Elgar. Correspondents frequently seek to amuse one another, not only by trying, in a fashion inherited from their reading in popular fiction, to be facetious (a common and, to the eye of a third party, often a lamentably thwarted ambition) but also by jokes and teases that depend on a prior intimacy but can sometimes be enjoyed by the voyeur; so, in the cause of such innocent amusement, there are included here a few mildly baffling letters, cryptograms, and bagatelles, and even a poem or two.

However, letter-writing, whether for business or pleasure, whether sprightly or dull, has normally served less frolicsome intentions. Nowadays business letters are purposeful but often dull and almost illiterate, and they certainly lack sudden rash half-caprioles of wit. Probably only the pleasures of love and friendship now warrant epistolary excesses of fancy or imagination. The technological interventions of the early years of the century have been enormously developed; even more of the burden of business communication, perhaps also of gossip, is now borne by the increasingly sophisticated telephone (telephones communicate with one another even when there are no humans around to join in; people talk on the telephone while walking down the street or driving their cars). The fax machine eliminates that delay between letter and reply which is a seemingly minor but in truth an essential part of the pleasures and the related pains of traditional correspondence, as all who have made love by mail will be aware. And now that all self-respecting and literate persons have computers, much as they used to have good fountain-pens, E-mail, whether seen as curse or blessing, fosters promiscuous communication and a lack of that privacy formerly taken for granted as a natural condition of letter-writing.

These various instantaneities make it harder than ever for us to imagine the pleasure of a long manuscript letter, probably crossed and hard to decipher, but worth the trouble and the money you paid to receive it if your correspondent did not know an MP or somebody else who could provide a frank. The sender, who would be conscious of the fact that the recipient would have to pay for the pleasure of reading the letter, took pains over its quality and was also keen to give good measure; he, or more probably she, would write diagonally across a completed page in order to save postage, which was charged at so much per sheet. These curious arrangements should have ended when it became possible for the sender to prepay the postage by affixing a stamp; in fact they lingered a while, whether out of habit or for the slow simple satisfactions of decipherment it is hard to say. (It is a curious fact that until quite recently, at any rate in Britain, it was thought rather disgraceful to type a personal letter, as if an idiosyncratic and possibly half-illegible script were an important part of the message, or at any rate of the solicitude that must attend its reading as well as its writing.)

In the middle of the last century the frank disappeared and the post, now stamped, was carried by rail, and delivered according to the prescriptions of the efficient Anthony Trollope. Far more people could now afford to use it, and far more became literate enough to do so. There ensued a brief golden age of popular correspondence. Millions of letters were of course inescapably ephemeral, doing what we now think of as the work of the telephone—arranging meetings, altering plans, congratulating, condoling, gossiping—and they did it well and promptly, for there were many collections and deliveries a day, including some on Sundays. Trollope would probably have considered our modern postal arrangements meagre and expensive.

The experience of receiving and reading a letter conveyed by these means already differed greatly from the old pleasure of poring over a 'cross' carried by mail coach. A letter posted in the City in the morning would reach a suburban address in time to announce that one would not be home to dinner. Presumably most communications of that kind perished instantly, but they shared the post with others of more substance, and survivors of this class, though a tiny proportion of the whole, are still desperately numerous.

A moment's reflection will be sufficient to convince anybody that of the millions of letters in the world it would be possible to read a few thousand, as we have done, and produce an entirely different collection from ours. Even if there were a measure of agreement about the great ones, the remainder would reflect almost infinite variations of taste. Looking over the vast heap of rejected letters, one's eye is caught by some that cry aloud for admission; but decisions had to be ruthless and after a time irreversible.

There might also be different ideas as to how the chosen letters should be presented. Here the arrangement is broadly chronological, with the reservation that having once embarked on authors from whom more than one letter has been chosen it seems best to stay with them, keeping all their letters together even when some were much later than the date of the first. (By an extension of this practice we have sometimes, as in the case of Swift, included under the author's name letters which derive their interest solely from their connection with him.) The next letter after such a sequence is of course the one nearest in time to the first letter of the previous writer.

Our original intention was to begin with some letters from the great and often wonderful fifteenth-century Paston family collection, but it became obvious that they would be tediously difficult for most people to read without the help of much unsightly glossing, so the idea was regretfully given up. Consequently the volume opens in the time of Henry V, with a meagre selection of the enormous Lisle Family archive, and a letter of Sir Thomas More.

Dr Johnson's *Dictionary* (7th edn.) declares that '"literary" is not properly used of missive letters', and it is true that good letters are normally in a familiar or 'low' style, though how low depends to some extent on the social status and education of the writer; there is a difference between the manner of writers to whom the writing of a letter is a necessary and sometimes fearful chore, and those whose understanding of the familiar style is conditioned by their knowledge of more formal procedures. And even they may be compelled to be extremely plain, or even ugly (though not ungainly), by the nature of the occasion, which might be transient business or indignation; or the cause might be too urgent for conventional compliment or leisurely prose (see Sir Philip Sidney's note to Mr Molyneux). Others, however, are in a familiar style because they take the place of easy talk between friends. And it is remarkable how elegant such talk could be, especially in the age of Johnson himself. We have tried not to be wholly seduced by that blend of comfort and stylishness because we wanted to include letters written by people on a variety of occasions and under all manner of circumstances, including the strains of exile and warfare and the fear of death. Lest there be too much about these extremities we have tried to establish a balance by including several balloons and coronations.

It may be complained that even with these precautions, these excursions into gaiety, we betray a preference for the dark, for sorrow, for illness, for such horrors as public executions; and that on the whole we draw for this purpose on writers rather than non-writers—Dr Johnson on his stroke, Frances Burney on her mastectomy, Ivor Gurney and Wilfred Owen on the First World War. This is true, but as we remarked earlier it is not surprising that good writers write good letters, and have, rather more than most, the resources to deal with suffering and death. Yet we have done our best for others less practised in self-examination and lacking prior 'literary' claims.

One conclusion rather hard to escape is that a great many of the most accomplished letter writers have been women. Perhaps the eloquence of familiarity comes more naturally to them than it does to men; or perhaps they have, historically, had less occasion to write merely performative letters, letters which command, promise, or threaten, so that they can afford to be more interested in themselves than in the achievement of any practical purpose unrelated to the pleasure of writing, and the pleasure of giving pleasure.[2] Tom Paulin, reviewing a selection of the letters of the American poet Elizabeth Bishop, maintains that 'what we demand of a letter is writing rather than the written, speaking not the spoken, the mind in action not the mind at rest'. Certainly there will be, in what we most admire, an emphasis on the word itself rather than on its consequences; and there will be a familiar tone, a known accent, to enhance the pleasure of friendship—to convey the action of a perhaps admired or beloved mind that has its own forms, its own peculiar power over what is seen, heard, and reported. And it is in the business of such easy, delicate self-exposures that women seem to succeed best, all the more so perhaps in these latter days, when feminine sensibilities have so changed, and gained so in authority— as Bishop's justly admired letters may testify.

Yet this pre-eminence is not in itself a new thing. Whether living in London and writing—sometimes daily—to friends in the country, or travelling, or simply keeping in touch, aristocratic and middle-class women have written thousands of good letters, properly seen by their recipients to deserve preservation. Long and unpremeditated, such letters often served as newspapers, commenting on local events or relaying the news and gossip of the town. Horace Walpole was also of course a chronicler of this kind, but he wrote, however informally, with an eye on posterity and from a masculine perspective. Although he aimed at 'extempore conversation upon paper', Walpole himself admitted that women did this better than men: 'our sex is too jealous of the reputation of good sense, to condescend to hazard a thousand trifles and negligences, which give grace, ease, and familiarity to correspondence.' Women of rank might report the goings-on of the great, but they were also, as letter writers, domestic and so the blend of interests in their correspondence is distinctively feminine. Women used their letters to cultivate personal relationships, to talk about family—to 'hang out', as Americans say, with their confidantes, a process more likely to take place in our day on the telephone, leaving no permanent record. Lady Sarah Lennox, who in her youth came quite close to marrying the future George III, wrote to her best friend over an almost unbroken period of nearly sixty years, amid all manner of marital and domestic upheavals;

[2] 'Women's art was the art of letter writing, an occupation one could carry on at odd moments, by a father's sick bed, among a thousand interruptions, anonymously as it were . . .' Virginia Woolf, 'Dorothy Osborne's Letters', in *The Essays of Virginia Woolf*, ed. Andrew McNeillie (The Hogarth Press, 1994), iv. 554.

and though she wrote with unfailing elegance and spirit, she was always easy, unaffected, and intimate.

It would be impossible to compile such a book as this without giving way to prejudices, conscious or unconscious. We read at least twenty times as many letters as there are here, and copied at least twice as many, discarding the remainder with much reluctance and uncertainty; and it would be absurd to claim that at any stage of this process the right choices were invariably made and the avowed criteria observed. But there is so much good or at least interesting epistolary writing of all sorts that its mere volume should protect anthologists from their own mistakes.

One thing seems certain and sad enough: the number of future claimants for representation in such a collection as this is not going to grow very quickly. The great age of letter-writing was, roughly, 1700–1918. Of course there are many good letters after that—think only of D. H. Lawrence and Virginia Woolf—and as Yeats remarked, thinking of poetry, though the great song is heard no more there's keen delight in what we have. But by the time of the Second World War there were a lot of those telephones about, admittedly less handy than they are now; and the postal service had begun to shrink and slow down. And as we have sufficiently remarked, later in the century other technologies have exerted their restrictive pressures. It may in some ways be a blessing that it is now possible to transmit the written word instantaneously, but it is hard to imagine an anthology of faxes, and harder still to foresee an Oxford Book of E-mail—even though a rereading of *Clarissa* tempts one to think that Richardson, who used the letter with tireless virtuosity in his fiction, and also undertook to instruct others in the proper usages of epistolary correspondence, would have been delighted to have these techniques at his disposal. However, one suspects that Lovelace, though capable of writing urgent and well-formed manuscript letters in a dripping copse, would have settled for a mobile phone.

Note on the Texts

Where editions exist we have used them. This explains some variations of procedure, for editors have diverse views on how best to present their texts. Some offer transcriptions that are virtually diplomatic, others have practised degrees of modernization. In a few cases, where the orthography seemed unacceptably daunting, we ourselves have thought it best to modernize. Letters transcribed from manuscript retain the original orthography and punctuation.

As a rule we have chosen complete letters and have ourselves made a cut in only one instance, Letter 115, excerpted from a letter so long that we could not offer it in full. All other cuts were made by previous editors, either silently or with ellipses indicating that something has been omitted. Such inserted ellipses have usually, but not always, been enclosed in square brackets; and there are a few cases (e.g. Letter 292) in which ellipses used as a form of punctuation belonged to the original text. Letters 20 and 94 were printed as fragments by the previous editors.

We have silently corrected what we took to be a few obvious printer's errors in the source material. Except for omitting full stops after 'Mr.', 'Mrs.', 'Dr.' and normalizing some typographical peculiarities reflecting stylistic choices of previous publishers (e.g. the use of italic in superscriptions or subscriptions, or of angled rather than square brackets for editorial insertions), we have not otherwise interfered with our printed sources.

Biographical information is in some cases not given simply because we could not find it. In some others, where the writer is very well known, it seemed unnecessary to provide it.

THE LETTERS

LADY LISLE

Arthur Plantagenet, Viscount Lisle (148?–1542), an illegitimate son of Edward IV, was Lord Deputy of Calais from 1533 to 1540. Three thousand letters concerning his household survive, full of high (and ferocious) politics, as well as more domestic matters. Lady Lisle, his second wife, was a formidably powerful woman; Foxe described her as 'incomparably evil'.

1. Sir Antony Windsor to Lady Lisle, 26 March 1535

Windsor owned estates bordering on those for which Lord Lisle was responsible to the King (Henry VIII). He is hoping Lady Lisle will pass this news on to her husband in as conciliatory a manner as possible.

Right honourable,

After my most hearty manner, my duty remembered, I recommend me unto your Ladyship. Pleaseth you to understand that now of late Peter Norton, a very young man, one of Mr Richard Norton's sons, came to my house at East Meon a' Sunday was sennight, and so desired a servant of mine to go with him to Hambledon, the which servant came to me and desired me that he might so do and so to go home to his wife; and so I gave him leave. And the truth is, they went straight to the Forest of Bere, where my lord hath rule, and so inrushed in the said forest and missed, and as they went by the highway homewards a buck roused, and so with their greyhounds killed him; and by reason of such persons as looked upon the marks the keeper had word of it, and because my servant was known, he and Hayeward came to East Meon to my house at ix of the clock in the night, drawing with their hounds, insomuch that all the town did perceive it; and where that I nor none of my house, on my faith and truth, had no more knowledge of their being in the forest, nor of no deer killed at that time than the child tonight born. Howbeit, within ij hours after, the deer was brought into the town, and it was in the morning ere I had knowledge thereof, and so Peter Norton brought it into my house. And when I saw that it was in by chance, without consent of me or any of mine but only he that asked me leave to go to his wife, I took the one half of his gift and the other half he had home to his father. And I dare say for his father, [he] was as ignorant of the deed doing as I was. Also I thought the flesh as meet for us as for the keepers.

I know right well they will make a grievous matter to my lord of it and otherwise than the truth. Madame, as I will answer before God, this is the very truth of the killing of this deer. Good Madame, though my servant and this young man hath done lewdly and have deserved punishment, I beseech you, Madame, to desire my lord to be good lord to them, for if old Mr Norton know it his son shall need no other punishment; and as for my servant, if it shall please my lord that I shall have the punishment of him, I trust so to order him that he shall never offend his lordship again, and though having been lewd before time I trust to bring him to goodness. And thus the Holy Ghost preserve your ladyship with much honour. Written in haste the morrow after our Lady Day.

Your own assured with my service
Antony Windsor

Madame, I beseech your ladyship to send me an answer of this letter. I pray God that your keepers and the officers may be found as true unto my lord in all other things concerning the forest, both in word and deed, as they be in this. You shall know more hereafter if you keep this article secret.

2. Lord Edmund Howard to Lady Lisle, 1535?

Howard was the youngest brother of the Duke of Norfolk, described by Muriel St Clare Byrne as 'the despair of his family', and was father of the future Queen, Katharine Howard.

Madame,

So it is I have this night after midnight taken your medicine, for the which I heartily thank you, for it hath done me much good, and hath caused the stone to break, so that now I void much gravel. But for all that, your said medicine hath done me little honesty, for it made me piss my bed this night, for the which my wife hath sore beaten me, and saying it is children's parts to bepiss their bed. Ye have made me such a pisser that I dare not this day go abroad, wherefore I beseech you to make mine excuse to my Lord and Master Treasurer, for that I shall not be with you this day at dinner. Madame, it is showed me that a wing or a leg of a stork, if I eat thereof, will make me that I shall never piss more in bed, and though my body be simple yet my tongue shall be ever good, and especially when it speaketh of women; and sithence such a medicine will do such a great cure God send me a piece thereof.

all youres,
Edmund Howard

SIR THOMAS MORE

(1478–1535)

After a brilliant career under Henry VIII More fell foul of the King in the matter of the royal divorce. He was imprisoned in 1534 and beheaded on 6 July 1535. This was his last letter, written 'with a coal' to his daughter Margaret, wife of William Roper. Dorothy Coly and Joan Alleyne were Margaret Roper's maids.

3. To Margaret Roper, 5 July 1535

Our Lord bless you good daughter and your good husband and your little boy and all yours and all my children and all my godchildren and all our friends. Recommend me when you may to my good daughter Cecily, whom I beseech our Lord to comfort, and I send her my blessing and to all her children and pray her to pray for me. I send her an handkercher and God comfort my good son her husband. My good daughter Daunce hath the picture in parchment that you delivered me from my Lady Conyers, her name is on the back side. Show her that I heartily pray her that you may send it in my name to her again for a token from me to pray for me.

I like special well Dorothy Coly, I pray you be good unto her. I would wit whether this be she that you wrote me of. If not I pray you be good to the tother, as you may in her affliction and to my good daughter Joan Alleyne to give her I pray you some kind answer, for she sued hither to me this day to pray you be good to her.

I cumber you good Margaret much, but I would be sorry, if it should be any longer than tomorrow, for it is St Thomas's Eve, and the utas of St Peter and therefore tomorrow long I to go to God, it were a day very meet and convenient for me. I never liked your manner toward me better than when you kissed me last for I love when daughterly love and dear charity hath no leisure to look to worldly courtesy.

Farewell my dear child, and pray for me, and I shall for you and all your friends that we may merrily meet in heaven. I thank you for your great cost.

I send now unto my good daughter Clement her algorism stone and I send her and my good son and all hers God's blessing and mine.

I pray you at time convenient recommend me to my good son John More. I liked well his natural fashion. Our Lord bless him and his good wife my loving daughter, to whom I pray him to be good, as he hath great cause, and that if the land of mine come to his hand, he break not my will concerning his sister Daunce. And our Lord bless Thomas and Austen and all that they shall have.

St Thomas] à Becket.   Utas] octave.   Clement] his foster daughter Margaret Gigg, married to John Clement.   Algorism stone] a slate to do arithmetic.

MARY HART

Mary Hart was the wife of John Hart (d. 1574), who wrote books on the reform of English spelling and pronunciation. William Dethick was a courtier of exceptionally violent temper, notorious for many assaults, who nevertheless prospered under Elizabeth and James I, and in 1586 succeeded his father as Garter king-of-arms, the chief Herald. At the time of Mary Hart's complaint he was York Herald.

4. To Lord Burghley, May 1573

William Cecil, Lord Burghley (1520–98) was Queen Elizabeth's Minister of State.

To the Right Honourable and my singular good Lord the Lord High Treasurer of England etc.

May 1573. Chester the Herald's wife
    against Detheck
      Garter's son.

In most humble wise I beseech your Lordship of your goodness and even for God's sake to have the truth tried and the matter ended of York's great misusing me. May it please your Honour, I being alone in my chamber, he put me in fear of my life, and almost took my breath from me, in most vile sort. I was never well long together since. His cousin Richard Detheck of Polstead in Suffolk hearing his doings came in, and took him by the middle, and prayed him to be content. I feared York would have killed me else, he spurned me down with his foot so oft my head was very near the fire and my hair like to be burned as yet may appear by my cap, which I had next my hair. He put a deep coal basket lined with leather on my head with some coals and dust in it, and kept it so long about my head and shoulders that my breath was almost gone. Saving the reverence of your Lordship, my chamber pot of urine, he poured on my bare head and thereafter rubbed hot ashes into my hair and dipped a basin into a stand of new drink and flashed so much full on my face, that I could not see for a time. As soon as I came to myself, I got down even as I was, and would have gone forth to have showed myself to the Gentlemen of the Arches but my Lady Garter kept the gate, and kept me in perforce, and there I laid to his charges, how he had misused me, and called me (saving your Honour's reverence) pocky whore. He said before Richmond and Somerset Heralds that I lied like a pocky drab (or a quean) and would have runned on me again with his foot, but his mother held him back. He since confessed to my husband, that he took my hair out of the fire, and yet I understand that he denieth as well his words, as that he came in my chamber. Master Garter hath reported to my friends and me, that my husband was the cause of all, which I could never perceive, but this I know very well, that Master Garter and his wife hath sought to set discord betwixt my husband and me, that marvel it is we had not been asunder long since, and because I, upon York's further threatening of me, I took the peace of him, he took the peace of my husband and me, and for the two actions my husband hath taken against him, he hath surmised two others against my husband and me, to trouble us withal. If it shall please your Honour, if there be either man or woman, that is able justly to prove that ever I was the beginner of any falling out, with him or any other body, then I will be content to be used thereafter. I most humbly beseech your Lordship, to pardon me of my rude writing, for that I lack utterance of speech, and am the more this constrained to write, the matter hath been so long a time deferred, to my great grief. And such a shame on my head undeserved I cannot bear, for I would more gladly have forgiven him my death than it. But I trust when the matter is duly tried and ended I shall be restored to my good and honest name, which they have so much sought to take from me, and in effect from my husband. And for your Lordship's dealing in my right, I shall be most bound to pray God for you and yours during life. And so the Lord God bless and prosper you and them.

Your Lordship's most humble, and servant if I were worthy,

Mary Hart

The Court of Arches was an ecclesiastical court of appeal held in St Mary-le-Bow.   My Lady Garter] Dethick's mother.   Master Garter] Dethick's father, Garter king-of-arms.   Took the peace] to take the peace is to swear that someone whom one has cause to fear may be bound over to keep the peace.   Surmised] submitted charges.

SIR PHILIP SIDNEY
(1554–1586)

5. To Edmund Molyneux, 31 May 1578

Molyneux was secretary to Sidney's father, Sir Henry Sidney. Later in the summer of 1578 he convinced Sidney of his innocence.

Mr Molyneux,

Few words are best. My letters to my father have come to the eyes of some: neither can I condemn any but you for it. If it be so, you have played the very knave with me: and so I will make you know if I have good proof of it. But that for so much as is past. For that is to come, I assure you before God, that if ever I know you do so much as read any letter I write

to my father, without his commandment or my consent, I will thrust my
dagger into you. And trust to it, for I speak it in earnest. In the mean time,
farewell. From Court, this last of May 1578.

By me
Philip Sidney

JOHN STUBBS
(c.1541–1590)

6. To Lord Burghley, 31 August 1580

> In 1579 Stubbs published a pamphlet protesting against the proposed marriage of
> Queen Elizabeth to the Duc d'Alençon. For this he and his publishers were sen-
> tenced to have their right hands cut off with a butcher's knife and mallet. William
> Camden, who was present, remembered that Stubbs, 'after his right hand was cut
> off, put off his hat with his left, and said with a loud voice, "God save the Queen"'.
> This letter from the Tower was written with his left hand.

The glad tidings of Her Majesty's most gracious disposition to my liberty,
my good Lord, signified by Mr Secretary Wilson, did justly rejoice me,
after almost a whole year of many troubles, and half revived my wife almost
in a dying bed. Now for full recovery of this joy and life, which the
accomplishment hereof will bring respectively to us both; my next means,
after Her Majesty's natural clemency, is by that Christian furtherance of
great personages about Her Highness. And therefore by your Lordship's
good favor I press boldly to the same, praying the joining of your honorable
and helping hand to Her Majesty's royal heart, now inclining to the release
of these heavy bands of indignation. My poor wife, also, as her short
breathing will suffer her, doth instantly and humbly pray the same of your
Lordship, who, as she heretofore sued for me and my liberty, so now I find
it my duty to sue for her and her life. For truly, my Lord, even before God
and your Lordship, whom I would not dishonor with an untruth, I neither
feign nor enforce this pitiful motive for my delivery, but shall a thousand
times more willingly receive this or any other never so great benefit by her
sickness than ever any most covetous merchant did throw overboard his
most precious freight to save his own life. Good my Lord, therefore, bear
with me, if somewhat importunely I crave your Lordship's favor for her
life, and that in the Lord Jesus Christ's name. And for me it may please
you to testify that, as to Her Majesty, so hereby now to your Lordship, I
profess and lay forth a sorry and sorrowful heart, thus to have incurred Her
Majesty's great offense and judicial sentence of transgressing the law. Henceforth vowing that short remain of my life and that small of my poor service

wholly to Her Highness, at least to pray for her long life and blessed reign over us: and to your Lordship that you may in you and yours, in this life, be right happily honorable and right honorably happy. Tower, 31 August, 1580.

Your Lordship's suppliant, a most desolate prisoner with his sick fellow prisoner.

[John Stubbs]

ENDORSEMENT: Mr John Stubbs to my Lordship from the Tower for his enlargement in regard of his wife's sickness.

'EMANUEL PLANTAGENET' (MILES FRY)

7. To Lord Burghley, 27 June 1587

Burghley apparently had many such letters from lunatics.

To the right honorable the Lord Burley. Lord Tresorer of the Quene of England.

My Lord, I am sent an Embassador from God the Father unto the Quenes Highnes to declare unto her that I am the sonne of them both, and when she was delivered of me, I was taken from her by the Angel Gabriel and brought unto one Miztres Fry for to be kept; and the time of this keping is ended: and God my father hath sent me unto her Highnes to declare unto her that I am her sonne: and to signifi unto her that this Gabriel which she loketh for at this time shal not cum unto her until fifti yeres be expired. I prai you to signifi unto her Majeste that I her pore sonne do humble besech her to suffer me to declare my fathers embassage unto her, and to be merciful unto me which am in great extremiti and redi to perish for lak of helpe. This embassage did I signifi unto Syr Francis Walsingam, her Secretari, almost fower yeres past, who promised to helpe me unto the Quene, but did it not, and my sute during almost this fower yeres, I having written a letter unto my Ladi the Quene and another unto my Lords of her Councel, and sundri letters unto that her Secretary at sundri times, besids the spech of my mouth unto him at divers tymes: I am yet so far from helpe of my Ladi that I have not the favor of a subject in her relme though I be her sonne. And during this sute I have bin hardli used: and nowe do make this my last mone unto you that you wolde obtaine of my Ladi the Quene for to hire this embassage of me and to accept me for her sonne. I have bin this xxxv. yeres knowen by the name of Miles Fry; and have bin taken for the sonne of Mr John Fry and Mistres Jone Fry his wife. This Mr Fry your Honor knoweth wel, which nowe dwelleth at Dulses, in the parish of Kilmington or Axmizter, in Devonshire. At this Ynne it is not convenient for me to ztai ani time, and yf I would I have not where with al: and in this Citi I shal not get ani helpe: so that yf you do not presentli helpe me uppon the sight hereof I shal then presentli depart unto Devonshire againe: and yf I do so, as treweli as God liueth and as my Ladi doth live, immediatli uppon my returne thither I shall end my life: as by my letters unto my Ladi and her Councel I did signifi longe gon: and then will God punish this land. My calling is not to redeme the worlde, but to shew the end of generation and the love between Christ and his Church; which Salomon began to do, and did it amisse. My autorite is greater than Gabriels. I am the son, he is but a servant. I pray you upon the sight hereof to speake with me; that with my mouth I mai declare unto you that which here I have written with my hande: you have bin alwais a favorar of the complaints of the Quenes pore subjects; much more then, ought you of her sonne. Thus I prai God to preserve my Ladi the Quene, and to direct your Honor in the right wai. Written with my diing hand at the signe of the Rose and Crowne in Saint Johns Strete, beyond Smithfelde, in London, the xxvijth of June, 1587.

> Your Honors to use,
> Emanuel Plantagenet

QUEEN ELIZABETH I
(1533–1603)

Between 1582 and 1603, the year of her death, Queen Elizabeth wrote often to James VI of Scotland. Many of the letters are in the Queen's autograph, and in her characteristic manner, which is firm if not always clear. James was devious but not a match for her. She reproves his dissembling and stresses the dangers of his tenderness for the Scottish Catholic lords, supporters of the Spanish against the English cause. Several letters deal with the tricky question of the execution of Mary Queen of Scots, James's mother.

8. To James VI of Scotland, c.1 February 1586/7

This letter dismisses a proposal that Mary, long under arrest, should be given into the custody of a neutral prince.

Be not carried away, my dear brother, with the lewd persuasions of such as instead of informing you of my too needful and helpless cause of defending the breath that God hath given me, to be better spent than spilt by the bloody invention of traitors' hands, may perhaps make you believe that either the offence was not so great, or if that cannot serve them, for the over-manifest trial which in public and by the greatest and most in this land hath been manifestly proved, yet they will make that her life may be saved and mine safe, which would God were true, for when you make view of my long danger endured these four—well-nigh five—months time to make a taste of, the greatest wits amongst my own, and then of French, and last of you, will grant with me, that if need were not more than my malice she should not have her merit.

And now for a good conclusion of my long-tarried-for answer. Your commissioners tells me, that I may trust her in the hand of some indifferent prince, and have all her cousins and allies promise she will no more seek my ruin. Dear brother and cousin, weigh in true and equal balance whether they lack not much good ground when such stuff serves for their building. Suppose you I am so mad to trust my life in another's hand and send it out of my own? If the young master of Gray, for currying favour with you, might fortune to say it, yet old master Melvin hath years enough to teach him more wisdom than to tell a prince of any judgment such a contrarious frivolous maimed reason. Let your councillors, for your honour, discharge their duty so much to you as to declare the absurdity of such an offer; and, for my part, I do assure myself too much of your wisdom, as, though like a most natural son you charged them to seek all means they could devise with wit or judgment to save her life, yet I can not, nor do not, allege any fault to you of these persuasions, for I take it you will remember, that advice or desires ought ever agree with the surety of the party sent to and honour of the sender, which when both you weigh, I doubt not but your wisdom will excuse my need, and wait [weigh?] my necessity, and not accuse me either of malice or of hate.

And now to conclude. Make account, I pray you, of my firm friendship, love and care, of which you may make sure account, as one that never minds to fail from my word, nor swerve from our league, but will increase, by all good means, any action that may make true show of my stable amity; from which, my dear brother, let no sinister whispers, no busy troublers of princes' states, persuade to leave your surest, and stick to unstable stays. Suppose them to be but the echoes of those whose stipendiaries they be, and will do more for their gain than for your good. And so, God hold you ever in his blessed keeping, and make you see your true friends. Excuse my not writing sooner, for pain in one of my eyes was only the cause.

Your most assured loving sister and cousin,
Elizabeth R.

To my dear brother and cousin, the king of Scots.

9. To James VI of Scotland, August 1588

This urgent letter requiring James to deny succour to the routed Armada expresses alarm lest the Catholics, whom in Elizabeth's opinion he should have locked up, should help the Spaniards. The most powerful of them, George Gordon, 6th Earl of Huntly, did have Spanish sympathies, but James continued to favour him.

Now may appear, my dear brother, how malice conjoined with might strives to make a shameful end to a villainous beginning, for, by God's singular favour, having their fleet well-beaten in our narrow seas, and pressing, with all violence, to achieve some watering place, to continue their pretended invasion, the winds have carried them to your coasts, where I doubt not they shall receive small succour and welcome; unless those lords that, so traitor-like, would belie their own prince, and promise another king relief in your name, be suffered to live at liberty, to dishonour you, peril you, and advance some other (which God forbid you suffer them live to do). Therefore I send you this gentleman, a rare young man and a wise, to declare unto you my full opinion in this great cause, as one that never will abuse you to serve my own turn; nor will you do aught that myself would not perform if I were in your place. You may assure yourself that, for my part, I doubt no whit but that all this tyrannical proud and brainsick attempt will be the beginning, though not the end, of the ruin of that king that, most unkingly, even in midst of treating peace, begins this wrongful war. He hath procured my greatest glory that meant my sorest wreck, and hath so dimmed the light of his sunshine, that who hath a will to obtain shame let him keep his forces company. But for all this, for yourself sake, let not the friends of Spain be suffered to yield them force; for though I fear not in the end the sequel, yet if, by leaving them unhelped, you may increase the English hearts unto you, you shall not do the worst deed for your behalf; for if aught should be done, your excuse will play the *boiteux*; if you make not sure work with the likely men to do it. Look well unto it, I beseech you.

The necessity of this matter makes my scribbling the more spidy [spidery?], hoping that you will measure my good affection with the right balance of my actions, which to you shall be ever such as I have professed, but doubting of the reciproque of your behalf, according as my last messenger unto you hath at large signified, for the which I render you a million of grateful thanks together, for the last general prohibition to your subjects not to foster nor aid our general foe, of which I doubt not the observation if the ringleaders be safe in your hands; as knoweth God, who ever have you in his blessed keeping, with many happy years of reign.

Your most assured loving sister and cousin,

Elizabeth R.

To my very good brother the king of Scots.

Traitor-like] Earl Huntly and his associates are the traitorous lords.   This gentleman]
Elizabeth's messenger was Sir Robert Sidney.   The ruin of that king] Philip of Spain.
Play the *boiteux*] make a lame excuse.

10. To Lord Mountjoy, 3 December 1600

Mountjoy enjoyed much needed military success when he succeeded Essex as Lord
Deputy in Ireland, but wrote to the Queen complaining that he was treated no better
than a scullion. The Queen, needing him to keep up the good work, replies in jocular
vein.

Mistress Kitchenmaid,

I had thought that precedency had been ever in question but among the
higher and greater sort; but now I find good proof that some of more
dignity and greater calling may by good desert and faithful care give the
upper hand to one of your faculty, that with your frying and other kitchen
stuff have brought to their last home more rebels, and passed greater
breakneck places, than those promised more and did less. Comfort yourself
therefore in this, that neither your careful endeavour, nor dangerous tra-
vails, nor heedful regards to our service, without your own by-respects,
could ever have been bestowed upon a Prince that more esteems them,
considers and regards them than she for whom chiefly I know all this hath
been done, and who keeps this verdict ever in store for you; that no
vainglory, nor popular fawning can ever advance you forward, but true vow
of duty and reverence of Prince, who two afore your life I see you do
prefer.

And though you lodge near Papists, and doubt you not for their infection, yet I fear you may fall in an heresy which I hereby do conjure you
from; that you suppose you to be back-bited by some to make me think you
faulty of many oversights and evil defaults in your government. I would
have you know for certain that as there is no man can rule so great a charge
without some errors, yet you may assure yourself I have never heard of any
had fewer; and such is your good luck that I have not known them, though
you were warned of them.

And learn this of me, that you must make difference betwixt admoni-
tions and charges, and like of faithful advices as your most necessariest
weapons to save you from blows of Princes' mislike. And so I absolve you
a poena et culpa if this you observe. And so God bless and prosper you as
if ourself were where you are.

Your Sovereign that dearly regards you.

Sir Walter Ralegh

(1554?–1618)

11. To his wife, December 1603

This letter was written while Ralegh was in the Tower awaiting trial. It suggests that he attempted suicide. Though probably innocent of all the charges, he was convicted on 17 Nov. of plotting against James I and accepting Spanish bribes. He was ordered to be executed on 11 Dec., and on the previous day wrote another famous farewell letter to his wife. He was reprieved but remained a prisoner in the Tower till 1616, when he was released on his promise to exploit a gold mine in Guiana (Venezuela). The expedition failed, and he was executed in 1618.

Ralegh's wife survived till 1647. The son here mentioned, Walter, born in 1593, was killed during the Guiana expedition. Nothing seems to be known of the presumably illegitimate daughter. The authenticity of this letter has been questioned.

Receive from thy unfortunate husband these his last lines, these the last words that ever thou shalt receive from him. That I can live to think never to see thee and my child more I cannot, I have desired God and disputed with my reason, but nature and compassion hath the victory. That I can live to think how you are both left a spoil to my enemies, and that my name shall be a dishonour to my child, I cannot, I cannot endure the memory thereof. Unfortunate woman, unfortunate child, comfort yourselves, trust God, and be contented with your poor estate; I would have bettered it if I had enjoyed a few years. Thou art a young woman, and forbear not to marry again; it is now nothing to me, thou art no more mine, nor I thine. To witness that thou didst love me once, take care that thou marry not to please sense, but to avoid poverty and to preserve thy child. That thou didst also love me living, witness it to others, to my poor daughter, to whom I have given nothing, for his sake who will be cruel to himself to preserve thee. Be charitable to her, and teach thy son to love her for his father's sake. For myself, I am left of all men that have done good to many. All my good turns forgotten, all my errors revived and expounded to all extremity of ill. All my services, hazards and expenses, for my country plantings, discoveries, fights, counsels, and whatever else, malice has now covered over; I am now made an enemy and traitor by the word of an unworthy man. He hath proclaimed me to be a partaker of his vain imaginations, notwithstanding the whole course of my life hath approved the contrary, as my death shall approve it. Woe, woe, woe be unto him by whose falsehood we are lost! He hath separated us asunder, he hath slain my honour, my fortune; he hath robbed thee of thy husband, thy child of its father, and me of you both. O God, thou dost know my wrongs, know then thou, my wife and child, know then thou my Lord and King, that I ever thought them too honest to betray, and too good to conspire against. But my wife, forgive thou all, as I do; live humble, for thou hast but a time also. God forgive my lord Harry, for he was my heavy enemy. And for my lord Cecil, I thought he would never forsake me in extremity; I would not have done it him, God knows. But do not thou know it, for he must be master of thy child, and may have compassion of him. Be not dismayed that I died in despair of God's mercies; strive not to dispute it, but assure thyself that God hath not left me, nor Satan tempted me. Hope and despair live not together. I know it is forbidden to destroy ourselves, but I trust it is forbidden in this sort, that we destroy not ourselves despairing of God's mercy.

The mercy of God is immeasurable, the cogitations of men comprehend it not. In the Lord I have ever trusted, and I know that my redeemer liveth. Far is it from me to be tempted with Satan; I am only tempted with sorrow, whose sharp teeth devour my heart. O God that art goodness itself, thou canst not be but merciful to me. For my estate, it is conveyed to feoffees, to your cousin Brett and others; I have but a bare estate for a short life. My plate is at gage in Lombard Street, my debts are many. To Peter Vanlore some £600, to Antrobus as much, but Compton is to pay £300 of it. To Michael Hext £100, to George Carew £100, to Nicholas Sanders £100, to John FitzJames £100, to Master Waddon £100, to a poor man one Hawker for horses £70, to a poor man called Hance £20; take first care of those, for God's sake. To a brewer at Weymouth, and a baker, for my Lord Cecil's ship and mine, I think some £80; John Reynolds knoweth it. And let that poor man have his true part of my return from Virginia, and let the poor men's wages be paid with the goods, for the Lord's sake. O what will my poor servants think at their return, when they hear I am accused to be Spanish, who sent them, to my great charge, to plant and discover upon his territory! O intolerable infamy! O God, I cannot resist these thoughts; I cannot live to think how I am derided, to think of the expectation of my enemies, the scorns I shall receive, the cruel words of lawyers, the infamous taunts and despites, to be made a wonder and a spectacle. O death, hasten thee unto me, that thou mayst destroy the memory of these, and lay me up in dark forgetfulness! O death, destroy my memory, which is my tormentor! My thoughts and my life cannot dwell in one body. But do thou forget me, poor wife, that thou mayest live to bring up thy poor child. I recommend unto you my poor brother, A. Gilbert. The lease of Sandring is his and none of mine; let him have it for God's cause. He knows what is due to me upon it. And be good to Kemys, for he is a perfect honest man, and hath much wrong for my sake. For the rest, I commend me to them, and them to God. And the Lord knows my sorrow to part from thee and my poor child, but part I must, by enemies and injuries; part with shame, and triumph of my detractors. And therefore be contented with this work of God, and forget me in all things but thine own honour and the love of mine. I bless my poor child; and let him know his father was no traitor. Be bold of my innocency, for God, to whom I offer life and soul, knows it. And whosoever thou choose again after me, let him be but thy politic husband; but let thy son be thy beloved, for he is part of me, and I live in him, and the difference is but in the number and not in the kind. And the Lord for ever keep thee and them, and give thee comfort in both worlds.

My lord Harry] Lord Henry Howard, who, with Cecil and others, was part of the commission that examined Ralegh.   Feoffees] those to whom an estate is entailed.   Kemys] Lawrence Kemys accompanied Ralegh on both his Guiana expeditions, and was also imprisoned. He committed suicide in 1618 after the defeat in Guiana.

JAMES HOWELL
(1593–1666)

Howell, a Welshman, went to Jesus College, Oxford, travelled in Europe, and was tutor to the sons of Sir Thomas Savage. He was in Spain with Prince Charles and Buckingham in 1623–4, and later was MP for Richmond and a friend of Ben Jonson's. Having worked for royalist intelligence, he was detained in the Fleet 1642–50, and soon after the Restoration was appointed Historiographer Royal to Charles II. He wrote many books, including a French grammar, a tetraglot dictionary, and various histories and political pamphlets. Because the letters, published in his lifetime, between 1645 and 1655, contain some errors and discrepancies, their authenticity has been questioned, but it is likely they are substantially by Howell.

12. To Captain Thomas Porter, 10 July 1623

Noble Captain,

My last to you was in *Spanish*, in answer to one of yours in the same Language; and among that confluence of *English* Gallants who, upon the occasion of His Highness being here, are come to this Court, I fed myself with hopes a long while to have seen you; but I find now that those hopes were imp'd with false feathers. I know your heart is here, and your best affections; therefore I wonder what keeps back your Person: but I conceive the reason to be, that you intend to come like yourself, to come Commander-in-chief of one of the Castles of the Crown, one of the Ships Royal: If you come to this Shore-side, I hope you will have time to come to the Court; I have at any time a good Lodging for you, and my Landlady is none of the meanest, and her Husband hath many good parts: I heard her setting him forth one day, and giving this Character of him: *Mi marido es buen musico, buen esgrimidor, buen escrivano, excellente arithmetico, salvo que no multiplica;—* My Husband is a good Musician, a good Fencer, a good Horseman, a good Penman, and an excellent *Arithmetician*, only he cannot multiply. For outward usage, there is all industry used to give the Prince and his Servants all possible contentment; and some of the King's own Servants wait upon them at Table in the Palace, where, I am sorry to hear, some of them jeer at the *Spanish* fare, and use other slighting speeches and demeanor. There are many excellent Poems made here since the Prince's arrival, which are too long to couch in a Letter; yet I will venture to send you this one Stanza of *Lope de Vegas:—*

> *Carlos Estuardo Soy*
> *Que siendo* Amor *mi guia,*
> *Al cielo d'España voy*
> *Por ver mi Estrella* Maria.

There are Comedians once a week come to the Palace, where, under a great Canopy, the Queen and the *Infanta* sit in the middle, our Prince and *Don Carlos* on the Queen's right hand, the King and the little Cardinal on the *Infanta's* left hand. I have seen the Prince have his Eyes immoveably fix'd upon the *Infanta* half an hour together in a thoughtful speculative posture, which sure would needs be tedious, unless affection did sweeten it: it was no handsome comparison of *Olivares*, that he watch'd her as a cat doth a Mouse. Not long since the Prince, understanding that the *Infanta* was used to go some mornings to the *Casa de Campo*, a Summer-house the King hath on t'other side the River, to gather *May-dew*, he rose betimes and went thither, taking your Brother with him; they were let into the House, and into the Garden, but the *Infanta* was in the Orchard: and there being a high partition-wall between, and the door doubly bolted, the Prince got on the top of the wall, and sprung down a great height, and so made towards her; but she spying him first of all the rest, gave a shriek, and ran back: the old Marquis that was then her Guardian came towards the Prince, and fell on his knees, conjuring His Highness to retire, in regard he hazarded his Head if he admitted any to her company; so the door was open'd, and he came out under that wall over which he had got in. I have seen him watch a long hour together in a close Coach, in the open street, to see her as she went abroad: I cannot say that the Prince did ever talk with her privatly, yet publickly often, my Lord of *Bristol* being Interpreter; but the King always sat hard by to overhear all. Our Cousin *Archy* hath more privilege than any, for he often goes with his Fool's-coat where the *Infanta* is with her *Menina's* and Ladies of Honour, and keeps a-blowing and blustering among them, and flurts out what he lists.

One day they were discoursing what a marvellous thing it was that the
D. of *Bavaria* with less than 15,000 Men, after a long toilsome March,
should dare to encounter the *Palsgrave's* Army, consisting of above 25,000,
and to give them an utter discomfiture, and take *Prague* presently after:
Whereunto *Archy* answer'd, that he would tell them a stranger thing than
that: Was it not a strange thing, quoth he, that in the Year 88 there should
come a Fleet of 140 Sail from *Spain* to invade *England*, and that ten of
these could not go back to tell what became of the rest? By the next
opportunity I will send you the *Cordouan* Pockets and Gloves you writ for
of *Francisco Moreno's* perfuming. So may my dear Captain live long, and
love his—

J. H.

Imp'd] feathers were imped, that is, inserted into a bird's wing to improve its power of
flight.   Lope de Vega] the famous Spanish dramatist (1562–1635), who had some part in
the festivities during Prince Charles's visit to Madrid. The lines attributed to him are translated
by Howell's editor: 'Charles Stuart am I, | Love has guided me far, | To Spanish heaven I come
| To see Maria, my star.'   Archie] the court fool of James I, who went to Madrid with the
Prince.   Meninas] ladies in waiting.   The Palsgrave] here Frederick, the Count Palatine, married to James's daughter Elizabeth. He briefly usurped the kingdom of Bohemia but was
defeated at the battle of the White Mountain, after which a Spanish army invaded the
Palatinate.   Cordouan] fine Spanish leather from Cordoba.

13. To Sir I. S., 25 May 1628

At this moment England was uncomfortably at war with both Spain and France.
Ambrogio Spinola commanded the Spanish army in the Netherlands till 1627. Now
the men of Harwich can relax.

Sir,

You writ to me lately for a Footman, and I think this Bearer will fit you:
I know he can run well, for he hath run away twice from me, but he knew
the way back again. Yet tho' he hath a running head as well as running
heels (and who will expect a Footman to be a stay'd man?), I would not part
with him were I not to go Post to the *North*. There be some things in him
that answer for his waggeries; he will come when you call him, go when
you bid him, and shut the door after him; he is faithful and stout, and a
lover of his Master: He is a great enemy to all dogs, if they bark at him in
his running, for I have seen him confront a huge Mastiff, and knock him
down; when you go a country journey, or have him run with you a hunting,
you must spirit him with liquor; you must allow him also something
extraordinary for Socks, else you must not have him to wait at your Table;
when his grease melts in running hard, 'tis subject to fall into his toes. I
send him you but for a trial; if he be not for your turn, turn him over to
me again when I come back.

The best News I can send you at this time is, that we are like to have

Peace both with *France* and *Spain*; so that *Harwich* Men, your Neighbours, shall not hereafter need to fear the Name of *Spinola*, who struck such an Apprehension into them lately, that I understand they began to fortify.

I pray present my most humble Service to my good Lady, and at my return from the *North*, I will be bold to kiss her hands and yours. So I am——

Your much obliged Servitor,
J. H.

14. *To Lady Scroop, 25 August 1628*

Lady Scroop was sister of the Earl of Rutland and aunt of the Duke of Buckingham, who was assassinated on 23 Aug. by a disaffected lieutenant, John Felton.

Madam,

I lay yesternight at the Post-house at *Stilton*, and this morning betimes the Post-master came to my Bed's-head and told me the D. of *Buckingham* was slain: My Faith was not then strong enough to believe it, till an hour ago I met in the way with my Lord of *Rutland* (your Brother) riding Post towards *London*; it pleas'd him to alight, and shew me a Letter, wherein there was an exact relation of all the circumstances of this sad Tragedy.

Upon *Saturday* last, which was but next before yesterday, being *Bartholomew* Eve, the Duke did rise up in a well-dispos'd humour out of his bed, and cut a Caper or two, and being ready, and having been under the Barber's hand (where the murderer had thought to have done the deed, for he was leaning upon the window all the while), he went to breakfast, attended by a great company of Commanders, where *Mons. Soubize* came to him, and whisper'd him in the ear that *Rochel* was reliev'd: The Duke seem'd to slight the news, which made some think that *Soubize* went away discontented. After breakfast, the Duke going out, Col. *Fryer* stept before him, and stopping him upon some business, and Lieut. *Felton* being behind, made a thrust with a common tenpenny knife over *Fryer's* arm at the Duke, which lighted so fatally, that he slit his heart in two, leaving the knife sticking in the body. The Duke took out the knife, and threw it away; and laying his hand on his Sword, and drawn it half out, said, The Villain hath kill'd me (meaning, as some think, Col. *Fryer*), for there had been some difference 'twixt them; so, reeling against a chimney, he fell down dead. The Dutchess being with Child, hearing the noise below, came in her night-geers from her Bed-chamber, which was in an upper room, to a kind of rail, and thence beheld him weltering in his own blood. *Felton* had lost his hat in the croud, wherein there was a Paper sow'd, wherein he declar'd, that the reason which mov'd him to this Act was no grudge of his own, tho' he had been far behind for his pay, and had been put by his Captain's place twice, but in regard he thought the Duke an Enemy to the *State*, because he was branded in Parliament; therefore what he did was for the publick good of his Country. Yet he got clearly down, and so might have gone to his horse, which was ty'd to a hedge hard by; but he was so amaz'd that he miss'd his way, and so struck into the pastry, where, altho' the cry went that some *Frenchman* had done't, he thinking the word was *Felton*, boldly confess'd, 'twas he that had done the deed, and so he was in their hands. *Jack Stamford* would have run at him, but he was kept off by Mr *Nicholas*; so being carry'd up to a Tower, Capt. *Mince* tore off his Spurs, and asking how he durst attempt such an Act, making him believe the Duke was not dead, he answer'd boldly, that he knew he was dispatch'd, for 'twas not he, but the hand of Heaven that gave the stroke; and tho' his whole body had been cover'd over with Armour of Proof, he could not have avoided it. Capt. *Cha. Price* went post presently to the King four miles off, who being at prayers on his knees when it was told him, yet never stirr'd, nor was he disturb'd a whit till all divine service was done. This was the relation, as far as my memory could bear, in my Lord of *Rutland's* Letter, who will'd me to remember him to your Ladyship, and tell you that he was going to comfort your niece (the Dutchess) as fast as he could. And so I have sent the truth of this sad story to your Ladyship, as fast as I could by this Post, because I cannot make that speed myself, in regard of some business I have to dispatch for my Lord in the way: So I humbly take my leave, and rest—

Your Ladyship's most dutiful Servant,
J. H.

Soubize] Soubise was the leader of the Huguenot rebels.   Rochel was reliev'd] the report that La Rochelle, occupied by the Huguenots, had been relieved was false.   The pastry] presumably the kitchen.

15. To Lady Cornwallis, 2 June 1630

Madam,

You spoke to me for a Cook who had seen the world Abroad, and I think the Bearer hereof will fit your Ladyship's turn. He can marinate fish, make gellies; he is excellent for a *piquant* sauce, and the *Haugou*; besides, Madam, he is passing good for an *Ollia*: He will tell your Ladyship, that the reverend Matron the *Olla podrida* hath intellectuals and senses; Mutton, Beef, and Bacon, are to her as the Will, Understanding, and Memory, are to the Soul: Cabbage, Turnips, Artichocks, Potatoes, and Dates, are her five Senses, and Pepper the Common-sense; she must have Marrow to keep Life in her, and some Birds to make her light; by all means she must go adorn'd with chains of Sausages. He is also good at larding of Meat after the *Mode* of *France*. Madam, you may make proof of him, and if your Ladyship find him too saucy or wasteful, you may return him whence you had him. So I rest, Madam—

Your Ladyship's humble Servitor,

J. H.

Haugou] *haut goût*, a strong relish.   *Ollia*] stew.   *Olla podrida*] literally, 'rotten pot', but referring to a Spanish stew, the contents of which are here enumerated.

KING CHARLES I
(1600–1649)

16. To the Duke of Buckingham, 12 July 1626

> Charles succeeded his father James I in 1625, and soon after his accession married Henrietta Maria, sister of the French King. She retained control over her own household, and remained a Catholic. Many Catholic missionaries had been executed at Tyburn, near what is now Marble Arch. Charles had been told that the Queen had gone to Tyburn to pray for those who had died there. The Queen denied the accusation, but Charles expelled her French attendants. The breach caused by this early quarrel was mended, and the marriage was a happy one.

Steenie,

It is not unknown, both to the French King and his mother, what unkindnesses and distastes have fallen between my wife and me; which hitherto I have borne with great patience (as all the world knows), ever expecting and hoping an amendment; knowing her to be but young, and perceiving it to be the ill crafty counsels of her servants for advancing of their own ends, rather than her own inclination. For, at my first meeting of her at Dover, I could not expect more testimonies of respect and love than she showed; as, to give one instance. Her first suit was, that she being young, and coming to a strange country, both by her years and ignorance of the customs of the place, might commit many errors; therefore, that I would not be angry with her for her faults of ignorance, before I had, by my instructions, learned her to eschew them; and desired me, in these cases, to use no third person, but to tell her myself, when I found she did anything amiss. I both granted her request and thanked her for it; but desired that she would use me as she had desired me to use her; which she willingly promised me, which promise she never kept. For, a little after this, Madame St George, taking a distaste because I would not let her ride with us in the coach when there were women of better quality to fill her room, claiming it as her due (which in England we think a strange thing) set my wife in such a humour of distaste against me as, from that very hour to this, no man can say that ever she asked me, two days together, with so much respect as I deserved of her; but, on the contrary, has put so many disrespects on me, that it were too long to set down all.

Some I will relate. As I take it, it was at her first coming to Hampton Court I sent some of my Council to her with those orders that were kept in the Queen my mother's house, desiring she would command the Count of Tilliers that the same might be kept in hers. Her answer was, that she hoped I would give her leave to order her house as she list herself. Now if she had said that she would speak with me, not doubting to give me satisfaction in it, I could have found no fault with her, whatsoever she would have said of this to myself, for I could only impute it to ignorance. But I could not imagine that she would have affronted me in such a thing publicly. After I heard this answer, I took a time, when I thought we had both best leisure to dispute it, to tell her calmly both her fault in the public denial and her mistaking the business itself. She, instead of acknowledging her fault and mistaking, gave me so ill an answer that I omit (not to be tedious) the relation of that discourse; having too much of that nature hereafter to relate.

Many little neglects I will not take the pains to set down; as, her eschewing to be in my company; when I have anything to speak to her, I must means [i.e. use as a mediator] her servant first, else I am sure to be denied; her neglect of the English tongue, and of the nation in general. I will also omit the affront she did me, before my going to this last unhappy assembly of Parliament, because there has been talk enough of that already. The author of it is before you in France.

To be short, omitting all other passages, coming only to that which is most recent in memory: I having made a commission to make my wife's jointure, to assign her those lands she is to live on, and it being brought to such a ripeness that it wanted but my consent to the particulars they had chosen; she, taking notice that it was now time to name the officers for her revenue, one night, when I was in bed, put a paper into my hand, telling me it was a list of those that she desired to be of her revenue. I took it, and said I would read it next morning; but withal told her that, by agreement in France, I had the naming of them. She said, there were both English and French in the note. I replied, that those English I thought fit to serve her I would confirm; but for the French, it was impossible for them to serve her in that nature. Then she said, all those in the paper had breviates from her mother and herself, and that she could admit no other. Then I said, it was neither in her mother's power nor hers to admit any without my leave; and that, if she stood upon that, whomsoever she recommended, should not come in. Then she bade me plainly take my lands to myself; for, if she had no power to put in whom she would in those places, she would have neither lands nor houses of me; but bade me give her what I thought fit in pension. I bade her then remember to whom she spoke; and told her she ought not to use me so. Then she fell into a passionate discourse, how miserable she was, in having no power to place servants, and that business succeeded the worse for her recommendation; which, when I offered to answer, she would not so much as hear me. Then she went on saying, she was not of that base quality to be used so ill. Then I made her both hear me, and end that discourse.

Thus, having had so long patience with the disturbance of that which should be one of my greatest contentments, I can no longer suffer those, that I know to be the cause and fomenters of these humours, to be about my wife any longer; which I must do, if it were but for one action which they made my wife do, which is, to make her go to Tyburn in devotion to pray: which action can have no greater invective made against it than the relation. Therefore, you shall tell my brother, the French King, as likewise his mother, that this being an action of so much necessity, I doubt not but he will be satisfied with it; especially since he hath done the like himself, not staying until he had so much reason. And, being an action that some may interpret to be of harshness to his nation, I thought good to give him an account of it; because that, in all things, I would preserve the good correspondency and brotherly affection that is between us. So I rest

Your loving, faithful, constant friend,

Charles R.

DUDLEY, LORD CARLETON
(1573–1632)

17. To Queen Henrietta Maria, 23 August 1628

Carleton was an associate of Buckingham, and on this occasion helped to prevent the crowd from tearing Felton to pieces. Parliament had been about to impeach Buckingham.

Maddam,

I am to trouble your Grace, with a most Lamentable Relation; This day betwixt nine and ten of the clock in the morning, the Duke of Buckingham then comming out of a Parlor, into a Hall, to goe to his coach and soe to the King, (who was four miles of) having about him diverse Lords, Colonells, and Captains, & many of his owne Servants, was by one Felton (once a Lieutenant of this our Army) slaine at one blow, with a dagger-knife. In his staggering he turn'd about, uttering onely this word, 'Villaine!' & never spake word more, but presently plucking out the knife from himselfe, before he fell to the ground, hee made towards the Traytor, two or three paces, and then fell against a Table although he were upheld by diverse that were neere him, that (through the villaines close carriage in the act) could not perceive him hurt at all, but guess'd him to be suddenly oversway'd with some apoplexie, till they saw the blood come gushing from his mouth and the wound, soe fast, that life, and breath, at once left his begored body.

Maddam, you may easily guesse what outcryes were then made, by us that were Commaunders and Officers there present, when wee saw him thus dead in a moment, and slaine by an unknowne hand; for it seemes that the Duke himselfe onely knew who it was that had murdered him, and by meanes of the confused presse at the instant about his person, wee neither did, nor could. The Souldiers feare his losse will be their utter ruine, wherefore att that instant the house and the court about it were full, every man present with the Dukes body, endeavouring a care of itt. In the meane time Felton pass'd the throng, which was confusedly great, not soe much as mark'd or followed, in soe much that not knowing where, nor who he was that had done that fact, some came to keepe guard at the gates, and others went to the ramports of the Towne; in all which time the villaine was standing in the kitchin of the same house, and after the inquiry made by a multitude of captaines and gentlemen then pressing into the house and court, and crying out a maine 'where is the villain? where is the butcher?' hee most audaciously and resolutely drawing forth his sword, came out and went amongst them, saying boldly, 'I am the Man, heere I am'; upon which diverse drew upon him, with an intent to have then dispatcht him; but Sr Thomas Morton, my selfe, and some others, us'd such means (though with much trouble and difficulty) that wee drew him out of their hands, and by order of my Lord High Chamberlaine, wee had the charge of keeping him from any comming to him untill a guard of musketeers were brought, to convey him to the Governor's House, where wee were discharg'd.

My Lord High Chamberlaine and Mr Secretary Cooke were then at the Governor's house, did there take his examination of which as yet there is nothing knowne, onely whilst he was in our custody I asked him several Questions, to which he answer'd; vizt. He sayd, he was a Protestant in Religion; hee also expressed himselfe that he was partly discontented for want of eighty pounds pay which was due unto him; and for that hee being Lieutenant of a company of foot, the company was given over his head unto another, and yet, hee sayd, that that did not move him to this resolution, but that he reading the Remonstrance of the house of Parliament it came into his mind, that in committing the Act of killing the Duke, hee should doe his Country great good service. And he sayd that to morrow he was to be pray'd for in London. I then asked him, att what Church, and to what purpose; hee told me at a Church by Fleet-Street-Conduit, and, as for a man much discontented in mind. Now wee seeing things to fall from him in this manner, suffer'd him not to bee further question'd by any, thinking it much fitter for the Lords to examine him, and to finde it out, and know from him whether he was encouraged and sett on by any to performe this wicked deed.

But to returne to the screeches made att the fatall blow given, the Duchesse of Buckingham and the Countesse of Anglesey came forth into a Gallery which look'd into the Hall where they might behold the blood of their deerest Lord gushing from him; ah poore Ladies, such was their screechings, teares, and distractions, that I never in my Life heard the like before, and hope never to heare the like againe. His Maties griefe for the losse of him, was express'd to be more then great, by the many teares hee hath shed for him, with which I will conclude this sad and untimely Newes.

Felton had sowed a writing in the crowne of his hatt, half within the lyning, to shew the cause why hee putt this cruell act in execution; thinking hee should have beene slaine in the place: and it was thus:

> 'If I bee slaine, let no man condemne me, but rather condemne himselfe; it is for our sinns that our harts are hardned, and become sencelesse, or else hee had not gone soe long unpunished.
>
> > JOHN FELTON.
>
> 'Hee is unworthy of the name of a Gentleman, or Soldier, in my opinion, that is afrayd to sacrifice his life for the honor of God, his King, and Country.
>
> > JOHN FELTON.

Maddam, this is the truth, the whole truth, and nothing but the truth, yet all too much too, if it had soe pleased God. I thought it my bounden duty howsoever to let your Matie have the first intelligence of it, by the hand of

Maddam

Yo^{r} sorrowfull servant

Dudley Carleton

ELIZABETH, QUEEN OF BOHEMIA
(1596–1662)

Elizabeth Stuart, daughter of James VI of Scotland and I of England, was married in 1613 to Frederick, Elector Palatine, a German Protestant prince (Donne wrote their Epithalamium). In 1619, Frederick accepted the crown of Bohemia from the insurgent Bohemian Protestants, mistakenly counting on the help of his father-in-law, among others, against Spain and Austria (the deposed King of Bohemia being head of the House of Habsburg). After his defeat in Nov. 1620, at the Battle of the White Mountain outside Prague, he took refuge in the The Hague, where Elizabeth continued to live after his death, returning to England at the Restoration. George I was her grandson.

18. To the Earl of Carlisle, 12 June 1630

James Hay (1580–1636), 1st Earl of Carlisle, was a Scottish favourite of James I who later served Charles I, Elizabeth's brother.

Thou ugly, filthy, camel's face, You chid me once for not writing to you; now I have my revenge, and more justly chide you, for not having heard from you so long as I fear you have forgot to write. I have charged this fat fellow to tell you all this, and that I cannot forget your villany. He can inform [you] how all things are here, and what they say to the peace with Spain; and though I confess I am not much rejoiced at it, yet I am so confident of my dear brother's love, and the promise he hath made me, not to forsake our cause, that it troubles me the less. I must desire your sweet face to continue your help to us, in this business which concerns me so near; and in spite of you, I am ever constantly

Your most affectionat frend
Elizabeth

JOHN WINTHROP
(1588–1649)

Winthrop was an English Puritan lawyer who became governor of the Massachusetts Bay Company; he sailed in the *Arbella* in 1630. His anti-democratic attitude got him into trouble with the other colonists but he survived and remained governor till his death. He figures in Hawthorne's *The Scarlet Letter* (1850).

19. To Margaret Winthrop, 9 September 1630

Winthrop and his third wife, Margaret Tyndale, who was pregnant and remained for the moment in England, had agreed times, Fridays and Mondays, when they would seek spiritual communion with each other. She joined him in 1631, but the baby died on the passage.

My dear wife,

The blessing of God all-sufficient be upon thee and all my dear ones with thee forever.

I praise the good Lord, though we see much mortality, sickness, and trouble, yet (such is His mercy) myself and children with most of my family are yet living and in health and enjoy prosperity enough, if the afflictions of our brethren did not hold under the comfort of it. The Lady Arbella is dead, and good Mr Higginson, my servant old Waters of Neyland, and many others. Thus the Lord is pleased still to humble us; yet he mixes so many mercies with His corrections as we are persuaded He will not cast us off, but in His due time will do us good, according to the measure of our afflictions. He stays but till He hath purged our corruptions and healed the hardness and error of our hearts and stripped us of our vain confidence in this arm of flesh that He may have us rely wholly upon Himself.

The French ship so long expected and given for lost is now come safe to us about a fortnight since, having been twelve weeks at sea, and yet her passengers (being but few) all safe and well but one, and her goats but six living of eighteen. So as now we are somewhat refreshed with such goods and provisions as she brought, though much thereof hath received damage by wet. I praise God, we have many occasions of comfort here and do hope that our days of affliction will soon have an end and that the Lord will do us more good in the end than we could have expected. That will abundantly recompense for all the trouble we have endured. Yet we may not look at great things here. It is enough that we shall have Heaven, though we should pass through Hell to it. We here enjoy God and Jesus Christ; is not this enough? What would we have more? I thank God, I like so well to be here as I do not repent my coming, and if I were to come again, I would not have altered my course, though I had foreseen all these afflictions. I never fared better in my life, never slept better, never had more content of mind, which comes merely of the Lord's good hand, for we have not the like means of these comforts here which we had in England, but the Lord is all-sufficient, blessed be His holy name. If He please, He can still uphold us in this estate. But if He shall see good to make us partakers with others in more affliction, His will be done. He is our God and may dispose of us as He sees good.

I am sorry to part with thee so soon, seeing we meet so seldom, and my much business hath made me too oft forget Mondays and Fridays. I long for the time when I may see thy sweet face again and the faces of my dear children. But I must break off and desire thee to commend me kindly to all my good friends and excuse my not writing at this time. If God please once to settle me, I shall make amends. I will name now but such as are nearest to thee: my brother and sister Gost[lin], Mr Leigh, etc., Castleins, my neighbor Cole and his good wife, with the rest of my good neighbors, tenants, and servants. The good Lord bless thee, and all our children and family. So I kiss my sweet wife and my dear children and rest.

Thy faithful husband,
Jo: Winthrop

I would have written to Maplestead if I had time. Thou must excuse me and remember me kindly to them all.

This is the third letter I have written to thee from n[ew] England. September 9, 1630.

ANTHONY THACHER

20. *To Peter Thacher, September 1635*

Thacher, a tailor, arrived in Massachusetts in June 1635. The hurricane of 16 Aug. 1635 left its mark in the literature of the colony. In this fragment of a letter to his brother back in England, Thacher describes the storm and his shipwreck. The island reached by Thacher and his wife is still known as Thacher's Island. He lived on into his eighties.

But now with the leaf I must alter my matter and subject and turn my drowned pen with my shaking hand to write other news and to rouse up my heavy heart and sadded spirits to indite the story of such sad news as never before this happened in New England and been lamented both in the public on the pulpit and concourse of the people and in private in the closet and in the same places hath God's name been magnified for his great mercy and wonderful deliverance of me out of the bottom of the angry sea.

The story is thus. First there was a league of perennial friendship solemnly made between my cousin Avary and myself made in Mr Graves his ship never to forsake each other to the death but to be partaker each of other's misery or welfare as also of habitation in one place. Now it pleased God immediately on our arrival unto New England there was an offer made unto us, and my cousin Avary was invited to Marblehed by the men of that place to be their pastor, there being as yet no church there planted but there a town appointed by the whole country to be planted there, intended for the good of the whole country to set up the trade of fishing. Now because that many there (the most being fishers) were something loose and remiss in their carriage and behavior, my cousin was unwilling to go thither, and so refusing it we went to Newberry to Mr Parker and others of his acquaintance, intending there to sit down and plant, but being solicited so often both by the men of the place and by the magistrates, and counselled to it by Mr Cotten and most of the ministers in the patent, alleging what a benefit we might do both to the people there and also unto the country and commonweal to settle there a plantation, at length we embraced it and there consented to go. The men of Marblehed forthwith sent a pinnace for us and our goods, and we were at Ipswich on Tuesday the twelfth of August, 1635, embarked ourselves and all and every one of our families with all our goods and substance for Marblehed, we being in all twenty-three souls, to wit eleven in my cousin's family and seven in mine and one Master William Elliott and four mariners. Whence the next morning having recommended ourselves unto the Lord with cheerful and contented hearts we hoisted sail for Marblehed.

But the Lord suddenly turned our cheerfulness into mourning and sad lamentation. Thus on Friday the fourteenth of August 1635 in the evening about ten of the clock our sails being old and torn, we, having a fine fresh gale of wind, were split. Our sailors, because it was something dark would not put on new sails presently but determined to cast their sheet anchor and so to ride at anchor until the next morning and then to put [them] on. But before daylight it pleased God to send so mighty a storm as the like was never felt in New England since the English came there nor in the memory of any of the Indeans. It was [so] furious that our anchor came home, whereupon our mariners let slip more cable, yea, even to the utmost end thereof, and so made it fast only about the bit, whence it slipped away end for end. Then our sailors knew not what to do but were driven as pleased the storm and waves. My cousin and we, perceiving our danger, solemnly recommended ourselves to God, the Lord both of earth and seas, expecting with every wave to be swallowed up and drenched in the deeps. And as my cousin, his wife and children and maid servant, my wife and my tender babes sat comforting and cheering on the other in the Lord against ghastly death, which every moment stares us in the face and sat triumphingly on each other's forehead, we were by the violence of the waves and fury of the winds by the Lord's permission lifted up upon a rock between two high rocks yet all was but one rock but ragged, with the stroke whereof the water came into the pinnace. So as we were presently up to the middle in water as wet, the waters came furiously and violently over us and against us but by reason of the rock's proportion could not lift us off but beat her all to pieces. Now look with me upon our distresses and consider of my misery, who beheld the ship broken, the water in her and violently overwhelming us, my goods and provision swimming in the seas, my friends almost drowned and mine own poor children so untimely (if I may so term it without offence) before mine eyes half drowned and ready to be swallowed up and dashed to pieces against the rocks by the merciless waves and myself ready to accompany them.

But I must go on to an end of this woeful relation. In the same room with us sat he that went master of the pinnace, not knowing what to do. Our foremast was cut down, our mainmast broken in three pieces, the forepart of our pinnace beaten away, our goods swimming about the seas, my children bewailing me as not pitying themselves, and myself bemoaning

them, poor souls whom I had occasioned to such an end in their tender
years whenas they could scarce be sensible of death. And so likewise my
cousin, his wife and his children and both of us bewailing each other in Our
Lord and only Savior Jesus Christ, in whom only we had comfort and
cheerfulness, insomuch that from the greatest to the least of us there was
not one screech or outcry made, but all as silent sheep were contentedly
resolved to die together lovingly as since our acquaintance we had lived
together friendly.

Now as I was sitting in the cabinroom door, lo, one of the sailors by a
wave being washed out of the pinnace was gotten in again, and coming into
the cabinroom over my back, cried out, 'oh, we are all cast away. Lord,
have mercy on us. I have been washed overboard into the sea and am
gotten in again.' His speeches made me look forth, and looking toward the
sea and seeing how we were, I turned myself toward my cousin and the rest
and these words, 'Oh, cousin, it hath pleased God here to cast us between
two rocks, and the shore not far off from us, for I saw the top of trees when
I looked forth.' Whereupon the said master of the pinnace, looking up at
the s[c]uttle hole of the half deck went out of it, but I never saw him
afterward. Then he that had been in the sea went out again by me and
leaped overboard toward the rock, whom afterward also I could never see.

Now none were left in the bark that I knew or saw, but my cousin and
his wife and children, myself and mine and his maidservant. I put [on] my
great coat, a waistcoat of cotton but had neither sleeves nor skirts, a thin
pair of breeches, a pair of boots without stockings. My coat I put off me
and laid it under my poor babe's feet to raise it out of the water (a poor
supporter), but my cousin thought I would have fled from him and said
unto me, 'Oh, cousin, leave us not. Let us die together,' and reached forth
his hand unto me. Then I, letting go my son Peter's hand, took him by the
hand and said to him, 'I purpose it not whither shall I go. I am willing and
ready here to die with you. And my poor children, God be merciful to us,'
adding these words, 'The Lord is able to help and to deliver us.' He
replied, saying, 'True, cousin, but what His pleasure is, we know not; I fear
we have been too unthankful for former mercies. But He hath promised to
deliver us from sin and condemnation, through the all–sufficient satisfaction of Jesus Christ. This, therefore, we may challenge of him.' To which
I, replying, said, 'That is all the deliverance I now desire and expect,'
which words I had no sooner spoken but by a mighty wave I was with a
piece of the bark washed out upon part of the rock, where the wave left me
almost drowned. But recovering my feet, [I] saw above me on the rock my
daughter Mary, to whom I was no sooner gotten but my cousin Avary and
his eldest son came to us, being all four of us washed out with one and the
same wave. We went all into a small hole on the top of the rock, whence we

called to those in the pinnace to come unto us. Supposing we had been in more safety than they were in, my wife, seeing us there, was crept into the scuttle of the half deck to come unto us, but presently another wave dashing the pinnace all to pieces carried away my wife in the scuttle as she was with the greater part of the half deck [carried] to the shore, where she was safely cast, but her legs were something bruised, and much timber of the vessel being there also cast, she was some time before she could get away, washed with the waves. All the rest that were in the bark were drowned in the merciless seas.

We four by that wave were clean swept away from off the rock also into the sea, the Lord in one instant of time disposing of the souls of us to his good pleasure and will. His wonderful mercy to me was thus. Standing on the rock as before you heard with my eldest daughter, my cousin, and his eldest son, [I was] looking upon and talking unto them in the bark whenas we were by that cruel wave washed off the rock as before you heard. God in his mercy caused me to fall by the stroke of the wave flat on my face, for my face was toward the sea insomuch that I was sliding down the rock into the sea. The Lord directed my toes into a joint in the rock's side as also the tops of some of my fingers with my right hand by means whereof, the waves leaving me, I remained so, having only my head above the water. On my left hand I espied a board or plank of the pinnace, and as I was reaching out my left hand to lay hold on it, by another wave coming on the top of the rock I was washed away from the rock and by the violence of the waves was driven hither and thither in the sea a great while and had many dashes against the rocks. At length past hope of life and wearied both in body and spirit I even gave out to nature, and being ready to receive in the waters of death I lifted up both my heart and hands to the God of heaven (for, note, I had my senses remaining and perfect with me all the time I was under and in the water), who at that instant lifted my head clean above the top of waters that so I might breathe without hindrance by the waters. I stood bolt upright as if I stood upon my feet but I felt no bottom nor had any footing for to stand upon but the waters. While I was thus above the waters I saw a piece of the mast as I supposed about three foot long which I labored to catch into my arms, but suddenly I was overwhelmed with water and driven to and fro again and at last I felt the ground with my right foot. Immediately I was violently thrown groveling on my face. When presently I recovered my feet [I] was in the water up to my breast and through God's great mercy had my face to the shore and not to the sea. I made haste to get out but was thrown down on my hands with the waves and so with safety crept forth to the dry shore, where, blessing God, I turned about to look for my children and friends but saw neither them nor any part of the pinnace where I left them as I supposed, but I saw my wife about a butt-length from me, getting herself forth from amongst the timber of the broken bark, but before I could get unto her she was gotten to the shore. When we were come each to other we went up into the land and sat us down under a cedar tree, which the winds had thrown down, where we sat about an hour, even dead with cold, for I was glad to put off my breeches, they being rent all to pieces in the rocks.

But now the storm was broken up and the wind was calm, but the sea remained rough and fearful to us. My legs was much bruised and so was my heart, and other hurt had I none, neither had I taken in much water. But my heart would not suffer me to sit still any longer, but I would go to see if any more was gotten to the land in safety, especially hoping to have met with some of mine own poor children, but I could find none, neither dead nor yet living. You condole with me my further miseries, who now began to consider of my losses. Now [I] called to my remembrance the time and manner how and when I last saw and left my children and friends. One was severed from me sitting on the rock at my feet, the other three in the pinnace, my little babe (ah, poor Peter) sitting in his sister Edith's arms, who to the utmost of her power sheltered him out of the waters, my poor William standing close unto her, all three of them looking ruefully on me on the rock, their very countenance calling unto me to help them, whom I could not go unto, neither could they come unto me, neither could the merciless waves afford me space or time to use any means at all, either to help them or myself.

Oh I yet see their cheeks, poor, silent lambs, pleading pity and help at my hands. Then on the other side to consider the loss of my dear friends with the spoil and loss of all our goods and provisions, myself cast upon an unknown land in a wilderness, I know not where, and how to get there we did not know. Then it came into my mind how I had occasioned the death of my children, who had occasioned them out of their native land, who might have left them there, yea and might have sent some of them back again and cost me nothing. These and many such thoughts do press down my heavy heart very much, but I leave this till I see your face, before which time I fear I shall never attain comfort. Now having no friend to whom I can freely impart myself, Mr Cotten is now my chiefest friend to whom I have free welcome and access, as also Mr Mavericke, Mr Warde, Mr Ward, Mr Hocker, Mr Weles, Mr Warhad, and Mr Parker also, Mr Noyes, who use me friendly. This is God's goodness to me, as also to set the eyes of all the country on me, especially of the magistrates who much favor and comfort me.

But I let this pass and will proceed on in the relation of God's goodness unto me. While I was in that desolate island on which I was cast, I and my wife were almost naked, both of us, and wet and cold even unto death.

When going down to the shore as before I said I found cast on the shore a snapsack in which I had a steel and a flint and a powder horn. Going further I found a drowned goat. Then I found a hat and my son Will's coat, both which I put on. My wife found one of her own petticoats which she put on. I found also two cheeses and some butter driven ashore. Thus the Lord sent us some clothes to put on and food to sustain our new lives which he had given lately unto us, and means also to make fire, for in my horn I had some gunpowder, which to my own and other men's admiration was dry. So, taking a piece of my wife's neckcloth, which I dried in the sun, I struck fire and so dried and warmed our wet bodies, and then skinned the goat, and having found a small brass pot we boiled some of it. Our drink was brackish water. Bread we had none. There we remained until the Monday following, where about three o'clock in the afternoon in a boat that came that way, we went off that desolate island, which I named after my own name, 'Thacher's Woe,' and the rock I named 'Avary his Fall,' to the end their fall and loss and mine own might be had in perpetual remembrance. In the island lieth buried the body of my cousin's eldest daughter, whom I found dead on the shore. On the Tuesday following in the afternoon we arrived at Marblehead, where I am now remaining in health and good respect though very poor, and thus you have heard such relation as never before happened in New England, and as much bewailed as it was strange. What I shall do or what course I shall take I know not. The Lord in his mercy direct me that I may so lead the new life which he hath given me as may be most to his own glory.

Praise God and pray to God for me.

Avary] John Avery had been a Wiltshire clergyman.

JOSEPH KENT

21. To ——, 11 March 1649

The report was untrue in respect of Lord Goring. George Joyce, a colonel in the Cromwellian army who had strongly advocated the trial of the King, was rumoured to have performed the beheading, with Hugh Peters, a junior officer, assisting. There were other suspects, but the executioner was probably Brandon, the common hangman. The story about the Duke of Gloucester has no foundation in fact. Prince Rupert (of the Rhine) was the King's nephew and a dashing warrior.

Noble Sir,

I humbly beg your pardon for my last weeks silence, for I vow to God I was so strangely surprised with grief, that I could not prevaile with my troubled minde for half an hours repose, to give you some relation of the sad and unexemplary murther of our Soveraign, whose soul is at rest.

The Antwerp Post came this morning, but without any Letters from our scandalous Island. I will impart with you what I have learnt from thence and Holland, concerning it.

Its written to several merchants of my acquaintance in Town that the Marquiss Hamilton and Lord Goring were, two days after His Majesty's execution, shot to death; some say they were beheaded, but all conclude they are dead.

Gregory the ordinary hangman of London was commanded to assist to the Kings death, which he refused, but to invite him to it he was proffered two hundred pounds, which he would not hear of; then they threatened to burn him, and at last imprisoned him, because he would not consent to so great a wickedness; but a Judas will never be wanting, a Collonel formerly a brazier (to the great dishonour of the noble military art) with his servant a minister, both masked, were those who cut the thread of His Majestie's life, and, in it, his loyal subjects happiness. A rogue of a minister, after his head was severed from his sacred body, elevated it publicly to the people; and which is more inhuman, its written that the little Duke of Gloucester was placed against the scaffold to see his royal father sacrificed.

P. Rupert is joyned with the English, I meane the Irish frigates and ships, and are betwixt Dover and Calais. They have taken many small vessels coming and going to London, and one of the Parliaments men of war. In brief, without the immediate help from God we are a lost nation, and already pointed at by all that are Christians.

My humble duty and respects to noble Sir R. Wyllis, and all the other gentlemen of the nation, to whom I know you will impart this, although most horrid news; and I beseech you tell Mr Worth I have receaved his Letters, which I answer not until tomorrow, because if I canne learn any thing else of news, I will add to him. Mr Bayly very affectionately salutes Sir Richard and your noble self, to whom I will ever continue,

Noble Sir, | Your most affectionate and | most humble servant

Jos. Kent

JAMES STANLEY, 7TH EARL OF DERBY
(1607–1651)

The Stanleys were hereditary rulers of the Isle of Man. Stanley commanded a royalist garrison there; when its surrender was demanded by Parliament he sent this defiant letter. He fought for Charles II, was captured after a battle at Wigan, Lancs., in 1651, and was executed on a charge of high treason.

22. To General Henry Ireton, July 1649

Ireton (1611–51) was Cromwell's deputy.

Sir,

I have received your letter with indignation, and with scorn return you this answer, that I cannot but wonder whence you should gather any hopes that I should prove like you, treacherous to my sovereign; since you cannot be ignorant of the manifest candour of my former actings in his late Majesty's service, from which principles of loyalty I am not a whit departed. I scorn your proffer; I disdain your favour; I abhor your treason; and am so far from delivering up this island to your advantage, that I shall keep it to the utmost of my power, and, I hope, to your destruction. Take this for your final answer, and forbear any further solicitations; for if you trouble me with any more messages of this nature, I will burn your paper, and hang up your messenger. This is the immutable resolution, and shall be the undoubted practice, of him who accounts it his chiefest glory to be his Majesty's most loyal and obedient subject,

Derby

MARGARET, DUCHESS OF NEWCASTLE
(1623?–1674)

Margaret Lucas was maid of honour (1643–5) to Queen Henrietta Maria, whom she accompanied to Paris, where in April 1645 she met William Cavendish, Marquis and subsequently Duke of Newcastle, an exiled royalist general, writer, and expert horseman (1592–1676). They married in the same year, and returned to England at the Restoration. Their marriage prospered despite the discrepancy of their ages. An eccentric and romantic figure, she was sometimes ridiculed. She produced many books, including much poetry and several works of philosophy; the most celebrated of her writings are a life of her husband (1667) and an autobiography (1655).

23. To William Cavendish, 1645

My Lord,

I wounder not at my loue, but at yours, becaus the obiet of mine is good. I wish the obiet of yours wer so, yet me thinkes, you should loue nothing that were ill, therefore if I haue any part of good tis your loue makes me so, but loued I nothing elles but you, I loue all that is good, and louing nothing aboue you I haue loues recompens. My lord, I haue not had much expereanse of the world, yet I haue found it such as I could willinly part with it, but sence I knew you, I fear I shall loue it to well, becaus you are in it, and yet, me thinkes, you are not in it, because you are not of it, a strong enchantment, but pray loue so as you may haue me long, for I shall euer be, my lord, your most humble seruant

Margreat Lucas

my lord, they say the qeen comes to morrow

ANNA CARR

Anna Carr was the second wife of Henry Cromwell, cousin of Oliver, and widow of Sir Edward Carr (d. 1640). She was a patient and correspondent of Dr John Symcotts (1592?–1662), who practised in the county of Huntingdon; he had treated Oliver Cromwell, whom he described as *valde melancholicus*, intensely melancholic. Doctors of the time often accepted 'recipes' from ladies who had experience of treating common ailments in families.

24. To Dr Symcotts, c.1650

Mr Symcotes,

I heartily thank you for your choice receipts which I highly esteem of, for, with my poor judgement, I am able to say they are excellent, and truly I never had any of them but the last, which you called the precious water for sores and wounds, and that I had afore.

Now for a bruise take this following:

Common wormwood either green or dry; strip it clean from the stalks; fry them in sweet butter; so as hot as may be apply it outwardly to the bruised place morning and evening. This will cure though the flesh be torn to the bone. Inwardly, take red comfrey leaves and flowers dried and beaten to powder, soaked in warm posset drink, fasting and last to bedward. Do these two till you be well.

If it were for my life I would not use anything else, for with this only I have cured those that carts have gone over, whose water has been gore blood; one that a loaded cart pressed in that sort that blood issued out at all passable places; an old man that was by a bull tossed up, and by the fall lighting on his head and neck, and both made and spat blood; and I think I may safely say first and last a hundred.

I pray God bless it to you in your application. I have sent you the calcined toad. (*Marg.* This is all that came of a great one.) If I can pleasure you, command it, for I will be no less wanting in that than in being

Your assured true friend
Anna Carr

I pray send me word what powder of toads calcined is good for. I only use it to staunch blood, but then I do not calcine them.

(*Marg.* Tell Mr Fullwood I received 3 doz. of vial glasses and 2 doz. pots. Commend me I pray to him and Mrs Fullwood, and tell him I rely upon him for Mr Cromwell's tobacco, hoping he will be careful both for weight and goodness.)

[*Addendum pasted in:*] The use to staunch bleeding is by holding it in the party's hand, so smelling to it; or else hanging it against the pit of the stomach. (*Marg. in the hand of J.S.* Bufo in furno exiccatus.) So ill I am as not able scarcely to write this.

Anna Carr

To my assured good friend Mr Symcotes.

DOROTHY OSBORNE
(1627–1695)

Dorothy Osborne met Sir William Temple (1628–99), the future patron of Swift, in 1648; the families of each had other plans for them, but they were eventually married in 1655, Dorothy having by that time lost her beauty after a bout of smallpox. Her letters to Temple in the years 1652–4, mostly from her father's house in Bedfordshire, were discovered in the nineteenth century; an edition appeared in 1888. Temple's replies have not been preserved.

25. To William Temple, September 1653

S^r,

Pray let not the aprehension that other's say finer things to mee make you [*sic*] letters at all the shorter, for if it were soe; I should not think they did, and soe Long you are safe. My Brother P. indeed do's somtim's send mee letters that may bee Excelent for ought I know, and the more likely because I doe not understand them, but I may say to you (as to a friend) I doe not like them, and have wonderd that my Sister whoe (I may tell you too and you will not think it Vanity in mee) had a great [deale] of Witt and was thought to write as well as most Women in England; never perswaded him to Alter his Stile and make it a litle more Intelligeble. Hee [is] an honnest Gentleman in Earnest, has understanding enough, and was an Excelent husband to two very different Wives, as two good on's could bee; My Sister was a melancholy retir'd woman, and besydes the Company of her husband and her book's, never sought any, but could have spent a life much longer then hers was in lookeing to her house and her Children; This Lady is of a free Jolly humor, loves cards and company and is never more pleased then when she see's a great many Others that are soe too; now with both these hee soe perfectly complyed that tis hard to guesse, wch humor

hee is more inclined to in himself, perhaps to neither, wch makes it soe
much ye more strange. his kindenesse to his first wife, may give him an
Esteem for her Sister, but hee was too much smitten with this Lady to
think of marryeng any body else, and seriously I could not blame him, for
she had, and has yet, great Lovlinesses in her, she was very handsom and
is very good, one may read it in her face at first sight; a Woman that is
hugely Civill to all People, and takes as Generaly as any body that I know.

but not more then my Cousen M: letters doe, wch yet you doe not like
you say, nor I neither i'le swere, and if it bee ignorance in us both we'el
forgive it one another. in my Opinion these great Schollers are not the best
writer's (of Letters I mean, of books perhaps they are). I never had I think
but one letter from Sr Jus: but twas worth twenty of any body's else to
make mee sport, it was the most sublime nonsense that in my life I ever
read, and yet I beleeve hee decended as low as hee could to come neer my
weak understanding; twill bee noe Complement after this to say I like your
letters in themselv's, not as they come from one that is not indifferent to
mee; but seriously I doe. all Letters mee thinks should bee free and Easy
as ones discourse, not studdyed, as an Oration, nor made up of hard words
like a Charme; tis an admirable thing to see how some People will labour
to finde out term's that may Obscure a plaine sence, like a gentleman I
knew, whoe would never say the weather grew cold, but that Winter began
to salute us. I have noe patience for such Coxcomb's and cannot blame an
old Uncle of mine that threw the Standish at his mans head because he
writt a letter for him where instead of sayeing (as his Master bid him) that
hee would have writ himself but that hee had the Goute in his hand; hee
sayed that the Goute in his hand would not permitt him to put pen to
paper; the ffellow thought hee had mended it Mightily and that putting
pen to paper was much better then plaine writeing. I have noe Patience
neither for these Translatours of Romances; I mett with Polexandre and
L'Illustre Bassa, both soe disguised that I who am theire old acquaintance
hardly knew them, besydes that they were still soe much french in words
and Phrases that twas imposible for one that understood not french to
make any thing of them. if Poore Prazimene bee in the same dresse, I
would not see her for the worlde, she has sufferd enough besydes; I never
saw but 4 Tomes of her and was told the Gentleman that writt her Storry
dyed when those were finnish'd, I was very sorry for it I remember, for I
liked soe farr as I had seen of it Extreamly. is it not my Good Lord of
Monmouth or some such honourable personage that presents her to the
English Lady's? I have heard many People wonder how hee spends his
Estate, I beleeve hee undo's himself with Printing his Translations, nobody
else will undergoe the Charge because they never hope to sell enough of

them to pay themselv's withall; I was lookeing tother day in a book of his where hee Translates Pipeur, a Piper and twenty words more that are as false as this. My Lord Broghill sure will give us somthing worth the reading; My Lord Saye I am tolde has writ a Romance Since his retirement in the Isle of Lundee, and Mr Waller they say is makeing one of Our Warr's, wch if hee do's not mingle with a great deal of pleasing fiction cannot bee very diverting sure, the Subject is soe sad.

but all this is nothing to my comeing to Towne You'le say, tis confest, and that I was willing as long as I could to avoyde sayeing any thing when I had nothing to say worth your knoweing. I am still Obliged to wayte my Brother P. and his Lady's comeing, I had a letter from him this week wch I will send you that you may see what hopes hee gives. as litle Roome as I have left too, I must tell you what a present I had made mee to day, two the finest Young Ireish Greyhounds that ere I saw, a Gentleman that serv's the Generall sent them mee; they are newly come over and sent for by H. C. hee tels mee, but not how hee gott them for mee. however I am glad I have them and much the more because it dispenses wth a very unfitt imployment that your father out of his kindenesse to you & his Civility to mee was content to take upon him.

Good Sister

I am very sorrie to heare of the losse of our good Brother whose short time gives us a sad example of o^r fraile condition. But I will say the lesse, knowing whom I write to; whose religion & wisedome is a present stay & support in all worldly accidents.

Tis long since wee resolved to have given you a visit, & have releived you of my Daughter. But I have had ye following of a most laborious affaire, which hath cost mee the travelling, though in o^r owne Country still, fifty miles a weeke; & have bin lesse at home then elsewhere ever since I came from London: which hath vext mee ye more in regard I have bin detayned from ye desires I had of being with you before this time. Such entertainment however must all those have that have to doe with such a purse-strong & willfull person as Sr Edw. Hales. This next weeke being Michaelmas weeke wee shall end all, & I bee at liberty I hope to consider my owne contentments. In ye meane time I knowe nott what excuses to make for ye trouble I have putt you to already, of which I growe to bee ashamed; & should much more bee soe, if I did not knowe you to bee as Good as you are Faire: in both which regards I have a great Honour to be esteemed

My good Sister | Your faithfull Brother & Servant
Thomas Peyton

[Written at back of Sir T. Peyton's letter]

Nothing that is paper can scape mee when I have time to write and tis to you; But that I am not willing to Excite your Envy, I would tell you how many Letters I have dispatch'd since I Ended yours, and if I could shew them you, twould bee a certaine Cure for it, for they are all very short on's and most of them meerly complement wch I am sure you care not for. I had forgott in my Other to tell you what Jane requir's for the Sattisfaction of what you confesse you owe her, You must promise her to bee merry and not to take Colde when you are at ye Tennis Court, for there shee hear's you were founde.

Because you mention my Lord Broghill and his witt I have sent you some of his Verses. My B. urged them against mee one day in a dispute where hee would needs make mee confesse that noe Passion could bee long lived and that such as were most in love forgott that ever they had bin soe within a twelve month after they were Marryed, and in Earnest the want of Examples to bring for the Contreary puzled mee a litle, soe that I was faine to bring out these Pittifull Verses of my Lord Biron to his wife, wch was soe poore an Agument [*sic*] that I was e'en ashamed on't my self, and hee quickly Laught mee out of Countenance with sayeing they were Just such as a marryed mans flame would produce, and a wife inspire. I send you a Love Letter too, wch simple as you see it was sent in very good Earnest, and to a person of quality as I was told. if you read it when you goe to bed twill certainly make you sleep, aproved.

I am Yours

Finer things] in an earlier letter she mentioned that a Mr Freeman had said fine things to her; Temple must have taken this up in his reply.   My brother P.] Thomas Peyton, brother-in-law.   Cousen M] Molle.   Sr Jus] Sir Justinian Isham, another suitor.   Polexandre] romance by Marin le Roy de Gomberville, 1632, translated 1647.   L'Illustre Bassa] romance by Georges de Scudéry, 1641, translated 1652.   Prazimene] by Le Maire, 1643. Monmouth] a translator, apparently a bad one.   Broghill] Roger Boyle, third son of the Earl of Cork, later Earl of Orrery, dramatist; author of the huge romance *Parthenissa*, 1654. Saye] Lord Saye and Sele; the romance is not known.   Waller] Sir Edmund Waller, the poet; no romance is known.   H. C.] Henry Cromwell, fourth son of the Protector—another suitor—who procured her these dogs from Ireland. She had asked Temple to do likewise, through his father; the favour was no longer needed.   Brother] Robin Osborne, died aged 27 on 26 Aug.   Hales] died in 1654; a difficult man, who lived close to Peyton.   Jane] the maid who had sent Temple a box containing quince marmalade.   Biron] John, Lord Byron, d. 1652; not known as a poet.   Aproved] 'I've tried the prescription and recommend it.'

SIR JOHN EVELYN

(1620–1706)

Evelyn was a founder-member of the new Royal Society and a man of many accomplishments—a virtuoso and the friend of other virtuosi, including Pepys. He wrote a celebrated Diary but also published on gardening, sculpture and architecture. Of his six sons only one survived infancy.

26. To Sir Richard Browne, 14 February 1658

Browne (d. 1669) had been a parliamentary general who changed sides and welcomed the returning Charles II. He was Lord Mayor of London in 1660. Evelyn married his only daughter Mary. Their son Richard, who died aged 5 on 27 Jan. 1658, was regarded as exceptionally precocious.

S^r,

By the reverse of this medall, you will perceive how much reason I had to be affraid of my felicity, and how greatly it did import to me to do all that I could to prevent what I have apprehended, what I deserved, and what now I feele. God has taken from us that deare childe, y^r grandson, your godsonn, and with him all the joy and satisfaction that could be derived from the greatest hopes. A losse, so much the more to be deplored, as our contentments were extraordinary, and the indications of his future perfections as faire & legible as, yet, I ever saw, or read of in one so very young: you have, Sir, heard so much of this, that I may say it with the lesse crime & suspicion. And indeed his whole life was from the beginning so greate a miracle, that it were hard to exceede in the description of it, and which I should here yet attempt, by sum'ing up all the prodigies of it, and what a child at 5 yeares old (for he was little more) is capable of, had I not given you so many minute and particular accounts of it, by several expresses, when I then mentioned those things with the greatest joy, which now I write with as much sorrow and amasement. But so it is, that has pleased God to dispose of him, and that blossome (fruit, rather I may say) is fallen; a six days quotidian having deprived us of him; an accident that has made so greate a breache in all my contentments, as I do never hope to see repaired: because we are not in this life to be fed with wonders: and that I know you will hardly be able to support the affliction & the losse, who beare so greate a part in every thing that concernes me. But thus we must be reduced when God sees good, and I submitt; since I had, therefore, this blessing for a punishment, & that I might feele the effects of my great unworthynesse. But I have begged of God that I might pay the fine heare, and if to such belonged the kingdome of heaven, I have one depositum there. *Dominus dedit, Dominus abstulit*: blessed be his name: since without that consideration it were impossible to support it: for the stroke is so severe, that I find nothing in all philosophy capable to allay the impression of it, beyond that of cutting the channell and dividing with our friends, who really sigh on our behalfe, and mingle with our greater sorrows in accents of piety and compassion, which is all that can yet any ways alleviate the sadness of, Deare Sir, Y^r &c.

Quotidian] a fever that recurs daily.   *Dominus dedit, Dominus abstulit*] the Lord gave, and
the Lord hath taken away (Job 1: 21).

27. To Dr Christopher Wren, 4 April 1665

The letter concerns the surviving son John (1655–99). The 'Parallel' was Roland Fréat's *A Parallel of the Ancient Architecture with the Modern*, translated by Evelyn (1664).

S^r,

You may please to remember that some tyme since I begg'd a favour of you in behalfe of my little boy: he is now susceptible of instruction, a pleasant, and (though I speake it) a most ingenious and pregnant child. My designe is to give him good education; he is past many initial difficulties, and conquers all things with incredible industry: do me that eternal obligation, as to enquire out and recom'end me some young man for a preceptor. I will give him £20 per ann. sallary, and such other accom'odations as shall be no ways disagreeable to an ingenuous spirit; and possibly I may do him other advantages: in all cases he will find his condition with us easy, his scholar a delight, & the conversation not to be despised: this obliges me to wish he may not be a morose, or severe person, but of an agreeable temper. The qualities I require are, that he be a perfect Grecian, and if more than vulgarly mathematical, so much the more accomplish'd for my designe: myne owne defects in ye Greeke tongue and knowledge of its usefulnesse, obliges me to mention that particular with an extraordinary note: in sum I would have him as well furnish'd as might be for the laying of a permanent & solid foundation: the boy is capable beyond his yeares; and if you encounter one thus qualified, I shall receive it amongst the greate good fortunes of my life that I obtain'd it by the benefit of y^r friendship, for which I have ever had so perfect an esteeme. There is no more to be said, but that when you have found the person, you direct him im'ediately to me, that I may receive, and value him.

S^r, I am told by S^r Jo: Denham that you looke towards France this somer: be assur'd I will charge you wth some addresses to friends of mine there, that shall exceedingly cherish you; and though you will stand in no neede of my recom'endations, yet I am confident you will not refuse the offer of those civilities which I shall bespeake you.

There has layne at Dr Needham's a copy of ye Parallel bound up for you, & long since design'd you, which I shall entreate you to accept; not as a recompence of your many favours to mee, much lesse a thing in the least assistant to you (who are y^rselfe a master), but as a toaken of my respect, as the booke itselfe is of the affection I beare to an art which you so happily cultivate.

Dear S^r, I am | Y^r &c.

JOHN STRYPE
(1643–1737)

Strype was an ecclesiastical historian. His father was an immigrant from Brabant, with a business in Petticoat Lane. Here he reports his early days at Cambridge.

28. To his mother, October? 1662

Good Mother,

Yours of the 24th instant I gladly received, expecting indeed one a Week before, but I understand both by Waterson and yourself of your indisposednesse then to write. The reason you receive this no sooner is, because I had a mind (knowing of this honest woman's setting out so suddenly for London from hence, and her businesse laying so neer to Petticote Lane,) that she should deliver it into your hands, that so you may the better, and more fully heare of me, and know how it fareth with me. She is my laundresse; make her welcome, and tell her how you would have my linen washed, as you were saying in your Letter. I am very glad to hear that you and my brother Johnson do agree so well, that I believe you account an unusual courtesie, that he should have you out to the Cake-House. However, pray Mother, be careful of yourself and do not over-walke yourself, for that is wont to bring you upon a sick bed. I hear also my brother Sayer is often a visitor: truly I am glad of it. I hope your Children may be comforts to you now you are growing old. Remember me back again most kindly to my brother Sayer.

Concerning the taking up of my Things, 'tis true I gave one shilling too much in the hundred: but why I gave so much, I thought indeed I had given you an account in that same letter: but it seems I have not. The only reason is, because they were a Scholar's goods: it is common to make them pay one shilling more than the Town's people. Dr Pearson himself payed so, and several other lads in this College: and my Tutor told me they would expect so much of me, being a Scholar: and I found it so.

Do not wonder so much at our Commons: they are more than many Colleges have. Trinity itself (where Herring and Davies are) which is the famousest College in the University, have but three half-pence. We have roast meat, dinner and supper, throughout the weeke; and such meate as you know I not use to care for; and that is Veal: but now I have learnt to eat it. Sometimes, neverthelesse, we have boiled meat, with pottage; and beef and mutton, which I am glad of; except Fridays and Saturdays, and sometimes Wednesdays; which days we have Fish at dinner, and tansy or pudding for supper. Our parts then are slender enough. But there is this remedy; we may retire unto the Butteries, and there take a half-penny loafe and butter or cheese; or else to the Kitchen, and take there what the Cook hath. But, for my part, I am sure, I never visited the Kitchen yet, since I have been here, and the Butteries but seldom after meals; unlesse for a Ciza, that is for a Farthing-worth of Small-Beer: so that lesse than a Peny in Beer doth serve me a whole Day. Neverthelesse sometimes we have Exceedings: then we have two or three Dishes (but that is very rare): otherwise never but one: so that a Cake and a Cheese would be very welcome to me: and a Neat's tongue, or some such thing, if it would not require too much money. If you do intend to send me any thing, do not send it yet, until you hear further of me: for I have many things to send for, which may all I hope be put into that Box you have at home: but what they are, I shall give you an account of hereafter, when I would have them sent: and that is, when I have got me a Chamber: for as yet, I am in a Chamber that doth not at all please me. I have thoughts of one, which is a very handsome one, and one pair of stairs high, and that looketh into the Master's garden. The price is but 20ˢ per annum, ten whereof a Knight's son, and lately admitted into this College, doth pay: though he did not come till about Midsummer, so that I shall have but 10ˢ to pay a year: besides my income, which may be about 40ˢ or thereabouts. Mother, I kindly thank you for your Orange pills you sent me. If you are not too straight of money, send me some such thing by the woman, and a pound or two of Almonds and Raisons. But first ask her if she will carry them, or if they be not too much trouble to her. I do much approve of your agreeing with the Carrier quarterly: he was indeed telling me of it, that you had agreed with him for it: and I think he means both yours and mine. Make your bargain sure with him.

I understand by your Letter that you are very inquisitive to know how things stand with me here. I believe you may be well enough satisfied by the Woman. My breakings-out are now all gone. Indeed I was afraid at my first coming it would have proved the Itch: but I am fairly rid on it: but I fear I shall get it, let me do what I can: for there are many here that have it cruelly. Some of them take strong purges that would kill a horse, weeks together for it, to get it away, and yet are hardly rid of it. At my first Coming I laid alone: but since, my Tutor desired me to let a very clear lad lay with me, and an Alderman's son of Colchester, which I could not deny, being newly come: he hath laid with me now for almost a fortnight, and will do till he can provide himself with a Chamber. I have been with all my Acquaintance, who have entreated me very courteously, especially Jonathan Houghton. I went to his Chamber the Friday night I first came, and there he made me stay and sup with him, and would have had me laid with him that night, and was extraordinary kind to me. Since, we have been together pretty often. He excused himselfe, that he did not come to see me before he went; and that he did not write to me since he had been come. He hath now, or is about obtaining, £10 more from the College.

We go twice a day to Chapel; in the morning about 7, and in the Evening about 5. After we come from Chapel in the morning, which is towards 8, we go to the Butteries for our breakfast, which usually is five Farthings; an halfepenny loaf and butter, and a cize of beer. But sometimes I go to an honest House near the College, and have a pint of milk boiled for my breakfast.

Truly I was much troubled to hear that my Letter for Ireland is not yet gone. I wish if Mr Jones is not yet gone, that it might be sent some other way. Indeed I wish I could see my cousin James Bonnell here within three or four years: for I believe our University is less strict to observe lads that do not in every point conforme, than theirs at Dublin: though ours be bad enough. Pray remember me to my Uncle, and all my friends there, when you write. Remember me to my cousin James Knox. I am glad he is recovered from his dangerous sickness, whatsoever it is; for I cannot make any thing of it, as you have written it. And thus, for want of Paper, I end, desiring heartily to be remembered to all my Friends. Excuse me to my Brother and Sister that they have not heard from me yet. Next week I hope to write to them both. Excuse my length, I thought I would answer your Letter to the full.

I remaine your dutiful Son,
J. Strijp

These for his honoured Mother
    Mrs Hester Stryp widdow,
    dwelling in Petticoat Lane, right over against the Five Ink-Hornes, without Bishops-Gate, in London.

Cake-House] a shop where cakes are sold.   Tansy] omelette or pudding flavoured with the juice of the potentilla or similar plant.   Ciza] assize or size—a measure of food or drink.   Exceedings] extra rations on festive occasions.   Orange] dried orange peel (?).

J. TILLISON

29. To Dr Sancroft, 14 September 1665

William Sancroft (1617–93), archbishop of Canterbury, at this time dean of St Paul's. He had left London to avoid the plague. Later he worked with Wren on the new cathedral.

Reverend Sir,

We are in good hopes that God in his mercy will put a stop to this sad calamity of Sickness; but the desolation of the City is very great. That heart is either steel or stone that will not lament this sad Visitation, and will not bleed for those unutterable sorrows.

It is a time, God knows, that one woe courts another; those that are sick are in extreme sorrow; the poor are in need; those that are in health are in fear of infection on the one side, and the wicked inventions of hellish rebellious spirits to put us in an uproar on the other side.

What eye would not weep to see so many habitations uninhabited; the poor sick not visited; the hungry not fed; the Grave not satisfied! Death stares us continually in the face in every infected person that passeth by us; in every coffin which is daily and hourly carried along the streets. The bells never cease to put us in mind of our mortality.

The custom was, in the beginning, to bury the dead in the night only; now, both night and day will hardly be time enough to do it.

For the last week, mortality did too apparently evidence that, that the dead was piled in heaps above ground for some hours together, before either time could be gained or place to bury them in.

The Quakers (as we are informed) have buried in their piece of ground a thousand for some weeks together last past.

Many are dead in Ludgate, Newgate, and Christ Church Hospital, and many other places about the town which are not included in the bill of mortality.

The disease itself (as is acknowledged by our practitioners in physic) was more favourable in the beginning of the contagion; now more fierce and violent; and they themselves do likewise confess to stand amazed to meet with so many various symptoms which they find amongst their patients. One week the general distempers are botches and boils; the next week as clear-skinned as may be; but death spares neither. One week, full of spots and tokens; and perhaps the succeeding, none at all. Now taken with a vomiting and looseness, and within two or three days almost a general raging madness. One while patients used to linger four or five days, at other times not forty-eight hours; and at this very time we find it more quick than ever it was. Many are sick, and few escape. Where it has had its fling, there it decreases; where it has not been long, there it increases. It reigned most heretofore in alleys, &c. now it domineers in the open streets. The poorer sort was most afflicted; now the richer bear a share.

Captain Colchester is dead. Fleetham and all his family are clearly swept away, except one maid. Dr Burnett, Dr Glover, and one or two more of the College of Physicians, with Dr O' Dowd, which was licensed by my Lord's Grace of Canterbury, some surgeons, apothecaries, and Johnson the chemist, died all very suddenly. Some say (but God forbid that I should report it for truth) that these, in a consultation together, if not all, yet the greatest part of them, attempted to open a dead corpse which was full of the tokens; and being in hand with the dissected body, some fell down dead immediately, and others did not outlive the next day at noon.

All is well and in safety at your house, God be thanked. Upon Tuesday last I made it my day's work to kindle fires in every room of the house where I could do it, and aired all the bedclothes and bedding at the fires, and so let them all lie abroad until this morning; the feather bed in the back chamber was almost spoiled with the heavy weight of carpets and other things upon it. I am afraid I have been too tedious, and therefore beg your pardon and take my leave, who am,

Reverend Sir, | your most faithful humble servant,

Jo. Tillison

Brimstone, hops, pepper, and frankincense, &c. I use to fume the rooms with.

For yourself. [For your eyes only?]

Mary Evelyn

(1635–1709)

Mary Evelyn was the daughter of Sir Richard Browne and the wife of John Evelyn (see above, Letter 26).

30. To her son, c.1673

I haue received y^r letter, and request for a supply of mony; but none of those you mention which were bare effects of y^r duty. If you were so desirous to answer our expectations as you pretend to be, you would give those tutors and overseers you think so exact over you lesse trouble then I feare they have with you. Much is to be wished in yor behalfe: that y^r temper were humble and tractable, y^r inclinations virtuous, and that from choice not compulsion you make an honnest man. Whateuer object of vice comes before you, should haue the same effect in y^r mind of dislike and aversion that drunkenesse had in the youth of Sparta when their slaves were presented to them in that brutish condition, not only from the deformity of such a sight, but from a motive beyond theirs, the hope of a future happinesse, which those rigorous heathens in morall virtue had little prospect of, finding no reward for virtue but in virtue itselfe. You are not too young to know that lying, defrauding, swearing, disobedience to parents and persons in authority, are offences to God and man: that debauchery is injurious to growth, health, life, and indeed to the pleasures of life: therefore now that you are turning from child to man endeavour to follow the best precepts, and chuse such wayes as may render you worthy of praise and love. You are assured of y^r Fathers care and my tendernesse: no mark of it shall be wanting at any time to confirme it to you, with this reserve only, that you strive to deserve kindnesse by a sincere honest proceeding, and not flatter y^r selfe that you are good whilst you only appeare to be so. Fallacies will only passe in schools. When you throughly weigh these considerations, I hope you will apply them to your owne advantage, as well as to our infinite satisfaction. I pray dayly God would inspire you with his grace, and blesse you.

I am, | Y^r louing mother,
M. Evelyn

CHRISTOPHER HATTON
(1632–1706)

Hatton was a soldier and a scholar—he presented the Bodleian Library with valuable Anglo-Saxon manuscripts.

31. *To his brother, 25 May 1676*

Here hath of late generall outrages been committed by our military officers at Plymouth. Coll. Piper, ye Deputy Governor, hath been basely assaulted by one Morris, a cap^t in S^r Ch. Littletons regiment, and soe wounded y^t it is beleeved he will not recover of his wounds. Morris invited ye Coll. and one Capt Morgan to a collation, and, Morgan profering to sell a horse to Morris, he asked him whither he wou'd warrant him sound. He s^d: 'Yes, upon his reputation.' 'What!' said Morris, 'upon such a reputation as our

Govr sold his?' (It seemes Coll. Piper had sold a horse, wch he warranted sound but happened to prove otherwise.) Herupon Piper asked Morris whither or noe he questioned his repuatation, wch certainly was as good as Morris his. Wherupon Morris giving him very foul language, Piper withdrew, telling [him] he supposed he wase in drinke, and y^t, when he wase sober, he wou'd be of another mind. Morris followed him, and, before Piper cou'd draw his sword, Morris run him through the thigh, and, making a 2 pass at him, Piper, putting by ye thrust wth his hand, is soe wounded in ye hand it is thought, if he recovers, he will loose ye use of his fingers. After this, Piper's man, coming to his masters assistance, wase wounded by Morris, who still thrusting at Piper, he catched hold of his sword and broke it short of; but, having lost much blood, he fell down, and Morris attempted to make his escape, but wase taken and committed to ye gaole at Plymouth. At Chichester, very lately, a cornet in my L^d of Oxfords regiment, quarelling wth a country gentleman, he challenged ye country gentleman into ye feild, who fought and disarmed ye cornet; after w^h, they were in appearance good friends and went together to ye tavern, wher ye cornet left him and went into ye town, called his corporal and one of his soldiers, whom he met in ye streete, to him, and commanded them to follow him; and he went to ye place wher he left ye gentleman, and, finding him ther, commanded the corporal to disarme him; but ye corporal, distrusting his command, he threatned him, and ye gentleman himselfe tooke his sword in ye scabbard, telling ye cornet y^t, to prevent his fury against his corporal, he wou'd disarme himself, and y^t he looked upon him as a gentleman who wou'd not doe a base act, and therefore he rendred him his sword, wch ye cornet snatched out of his hand and immediately run him through wth it, soe y^t he dyed on ye place, and ye cornet wase seized on and sent to ye county goale.

Y^r truly affectionat Brother to serve you,

C. Hatton

COTTON MATHER
(1663–1728)

As the gifted eldest son of Increase Mather, so powerful in Boston, Mather had great influence and defended the Salem witch trials. He shared the prejudice of New England Congregationalist Puritans against the Quakers.

32. To the Aged and Beloved, Mr John Higginson, 1682

William Penn (1644–1718) founded Pennsylvania in 1681. The New England colonies, except for Rhode Island, persecuted Quakers attempting to enter their territories, as they had done persistently since the 1650s.

There be now at sea a ship called Welcome, which has on board 100 or more of the heretics and malignants called Quakers, with W Penn, who is the chief scamp, at the head of them. The General Court has accordingly given sacred orders to Master Malachi Huscott, of the brig Porpoise, to waylay the said Welcome slyly as near the Cape of Cod as may be, and make captive the said Penn and his ungodly crew, so that the Lord may be glorified and not mocked on the soil of this new country with the heathen worship of these people. Much spoil can be made of selling the whole lot to Barbados, where slaves fetch good prices in rum and sugar, and we shall not only do the Lord great good by punishing the wicked, but we shall make great good for His Minister and people.

Yours in the bowels of Christ,
Cotton Mather

SIR JAMES DICK
(1644–1728)

Dick was Lord Provost of Edinburgh, 1679–81. He lost, on a charge of bribery, his job as Commissioner for Edinburgh.

33. To Mr Ellies, 9 May 1682

The wreck occurred on 5 May. Less sympathetic accounts suggest that the future James II was more anxious to save his 'dogs and priests' than anybody else, and swimmers trying to board the boat, said not to be full, were thrust off.

Dear Sir,

Upon Sunday, at eight o'clock at night, his Royal Highness with his retinue arrived safe here, there being a most sad disaster upon the Saturday before, at eleven o'clock in the morning; the man of war called the Gloster, Sir John Barrie Captain, wherein his Highness was, and a great retinue of noblemen and gentlemen, whereof I was one, the said ship did strike in pieces and did wholly sink in a Bank of sand called the Lemon and Ore, about twelve leagues from Yarmouth. This was occasioned by the wrong calcul and ignorance of a Pilot, and put us all in such consternation that we knew not what to do: the Duke and all that were with him being in bed when she first struck. The helm having broke, the man was killed by the force thereof at the first shock.

When the Duke got his clothes on and inquired how things stood, she had nine feet water in her hold, and the sea fast coming in at the gun-ports; the seamen and passengers were not at command, every man studying his own safety. This forced the Duke to go out at the large window of the cabin where his little boat was ordered quietly to attend him, lest the passengers and seamen should have thronged so in upon him, as to overset his boat. This was accordingly so conducted as that none but Earl Winton and the President of the Session, with two of the bed-chamber men, went with him. They were forced to draw their swords to hold people off.

We seeing they were gone, did cause tackle out with great difficulty the Ship's boat, wherein the Earl of Perth got, and then I went by jumping off the shrouds; the Earl of Middleton immediately after me did jump in upon my shoulders; withal there came the Laird of Touch with several others, besides the seamen that were to row, which was thought a sufficient number for her loading, considering there was going so great a sea, occasioned by the wind at North East; and we seeing that at the Duke's boat side, there was one overwhelmed by reason of the greatness of the sea, which drowned the whole in her except two men, whom we saw riding on her keel. This made us desire to be gone, but before we were loose, there leaped from the shrouds about twenty or twenty-four seamen in upon us, which made all the spectators and ourselves to think we would sink, and all having given us over for lost, did hinder an hundred more from leaping in upon us.

With those that were left was Lord Roxburgh and Laird Hopton, and Mr Littledel, Roxburgh's servant, Doctor Livingston, and the President of the Sessions' man, and my servant. They all being at the place when I jumped would not follow, because it seems they concluded it more safe to stay in the vessel than to expose themselves to our hazard; all which persons in an instant were washed off and drowned.

There will be perished in this disaster above two hundred persons, for I reckon there were two hundred and fifty seamen, and I am sure there were eighty noblemen, gentlemen, and their servants; my computation was that there were three hundred and thirty in all, of which I cannot learn that a hundred and thirty are found alive.

Our difficulties and hazards that were in this boat were wonderful. If the rest had not thought us all dead men, I am sure many more would have jumped in upon us. We were so thronged we had no room to stand, and when we were forcing ourselves from the ship, she being sinking by degrees all the time; and besides the surfs were so boisterous that we were like to be struck in pieces upon the wreck so sinking, it was not but with great difficulty that we forced out the boat from the ship; and when we came to row to the nearest yacht, the waves were such, we being overloaded, that every moment we thought to have been drowned; and being about midway to the yachts, there were a great many swimming for their lives, who caught a dead gripe of our boat, holding up their heads above the water and crying for help; which hinderance was put off and their hands loosed, by telling them they would both lose themselves and us; yet this would not do to make them loose their gripe, till they were forced off by several in our boat, except one that took hold of me, whom I caused catch into the boat, lest I should have been pulled out by him; and when it pleased God to bring us wonderfully to one of the yacht's side, being not less than a quarter of a mile distant from our ship, they not daring to come nearer by reason of the sand bank upon which we were wrecked; and if we had not shot off guns, shewing them our distress, the other men of war that were immediately following would have met with the same disaster; but they immediately bore off. The four yachts came as near as they could, and put off their boats to help us, but all that could be done could not prevent this great loss of about two hundred men. I was in my gown and slippers, lying in bed, when she first struck, and did escape in that condition; and when unexpectedly and wonderfully we came to the yacht's side, called Captain Saunders, we were like to be crushed to pieces by it, which by reason of the great sea was like to run us down.

At last a rope was cast, which was so managed that we were brought to the lee side, then every man climbed for his life, and so did I, taking hold of a rope, and made shift upon the side till I came within men's reach, and was hauled in; and I then looked back but could not see one bit of our Great Ship above water, but about a Scots ell long of the staff upon which the Royal Standard stood; for with her striking she had come off the sand bank which was but three fathoms, and her draught was eighteen feet. There was eighteen fathoms water upon each side when she struck, and so did sink in the deepest place. Now if she had continued upon the three fathoms, and broke in pieces there, all would have had time to have saved themselves; but such was the misfortune, that she was wholly overwhelmed, and all washed into the sea that were upon her decks. There would have been relief by boats if she had stood half an hour longer.

So to conclude this melancholy account, all the above persons, our countrymen, that were of respect, are as I have told. Of Englishmen of respect there were lost Lord O'Brien and Lord Hyde's brother, who was lieutenant of the ship; and a number of noblemen and gentlemen's servants, which I cannot name. I can hardly speak with any that were aboard with the Duke but they have lost of servants more or less. God make me thankful for this wonderful deliverance.

I believe I shall have trouble now that both my Lord Roxburgh and his man are lost, to recover payment of these bills: all my clothes and papers are lost, having nothing saved but the twenty guineas which were in my little pocket with my watch, and the little box with my wife's ring and necklace; but for my papers, I rolled them up in a handkerchief, and put them off me, so that both the King's letter for the £1,200 sterling, and the accompt I filed with you, are gone.

Yesterday his Royal Highness called the King's Council, and there the King's will was declared as to his Chancellor, who was the President of the Session; my Lord Queensberry for Treasurer, and Lord Perth Justice-General which Queensberry had before.

Notwithstanding the disaster his Highness met with in this last sea voyage, yet he is within five or six days, with his Duchess and the Lady Anne, to take shipping for London.

James Dick

SIR GEORGE ETHEREGE
(1634?–1691)

Etherege was a Restoration dramatist (*The Man of Mode*, 1676) and diplomat, and a friend of Rochester and Sedley. He was the envoy of James II at Ratisbon, where, according to *The Dictionary of National Biography*, 'he continued his habits of squalid debauchery'.

34. To the Duke of Buckingham, March 1687?

Etherege's editor dates this letter before 19 May 1687, by which time Etherege knew of Buckingham's death the previous month; it follows that the third paragraph is a later insertion, written not later than the spring of 1688, the date of the plays by Durfey and Shadwell (*Three Dukes of Dunstable* and *The Squire of Alsatia*) there mentioned.

My Lord,

I never enjoy my self so much as when I can steal a few Moments, from the Hurry of public Business, to write to my Friends in England; and as there is none there to whom I pay a profounder Respect than to your Grace, wonder not if I afford my self the Satisfaction of conversing with you by way of Letters, (the only Relief I have left me to support your Absence at this distance) as often as I can find an opportunity.

You may guess by my last, whether I don't pass my Time very comfortably here; forc'd as I am by my Character, to spend the better part of my time in Squabling and Deliberating with Persons of Beard and Gravity, how to preserve the Ballance of Christendome, which would go well enough of its self, if the Divines and Ministers of Princes would let it alone: And when I come home spent and weary from the Diet, I have no Lord D[orse]t's, or Sir Charles S[edle]y's to sport away the Evening with; no Madam I——, or my Lady A——'s; in short, none of those kind charming Creatures

London affords, in whose Embraces I might make my self amends for so many Hours murdered in impertinent Debates; so that not to magnifie my sufferings to your Grace, they really want a greater stock of Christian Patience to support them, than I can pretend to be Master of.

I have been long enough in this Town (one would think) to have made Acquaintance enough with Persons of both Sexes, so as never to be at a loss how to pass the few vacant Hours I can allow my self: But the terrible Drinking that accompanies all our Visits, hinders me from Conversing with the Men so often as I would otherwise doe; and the German Ladies are so intollerably reserv'd and virtuous, (with Tears in my eyes I speak it to your Grace) that 'tis next to an impossibility to carry on an Intrigue with them: A Man has so many Scruples to conquer, and so many Difficulties to surmount, before he can promise himself the least Success, that for my part I have given over all Pursuits of this Nature: Besides, there is so universal a Spirit of Censoriousness reigns in this Town, that a Man and a Woman cannot be seen at Ombre or Picquet together, but 'tis immediately concluded some other Game has been played between them; and as this renders all manner of Access to the Ladies almost impracticable, for fear of exposing their Reputation to the Mercy of their ill-natur'd Neighbours, so it makes an innocent Piece of Gallantry often pass for a criminal Correspondence.

So that to deal freely with your Grace among so many noble and wealthy Families as we have in this Town, I can only pretend to be truly acquainted but with one: The Gentleman's Name was Monsieur Hoffman, a frank, hearty, jolly Companion; his Father, one of the most eminent Wine-merchants of the City, left him a considerable Fortune, which he improved by marrying a French Jeweller's Daughter of Lyons: To give you his Character in short, he was a sensible ingenious Man, and had none of his Country Vices, which I impute to his having travelled abroad and seen Italy, France, and England. His Lady is a most accomplish'd ingenious Person, and notwithstanding she is come in to a Place where so much Formality and Stiffness are practiced, keeps up all the Vivacity, and Air, and good Humor of France.

I had been happy in my Acquaintance with this Family for some Months, when an ill favour'd Accident rob'd me of the greatest Happiness I had hitherto enjoy'd in Germany the loss of which I can never sufficiently regret. Monsieur Hoffman, about three Weeks ago, going to make merry with some Friends (at a Village some three Leagues from this Place) upon the Danube, by the Unskillfulness or Negligence of the Watermen, the Boat, wherin he was, unfortunately chanced to over-set, and of some twenty Persons, not one escaped to bring home the News but a Boy that miraculously saved himself by holding fast to the Rudder, and so by the Rapidity of the Current was cast upon the other Shore.

I was sensibly afflicted at the Destiny of my worthy Friend, and so indeed were all that had the Honour of knowing him; but his Wife took on so extravagantly, that she (in a short Time) was the only talk both of City and Country; she refus'd to admit any Visits from her nearest Relations, her Chamber, her Antichamber, and Pro-antichamber were hung with Black, nay the very Candles, her Fans, and Tea-table wore the Livery of Grief; she refus'd all manner of Sustenance, and was so averse to the Thoughts of Living, that she talk'd of nothing but Death; in short, you may tell your injenious Friend Monsieur de Saint Evremont, that Petronius's Ephesian Matron, to whose Story he has done so much Justice in his noble Translation, was only a Type of our more obstinate, as well as unhappy German Widow.

About a Fortnight after this cruel Loss (for I thought it would be Labour lost to attack her Grief in its first Vehemence) I thought my self obliged, in Point of Honour and Gratitude to the Memory of my deceased Friend, to make her a small Visit, and condole her Ladyship upon this unhappy Occasion: And tho' I had been told that she had refused to see several Persons who had gon to wait on her with the same Errand, yet I presumed so much upon the Friendship her late Husband had always express'd for me, (not to mention the particular Civilities I had received from her self) as to think I wou'd be admitted to have a sight of her: Accordingly I came to her House, sent up my Name, and word was immediately brought me, that if I pleas'd I might go up to her.

When I came into the Room, I fancy'd my self in the Territories of Death, every thing looked so gloomy, so dismal, and so melancholly. There was a grave Lutheran Minister with her, that omitted no Arguments to bring her to a more composed and more Christian Disposition of Mind. Madam (says he) you don't consider that by abandoning your self thus to Despair, you actually rebel against Providence; I cann't help it, (says she) Providence may e'en thank it self, for laying so insupportable a Load upon me: O fye, Madam, (cries the other) this is down right impiety; What would you say now, if Heaven should punish it by some more exemplary Visitation? That is impossible, replies the Lady sighing, and since it has rob'd me of the onely Delight I had in this World, the only Favour it can do me is to level a Thunderbolt at my Head, and put an end to all my Sufferings. The Parson finding her in this extravagant Strain, and seeing no likelihood of Perswading her to come to a better Temper, got up from his Seat and took his leave of her.

It came to my turn now to try whether I was not capable of comforting her, and being convinced by so late an Instance that Arguments brought from Religion were not like to work any extraordinary Effects upon her, I resolved to attack her Ladiship in a more sensible part, and represent to her

the great inconveniences (not which her Soul, but) her Body received from
this inordinate Sorrow.

Madam, saies I to her, next to my Concern for your worthy Husband's
untimely Death, I am griev'd to see what an Alteration the Bemoaning of
his Loss has occasion'd in you: These Words raising her Curiosity to know
what this Alteration was, I thus continu'd my Discourse; In endeavouring,
Madam, to extinguish, or at least to alleviate your Grief, than which nothing can be more prejudicial to a beautiful Woman, I intend a publick
Benefit, for if the Public is interested, as most certainly it is, in the preserving of a beautiful Face, that Man does the Public no little Service who
contributes most to its Preservation.

This odd Beginning operated so wonderfully upon her, that she desired
me to leave this general Road of Complements, and explain my self more
particularly to her. Upon this (delivering my self with an unusual Air of
Gravity, which your Grace knows I seldom carry about me in the Company of Ladies) I told her, that Grief ruines the finest Faces sooner than
any thing whatever; and that as envy it self could not deny her Face to be
the most charming in the Universe, so if she did not suffer her self to be
comforted, she must soon expect to take her Farewel of it. I confirm'd this
Assertion, by telling her of one of the finest Women we ever had in
England who did her self more injury in a Fortnight's time by lamenting
her only Brother's Death, than ten Years could possibly have done; that I
had heard an eminent Physician at Leyden say, That Tears (having abundance of saline Particles in them) not only spoild the Complexion, but
hastned Wrinkles: But, Madam, concluded I, why should I give my self the
trouble to confirm this by foreign instances, and by the Testimonies of our
most knowing Doctors, when alas! your own Face so fully justifies the
Truth of what I have said to you.

How! reply'd our disconsolate Widow, with a Sigh that came from the
Bottom of her Heart, And is it possible that my just concern for my dear
Husband, has wrought so cruel an Effect upon me in so short a Time?
With that she order'd her Gentlewoman to bring the Lookinglass to her,
and having survey'd her self a few Minutes in it, she told me she was
perfectly convinced that my Notions were true; but, cries she, what would
you have us poor Women do in these Cases? For something, continues she,
we owe to the Memory of the Deceased, and something too to the World,
which expects at least the common Appearances of Grief from us.

By your leave, Madam, saies I, all this is a Mistake, and no better; you
owe nothing to your Husband, since he is dead, and knows nothing of your
Lamentation; besides, cou'd you shed an Ocean of Tears upon his Hearse,
it would not do him the least Service; much less do you lye under any such
Obligations to the World, as to spoil a good Face only to comply with its

tyrannic Customs: No, Madam, take care to preserve your Beauty, and then let the World say what it pleases, your Ladyship may be revenged upon the World whene'er you see fit. I am resolved, answers she, to be intirely govern'd by you, therefore tell me frankly what sort of a Course you'd have me steer? Why, Madam, saies I, in the first place forget the Defunct; and in order to bring that about, relieve Nature, to which you have been so long unmerciful, with the most exquisit Meats and the most generous Wines. Upon Condition you'll sup with me, cries our afflicted Lady, I will submit to your prescription. But why should I trouble your Grace with a Narration of every Particular? In short, we had a noble Regale that Evening in her Bed-chamber, and our good Widow push'd the Glass so strenuously about, that her Comforter (meaning my self) could hardly find the way to his Coach. To conclude this Farce (which I am afraid begins now to be too tedious to your Grace) this Phoenix of her Sex, this Pattern of Conjugal Fidelity, two Mornings ago was marry'd to a smooth-chind Ensign of Count Trautmandorf's Regiment, that had not a farthing in the World but his Pay to depend upon: I assisted at the Ceremony, tho' I little imagin'd the Lady wou'd take the Matrimonial Receit so soon.

I was the easier perswaded to give your Grace a large Account of this Tragi-comedy, not only because I wanted better Matter to entertain you with at this Lazy Conjuncture, but also to show your Grace, that not only Ephesus in ancient, and England in later Times, have afforded such fantastical Widows, but even Germany it self; where, if the Ladies have not more Virtue than those of their Sex in other Countries, yet they pretend at least a greater Management of the outside of it.

By my last Pacquet from England, among a heap of nauseous Trash, I received the Three Dukes of Dunstable, which is really so monstrous and insipid, that I am sorry Lapland or Livonia had not the Honour of producing it; but if I did Pennance in reading it, I rejoyced to hear that it was so solemnly interr'd to the Tune of Catcalls. The 'Squire of Alsatia, however, which came by the following Post, made me some amends for the cursed impertinence of the Three Dukes; and my witty Friend Sir C[harles] S[edle]y's Bella mira gave me that intire Satisfaction that I cannot read it over too often.

They tell me my old Acquaintance Mr Dryden has left off the Theatre, and wholly applies him self to the Study of the Controversies between the two Churches. Pray Heaven! this strange alteration in him portends nothing disastrous to the State; but I have all along observed, That Poets do Religion as little Service by drawing their Pens for it, as the Divines do Poetry by pretending to Versification.

But I forget how troublesome I have been to your Grace, I shall therefore conclude with assuring you that I am, and to the last Moment of my

Life shall be ambitious of being, My LORD, Your Grace's most obedient,
and most obliged Servant,

G. Etherege

Regale] banquet.   Dryden] John Dryden (1631–1700) was working on his poem *The Hind
and the Panther* about 'the Controversies between the two Churches'.

LADY MARY WORTLEY MONTAGU
(1689–1762)

Daughter of the 5th Earl and 1st Duke of Kingston, Lady Mary was prominent
in London social and literary life. A close friend, later an enemy of Pope's, she was
a poet, but is best remembered, as she expected, for her letters. In 1712 she defied
her father and secretly married Edward Wortley Montagu (1678–1761). In 1716 she
accompanied him to Constantinople, where he was ambassador. Thence came the
'Turkish Embassy' letters which, when published in 1763, made her posthumously
famous. In Turkey she also learned of the practice of inoculation against smallpox,
and it was through her efforts that it was introduced in England. In 1739 she left
England alone and spent the next twenty-three years in Italy and France, returning
to England only after her husband's death in 1761.

35. *To Edward Wortley Montagu, c.26 July 1712*

Lady Mary's father wanted her to marry Clotworthy Skeffington, heir of an Irish
peer, but she had become attached to Montagu, an MP and friend of Addison. They
eloped in Aug. 1712.

I am going to write you a plain long letter. What I have allready told you
is nothing but the truth. I have no reason to beleive I am going to be
otherwaies confine'd than by my Duty, but I, that know my own Mind,
know that is enough to make me miserable. I see all the Misfortune of
marrying where it is impossible to Love. I am going to confesse a weaknesse
[that] may perhaps add to your contempt of me. I wanted courrage to resist
at first the Will of my Relations, but as every day added to my fears, Those
at last grew strong enough to make me venture the disobliging them. A
harsh word damps my Spirits to a degree of Silenceing all I have to say. I
knew the folly of my own temper, and took the Method of writeing to the
disposer of me. I said every thing in this Letter I thought proper to move
him, and proffer'd in attonement for not marrying whom he would, never
to marry at all. He did not think fit to answer this letter, but sent for me
to him. He told me he was very much surpriz'd that I did not depend on
his Judgment for my future happynesse, that he knew nothing I had to
complain of etc., that he did not doubt I had some other fancy in my head

which encourrag'd me to this disobedience, but he assur'd me if I refus'd
a settlement he has provided for me, he gave me his word, whatever
proposalls were made him, he would never so much as enter into a Treaty
with any other; that if I founded any hopes upon his death, I should find
my selfe mistaken—he never intended to leave me any thing but an Annu-
ity of £400; that tho' another would proceed in this manner, after I had
given so just a pretence for it, yet he had goodnesse to leave my destiny yet
in my own choice;—and at the same time commanded me to communicate
my design to my Relations and ask their Advice.—

As hard as this may sound, it did not shock my resolution. I was pleas'd
to think at any price I had it in my power to be free from a Man I hated.
I told my Intention to all my nearest Relations; I was surpriz'd at their
blameing it to the greatest degree. I was told they were sorry I would ruin
my selfe, but if I was so unreasonable they could not blame my F[ather]
whatever he inflicted on me. I objected I did not love him. They made
answer they found no Necessity of Loveing; if I liv'd well with him, that
was all was requir'd of me, and that if I consider'd this Town I should find
very few women in love with their Husbands and yet a manny happy. It
was in vain to dispute with such prudent people; they look'd upon me as
a little Romantic, and I found it impossible to perswade them that liveing
in London at Liberty was not the height of happynesse. However, they
could not change my thought, tho' I found I was to expect no protection
from them. When I was to give my final answer to [my Father] I told him
that I prefer'd a single life to any other, and if he pleas'd to permit me, I
would take that Resolution. He reply'd, he could not hinder my resolu-
tions, but I should not pretend after that to please him, since pleaseing him
was only to be done by Obedience; that if I would disobey, I knew the
consequences—he would not fail to confine me where I might repent at
Leisure; that he had also consulted my Relations and found them all agreeing in his Sentiments.

He spoke this in a manner hinder'd my answering. I retir'd to my
chamber, where I writ a letter to let him know my Aversion to the Man
propos'd was too great to be overcome, that I should be miserable beyond
all things could be imagin'd, but I was in his hands, and he might dispose
of me as he thought fit.—He was perfectly satisfy'd with this Answer, and
proceeded as if I had given a willing consent.—I forgot to tell you he
name'd you, and said if I thought that way, I was very much mistaken, that
if he had no other Engagements, yet he would never have agreed to your
proposalls, haveing no Inclination to see his Grandchildren beggars.

I do not speak this to endeavor to alter your opinion, but to shew the
improbabillity of his agreeing to it. I confesse I am entirely of your Mind.
I reckon it among the absurditys of custom that a Man must be oblig'd to

settle his whole Estate on an eldest Son, beyond his power to recall, whatever he proves to be, and make himself unable to make happy a younger Child that may deserve to be so. If I had an Estate my selfe, I should not make such ridiculous settlements, and I cannot blame you for being in the right.

I have told you all my Affairs with a plain sincerity. I have avoided to move your compassion, and I have said nothing of what I suffer; and I have not perswaded you to a Treaty which I am sure my familly will never agree to. I can have no fortune without an entire Obedience.

Whatever your busynesse is, may it end to your Satisfaction. I think of the public as you do. As little as that is a Woman's care, it may be permitted into the Number of a Woman's fears. But wretched as I am, I have no more to fear for my selfe. I have still a concern for my freinds, and I am in pain for your danger. I am far from takeing ill what you say. [I] never valu'd my selfe as the daughter of ——, and ever dispis'd those that esteem'd me on that Account. With pleasure I could barter all that, and change to be any Country Gentleman's daughter that would have reason enough to make happynesse in privacy.

My Letter is too long. I beg your pardon. You may see by the situation of my affairs tis without design.

36. To Edward Wortley Montagu, c.24 September 1714

Thô I am very impatient to see you, I would not have you by hastening to come down lose any part of your Interest. I am surpriz'd you say nothing of where you stand. I had a letter from Mrs Hewet last post who said she heard you stood at Newark and would be chose without opposition, but I fear her Inttelligence is not at all to be depended on. I am glad you think of serving your freinds; I hope it will put you in mind of serving your selfe.

I need not enlarge upon the Advantages of Money. Every thing we see and every thing we hear puts us in remembrance of it. If it was possible to restore Liberty to your Country or limit the Encroachments of the Pre[rogati]ve by reduceing your selfe to a Garret, I should be pleas'd to share so glorious a poverty with you, but as the World is and will be, tis a sort of Duty to be rich, that it may be in one's power to do good, Riches being another word for Power, towards the obtaining of which the first necessary qualification is Impudence, and (as Demosthenes said of Pronunciation in Oratory) the 2nd is Impudence, and the 3rd, still, Impudence. No modest Man ever did or ever will make his Fortune. Your freind Lord H[alifa]x, R[obert] W[alpo]le and all other remarkable instances of quick Advancement have been remarkably Impudent. The Ministry is like a play at Court. There's a little door to get in, and a great Croud without, shoveing and thrusting who shall be foremost; people that knock others with their Elbows, disregard a little kick of the shinns, and still thrust heartily forwards are sure of a good place. Your modest man stands behind in the Croud, is shov'd about by every body, his Cloaths tore, allmost squeez'd to death, and sees a 1,000 get in before him that don't make so good a figure as him selfe. I don't say tis impossible for an Impudent Man not to rise in the World, but a Moderate Merit with a large share of Impudence is more probable to be advance'd than the greatest Qualifications without it.

If this Letter is impertinent it is founded upon an opinion of your merit, which if tis a mistake I would not be undeceiv'd in. Tis my Interest to beleive (as I do) that you deserve every thing, and are capable of every thing, but no body else will beleive it if they see you get nothing.

37. To Lady ——, 16 August 1716

This, like the other Turkish letters, is not as it was first sent, but an edited version made by Lady Mary with a view to posthumous publication. Cologne, known as the Rome of Germany, venerated the relics of St Ursula, a British princess supposed to have been murdered there, along with the 11,000 virgins in her train, on her return from a pilgrimage to Rome.

If my Lady —— could have any Notion of the Fatigues that I have suffer'd this last 2 days, I am sure she would own it a great proofe of regard that I now sit down to write to her. We hir'd Horses from Nimeguen hither, not having the conveniency of the post, and found but very indifferent accomodation at Reinberg, our first stage, but that was nothing to what I suffer'd yesterday. We were in hopes to reach Collen. Our horses tir'd at Stamel 3 hours from it, where I was forc'd to pass the night in my Cloths in a room not at all better than a Hovel, for thô I have my own bed, I had no mind to undress where the wind came in from a thousand places. We left this wretched lodging at day break and about 6 this morning came safe here, where I got immediately into bed and slept so well for 3 hours that I found my selfe perfectly recover'd and have had Spirits enough to go see all that is curious in the Town, that is to say, the churches, for here is nothing else worth seeing, tho it is a very large Town, but most part of it old built.

The Jesuits' church is the neatest, which was shew'd me in a very complaisant Manner by a handsome young Jesuit, who, not knowing who I was, took a Liberty in his complements and railerys which very much diverted me. Having never before seen any thing of that nature, I could not enough admire the magnificence of the altars, the rich Images of the Saints (all massy silver) and the enchasures of the Relicks, thô I could not help murmuring in my heart at that profusion of pearls, Diamonds and Rubys bestow'd on the adornment of rotten teeth, dirty rags, etc. I own that I had wickedness enough to covet St Ursula's pearl necklace, thô perhaps it was no wickedness at all, an Image not being certainly one's Neighbour; but I went yet farther and wish'd even she her selfe converted into dressing plate, and a great St Christopher I imagin'd would have look'd very well in a Cistern. These were my pious refflexions, thô I was very well satisfy'd to see, pil'd up to the Honnour of our Nation, the Skulls of the 11,000 Virgins. I have seen some Hundreds of Relicks here of no less consequence, but I will not imitate the common stile of Travellers so far as to give you a list of 'em, being perswaded that you have no manner of curiosity for the Titles given to Jaw bones and bits of worm eaten wood.

—Adeiu. I am just going to supper where I shall drink your Health in an admirable sort of Lorrain Wine, which I am sure is the same you call Burgundy in London.

38. To Lady ——, 1 April 1717

Robert Halsband, editor of *The Complete Letters* of Lady Mary, remarks that Ingres's *Le Bain turc* in the Louvre shows the influence of this passage.

I am now got into a new World where every thing I see appears to me a change of Scene, and I write to your Ladyship with some content of mind, hoping at least that you will find the charm of Novelty in my Letters and no longer reproach me that I tell you nothing extrodinary. I won't trouble you with a Relation of our tedious Journey, but I must not omit what I saw remarkable at Sophia, one of the most beautifull Towns in the Turkish Empire and famous for its Hot Baths that are resorted to both for diversion and health. I stop'd here one day on purpose to see them. Designing to go incognito, I hir'd a Turkish Coach. These Voitures are not at all like ours, but much more convenient for the Country, the heat being so great that Glasses would be very troublesome. They are made a good deal in the manner of the Dutch Coaches, haveing wooden Lattices painted and gilded, the inside being painted with baskets and nosegays of Flowers, entermix'd commonly with little poetical mottos. They are cover'd all over with scarlet cloth, lin'd with silk and very often richly embroider'd and fring'd. This covering entirely hides the persons in them, but may be thrown back at pleasure and the Ladys peep through the Lattices. They hold 4 people very conveniently, seated on cushions, but not rais'd.

In one of these cover'd Waggons I went to the Bagnio about 10 a clock. It was allready full of Women. It is built of Stone in the shape of a Dome with no Windows but in the Roofe, which gives Light enough. There was 5 of these domes joyn'd together, the outmost being less than the rest and serving only as a hall where the portress stood at the door. Ladys of Quality gennerally give this Woman the value of a crown or 10 shillings, and I did not forget that ceremony. The next room is a very large one, pav'd with Marble, and all round it rais'd 2 Sofas of marble, one above another. There were 4 fountains of cold Water in this room, falling first into marble Basins and then running on the floor in little channels made for that purpose, which carry'd the streams into the next room, something less than this, with the same sort of marble sofas, but so hot with steams of sulphur proceeding from the baths joyning to it, twas impossible to stay there with one's Cloths on. The 2 other domes were the hot baths, one of which had cocks of cold Water turning into it to temper it to what degree of warmth the bathers have a mind to.

I was in my travelling Habit, which is a rideing dress, and certainly appear'd very extrodinary to them, yet there was not one of 'em that shew'd the least surprize or impertinent Curiosity, but receiv'd me with all the obliging civillity possible. I know no European Court where the Ladys would have behav'd them selves in so polite a manner to a stranger.

I beleive in the whole there were 200 Women and yet none of those disdainfull smiles or satyric whispers that never fail in our assemblys when any body appears that is not dress'd exactly in fashion. They repeated over and over to me, Uzelle, pek uzelle, which is nothing but, charming, very charming. The first sofas were cover'd with Cushions and rich Carpets, on which sat the Ladys, and on the 2nd their slaves behind 'em, but without any distinction of rank by their dress, all being in the state of nature, that is, in plain English, stark naked, without any Beauty or deffect conceal'd yet there was not the least wanton smile or immodest Gesture amongst 'em. They Walk'd and mov'd with the same majestic Grace which Milton describes of our General Mother. There were many amongst them as exactly proportion'd as ever any Goddess was drawn by the pencil of Guido or Titian, and most of their skins shineingly white, only adorn'd by their Beautifull Hair divided into many tresses hanging on their shoulders, braided either with pearl or riband, perfectly representing the figures of the Graces. I was here convinc'd of the Truth of a Refflexion that I had often made, that if twas the fashion to go naked, the face would be hardly observ'd. I perceiv'd that the Ladys with the finest skins and most delicate shapes had the greatest share of my admiration, thô their faces were sometimes less beautifull than those of their companions. To tell you the truth, I had wickedness enough to wish secretly that Mr Gervase could have been there invisible. I fancy it would have very much improv'd his art to see so many fine Women naked in different postures, some in conversation, some working, others drinking Coffee or sherbet, and many negligently lying on their Cushions while their slaves (generally pritty Girls of 17 or 18) were employ'd in braiding their hair in several pritty manners. In short, tis the Women's coffee house, where all the news of the Town is told, Scandal invented etc. They gennerally take this Diversion once a week, and stay there at least 4 or 5 hours without geting cold by immediate coming out of the hot bath into the cool room, which was very surprizing to me. The Lady that seem'd the most considerable amongst them entreated me to sit by her and would fain have undress'd me for the bath. I excus'd my selfe with some difficulty, they being all so earnest in perswading me. I was at last forc'd to open my skirt and shew them my stays, which satisfy'd 'em very well, for I saw they beleiv'd I was so lock'd up in that machine that it was not in my own power to open it, which contrivance they attributed to my Husband. I was charm'd with their Civillity and Beauty and should have been very glad to pass more time with them, but Mr W[ortley] resolving to persue his Journey the next morning early, I was in haste to see the ruins of Justinian's church, which did not afford me so agreable a prospect as I had left, being little more than a heap of stones.

Adeiu, Madam. I am sure I have now entertaind you with an Account of such a sight as you never saw in your Life and what no book of travells could inform you of. 'Tis no less than Death for a Man to be found in one of these places.

Milton] *Paradise Lost*, iv. 304–18.

39. To Lady Mar, 23 June 1727

Lady Mar was Lady Mary's sister, who lived in Paris and suffered from melancholia.

I am allways pleas'd to hear from You (Dear Sister), particularly when you tell me you are well. I beleive you'l find upon the whole my Sense is right, that Air, Exercise and Company are the best med'cines, and Physic and Retirement good for nothing but to break Hearts and spoil Constitutions.

I was glad to hear Mr Remond's History from you, thô the newspaper had given it me en gros and my Lady Stafford in detail some time before. I will tell you in return, as well as I can, what happens amongst our Acquaintance here. To begin with family affairs: the Dutchess of Kingston grunts on as usual, and I fear will put us in black Bombazine soon, which is a real greife to me. My dear Aunt Cheyne makes all the money she can of Lady Francesse, and I fear will carry on those Politics to the last point, thô the Girl is such a fool, tis no great matter. I am going within this halfe hour to call her to Court.

Our poor Cousins the Fieldings are grown yet poorer by the loss of all the little money they had, which in their Infinite wisdom they put into the hands of a rogueish Broker who has fairly walk'd off with it.

The most diverting story about Town at present is in relation to Edgecombe, thô youre not knowing the people concern'd as well as I do will, I fear, hinder you from being so much entertain'd by it. I can't tell whither you know a Tall, musical, silly, ugly thing, niece to Lady Essex Roberts, who is call'd Miss Leigh. She went a few days ago to visit Mrs Betty Titchburne, Lady Sunderland's sister, who lives in the House with her, and was deny'd at the door; but with the true manners of a great Fool told the porter that if his Lady was at home she was very positive she would be very glad to see her. Upon which she was shew'd up stairs to Miss Titchburne, who was ready to drop down at the sight of her, and could not help asking her in a grave way how she got in, being deny'd to every mortal, intending to pass the Evening in devout preparations. Miss Liegh [*sic*] said she had sent away her chair and servants with intent of staying till 9 o'clock. There was then no Remedy and she was ask'd to sit down, but had not been there a quarter of an hour when she heard a violent rap at the door, and somebody vehemently run up stairs. Miss Titchburne seem'd much surprizd and said she beleiv'd it was Mr Edgcombe, and was quite amaz'd how he took it into his Head to visit her. During these Excuses, enter Edgcombe, who appear'd frighted at the sight of a third person. Miss Titchburne told him almost at his Entrance that the Lady he saw there was a perfect mistriss of music, and as he passionately lov'd it she thought she could not oblige him more than by desiring her to play. Miss Leigh very willingly sat to the Harpsicord, upon which her Audience decamp'd to the Bed Chamber, and left her to play over 3 or 4 lessons to her selfe. They return'd, and made what excuses they could, but said very frankly they had not heard her performance and begg'd her to begin again, which she comply'd with, and gave them the opertunity of a second retirement. Miss Leigh was by this time all Fire and Flame to see her heavenly Harmony thus slighted, and when they return'd told them she did not understand playing to an empty room. Mr Edgecombe begg'd ten thousand pardons, and said if she would play Godi, it was a Tune he dy'd to hear, and it would be an Obligation he should never forget. She made answer, she would do him a much greater Obligation by her Absence, which she suppos'd was all that was wanting at that Time, and run down stairs in a great Fury, to publish as fast as she could, and was so indefatigable in this pious design that in 4 and twenty hours all the people in Town had heard the story, and poor Edgcombe met with nothing where ever he went but complements about his third Tune, which is reckon'd very handsome in a Lover past forty.

My Lady Sunderland could not avoid hearing this Galant History, and 3 days after invited Miss Leigh to dinner, where in the presence of her Sister and all the servants in waiting, she told her she was very sorry she had been so rudely treated in her House; that it was very true Mr Edgecombe had been a perpetual Companion of her sister's this 2 year, and she thought it high time he should explain himself; and she expected her sister should act in this matter as discreetly as Lady K. Pelham had done in the like case, who she heard had given Mr Pelham 4 months to resolve in, and after that he was either to marry or lose her for ever. Sir Robert Sutton intterupted her by saying that he never doubted the Honour of Mr Edgecombe and was persuaded he could have no ill design in his Family. The Affair stands thus, and Edgecombe has 4 months to provide him selfe elsewhere, during which time he has free egress and regress, and tis seriously the opinion of many that a wedding will in good earnest be brought about by this admirable Conduct.

I send you a novell instead of a Letter, but as it is in your power to shorten it when you please by reading no farther than you like, I will make no Excuses for the length of it.

Remond] Rémond's history of his passion for a jeweller's daughter.　　Edgecombe] Richard Edgcumbe (1680–1758) was a politician.　　Miss Leigh] Elizabeth Leigh (d. 1734) was described by Horace Walpole as 'a virtuosa, a musician, a madwoman'. She was in love with Handel.　　Godi] 'Godi l'alma' is an air from Handel's *Ottone*.　　Wedding] Edgcumbe, a widower, never remarried.

40. To Lady Pomfret, March 1739

Henrietta Louisa, Countess of Pomfret (d. 1761), a Lady of the Bedchamber to Queen Caroline, was much ridiculed for her dullness and affectation of learning.

I am so well acquainted with the lady you mention, that I am not surprized at any proof of her want of judgment; she is one of those who has passed upon the world vivacity in the place of understanding; for me, who think with Boileau

Rien n'est beau que le vrai, le vrai seul est aimable,

I have always thought those geniuses much inferior to the plain sense of a cook-maid, who can make a good pudding and keep the kitchen in good order.

Here is no news to be sent you from this place, which has been for this fortnight and still continues overwhelmed with politicks, and which are of so mysterious a nature, one ought to have some of the gifts of Lilly or Partridge to be able to write about them; and I leave all those dissertations to those distinguished mortals who are endowed with the talent of divination; though I am at present the only one of my sex who seems to be of that opinion, the ladies having shewn their zeal and appetite for knowledge in a most glorious manner. At the last warm debate in the House of Lords, it was unanimously resolved there should be no crowd of unnecessary auditors; consequently the fair sex were excluded, and the gallery destined to the sole use of the House of Commons. Notwithstanding which determination, a tribe of dames resolved to shew on this occasion, that neither men nor laws could resist them. These heroines were Lady Huntingdon, the Duchess of Queensbury, the Duchess of Ancaster, Lady Westmoreland, Lady Cobham, Lady Charlotte Edwin, Lady Archibald Hamilton and her daughter, Mrs Scott, and Mrs Pendarvis, and Lady Frances Saunderson. I am thus particular in their names since I look upon them to be the boldest assertors, and most resigned sufferers for liberty, I ever read of. They presented themselves at the door at nine o'clock in the morning, where Sir William Saunderson respectfully informed them the [Lord] Chancellor had made an order against their admittance. The Duchess of Queensbury, as head of the squadron, pished at the ill-breeding of a mere lawyer, and desired him to let them up stairs privately. After some modest refusals he swore by G—— he would not let them in. Her grace, with a noble warmth, answered, by G—— they would come in, in spite of the Chancellor and the whole House. This being reported, the Peers resolved to starve them out; an order was made that the doors should not be opened till they had raised their siege.

These Amazons now shewed themselves qualified for the duty even of foot-soldiers; they stood there till five in the afternoon, without either sustenance or evacuation, every now and then playing vollies of thumps, kicks, and raps, against the door, with so much violence that the speakers in the House were scarce heard. When the Lords were not to be conquered by this, the two Duchesses (very well apprized of the use of stratagems in war) commanded a dead silence of half an hour; and the Chancellor, who thought this a certain proof of their absence, (the Commons also being very impatient to enter) gave order for the opening of the door; upon which they all rushed in, pushed aside their competitors, and placed themselves in the front rows of the gallery. They stayed there till after eleven, when the House rose; and during the debate gave applause, and showed marks of dislike, not only by smiles and winks (which have always been allowed in these cases), but by noisy laughs and apparent contempts; which is supposed the true reason why poor Lord Hervey spoke miserably. I beg your pardon, dear madam, for this long relation; but 'tis impossible to be short on so copious a subject; and you must own this action very well worthy of record, and I think not to be paralleled in any history, ancient or modern. I look so little in my own eyes (who was at that time ingloriously sitting over a tea-table), I hardly dare subscribe myself even,

Yours.

Lilly and Partridge] almanac makers.   Sir William Saunderson] was Black Rod.

JONATHAN SWIFT
(1667–1745)

As a young man, Swift served Sir William Temple, and wrote his early works at
Moor Park, Temple's house. He was ordained in 1694. Though he spent some time
in Ireland he became a familiar figure in London and a friend of Addison and Steele.
But in 1710 he abandoned the Whigs and, having joined with the Tories, became a
friend of Pope, Gay, and Arbuthnot—members of the Scriblerus Club, a group of
writers determined to satirize 'all the false tastes of learning'—and a close associate
of the Tory leaders Bolingbroke and Oxford. In 1713, with the Tory ministry in
trouble and Bolingbroke and Oxford bitterly at odds, Swift professed that he would
not remain in service with the survivor of the two. In that year he was made dean of
St Patrick's, Dublin. Queen Anne dismissed Oxford in July 1714, a few days before
her death. The succession of George I meant the end of the Tory regime, and Swift
thenceforth was mostly in Ireland.

41. To Lord Oxford, 21 November 1713

Oxford's daughter Elizabeth had died the day before.

My Lord,

Your Lordship is the person in the world to whom every body ought to
be silent upon such an occasion as this, which is only to be supported by
the greatest wisdom and strength of mind: wherein, God knows, the wisest
and best of us, who would presume to offer their thoughts, are far your
inferiors. It is true, indeed, that a great misfortune is apt to weaken the
mind, and disturb the understanding. This, indeed, might be some pretence to us to administer our consolations, if we had been wholly strangers
to the person gone. But, my Lord, whoever had the honour to know her,
wants a comforter as much as your Lordship; because, though their loss is
not so great, yet they have not the same firmness and prudence, to support
the want of a friend, a patroness, a benefactor, as you have to support that
of a daughter. My Lord, both religion and reason forbid me to have the
least concern for that Lady's death, upon her own account, and he must be
an ill Christian, or a perfect stranger to her virtues, who would not wish
himself, with all submission to God Almighty's will, in her condition. But
your Lordship, who hath lost such a daughter, and we, who have lost such
a friend, and the world, which hath lost such an example, have, in our
several degrees, greater cause to lament, than, perhaps, was ever given by
any private person before. For, my Lord, I have sat down to think of every
amiable quality that could enter into the composition of a lady, and could
not single out one, which she did not possess in as high a perfection as
human nature is capable of. But, as to your Lordship's own particular, as

it is an unconceivable misfortune to have lost such a daughter, so it is a possession which few can boast of, to have had such a daughter. I have often said to your Lordship, that I never knew any one, by many degrees, so happy in their domestic as you; and I affirm you are so still, though not by so many degrees: From whence it is very obvious, that your Lordship should reflect upon what you have left, and not upon what you have lost.

To say the truth, my Lord, you began to be too happy for a mortal; much more happy than is usual with the dispensations of Providence long to continue. You had been the great instrument of preserving your country from foreign and domestic ruin: You have had the felicity of establishing your family in the greatest lustre, without any obligation to the bounty of your Prince, or any industry of your own: You have triumphed over the violence and treachery of your enemies, by your courage and abilities; and, by the steadiness of your temper, over the inconstancy and caprice of your friends. Perhaps your Lordship has felt too much complacency within yourself, upon this universal success: and God Almighty, who would not disappoint your endeavours for the public, thought fit to punish you with a domestic loss, where he knew your heart was most exposed; and, at the same time, has fulfilled his own wise purposes, by rewarding in a better life, that excellent creature he has taken from you.

I know not, my Lord, why I write this to you, nor hardly what I am writing. I am sure, it is not from any compliance with form; it is not from thinking that I can give your Lordship any ease. I think it was an impulse upon me that I should say something: And whether I shall send you what I have written, I am yet in doubt, &c.

42. To Robert Percival, 3 January 1730

Percival (1683–1748) was a squire and son of a former neighbour of Swift's.

S^r,

Seeing your frank on the outside, and the address in the same hand, it was obvious who was the writer, and before I opened it, a worthy friend being with me, I told him the subject of the difference between us: That your Tythes being generally worth 5 or 6ll a year, and by the terror of your Squireship frighting my Agent, to take what you graciously thought fit to give, you wronged me of half my due every year . . . That having held from your father an Island worth three pence a year, which I planted, and pay^d two Shillings annually for, and being out of possession of the s^d Island seven or eight years, there could not possibly be above 4^s due to you; for which you have thought fit to stop 3 or 4 years of Tyth at your own rate of 2^{ll}–5^s a year (as I remember) and still continue to stop it, on pretence that the s^d Island was not surrendered to you in form; although you have cutt down more Plantations of Willow and Abeilles than would purchase a dozen such Islands. I told my friend, that this talent of Squires formerly prevayled very much in the County of Meath; that as to your self, from the badness of your Education against all my advice and endeavors, and from the case of your Nature, as well as another circumstance which I shall not mention, I expected nothing from you that became a Gentleman. That I had expostulated this scurvy matter very gently with you, that I conceived this letter was answer: that from the prerogative of a good estate the practice of lording over a few Irish wretches, and from the naturall want of better thinking, I was sure your answer would be extremely rude and stupid, full of very bad language in all senses: That a Bear in a wilderness will as soon fix on a Philosopher as on a Cotteger; and a Man wholly voyd of education, judgment, or distinction of person has no regard in his insolence but to the passion of fear; and how heartily I wished, that to make you shew your humility, your quarrell had been rather with a Captain of Dragoons than the Dean of St Patricks.

All this happened before my opening your Letter; which being read, my friend told me I was an ill guesser . . . That you affirm you despise me onely as a Clergy-man, by your own Confession: And that you had good reason, because Clergymen pretend to learning, wherein you value your self as what you are an utter Stranger to.

I took some pains in providing and advising about your Education, but since you have made so ill use of my rules; I cannot deny according to your own Principles that your usage of me is just . . . You are wholly out of my danger; the weapons I use will do you no hurt, and to that which would keep a nicer man in aw, you are insensible. A needle against a stone wall can make no impression. Your faculty lyes in making bargains: stick to that; leave your Children a better estate than your father left you; as he left you much more than your Grandfather left him. Your father and you are much wiser than I, who gave amongst you fifty years purchase for land, for which I am not to see one farthing. This was intended as an Encouragement for a Clergyman to reside among you, whenever any of your posterity shall be able to distinguish a Man from a Beast. One thing I desire you will be set right in; I do not despise All Squires. It is true I despise the bulk of them. But, pray take notice, that a Squire must have some merit before I shall honor him with my contempt. For, I do not despise a Fly, a Maggot, or a Mite.

If you send me an answer to this, I shall not read it, but open it before company, and in their presence burn it; for no other reason but the detestation of bad spelling, no grammar, and that pertness which proceeds from ignorance and an invincible want of tast.

I have ordered a Copy of this Letter to be taken with an intention to print it, as a mark of my esteem for you; which however perhaps I shall not pursue; For I could willingly excuse our two names from standing in the same paper, since I am confident you have as little desire of Fame, as I have to give it you.

I wish many happy new years to you and your family and am with truth | Your friend and humble Servt

J: Swift

Let me add something serious; that, as it is held an imprudent thing to provoke valour, so I confess it was imprudent in me to provoke rudeness: which, as it was my own standing rule never to do except in cases where I had power to punish it, so my error proceeded from a better opinion of you than you have thought fit to make good . . . for with every fault in your Nature, your education, and your understanding, I never imagined you so utterly devoyd of knowing some little distinction between persons.

Island] a plot of land rising above marsh or bog   Abeilles] more commonly 'abeles', poplars.

43. To John Gay, 4 May 1732

Gay (1685–1732) was a wit, playwright, and friend of Pope and Swift. He lost a fortune in the South Sea Company (founded by Oxford in 1711; the Bubble burst in 1720) and made another with *The Beggar's Opera* (1728).

I am now as lame as when you writ your Letter, and almost as lame as your letter it Self, for want of that limb from my Lady Dutchess, which you promised, and without which I wonder how it could limp hither. I am not in a condition to make a *true* Step even on Amesbury Downs, and I declare that a corporeal false Step is worse than a political one; nay worse than a thousand politicall ones, for which I appeal to Courts and Ministers who hobble on and prosper without the Sense of feeling, To talk of riding and walking is insulting to me, for, I can as soon fly as do ether, I desire you will manage my South-Sea estate, as you would do if it were your own, I mean in every circumstance except gaming with the public, that is buying or Selling lottery tickets, as you once proposed to me from your own practice. I love Mr Lewis's Device; Piano piano. It is your pride or lazyness more than Chair-hire, that make the town expensive. No honer is lost by walking in the dark, and in the day, you may becken a blackguard boy under a gate, near your visiting place (experto crede) Save eleven pence; and get half a crowns worth of health, The worst of my present misfortune is, that I eat and drink, and can digest neither for want of exercise; and to encrease my misery the knaves are Sure to find me at home, and make huge voyd Spaces in my Cellars, I congratulate with you for losing your *great* acquaintance, in Such a case philosophy teaches that we must Submit, and be content with *good* ones, I like Lord Cornbury's refusing his pension, but demur at his being elected for Oxford, which I conceive is wholly changed, and entirely, devoted to new Principles, directly contrary to those for which Lord Cornbury refused a pension, and appeared to me a most corrupt Seminary the two last times I was there.

I find by the whole cast of your letter that you are as giddy and as volatile as ever; just the reverse of Mr Pope, who hath always loved a domestick life from his youth. I was going to wish you had Some little place that you could call your own, but I profess I do not know you well enough to contrive any one Systeem of life that would please you, You pretend to preach up riding and walking to the Dutchess, yet from my knowledge of you after twenty years, you allways Joyned a violent desire of perpetually Shifting places and company, with a rooted Lazyness, and an utter impatience of fatigue. A coach and Six horses is the utmost exercise you can bear, and this onely when you can fill it with Such company as is best Suited to your tast, and how glad would you be if it could waft you in the air to avoyd jolting; while I who am So much later in life can or at least would ride 500 miles on a trotting horse, You mortaly hate writing onely because it is the thing you chiefly ought to do as well to keep up the vogue you have in the world, as to make you easy in your fortune; you are mercifull to every thing but money, your best friend, whom you treat with inhumanity;—Be assured, I will hire people to watch all your motions, and to return me a faithfull account. Tell me, have you cured your absence of mind? Can you attend to trifles? Can you at Amesbury write domestick libels to divert the family and the Neighboring Squires for five-miles round; or venture So far on Horseback without apprehending a Stumble at every Step? Can you Set the footman laughing as they wait at dinner; and do the Dutchess's women admire your Wit? In what esteem are you with the Vicar of the Parish? can you play with him at Back-gammon? Have the Farmers found out that you cannot distinguish Rye from Barly, or an Oak from a crab-tree? You are Sensible that I know the full extent of your country Skill is in fishing for Roches, or Gudgeons at the highest.

I love to do you good offices with your friends; and therefore desire you will Show this letter to the Dutchess, to improve Her Graces good opinion of your qualifications, and convince her how usefully you are like to be in the family. I suppose you have Seen Dr Delany who hath been long amongst you, And we hear is printing many Sermons against free thinkers, besides one or more against eating blood. I advised him against preaching on those Subjects to plain believing Christians, but that he might print if he pleas'd, This I Suppose hindred him from taking me as his adviser, & he rather chose Lord Bolingbroke. We hear he has published a Poem inscribed to one of the Princesses. Pray how does Dr Berkeleys book pass amongst you; It is too Speculative for me, I hope you Still See Ldy S—— in her grandeur and think her as much your friend as ever; in which you do her justice. I desire to present my most humble respects to the Duke and Dutchess. Her Grace shall have the honor of my correspondance again, when She goes to Amesbury. Hear a piece of Irish news, I buryed the famous General Meredyth's father last night in my Cathedral, he was 96 years old: So that Mrs Pope may live Seven years longer. You saw Mr Pope in health, pray is he generally more healthy than when I was amongst you, I would know how your own health is, and how much wine you drink in a day. My Stint in company is a pint at noon, and half as much at night, but I often dine alone like a Hermit, and then I drink little or none at all, yet I differ from you for I would have Society if I could get what I like, people of middle understanding middle rank, very complying, and consequently Such as I can govern. Lord knows where this letter will find you, but I think your will is that I Should always direct to the Dukes in Burlington Gardens. There's a Lord for you wholly out of my favor whom I will use as I did Schomberg's Heiresses.

So adiu | ever your &c. | ex

Lewis] Erasmus Lewis was Oxford's secretary.　　Experto crede] 'believe me, I've experienced it.'　　Dr Delany] Patrick Delany (1685–1768), long a close friend of Swift's, though the friendship cooled before Swift's death.　　Dr Berkeley] George Berkeley (1685–1753), bishop of Cloyne, the most distinguished philosopher of the age. The book was presumably *Alciphron* (1632), which had its origin in a visit to New England.　　Ldy S——] Henrietta Howard (1681–1767), mistress of George II, Duchess of Suffolk; widowed, she married into the Berkeley family.　　Duke and Dutchess] the Duke and Duchess of Queensbury were Gay's protectors.　　Mrs Pope] Pope's mother was almost 90 at the date of this letter.　　A Lord] Lord Burlington lost favour with Swift when he neglected to assist him in the raising of a monument to the Duke of Schomberg, Protestant hero of the Battle of the Boyne, as, apparently, did Schomberg's heirs.

ALEXANDER POPE (1688–1744) AND JOHN ARBUTHNOT (1667–1735)

Arbuthnot was physician to Queen Anne, a wit, a leading member of the Scriblerus Club, and a close friend of Gay, Pope, and Swift.

44. To Jonathan Swift, 5 December 1732

Gay died on 4 Dec.

It is not a time to complain that you have not answered me two letters (in the last of which I was impatient under some fears) It is not now indeed a time to think of one's self when one of the nearest and longest tyes I have ever had, is broken all on a sudden, by the unexpected death of poor Mr

Gay. An inflammatory fever hurried him out of this life in three days. He died last night at nine a clock, not deprived of his senses entirely at last, and possessing them perfectly till within five hours. He asked of you a few hours before, when in acute torment by the inflammation in his bowels and breast. His effects are in the Duke of Queensbury's custody. His sisters, we suppose, will be his heirs, who are two widows; as yet it is not known whether or no he left a will—Good God! how often are we to die before we go quite off this stage? in every friend we lose a part of ourselves, and the best part. God keep those we have left! few are worth praying for, and one's self the least of all.

I shall never see you now I believe; one of your principal Calls to England is at an end. Indeed he was the most amiable by far, his qualities were the gentlest, but I love you as well and as firmly. Would to God the man we have lost had not been so amiable, nor so good! but that's a wish for our own sakes, not for his. Sure if Innocence and Integrity can deserve Happiness, it must be his. Adieu. I can add nothing to what you will feel, and diminish nothing from it. Yet write to me, and soon. Believe no man now living loves you better, I believe no man ever did, than A. Pope.

Dr Arbuthnot, whose humanity you know, heartily commends himself to you. All possible diligence and affection has been shown, and continued attendance on this melancholy occasion. Once more adieu, and write to one who is truly disconsolate.—

Dear Sir,

I am sorry that the renewal of our correspondence should be upon such a melancholy occasion. poor Mr Gay dy'd of an inflammation, and I believe at last a mortification of the bowels; it was the most precipitate case I ever knew, having cut him off in three days. He was attended by two Physicians besides my self. I believed the distemper mortal from the beginning. I have not had the pleasure of a line from you these two years; I wrote one about your health, to which I had no answer.

I wish you all health and happiness, being with great affection and respect, Sir, Your, &c.

THOMAS SHERIDAN
(1687–1735)

The Revd Thomas Sheridan was a Dublin schoolmaster and grandfather of the dramatist Richard Brinsley Sheridan. Like Swift, he loved jokes, puns, and 'bagatelles' of all sorts.

45. *To Jonathan Swift, 15 July 1735*

For those who find the 'Latin' too laborious we append the translation of Sir Walter Scott.

De armis ter De An,

Urit tome sum time ago an diam redito anser it thus. A lac a de mi illinc, ducis in it, is notabit fit fora de an; it is more fit fora puppi. I lusit toti. Irritato ripam flet an Dicti toral e ver ibit. Dic is abest. Dic is a serpenti se. Dic is a turdi se. Dic is a fartor. Dic is pisti se. Dic is a vix en. Dic is as qui ter in nasti fusti musti cur. Dic is arantur. Dic is ab a boni se. Sed Ito Dicti cantu cum in as a dans in mas ter an dans ab ori ora minuet. Da me I fido sed Dic. Quis mi ars se diu puppi. Ure as turdi rufi an sed I. Ure a tori villa in sed Dic. Ure fit fora gallus sed I; an dume dia dans in. Ure aras calli cur sed Dic. Dicti sed I ure regis a farto me.

> Tanti vi sed I tanti vi
> Hi fora Dic in apri vi.

Ime Dic as te mas amo use foralis angor. I recollecta piper, sed I, an dat rumpetur, an da sume cur, an ad rumor, an das qui re, an ab lac a more in ure cum pani, an da de al more me ac in a gesto uti. It is ali ad a me sed Dic, as suras istinc. Sensu caseso I caeno more.

I cum here formo ni. Itis apparent I canta ve mi maerent, mi tenentis tardi. I cursim e veri de nota peni cani res. I ambit. Mi stomachis a cor morante ver re ad ito digesta me ale in a minute. I eat nolam, nôram, no dux, I generali eat a quale carbone dedat super an da qualis as fine abit as arabit. I es ter de I eat atro ut at abit. De vilis in mi a petite. A crustis mi de lite. (I neu Eumenides ago eat tuenti times more.) As unde I eat offa buccas fatas mi arsis. On nam unde I eat sum pes. A tu es de I eat apud in migra num edit. A venis de I eat sum pasti. Post de notabit. Afri de abit ab re ad. A Satur de sum tripes.

Luis is mus ter in an armi an de sines carri in it as far as I tali, sum se germani. It do es alarum mus; De vel partum. I fani nues is fito ritu me directo me at cava ni Virgini a. Miser vice tomi da ter an, Capta in Pari, Doctor de lanij, Major Folli ut; an mi complemento mi de armis tresses, especiali fiRLL.

I amat ure re verens his cervice forever an de ver.

Dear Mister Dean,

You writ to me some time ago, and I am ready to answer it thus. Alack-a-day, my ill ink, deuce is in it, is not a bit fit for a Dean; it is more fit for a puppy. I'll use it to Tighe. I writ a Tory pamphlet, and Dick Tighe tore all, every bit. Dick is a beast. Dick is a serpent, I say, Dick is a turd, I say.

Dick is a farter. Dick is pist, I say. Dick is a vixen. Dick is a squittering, nasty, fusty, musty cur. Dick is a ranter. Dick is a baboon, I say. Said I to Dick Tighe, can't you come in as a dancing-master, and dance a bory or a minuet? Damme if I do, said Dick. K—— my a——, said I, you puppy. You're a sturdy ruffian, said I. You're a Tory villain, said Dick. You're fit for a gallows, said I, and you may die a-dancing. You're a rascally cur, said Dick. Dick Tighe, said I, your rage is a fart to me.

> Tantivy, said I, tantivy,
> Hy! for a Dick in a privy.

I made Dick as tame as a mouse for all his anger. I recollect a piper, said I, and a trumpeter, and a shoemaker, and a drummer, and a squire, and a blackamore in your company, and a deal more making a jest o' you, Tighe. It is all a lie, a damme, said Dick, as sure as I stink. Since you say so, I say no more.

I come here for money. It is apparent I can't have my May-rent, my tenant is tardy. I curse him every day, not a penny can I raise. I am bit. My stomach is a cormorant, ever ready to digest a meal every minute. I eat no lamb, no ram, no ducks. I generally eat a quail carbonaded at supper, and a quail is as fine a bit as a rabbit. Yesterday I eat a trout at a bit. Devil is in my appetite. A crust is my delight. I knew you, many days ago, eat twenty times more. A' Sunday I eat of a buck as fat as my —— is; on a Monday I eat some peas; a' Wednesday I eat some pasty; Post-day not a bit; a' Friday a bit of bread; a' Saturday, some tripes.

Lewis is mustering an army, and designs carrying it as far as Italy, some say Germany. It does alarm us; devil part 'em. If any news is fit to write, you may direct to me at Cavan in Virginia. My service to my daughter Anne, Captain Parry, Doctor Delany, Major Ffolliott; and my compliment to my dear mistresses, especially Worrall.

I am at your Reverence his service for ever and ever.

46. To Jonathan Swift, 13 August 1735

Dear Sir,

Because of some dropping young lads coming to me, and because it was impossible for me to get any money before the 23rd of this month, I could not fix my vacation. Now I do. On *Saturday* se'nnight, the 23d, I set out for *Dublin* to bring you home: and so, without Ifs, Ands, and Ors, get ready before our fields be stript of all their gaiety. I thank God, I have every good thing in plenty but money; and that, as affairs are likely to go, will not be my complaint a month longer. *Belturbet* fair will make me an emperor. I have all this town, and six men of my own, at work at this juncture, to make you a winter walk by the river side. I have raised mountains of gravel, and diverted the river's course for that end—*Regis Opus*, you will wonder and be delighted when you see it. Your works at *Quilca* are to be as much inferior to ours here, as a sugar loaf to an *Egyptian* pyramid. We had a county of *Armagh* rogue, one *Mackay*, hanged yesterday: *Griffith* the player never made so merry an exit. He invited his audience the night before, with a promise of giving them such a speech from the gallows as they never heard: and indeed he made his words good; for no man was ever merrier at a christening than he was upon the ladder.

When he mounted to his proper height, he turned his face to each side of the gallows, and said, in a chearful manner, Hah, my friend, am I come to you at last! Then turning to the people, Gentlemen, you need not stand so thick, for the farthest shall hear me as easily as the nearest. Upon this a fellow interrupted him, and asked him, Did he know any thing of a grey mare which was stolen from him? Why, what if I should, would you pay for a mass for my soul? Ay, by G——, said the fellow, will I pay for seven. Why then, said the criminal laughing, I know nothing of your mare. After this he entertained the company with two hours history of his villanies, in a loud unconcerned voice. At last he concluded with his humble service to one of the inhabitants of our town, desiring that he would give him a single night's lodging, which was all he would trouble him for. He was not the least touched with any liquor; but soberly and intrepidly desired the hangman to do his office: and at last went off with a joke. Match me this with any of your *Englishmen*, if you can. I have no more news from *Cavan*, but that you have all their hearts, and mine among the rest, if it be worth any thing. My love and service to Mrs *Whiteway*, and all friends.

> I am, dear Sir, your most obedient and very humble servant,
> Thomas Sheridan

Quilca] in Co. Cavan; the home of Sheridan's wife Elizabeth, and a place apparently detested equally by Sheridan and Swift.   Griffith] Thomas Griffith was a well-known Dublin actor.

MRS WHITEWAY

Mrs Whiteway was a much younger cousin of Jonathan Swift's who looked after him devotedly in his later years. John Boyle, 5th Earl of Cork and Orrery (1707–62), wrote a book on Swift (1752) and printed this letter.

47. To the Earl of Orrery, 22 November 1742

My Lord,

The easy manner, in which you reproach me for not acquainting you with the poor Dean's situation, lays a fresh obligation upon me; yet mean as an excuse is for a fault, I shall attempt one to your Lordship, and only for this reason, that you may not think me capable of neglecting any thing

you could command me. I told you in my last letter, the Dean's understanding was quite gone, and I feared the farther particulars would only
shock the tenderness of your nature, and the melancholy scene make your
heart ach, as it has often done mine. I was the last person whom he knew,
and when that part of his memory failed, he was so outragious at seeing any
body, that I was forced to leave him, nor could he rest for a night or two
after seeing any person: so that all the attendance I could pay him was
calling twice a week to enquire after his health, and to observe that proper
care was taken of him, and durst only look at him while his back was turned
towards me, fearing to discompose him. He walked ten hours a day, would
not eat or drink if his servant stayed in the room. His meat was served up
ready cut, and sometimes it would lie an hour on the table before he would
touch it, and then eat it walking. About six weeks ago, in one night's time,
his left eye swelled as large as an egg, and the lid Mr NICHOLS (his surgeon)
thought would mortify, and many large boils appeared under his arms and
body. The torture he was in, is not to be described. Five persons could
scarce hold him for a week, from tearing out his own eyes: and, for near a
month, he did not sleep two hours in twenty four: yet a moderate appetite
continued; and what is more to be wondered at, the last day of his illness,
he knew me perfectly well, took me by the hand, called me by my name,
and shewed the same pleasure as usual in seeing me. I asked him, if he
would give me a dinner? He said, to be sure, my old friend. Thus he
continued that day, and knew the Doctor and Surgeon, and all his family
so well, that Mr NICHOLS thought it possible that he might return to a share
of understanding, so as to able to call for what he wanted, and to bear some
of his old friends to amuse him. But alas! this pleasure to me was but of
short duration; for the next day or two it was all over, and proved to be
only pain that had rouzed him. He is now free from torture: his eye almost
well; very quiet, and begins to sleep, but cannot, without great difficulty,
be prevailed on to walk a turn about his room: and yet in this way the
Physicians think he may hold out for some time.

I amm my Lord, | Your Lordship's most obedient | humble servant,
M. Whiteway

DEANE SWIFT
(1706–1783)

Deane Swift was the son of a cousin of Swift's. He inherited and published several
of the author's posthumous works. He married Mrs Whiteway's daughter. This
letter was printed by Orrery.

48. To the Earl of Orrery, 4 April 1744

My Lord,

As to the story of *O poor old man!* I enquired into it. The Dean did say something upon seeing himself in the glass, but neither Mrs *Ridgeway*, nor the lower servants could tell what it was he said. I desired them to recollect it, by the time when I should come again to the deanery. I have been there since, they cannot recollect it. A thousand stories have been invented of him within these two years, and imposed upon the world. I thought this might have been one of them: and yet I am now inclined to think, there may be some truth in it: for on Sunday the 17th of March, as he sat in his chair, upon the housekeeper's moving a knife from him as he was going to catch at it, he shrugged his shoulders, and, rocking himself, said, *I am what I am, I am what I am*: and, about six minutes afterwards, repeated the same words two or three times over.

His servant shaves his cheeks, and all his face as low as the tip of his chin, once a week: but under the chin, and about the throat, when the hair grows long, it is cut with scissars.

Sometimes he will not utter a syllable: at other times he will speak incoherent words: but he never yet, as far as I could hear, talked nonsense, or said a foolish thing.

About four months ago he gave me great trouble: he seemed to have a mind to talk to me. In order to try what he would say, I told him, I came to dine with him, and immediately his housekeeper, Mrs *Ridgeway*, said, *Won't you give Mr Swift a glass of wine, Sir?* he shrugged his shoulders, just as he used to do when he had a mind that a friend should spend the evening with him. Shrugging his shoulders, your Lordship may remember, was as much as to say, 'You'll ruin me in wine.' I own, I was scarce able to bear the sight. Soon after, he again endeavoured, with a good deal of pain, to find words to speak to me: at last, not being able, after many efforts, he gave a heavy sigh, and, I think, was afterwards silent. This puts me in mind of what he said about five days ago. He endeavoured several times to speak to his servant (now and then he calls him by his name): at last, not finding words to express what he would be at, after some uneasiness, he said 'I am a fool'. Not long ago, the servant took up his watch that lay upon the table to see what o'clock it was, he said, 'Bring it here:' and when it was brought, he looked very attentively at it: some time ago, the servant was breaking a large stubborn coal, he said, 'That's a stone, you blockhead.'

In a few days, or some very short time, after guardians had been appointed for him, I went into his dining room, where he was walking, I said something to him very insignificant, I know not what; but, instead of making any kind of answer to it, he said, 'Go, Go,' pointing with his hand to the door, and immediately afterwards, raising his hand to his head, he said, 'My best understanding,' and so broke off abruptly, and walked away.

I am, my Lord, | Your Lordship's most obedient, |
and most humble servant,
Deane Swift

ALEXANDER POPE
(1688–1744)

In the course of what he called 'this long disease, my life', Pope, though affected physically and mentally by his illnesses, made many friends. This selection of his voluminous (and carefully edited) correspondence represents a tribute to an early friendship and a communication, made within ten weeks of his death, to another friend of long standing.

49. To Martha Blount, November 1714

Martha Blount (1690–1763) and her sister Teresa (1688–1759) of Mapledurham, on the Thames near Reading, were Catholic friends from the childhood of Pope. Martha was his chief legatee.

Most Divine!

'Tis some proof of my sincerity towards you that I write when I am prepared by drinking to speak truth, and sure a letter after twelve at night must abound with that noble ingredient. That heart must have abundance of flames which is at once warmed by wine and you; wine awakens and refreshes the lurking passions of the mind, as varnish does the colours that are sunk in a picture, and brings them out in all their natural glowings. My good qualities have been so frozen and locked up in a dull constitution at all my former sober hours, that it is very astonishing to me, now I am drunk, to find so much virtue in me.

In these overflowings of my heart I pay you my thanks for those two obliging letters you favoured me with of the 18th and 24th instant. That which begins with 'Dear Creature', and 'my charming Mr Pope', was a delight to me beyond all expression. You have at last entirely gained the conquest over your fair sister; 'tis true you are not handsome, for you are a woman and think you are not; but this good humour and tenderness for me has a charm that cannot be resisted. That face must needs be irresistible which was adorned with smiles even when it could not see the Coronation.

I must own I have long been shocked at your sister on several accounts, but above all things at her prudery: I am resolved to break with her for ever; and therefore tell her I shall take the first opportunity of sending back all her letters.

I do suppose you will not show this epistle out of vanity, as I doubt not your said sister does all I writ to her. Indeed to correspond with Mr Pope may make anyone proud who lives under a dejection of heart in the country. Every one values Mr Pope, but every one for a different reason. One for his firm adherence to the Catholic faith, another for his neglect of Popish superstition, one for his grave behaviour, another for his whimsicalness. Mr Tidcombe for his pretty atheistical jests, Mr Caryll for his moral and Christian sentences, Mrs Teresa for his reflections on Mrs Patty, and Mrs Patty for his reflections on Mrs Teresa.

My acquaintance runs so much in an anti-Catholic channel, that it was but t'other day I heard of Mrs Fermor's being actually, directly, and consummatively, married. I wonder how the guilty couple and their accessories at Whiteknights look, stare, or simper, since that grand secret came out which they so well concealed before. They concealed it as well as a barber does his utensils when he goes to trim upon a Sunday and his towels hang out all the way: or as well as a friar concealed a little wench, whom he was carrying under his habit to Mr Colingwood's convent; 'Pray, Father', said one in the street to him, 'what's that under your arm?' 'A saddle for one of the brothers to ride with', quoth the friar. 'Then Father', cried he, 'take care and shorten the stirrups'—For the girl's legs hung out—

You know your doctor is gone the way of all his patients, and was hard put to it how to dispose of an estate miserably unwieldy, and splendidly unuseful to him. Sir Sam. Garth says, that for Radcliffe to leave a library was as if an eunuch should found a seraglio. Dr Shadwell lately told a lady he wondered she could be alive after him; she made answer she wondered at it too, both because Dr Radcliffe was dead, and because Dr Shadwell was alive.

Poor Parnell is now on the briny ocean which he increases with his briny tears for the loss of you etc. Pray for him, if you please, but not for me. Don't so much as hope I may go to Heaven: 'tis a place I am not very fond of, I hear no great good of it. All the descriptions I ever heard of it amount to no more than just this: it is eternal singing, and piping, and sitting in sunshine. Much good may it do the saints; and those who intend to be saints. For my part I am better than a saint, for I am, Madam, Your most faithful admirer, friend, servant, anything.

I send you Gay's poem on the Princess. She is very fat. God keep her husband.

Coronation] Martha was prevented from attending the coronation of George I by an attack of smallpox.   Caryll] John Caryll, another Catholic, was a lifelong friend.   Mrs Patty] Martha.   Mrs Fermor] Arabella Fermor, immortalized as Belinda in *The Rape of the Lock* (1712, 1714).   Radcliffe] Dr John Radcliffe, a rich doctor, left a large bequest to Oxford University.   Parnell] Thomas Parnell (1679–1718), Irish poet and member of the Scriblerus Club.

50. *To Hugh Bethell, 19 March 1744*

Bethell (1689–1747) was a Yorkshireman, an MP in Burlington's circle.

I am very solicitous to know how you proceed in your health, and these inveterate north-easterly winds give me much apprehension for yours, as they very greatly affect mine. Within these three weeks I have been excessive ill. The asthma in every symptom increased, with a swelling in my legs and a low fever. I have been so long and yet am confined to my chamber at Twitnam and the whole business of my two servants night and day to attend me. Dr Burton is very watchful over me, he changed the warm pills into a cooler regimen. I drink no wine, and take scarce any meat. Asses' milk twice a day. My only medicines are millepedes and garlic, and horehound tea. He is against crude quicksilver till he is sure there is no fever, but prescribes alkalized mercury in five pills a day: and proposes an issue, which I fear may drain and waste me too much, it can't be imagined how weak I am, and how unable to move, or walk, or use any exercise, but going in a coach, for which the weather is yet too cold. These are all discouraging things, to cure me of buying houses, so I've determined not to purchase this, which will cost me £1,200 and instead of it to lay out three upon a cheap one in London, seated in an airy high place. If I live but five months I shall never be able to live about, as I used, in other peoples houses, but quite at ease, to keep my own hours, and with my own servants: and if I don't live there, it will do for a friend, which Twitnam would not suit at all. Give me leave therefore to pay in to your brother what I don't want of the sum I drew upon him by your kind order.—I told you in my last how very welcome was your kind present of your picture which he transmitted very safe. The last thing I did before I was confined, was to sit the first time to Mr Kent, for you: it wants but one sitting more, and pray tell me, where, or with whom it shall be left for you?

Now I have said a great deal, all I could, of my own state, pray be as particular as to yours. I every morning and night see you in my bedchamber and think of you: nothing can be more resembling, but I wish your complexion be in reality as healthy. Dear Sir, if you are not worse, do not let me wait long for the comfort of knowing it, though you employ any hand, and spare your own eyes. Above all, what is your scheme, as to coming to London, and when? Me you cannot miss; and we may truly say of each other, that we shall be friends to the last breath. Pray remember me to Mr Moyser.

Ever yours
A. Pope

I must desire you to say nothing of what I tell you concerning my purchase of the house in town, which is done in another's name.

Dr Burton] a well-known physician.   Garlic ... mercury] garlic, horehound, asses' milk, and preparations of mercury were in the pharmacopoeia of the period.   Brother] Bethell's brother Slingsby was a city merchant and MP.   Say nothing] Roman Catholics were barred from owning real estate, and subterfuges of this kind were not unusual.

LORD HERVEY
(1696–1743)

John Hervey, Baron Hervey of Ickworth, was a courtier, politician, and writer, and a friend of Lady Mary Wortley Montagu. He was violently attacked by Pope as an effeminate mischief-maker ('Lord Fanny' and 'Sporus', 'this painted child of dirt that stinks and stings').

51. To Stephen Fox, 7 September 1730

Sir Stephen Fox (1704–74), later Earl of Ilchester and brother of Henry, 1st Lord Holland, was a friend of Hervey and Horace Walpole. Hervey had travelled in Italy with Fox.

There is no part of my time I repine so much at not being master of, as the hours I wish to dedicate to you; and though this is a misfortune that happens to me every post day, it is one I am as impatient under as if I was not accustomed to it. The King is this moment come from a horse-race, where popularity I believe carried him, as it does a stag-hunting; for sure the pleasure of both these entertainments were calculated for much better eyes than His Majesty's. The last letters bring but indifferent accounts of the poor P. of Prussia; his father's severities increase daily towards him and all his adherents; in so much that I should not be at all surprised to hear of his having proceeded to extremities for which I know but one example. I shall never have done wondering at the K. of Sardinia; he is as incomprehensible as the Trinity.

I cannot resist giving you an account of the Princess of Holstein's wedding. I read it in a private letter from one of the King of Poland's family, who was present at it, to an Hanoverian officer now at Windsor. She was called Countess of Rosinski [*sic*], is natural daughter to his Polish Majesty, his declared mistress, and privately well with her brother the Count Rotoski. The King, tired of her, insisted on her marrying this Prince of Holstein; and he, tired of being poor, consented to take her with a pension of 12,000 German crowns which her father offered to get rid of her. The lady, who liked being a w—— in jack-boots better than a Princess in petticoats, and preferred drinking in a camp to curtseying in a Drawing Room, told her future spouse, that though he did marry her, she would not only continue to lie with those she liked, but would upon no terms ever consent to lie with one she did not, and that inflicting his name upon her should never be a plea for his inflicting his person. The wise Prince, thinking of nothing but the 12,000 crowns, very loyally and philosophically told her that he thought himself obliged to obey his King, and would trust to her goodness and his own unwearied endeavours to please her for the reversal of so hard a sentence as what she then pronounced. Upon these terms the nuptials were solemnised in the most pompous manner. The day passed in feasting, balls, shows, etc. At night the lady was laid with the usual ceremonies in bed; the husband was afterwards brought dead drunk by the bride-grooms (whom she had bribed with gold or beauty to make him so), and laid in the bed by her. The company was no sooner gone out of the room, but she rose, went into another apartment, and slept very quietly all night. The husband waking in the morning would have followed her, but found the room fortified, the lady determined not to capitulate, and so was forced to raise the siege. She told him, as Evadne does Amintor, this was no affected coyness for a night, but that he was never to expect more favour at her hands; and his inclination being much weaker than her aversion, and his love of 12,000 crowns so much stronger than that he had for her person, he submitted: and said since she insisted upon it, he saw no great difference between beginning the part of a husband at the fifth act or the first. And since the indifference they felt for one another was what all married people must come to, he thought a little sooner or a little later would make no great odds in their happiness, and that very possibly their having never been fond, might make them civil with less constraint. The truth of this was soon proved, by his going in two days with her to a convent, to see a natural child she had there at nurse, with as much sang-froid as if he had begot it. Adieu, this history perhaps may tire you, but it entertained me.

P. of Prussia] Frederick Louis, Prince of Prussia (1707–51), now Prince of Wales, son of George II; killed by a tennis ball, he did not live to succeed his father, with whom he did not get on. He came to England from Hanover in 1728 and was narrowly prevented from secretly marrying Lady Diana Spencer.   K. of Sardinia] the King of Sardinia had abdicated in favour of his son.   Rosinski] Countess Orzelska (Rosinski) was one of the King of Poland's 364 children. Carlyle in his *Frederick the Great* remarks that she might well not have known Rotoski was her brother, but adds that 'her history is not to be touched, except upon compulsion, as if with a pair of tongs'.   Evadne] Evadne ('a maidenhead, Amintor, at my years?') and Amintor are in Beaumont and Fletcher's *The Maid's Tragedy* (1619).

52. *To Stephen Fox, 14 November 1732*

Excepting the agreeable days I have pass'd alone with you, I never spent one in a more pleasant male tête à tête than I did yesterday. Ld. Chesterfield came early in the morning to breakfast with me. We went together to make our court at Richmond, came back together, and dined together alone afterwards *à petit couvert* in his library. I have not known him in so good humour and spirits of several years. He was incessantly entertaining; and though naturally I know your taste is not turned to romances, but that truths and facts are your search, yet the historical, political, amorous, familiar, foreign and domestic novels which he told, were related in so compendious a manner and so lively a style, that I am sure you would have been infinitely pleased to have been an invisible auditor. I always listen to him as I read poetry, without hoping for a word of truth; and no more consider any thing he says in the light of truth or falsehood than I do any thing that Ariosto writes. If ever I do think of it upon that foot, it is only to admire the fertility of his imagination and the luxuriancy of his invention; and, as one values other people in proportion to their adherence to truth, one admires him most when he deviates most from it. With all this he is positively no liar; a liar, if I understand the definition of one, being a man that tells things as true, which he knows to be false in order to deceive. Now his Lordship never thinks of the things he tells being either true or false, and [as] for deceiving you, provided he is sure you like his manner of telling them, he concerns himself no more about the credit you give to his narrations than he does about the authority he has for them. He is a most wonderful composition.

I concluded the day at Miss Skeritt's. Our Naples friend Celestina sung and supped there with her husband, Mr Hempson, another of our Naples friends, who used to live with the Consul and play upon the flute. There was no body there besides, excepting Lady Susan Hamilton and our Florence acquaintance, Sir Robert Morton, who is just come over, and, moyennant Lady Susan Hamilton by a Scotch nationality, was brought thither under her wing. Voilà la Gazette de hier. Adio, caro & carissimo & sempre caro. Pray tell the Count that I hear by a letter the Duke of Richmond wrote to me last post, that he had written that day to invite his Countship to Goodwood. I hope he intends to accept the invitation; and since we could not be all together in Somersetshire, that we shall be so at least in Sussex, though that will not be half so well.

I desire you would always put your letters in covers, for at best they are not very legible; and when they are nudities, I tear them all to pieces in opening, which makes the deciphering of them so infinitely difficult and laborious, that I am sure it would pose Mr Wills himself.

Ld. Chesterfield] (1694–1773) is best known for his letters on etiquette to his natural son Philip, and for the reproof he received from Dr Johnson. Miss Skeritt] Maria Skerrett was Walpole's mistress and later his wife; he thought she was caricatured as Polly in Gay's *The Beggar's Opera*, and suppressed its sequel, *Polly*.

THOMAS GRAY
(1716–1771)

The poet Gray was at Eton with Walpole and later toured with him in Italy; he was an undergraduate at Peterhouse, Cambridge, and from 1742 a Fellow. He moved to Pembroke College in 1756.

53. To Horace Walpole, 31 October 1734

For Walpole, see Letters 55–60. Gray writes as a freshman of three weeks' standing at Peterhouse.

For Gods sake send me your Quære's, & I'll do my best to get information upon those Points, you don't understand: I warrant, you imagine that People in one College, know the Customs of others; but you mistake, they are quite little Societies by themselves: yᵉ Dresses, Language, Customs &c are different in different Colledges: what passes for Wit in one, would not be understood if it were carried to another: thus the Men of Peter-house, Pembroke & Clare-hall of course must be Tories; those of Trinity, Rakes; of Kings, Scholars; of Sidney, Wigs; of Sᵗ Johns, Worthy men & so on: now what to say about this Terra Incognita, I don't know; First then it is a great old Town, shaped like a Spider, with a nasty lump in the middle of it, & half a dozen scambling long legs: it has 14 Parishes, 12 Colledges, & 4 Halls, these Halls only entertain Students, who after a term of years, are elected into the Colledges: there are 5 ranks in the University, subordinate to the Vice-chancellour, who is chose annually: these are Masters, Fellows, Fellow-Commoners, Pensioners, & Sizers; The Masters of Colledges are twelve grey-hair'd Gentlefolks, who are all mad with Pride; the Fellows are sleepy, drunken, dull, illiterate Things; the Fellow-Com: are imitatours of the Fellows, or else Beaux, or else nothing: the Pension: grave, formal Sots, who would be thought old; or else drink Ale, & sing Songs against yᵉ Excise. The Sizers are Graziers Eldest Sons, who come to get good Learning, that they may all be Archbishops of Canterbury: these 2 last Orders are qualified to take Scholarships; one of which, your humble Servᵗ has had given him: first they led me into the hall, & there I swore Allegiance to yᵉ King; then I went to a room, where I took 50000 Latin Oaths, such as, to wear a Square Cap, to make 6 verses upon the Epistle or Gospel every Sunday morning, to chant very loud in Chappel, to wear a clean Surplice, &c: &c: Now as to eating: the Fellow-Com: dine at the Fellows Table, their Commons is worth 6ˢ-4ᵈ a-week, the Pensioners pay but 2ˢ-4ᵈ; if any body don't like their Commons, they send down into the Kitchen to know, what's for Sizing: the Cook sends up a Catalogue of what there is; & they chuse, what they please: they are obliged to pay for Commons, whither they eat it, or no: there is always Plenty enough: the Sizers feast upon the leavings of the rest; as to dress, the Fell: Commoners usually wear a Prunella Gown with Sleeves, a hat & no band; but their proper habit has its Sleeves trimmed with Gold-lace, this they only wear at publick Ceremonies; neither do the Noblemen use their pr: Habit commonly, but wear only a black Padesoy Gown: the Men of Kings are a sort of University by themselves; & differ in Customs from all the rest; every body hates 'em & when Almanzor comes to me, our Peoples stare at him, like a Lord-mayors Show, & wonder to see a human Creature among them: if I tell you, I never stirr out, perhaps you won't believe me; especially when you know, there's a Club of Wits kept at the Mitre, all such as come from Eton; where Alm: would introduce me, if I so pleased:—yet you will not think it strange, that I don't go abroad, when I tell you, that I am got into a room; such a hugeous one, that little i is quite lost in it; so that when I get up in the morning, I begin to travel towards the middle of it with might & main, & with much ado about noon bate at a great Table, which stands half-way it: so then, by that time, (after having pursued my journey full speed); that I arrive at the door, it is so dark & late, & I am so tired, that I am obliged to turn back again: so about Midnight I get to the bedside: then, thinks you, I suppose, he goes to sleep: hold you a bit; in this Country it is so far from that, that we go to bed to wake, & rise to sleep: in short, those that go along the street, do nothing but walk in their sleep: they run against every Post they meet: but I beg pardon, for talking so much of myself, since that's not, what you care for—(To be continued)

Sizing] an extra dish, paid for separately.   Prunella] worsted stuff used for gowns.
Padesoy] Paduasoy, stuff of strong silk.   Almanzor] a character in Dryden's *Conquest of Granada* (1670), but here Thomas Ashton, now an undergraduate at King's; he had been at Eton with Gray.

54. To James Brown, 24 September 1761

James Brown (1709–84) was a Fellow, and later Master, of Pembroke College, Cambridge.

Dear S^r,

I set out at half an hour past four in the morning for the Coronation, & (in the midst of perils & dangers) arrived very safe at my Ld Chamberlain's Box in Westminster Hall. it was on the left hand of the throne over that appropriated to the Foreign Ministers. opposite to us was the Box of the Earl Marshal, & other Great Officers, & below it that of the Princess, & younger Part of the Royal Family. next them was the royal sideboard. then below the steps of the Haut-pas were the tables of the Nobility on each side quite to the door, behind them boxes for the sideboards, over these the galleries for the Peers Tickets, & still higher the boxes of the Auditor, the board of Green-Cloth, &c: all these throng'd with people head above head, all dress'd, & the Women with their Jewels on. in the front of the throne was a Triomfe of foliage & flowers, resembling nature, placed on the royal table, & rising as high as the canopy itself. the several bodies, that were to form the procession, issued from behind the throne gradually & in order, and proceeding down the steps were ranged on either side of the hall, all the Privy-Councellors, that are Commoners, (I think) were there, (except Mr Pitt), mightily dress'd in rich stuffs of gold & colours with long flowing wigs, some of them comical figures enough. the Kn:^{s} of the Bath with their high plumage were very ornamental, of the Scotch Peers or Peeresses, that you see in the list, very few walk'd; & of the English Dowagers as few, tho' many of them were in Town & among the Spectators. the noblest and most graceful figures among the Ladies, were the Marchioness of Kildare (as Viscountess Leinster) Visc:^{ss} Spencer, Countesses of Harrington, Pembroke & Strafford, & the Duchess of Richmond. of the older sort (for there is a grace, that belongs to age too) the Countess of Westmoreland C:^{ss} of Albermarle, & Dutchess of Queensberry. I should mention too the odd and extraordinary appearances: they were the Visc:^{ss} Say & Sele, Countesses of Portsmouth, & another that I do not name, because she is said to be an extraordinary good woman, Countess of Harcourt, & Dutchess of St Albans. of the Men doubtless the noblest and most striking figure was the Earl of Errol, & after him the Dukes of Ancaster, Richmond, Marlborough, Kingston; Earl of Northampton, Pomfret, Visc:^{t} Weymouth, &c: the comical Men were the Earl Talbot (most in sight of anybody) Earls of Delawere & Macclesfield, Lords Montfort & Melcombe. all these I beheld at great leisure. then the Princess and Royal Family enter'd their Box; the Queen, & then the King, took their places in their chairs of state, glitt'ring with jewels (for the hire of w^{ch}, beside all his own, he paid 9000£) & the Dean & Chapter (who had been waiting without doors a full hour & half) brought up the Regalia, wch the D. of Ancaster received and placed on the Table. here ensued great confusion in the delivering them out to the Lords, who were appointed to bear them. the Heralds were stupid; the Great Officers knew nothing they were doing; the B^p. of Rochester would have drop'd the Crown, if it had not been pin'd to the Cushion, & the King was often obliged to call out, & set matters right: but the Sword of State had been entirely forgot; so Ld Huntingdon was forced to carry the Ld Mayor's great two-handed sword instead of it. this made it later than ordinary, before they got under their canopies, & set forward. I should have told you, that the old B^p of Lincoln with his stick went doddling by the side of the Queen, & the B^p of Chester had the pleasure of bearing the gold paten.

when they were gone we went down to dinner, for there were three rooms
below, where the Duke of Devonshire was so good to feed us with great
cold Sirloins of beef, legs of mutton, fillets of veal, & other substantial
viands, and liqueurs, w:^{ch} we devour'd all higgledy-piggledy like Porters.
after w:^{ch} every one scrambled up again & seated themselves. the tables
were now spread, the cold viands set on & at the Kings table & side-board
a great show of gold-plate, & a desert representing Parnassus with abundance of figures of Muses, Arts, &c. design'd by Ld Talbot: this was so
high, that those at the end of the Hall could see neither K: nor Queen at
supper. when they return'd, it was so dark, that the People without doors
scarce saw anything of the procession, & as the Hall had then no other light
than two long ranges of candles at each of the Peers tables, we saw almost
as little as they; only one perceived the L^{ds} & Ladies sidleing in & taking
their places to dine, but the instant the Queen's Canopy enter'd, fire was
given to all the Lustres at once by trains of prepared flax, that reached from
one to the other. to me it seem'd an interval of not half a minute, before the
whole was in a blaze of splendor. it is true, that for that half minute it
rain'd fire upon the heads of all the spectators (the flax falling in large
flakes) & the Ladies (Queen & all) were in no small terrors, but no mischief
ensued. it was out as soon as it fell, & the most magnificent spectacle, I ever
beheld remain'd. the K: (bowing to the Lords as he pass'd) with his crown
on his head, & the sceptre & orb in his hands, took his place with great
majesty & grace: so did the Q: with her crown, sceptre & rod. then supper
was served in gold plate, the Earl Talbot, D: of Bedford, & E: of Effingham,
in their robes, all three on horseback prancing & curvetting, like the hobby-
horses in the Rehearsal, usher'd in the courses to the foot of the haut-pas.
between the courses the Champion performed his part with applause. the
E. of Denbigh carved for the King, E. of Holdernesse for the Queen: they
both eat like farmers. at the board's end on the right sup'd the D^s: of York
& Cumberland, on the left Lady Augusta, all of them very rich in jewels.
the maple cups, the wafers, the faulcons, &c: were brought up & presented
in form, 3 persons were knighted, & before 10 the K: & Q: retired. then I
got a scrap of supper, & at one o'clock I walk'd home. so much for the
spectacle, wch in magnificence surpass'd every thing I have seen. next I
must tell you, that the Barons of the Cinque-ports, who by ancient right
should dine at a table on the Haut-pas at the right hand of the throne,
found that no provision at all had been made for them, & representing their
case to Earl Talbot, he told them Gentlemen, if you speak to me as High-
Steward I must tell you, there was no room for you: if as Ld Talbot, I am
ready to give you satisfaction in any way you think fit. they are several of
them Gentlemen of the best families, so this has bred ill blood. in the next
place the City of London found they had no table neither; but Beckford

bullied my Ld High Steward, till he was forced to give them that intended for the Kn:^{ts} of the Bath & instead of it they dined at the entertainment prepared for the Great Officers. 3dly & lastly (this is fact) when the Queen retired while she was in the Abbey, to a sort of closet furnish'd with necessary conveniences, one of the Ladies opening the door to see all was right, found the D:^{e} of Newcastle perk'd up & in the very act upon the anointed velvet closestool. Do not think I joke, it is literally true.

Bussy was not at the ceremony: he is just setting out for France. Spain has supplied them with money, & is picking a quarrel with us about the fishery & the logwood. Mr Pitt says, so much the better! & was for recalling Ld Bristol directly: however a flat denial has been return'd to their pretentions.

When you have read this send it to Pa:

The Coronation] of George III.   Haut-pas] dais.   Auditor] of the Exchequer. Green-Cloth] Lord Steward of the Household.   Triomfe] arch.   Ancaster] the Duke of Ancaster was Lord Great Chamberlain.   Devonshire] the Duke of Devonshire was Lord Chamberlain.   Bedford] the Duke of Bedford was Lord High Constable.   Rehearsal] in the Duke of Buckingham's play *The Rehearsal* (1671) there is a battle involving hobby-horses. Champion] the Champion issues a challenge on behalf of the monarch; this time, according to Horace Walpole, Lord Talbot had trained his horse to go backward so as not to turn its rump to the King.   Beckford] MP for the City of London.   Bussy] the Abbé de Bussy was in town to negotiate a peace.   Bristol] Lord Bristol was ambassador in Madrid.

HORACE WALPOLE

(1717–1797)

Horace Walpole was the son of Sir Robert, owner of the Gothic house Strawberry Hill, at Twickenham, and the author of the Gothic novel *The Castle of Otranto* (1764). His letters, written for eventual publication, require forty-eight volumes in the edition of W. S. Lewis. Correspondents included his friend the poet Gray, Horace Mann, the Countess of Ossory, George Montagu, and Mary Berry, one of the two sisters on whom he came to depend in later life.

55. *To Richard West, 27 February 1740*

Walpole, writing from Florence, was making the grand tour with Thomas Gray. Richard West (1716–42) was an Eton friend of Gray and Walpole.

Well, West, I have found a little unmasqued moment to write to you; but for this week past I have been so muffled up in my domino, that I have not had the command of my elbows. But what have you been doing all the mornings? Could you not write then?—No, then I was masqued too; I have done nothing but slip out of my domino into bed, and out of bed into my domino. The end of the Carnival is frantic, bacchanalian; all the morn one

makes parties in masque to the shops and coffee-houses, and all the evening
to the operas and balls. *Then I have danced, good gods! how have I danced!*
The Italians are fond to a degree of our country dances: *Cold and raw* they
only know by the tune; *Blowzybella* is almost Italian, and *Buttered peas* is
Pizelli al buro. There are but three days more; but the two last are to have
balls all the morning at the fine unfinished palace of the Strozzi; and the
Tuesday night a masquerade after supper: they sup first, to eat *gras*, and
not encroach upon Ash-Wednesday. What makes masquerading more agreeable here than in England, is the great deference that is shown to the
disguised. Here they do not catch at those little dirty opportunities of
saying any ill-natured thing they know of you, do not abuse you because
they may, or talk gross bawdy to a woman of quality. I found the other day,
by a play of Etheridge's, that we have had a sort of Carnival even since the
Reformation; 'tis in *She would if She could*, they talk of going a-mumming
in Shrove-tide.——

After talking so much of diversions, I fear you will attribute to them the
fondness I own I contract for Florence; but it has so many other charms,
that I shall not want excuses for my taste. The freedom of the Carnival has
given me opportunities to make several acquaintances; and if I have not
found them refined, learned, polished, like some other cities, yet they are
civil, good-natured, and fond of the English. Their little partiality for
themselves, opposed to the violent vanity of the French, makes them very
amiable in my eyes. I can give you a comical instance of their great prejudice about nobility; it happened yesterday. While we were at dinner at
Mr Mann's, word was brought by his secretary, that a cavalier demanded
audience of him upon an affair of honour. Gray and I flew behind the
curtain of the door. An elderly gentleman, whose attire was not certainly
correspondent to the greatness of his birth, entered, and informed the
British minister, that one Martin, an English painter, had left a challenge
for him at his house, for having said Martin was no gentleman. He would
by no means have spoke of the duel before the transaction of it, but that his
honour, his blood, his &c. would never permit him to fight with one who
was no cavalier; which was what he came to inquire of his excellency. We
laughed loud laughs, but unheard: his fright or his nobility had closed his
ears. But mark the sequel: the instant he was gone, my very English
curiosity hurried me out of the Gate St Gallo; 'twas the place and hour
appointed. We had not been driving about above ten minutes, but out
popped a little figure, pale but cross, with beard unshaved and hair un-
combed, a slouched hat, and a considerable red cloak, in which was wrapped
under his arm, the fatal sword that was to revenge the highly injured Mr
Martin, painter and defendant. I darted my head out of the coach, just
ready to say, 'Your servant, Mr Martin,' and talk about the architecture of
the triumphal arch that was building there; but he would not know me, and

walked off. We left him to wait for an hour, to grow very cold and very valiant the more it grew past the hour of appointment. We were figuring all the poor creature's huddle of thoughts, and confused hopes of victory or fame, of his unfinished pictures, or his situation upon bouncing into the next world. You will think us strange creatures; but 'twas a pleasant sight, as we knew the poor painter was safe. I have thought of it since, and am inclined to believe that nothing but two English could have been capable of such a jaunt. I remember, 'twas reported in London, that the plague was at a house in the city, and all the town went to see it.

I have this instant received your letter. Lord! I am glad I thought of those parallel passages, since it made you translate them. 'Tis excessively near the original; and yet, I don't know, 'tis very easy too.—It snows here a little to-night, but it never lies but on the mountains. Adieu!

Yours ever.

P.S.—What is the history of the theatres this winter?

Domino] mask.   Etheridge] Sir George Etherege (1634–91), whose play *She Wou'd if she Cou'd* was performed in 1668.   Mr Mann] Horace Mann.

56. To Horace Mann, 21 August 1746

Sir Horace Mann (1701–86) was the British envoy in Florence with a special charge to watch the doings of the Young Pretender, the execution of whose supporters, the Jacobite leaders of the Forty-Five, is the main topic of this letter. His correspondence with Walpole is so voluminous that the latter said it was 'not to be paralleled in the history of the post-office'. Mann's share is generally regarded as of little interest. The Jacobites described in this letter include Lord Balmerino (1688–1746), who had been a Jacobite in exile, but returned in 1733 with a pardon; when Prince Charles arrived in Scotland in 1745 he at once joined him. Captured after Culloden, Balmerino was tried for high treason (Walpole was there, and described the occasion to Mann, calling Balmerino 'the most natural brave old gentleman I have ever seen'). Unlike Lord Kilmarnock, he declined to sue for mercy. Kilmarnock (1704–46), who had only recently defected to the Jacobite side, was wrongly suspected of ordering the massacre of English prisoners at Culloden. The animosity of the Duke of Cumberland ('the Duke') ensured that he was not, like Lord Cromarty, granted mercy.

You will perceive by my date that I am got into a new scene [Windsor], and that I am retired hither like an old summer dowager; only that I have no toad-eater to take the air with me in the back part of my lozenge-coach, and to be scolded. I have taken a small house here within the castle, and propose spending the greatest part of every week here till the Parliament meets; but my jaunts to town will prevent my news from being quite provincial and marvelous. Then I promise you, I will go to no races nor assemblies, nor make comments upon couples that come in chaises to the White Hart.

I came from town (for take notice, I put this place upon myself for the country) the day after the execution of the rebel lords: I was not at it, but had two persons come to me directly who were at the next house to the scaffold: and I saw another who was upon it, so that you may depend upon my accounts.

Just before they came out of the Tower, Lord Balmerino drank a bumper to King James's health. As the clock struck ten, they came forth on foot, Lord Kilmarnock all in black, his hair unpowdered in a bag, supported by Forster, the great Presbyterian, and Mr Home, a young clergyman, his friend. Lord Balmerino followed, alone, in a blue coat, turned up with red (his rebellious regimentals), a flannel waist coat, and his shroud beneath; their hearses following. They were conducted to a house near the scaffold: the room forwards had benches for spectators, in the second Lord Kilmarnock was put, and in the third backwards Lord Balmerino: all three chambers hung with black. Here they parted! Balmerino embraced the other and said, 'My lord, I wish I could suffer for both!' He had scarce left him, before he desired again to see him, and then asked him, 'My Lord Kilmarnock, do you know anything of the resolution taken in our army, the day before the battle of Culloden, to put the English prisoners to death?' He replied, 'My Lord, I was not present; but since I came hither, I have had all the reason in the world to believe that there was such order taken; and I hear the Duke has the pocket-book with the order.' Balmerino answered, 'It was a lie raised to excuse their barbarity to us.'—Take notice, that the Duke's charging this on Lord Kilmarnock (certainly on misinformation) decided this unhappy man's fate! The most now pretended is, that it would have come to Lord Kilmarnock's turn to have given the word for the slaughter, as lieutenant-general, with the patent for which he was immediately drawn into the Rebellion, after having been staggered by his wife, her mother, his own poverty, and the defeat of Cope. He remained an hour and a half in the house, and shed tears. At last he came to the scaffold, certainly much terrified, but with a resolution that prevented his behaving in the least meanly or unlike a gentleman. He took no notice of the crowd, only to desire that the baize might be lifted up from the rails, that the mob might see the spectacle. He stood and prayed some time with Forster, who wept over him, exhorted and encouraged him. He delivered a long speech to the Sheriff, and with a noble manliness stuck to the recantation he had made at his trial; declaring he wished that all who embarked in the same cause might meet the same fate. He then took off his bag, coat and waistcoat, with great composure, and after some trouble put on a napkin-cap, and then several times tried the block; the executioner, who was in white, with a white apron, out of tenderness concealing the axe behind himself. At last the Earl knelt down, with a visible unwillingness to depart, and after five minutes dropped his handkerchief, the signal, and his head was cut off at once, only hanging by a bit of skin, and was received in a scarlet cloth by

four of the undertaker's men kneeling, who wrapped it up and put it into
the coffin with the body; orders having been given not to expose the heads,
as used to be the custom.

The scaffold was immediately new-strewed with sawdust, the block
new-covered, the executioner new-dressed, and a new axe brought. Then
came old Balmerino, treading with the air of a general. As soon as he
mounted the scaffold, he read the inscription on his coffin, as he did again
afterwards: he then surveyed the spectators, who were in amazing numbers, even upon masts of ships in the river; and pulling out his spectacles
read a treasonable speech, which he delivered to the Sheriff, and said the
young Pretender was so sweet a Prince, that flesh and blood could not resist
following him; and lying down to try the block, he said, 'If I had a thousand
lives, I would lay them all down here in the same cause.' He said, if he had
not taken the sacrament the day before, he would have knocked down
Williamson, the Lieutenant of the Tower, for his ill usage of him. He took
the axe and felt it, and asked the headsman how many blows he had given
Lord Kilmarnock; and gave him three guineas. Two clergymen, who attended him, coming up, he said, 'No, gentlemen, I believe you have already
done me all the service you can.' Then he went to the corner of the
scaffold, and called very loud for the warder, to give him his perriwig,
which he took off, and put on a night-cap of Scotch plaid, and then pulled
off his coat and waistcoat and lay down; but being told he was on the wrong
side, vaulted round, and immediately gave the sign by tossing up his arm,
as if he were giving the signal for battle. He received three blows, but the
first certainly took away all sensation. He was not a quarter of an hour on
the scaffold; Lord Kilmarnock above half a one. Balmerino certainly died
with the intrepidity of a hero, but with the insensibility of one too. As he
walked from his prison to execution, seeing every window and top of house
filled with spectators, he cried out, 'Look, look, how they are all piled up
like rotten oranges!'

My Lady Townshend, who fell in love with Lord Kilmarnock at his
trial, will go nowhere to dinner, for fear of meeting with a rebel-pie; she
says everybody is so bloody-minded that they eat rebels! The Prince of
Wales, whose intercession saved Lord Cromartie, says he did it in return
for old Sir W. (Lady Cromartie's father) coming down out of his death-bed
to vote against my father in the Chippenham election. If his Royal Highness had not countenanced inveteracy like that of Sir Gordon, he would
have no occasion to exert his gratitude now in favour of rebels. His brother
has plucked a very useful feather out of the cap of the ministry, by forbid-
ding any application for posts in the army to be made to anybody but
himself: a resolution, I dare say, he will keep as strictly and minutely as he
does the discipline and dress of the army.   Adieu!

P.S. I have just received yours of Aug. 9th. You had not then heard of the second great battle of Placentia, which has already occasioned new instructions, or in effect, a recall being sent after Lord Sandwich.

Lozenge-coach] bearing the arms of a maiden lady.   Cope] Sir John Cope was defeated by Prince Charles at Prestonpans (1745).   Chippenham] where Sir Robert Walpole lost an election in 1742.   Placentia] in Lombardy. The Austrians defeated the Spanish there in June 1746. Lord Sandwich had been trying to negotiate a peace.

57. To George Montagu, 13 November 1760

Montagu and Walpole were close friends at Eton. This letter describes the conduct of the new king, George III, and the funeral of the old.

Even the honeymoon of a new reign don't produce events every day. There is nothing but the common toying of addresses and kissing hands. The chief difficulty is settled; Lord Gower yields the Mastership of the Horse to Lord Huntingdon, and removes to the Great Wardrobe, from whence Sir Thomas Robinson was to have gone into Ellis's place, but he is saved, and Sir Thomas remains as lumber, not yet disposed of. The City however have a mind to be out of humour; a paper has been fixed on the Royal Exchange with these words, 'No petticoat government, no Scotch minister, no Lord George Sackville.' Two hints totally unfounded, and the other scarce true. No petticoat ever governed less; it is left at Leicester-house; Lord George's breeches are as little concerned; and except Lady Susan Stuart, and Sir Harry Erskine, nothing has yet been done for any Scots. For the King himself he seems all good-nature, and wishing to satisfy everybody. All his speeches are obliging. I saw him again yesterday, and was surprised to find the levee room had lost so entirely the air of the lion's den. This young man don't stand in one spot, with his eyes fixed royally on the ground, and dropping bits of German news. He walks about and speaks to everybody. I saw him afterwards on the throne, where he is graceful and genteel, sits with dignity, and reads his answers to addresses well. It was the Cambridge address, carried by the Duke of Newcastle in his Doctor's gown, and looking like the *médecin malgré lui*. He had been vehemently solicitous for attendance, for fear my Lord Westmorland, who vouchsafes himself to bring the address from Oxford, should outnumber him. Lord Litchfield and several other Jacobites have kissed hands; George Selwyn says they go to St James's, because now there are so many *Stuarts* there.

Do you know I had the curiosity to go to the burying t'other night; I had never seen a royal funeral. Nay, I walked as a rag of quality, which I found would be, and so it was, the easiest way of seeing it. It is absolutely a noble sight. The Prince's Chamber hung with purple and a quantity of silver lamps, the coffin under a canopy of purple velvet, and six vast chandeliers of silver on high stands had a very good effect: the ambassador from

Tripoli and his son were carried to see that chamber. The procession through a line of foot-guards, every seventh man bearing a torch, the horse-guards lining the outside, their officers with drawn sabres and crape sashes, on horseback, the drums muffled, the fifes, bells tolling and minute guns, all this was very solemn. But the charm was the entrance of the Abbey, where we were received by the Dean and chapter in rich copes, the choir and almsmen all bearing torches; the whole Abbey so illuminated, that one saw it to greater advantage than by day; the tombs, long aisles, and fretted roof all appearing distinctly, and with the happiest chiaroscuro. There wanted nothing but incense, and little chapels here and there with priests saying mass for the repose of the defunct—yet one could not complain of its not being Catholic enough. I had been in dread of being coupled with some boy of ten years old—but the heralds were not very accurate, and I walked with George Grenville, taller and older enough to keep me in countenance. When we came to the chapel of Henry VII all solemnity and decorum ceased—no order was observed, people sat or stood where they could or would, the yeomen of the guard were crying out for help, oppressed by the immense weight of the coffin, the Bishop read sadly, and blundered in the prayers, the fine chapter, *Man that is born of a woman*, was chanted not read, and the anthem, besides being unmeasurably tedious, would have served as well for a nuptial. The real serious part was the figure of the Duke of Cumberland, heightened by a thousand melancholy circumstances. He had a dark brown adonis, and a cloak of black cloth with a train of five yards. Attending the funeral of a father, how little reason soever he had to love him, could not be pleasant. His leg extremely bad, yet forced to stand upon it near two hours, his face bloated and distorted with his late paralytic stroke, which has affected too one of his eyes, and placed over the mouth of the vault, into which in all probability he must himself so soon descend—think how unpleasant a situation! He bore it all with a firm and unaffected countenance. This grave scene was fully contrasted by the burlesque Duke of Newcastle—he fell into a fit of crying the moment he came into the chapel and flung himself back in a stall, the Archbishop hovering over him with a smelling bottle—but in two minutes his curiosity got the better of his hypocrisy and he ran about the chapel with his glass to spy who was or was not there, spying with one hand and mopping his eyes with t'other. Then returned the fear of catching cold, and the Duke of Cumberland, who was sinking with heat, felt himself weighed down, and turning round, found it was the Duke of Newcastle standing upon his train to avoid the chill of the marble. It was very theatric to look down into the vault, where the coffin lay, attended by mourners with lights. Clavering, the Groom of the Bedchamber, refused to sit up with the body, and was dismissed by the King's order.

I have nothing more to tell you but a trifle, a very trifle—the King of Prussia has totally defeated Marshal Daun. This which would have been prodigious news a month ago, is nothing today; it only takes its turn among the questions, 'Who is to be Groom of the Bedchamber?' 'What is Sir T. Robinson to have?' I have been at Leicester Fields today; the crowd was immoderate; I don't believe it will continue so. Good night.

Yours ever
H. W.

Petticoat government] George III was brought up by his mother, the Dowager Princess Augusta.   Scotch minister] the Earl of Bute (1713–92), who had been adviser to the King when Prince of Wales.   Sackville] Viscount Sackville (1716–85) was in disgrace at the time, following a court martial.   Rag of quality] an earl's younger son.   Duke of Cumberland] (1721–65), uncle of George III.   Adonis] wig.   Newcastle] (1693–1768), a corrupt minister disliked by George III.

58. *To George Montagu, 2 February 1762*

I scolded you in my last, but I shall forgive you, if you return soon to England, as you talk of doing, for though you are an abominable correspondent, and only write to beg letters, you are good company, and I have a notion, I shall still be glad to see you.

Lady Mary Wortley is arrived; I have seen her; I think her avarice, her dirt, and her vivacity are all increased. Her dress, like her languages, is a galimatias of several countries; the groundwork, rags; and the embroidery, nastiness. She wears no cap, no handkerchief, no gown, no petticoat, no shoes. An old black laced hood represents the first, the fur of a horseman's coat, which replaces the third, serves for the second; a dimity petticoat is deputy and officiates for the fourth, and slippers act the part of the last. When I was at Florence, and she was expected there, we were drawing *Sortes Virgilianas*—for her, we literally drew

Insanam vatem aspices—

it would have been a stronger prophecy now, even than it was then.

You told me not a word of Mr McNaghton, and I have a great mind to be as coolly indolent about our famous ghost in Cock Lane—why should one steal half an hour from one's amusements to tell a story to a friend in another island? I could send you volumes on the ghost, and I believe if I was to stay a little, I might send you its *Life*, dedicated to my Lord Dartmouth, by the Ordinary of Newgate, its two great patrons. A drunken parish clerk set it on foot out of revenge, the Methodists have adopted it, and the whole town of London think of nothing else. Elizabeth Canning and the rabbit-woman were modest impostors in comparison of this, which goes on without saving the least appearances. The Archbishop, who would

not suffer *The Minor* to be acted in ridicule of the Methodists, permits this
farce to be played every night, and I shall not be surprised if they perform
in the great hall at Lambeth. I went to hear it—for it is not an *apparition*,
but an *audition*—We set out from the opera, changed our clothes at Northumberland House, the Duke of York, Lady Northumberland, Lady Mary
Coke, Lord Hertford and I, all in one hackney-coach and drove to the spot;
it rained torrents; yet the lane was full of mob, and the house so full we
could not get in—at last they discovered it was the Duke of York, and the
company squeezed themselves into one another's pockets to make room for
us. The house, which is borrowed, and to which the ghost has adjourned,
is wretchedly small and miserable; when we opened the chamber, in which
were fifty people, with no light but one tallow candle at the end, we
tumbled over the bed of the child to whom the ghost comes, and whom
they are murdering there by inches in such insufferable heat and stench. At
the top of the room are ropes to dry clothes—I asked, if we were to have
rope-dancing between the acts?—We had nothing; they told us, as they
would at a puppet-show, that it would not come that night till 7 in the
morning—that is, when there are only prentices and old women. We stayed
however till half an hour after one. The Methodists have promised them
contributions; provisions are sent in like forage, and all the taverns and
alehouses in the neighbourhood make fortunes. The most diverting part, is
to hear people wondering *when it will be found out*—as if there was anything
to find out; as if the actors would make their noises where they can be
discovered. However as this pantomime cannot last much longer, I hope
Lady Fanny Shirley will set up a ghost of her own at Twickenham, and
then you shall *hear* one. The Methodists, as Lord Aylsford assured Mr
Chute two nights ago at Lord Dacre's, have attempted ghosts three times
in Warwickshire. There! How good I am!

Yours ever
H. W.

Galimatias] medley.   *Sortes Virgilianas*] the practice of opening the *Aeneid* at random to
find one's fate.   *Insanam . . .*] 'Behold the crazy prophetess!'   Ordinary] chaplain.
Elizabeth Canning] convicted of perjury for a false claim that she had been kidnapped.   The
rabbit-woman] Mary Toft claimed in 1726 to have given birth to rabbits.   *The Minor*]
Samuel Foote's play *The Minor* (1760) satirized George Whitefield the Methodist.   *Found
out*] Dr Johnson wrote a brief 'Account of the Detection of the Imposture in Cock-Lane'.

59. To the Countess of Upper Ossory, 8 April 1779

Anne Liddell (*c*.1738–1804) married the 2nd Earl of Ossory *en secondes noces*; she
became the favoured recipient of Walpole's letters 'on the great world'.

I did not answer your Ladyship's letter, as I generally do, the moment I
received it, because I had nothing to tell you about the remnant of myself,

which is the worst subject in the world. I have been six days at Strawberry Hill, and I think the soft south-west did me good; but I have a constant feverish heat that seems to be undermining my ruins; however, its progress is very slow; and so if you please we will say no more of it; but your goodness in inquiring is written on my heart's last tablet. Mr Mason was with me for two days: he is printing the third book of his *Garden*.

Lord Harrington is gathered to his fathers, or rather, is taken from his *mothers*. Lord Beauchamp's son is well again. Lord Harrington has left my Lady 2,500*l*. besides her jointure of 1,500*l*. a year; to Lady Anna Maria 6,000*l*.; 5,000*l*. to Mr Stanhope, and an estate of 150*l*. a year; but there are so many debts that the legacies are more magnificent than generous. The charming house at St James's is to be sold; but it is supposed the present Earl will purchase it.

This is all I have heard, Madam, since I came to town yesterday, which is perfectly empty; the grass grows in the streets, though nowhere else, for the climate is turned as Asiatic as the government; and it is to be hoped that in time there will be elephants and tigers of our own growth in the Sultan's gardens, to the great satisfaction of Sir William Chambers. I was pleased yesterday to see that, though everything old-fashioned is going out of date, we have still resources. If our trade decays we have new handicrafts: at Turnham Green I read on a large board—*manufacture of temples*. I suppose the Archbishop of York will set up looms in his diocese for Popish chapels, and Manchester weave dungeons for the Inquisition. The Pope's bull against the Dissenters' Bill is actually issued from the Clarendon printing-house. I was interrupted by the strangest story I ever heard, and which I cannot yet believe, though it is certainly true. Last night as Miss Wray was getting into her coach in Covent Garden from the play, a clergyman shot her through the head, and then himself. She is dead; but he is alive to be hanged—in the room of Sir Hugh Palliser. Now, Madam, can one believe such a tale? How could poor Miss Wray have offended a divine? She was no enemy to the church militant or naval, to the Church of England, or the church of Paphos. I do not doubt but it will be found that the assassin was a Dissenter, and instigated by the Americans to give such a blow to the state. My servants have heard that the murderer was the victim's husband: methinks his jealousy was very long-suffering! *Tantaene animis caelestibus irae!* and that he should not have compounded for a deanery! What trials Lord Sandwich goes through! he had better have one for all.

Friday, 9th

I gave David this letter yesterday, and had forgotten to seal it, which he did not perceive till I was gone out for the evening. Instead of sealing it he kept it for me till this morning after I had written my second. I send both to show I have been punctual, though all the novelty is evaporated, and my intelligence is not worth a farthing more than the newspaper.

Ladies, said a certain philosopher, always tell their minds in the postscript. As that is the habitation of truth, I send you, Madam, a little more truth than there was in my narrative of yesterday, which was warm from the first breath of rumour: yet though this is only a postscript I will not answer for its perfect veracity. It is the most authentic account I have yet been able to collect of so strange a story, of which no doubt you are curious to know more.

The assassin's name is Hackman; he is brother to a reputable tradesman in Cheapside, and is of a very pleasing figure himself, and most engaging behaviour. About five years ago he was an officer in the 66th Regiment, and being quartered at Huntingdon, pleased so much as to be invited to the oratorios at Hinchinbrook, and was much caressed there. Struck with Miss Ray's charms he proposed marriage, but she told him she did not choose to carry a knapsack. He went to Ireland, and there changed the colour of his cloth, and at his return, I think not long ago, renewed his suit, hoping a cassock would be more tempting than a gorget; but in vain. Miss Wray, it seems, has been out of order, and abroad but twice all the winter. She went to the play on Wednesday night for the second time with Galli the singer. During the play the desperate lover was at the Bedford Coffee House, and behaved with great calmness, and drank a glass of capillaire. Towards the conclusion, he sallied into the piazza, waiting till he saw his victim handed by Mr Macnamara. He came behind her, pulled her by the gown, and on her turning round, clapped the pistol to her forehead, and shot her through the head. With another pistol he then attempted to shoot himself, but the ball only grazing his brow, he tried to dash out his own brains with the pistol, and is more wounded by those blows than by the ball.

Lord Sandwich was at home expecting her to supper at half an hour after ten. On her not returning an hour later, he said something must have happened: however, being tired, he went to bed at half an hour after eleven, and was scarce in bed before one of his servants came in and said Miss Ray was shot. He stared, and could not comprehend what the fellow meant; nay, lay still, which is full as odd a part of the story as any. At twelve came a letter from the surgeon to confirm the account; and then he was extremely afflicted.

Now, upon the whole, Madam, is not the story full as strange as ever it was? Miss Ray has six children, the eldest son is fifteen, and she was at least three times as much. To bear a hopeless passion for five years, and then murder one's mistress—I don't understand it! If the story clears up at all, your Ladyship shall have a sequel. These circumstances I received from

Lord Hertford, who heard them at court yesterday from the Lords of the Admiralty. I forgot that the Galli swooned away on the spot.

I do not love tragic events *en pure perte*. If they do happen, I would have them historic. This is only of kin to history, and tends to nothing. It is very impertinent in one Hackman, to rival Herod, and shoot Mariamne—and *that* Mariamne a kept mistress! and yet it just sets curiosity agog, because she belongs to Lord Sandwich, at a critical moment—and yet he might as well have killed any other inhabitant of Covent Garden.

Mason] William Mason (1725–97), poet and close friend of Thomas Gray, wrote *The English Garden*, a poem in four books (1771–81). Sir William Chambers] architect (1726–96) who fostered a taste for oriental styles, as in the pagoda at Kew. The Dissenters' bill] intended to excuse Dissenting ministers from subscribing to the articles of the established Church. Miss Wray] Martha Wray (or Ray) was the mistress of Lord Sandwich. The murder, a momentary sensation, is also discussed by Lady Sarah Lennox in a letter of 21 Apr.: 'Don't you pity that poor devil Lord Sandwich just now, & the poor girl too & I think the poor man too: tho' I think it quite right he should be hanged, I pity him monstrously.' *Tantaene* . . .] 'Were the spirits of the gods so full of anger?' (Virgil). Gorget] a military badge worn round the neck. Capillaire] an infusion of maidenhair fern.

60. *To the Countess of Upper Ossory, 3 June 1780*

Lord George Gordon (1751–93) was president of the Protestant Association, which wanted the repeal of the Roman Catholic Relief Act of 1778. When he presented a petition to Parliament requiring the repeal, thousands marched on Westminster. At first orderly, the crowd grew riotous as dark came on, and spread into London, wrecking and burning. The disturbances lasted until 9 June.

I know that a governor or a gazetteer ought not to desert their posts, if a town is besieged, or a town is full of news; and therefore, Madam, I resume my office. I smile today—but I trembled last night; for an hour or more I never felt more anxiety. I knew the bravest of my friends were barricaded into the House of Commons, and every avenue to it impossible. Till I heard the Horse and Foot Guards were gone to their rescue, I expected nothing but some dire misfortune; and the first thing I heard this morning was that part of the town had had a fortunate escape from being burnt after ten last night. You must not expect order, Madam; I must recollect circumstances as they occur; and the best idea I can give your Ladyship of the tumult will be to relate it as I heard it.

I had come to town in the morning on a private occasion, and found it so much as I left it, that though I saw a few blue cockades here and there, I only took them for new recruits. Nobody came in; between seven and eight I saw a hack and another coach arrive at Lord Shelburne's, and thence concluded that Lord George Gordon's trumpet had brayed to no purpose. At eight I went to Gloucester House; the Duchess told me there had been a riot, and that Lord Mansfield's glasses had been broken, and a bishop's, but that most of the populace were dispersed. About nine his

Royal Highness and Colonel Heywood arrived; and then we heard a much more alarming account. The concourse had been incredible, and had by no means obeyed the injunctions of their apostle, or rather had interpreted the spirit instead of the letter. The Duke had reached the House with the utmost difficulty, and found it sunk from the temple of dignity to an asylum of lamentable objects. There were the Lords Hillsborough, Stormont, Townshend, without their bags, and with their hair dishevelled about their ears, and Lord Willoughby without his periwig, and Lord Mansfield, whose glasses had been broken, quivering on the woolsack like an aspen. Lord Ashburnham had been torn out of his chariot, the Bishop of Lincoln ill-treated, the Duke of Northumberland had lost his watch in the holy hurly-burly, and Mr Mackenzie his snuff-box and spectacles. Alarm came that the mob had thrown down Lord Boston, and were trampling him to death; which they almost did. They had diswigged Lord Bathurst on his answering them stoutly, and told him he was the Pope, and an old woman; thus splitting Pope Joan into two. Lord Hillsborough, on being taxed with negligence, affirmed that the Cabinet had the day before empowered Lord North to take precautions; but two Justices that were called denied having received any orders. Colonel Heywood, a very stout man, and luckily a very cool one, told me he had thrice been collared as he went by the Duke's order to inquire what was doing in the other House; but though he was not suffered to pass he reasoned the mob into releasing him,—yet, he said, he never saw so serious an appearance and such determined countenances.

About eight the Lords adjourned, and were suffered to go home; though the rioters declared that if the other House did not repeal the bill, there would at night be terrible mischief. Mr Burke's name had been given out as the object of resentment. General Conway I knew would be intrepid and not give way; nor did he, but inspired the other House with his own resolution. Lord George Gordon was running backwards and forwards, from the windows of the Speaker's Chamber denouncing all that spoke against him to the mob in the lobby. Mr Conway tasked him severely both in the House and aside, and Colonel Murray told him he was a disgrace to his family. Still the members were besieged and locked up for four hours, nor could divide, as the lobby was crammed. Mr Conway and Lord Frederick Cavendish, with whom I supped afterwards, told me there was a moment when they thought they must have opened the doors and fought their way out swords in hand. Lord North was very firm, and at last they got the Guards and cleared the pass.

Blue banners had been waved from tops of houses at Whitehall as signals to the people, while the coaches passed, whom they should applaud or abuse. Sir George Savile's and Charles Turner's coaches were demolished. Ellis, whom they took for a Popish gentleman, they carried prisoner to the

Guildhall in Westminster, and he escaped by a ladder out of a window. Lord Mahon harangued the people from the balcony of a coffee-house and begged them to retire; but at past ten a new scene opened. The mob forced the Sardinian minister's chapel in Lincoln's Inn Fields, and gutted it. He saved nothing but two chalices; lost the silver lamps, &c., and the benches being tossed into the street, were food for a bonfire, with the blazing brands of which they set fire to the inside of the chapel, nor, till the Guards arrived, would suffer the engines to play. My cousin, T. Walpole, fetched poor Madam Cordon, who was ill, and guarded her in his house till three in the morning, when all was quiet.

Old Haslang's chapel has undergone the same fate, all except the ordeal. They found stores of mass-books and run tea.

This is a slight and hasty sketch, Madam. On Tuesday the House of Commons is to consider the Popish laws. I forgot to tell you that the bishops not daring to appear, the Winchester bill, which had passed the Commons, was thrown out.

No saint was ever more diabolic than Lord George Gordon. Eleven wretches are in prison for the outrage at Cordon's and will be hanged instead of their arch-incendiary. One person seized is a Russian officer, who had the impudence to claim acquaintance with the Sardinian minister, and desired to be released. Cordon replied, 'Oui, Monsieur, je vous connoissois, mais je ne vous connois plus.' I do not know whether he is an associate of Thalestris, who seems to have snuffed a revolution in the wind.

I hear there are hopes of some temperament in Ireland. Somebody, I forget who, has observed that the English government pretends not to *quarter* soldiers in Ireland, and therefore must be glad of a bill. It is time some of our wounds should close; or, I believe, I shall soon have too much employment, instead of wanting materials for letters.

Blue cockade] the badge of the Protestant Association.   Bags] wigs.   Run tea] the Bavarian minister Haslang apparently smuggled tea.   Cordon] the Sardinian minister. Thalestris] an Amazon queen who marched to meet Alexander the Great with 300 women. Ireland] there were some threats of rebellion, with French assistance, in Ireland, and some economic concessions were made.

SAMUEL RICHARDSON
(1689–1761)

In addition to his epistolary novels, which included *Pamela* (1740) and *Clarissa* (1747–8), Richardson produced other books of moral and social instruction. *Letters Written to and for Particular Friends, Directing the Requisite Style and Forms to be Observed in Writing Familiar Letters* appeared in many editions between 1741 and 1755.

61. From a mother to a daughter jealous of her husband

Dear Bet,

What I wrote in my former, was on a supposition that you had too much reason to be uneasy at your husband's conduct.

I will now pursue the subject, and put the case that you have no *proof* that he is guilty, but your surmizes, or, perhaps, the busy *whisperings* of officious *make-debates*. In this case, take care, my Betsey, that you don't, by the violence of your passions, precipitate him on the course you dread, and that you alienate not, by unjust suspicion, his affections from you; for then perhaps he will be ready *indeed* to place them somewhere else, whence you may not so easily draw him off; for he will, may be, think, as to *you* (if he be devoid of *superior* considerations), that he may as well *deserve* your suspicions, as be teized with them *without* deserving them.

I know it is a most shocking thing to a sober young woman, to think herself obliged to *share* those affections which ought to be *all her own*, with a *vile prostitute*, besides the danger, which is not small, of being intirely circumvented in her husband's *love*, and perhaps have only his *indifference*, if not *contempt*, instead of it. But, my dear, at the worst, comfort yourself that *you* are not the guilty person; for one day he will, perhaps, fatally find his error. And consider, besides, my Betsey, that your case, from an un-faithful *husband*, is not near so bad as his would be from an unfaithful *wife*: For, child, he cannot make the progeny of a *bastard race* succeed to his and your estate or chattels, in injury of your *lawful children*. If any such he should have, the law of the land *brands* them: Whereas a *naughty wife* often makes the children of *another man* heirs of her husband's estate and for-tune, in injury of his *own children* or *family*. So, tho' the crime may be equal in *other respects*, yet this makes the injury of the woman to the man, greater than *his* can be to *her*.

These thoughts I have thrown together, as they occurred, in two letters, that I might not tire you with a length, that, yet, the important subject required. Let me briefly sum up the contents.

If he be *guilty*, try by softness and kind expostulation to reclaim him, before the vice be rooted in him. If it be so rooted, as that he cannot be drawn off, you know not what God may do for you, if you trust in him, and take not upon yourself, by giving up your mind to violence, to be your own avenger. A *sick bed*, a *tender conduct* in you, *a sore disaster* (and who that lives is not liable to such?) may give him to see the error of his ways, and shew him the foulness of his crime; which your good usage will aggravate, upon his sober reflection, with the no weak addition of *ingratitude* to so good a wife. The *wretch* he has chosen for a partner in his guilt, may, by her sordid ways, *awake* him; by her libidinous deportment, *satiate* him; by her

detected commerce with *others* (for such creatures, having once given themselves up to vice, know no bounds), make him abhor her: And then he will
see the difference between such an one, and a chaste wife, whose *interests*
are bound up in *his own*, and will admire you more than ever he did; And
you'll have the pleasure, besides, in all probability, of saving a soul that
stands in so near a relation to your own.

But if your uneasiness be owing to *private tale-bearers*, and *busy
intermeddlers*; take care, my dear, you are not made a property of by such
mischievous people. Take care that you make not your own *present peace*,
and your *future good*, and that of your *family*, and of *him* your injur'd
husband, the sacrifice to such pernicious busy-bodies.

Consider, my dear, all I have said, and God bless you with a conduct and
discretion suitable to the occasion before you, and, at the worst, give you
comfort and patience in *your own* innocence. For such is this transitory life,
that all the ill or good we receive, will be *soon over with us*; and then the
punishment of the *former*, and the *reward* of the *latter*, will make *all scores
even*, and what is *past* appear as *nothing*. Mean time I can but pray for you:
As, my dear child, becomes

Your ever affectionate Mother.

62. *A gentleman to a lady, who humorously resents his mistress's fondness of
a monkey, and indifference to himself*

Madam,

I must be under the less regret, for the contempt with which you receive
my addresses, when your favour is wholly engrossed by so wretched a rival:
For ought a *rational man* to wonder he is received with neglect and slight
by a lady who can be taken up with the admiration of a *chattering* monkey?
But pray be so good as to permit me to reason the matter a little with you.
I would ask you then, By what extraordinary endowment this happy creature has found means to engross your favour? Extravagance is never commendable. But while I am dying beneath your frowns, how can you be
profuse in your caresses to so mean a competitor? Condescend to view us
in the same light: What valuable qualification is Mr Pug endowed with,
which I am destitute of? What can he do, which I cannot perform, tho'
with less agility, to full as good purpose? Is it a recommendation in him,
that he wears no breeches? For my part, I will most willingly surrender
mine at your feet. Be impartial for once: Place us together before you: View
our faces, our airs, our shapes, and our language. If he be handsomer than
I, which, on a strict scrutiny, I hope will not be allowed him neither, pray
try our wits: However acute he may be, I can assure you I reckon myself no
fool; for if I was, I should less resent the preference you give against me.

I will sing or dance with him for his ears: Turn him loose to me, I will fight him, if that be necessary to obtain your favour; or do anything in the world to show you how much I am, and shall ever be, if you'll permit it,

Your very humble Admirer.

63. From a country gentleman in town, to his brother in the country, describing a public execution in London

Dear Brother,

I have this day been satisfying a curiosity, I believe natural to most people, by seeing an execution at Tyburn: The sight has had an extraordinary effect upon me, which is more owing to the unexpected oddness of the scene, than the affecting concern which is unavoidable in a thinking person, at a spectacle so awful, and so interesting, to all who consider themselves of the same species with the unhappy sufferers.

That I might the better view the prisoners, and escape the pressure of the mob, which is prodigious, nay, almost incredible, if we consider the frequency of these executions in London, which is once a month; I mounted my horse, and accompanied the melancholy cavalcade from Newgate to the fatal tree. The criminals were five in number. I was much disappointed at the unconcern and carelessness that appeared in the faces of three of the unhappy wretches: The countenances of the other two were spread with that horror and despair which is not to be wonder'd at in men whose period of life is so near, with the terrible aggravation of its being hastened by their own voluntary indiscretion and misdeeds. The exhortation spoken by the bell-man, from the wall of St Sepulchre's churchyard, is well intended; but the noise of the officers, and the mob, was so great, and the silly curiosity of people climbing into the cart to take leave of the criminals, made such a confused noise, that I could not hear the words of the exhortation when spoken; tho' they are as follow:

'All good people pray heartily to God for these poor sinners, who now are going to their deaths; for whom this great bell doth toll.

You that are condemned to die, repent with lamentable tears. Ask mercy of the Lord for the salvation of your own souls, thro' the merits, death, and passion, of Jesus Christ, who now sits at the right-hand of God, to make intercession for as many of you as penitently return unto him.

Lord have mercy upon you! Christ have mercy upon you!'—Which last words the bell-man repeats three times.

All the way up Holborn the croud was so great, as, at every twenty or thirty yards, to obstruct the passage; and wine, notwithstanding a late good order against that practice, was brought the malefactors, who drank greedily of it, which I thought did not suit well with their deplorable circumstances: After this, the three thoughtless young men, who at *first* seemed not enough concerned, grew most shamefully daring and wanton; behaving themselves in a manner that would have been ridiculous in men in any circumstance whatever: They swore, laugh'd, and talked obscenely; and wish'd their wicked companions good luck, with as much assurance as if their employment had been the most lawful.

At the place of execution, the scene grew still more shocking; and the clergyman who attended was more the subject of ridicule, than of their serious attention. The psalm was sung amidst the curses and quarrelling of hundreds of the most abandon'd and profligate of mankind: Upon whom (so stupid are they to any sense of decency) all the preparation of the unhappy wretches seems to serve only for the subject of a barbarous kind of mirth, altogether inconsistent with humanity. And as soon as the poor creatures were half-dead, I was much surprised, before such a number of peace-officers, to see the populace fall to haling and pulling the carcases with so much earnestness, as to occasion several warm rencounters, and broken heads. These, I was told, were the friends of the persons executed, or such as, for the sake of tumult, chose to appear so, and some persons sent by private surgeons to obtain bodies for dissection. The contests between these were fierce and bloody, and frightful to look at: so that I made the best of my way out of the croud, and, with some difficulty, rode back among a large number of people, who had been upon the same errand with myself. The face of every one spoke a kind of mirth, as if the spectacle they had beheld had afforded pleasure instead of pain, which I am wholly unable to account for.

In other nations, common criminal executions are said to be little attended by any beside the necessary officers, and the mournful friends, but here, all was hurry and confusion, racket and noise, praying and oaths, swearing and singing psalms; I am unwilling to impute this difference in our own from the practice of other nations, to the cruelty of our natures; to which, foreigners, however, to our dishonour, ascribe it. In most instances, let them say what they will, we are humane beyond what other nations can boast; but in this, the behaviour of my countrymen is past my accounting for; every street and lane I passed through, bearing rather the face of a holiday, than of that sorrow which I expected to see, for the untimely deaths of five members of the community.

One of their bodies was carried to the lodging of his wife, who not being in the way to receive it, they immediately hawked it about to every surgeon they could think of, and when none would buy it, they rubb'd tar all over it, and left it in a field hardly cover'd with earth.

This is the best description I can give you of a scene that was no way entertaining to me, and which I shall not again take so much pains to see. I am, dear brother,

Yours affectionately.

From Newgate] Felons were carted across London from Newgate gaol to Tyburn for execution.

DAVID GARRICK
(1717–1779)

Garrick was the greatest actor of his time, and a lifelong friend of Dr Johnson.

64. *To the Countess of Burlington, 21 July 1755*

Lady Burlington was the daughter of Lord Halifax and wife of Lord Burlington, famous for his interest in architecture and the arts; she was also a patroness of music.

Madam,

Tho y^r Lady$^{p's}$ Letter was directed to Mrs Garrick, yet as it chiefly concerns Me, I must beg leave to answer it with that truth & freedom, which I hope will be always seen in my words & actions.

I must confess that in my late Attendances upon Your Lad^p, I have not felt that pleasure & Satisfaction which I have heretofore Enjoy'd so often in Y^r Family. many are indeed ye Reasons for this alteration; & I would willingly have given way to some inconveniences for ye honor of paying my Duty to You; but when Malice, Meanness & Folly (for Fools will be Ever Mischievous) are Endeavouring to attack my Integrity, & belye my Actions, I cannot tamely support this Injury; & I will rather forego the Loss of any thing, nay Every thing, than that of my Reputation.

The Arrows that fly by Night, have been abroad for Some time, but I secretly despis'd them, imagining that Your Lad$^{p's}$ Good Sense & former Good Will to Me & my Wife would have been my Shield & defence; but when I find, that my once best Friend (in y^r Lady$^{p's}$ Breast), has deserted Me; it is high time to gird on my Sword & rely on y^e Strength of my own Arm. I have hitherto curb'd my resentments in deference to Your Ladyship, but as my passiveness is only a stronger incitement to Malice & Slander, I am resolv'd (to speak in y^e Scripture Phrase again) *that ye Mischief of their Lips shall fall upon their own heads*:

The Accusation against Me (wch clos'd ye Entertainment of Yesterday) was, that I had spirited away one of Your Servants, that I had promis'd to provide for him, & as an Encouragement for joining Me in this Plot, I had brib'd him with the Sum of two Shill^{gs} & Sixpence! was this Madam (after what has pass'd) a proper Subject for my *Smiles*? this vile mean Falsehood?

The mere malice & wickedness of it, I could have laugh'd at & despis'd; but when y^r Lady^p contrary to y^r usual greatness & strength of Mind, & let me add Affection too, seem'd to credit this of Me; I was no longer Myself— I was torn to pieces—& I felt more at ye time, than I would feel again, for double what y^e Inventors of this Falsehood imagine they are to reap from it—

I spoke this Morning with *Roger*, & I sent to Mr *Ferret*: The *Last* absolutely denies, that *Roger* ever Said that he was advis'd by any one to leave his place, & the Lad vows & protests that it was *chiefly* his losing y^r Lad$^{p's}$ place & Livery that induc'd him to give Warning; he says indeed, (for wch I am greatly Oblig'd to my Friend Mr Cumberlidge) that he was often Examin'd by him; whether Mr *Garrick* or y^r Lady$^{p's}$ Coachman, or Chairman, or any other Person with whom he was pleas'd to Yoke Me, had Ever advis'd him to quit his place—nay some other things were said about M^r & Mrs *Garrick*, much below Your hearing or my Notice, & wch are of very little consequence, but as they too plainly prove, that they may venture to make free wth Us, & that we are Sunk in Y^r Ladyship's Barometer from very Warm, to Extream cold. *Roger* has more things to Say, which I don't care to repeat, & wch I suppose, he makes no Secret of; He will be ready at any time to attend y^r Commands, whenever You please to hear his Reasons at large for quitting Your Service—and now Madam, let me be permitted *calmly* to ask; Why am I, who never (but innocently or when Employ'd by You) concern'd myself with y^r Ladyship's Family, drawn again into an Altercation about Y^r Servants?—Was it not most undeniably prov'd (at ye late bustle about ye Note) that neither my wife or I *directly* or *indirectly* Endeavor'd to prejudice y^r Lad^p against any Person whatsoever?

Can it be said that Either of Us has been wanting at any time, & to y^e Utmost of our Power, to express our warmest duty & Obedience consistently wth truth & Justice? can any one instance be produc'd of our injuring, belying, back biting or betraying any of y^r Lady$^{p's}$ Friends, Relations or Servants? Tho we are much fall'n in y^r Esteem, yet we can (let what will happen) lay our hands upon our hearts & openly avow *this*, to all y^e world & in y^e face of Day!

> Le Vrai, Madame, toujours du Mensonge Vainqueur,
> *Par tout* se montre aux Yeux, et va saisir le Cœur.

As I am fully convinc'd from our Yesterday's conversation What is ye Point in view, & as I can no longer with pleasure to you, or with safety & satisfaction to Myself pay my duty at Chiswick, I must beg leave to withdraw Myself (only) from ye honor & happiness which I have Enjoy'd so many Years—and I most sincerely wish that No One may Ever disturb or Embroil y^r Family more than I have done, & that for y^r future Entertainment

& Content, you may never have persons less wise & Good than those which are at present about You—

   I am, Ever was, & Ever will be, Y^r Lady^{p's} most humble & most
                   dutifull Servant
                      D: Garrick

P.S. I return your Lady^p my most grateful acknowledgments for ye Money my Wife has receiv'd—

The Arrows . . .] Ps. 91: 5. *y^f Mischief* . . .] Ps. 140: 9 *Le Vrai* . . .] adapted from Boileau. Money] the editor suggests that some of Mrs Garrick's dowry was invested in one of Lady Burlington's estates.

65. *To the Marquis of Hartington, 2 August 1755*

Hartington (1720–64) was Prime Minister in 1756–7, and was soon to succeed his father as Duke of Devonshire at the time of this letter.

My Lord,

 According to my Promise I have sent y^r Lord^p the Copies of ye two Letters I mention'd in my last. I can Easily imagine that my Behaviour on this Occasion may be misrepresented, & therefore I send my Credentials, fully satisfy'd that y^r Lord^{p's} Candour & Justice will not misjudge Me. Lady B[urlington] has been most particularly kind to my Wife since this Accident; & tho I have not yet Seen her since ye fracas; Some small tokens of affection have been sent to Me, in ye Shapes of Pine Apples, Apricots, &c. The Subject of ye following Letters was related in my Last, & my warmth (particularly) upon being tax'd as ye Seducer of *Roger*, occasion'd this Letter from her Lad^p to Mrs Garrick.

                    Monday Morn^g
Dear Mrs Garrick

 I was most extreamly shock'd, & am very much concern'd at the Sudden Passion Mr Garrick fell into last Night, upon my beginning to Speak upon a most insignificant Subject—which I was only about to give him an Account of, as thinking (if he had heard me out) it might have made him Smile; or perhaps have mov'd his Pity, to hear, how very absurd some People were capable of being.

 I am sure You can acquit Me of intending to hurt, or deceive any body by misreport: so that whenever I am Either mistaken Myself, or deceiv'd by others, Nobody more ready or desirous of being rightly inform'd—if therefore (as he said) I have wicked People about Me, How kind would it be in him, to tell me by whom, & in what particulars I am impos'd upon—for Whilst I remain in Ignorance, it is impossible for Me to alter, correct or amend. As for domestick Quarrels, I love quiet too well to give much attention to them, having had long

Experience that it is of no Use, but adding trouble to one's self—& I think, I
have had too many real Griefs, to create to Myself Imaginary ones.

I am very truly Y^{rs}
D B

[A copy of the letter to Lady Burlington]

The above were ye Letters pass'd between Us: I hope Y^r Lord^p does not
think I carry'd my feeling too far; indeed there was no going on wth such
continual Suspicions & oddness of Behavior—It is my opinion this affair
with *Me*, will have very good Effects—for my being disgrac'd is of little
Consequence; & If it makes her Lad^p a little more carefull of her Behavior
with those of more Consequence, it is not without It's advantages—Miss
And——n has been much more graciously rec'd since this Bustle—M^{rs}
Garrick is to dine at Chiswick to day, If any thing Extraordinary should
occur, I will add it to this Letter, & so I shall leave off till I see her at
Night—

Mrs Garrick is return'd, & says She found my Lady Well & most affectionate—She ask'd her when I would come? My Wife answer'd, that I sh^d
always obey her commands—a few Tears Ensu'd; join'd wth some kind
Expressions towards Me—so that (I imagine) another Week will bring
about a Coalition of Parties.

Master Dicky had not been Well, & was Yesterday very indifferent—
Terry alone attended, but by M^{rs} G's pressing it, Dr Taylour was sent for
last Night—& I hope all will be right again in a day or two. Miss Anderson
whisper'd my wife & told her My L^y was quite alter'd for ye better to her
Since my Bustle. I hope Y^r L^p is well & happy.

I am Ever Y^r Excellency's most dutifull
D Garrick.

Chiswick] Burlington's Palladian country house there.

66. To Peter Garrick, 6 November 1762

Peter was Garrick's brother, still living in their home town of Lichfield.

My dear Peter,

I receiv'd Your Letter, in Which was Enclos'd a Draught from My
Brother [Docksey] & for Which I have Enclos'd my receipt.

I am very glad that You are all so merry at Lichfield with Your Balls,
Players &c for my part I detest Balls, & the name of Players makes me
Sick—I have a goodly parcel of 'Em Myself, & a pretty choice set of Devils
they are; however they are less damnable with Me, than Any body Else; but
Woe to ye Manager who is not the first Actor in his Company. I don't know

how it is, but the Strollers are a hundred years behind hand—We in Town are Endeavouring to bring the Sock & Buskin down to Nature, but *they* still keep to their Strutting, bouncing & mouthing, that with Whiskers on, they put me in mind of ye late Czar of Russia, who was both an Ideot & a Madman—I have made an Observation, which has been confirm'd by Every Example in my Knowledge, that Conceit utterly destroys all feeling, & it is as impossible to be an Actor with a Grain of it in ye Composition; as to make an agreeable Marmalade with [*deleted*] and I never saw one Stroller in my Life, that was not a little [*deleted*], & therefore can never be a Sweet meat. our Theatre is most amazingly improv'd, & I really think it the first Playhouse in Europe. You will say so, whenever You can rouze from y^r Lichfield Lethargy, & make us a Visit—I have seen this day a Surgeon whose Name is Wyat—a Staffordshire Man & recommended to Me by Mr Levett. I shall do him all ye Service in my Power, & I believe I can do him Some—If you See Mr Levett You may tell him So, & make my Comp^ts to him—

My Love to Sisters, & Brother D[ocksey] & believe Me | Most affectionatly & Ever Yours

D: Garrick

My Wife sends her best love to you all. & she is most particularly Oblig'd to You for Your Elegant Present—

Docksey] Thomas Docksey was Garrick's brother-in-law.   Czar] Peter III (1728–62); he was deposed and murdered.   Levett] presumably Robert Levett (1705–82), Dr Johnson's friend and lodger.

GEORGE BURTON
(1717–1791)

Burton was a 'chronologer', a specialist in obscure biblical mathematics, and, as appears from this and another letter to Stukeley (the antiquary and Stonehenge specialist), a fervent anti-Methodist. At this period some expressions of Methodist religious fervour took extravagant forms, and some were regarded as socially dangerous.

67. To the Revd Dr William Stukeley, 14 April 1758

We have got a furious hot Methodist come amongst us, who has already scattered so much of his hellebore as to raise a conventicle of about four-score, & a love-feast once a week, where the effects of their works of darkness, I suppose, will become visible some nine months hence. If some stop is not put to the proceedings of these people, they will in time throw us into confusion, for they attack us very forcibly by stealing into Orders;

& under a sanction of that, & by the help of the Act of Toleration, they bid us defiance, & even promise salvation to their converts, & defame and misrepresent us & our best performances. In short, I know not what you do with them in London, but we have a melancholy prospect from them in the country, for what with fondness for novelty, their encouragements to sloth, & a reliance on Providence for support, & their largesses to the poor, as our poor where they come are no longer in danger of being starved, there is likely to be nothing but psalm-singing coblers & spiritual taylors amongst us shortly; & a cobler's bastard will by & by be employed upon the bench in splitting a text instead of an hair to lengthen out his end with. What a miserable infatuation has Providence laid us under for our long insensibility & irreligion, when I consider the growing charge of our ministry. It sometimes shocks me to think what must be the end of it. There seems to be a general insensibility to goodness, & conscience, like the venerable dress of our wise forefathers, is become the jest of fools—the cloak of villany. How deplorable is it to say thus of one's native country; that country which possesses every thing that this life can make dear to us. But how much more deplorable is it to know this to be a real fact. The old maxim is now reversed. We cannot say Decipimur *specie* recti; for the modern libertines glory in their shame. They boldly thrust themselves forward in defence of vice & immorality, & tell you down right that the best way to live is to stop at no villany; the relenting sinner is a disgrace to manhood, and reason was designed as a bawd to vice. Was Don Quevedo's Chymist to pop out of his bottle in these days, I think he would be for doubling his haste to be corked up again, & beg likewise to have his cork tied down and sealed, too, for fear of an unexpected explosion. But however bad the world grows, let us hope we are not without a remnant, small as it is, to save us, that may avert the threatened blow, & teach us in time to be wiser.

I am, &c.,

G. Burton

Decipimur . . .] we are deceived by the mere appearance of right (Horace, *Ars Poetica*, 25).
Quevedo] Francisco Quevedo y Villegas (1580–1645), satirist.

LADY SARAH LENNOX
(1745–1826)

Lady Sarah Lennox was a daughter of the Duke of Richmond and thought to be the last surviving great-granddaughter of Charles II. At 17 she came close to marrying George III but was eventually a bridesmaid at his wedding. Her sister Georgiana married Henry Fox, 1st Lord Holland (1706–74), so she was often at Holland House, where George III in 1761, on his way to Hammersmith, would stop and find her fetchingly making hay in the grounds. She married Sir Charles Bunbury but was divorced in 1776 and resumed her maiden name; secondly she married Colonel George Napier (1751–1804) in 1782. His military career was spent mostly in Ireland, and many of her voluminous letters were written from there. She died, totally blind from cataract, in 1826.

68. To Lady Susan Fox Strangways, 7 July 1761

Lady Susan (later Lady Susan O'Brien) (1745–1823) was a lifelong correspondent, the daughter of the Earl of Ilchester. In 1764 she married without parental consent the actor William O'Brien, and lived with him for some years in America.

My dearest Susan,

I return you Tony Martin, in perfect health, I hope. I take the opportunity of writing by him, as I think this should not be trusted to the post. To begin to astonish you as much as I was, I must tell you that the [King] is going to be married to a Princess of Mecklenburg, & that I am sure of it. There is a Council to-morrow on purpose, the orders for it are *urgent &* *important* business; does not your chollar rise at hearing this; but you think I daresay that I have been doing some terrible thing to deserve it, for you won't be easily brought to change so totaly your opinion of any person; but I assure you I have not. I have been very often since I wrote last, but tho' nothing was said, he always took pains to shew me some prefference by talking twice, and mighty kind speeches and looks; even last Thursday, the day after the orders were come out, the hipocrite had the face to come up & speak to me with all the good humour in the world, & seemed to want to speak to me but was afraid. There is something so astonishing in this that I can hardly believe, but yet Mr Fox knows it to be true; I cannot help wishing to-morrow over, tho' I can expect nothing from it. He must have sent to this woman before you went out of town; then what business had he to begin again? In short, his behaviour is that of a man who has neither *sense, good nature*, nor *honesty*. I shall go Thursday sennight; I shall take care to shew that I am not mortified to anybody, but if it is true that one can vex anybody with a reserved, cold manner, he shall have it I promise him.

Now as to what I think about it as to myself, excepting this little revenge, I have almost forgiven him; luckily for me I did not love him, & only liked him, nor did the title weigh anything with me; so little at least, that my disappointment did not *affect* my spirits above one hour or two I believe.

I did not cry I assure you, which I believe you will, as I know you were more set upon it than I was. The thing I am most angry at, is looking so like a fool, as I shall for having gone so often for nothing, but I don't much care; if he was to change his mind again (which can't be tho'), & not give me a *very* good reason for his conduct, I would not have him, for if he is so weak as to be govern'd by everybody I shall have but a bad time of it. Now I charge you, dear Lady Sue, not to mention this to anybody but Ld and Ly Ilchester, & desire them not to speak of it to any mortal, for it will be said we invent storries, & he will hate us all anyway, for one generally hates people that one is in the wrong with and that knows one has acted wrong, particularly if they speak of it, and it might do a great deal of harm to all the rest of the family, & do me no good. So pray remember this, for a secret among many people is very bad and I must tell it some.

Ste. is come; he is very much improved, but looks as he did only taller & thinner.

My love & compts to every body at Redlinch.

Adieu, dear Susan. Yours sincerely,
S. Lennox

We are to act a play, and have a little ball; I wish you were here to enjoy them, but they are forwarded for Ste., & to shew that we are not so melancholy quite.

I have taken a fancy to Lord Litchfield for looking shocked to see Lady A. & Lady S.S. burst out laughing in my face to put me out when the former's brother was speaking to me last time.

Ste.] Stephen Fox, eldest son of Henry.　　Compts] compliments.　　Lady A.] Princess Augusta, the King's sister.　　Lady S.S.] Lady Susan Stuart.　　Lord Lichfield] (1718–72) was at this time Lord of the Bedchamber.

69. To Lady Susan O'Brien, 9 January 1766

I can conceive the pleasure my letter gave to my sweet little Netty, by what I felt myself when I got your two letters almost at the same time; sure the pleasure one feels at such a time fully makes up for anything one can suffer, & I intirely agree with Mr O'Brien that it is like lovers. Indeed I cannot enough thank you for the eagerness you shew to make it up, & I am very well content never to name it more, as it is very much for my interest that it should not be thought of more. I named it to nobody but Sr Charles, who knows my countenance too well for me to impose upon him, & he could not avoid seeing that I was very unhappy. . . .

I am very glad you told me about the horse, for I am so horse mad that I thought it was impossible but you must like it, & had got one for you. I allow the chaise is much more usefull & have ordered one, but Mr Buttler does not recolect making any for Wormly, so I am affraid we must trust to chance for it's being right. They are very common here, & almost all the same, so I hope it won't be wrong; you shall receive it at New York as soon as possible with the harness, & the carriage paid for.

I find my sister Holland has sent you the flowers, but indeed I have a thousand pardons to ask you, for I own I had totally forgot them, but if you will write me word if you want the narcissuses & hyacinths, I will take care that you shall have them with the pots for next year.

I was vastly diverted with my *friendship* with Mrs Cary: you know she dined one day at the Pay Office. I saw her at Ranelagh one night this year, & went up to make her a civil speech: & that is our friendship. As to her fashions, I am sorry to say they are but too true among the common run of people here, for such figures as one sees at publick places is not to be described; I am sorry for our English taste, but so it is. However it is, as you may immagine, very *vulgar* to dress so. I think that by degrees the French dress is coming into fashion, tho' 'tis almost impossible to make the ladies understand that heads bigger than one's body are ugly; it is growing the fashion to have the heads *moutoné*; I have cut off my hair, & find it very convenient in the country without powder, because my hair curls naturally, but it's horrid troublesome to have it well curled; if it's big it's frightful. I wear it very often with three rows of curls behind, & the rest smooth with a fruzed *toupé*, & a cap, that is, *en paresseuse*. There is nobody but Ly Tavistock, who does not dress French, who is at all genteel, for if they are not French they are so very illdressed, it's terrible. Almost everybody powders now, & wear a little hoop; hats are vastly left off; the hair down on the forehead belongs to the short waist, & is equally vulgar with poppons, trimmings, beads, garnets, flying caps, & false hair. To be perfectly genteel you must be dress'd thus. Your hair need not be cut off, for 'tis much too pretty, but it must be powdered, curled in very small curls, & altogether be in the style of Ly Tavistock's, *neat*, but it must be high before & give your head the look of a sugar loaf a little. The roots of the hair must be drawn up straight, & not fruzed at all for half an inch above the root; you must wear no cap, & only *little little* flowers dab'd in on the left side; the only feather permited is a black or white sultane perched up on the left side, & your diamond feather against it. A broad, puff'd ribbon collier with a tippet ruff, or only a little black handkerchief very narrow over the shoulders; your stays very high & pretty tight at bottom; your gown trimmed with the same straight down the robings, & a narrow flounce at bottom to button with a *compère*, & to be loose at the fore part of your robing. The sleeves long and loose, the waist very long, the flounces & ruffles of a decent length, not too long, nor so hideously short as they now wear them. No trimming on the sleeve but a ribbon knot tied to hang on the ruffles. The men's dress is exactly what they used to wear latterly; that is 3 or 4 curls high at the sides. Some people wear it cut short before & comed up *en brosse* very high upon the top of the head, it's called *à la greque*, & is very pretty when well done. Mr Robinson says that everybody now dresses their hair so well that the old Makaronis must be quite plain to distinguish themselves, & indeed it's true, tho' I think this style much prettier than the hair down at the ears in Sr Charles' style. I have given you a pretty good boar upon dress, but I was provoked at Mrs Cary setting such vulgar fashions. I will now tell you all the chit-chat I know; tho' it seems so stupid to me, I believe you had rather hear it, as it gives you knowledge of more people & things. I told you the word 'boar' is a fashionable expression for tiresome people & conversations, & is a very good one & *very* useful, for one may tell anybody (Ld G. Cavendish for example), 'I am sure this will be a boar, so I must leave you, Ld George.' If it was not the fashion it would be very rude, but I own I encourage the fashion vastly, for it's delightful I think; one need only name a pig or pork, & nobody dares take it ill but hold their tongues directly. To 'grub up such a one' is also a new expression, which cannot be better illustrated to you, than by suposing you were talking to Mr Robinson, who diverted you very much, in comes the D. of York or Gloucester, & by sitting down by you 'grubs up' poor Mr Robinson, perhaps for the whole evening. The Dukes will either of them serve for an example of a boar too, also Ld Clanbrassil. When you know what 'lending a tascusa' is, you are *au fait* of the *bon ton*. You have lent that puppy Major Walpole many a 'tascusa', & indeed I think you have the knack of lending them better than anybody, so when you are *glumpy* & that some puppy comes & talks to you, the snub that they will get from you is exactly a tascusa in its full force. Take notice the word, tho' it appears Italian, has no meaning of its own; it's like 'chiquinno,' which is used for any card under a 5 at quinze. By way of new married folks, Ld Newnham & Mr Mackenzie are the only people I think; Ly Newnham was a Miss Vernon, she is not pretty but as Ld N. makes her wear rouge & dresses her very well, she is very tollerable. Mr Mack. is a very pretty young man, & they seem very happy.

The new importation of this year for young men is Ld Mount-Stuard, Ld Ossory, & Ste., who is come to stay in England. Ld Mount is tall, well made, & very handsome; he is sensible, and 'tis the fashion to cry him up; I think he is very conceited, & seems to me to be very proud & vain, but yet is very well bred, and does vastly well for a beau. Ld Ossory I doat upon, tho' he is not handsome or conceited, but I know him to have so aimable a character from Sr Charles, whose greatest friend he is, that I like every thing he does. I am grown to love Ste. excessively; in my journey to Paris I grew to know him better, & I really love him dearly now. (Charles was very jealous of him). I find he is vastly liked in general. Miss Greville's match with him is quite off, why I don't know; but he never proposed, tho' he liked her. I think he takes to Ly Mary FitzPatrick most; I wish it might succeed, for he will make any woman happy, if his figure can be got over,

& I do love my sweet dear little Ly Mary to distraction: how happy I should be to have it in my power to make a stronger friendship with her, for tho' I am very well at B. House, yet as long as she lives with people whose characters I cannot esteem, I cannot have that confidence & openness with her that I should wish. The 1st thing that made me love her was her good nature about you, & I cannot find that she varys the least from the sweet character I had formed to myself from her conversation about you, as well as on other subjects. Ly Harrington wanted to get Ste. for Ly Bell, but it would not do. I own I wonder at it, for 'tis not possible to see any woman more beautiful, tho' many are more regularly handsome & more pleasing. Her face is very expressive & lively, & she has more *éclat* than any woman I ever saw; she seems of an oppen, good-humoured disposition, has a very good understanding, & behaves herself perfectly well. Notwithstanding this, the dislike of her mother is so prevalent that it hurts her, & none of the young men have spirit enough to take her out of her mother's hands. Miss Conway is come about, she is grown very pretty & agreable. A Miss Sophia Finch, a daughter of Ly Charlotte's, is a sweet girl also. Miss Greville is vastly improved & is prettier than ever; she & her mother go to Munich next spring; Mr Greville is Envoy there, & goes immediately. I hope she will be married tho', for if once she goes abroad, nobody knows how long she may stay, & if her beauty goes off her money won't get her married. The D. of Beaufort I forgot to name; he is an admirer of Miss G.'s, but the folks are so stupid now a days, they make such prudent matches that I don't think their is one of them that deserves a very aimable, handsome girl. Mr Crew is a fine catch for any Miss, he is very rich & is a very good kind of man, but he is so prodigiously affraid of being married too that he won't speak to a Miss.

I wonder they don't comfort themselves, as Joseph Andrews did, & take courage to speak. I do not find that it's true that 17 people are to be parted, as the newspapers said, but there has been as many reports to the full; however I think none is fixed but Ld & Ly Bollingbroke, Mr Finch and Ly Charlotte, & Ld & Ly Fortescue; the 2 latter are because the husbands are stark staring mad, & have attempted to kill their wives & children. The former is because both sides are mad I believe; but seriously speaking I believe Ld B. is much the same as mad when he is drunk, & that he is generally. Ly B.'s reason for parting is that she cannot live with him with safety to her health; Ld B. is very penitent & wants her to come back, but she won't trust him. Her reason is a very good one, but whether she ought to forgive him or not depends on circumstances & tempers, which nobody but themselves can be judge of; he says he is more in love with her than ever, & would marry her now if she was Ly Die Spencer. Everybody that don't love her pities him, but as I heard he had got a woman in the house already I can't say I do, for if he was unhappy at the thoughts of having used her so cruelly as he has done surely a man that had any feeling would not recover his spirits so easily. If he feels that at all, he must feel it very strongly. I own I am partial to her, & have taken a great fancy to her lately: not but I think she may be very much to blame too. She is in great spirits & seems to be very glad that she has got rid of him. I was in town for a week at the meeting of the parliament; Sr Charles goes again next week. I don't propose leaving this sweet place till the end of Febry, for what with my journey to Paris which lasted till June, my visits to Lady Ilchester & my brother, the time of that angel George's illness that I was in town, & my journey to Ireland, I have not rested a moment nor enjoyed Barton in comfort. Mr & Mrs Soame have promised to come; I expect them to-morrow, & hope they will stay here till I go. I divert myself so much here that I have not a minute on my hands, & I long to be here almost alone for some time. I propose reading a vast deal, I have left off riding a good deal & I have taken to drawing. If I can finish a little drawing I will send you one, tho' 'tis not worth it, for I can only coppy prints, & I have not patience to do more than a head, but it diverts me vastly. Sr Charles has promised to come and see me in Feb. if I don't come to town before, for he fancies I shall grow tired; I certainly will go the moment I am tired, but as I know I may go I fancy I shall not be in a hurry if he will come to me, for I think the winters are too long generally.

Do you know that I feel quite frightened about these rebellions at New York. Sure, my dearest Netty, you won't be such a goose as not to do as you are bid, & run any risk to keep up your character of courage. I don't to this minute understand anything about the cause of it all; I am so far from a pollitician, that I never should have ask'd if you had not been there, & when I did, I was not the wiser for it. You are very good to be anxious about Sr Charles, believe me he & I both thought with pleasure of being of use to you & Mr O'Brien, & I look'd upon it as one of the greatest pleasures of the place; but the time will come perhaps that we may still be of use to you.

I must tell you that I was talking to Charles about Lord Stavordale's neglect of you, & he told me I accused him unjustly, for that he enquired of him perpetually of you, & that he would have wrote, but that *he*, Charles, advised him not at first. I am glad I can justify him from a fault I thought a great one, & at the same time give you great pleasure. As for your father, I cannot recover my astonishment at his perfect ease on your account, and I can attribute it to nothing but his having a great deal of unfeelingness in his character, which, from what I know of him now, I think is very plain. I only wonder you did not know it, that are so plain-sighted. I believe their will be no end of my letter, if I let myself write as much as I would, but I fear I shall miss the packet if this don't go to-night, so adieu, my dearest Netty.

Yours ever affecately & sincerely,
Sarah Bunbury

Sr Charles] Lady Sarah's first husband.   *Moutoné*] rounded like a sheep's back.
Fruzed] frizzed.   *En paresseuse*] informally.   Poppons] beads(?).   Sultane] here, presumably, a feather from the sultan-bird (a kind of domestic fowl); more commonly, a richly ornamented gown.   Makaronis] dandies formerly distinguished by their elaborate fashions.
Chiquinno] chequeen, chequin, from Italian *zecchino*, a coin.   Ly Mary FitzPatrick] Stephen Fox did marry her.   Joseph Andrews] the naïve hero of Fielding's novel of the same name (1742).   Bollingbroke] Lady Bolingbroke was Lady Diana Spencer, daughter of the Duke of Marlborough; she was divorced from her husband in 1768 and two days later married Topham Beauclerk, friend of Dr Johnson.   Rebellions] these were American agitations against the Stamp Act, imposing taxes on legal transactions and newspapers; it was enacted but soon repealed.

70. To Lady Susan O'Brien, February 1779

I am sure, my dear Ly Susan, you know enough of human nature not to be surprised that a little flattery always takes effect, & therefore I may as well confess that, hearing my letters can in any degree contribute to your amusement encourages me to sit down & write the moment I have received yours. But yet I am not so vain as to undertake a letter visibly design'd to entertain, without some more subjects than my own ideas afford, & the court-martial quite seems calculated for the purpose as it interests the feelings, as well as astonishes & amuses the publick. I must, however, prefface that the *Genl Advertiser's* account by express is very accurate (except for the first day or two of the trial), so that it will tell you more than I can; my brother attends the trial & will be at home to-night, so I can tell you the freshest news perhaps. *En attendant*, what do you think of Sir Hugh's complaining to the court that Mr Keppell laugh'd? *His* answer was 'I assure you I don't *put on* a laugh, it's quite natural to me, & I can't help it.'

You will find by Saturday's account they have fallen into their own netts at every step. It is generally believed that the first villany about Captain Hood's logbook coming out so early in the tryal, & meeting with such general detestation, has silenced all the roguery that was fabricating against the Admiral, who owes the glorious result of this tryal to the pleasantest of all reasons; first, to truth, 2ndly, to the uprightness of his judges; 3rdly, to the general high esteem & respect of all sea officers; & 4thly, to the fears of guilty wretches who are daunted by his plain dealing. What a satisfied conscience must a man have whose character is thus raised by his enemies. *Don't* you doat upon Adl Montague?

Your anxiety about poor Ly Albemarle is very kind & just, for she has indeed suffered a great deal, not from fear of her son's *demerit*, but from fear of vilany; however, she now begins to recover her spirits which were terribly hurt, & now she will I hope fill up all the *chinks* of fear with anger, a much better companion for the dear old soul, who is more affectionate, more delightfull to all her relations than it's possible to describe; indeed, they all deserve it of her except me, who have no other title to her goodness but my love for her. However she makes no difference but treats me just as she does the rest. I must give you an instance of it. My brother was so ill that I went up to town *de mon chef* with my girl, & fearing my sudden appearance should startle him, I debarqued at 11 o'clock at night in Ly Albemarle's house: she was out, so I established myself there, & at 12 she arrived, & stopped all my speeches with, 'Child, hold your tongue, what's an old aunt fit for in this world but to make those she loves comfortable? You have obliged me beyond immagination, for now I know you are convinced you are welcome.' She show'd me every attention & kindness it is possible, & now I leave you (who know the regularity of old ladies & the great fuss they make with little things) to judge if she is not a most delightful old lady. But to return to her son, he is in very good health, which is a most happy circumstance; I'm told his behaviour is the most gentlemanlike, proper manner in the world, & the very opposite of his enemys. Mr Jackson the Advocate is a dirty fellow, who takes every little mean advantage of his own ignorance of sea terms, & the Adl *set him right* with a patience & goodhumour that is amusing.

It is very true that poor unfortunate Captain Hood is generally shunned, *he is sent to Coventry* by all the officers; I pity him because he *was* an honest man, tho' he has so far gone from the road of honesty. I even pity Sir Hugh, because I cannot persuade myself he won't be tried & shot, & yet if anything can blunt the feelings of humanity, it is his unparallel'd badness of heart. Most of the sea officers of character have held a very high language in the publick coffee houses at Portsmouth, declaring they would throw up their commissions if the least harm happened to Mr Keppel, & *abusing* others at such a rate, that unless his success softens their tempers a little, many duels are likely to ensue.

Now if I was not afraid of running into the spirit of scandal, I would tell you all the chitchat that comes round to me, but I have a constant monitor that tells me for ever, 'Would you like to have all your faults the topick of conversation?' & this same whisper checks me. However, it is no scandal to tell you it is immagined the D. of Dorset will marry Lady Derby, who is now in the country keeping quiet & out of the way. There is a sort of party in town of who is to visit her & who is not, which creates great squabbles, as if the curse or blessing of the poor woman depended on a few tickets more or less; I don't know her enough to guess how far this important point concerns her, but I'm told she has been & is still most thoroughly attached to the D. of Dorset, & if so I should supose she will be very happy, if the lessening of her visiting list is her only misfortune, & what with giving up her children, sorrow for a fault, dread of not preserving his affection, I think she is much to be pitied. This subject leads me to one I wish to tell you of in case you should hear of it, & be surprised at my making a secret of it to you, which is not my intention, as I hope you won't laugh at me for the wish I have long had to see Sir Charles again. I hope my dear Ly Susan knows me enough to comprehend that I never could return all the goodness of Sir Charles to me by the least grain of dislike; I was *indifferent*, & that has always been the cause of my ingratitude, which never proceeded from anger or dislike; with this same indifference as to love, I have always had an interest in everything that concerned him, & I never felt satisfied not to have received his pardon. When I was in town last he was there too, & wrote to ask to see me; I was delighted at the offer, & accepted it. The first day I saw him, I was too much overcome to have the least conversation with him, but his extreme delicacy in avoiding to give the least hint about my conduct, & the ingenious manner in which he contrived to give me comfort by talking of Ly Derby's conduct just as I would wish him to talk about mine, did at last restore my spirits in some degree, & when he came the next day to see me I had a very long conversation with him, during which without naming my faults or the word forgiveness, he contrived to convince me he looked upon me as his friend & one whose friendship he was pleased with. I cannot describe to you how light my heart has felt since this meeting, & *that* will fully convince you that all love is out of the question, for I don't know what effect it may have on others, but love has ever given me a heavy heart. The very friendly manner in which he treated me gives me the most *comfortable* feel, & to add to my satisfaction he has shewn all sorts of kindness to my dear little Louisa, whom he told me he liked vastly, & has invited her to come to him whenever she is in town. I am sure the pleasure this has given me will give you some for my sake. I had the very great satisfaction of seing him look in remarkable good health & spirits, which latter he carried so far as to laugh at me for being ashamed to see him, even before the servants. He said he saw no sort of reason why he might not see me just when he pleased, nor why it was to put me out of countenance. I could not *argue* that point with him, but I told him how glad I was that he could see me with such goodhumour, to which he answered, 'Why should not I? You know I'm not apt to bear malice!' This set me into such a fit of crying again that he told me I *drove* him from me, & that if his earnest wish to see me happy & comfortable only made me reproach myself he would keep away; & so we parted the best of friends in the world, but it is very true that every mark of his forgiveness is like a dagger to my heart.

The court-martial] Admiral Augustus Keppel (1725–86) was court-martialled on a charge of misconduct and neglect of duty in an engagement with the French fleet. A verdict of guilty would have entailed capital punishment, but the accusation, supported by his second-in-command Sir Hugh Palliser, was malicious, and the court found it to be so. There were great popular celebrations.   Logbook] Captain Alexander Hood, brother of the more famous admiral, admitted, in giving evidence against Keppel, that he had altered the log of the *Robust* before the court-martial, saying that he had only done so to tidy it up.   Montague] Admiral John Montagu was the president of the court-martial.   Ly Albemarle] Keppel's mother.   *De mon chef*] on my own initiative.   Dorset] the Dorset–Derby marriage did not happen. Sir Charles] Lady Sarah's first husband.

71. To Lady Susan O'Brien, 29 September 1815

The first impulse of my heart was to set off & travel above 150 miles to go to my dear afflicted friend, & I believe the great agitation I remained in for some days brought on a fever, which lasted but a few days & ended in an erysipelas in my leg after having threatened my head. But it is all gone now, & is so constantly the attendant on agitation with me that I am used to it, & am really not at all now the worse for it, for it taught me to reflect on the difficulty attending my wishes. The bars are many; 70 years of age acting on me like 80; blindness, which makes me so helpless & dependant on friends & servants, for I require both; a very scanty purse, which obliges me to travel in hired chaises; all these seemed insurmountable in winter, and when I came to consider what the only use friends can be to you is active chearfulness to excite you to keep up the natural firmness of your mind, what am I to undertake such a task? Why a mere log, totally incapable of helping anybody, & nothing but your friendship could make you bear such a burthen at a time, when you require all the energy of your mind, & all the assistance of active young friends to support you. Thus, my dearest Ly Susan, do I see with reason both your situation & my own, & I shall act as I ought to do, that is to be content with hearing of you, & requesting to be told if I can in any way contribute my small share of power to your service in any way; but how I can be of use to you, I know not. I am a sort of vagabond this year having let my house; I visit in a small circle within my means among my kindred. I am now with Charles here at Wm's house, while he & his wife are at Paris; I am going next week to Twickenham to stay with George & his wife, being now well enough to move. I have made roundabout enquiries about you, sure that at first there could be nothing told me I did not guess, & since your health is not hurt I wait to learn such particulars of you as time alone can develop, even to yourself. I wait without impatience but not without the greatest anxiety to learn more of you, for I can no longer bear with this seeming silence between us while I feel our hearts must be in unison with each other. I hear you have an old friend with you, may I not call her mine since she is yours, & will she indulge me with a letter written as if we were acquainted, & that she knew all details relating to you interest me too warmly not to be welcome however minute they may be? Pray ask this favor of her, & get it directed to me at Lt.-Col. G. Napier's at Twickenham, where it will find me. Do not mind a frank, tho' I delay this to find one for you, as my scrawl covers so much paper. I must insist on your not attempting to write to me yourself, for I well know how such an exertion produces unnecessary emotion which ought to be avoided. Alas, it will come too frequently unbid. God bless you, my dear, my first, my constant friend, remember how unalterably I am yours.

S. Napier.

Afflicted friend] Lady Susan's husband died 3 Sept. 1815.　　Charles . . .] Charles, William, and George were three of Lady Sarah's five sons by Napier, who died in 1804, when George III granted her a pension of £1,000 a year.　　Do not mind a frank] do not let it trouble you that I should have to pay postage on the letter. She, however, has obtained one, from somebody entitled to a free post (e.g. an MP), to save Lady Susan money.

72. Changes between 1760 and 1818

This is not strictly a letter but a sort of memorandum, by Lady Napier's correspondent, on changes in society observed during her long life.

Court.—Drawing-rooms once a week. Very select company: that is, few without titles or offices or connexions at Court; on some occasions crowded drawing-rooms, but in general a well-regulated & elegant assembly of the best company.

Now held but 3 or 4 times a year, & every body man or woman that assumes the name of gentleman or lady go to it. The crowds are so great & so little decorum attended to, that people's clothes are litterally torn to pieces.

Theatres.—Were generally well attended by people of fashion. They were well regulated; of size to see & hear the performers; the access easy and safe; every lady went to her box without interruption or offence, & return'd equally safe, whether attended or otherwise. There were always boxes upstairs set apart, & generally occupy'd by women of bad character.

Now ladies of character can't go to the Play without gentlemen to take care of them, to guard them, to remain with them in their boxes. The avenues are filled with prostitutes & men that go to meet & talk to them, & people are liable to see & hear very improper things. The new theatres are built with a view to this, & apartments fitted up for company that never think of seeing the Play. The side boxes, which were always filled with the best company, are now frequently occupied by prentices, valets, & every body that can pay. A man who had offer'd as a cook in the morning was seen by the gentleman who had refused to hire him sitting in the side box near him with some *ladies* in the evening.

Assemblys.—There were but few that were call'd great or very numerous: Bedford House, Northumberland House, Norfolk House, Lady Hilsborough's, Lady Shelburne's, & perhaps one or two more where foreigners were acquainted & received; others had their own acquaintance in such partys as their house cd accomodate agreeably, always according to the card-tables—for cards were indispensible in all partys. Balls were few. One place in an eveng was an engagement, & sufficient amusement.

Now assemblys are become so numerous that 2 or 3 of a night it is common to go to. The size of the house is not thought of much consequence, as if it is not quite crowded it is not thought good or agreeable; more people can be contained in a large one, but the crowd must be equal everywhere. No cards are admitted. Music, in which all are proficients, has taken their place. Balls extremely numerous.

Hours.—They are so changed that the change has occasioned many others. The Houses of Parlt met early, & when no particular business was expected, were up time enough for the dinner-hour, universally four o'clock. This allowed for going easily to the Play, Opera or to card-partys, & for keeping early hours at night; long speeches were very rare, even with the great orators.

Now Parlt does not meet till 4 or 5 o'clock; long speeches are in daily practice on every topic, & by everybody. All are orators. This mania has occasion'd the lateness of every amusement & every topic & family transaction—dinner 7 or 8 o'clock, partys beginning at ten, balls at eleven or twelve. Thus everything is done by candle-light, which adds greatly to the expense in large familys, is hurtful to the health of young persons, & the morals of the lower classes.

Manners.—Great civility was general in all ranks. Form was much abated; none remained that was troublesome, yet there was a sort of respect shewn to elderly people & those of high rank greater than to those more on equality. Titles were used in common, & none but by parents or the greatest intimates were ever call'd by their Christian names. Servants always call'd those they served My Lord or My Lady, My Master or My Mistress. They were in general respectful & anxious to please, & continued in the same service.

Now there is a certain rudeness or carelessness of manners affected both by men and women. Ladies pretty and young may go and seek their own carriages, & meet with no assistance; persons with or without titles are called by their Xtian names, Mary P., Louisa S., etc. *Misses* likewise give up their *titles*, Maria H., Emily B.; all follow this laudable humility, & every rank contributes its mite to equality. Every man, tradesman, or farmer is Esqr., & every prentice girl a young lady. Servants speak of their masters in the third person, Ld I. or Mr F. There are fewer lady's good horsewomen owing to their driving much in open carriages, which makes them greater rovers about the kingdom than formerly.

Language—has been always changing, & it has been said, as morals grow worse language grows more refined. No one can say 'breeding' or 'with child' or 'lying in,' without being thought indelicate. 'In the family way' & 'confinement' have taken their place. 'Cholic' & 'bowels' are exploded words. 'Stomach' signifies everything. This is delicate, but to very many unintelligible, & in writing wd be entirely so, very difficult for a foreigner to translate, or a medical man to understand that was not in the high *ton*; 'fair Cyprians,' & 'tender' or 'interesting connexions,' have succeeded to 'women on the town,' & 'kept mistresses.'

Trade—will be & was always in this country consider'd respectable as well as profitable; an English merchant was a high character. He felt responsible for his merchandise.

Now the change has been very great. Every adventurer, every speculator is a merchant, & all whose gains do not answer their mad expectations become bankrupts, wh being so common seems hardly to have any reproach. All are distress'd by this proceeding, but greedyness has no bounds; character is little attended to, & the cheating swindler has sometimes more advantages than the honest trader.

Character.—A woman of doubtful character was shy'd; if bad, decidedly avoided.

Now the very worst are countenanced by many. It is difficult to say where any line is drawn; & the number of ladies who choose to have particular attendants suppos'd for them proves that neglect or contempt do not follow such conduct. This is one of the changes of manners in the period. *Virtue* may, as some say, have been pretty much the same; *character* is certainly much less attended to.

Politicks.—Whig & Tory, peace & war, lamentations about the taxes, or a general election were the subjects that occupy'd the politicians. Englishmen admired the Constitution as much as all but Englishmen do at present.

Now since the French Revolution the topic is become universal. No man of any degree but reads, studys the newspapers, to form a creed for themselves. No ale-house club but meets to descant on the conduct of the Royal Family, or the Constitution, the state of representation, the use that Kings are of to the people, the inequality of ranks & riches, & everything that can tend to raise discontent in minds quite unfit for such discussions. Every parish has its commitee to arrange something or other. No commitee but call themselves gentlemen, thank their chairman, & ape every thing of this kind in their superiors. At present (as once before) the kingdom is governed by commitees. The consequences may probably be the same.

Religion—was injured & opinions shaken by the writings of the

philosophers in fashion. This mischief was not so counteracted as might
have been expected; the Bishops were too negligent of the conduct &
character of their clergy, & the clergy of their parishes: this gave great
openings for the introduction of Methodists, who are indefatiguable in
their pursuits.

Susan O'Brien

Drawing-rooms] formal receptions at court.   As once before] during the Commonwealth
period (?).   The philosophers] the Deists, who argued for rational as against revealed religion.

SAMUEL JOHNSON
(1709–1784)

73. To the Earl of Bute, 3 November 1762

Bute (1713–92) was First Lord of the Treasury (Prime Minister) in 1762–3 when he
sent word to Johnson that the crown wished to grant him a pension of £300 per
annum. Johnson's *Dictionary* defines 'pension' as 'in England . . . pay given to a state
hireling for treason to his country', and Bute had been criticized for granting pen-
sions to fellow Scots. Johnson's friends, and Bute himself, convinced him that the
award was entirely in respect of his merit, so he accepted the pension in July. One
instalment was paid in July, but the Sept. payment had not followed.

My Lord,
    That generosity by which I was recommended to the favour of his
Majesty, will not be offended at a solicitation necessary to make that favour
permanent and effectual.
    The pension appointed to be paid me at Michaelmas I have not received,
and know not where or from whom I am to ask it. I beg therefore that your
Lordship will be pleased to supply Mr Wedderburne with such directions
as may be necessary, which I believe his friendship will make him think it
no trouble to convey to me.
    To interrupt your Lordship at a time like this with such petty difficulties
is improper and unseasonable, but your knowledge of the world has long
since taught you, that every man's affairs, however little, are important to
himself. Every Man hopes that he shall escape neglect, and with reason
may every man, whose vices do not preclude his claim, expect favour from
that beneficence which has been extended to
My Lord Your Lordship's most obliged and most humble Servant
Sam: Johnson

Wedderburne] Alexander Wedderburne (1733–1805), a Scottish lawyer employed by Bute.

74. (Probably) to William Strahan, 7 March 1774

Strahan (1715–85) was the King's printer and a friend of Johnson's. Strahan seems to have been seeking support for a protest against the ruling that literary copyright was not the perpetual possession of the original owner. The Lords decided against this view. Johnson's opinion is approximately what prevailed.

Sir,

I will tell you in a few words, what is, in my opinion, the most desirable state of Copyright or literary Property.

The Authour has a natural and peculiar right to the profits of his own work.

But as every Man who claims the protection of Society, must purchase it by resigning some part of his natural right, the authour must recede from so much of his claim, as shall be deemed injurious or inconvenient to Society.

It is inconvenient to Society that an useful book should become perpetual and exclusive property.

The Judgement of the Lords was therefore legally and politically right.

But the Authours enjoyment of his natural right might without any inconvenience be protracted beyond the term settled by the statute. And it is, I think, to be desired

1 That an Authour should retain during his life the sole right of printing and selling his work.

This is agreeable to moral right, and not inconvenient to the publick, for who will be so diligent as the authour to improve the book, or who can know so well how to improve it?

2 That the authour be allowed, as by the present act, to alienate his right only for fourteen years.

A shorter time would not procure a sufficient price, and a longer would cut off all hope of future profit, and consequently all solicitude for correction or addition.

3 That when after fourteen years the copy shall revert to the authour, he be allowed to alienate it again only for seven years at a time.

After fourteen years the value of the work will be known, and it will be no longer bought at hazard. Seven years of possession will therefore have an assignable price. It is proper that the authour be always incited to polish and improve his work, by that prospect of accruing interest which those shorter periods of alienation will afford him.

4 That after the Authours death his work should continue an exclusive property capable of bequest and inheritance, and of conveyance by gift or sale for thirty years.

By these regulations a book may continue the property of the authour or of those who claim from him about fifty years, a term sufficient to reward the writer without any loss to the publick. In fifty years far the greater number of books are forgotten and annihilated, and it is for the advantage of learning that those which fifty years have not destroyed should become bona communia, to be used by every scholar as he shall think best.

In fifty years almost every book begins to require notes either to explain forgotten allusions and obsolete words; or to subjoin those discoveries which have been made by the gradual advancement of knowledge; or to correct those mistakes which time may have discovered.

Such Notes cannot be written to any useful purpose without the text, and the text will frequently be refused while it is any man's property.

I am Sir Your humble servant,
Sam: Johnson

75. To James Macpherson, 20 January 1775

Macpherson (1736–96) was a Scottish poet in the authenticity of whose supposed translations of the ancient Gaelic poet Ossian Johnson declined to believe. He said so in his *Journey to the Western Isles* (1775). Macpherson, having failed to persuade the publisher to cancel the passage, wrote Johnson a threatening letter, to which this is the reply. Johnson also bought himself a stout oaken stick. Macpherson published in 1773 a translation of the *Iliad* in Ossianic prose.

Mr James Macpherson,

I received your foolish and impudent note. Whatever insult is offered me I will do my best to repel, and what I cannot do for myself the law will do for me. I will not desist from detecting what I think a cheat, from any fear of the menaces of a Ruffian.

You want me to retract. What shall I retract? I thought your book an imposture from the beginning, I think it upon yet surer reasons an imposture still. For this opinion I give the publick my reasons which I here dare you to refute.

But however I may despise you, I reverence truth and if you can prove the genuineness of the work I will confess it. Your rage I defy, your abilities since your Homer are not so formidable, and what I have heard of your morals disposes me to pay regard not to what you shall say, but to what you can prove.

You may print this if you will.
Sam: Johnson

76. To Hester Thrale, 27 October 1777

Mrs Thrale (1741–1821), wife of a wealthy brewer, became one of Johnson's closest friends, but her second marriage, in 1784, to Gabriel Piozzi, an Italian musician, shocked him and effectively ended their friendship.

Dear Madam,

You talk of writing and writing as if you had all the writing to yourself. If our Correspondence were printed I am sure Posterity, for Posterity is always the authours favourite, would say that I am a good writer too. Anch' io sonô Pittore. To sit down so often with nothing to say, to say something so often, almost without consciousness of saying, and without any remembrance of having said, is a power of which I will not violate my modesty by boasting, but I do not believe that every body has it.

Some when they write to their friends are all affection, some are wise and sententious, some strain their powers for efforts of gayety, some write news, and some write secrets, but to make a letter without affection, without wisdom, without gayety, without news, and without a secret is, doubtless, the great epistolick art.

In a Man's Letters you know, Madam, his soul lies naked, his letters are only the mirrour of his breast, whatever passes within him is shown undisguised in its natural process. Nothing is inverted, nothing distorted, you see systems in their elements, you discover actions in their motives.

Of this great truth sounded by the knowing to the ignorant, and so echoed by the ignorant to the knowing, what evidence have you now before you. Is not my soul laid open in these veracious pages? do not you see me reduced to my first principles? This is the pleasure of corresponding with a friend, where doubt and distrust have no place, and everything is said as it is thought. The original Idea is laid down in its simple purity, and all the supervenient conceptions, are spread over it stratum super stratum, as they happen to be formed. These are the letters by which souls are united, and by which Minds naturally in unison move each other as they are moved themselves. I know, dearest Lady, that in the perusal of this such is the consanguinity of our intellects, you will be touched as I am touched. I have indeed concealed nothing from you, nor do I expect ever to repent of having thus opened my heart.

I am, Madam, Your most humble servant,
Sam: Johnson

Anch' io sonô Pittore] 'I too am a painter'—a remark traditionally though incorrectly attributed to Correggio on his looking at a painting of Raphael's.

77. To James Boswell, 14 March 1781

Boswell had written in Feb. to say he was perplexed by this problem.

Dear Sir,

I hoped you had got rid of all this hypocrisy of misery. What have you to do with Liberty and Necessity? Or what more than to hold your tongue about it? Do not doubt but I shall be most heartily glad to see you here again, for I love every part about you but your affectation of distress.

I have at last finished my Lives, and have laid up for you a load of copy, all out of order, so that it will amuse you a long time to set it right. Come to me, my dear Bozzy, and let us be as happy as we can. We will go again to the Mitre, and talk old times over.

I am, dear Sir, Yours, affectionately,
Sam. Johnson

My Lives] Johnson's *Lives of the Poets* (1779–81).

78. *To Hester Thrale, 19 June 1783*

Mrs Thrale was already cooling.

Dear Madam,

I am sitting down in no chearful solitude to write a narrative which would once have affected you with tenderness and sorrow, but which You will perhaps pass over now with the careless glance of frigid indifference. For this diminution of regard however, I know not whether I ought to blame You, who may have reasons which I cannot know, and I do not blame myself who have for a great part of human life done You what good I could, and have never done you evil.

I had been disordered in the usual way, and had been relieved by the usual methods, by opium and catharticks, but had rather lessened my dose of opium.

On Monday the 16 I sat for my picture, and walked a considerable way with little inconvenience. In the afternoon and evening I felt myself light and easy, and began to plan schemes of life. Thus I went to bed, and in a short time waked and sat up as has been long my custom when I felt a confusion and indistinctness in my head which lasted, I suppose about half a minute. I was alarmed and prayed God, that however he might afflict my body he would spare my understanding. This prayer, that I might try the integrity of my faculties I made in Latin verse. The lines were not very good, but I knew them not to be very good, I made them easily, and concluded myself to be unimpaired in my faculties.

Soon after I perceived that I had suffered a paralytick stroke, and that my Speech was taken from me. I had no pain, and so little dejection in this dreadful state that I wondered at my own apathy, and considered that perhaps death itself when it should come, would excite less horrour than seem[s] now to attend it.

In order to rouse the vocal organs I took two drams, Wine has been celebrated for the production of eloquence; I put myself into violent motion, and, I think, repeated it. But all was vain; I then went to bed, and, strange as it may seem, I think, slept. When I saw light, it was time to contrive what I should do. Though God stopped my speech he left me my hand, I enjoyed a mercy which was not granted to my Dear Friend Laurence, who now perhaps overlooks me as I am writing and rejoices that I have what he wanted. My first note was necessarily to my servant, who came in talking, and could not immediately comprehend why he should read what I put into his hands.

I then wrote a card to Mr Allen, that I might have a discreet friend at hand to act as occasion should require. In penning this note I had some difficulty, my hand, I knew not how nor why, made wrong letters. I then wrote to Dr Taylor to come to me, and bring Dr Heberden, and I sent to Dr Brocklesby, who is my neighbour. My Physicians are very friendly and very disinterested, and give me great hopes, but You may imagine my situation. I have so far recovered my vocal powers, as to repeat the Lord's Prayer with no very imperfect articulation. My memory, I hope, yet remains as it was. But such an attack produces solicitude for the safety of every Faculty.

How this will be received by You I know not, I hope You will sympathise with me, but perhaps

> My Mistress gracious, mild, and good,
> Cries, Is he dumb? 'tis time he shou'd.

But can this be possible, I hope it cannot. I hope that what, when I could speak, I spoke of You, and to You, will be in a sober and serious hour remembred by You, and surely it cannot be remembred but with some degree of kindness. I have loved you with virtuous affection, I have honoured You with sincere Esteem. Let not all our endearment be forgotten, but let me have in this great distress your pity and your prayers. You see I yet turn to You with my complaints as a settled and unalienable friend, do not, do not drive me from You, for I have not deserved either neglect or hatred.

To the Girls, who do not write often, for Susy has written only once, and Miss Thrale owes me a letter, I earnestly recommend as their Guardian and Friend, that They remember their Creator in the days of their Youth.

I suppose You may wish to know how my disease is treated by the physitians. They put a blister upon my back, and two from my ear to my throat, one on a side. The blister on the back has done little, and those on the throat have not risen. I bullied, and bounced, (it sticks to our last sand) and compelled the apothecary to make his salve according to the Edinburgh dispensatory that it might adhere better. I have two on now of my own prescription. They likewise give me salt of hartshorn, which I take with no great confidence, but am satisfied that what can be done, is done for me.

O God, give me comfort and confidence in Thee, forgive my sins, and if it be thy good pleasure, relieve my diseases for Jesus Christs sake, Amen.

I am almost ashamed of this querulous letter, but now it is written, let it go. I am, Madam Your most humble servant,

Sam: Johnson

Picture] the painter was Frances Reynolds, sister of Sir Joshua.　　Latin verse] the Latin
prayer, in which he asks God to spare his intellect, 'the only faculty with which I may hope to
please thee', survives.　　Laurence] Dr Thomas Laurence (or Lawrence) (1711–83) died on
6 June of a palsy which had prevented his writing.　　Allen] Edmund Allen (1726–84),
another friend, a printer who lived in Bolt Court.　　My Mistress . . .] Swift, 'Verses on the
Death of Dr S[wift]': 'The Queen, so Gracious, Mild, and Good, | Cries, "Is he gone? 'Tis time
he shou'd." '　　Our last sand] Pope, *Epistle to Cobham*: 'Time, that on all things lays his
lenient hand, | Yet tames not this; it sticks to our last sand.'

JAMES BOSWELL
(1740–1795)

Boswell, the Scottish lawyer and author, is known especially for his *Life of Samuel
Johnson* (1791). He met Johnson in 1763. He then travelled in Europe and met
Voltaire and Rousseau, who had a powerful effect on him, though Johnson remained
his 'unalterable friend'.

79. To Samuel Johnson, 30 September 1764

Boswell did not send this letter for years; Johnson acknowledged receipt on 28 June
1777.

My ever dear and much-respected Sir,

You know my solemn enthusiasm of mind. You love me for it, and I
respect myself for it, because in so far I resemble Mr Johnson. You will be
agreeably surprised, when you learn the reason of my writing this letter. I
am at Wittemberg in Saxony. I am in the old church where the Reformation was first preached, and where some of the reformers lie interred. I
cannot resist the serious pleasure of writing to Mr Johnson from the tomb
of Melancthon. My paper rests upon the gravestone of that great and good
man, who was undoubtedly the worthiest of all the reformers. He wished
to reform abuses which had been introduced into the Church; but had no
private resentment to gratify. So mild was he, that when his aged mother
consulted him with anxiety on the perplexing disputes of the times, he
advised her 'to keep to the old religion'. At this tomb, then, my ever dear
and respected friend! I vow to thee an eternal attachment. It shall be my
study to do what I can to render your life happy: and if you die before me,
I shall endeavour to do honour to your memory; and, elevated by the
remembrance of you, persist in noble piety. May God, the Father of all
beings, ever bless you! and may you continue to love

Your most affectionate friend, and devoted servant,

James Boswell

Melanchthon] Philip Melanchthon (1497–1560), scholar, Luther's deputy, and a force for mod-
eration in Reform.

80. To the Revd William Temple, 8 February 1768

Temple (1739–96) was a fellow-student of Boswell's at Edinburgh, and they remained close friends and correspondents till Boswell's death. Catherine Blair (1750–
98)—'the finest woman I have ever seen', and an heiress—married a cousin, Sir
William Maxwell, in 1776.

My dear friend,

All is over between Miss Blair and me. I have delayed writing till I could
give you some final account. About a fortnight after she went to the country, a report went that she was going to be married to Sir Alexander
Gilmour, Member of Parliament for the county of Midlothian, a young
man about thirty, who has £1,600 a year of estate, was formerly an officer
in the guards, and is now one of the Clerks of the Board of Green Cloth,
£1,000 a year—in short a noble match, though a man of expence and
obliged to lead a London life. After the fair agreement between her and me,
which I gave you fully in my last, I had a title to know the truth. I wrote
to her seriously and told her that if she did not write me an answer I should
believe the report to be true. After three days, I concluded from her silence
that she was at last engaged. I endeavoured to laugh off my passion and I
got Sir Alexander Gilmour to frank a letter to her, which I wrote in a
pleasant strain, and amused myself with the whim. Still, however, I was not
absolutely certain, as her conduct has been so prudent all along. At last she
comes to town, and who comes too but my old rival the Nabob? I got
acquainted with Mr Fullarton, and he and I joked a good deal about our
heiress. Last night he proposed that he and I should go together and pay
her a visit for the first time after her return from the country. Accordingly
we went and I give you my word, Temple, it was a curious scene. However,
the Princess behaved exceedingly well, though with a reserve more than
ordinary. When we left her, we both exclaimed, 'Upon my soul, a fine
woman!' I began to like the Nabob much; so I said to him, 'I do believe, Mr
Fullarton, you and I are in the same situation here. Is it possible to be upon
honour, and generous in an affair of this kind?' We agreed it was. Each
then declared he was serious in his love for Miss B. and each protested he
never before believed the other in earnest. We agreed to deal by one
another in a fair and candid manner. I carried him to sup at a lady's, a
cousin of mine, where we stayed till half an hour past eleven. We then went
to a tavern and the good old claret was set before us. He told me that he
had been most assiduous in attending Miss Blair; but she never gave him
the least encouragement and declared he was convinced she loved me as
much as a woman could love a man. With equal honesty I told all that has
past between her and me, and your observation on the *wary mother*. 'What,'
said he, 'did Temple say so? If he had lived twenty years in the country

with them, he could not have said a better thing.' I then told him Dempster's humorous saying that all Miss B's connections were in an absolute confederacy to lay hold of every man who has a £1,000 a year, and how I called their system a *Salmond Fishing*. 'You have hit it,' said he, 'we're all kept in play; but I am positive you are the fish and Sir Alexander is only a mock salmon to force you to jump more expeditiously at the bait.' We sat till two this morning. We gave our words as men of honour that we would be honest to each other; so that neither should suffer needlessly and, to satisfy ourselves of our real situation, we gave our words that we should both ask her this morning, and I should go first. Could there be anything better than this? The Nabob talked to me with the warmth of the Indies, and professed the greatest pleasure on being acquainted with me.

Well, Temple, I went this morning and she made tea to me alone. I then asked her seriously if she was to be married to Sir Alexander. She said 'it was odd to believe every thing people said, and why did I put such question? &c.' I said that she knew very well I was much in love with her, and that if I had any chance I would take a good deal of trouble to make myself agreable to her. She said I need not take the trouble, and I must not be angry, for she thought it best to tell me honestly. 'What then,' said I, 'have I no chance?' 'No,' said she. I asked her to say so upon her word and upon honour. She fairly repeated the words. So I think, Temple, I had enough.

She would not tell me whether she was engaged to the knight. She said she would not satisfy an idle curiosity. But I own I had no doubt of it. What amazed me was that she and I were as easy and as good friends as ever. I told her I have great animal spirits and bear it wonderfully well. But this is really hard. I am thrown upon the wide world again. I don't know what will become of me.

Before dinner, the Nabob and I met, and he told me that he went and, in the most serious and submissive manner, begged to know if she was engaged. She would give him no satisfaction and treated him with a degree of coldness that overpowered him quite, poor man.

Such is the history of the lovers of this cruel Princess, who certainly is a lucky woman to have had a sovereign sway over so many admirers. I have endeavoured to make merry on my misfortune.

A Crambo Song on losing my Mistress.

Although I be an honest *Laird*,
In person rather strong and brawny,
For me the Heiress never car'd,
For she would have the Knight, Sir Sawney.

And when with ardent vows, I swore
Loud as Sir Jonathan Trelawney,

The Heiress shewed me to the door,
And said, she'd have the Knight, Sir Sawney.

She told me, with a scornful look,
I was as ugly as a Tawney;
For she a better fish could hook,
The rich and gallant Knight, Sir Sawney.

N.B. I can find no more rhimes to Sawney.

Now that all is over, I see many faults in her, which I did not see before. Do you not think she has not feeling enough, nor that ingenuous spirit which your friend requires? The Nabob and many other people are still of opinion that she has not made sure of Sir Sawney, and that all this may be finesse. But I cannot suspect so young a creature of so much artifice and whatever may be in it, I am honourably off, and you may wonder at it, but I assure you I am very easy and chearful. I am, however, resolved to look out for a good wife, either here or in England. I intend to be in London in March. My address will be at Mr Dilly's, Bookseller. But I expect to hear from you before I set out, which will not be till the 14th of March. I rejoice to hear that Mrs Temple is in a good way. My best wishes ever attend you and her.

I am your most affectionate friend,
James Boswell

11 February. I have allowed my letter to lie by till this day. The heiress is a good Scots lass. But I must have an English woman. My mind is now twice as enlarged as it has been for some months. You cannot say how fine a woman I may marry, perhaps a Howard or some other of the noblest in the kingdom.

Board of Green Cloth] Counting House of the King's Household.   Frank] Gilmour would have franks as a court official.   Nabob] William Fullarton, a surgeon returned from India.   Dempster] George Dempster, MP, was a young Edinburgh advocate.   Crambo] a word game in which one has to answer a line with another that rhymes; here Boswell plays it by himself.   Sawney] nickname for a Scotsman; a simpleton.   Trelawney] Sir Jonathan Trelawny (1650–1721) was an important bishop, but bad-tempered and given to drink. Tawney] a Moor.

SIR JOSHUA REYNOLDS

(1723–1792)

Reynolds was a portrait painter and first president of the Royal Academy. During his two years in Rome he did much copying but not of Michelangelo, whom he most admired.

81. To James Barry, 1769

Barry (1741–1806), an Irish painter, went to Rome on the advice of Reynolds and with the support of Burke. A quarrelsome man, he later became professor of painting at the Academy but used his lectures to attack Reynolds. They were later reconciled, but another row resulted in his expulsion from the Academy. The 'temporary matters' mentioned here seem to have been quarrels with picture dealers in Rome.

Dear Sir,

I am very much obliged to you for your remembrance of me in your letter to Mr Burke, which, though I have read with great pleasure, as a composition, I cannot help saying with some regret, to find that so great a portion of your attention has been engaged upon temporary matters, which might be so much more profitably employed upon what would stick by you through your whole life.

Whoever is resolved to excel in painting, or indeed any other art, must bring all his mind to bear upon that one object, from the moment he rises till he goes to bed; the effect of every object that meets a painter's eye, may give him a lesson, provided his mind is calm, unembarrassed with other subjects, and open to instruction. This general attention, with other studies connected with the art, which must employ the artist in his closet, will be found sufficient to fill up life, if it was much longer than it is. Were I in your place, I would consider myself as playing a great game, and never suffer the little malice and envy of my rivals to draw off my attention from the main object, which, if you pursue with a steady eye, it will not be in the power of all the Cicerones in the world to hurt you. Whilst they are endeavouring to prevent the gentlemen from employing the young artists, instead of injuring them, they are in my opinion doing them the greatest service. Whilst I was at Rome I was very little employed by them, and that little I always considered as so much time lost: copying those ornamental pictures which the travelling gentlemen always bring home with them as furniture for their houses, is far from being the most profitable manner of a student spending his time. Whoever has great views, I would recommend to him whilst at Rome, rather to live on bread and water than lose those advantages which he can never hope to enjoy a second time, and which he will find only in the Vatican, where, I will engage no Cavalier sends students to copy for him. I do not mean this as any reproach to the gentlemen; the works in that place, though they are the proper study of an artist, make but an aukward figure painted in oil, and reduced to the size of easel pictures. The Capella Sistina is the production of the greatest genius that ever was employed in the arts; it is worth considering by what principles that stupendous greatness of style is produced; and endeavouring to produce something of your own on those principles will be a more advantageous method of study than copying the St Cecilia in the Borghese, or the

Herodias of Guido, which may be copied to eternity without contributing one jot towards making a man a more able painter.

If you neglect visiting the Vatican often, and particularly the Capella Sistina, you will neglect receiving that peculiar advantage which Rome can give above all other cities in the world. In other places you will find casts from the antique, and capital pictures of the great painters, but it is *there* only that you can form an idea of the dignity of the art, as it is there only that you can see the works of Michael Angelo and Raffael. If you should not relish them at first, which may probably be the case, as they have none of those qualities which are captivating at first sight, never cease looking till you feel something like inspiration come over you, till you think every other painter insipid in comparison, and to be admired only for petty excellencies.

I suppose you have heard of the establishment of a royal academy here; the first opportunity I have I will send you the discourse I delivered at its opening, which was the first of January. As I hope you will hereafter be one of our body, I wish you would, as opportunity offers, make memorandums of the regulations of the academies that you may visit in your travels, to be engrafted on our own, if they should be found useful.

I am, with the greatest esteem, yours,

J. Reynolds

Cicerones] guides (to gentlemen making the grand tour).

82. To Valentine Green, 1 June 1783

Green (1739–1813) was an engraver. The cause of his complaint is clear from Reynolds's reply. Mrs Siddons (1755–1831), the great tragic actress, wanted Francis Howard to do the engravings; her note to Reynolds survives.

Sir,—

You have the pleasure, if it is any pleasure to you, of reducing me to a most mortifying situation: I must either treat your hard accusations of being a liar, with the contempt of silence (which you and your friends may think implies guilt) or I must submit to vindicate myself, like a criminal, from this heavy charge. I mentioned in conversation, when I had the honour of seeing you last at my house, that Mrs Siddons had wrote a note to me respecting the print. When I assert any thing, I have the happiness of knowing that my friends believe what I say, without being put to the blush, as I am at present, by being forced to produce proofs, since you tell me in your letter, that *Mrs Siddons never did write or even speak to me in favour of any other artist.*

But supposing Mrs Siddons out of the question, my words (on which you grounded your *demand as right, and not as a favour*) I do not see can any way be interposed as such an absolute promise; I intended it to mean only, that you having made the first application, should be remembered by me, and that it should turn the scale in your favour, supposing equality in other respects. You say you wait the result of my determination; what determination can you expect after such a letter?

You have been so good as to recommend to me *to give for the future unequivocal answers*. I shall immediately follow your advice, and do now in the most unequivocal manner inform you, that you shall NOT do the print.

I am, Sir, with all humility, and due acknowledgment of your dignity,

Your most humble Servant,

Joshua Reynolds

83. To James Boswell, 7 July 1785

This is a draft. On 6 July Reynolds and Boswell attended the hanging of, among others, Peter Shaw, a servant of Edmund Burke, for robbery. They appeared on the scaffold, and were reproved in the *Morning Chronicle* of 8 July.

... I am obliged to you for carrying me yesterday to see the execution at Newgate of the five malefactors. I am convinced it is a vulgar error, the opinion that it is so terrible a spectacle, or that it any way implies a hardness of heart or cruelty of disposition, any more than such a disposition is implied in seeking delight from the representation of a tragedy. Such an execution as we saw, where there was no torture of the body or expression of agony of the mind, but where the criminals, on the contrary, appeared perfectly composed, without the least trembling, ready to speak and answer with civility and attention any question that was proposed, neither in a state of torpidity or insensibility, but grave and composed ... I am convinced from what we saw, and from the report of Mr Akerman, that it is a state of suspense that is the most irksome and intolerable to the human mind, and that certainty, though of the worst, is a more eligible state; that the mind soon reconciles itself even to the worst, when that worst is fixed as fate. Thus bankrupts ... I consider it is natural to desire to see such sights, and, if I may venture, to take delight in them, in order to stir and interest the mind, to give it some emotion, as moderate exercise is necessary for the body. This execution is not more, though I expected it to be too much. If the criminals had expressed great agony of mind, the spectators must infallibly sympathise; but so far was the fact from it, that you regard with admiration the serenity of their countenances and whole deportment. ...

Akerman] Keeper of Newgate.

CAPTAIN W. G. EVELYN
(1742–1776)

William Glanville Evelyn fought with his British regiment in the American War of Independence and died of wounds received on 22 Aug. 1776.

84. To the Hon. Mrs Leveson Gower, 19 August 1775

Kinswoman of Granville Leveson Gower (see below, Letters 101–4), Mrs Leveson Gower was Evelyn's cousin.

Dear Madam,

The 'Charming Nancy' returns once more to visit you, and carries with her Mrs Gage, and others of less note, whose curiosity as to the business of war is, I believe, sufficiently satisfied, and who begin to discover that a winter may be full as agreeable in London as in a town invested on all sides by thousands of armed men, cut off from all resources (I may almost say) by sea as well as by land, and threatened every day to be attacked with fire and sword. With you, who are so jealous of the honour of the British flag, I shall risk my credit, if I tell you what insults have been offered to it with impunity; but indeed they are too many to relate.

The Yankey fishermen in their whale-boats have repeatedly drove off the stock, and set fire to the houses on islands, under the guns of the fleet. They have killed a midshipman of the Admiral's (Brown), and destroyed the sloop he commanded. They have burned the lighthouse at the entrance of the harbour, killed Lieutenant Colthurst (who commanded thirty Marines), some of his men, and took the rest prisoners.

They have burned an armed sloop belonging to the 'Rose' man-of-war, and we hear have taken another, called the 'Diligence,' belonging to the Admiral, and lastly have cut off nine-and-thirty of the 'Falcon's' crew, and have taken all her boats except one; the Lieutenant has made his escape, much wounded. And to complete all, the Admiral has had a boxing-match in the streets, has got his eyes blackened, and his sword broke by a gentleman of the town, whom he had used very ill, and struck repeatedly, before he returned his blows.

A few nights ago General Clinton had laid the plan of giving the rebels a general *alerte*, which was to have begun at twelve o'clock, by surprising and attacking all their outposts at the same instant; and the Admiral was at the same time to have made a descent, and burned a small town on the coast. Our part succeeded as well as we could wish, indeed better, for with a few men of our regiment I had the honour of burning an advanced post of the rebels, which was more than was intended in the original plan. The Admiral's part miscarried, but for what reason I do not know. The truth is, there is no good understanding between him and the General, and he endeavours to counteract the General wherever he is concerned. Every man both in the army and navy wishes him recalled, as the service must always suffer where there is such disagreement betwixt the leaders.

Our situation has undergone very little change since the affair of the 17th of June, except the daily loss of men and officers in the hospitals. I suppose the accounts of that transaction did not meet with credit in England, and that it could not be believed that a thousand men and officers of the bravest troops in the world could in so short a time be cut off by irregulars. After two or three such instances, you good people of old England will find out that five or six thousand men are not sufficient to reduce a country of 1500 miles in extent, fortified by nature, and where every man from fifteen to fifty is either a volunteer, or compelled to carry arms; amongst whom the number of our countrymen is very great, and they are the most dangerous enemies we have to encounter. [The people of England] will find out that some other mode must be adopted than gaining every little hill at the expense of a thousand Englishmen; and if they mean to continue masters of this country, they will lay aside that false humanity towards these wretches which has hitherto been so destructive to us. They must lay aside the notion that hurting America is ruining Great Britain, and they must permit us to restore to them the dominion of the country by laying it waste, and almost extirpating the present rebellious race, and upon no other terms will they ever possess it in peace.

Major Bishop's state of health making it necessary for him to go home, I think I shall take the liberty of troubling him with this letter, though I believe he cannot get a passage in the 'Charming Nancy,' but goes in another which sails at the same time. I fancy George writes by him, and to his information I refer you for particulars as to us and our situation. I dare say this report of George will give you satisfaction. I shall only say in general, that he continues to improve. I dare say you are in some concern for us, from the idea of our being obliged to live upon salt pork and pease. Fresh provision is in general rather scarce, very dear, and not of the best kind; but we come in for a share now and then. We have had a good recruit within these few days; our transports having brought in upwards of two thousand sheep from some islands near New York, which is a very seasonable relief to our sick and wounded. George and I come in sometimes for a good dinner among the great people, and are particularly indebted to Lord Percy and General Clinton. We have not the honour of an introduction to General Burgoyne.

I am strictly enjoined, whenever I write to you, not to omit presenting

Adair's most respectful compliments to you and Captain Leveson. He is much taken notice of here, and in great repute from having been one of the first men who entered the enemy's works on the 17th of June. He is strongly recommended for a company, and I hope will get one, as there has been a great mortality among the Marine captains; five or six of them being already dead.

My best wishes attend you and Captain Leveson, and little family.

I am, dear Madam, | With the greatest esteem, Your faithful and
obedient servant,
W. G. Evelyn

Little hill] Bunker Hill. The battle of 17 June had cost the British 1,054 killed and wounded.   Lord Percy] (1742–1817) commanded the British camp at Boston.   General Clinton] (1738?–95) was later commander-in-chief.   General Burgoyne] (1722–92) later surrendered to the Americans at Saratoga (17 Oct. 1777).

JOHN AND ABIGAIL ADAMS
(1735–1826) (1744–1818)

John Adams was the second President of the United States (1797–1801). He helped to draft the Declaration of Independence and to negotiate the peace with England, where, from 1785, he was the United States ambassador. Abigail was a notable letter writer, especially to her husband, from whom she was separated for long periods during the Revolution.

85. Abigail to John Adams, 31 March 1776

I wish you would ever write me a Letter half as long as I write you; and tell me if you may where your Fleet are gone? What sort of Defence Virginia can make against our common Enemy? Whether it is so situated as to make an able Defence? Are not the Gentery Lords and the common people vassals, are they not like the uncivilized Natives Brittain represents us to be? I hope their Riffel Men who have shewen themselves very savage and even Blood thirsty; are not a specimen of the Generality of the people.

I am willing to allow the Colony great merrit for having produced a Washington but they have been shamefully duped by a Dunmore.

I have sometimes been ready to think that the passion for Liberty cannot be Eaquelly Strong in the Breasts of those who have been accustomed to deprive their fellow Creatures of theirs. Of this I am certain that it is not founded upon that generous and christian principal of doing to others as we would that others should do unto us.

Do not you want to see Boston; I am fearfull of the small pox, or I should have been in before this time. I got Mr Crane to go to our House and see what state it was in. I find it has been occupied by one of the Doctors of a Regiment, very dirty, but no other damage has been done to it. The few things which were left in it are all gone. Cranch has the key which he never deliverd up. I have wrote to him for it and am determined to get it cleand as soon as possible and shut it up. I look upon it a new acquisition of property, a property which one month ago I did not value at a single Shilling, and could with pleasure have seen it in flames.

The Town in General is left in a better state than we expected, more oweing to a percipitate flight than any Regard to the inhabitants, tho some individuals discoverd a sense of honour and justice and have left the rent of the Houses in which they were, for the owners and the furniture unhurt, or if damaged sufficent to make it good.

Others have committed abominable Ravages. The Mansion House of your President is safe and the furniture unhurt whilst both the House and Furniture of the Solisiter General have fallen a prey to their own merciless party. Surely the very Fiends feel a Reverential awe for Virtue and patriotism, whilst they Detest the paricide and traitor.

I feel very differently at the approach of spring to what I did a month ago. We knew not then whether we could plant or sow with safety, whether when we had toild we could reap the fruits of our own industery, whether we could rest in our own Cottages, or whether we should not be driven from the sea coasts to seek shelter in the wilderness, but now we feel as if we might sit under our own vine and eat the good of the land.

I feel a gaieti de Coar to which before I was a stranger. I think the Sun looks brighter, the Birds sing more melodiously, and Nature puts on a more chearfull countanance. We feel a temporary peace, and the poor fugitives are returning to their deserted habitations.

Tho we felicitate ourselves, we sympathize with those who are trembling least the Lot of Boston should be theirs. But they cannot be in similar circumstances unless pusilanimity and cowardise should take possession of them. They have time and warning given them to see the Evil and shun it.—I long to hear that you have declared an independancy—and by the way in the new Code of Laws which I suppose it will be necessary for you to make I desire you would Remember the Ladies, and be more generous and favourable to them than your ancestors. Do not put such unlimited power into the hands of the Husbands. Remember all Men would be tyrants if they could. If perticuliar care and attention is not paid to the Laidies we are determined to foment a Rebelion, and will not hold ourselves bound by any Laws in which we have no voice, or Representation.

That your Sex are Naturally Tyrannical is a Truth so thoroughly established as to admit of no dispute, but such of you as wish to be happy willingly give up the harsh title of Master for the more tender and endearing one of Friend. Why then, not put it out of the power of the vicious and the Lawless to use us with cruelty and indignity with impunity. Men of Sense in all Ages abhor those customs which treat us only as the vassals of your Sex. Regard us then as Beings placed by providence under your protection and in immitation of the Supreem Being make use of that power only for our happiness.

Braintree] the modern Quincy, Mass.; the birthplace of John Adams.   Washington] John Adams was responsible for the appointment of Washington, a Virginian, as commander-in-chief, though the campaign was in New England, hoping thus to associate Virginia more strongly with the revolutionary cause.   Dunmore] John Murray, Earl of Dunmore (1732–1809), governor of Virginia (1770–76), took the Loyalist side in the Revolutionary War.   Flight] the British evacuated Boston on 17 Mar.

86. John to Abigail Adams, 14 April 1776

You justly complain of my short Letters, but the critical State of Things and the Multiplicity of Avocations must plead my Excuse.—You ask where the Fleet is. The inclosed Papers will inform you. You ask what Sort of Defence Virginia can make. I believe they will make an able Defence. Their Militia and minute Men have been some time employed in training them selves, and they have Nine Battallions of regulars as they call them, maintained among them, under good Officers, at the Continental Expence. They have set up a Number of Manufactories of Fire Arms, which are busily employed. They are tolerably supplied with Powder, and are successfull and assiduous, in making Salt Petre. Their neighbouring Sister or rather Daughter Colony of North Carolina, which is a warlike Colony, and has several Battallions at the Continental Expence, as well as a pretty good Militia, are ready to assist them, and they are in very good Spirits, and seem determined to make a brave Resistance.—The Gentry are very rich, and the common People very poor. This Inequality of Property, gives an Aristocratical Turn to all their Proceedings, and occasions a strong Aversion in their Patricians, to Common Sense. But the Spirit of these Barons, is coming down, and it must submit.

It is very true, as you observe they have been duped by Dunmore. But this is a Common Case. All the Colonies are duped, more or less, at one Time and another. A more egregious Bubble was never blown up, than the Story of Commissioners coming to treat with the Congress. Yet it has gained Credit like a Charm, not only without but against the clearest Evidence. I never shall forget the Delusion, which seized our best and most sagacious Friends the dear Inhabitants of Boston, the Winter before last. Credulity and the Want of Foresight, are Imperfections in the human Character, that no Politician can sufficiently guard against.

You have given me some Pleasure, by your Account of a certain House in Queen Street. I had burned it, long ago, in Imagination. It rises now to my View like a Phœnix.—What shall I say of the Solicitor General? I pity his pretty Children, I pity his Father, and his sisters. I wish I could be clear that it is no moral Evil to pity him and his Lady. Upon Repentance they will certainly have a large Share in the Compassions of many. But let Us take Warning and give it to our Children. Whenever Vanity, and Gaiety, a Love of Pomp and Dress, Furniture, Equipage, Buildings, great Company, expensive Diversions, and elegant Entertainments get the better of the Principles and Judgments of Men or Women there is no knowing where they will stop, nor into what Evils, natural, moral, or political, they will lead us.

Your Description of your own Gaiety de Coeur, charms me. Thanks be to God you have just Cause to rejoice—and may the bright Prospect be obscured by no Cloud.

As to Declarations of Independency, be patient. Read our Privateering Laws, and our Commercial Laws. What signifies a Word.

As to your extraordinary Code of Laws, I cannot but laugh. We have been told that our Struggle has loosened the bands of Government every where. That Children and Apprentices were disobedient—that schools and Colledges were grown turbulent—that Indians slighted their Guardians and Negroes grew insolent to their Masters. But your Letter was the first Intimation that another Tribe more numerous and powerfull than all the rest were grown discontented.—This is rather too coarse a Compliment but you are so saucy, I wont blot it out.

Depend upon it, We know better than to repeal our Masculine systems. Altho they are in full Force, you know they are little more than Theory. We dare not exert our Power in its full Latitude. We are obliged to go fair, and softly, and in Practice you know We are the subjects. We have only the Name of Masters, and rather than give up this, which would compleatly subject Us to the Despotism of the Peticoat, I hope General Washington, and all our brave Heroes would fight. I am sure every good Politician would plot, as long as he would against Despotism, Empire, Monarchy, Aristocracy, Oligarchy, or Ochlocracy.—A fine Story indeed. I begin to think the Ministry as deep as they are wicked. After stirring up Tories, Landjobbers, Trimmers, Bigots, Canadians, Indians, Negroes, Hanoverians, Hessians, Russians, Irish Roman Catholicks, Scotch Renegadoes, at last they have stimulated the   to demand new Priviledges and threaten to rebell.

Ochlocracy] mob rule.   Stimulated the   ] the missing word can easily be supplied.

ERASMUS DARWIN (1731–1802) AND ANNA SEWARD (1747–1809)

Anna Seward's *Memoir of the Life of Dr Darwin* (1804), from which this correspondence is drawn, contains some material unfavourable to the poet–doctor, but it was shown to be false and attributed to Miss Seward's disappointment when the widowed Darwin did not marry her. Darwin was a distinguished doctor and the author of the strange didactic poem *The Botanic Garden* (1791). His theories of evolution in some respects anticipated those of his grandson Charles. Seward, known as 'the Swan of Lichfield', was also a poet. In Sept. 1780 'a playful correspondence passed between Dr Darwin and Miss Seward, in the name of their respective cats' (*Memoir*, 96).

87. From the Persian Snow, at Dr Darwin's, to Miss Po Felina, at the Palace, Litchfield, 7 September 1780, with her answer

Dear Miss Pussey,

As I sat, the other day, basking myself in the Dean's Walk, I saw you in your stately palace, washing your beautiful round face, and elegantly brinded ears, with your velvet paws, and whisking about, with grateful sinuosity, your meandering tail. That treacherous hedgehog, Cupid, concealed himself behind your tabby beauties, and darting one of his too well-aimed quills, pierced, O cruel imp! my fluttering heart.

Ever since that fatal hour I have watched, day and night, in my balcony, hoping that the stillness of the starlight evenings might induce you to take the air on the leads of the palace. Many serenades have I sung under your windows; and when you failed to appear, made the sound of my voice to re-echo through all its winding lanes and dirty alleys. All heard me but my cruel Fair-one; she, wrapped in fur, sat purring with contented insensibility, or slept with untroubled dreams. Though I cannot boast those delicate varieties of melody with which you sometimes ravish the ear of night, and stay the listening stars; though you sleep hourly on the lap of the favourite of the muses and are patted by those fingers which hold the pen of science; and every day, with her permission, dip your whiskers in delicious cream, yet am I not destitute of all advantages of birth, education and beauty. Derived from Persian kings, my snowy fur yet retains the whiteness and splendour of their ermine.

This morning, as I sat upon the Doctor's tea-table and saw my reflected features in the slop-basin, my long white whiskers, ivory teeth, and topaz eyes, I felt an agreeable presentiment of my suit; and certainly the slop-basin did not flatter me, which shews the azure flowers on its borders less beautiful than they are.

You know not, dear Miss Pussey Po, the value of the address you neglect.

New milk have I, in flowing abundance, and mice pent up in twenty garrets, for your food and and amusement,

Permit me this afternoon, to lay at your divine feet the head of an enormous Norway rat, which has even now stained my paws with its gore. If you will do me the honor to sing the following song, which I have taken the liberty to write, as expressing the sentiments I wish you to entertain, I will bring a band of catgut and catcall, to accompany you in chorus.

AIR: . . . SPIRITUOSÓ

Cats I scorn, who sleek and fat,
Shiver at a Norway rat;
Rough and hardy, bold and free,
Be the cat that's made for me!
He, whose nervous paws can take
My lady's lapdog by the neck;
With furious hiss attack the hen,
And snatch a chicken from the pen.
If the treacherous swain should prove
Rebellious to my tender love,
My scorn the vengeful paw shall dart,
Shall tear his fur, and pierce his heart.

CHORUS

Qu-ow wow, quall, wawl, moon.

Deign, most adorable charmer, to pur your assent to this request, and believe me to be with the profoundest respect, your true admirer.

Snow*

*The cat, to whom the above letter was addressed, had been broken of the propensity to kill birds, and lived several years without molesting a dove, a tame lark, a redbreast, all of which used to fly about the room where the cat was daily admitted. The dove frequently sat on pussey's back, and the little birds would peck fearlessly from the plate from which she was eating.

Answer, from the Palace, Litchfield, 8 September 1780

I am too sensible of the charms of Mr Snow; but while I admire the spotless whiteness of his ermine, and the tyger-strength of his commanding form, I sigh in secret, that he who sucked the milk of benevolence and philosophy should yet retain the extreme of that fierceness, too justly imputed to the Grimalkin race. Our hereditary violence is perhaps commendable when we exert it against the foes of our protectors, but deserves much blame when it annoys their friends.

The happiness of a refined education was mine; yet dear Mr Snow my advantages in that respect were not equal to what yours might have been;

but, while you give unbounded indulgence to your carnivorous desires, I have so far subdued mine, that the lark pours his mattin song, the canary-bird warbles wild and loud, and the robin pipes his farewell song to the setting sun, unmolested in my presence; nay, the plump and tempting dove has reposed securely upon my soft back, and bent her glossy neck in graceful curves as she walked around me.

But let me hasten to tell thee how my sensibilities in thy favour were, last month, unfortunately repressed. Once, in the noon of one of its most beautiful nights, I was invited abroad by the serenity of the amorous hour, secretly stimulated by the hope of meeting my admired Persian. With silent steps I passed around the dimly-gleaming leads of the palace. I had acquired a taste for scenic beauty and poetic imagery by listening to ingenious observations upon their nature from the lips of thy own lord, as I lay purring at the feet of my mistress.

I admired the lovely scene, and breathed my sighs for thee to the listening moon. She threw the long shadows of the majestic cathedral upon the silvered lawn. I beheld the pearly meadows of Stow Valley, and the lake in its bosom, which, reflecting the lunar rays, seemed a sheet of diamonds. The trees of the Dean's Walk, which the hand of Dulness had been restrained from torturing into trim and detestable regularity, met each other in a thousand various and beautiful forms. Their liberated boughs danced on the midnight gale, and the edges of their leaves were whitened by the moon beams. I descended to the lawn, that I might throw the beauties of the valley into perspective through the graceful arches, formed by their meeting branches. Suddenly my ear was startled, not by the voice of my lover, but by the loud and dissonant noise of the war-song, which six black grimalkins were raising in honor of the numerous victories obtained by the Persian, Snow; compared with which, they acknowledged those of English cats had little brilliance, eclipsed, like the unimportant victories of the Howes, by the puissant Clinton and Arbuthnot, and the still more puissant Cornwallis. They sung that thou didst owe thy matchless might to thy lineal descent from the invincible Alexander, as he derived his more than mortal valour from his mother Olympia's illicit commerce with Jupiter. They sung that, amid the renowned siege of Persepolis, while Roxana and Satira were contending for the honor of his attentions, the conqueror of the world deigned to bestow them upon a large, white female cat, thy grandmother, warlike Mr Snow, in the ten thousandth and ninety-ninth ascent.

Thus far their triumphant din was music to my ear, even when it sung that lakes of milk ran curdling white whey, within the ebon conclave of their pancheons, with terror at thine approach; that mice squealed at them from all the neighbouring garrets; and that whole armies of Norway rats, crying out amain, 'the devil take the hindmost,' ran violently into the minster-pool, at the first gleam of thy white mail through the shrubs of Mr Howard's garden.

But O! when they sung, or rather yelled, of larks warbling on sunbeams, fascinated suddenly by the glare of thine eyes, and falling into thy remorseless talons; of robins, warbling soft and solitary upon the leafless branch, till the pale cheek of winter dimpled with joy; of hundreds of those bright-breasted songsters, torn from their barren sprays by thy pitiless fangs! . . . Alas! my heart died within me at the idea of so preposterous a union!

Marry you, Mr Snow, I am afraid I cannot; since, though the laws of our community might not oppose our connection, yet those of principle, of delicacy, of duty to my mistress, do very powerfully oppose it.

As to presiding at your concert, if you extremely wish it, I may perhaps grant your request; but then you must allow me to sing a song of my own composition, applicable to our present situation, and set to music by sister Sophy at Mr Brown's the organist's, thus,

AIR: . . . AFFETUOSO

He, whom Pussy Po detains,
A captive in her silken chains,
Must curb the furious thirst of prey,
Nor rend the warbler from his spray!
Nor let his wild, ungenerous rage
An unprotected foe engage.

O, should cat of Darwin prove
Foe to pity, foe to love!
Cat, that listens, day by day,
To mercy's wild and honied lay,
Too surely would the dire disgrace
More deeply brand our future race,
The stigma fix, where'er they range,
That cats can ne'er their nature change.

Should I consent with thee to wed,
These sanguine crimes upon thy head,
And ere the wish'd reform I see,
Adieu to lapping Seward's tea!
Charm'd as she quotes thy master's lays! . . .
Could I, alas, my kittens bring
Where sweet her plumy favorites sing,
Would not the watchful nymph espy
Their father's fierceness in their eye,
And drive us far and wide away,
In cold and lonely barn to stay?
Where the dark owl, with hideous scream,
Shall mock our yells for forfeit cream,

As on starv'd mice we swearing dine,
And grumble that our lives are nine.

CHORUS . . . LARGO
Waal, woee, trone, moas, mall, oll, moule

The still too much admired Mr Snow will have the goodness to pardon
the freedom of these expostulations, and excuse their imperfections. The
morning, O Snow! had been devoted to this my correspondence with thee,
but I was interrupted in that employment by the visit of two females of our
species, who fed my ill-starred passion by praising thy wit and endow-
ments, exemplified by thy elegant letter, to which the delicacy of my
sentiments obliges me to send so inauspicious a reply.

I am, Dear Mr Snow, | Your ever obliged,
Po Felina

Howes . . .] William and George Augustus Howe, Cornwallis, Arbuthnot, and Clinton were all
officers involved in the American War of Independence.   Pancheons] earthenware bowls.

GEORGE, PRINCE OF WALES
(LATER GEORGE IV)
(1762–1830)

88. To Prince Frederick, 17 July 1781

Prince Frederick, Duke of York (1763–1827), was the second son of George III. He
went to Hanover in 1780 to study French and German, and German military
manœuvres.

You will not wonder at my long silence when you know the cause of it. Ye
misery yt. I suffer is not to be believed. However, you must give yr. word
& honor as a gentleman before you begin to read ye sad tale I have to
unfold, yt. it must be buried in ye strictest silence, for reasons wh. will
strike you, & for others wh. I will mention to you. What I have suffered
ever since last Saturday was sennight, is beyond ye power of man to
describe. However, I will now begin.

Soon after I recovered my violent illness in ye winter I went to Court.
There I saw Monsieur Hardenberg. Madame was there also, but whether
on account of the crouds there were ye two ensuing Drawing Rooms, I
never saw her either yt. Drawing or any of ye other two, but being at St
James's ye ensuing Thursday, someone, upon my asking, shewed her to me
at ye other end of the room. I bowed to her but could not get up to speak
to her before ye. Court was over. However, I met her in ye evening in ye.

Queen's appartment, at a great concert we had there. I then was introduced to her. After having conversed with her some time I perceived yt. she was a very sensible, agreable, pleasant little woman, but devilish severe. I thought no more of her at yt. time. Busche having desired me to take notice of her husband as a very sensible honest man, I invited him to dinner, with a grande société, in order to shew him every civility & attention yt. was in my power, by introducing him to several people, in short, to as many as I possibly could, in order to encrease his acquaintance & make him known to some of ye. people of ye. first fashion here. He dined with me once or twice before I met him, *alone*, at ye. Lodge at Windsor, in order to hunt with our pack of hounds ye. next morning. The King invited him down twice in this manner in order to hunt. However, ye. third time he was invited down, he was ordered to make up ye. King's hunt, & desired to bring Madame with him. I had seen & met Madame only once since ye. first time I mentioned meeting her at ye. Queen's House, in ye. Queen's appartment, when I was set down to whist with a set of very good and consequently very grave players. She was set down at ye next table opposite to me to a commerce party with my sister, a thing I could easily perceive by her looks she disliked very much, not particularly because she was to play with those girls, but because, as I have since learnt from her, she hates all games at cards, as I do, unless they are games of chance, merely for ye sake of gambling. That night I thought her devinely pretty. My attention was naturally taken from the cards, & in short, I could not keep my eyes off her. One of my sisters who had undertaken to teach her ye. game, with wh. she was totally unacquainted, played her cards for her, & I observed her to be equally inattentive to her play, as I was, but I thought I met her eyes too frequently to fancy yt. it proceeded from inattention or common curiosity only. However, at yt. moment I was too much taken up with looking at her myself to be so observant, tho' it struck me afterwards. From that moment ye. fatal tho' delightful passion arose in my bosom for her, wh. has made me since, ye. most miserable & wretched of men. With whom should I so soon place my whole confidence & all my cares & misfortunes wh. have now brought me to ye. utmost pitch of misery, as with him who is ye. friend of my heart, who has always proved himself deserving of ye. confidence I have placed in him, my dearest brother? Yes, my beloved Frederick, with you I know this unhappy secret will be buried in eternal in eternal [*sic*] silence. O did you but know how I adore her, how I love her, how I would sacrifice every earthly thing to her; by Heavens I shall go distracted: my brain will split. But to return to our subject. I went down to Windsor. I met Mme Hardenberg there; she was to stay & did stay a fortnight there with us. During ye. first three or four days I shewed her every attention possible, & did not mention a word of love to her. However, within a day or two I said to her, after having shewn her very particular attentions, yt. it was a pity after having met so often at Windsor I could not have ye. satisfaction of seeing her so frequently in London, & asked her if she was not to be seen in town sometimes after eleven o'clock when her husband was out. She resented this with very great spirit saying she believed I had forgot whom I was speaking to, but, upon my making her strong excuses & saying I really did not mean to give her ye. smallest offence, she said she would forget all. But in order to shorten my dismal tale & not to stick upon minutiae I will tell you yt. [I] dropped every other connexion of whatever sort or kind, & devoted myself entirely to this angelick little woman. I grew more & more fond of her, & to so violent a degree did I doat upon her, yt. it impaired my health & constitution very much. Jebb was obliged to attend upon me. I have spit blood & am so much emaciated you would hardly know me again. This had a strong effect upon her. She began then to perceive how truly I was attached to her, & one morning when I called upon her at her house at Old Windsor while her husband was absent, after I had complained much of her coldness & cruelty to me, she thus spoke to me, 'I certainly am very much attached to you, & do love you most sincerely, & it affords me great delight to think yt. you are attached to me, but I must tell you yt. I was once very much attached to another person, & did think yt a woman never could love but once very sincerely during her life. If, after such a declaration, you can attach yourself to me, it will be an additional proof of your love, but should you not, for God's sake let us drop all thoughts of love & part very good friends'. I assured her yt. what she had said, so far from lessening my affection, encreased it if possible, & made me entertain a higher idea of her honor. I then continued visiting her two or three times more before she would consent to listen to any idea of compleating my happiness. However at last she did. O my beloved brother, I enjoyed beforehand ye. pleasures of Elyssium; but this is a secret wh. no one but Hulse & you know of. Thus did our connexion go forward in ye most delightful manner yt. you can form any idea to yourself of, till an unfortunate article in ye. *Morning Herald* appeared, saying yt. ye. German Baroness who had been imported by ye Queen, had taken a house next door to Perdita's in Cork Street, & yt. my carriage was seen constantly at her door. Ye. confusion wh. caused this article is yt. a Polish Countess, Countess Raouska, has taken ye. house next to Mrs. R[obinson]'s, & ye. Duke of Gloucester's carriage is very often, nay even every day seen at her door. Be this as it will, her husband, who had been put upon his guard by some servant in his family, came to her & told her yt. unless she immediately wrote a letter to me saying she would drop all connexion with me he should suppose she had cuckolded him. She endeavored to convince him concerning his absurdity about ye. newspaper, & at last grew angry.

However, he intim[id]ated her so much by his brutality yt. she was in a moment of fright weak enough to confess I had made proposals to her, tho' never had succeeded, & forced her to write ye. letter I have already mentioned to you, to me. He also wrote one to me wh. accompanied it. I almost fell into fits when I received the packet from him, & augured no good from it, but upon opening it I thought I should have run distracted, as I conceived her to be guilty of ye. blackest ingratitude & cruelty to me. However, I immediately sat down & wrote to them both saying to him yt. it was very true I was very strongly attached to his wife, but yt. I should be ye. most infamous of human beings if, after the proposals I had made her I should have a single doubt concerning his wife's character, for yt. she had always treated me with ye. utmost coolness & yt. I was ye. only person yt. he was to blame in ye. whole of this affair. As to her, I wrote her ye. most passionate of letters. I thought everything was then at an end, & I sent an express for Lord Southampton & desired he wld. go into ye. King & ask his permission for me to go abroad, as an unfortunate affair had of late happened to me wh. made me excessively miserable, & I wished by yt. means to try if I could not a little dissipate my thoughts; yt. it was not an affair yt. would ever come to ye. King's ears & yt. therefore I flattered myself I should receive his Majesty's leave to set out as soon as possible. The answer Southampton brought me was yt. the King cld. not at present think of my going abroad as it was during ye. war. This was on Sunday sennight in ye morning, & on Sunday at noon I received a letter from her, yt. she was forced to write ye. preceding one to me, reminding me of her attachment, saying she hoped I had not forgot all my vows, & would run off with her yt. night. Adoring her as I do, judge of ye. different combats my heart had to endure, ye. idea of ye. noise my flight would cause in ye. world, then ye. idea of being in possession of her who alone forms all my happiness. For some time I in a manner lost my senses entirely. However, I chanced to meet her & consented to ye. plot, but as soon as I had, reflection crouded itself on my mind. Ye. thought wh. then occurred to me was yt. although she was unhappy, nay miserable, with her husband, yet she would live as a woman in her situation in life ought to do; at least she could eat & she cld. drink & live, but had she been with me, you know our father's severe disposition; everything yt. was shocking is to be expected from him; & ye. very thought yt. I should perhaps see ye. object of all my tenderness, of all my love, in short, ye. only woman upon earth I can & do only love, perishing for want, is such an idea yt. it stabbed me to ye. very heart & staggered my resolution. I need not desire you, dearest Frederick, to feel for my sufferings. Yr. generous heart will sufficiently share ye. pangs & conflicts I have & still do endure; in short, my misery was such yt. I went under ye promise of ye greatest secrecy & threw myself at my mother's feet

& confessed ye. whole truth to her. I fainted. She cried excessively & felt for me very much. There was then but one thing to be done, & we sent Hulse to Mme. H. to tell her yt. nothing but an unforeseen accident wh. had happened cld. prevent my coming. Upon this ye. Queen only begged me to allow her to tell ye. King upon condition he took no part in it, what had been ye. subject of our conversation. Whether she was quite true to me or not I cannot say. However, all yt. I have now time to tell you is yt. my father sent for Hardenberg & yt. he went off with my little angel to Bruxelles on Thursday night, leaving me to all ye. agonies of misery & despair. I have not time, my best friend, to explain anything more to you at present, but will certainly by ye. very next post. I only now have to add yt. I trust so much to yr. honor (yt. supposing her to [be] capable of allowing of it, wh. I believe impossible but I say supposing yt. possible) yt. you would not add to my misery by making up to her or making love to her even in ye. most distant. If ever I should hear it you wld. be ye. cause of my death, but I cannot help upbraiding myself for want of confidence in yr. honor, so you are incapable of it, you wld. not hurt yr. brother who loves you so tenderly, in ye. most distant manner, however you must allow for ye. feelings of a lover. You will see ye. necessity for yr. secrecy. I will tell you & explain to you much more in my next, concerning all my plans & views wh. are ye. only things wh. now keep me alive. With regard to the King, you will not make any comments, I hope, upon any part of ye. business to him, only say you are sorry to hear of the affair & promise yr. secrecy upon ye. occasion. Adieu, dearest of brothers, my heart is ready to burst.

Queen's House, Friday, 20 July 1781

P.S. You will perceive my agitation by ye. horrid style & scrawl. You shall hear from me again almost immediately, as I have scarce any other satisfaction left than yt. of knowing I have a friend who will feel most truly for me. Once more, adieu, my dearest Frederick.

Hulse] The Prince's equerry.   Perdita] Mary Robinson, celebrated for her performance in *The Winter's Tale*, had been mistress to the Prince of Wales, who courted her as 'Florizel'.   Duke of Gloucester] a great-grandson of George II and, later, brother-in-law to the Prince of Wales.

89. Prince Frederick to the Prince of Wales, 30 July 1781

I cannot let General Freytag return to England without writing to you to thank you for your last letter, though I am sorry it was on so dismal an occasion. You, I am sure, are too fully persuaded of my affection for you not to know how much I felt upon reading your letter. As for the promise which you ask of me, I most willingly give it, for if you knew her as well as I do . . . you would be completely cured of any particular affection for her. Next letter I shall write to you, when I suppose your grief be a little subsided, I will send you an exact account of her behaviour to me, of which I have no doubt she spoke to you, though very possibly with not so exact a regard for truth as I will have. There is also another story of her which I know for a fact & which I will also send you, but which you must never mention.

I am just returned from a very agreeable party to Pyrmont, which is a sweet spot.

Pray send me back by the courier the new Army List. I have not time to add any more, only that I am, [etc.].

Pray write soon.

90. *The Prince of Wales to Princess Caroline, 30 April 1796*

> The heir to the throne, who had already entered a form of marriage with Mrs Fitzherbert, detested his wife, Princess Caroline of Brunswick, at first sight (1795) and separated from her after the birth of a daughter. This letter informed her of his decision to do so. In 1821 he barred her from his coronation.

Madam,

As Lord Cholmondeley informs me that you wish I would define, in writing, the terms upon which we are to live, I shall endeavour to explain myself with as much clearness, and with as much propriety as the nature of the subject will admit. Our inclinations are not in our power, nor should either of us be held answerable to the other, because nature has not made us suitable to each other. Tranquil and comfortable society is, however, in our power; let our intercourse, therefore, be restricted to that, and I will distinctly subscribe to the condition which you required, through Lady Cholmondeley, that even in the event of any accident happening to my daughter, which I trust Providence in his mercy will avert, I shall not infringe the terms of the restriction by proposing at any period, a connexion of a more particular nature. I shall now finally close this disagreeable correspondence trusting that as we have completely explained ourselves to each other, the rest of our lives will be passed in uninterrupted tranquility.

I am Madam, | With great truth, very sincerely yours,

George P.

BENJAMIN FRANKLIN
(1706–1790)

Franklin was ambassador to France at the time of writing. Banks (1743–1820), a naturalist, was president of the Royal Society.

91. To Sir Joseph Banks, 27 July 1783

Dear Sir,

I received your very kind letter by Dr Blagden, and esteem myself much honour'd by your friendly remembrance. I have been too much and too closely engag'd in public affairs since his being here, to enjoy all the benefit of his conversation you were so good as to intend me. I hope soon to have more leisure, and to spend a part of it in those studies that are much more agreeable to me than political operations.

I join with you most cordially in rejoicing at the return of Peace. I hope it will be lasting, and that mankind will at length, as they call themselves reasonable creatures, have reason and sense enough to settle their differences without cutting throats. For in my opinion *there never was a good War, or a bad Peace.*

What vast additions to the conveniences and comforts of living might mankind have acquired, if the money spent in wars had been employ'd in Works of public utility; what an extention of agriculture even to the tops of our Mountains; what Rivers rendered navigable, or joined by canals; what Bridges, Acqueducts, new Roads, and other public Works, Edifices, and Improvements, rendering England a compleat Paradise, might not have been obtain'd by spending those millions in doing good, which in the last War have been spent in doing mischief; in bringing misery into thousands of families, and destroying the lives of so many thousands of working people who might have perform'd the useful labour.

I am pleas'd with the late astronomical discoveries made by our Society. Furnish'd as all Europe now is with Academies of Science, with nice instruments and the spirit of Experiment, the progress of human knowledge will be rapid, and discoveries made of which we have at present no conception. I begin to be almost sorry I was born so soon, since I cannot have the happiness of knowing what will be known a hundred years hence.

I wish continued success to the labours of the Royal Society, and that you may long adorn their chair, being with the highest esteem,

Dear Sir, | your most obedient and most humble servant,

B. Franklin

Dr Blagden will acquaint you with the experiment of a vast Globe sent up into the air, much talk'd of here at present, and which if prosecuted may furnish means of new knowledge.

92. To Sir Joseph Banks, 30 November 1783

Dear Sir,

I did myself the honour of writing to you the beginning of last week, and I sent you by the Courier M. Faujas's Book upon the Balloons which I hope you have receiv'd. I did hope to have given you to day an Account of Mr Charles's grand Balloon, which was to have gone up yesterday; but the filling it with inflammable air having taken more time than had been calculated, it is deferred till to-morrow. I send you herewith a Paper in which you will see what was propos'd by Messrs Robert who constructed the Machine; and some other Papers relative to the same subject, the last of which is curious, as containing the Journal of the first Aërial Voyage perform'd by Men. I purpose being present to-morrow at the Experiment, and shall give you an Account of it by the Wednesday's Post. With sincere and great esteem, I have the honour, to be,

Sir, | Your most obed^t humble serv^t,
B. Franklin.

VINCENZO LUNARDI
(1759–1806)

93. To King George III, 16 September 1784

Lunardi was secretary to the Neapolitan ambassador Prince Caramanico. Two hundred thousand people witnessed his ascent, the first in England, in a 32-foot balloon filled with hydrogen. The King watched through a telescope from St James's. Lunardi finally landed at Ware. The heroine who held the rope was Elizabeth Brett, a farmer's servant, who declared on oath before William Baker, justice of the peace, that the men close at hand had declined to help, 'George Philips saying he was too short, and John Mills saying he did not like it'; but braver spirits, harvesting nearby, came to her help. Lunardi returned to London, with his balloon, amid loud acclamations.

Sire,

Full of thankfullness for the honor granted me, I beg to lay myself at your Majesty's feet, having no higher ambition than to obtain the approbation of a monarch no less admired by strangers than beloved by his people. I humbly beg leave to present to your Majesty a memoir of the first aerial voyage that hath been undertaken in your Majesty's dominions. And if I have the happiness to afford your Majesty any pleasure or entertainment, I have at least obtained one principal object which outweighs the hazard of the enterprise.

The 15th of September being fixed on for my embarcation from the artillery grounds, accompanied by a friend, an immense multitude assembled, of which many thousands were witnesses to the process and preparation for my departure. Though the utmost diligence had been used by myself and several ingenious friends to put the machine in a condition to be launched at the appointed hour, it was found impracticable: from the violent agitation it received from the wind, an aperture was made in the neck, which required a considerable delay to remedy. I determined therefore to embark in the state it then was, lest I should be exposed to the fury of the populace, who already betrayed symptoms of impatience and incredulity; and filled me with apprehensions of being treated as an impostor. A smaller gallery was, in consequence, suspended, and the ballast reduced; but the power of the balloon being still unequal to the weight of myself and my friend, I was obliged to forego the pleasure and advantage of his company on the voyage.

Exhausted with fatigue, and full of apprehension and anxiety, I was preparing to embark in the armory room, when intelligence was brought me that an accident had happened to the balloon, which in all probability would defeat the experiment. I now gave myself up for lost, and was reduced almost to a state of incapacity to undertake the voyage; however, I found the accident upon examination to be so trifling as to occasion very little delay.

All difficulties being at length overcome, I took my seat in the gallery, but in the hurry and discomposure which a combination of untoward circumstances had occasioned, I forgot some of the instruments necessary for my intended observations, which, added to the loss of a scientific companion, hath very much lessened the philosophic importance of my voyage.

The cords being divided, the balloon ascended with a slow and majestic motion amidst the shouts and acclamations of a numberless multitude, who liberally attoned for their suspicions of imposture by their unbounded admiration and applause. At the height of twenty yards the globe was suddenly depressed by the wind, but on discharging a part of the ballast it again ascended, and at the height of two hundred yards I repeated the salute of waving my flag, which I then threw down to convince such as were yet incredulous that I accompanied the balloon.

I now began to apply my oars, but one of them unfortunately broke, and fell from me; here likewise a pigeon escaped, which, with a cat and dog I had taken up as subjects of experimental observation.

The thermometer having now fallen from 68° to 61° I perceived a great difference in the temperature of the air; I became very sensible to cold, and found it necessary to take a few glasses of wine; I ate likewise the leg of a chicken, but my bread and other provisions were spoiled by mixing with the sand. When my thermometer was at 50° I felt the most delightful sensations, such I believe as are felt in no region upon earth. The stillness of the scene was inexpressibly awful; the prospect of London, with the surrounding country, in which trees and fields were distinguishable to a great extent, presented a picture of which the liveliest fancy can form no idea.

To prolong this exquisite enjoyment, I kept myself in the same parallel for at least half an hour, by working continually with my single oar, and again had recourse to my bottle, which I emptied to the health of my friends and benefactors in the lower world. All my affections were alive, but the sentiment that seemed most congenial to this enchanting region, was gratitude, which, irresistibly impelling me to address myself to my honoured friend and patron, I wrote four pages of observations, and pinning them to a napkin, consigned them to the zephyrs to waft them to the Prince Caramanico.

At this instant I heard the report of a gun, and examining my thermometer, it had fallen to 32°. The balloon was now so compleatly inflated, that to prevent its bursting, I slackened the neck, which I held in my hand, to give, if possible, a free passage to the inflammable air.

I here congratulated myself on the circumstances which had prevented the compleat filling of the globe previous to my departure; and which an hour before, I had reckoned the greatest misfortune that could befal me. The vapour about the neck of the balloon was quite frozen, though I was perfectly free from cold, owing to much labor, and the wine I had taken. The earth at this point appeared like a boundless plain, whose surface was variegated, but on which no objects could be distinguished.

I now descended by means of my oar, to about the distance of three hundred yards from the earth, and moving horizontally, spoke through my trumpet to some country-people, from whom I heard a confused noise in reply. At half past three I descended with much labour on a cornfield in the Common of North Mimms, where I landed my cat.[1] The poor animal had been sensibly affected by the cold during the greatest part of the time.

My general course from the artillery ground to this place, was something more than one point to the westward of the north. A gentleman on horseback approached me, but I could not speak to him, being intent on my reascention, which I effected after moving horizontally about forty paces. As I ascended one of the ballustrades of the gallery gave way, but no danger attended it; I threw out the remainder of my ballast and provisions, and again resumed my pen. My ascension was so rapid, that before half the page was filled, the thermometer had fallen to 29°. The drops of water that adhered to the neck of the globe, were congealed to a perfect chrystal. At this point of elevation, (which was the highest I attain'd) I finished my letter, and fastening it with a corkscrew to my handkerchief, threw it down. I likewise threw down the plates, knives and forks, with the little sand that remained of my ballast; and likewise an empty bottle, which I could plainly distinguish for some time before it totally disappeared.

I now prepared to write my last dispatch, which fixed to a leather belt,

---

[1] This field is called Etna in the manor of the Duke of Leeds, is about half a mile to the eastward of the 16 milestone on the road leading from London to Hatfield.

I sent towards the earth; it was visible to me on its passage for the space of several minutes. The earth appeared, as before, like an extensive plain, with the same variegated face.

Having no further object to pursue, I betook myself to the oar, in order to descend: with a quarter of an hour's hard labour, by which my strength was almost exhausted, I accomplished my descent. My chief care was to avoid too violent a concussion at my landing. In this my good fortune befriended me.

At twenty five minutes past four I descended on a spacious meadow, in the Parish of Standon,[2] in which some countrymen were at work. I requested their assistance, but no intreaties could prevail with them to approach me. I at last owed my deliverance to female heroism: a young woman, who was likewise in the field, took hold of a cord which I threw out, and calling to the men for their assistance, they yielded to her entreaties.

A crowd of country people were soon assembled, who very obligingly assisted me to disembark. General Smith, who had followed me on horseback, was the first gentleman that overtook me. I am much indebted to him for his great affability and politeness to me and his kind assistance in securing the balloon, which, after letting out the inflammable air by an incision, I committed to the care of Mr Hollingsworth, (who kindly offered his service for that purpose) and then proceeded with General Smith and several other gentlemen to the Bull Inn at Ware.

The general course of my second voyage was three points to the eastward of the north from the artillery ground, and about four points to the eastward of the north from the place at which I first descended.

On my arrival at Ware I had the honor to be introduced to William Baker, Esqr., late Member for Hertford, who conducted me to his seat at Bayford-bury and entertained me with an hospitality and politeness which I shall ever remember with gratitude, and excited my admiration of that liberality and beneficence which are the allowed characteristics of English gentlemen.

[2] About half a mile to the north west of the 24 milestone on the road that leads from London to Cambridge through Ware & Puckeridge.

JOHN NEWTON
(1725–1807)

After a career in the merchant marine which included service with slave-traders, Newton became a parson and settled at Olney under the patronage of the liberal Lord Dartmouth. He was a famous preacher, and a close friend of the poet William Cowper, with whom he collaborated on the *Olney Hymns* (1779).

94. John Newton to the Earl of Dartmouth, 22 September 1784

I durst not, therefore, upon my principles have accompanied Mr Lunardi in his late balloon expedition. I looked after him in his flight, with a mixture of admiration and compassion. How great the hazard, how poor the motives. A strange creature man is, his powers of invention, the ardour and enterprise of his spirit bespeak his original, but the misapplication of his powers loudly proclaim his depravity. He is continually making new discoveries, but to the need, and worth, and way of salvation he is blind and insensible. If gain or the applause of his fellow creatures be his prospect, he will venture the greatest risk, and expose himself to the greatest hardship, but a happiness suited to his nature and the approbation of God, are disregarded as trifles, unworthy of his pursuit. I was glad to hear that Mr Lunardi was again safe upon terra firma, but I hear he is meditating a new excursion and that many others animated by his success are eager to follow his example. I fear this balloon mania will not subside till some awful events put a stop to it. The Philosophers I am told are sanguine in their expectations of making this new art of flying more generally practicable, but I believe and hope they will not succeed. We are bad enough already, but were it possible for men to transport themselves at their pleasure through the air, how greatly would the mischiefs and missions of human life be multiplied. As the providence of God is concerned in all events, there must I think be some ends to be answered by this discovery and these attempts in the balloon way, but at present I can only moralize upon them. I would learn in the first place not to be peremptory in determining what is or what is not impossible. A while ago it would have been thought impossible for a man to travel through the air. Many things which at present appear equally inconceivable may in time be easy, for who can say what secret powers may be in the course of nature. The effects of gunpowder and of electricity were unknown for ages. Again, I observe, how preposterous is the judgment of men; a person is talked of and admired by thousands for venturing up with a balloon, though it is a mere point of curiosity, not likely to be productive of any benefit, while he who came down from Heaven to dwell for a time with men, and to die for them is slighted and disregarded.

GILBERT WHITE (OF SELBORNE)

(1720–1793)

A curate at Selborne, Hampshire, where he spent most of his life, White won distinction as a naturalist. His meteorological interests perhaps made him especially

susceptible to the charm of the balloon; on 24 Sept. 1784 he complained to his sister
Mary that she had said nothing about Lunardi's flight ('did it not affect you, to see
a poor human creature entering upon so strange and hazardous an exploit?'). He was
to see another such hero in the following month.

95. To Mrs Barker, 19 October 1784

Dear Sister,

From the fineness of the weather, and the steadiness of the wind to the
N.E. I began to be possessed with a notion last Friday that we should see
Mr Blanchard in his balloon the day following: and therefore I called on
many of my neighbours in the street, and told them my suspicions. The
next day proving also bright, and the wind continuing as before, I became
more sanguine than ever; and issuing forth in the morning exhorted all
those that had any curiosity to look sharp from about one o' the clock to
three towards London, as they would stand a good chance of being entertained with a very extraordinary sight. That day I was not content to call
at the houses only; but I went out to the plow-men and labourers in the
fields, and advised them to keep an eye to the N. and N.E. at times. I wrote
also to Mr Pink of Faringdon to desire him to look about him. But about
one o'clock there came up such a haze that I could not see the hanger.
However, not long after the mist cleared away in some degree, and people
began to mount the hill. I was busy in and out 'til a quarter after two; and
took my last walk along the top of the pound-field, from whence I could
discern a long cloud of London smoke, hanging to the N. and N.N.E. This
appearance, for obvious reasons, increased my expectation: yet I came
home to dinner, knowing how many were on the watch: but laid my hat
and surtout ready in a chair, in case of an alarm. At twenty minutes before
three there was a cry in the street that the balloon was come. We ran into
the orchard, where we found twenty or thirty neighbours assembled; and
from the green bank at the S.W. end of my house saw a dark blue speck at
a most prodigious height, dropping as it were from the sky, and hanging
amidst the regions of the upper air, between the weather-cock of the tower
and the top of the may-pole. At first, coming towards us, it did not seem
to make any way; but we soon discovered that its velocity was very considerable. For in a few minutes it was over the may-pole; and then over the
Fox on my great parlor chimney; and in ten minutes more behind my great
wallnut tree. The machine looked mostly of a dark blue colour; but some
times reflected the rays of the sun, and appeared of a bright yellow. With
a telescope I could discern the boat, and the ropes that supported it. To my
eye this vast balloon appeared no bigger than a large tea-urn. When we saw
it first, it was north of Farnham, over Farnham-heath; and never came, I
believe, on this side the Farnham-road; but continued to pass on the other
side of Bentley, Froil, Alton; and so for Medsted, Lord Northington's at

the Grange, and to the right of Alresford, and Winton; and to Rumsey, where the aerial philosopher came safe to the ground, near the Church, at about five in the evening. I was wonderfully struck at first with the phænomenon; and, like Milton's 'belated peasant', felt my heart rebound with fear and joy at the same time. After a while I surveyed the machine with more composure, without that awe and concern for two of my fellow-creatures, lost, in appearance, in the boundless depths of the atmosphere! for we supposed *then* that *two* were embarked in this astonishing voyage. At last, seeing with what steady composure they moved, I began to consider them as secure as a group of Storks or Cranes intent on the business of emigration, and who had—

> '. . . set forth
> Their airy caravan, high over seas
> Flying, and over lands, with mutual wing
> Easing their flight. . . .'

Mr Taylor, our new vicar, has taken possession of S[elborne] living; and I have reassumed the curacy, after an intermission of 26 years! Mrs Etty rents the vicarage house; but has been gone eight or nine weeks, and does not return 'til winter. Mr Yalden has gone to Bath in Company with Mr Budd. Brother Ben. and family are at Newton, but go next week. Brother Thomas has been expected here all the autumn, but is not yet come. Mrs H. White brought Lucy to my house lately, for change of air: the poor young woman is languid, and has over-grown her strength: but I perceive no bad symptoms. We have apples and pears innumerable, and *very* fine grapes. Mrs Clement is in a fair way, I suspect, to encrease her family. I wish you joy of your late grand-daughter, which makes my 41st nephew and niece! I have very dutiful nieces, that seem disposed to make me as *great* an uncle as they can. Mrs J. White joins in respects. I am with all due affection and regard,

Y^r loving brother,
Gil. White.

Sweet autumnal weather! we have had no rain since Septemr. 27th not enough to measure. I miss poor Mr Etty every day: he was a blameless man, without guile. His son Charles is in London making interest for an appointment to India. His escape off Ceylon was wonderful!

Mr Blanchard] a famous French balloonist who made the first channel crossing by balloon in 1785. He was killed in 1809 using a parachute he had invented.   Mr Pink] a neighbouring farmer, who decided that White had lost his mind: 'I had a letter from him yesterday, and what do you think he desired me to do?—he told me to look out sharp to the north-east between one and three o'clock today, and perhaps I should see two men riding in a balloon.' White had in fact alerted the whole village.   Hanger] a wooded hillside.   Milton] *Paradise Lost*, i. 783; vii. 427–30.

QUEEN CHARLOTTE SOPHIA
(1744–1818)

Charlotte Sophia was the queen of George III, and mother of his fifteen children.

96. To Prince William, August 1785

William (1765–1837) was the third son. He had a naval career and eventually (1830) succeeded to the throne as William IV.

I am very happy to find by both your letters that you are perfectly well & so much amused, but cannot help saying how sorry I am to see that you continue still to harbour such unaccountable dislikes to those about you. Your reasons for liking and disliking are in general so trifling and frivolous that the best judgement one could form upon them would be that of youthful volatility, but when one knows you to be twenty years of age this very month, this excuse can no longer be made & severer judgements must arise, which can be no less than the want of *a good heart*, want *of understanding, ambition, vanity, willfulness* & an uncommon share of caprice, which imperceptibly will lead you to be what you will be ashamed to hear, *a true trifling character*, which is the most despicable of all things in the world, & the higher the rank the more it is observed; & it is surprizing that with the proofs you give to the world of your *offensive pride* you do not feel the necessity of a proper behaviour. Want of decency is want of sense, & can there be a greater proof of that, than your shunning the company of those whose experience could alone direct & guide you, & the choice you make, in your acquaintance of every young man that comes to see Germany. Believe me, there is not so great a fool and so bad a man but he sees your faults & carries you as he finds you wherever he goes, & that is your case already, for it is amazing how your indifference of behaviour is talkd of both here & abroad, & the world so far is just in attributing it to your want of minding the advice of proper people, & the great opinion you have of yourself. Cease, I beseech you, to be a *great-little* man, which in reality is *nothing at all*, & return to those who are put about you in order to guide you. Do not think that all Princes share alike. The situation of some is unfortunately such, that they can never be in a way to hear their real faults as it is people's interest to keep them ignorant of it, but a younger brother can never be in that dilemma, for though you are the King's third son, brought up in an honorable profession, I do assure you you will not have it in your power to make people believe that your pretentions to a thing makes you worthy of it if you are not, nay, what is more to be feared is that they will encourage you to think so in order to make your fall the sorer, & in the end profit by your ignorance. Try for the future to be more reasonable. Make no promises but act a right, honorable, open part; think time is precious, what is lost cannot be recovered, & copy those who are good, seek their company, & leave vice & folly to those who think but of the present & not of hereafter. Choose to be a usefull member of society & make yourself more respected through your decency & good behaviour than by your rank. This respect of rank is like that paid to the idols, but that which is gained by a uniform continual upright conduct is everlasting. Whatever I can contribute to your reform I am very ready to do at all times, but I beseech you make no more promises, for they fill your letters but take no effect upon yourself. Before you answer I beg you will reflect a little and consider whether it is not more for your good to have recourse to Budé's advice & to follow it than to be directed by your own little nonsensical volatile head. *Adieu tout à vous* [etc.]

SIR WILLIAM HAMILTON
(1730–1803)

Hamilton was a diplomat, archaeologist, connoisseur, and husband of Lord Nelson's mistress Emma.

97. *To the Prince of Wales, 12 November 1788*

Your Royal Highness will I hope pardon the great liberty I have taken in sending you a case containing a colossal head in marble of an Augustus, of true Grecian sculpture which I discovered in an old tower in this city, and which, in the building thereof, had been made use of as a common stone. When the noble owner of the tower allowed me to have it extracted, I luckily found it infinitely beyond my expectation excellent, and (except a part of the nose, part of one ear and a lock of hair, which had been broken off) in good preservation. I sent it to Rome to have those parts properly restored, and I flatter myself that now your Royal Highness will not think this monument of antiquity unworthy of a place in Carleton House. I will tell your Royal Highness truly what induced me to think of taking so great a liberty. When I was last in England I perceived with pleasure that your Royal Highness had a great love for the Arts and a desire of acquiring a knowledge of them. The only method is to examine with attention such works of art as are avowedly & undoubtedly of the first class and compare them with others that only pretend to be so. I am convinced that when this bust is placed in a good light and at its proper height, and your Royal

Highness has been accustom'd to look upon it you will never bear the sight of a bust of indifferent sculpture. His Majesty, who is certainly a great lover of the Arts, and has given them great encouragement, for want of having formed his taste early on works of the first class, has never arrived at being sensible to what is properly call'd the sublime in the Arts.

This favorite subject of mine has I fear already carried me too far. May your R. Highness enjoy health and every happiness and that the Arts in Great Britain may flourish one day under the auspices of your Royal Highness to as great a degree of perfection as they did at Rome in the days of Augustus is the sincere wish of Sir [etc.].

EDMUND BURKE
(1729–1797)

Burke was celebrated for his parliamentary oratory, advocating conciliatory attitudes to the Americans and Catholic emancipation. He played a central part in the impeachment of Warren Hastings, and was most famous for his *Reflections on the Revolution in France* (1790), defended in this letter.

98. To Sir Philip Francis, 20 February 1790

Francis (1740–1818) was the supposed author of the 'Junius' Letters, anonymous attacks on corruption in public life (1769–72). He visited India, and being hostile to Hastings provided Burke with information against him, but he censured his friend for the celebrated and sentimental encomium of Marie Antoinette, seen in manuscript. Burke writes after a ball at Carlton House given by the Prince Regent.

My dear Sir,

I sat up rather late at Carlton House; and on my return hither I found your Letter on my Table. I have not slept since. You will therefore excuse me if you find any thing confused, or otherwise expressed than I could wish in speaking to you upon a matter which interests you from your regard to me. There are some things in your Letter for which I must thank you; there are others which I must answer; Some things bear the marks of friendly admonition; others bear some resemblance to the Tone of accusation.

You are the only friend I have who will dare to give me advice. I must then have something terrible in me, which intimidates all others who know me from giving me the only unequivocal mark of their regard. Whatever this Rough and menacing manner may be, I must search myself upon it; and when I discover it, old as I am, I must endeavour to correct it. I flatterd myself however, that you at least would not have thought my other friends altogether justified in withholding from me their services of this Kind. You certainly do not always convey to me your opinions with the greatest possible Tenderness, and management; and yet I do not recollect since I first had the pleasure of your acquaintance that there has been an heat or a coolness of a single days duration on my side during that whole time. I believe your memory cannot present to you an instance of it. I ill deserve friends, if I throw them away on account of the Candour and simplicity of their good nature. In particular you know, that you have in some instances favourd me with your Instructions relative to things I was preparing for the publick. If I did not in every instance agree with you, I think you had on the whole sufficient proofs of my docility to make you believe that I received your corrections not only without offence, but with no small degree of Gratitude.

Your remarks upon the two first Sheets of my Paris Letter relate to the Composition and the matter. The composition you say is loose; and I am quite sure it is. I never intended it should be otherwise; for purporting to be, what in Truth it originally was, a Letter to a friend, I had no Idea of digesting it in a Systematick order. The Style is open to correction, and wants it. My natural Style of writing is somewhat careless; and I should be happy in receiving your advice towards making it as little viscious as such a Style is capable of being made. The general Character and colour of a Style which grows out of the Writers peculiar Turn of mind and habit of expressing his thoughts must be attended to in all corrections. It is not the insertion of a piece of Stuff though of a better kind which is at all times an improvement.

Your main Objections are however of a much deeper Nature, and go to the Political opinions and moral Sentiments of the piece; in which I find, (though with no sort of surprise, having often talked with you on the Subject) that we differ only in every thing. You say 'The mischief you are going to do yourself is to my apprehension palpable. I snuff it in the wind; and my Taste sickens at it.' This anticipated Stench that turns your Stomach at such a distance must be nauseous indeed. You seem to think I shall incur great (and not wholly undeserved) infamy by this publication. This makes it a matter of some delicacy to me to suppress what I have written; for I must admit in my own feeling, and in that of those who have seen this piece, that my Sentiments and opinions deserve the infamy with which they are threatned. If they do not, I know nothing more than that I oppose the prejudices and inclinations of many people. This I was well aware of from the beginning, and it was in order to oppose those inclinations and prejudices, that I proposed to publish my Letter. I really am perfectly astonish'd how you could dream with my paper in your hand—that I found

no other Cause than the Beauty of the Queen of France (now I suppose
pretty much faded) for disapproving the Conduct which has been held
towards her, and for expressing my own particular feelings. I am not to
order the Natural Sympathies of my own Breast, and of every honest breast
to wait until the Tales and all the anecdotes of the Coffeehouses of Paris
and of the dissenting meeting houses of London are scoured of all the
slander of those who calumniate persons, that afterwards they may murder
them with impunity? I know nothing of your Story of Messalina. Am I
obliged to prove juridically the Virtues of all those I shall see suffering
every kind of wrong, and contumely, and risk of Life, before I endeavour
to interest others in their sufferings, and before I endeavour to excite an
horrour against midnight assassins at back stairs, and their more wicked
abettors in Pulpits? What, are not high Rank, great Splendour of descent,
great personal Elegance and outward accomplishments ingredients of
moment in forming the interest we take in the Misfortunes of Men? The
minds of those who do not feel thus are not even Dramatically right.
'Whats Hecuba to him or he to Hecuba that he should weep for her?' Why
because she was Hecuba, the Queen of Troy, the Wife of Priam, and
sufferd in the close of Life a thousand Calamities. I felt too for Hecuba
when I read the fine Tragedy of Euripides upon her Story: and I never
enquired into the Anecdotes of the Court or City of Troy before I gave way
to the Sentiments which the author wished to inspire; nor do I remember
that he ever said one word of her Virtues. It is for those who applaud or
palliate assassination, regicide, and base insults to Women of illustrious
place, to prove the Crimes in the sufferers which they allege to justifye
their own. But if they had proved fornication on any such Woman, taking
the manners of the world and the manners of France, I shall never put it
in a parralel with Assassination. No! I have no such inverted Scale of Faults
in my heart or my head. You find it perfectly ridiculous, and unfit for me
in particular, to take these things as my ingredients of Commiseration. Pray
why so? Is it absurd in me, to think that the Chivalrous Spirit which
dictated a veneration for Women of condition and of Beauty, without any
consideration whatsoever of enjoying them, was the great Scource of those
manners which have been the Pride and ornament of Europe for so many
ages? And am I not to lament that I have lived to see those manners
extinguishd in so shocking a manner by mean speculations of Finance and
the false Science of a sordid and degenerate Philosophy? I tell you again
that the recollection of the manner in which I saw the Queen of France in
the year 1774 and the contrast between that brilliancy, Splendour, and
beauty, with the prostrate Homage of a Nation to her, compared with the
abominable Scene of 1789 which I was describing did draw Tears from me
and wetted my Paper. These Tears came again into my Eyes almost as

often as I looked at the description. They may again. You do not believe this fact, or that these are my real feelings, but that the whole is affected, or as you express it, 'downright Foppery'. My friend, I tell you it is truth—and that it is true, and will be true, when you and I are no more, and will exist as long as men—with their Natural feelings exist. I shall say no more on this Foppery of mine.—Oh by the way—you ask me how long I have been an admirer of German Ladies? Always the same. Present me the Idea of such massacres about any German Lady here, and such attempts to assassinate her, and such a Triumphal procession from Windsor to the old Jewry—and I assure you I shall be quite as full of natural concern and just indignation. As to the other points they deserve serious consideration and they shall have it. I certainly cannot profit quite as much by your assistance as if we agreed. In that case every correction would be forwarding the design. We should work with one common View. But it is impossible that any man can correct a Work according to its true Spirit who is opposed to its object; or can help the expression of what he thinks ought not to be expressed at all.

I should agree with You about the vileness of the Controversy with such Miscreants as the Revolution society and the National assembly, and I know very well that they, as well as their Allies the Indian delinquents, will darken the air with their arrows. But I do not yet think, they have the advowson of reputation. I shall try that point. My dear sir you think of nothing but controversies. 'I challenge into the field of Battle and retire defeated' &ca &ca. If their having the last word be a defeat they most assuredly will defeat me. But I intend no controversy with Dr Price or Lord Shelburne or any other of their set. I mean to set in a full View the danger from their wicked principles and their black hearts; I intend to state the true principles of our constitution in Church and state—upon Grounds opposite to theirs. If any one be the better for the example made of them, and for this exposition, well and good. I mean to do my best to expose them to the hatred, ridicule, and contempt of the whole world; as I shall always expose such, calumniators, hypocrites sowers of sedition, and approvers of murder and all its Triumphs. When I have done that, they may have the field to themselves and I care very little how they Triumph over me, since I hope they will not be able to draw me at their heels and carry my head in Triumph on their Poles. I have been interrupted and have said enough. Adieu. Believe me always sensible of your friendship; though it is impossible that a greater difference can exist on Earth between any Sentiments on those Subjects than unfortunately for me there is between yours and mine.

The piece] the *Reflections*, published later in the same year.   Messalina] wife of the Emperor Claudius, famous for her sexual profligacy. Marie Antoinette's enemies said she had habits

of the same kind.   Midnight assassins] the mob which broke into the Queen's chamber on
6 Oct. 1789.   'Whats Hecuba . . .'] *Hamlet*, II. ii. 559–60.   Advowson] patronage.
Dr Price] a radical, friend of Benjamin Franklin.   Lord Shelburne] an old enemy of
Burke's.

RICHARD BURKE
(1758–?)

Richard was the son of Edmund Burke.

99. *To the King of France, 6 August 1791*

The younger Burke sent this letter from Brussels. Louis XVI endorsed it 'le fils de
Mr Burke'.

Sir,

A very humble stranger thinks it necessary, at this most important crisis,
to offer his opinion and advice. When such numbers go out of their rank
to do evil, It may be allowed to me to do so, with the hope of doing good.
One word of timely consolation, one ray of rational hope making its way—
from a new quarter—through the gloom of treasonable fraud and treasonable violence which surrounds you, may be necessary and may be sufficient
to save even a firm heart from sinking. As God is my Judge I would not
willingly deceive you with false hopes; and I have no interest in giving you
bad advice. My own opinion is of little importance, I give you that of my
father. You know what he has done for you and for the mighty interests
which are involved in yours. You know his wisdom also. The world fully
acknowledges it and I who know him better than any one, know that his
wisdom is beyond even what the world thinks of it. It is founded on the
profoundest meditation, the most intensive knowledge and the most various experience of men and things. His deliberate opinion, then, is this. In
the present state of things, You have nothing to hope *from the interior of
your dominions*. Nothing. Nothing. *For a long time to come*, it can be no
otherwise. It is *only* from abroad that relief can come; And *It is coming*.
Therefore, Sustain your courage. Above all things, remember that you are
surrounded by none but the most determin'd traitors; men who have no
other view—no other desire—no other interest than to destroy you. They
would not save you, much less serve you, if they could; But the situation
in which their execrable and depraved ambition has placed them, disables
them from doing it, if it was their desire, which it is not. If they promise
any thing, it will be only more effectually to deceive you. If they offer you
any alleviation of your sufferings, It will be only to ensure your ruin.

Therefore—Listen to no terms—to no compromise—to no proposition whatever. It is an indubitable truth written in the essence of things, that good cannot be extracted from bad men by any human device or be procured by any compromise with them. In your situation, it is, if possible, truer than truth itself. Lay it to your heart and it will prove your salvation. The bad men you have to deal with are the worst of all. I do not speak of your people in general; There are many—many good men amongst them, as you will find *at some future time*; but they cannot *now* be of the least use to you. Not one of them can *by any possibility* approach your person or stir a finger in your service, Untill the real patriots who are now driven out of France, come with foreign aid, to your and their assistance.—When I left my father (five days ago) he did not suppose it was possible to convey a letter to you; he therefore desired me to try, if a slip of paper could be conveyed, inscribed with these few words, which is the sum of his whole advice and which will preserve you, If Providence has decreed that you should be preserved. The words are these. 'Say Little. Write nothing. Promise nothing. Agree to nothing. Sustain your courage to the last. We are labouring to succour you'.—This is the substance of what I now say to you. I am to tell you that I have left England meerly to serve you—for no other reason. I am not employed by my country—but Individuals, aided by the conjuncture, can sometimes do a great deal. You have nothing to fear from England. Depend on that. All the other powers of Europe are for you. As far as I am able to judge the preparations making are *effectual* and cannot fail of success. I am also satisfied that your affairs are in good hands. Do not let the delay alarm you. It is necessary. I have only to add and to repeat again and again, Maintain your courage. Whatever you have suffer'd or may suffer, You will live to see better days. Let it be your consolation that you suffer for your virtues and your virtues only. Faults, I suppose you have, like all men; but it is your virtues which have render'd them prejudicial to you. You are therefore the martyr of your virtues—a true martyr. Bear yourself as such. Remember that not only your own life, but that the cause of virtue of Government, of religion and of all good men depends upon your firmness at this moment. God who has inflicted these trials, will be your comfort and supporter. I am younger than you, but I have seen sorrow and have lived to see better days afterwards. The condition from which you are fallen shows the instability of human things; that very instability ought now to be your consolation, Because your fall was once much more improbable than your perfect restoration is now. Again I repeat it, Your only hope, Your sure hope is Firmness and a *total* distrust of all things and all men that belong to the present system.—This is no time for ceremony. I write to you as from one man to another. You are nothing to me. I am not your subject; but I have thought for you and laboured for you and mean to do so in future, both on your own account and on account of your cause which is that of Religion and Government. The means of justice to God and Man. As far as my other duties will permit, I am devoted to your service. Humble as my means and qualifications are. If you are true to yourself, even I may be able to contribute something to your service.

I am &c &c
Richard Burke

MARY WOLLSTONECRAFT
(1759–1797)

Mary Wollstonecraft was the author of *A Vindication of the Rights of Woman* (1792). After an unhappy relationship with the American Gilbert Imlay she married, in 1797, the philosopher and novelist William Godwin and died giving birth to a daughter Mary, who was to be the wife of Shelley. This letter belongs to the period between the Imlay affair and the Godwin marriage, and protests against an officious attempt by an acquaintance to find her a husband and so restore her to respectability.

100. To ——, 1795

Sir,

It is inexpressibly disagreeable to me to be obliged to enter again on a subject, that has already raised a tumult of *indignant* emotions in my bosom, which I was labouring to suppress when I received your letter. I shall now *condescend* to answer your epistle; but let me first tell you, that, in my *unprotected* situation, I make a point of never forgiving a *deliberate insult*— and in that light I consider your late officious conduct. It is not according to my nature to mince matters—I will then tell you in plain terms, what I think. I have ever considered you in the light of a *civil* acquaintance—on the word friend I lay a peculiar emphasis—and, as a mere acquaintance, you were rude and *cruel*, to step forward to insult a woman, whose conduct and misfortune demand respect. If my friend, Mr Johnson, had made the proposal—I should have been severely hurt—have thought him unkind and unfeeling, but not *impertinent*.—The privilege of intimacy you had no claim to—and should have referred the man to myself—if you had not sufficient discernment to quash it at once. I am, sir, poor and destitute.— Yet I have a spirit that will never bend, or take indirect methods, to obtain the consequence I despise; nay, if to support life it was necessary to act contrary to my principles, the struggle would soon be over. I can bear any thing but my own contempt.

In a few words, what I call an insult, is the bare supposition that I could for a moment think of *prostituting* my person for a maintenance; for in that point of view does such a marriage appear to me, who consider right and wrong in the abstract, and never by words and local opinions shield myself from the reproaches of my own heart and understanding.

It is needless to say more—Only you must excuse me when I add, that I wish never to see, but as a perfect stranger, a person who could so grossly mistake my character. An apology is not necessary—if you were inclined to make one—nor any further expostulations.—I again repeat, I cannot over-look an affront; few indeed have sufficient delicacy to respect poverty, even where it gives lustre to a character—and I tell you sir, I am POOR—yet can live without your benevolent exertions.

Mary Wollstonecraft

HENRIETTA, COUNTESS BESSBOROUGH
(1761–1821)

Henrietta, Countess of Bessborough, was the sister of the Duchess of Devonshire and the mother of Lady Caroline Lamb, Byron's mistress and wife of William Lamb, later Lord Melbourne, Victoria's Prime Minister. Lord Granville (1773–1846) was a politician and diplomat; he served in Paris, Berlin, St Petersburg, and Brussels. He met Lady Bessborough in 1794 when in Naples with Lord Holland, and they re-mained friends till her death.

101. *To Granville Leveson Gower, 1796*

The reason I press you to write a little every day to me is from knowing how hurried you must be when the Courier sets off, which, of course, makes your writing to me what I never wish it to be, an unpleasant task. However, I must say, considering you did not do so, you have been very good this time, and written me a tolerable letter, which I thank you very much for. I envy your being at Paris and the people you see. Is Lodoiska handsome, clever, and amiable, and is Louvet pleasant in society? I expect you to give me a particular account of every thing and every body you meet with. I like your description of your little friend very much, and think what she says of Barrère excellent, and applicable to many people I have known. Mad. Tallien seems an extraordinary character, but the easiness with which she grants her favours now takes off a little from the merit of the sacrifice. Apparemment cela ne lui coutait pas beaucoup. De you mean in conse-quence of her beauty to declare yourself sur les rangs, and try what her humanity will do for you? Remember, I expect the truth, the *whole truth*. Pray bring me a wig (if you ever come back). I shall like to have it even if I do not wear it, and it would be remarkably convenient just now, for I have cut off all my hair. Your negotiations do not seem to advance much. How woefully disconcerted all the *old traders* must be with this new fashion of frankness after being so long accustom'd to Ministerial mystery. In fact, there is little difference, for it is only publishing at once what us'd always to be known in whispers. We go to town to morrow for a fortnight, and I have been leading such a recluse life at *Roe* that I cannot tell you a word of news of any sort or kind, I think. (Do you get the English papers at Paris? I mean without a Courier.) My sister's eye continues slowly mending; she is drove to town by the dry rot having broke out again at poor Chiswick; it is a sad pity. Anne very near kill'd herself the other day by taking some Laudanum by mistake; she has been very nervous ever since. *Soldini* is gone to Castle Howard, and has another brother or sister forthcoming soon. Ly. Sutherland has taken so violent a fit of kindness for me that I know not what to make of her. I cannot account for it any how, but we are like the people in the 'Roman comique,' comme si nous étions camarades depuis vingt ans. Ly. E. Monk is in town in most flaming beauty, and Ld. Boringdon, as he always is, good nature itself. I had always a great partiality for him, but now I have to add gratitude to partiality. I cannot explain this at this distance, but I will when we meet. I have not got the book you mention, which I am impatient for. I have been reading lately some very entertaining letters of Sr. C. H. Williams and the old Ld. Holland. Don't be shock'd if you have heard of them (they are Manuscript); there is but a small part improper, and that is so very bad that half of it I did not understand, and the other half I skipt from disgust. . . . The entertaining parts are accounts of his negotiations and of his writings. . . . I am sure I set you a good example, and write à tort et à travers four sides full; every opportunity you make me excuses for not having had time to *think of what you sh*^{d} *say.* Who ever thinks before hand of a letter? I am sure I should not know what to say if I did. Believe me, it is better to trust to chance, and write whatever comes uppermost at the moment. If I imagined you thought much about what you write to me I should have no pleasure in it, and never believe a word you said. . . . Are your Morals corrupted yet? You don't take one word of notice at my sermon. Is it innocence or guilt that makes you silent?

Granville had mentioned, among others, the Jacobins, J. B. Louvet, and Lodoiska. The 'little friend' was the wife of Talma the great tragic actor. Mme Tallien, a beauty supposed to have saved many from the guillotine by granting sexual favours, married Tallien with the same object; he divorced her in 1802.   Barrère] a Girondin and lover of Mme Tallien.   *Soldini*] 'small change', nickname of Lord Morpeth.

102. *To Granville Leveson Gower, 2 October 1805*

My whole day has been taken up by a horrible adventure. I found a little boy almost naked, crying bitterly and nursing a baby in his arms; he told me his Mammy was dying and had nobody to help her. I ask'd where she was; he got up and led the way to a miserable house, so miserable that I drew back unwilling to go in. The child held my gown, and looking up piteously, said, 'Won't you come?' in such a tone, that I reproach'd myself for my fine Ladyship in doubting, and forc'd myself to go on. Indeed, dear G., I could not have imagin'd a human being reduc'd to so much wretchedness: in a miserable hole on a rug on the stones lay a creature almost naked, almost a skeleton, distorted, hideous and disgusting to the most frightful degree, so helpless that her arms, face and bosom were cover'd with flies, which seem'd devouring her and which she had not strength to drive from her. She was groaning terribly, and to all appearance in the last agonies of death. I was so overcome, so shock'd, that my head swam. I totter'd against the door and for fear of fainting was moving out of the room, when in a hollow voice and rolling her great eyes towards me, she said: 'Have mercy upon me.' I cannot tell you how I felt, my heart sunk so within me. I went up to her and tried with my handkerchief to drive the flies away. She said several things I could not hear, but at last I heard she told me, 'I am a great Sinner—pray for my poor soul.' I knelt down almost mechanically and pray'd fervently (scarcely knowing what I did) for her and for myself, for I thought it presumption for *me* to pray for any one. She thanked me and said I was the only person that had pitied her. As soon as I got out, after charging the woman of the house to take care of her, I went to the apothecary's (but this house is next to a public house, and the noise of singing and drunkenness almost mixes with the groans of this poor dying creature). The man whom I made go with me came out almost as shock'd as I was, but told me a dreadful story. He knew the woman; he saw her five years ago—young, very pretty, and a decent kind of woman. She married a Soldier who got drunk, beat and abandon'd her, since when she gave herself up to every kind of vice; in short, her disorder is the consequence of her way of life. His expression to me was horrible, but, in short, that every part of her, inside and out, was decay'd, and for this last fortnight it seems she had been compleatly neglected.

Will you forgive me for this long story? J'en ai l'esprit frappé, and can think of nothing else. We go from hence Sunday to Compton place, Tuesday to the Pavilion, Friday to the Jersey's at Worthing, and Saturday to town.

Thursday, Oct. 3.

Only one line. First, my wretched woman is dead, et j'ai sur les bras a little child of four years old and another of one.

I saw the P. of Wales for a moment the other day, saying he knew all along Mr Pitt had no intention of proposing any thing, and full of a visit he had made to the Dr on his return from Weymouth.

103. To Granville Leveson Gower, 11 October 1808

Of all disappointments the worst disappointment is expecting a full post and finding none. Oh, the misery of depending on wind and weather for one's letters! We had a delightful day upon the lake, which is beautiful. I came back promising myself such a comfortable evening, with heaps of letters, when I was chill'd with 'No mail from England,' in answer to my eager enquiries. You are so much more patient than I am, that you do not know what it is to pester et endurer for an hour together about what cannot be help'd. I was so cross that I tore a letter I had begun writing, and threw it on to the fire from mere despite. I was interrupted and drawn to the window by the most discordant sounds I ever heard—long cries and groans, in short, the Irish Howl. It was a funeral passing, the coffin borne upon an open herse, at one end of which sat a woman with her back to the horses hanging over the coffin, sometimes throwing herself upon it, tearing her hair, beating her breast, with every appearance of despair, and making the most dismal scream I ever heard. I was quite affected with the excessive misery she express'd, when the waiter told me she was hired to do all this, and that it was a trade like any other. I cannot bear this. But sometimes they say it really is the nearest relation of the dead person. Every body who meets the funeral is expected (as a mark of respect to the dead) to turn and follow it a little way, so that the noise encreases every step they go and is really very extraordinary. The Lakes are as beautiful as it is possible for immense mountains, Rocks, woods and water to make them, and answer all that is said of them. As we row'd by a beautiful mountain Glen, the boatmen began lamenting themselves, shaking their heads and saying it was fine once but spoilt now—all *gone to England*. I could not understand till the Master of the Vessel explain'd to me that it had shar'd the fate of several other fine woods near, and what probably would soon render this as bare of trees as the rest of Ireland. Ld. Kenmare and Mr Herbert live in England; they make the most of Estates they never see: the trees are all to be cut down for timber, and the money sent to them, and this is pretty nearly the history of all the miseries in Ireland. Absentees in one shape or other spread distress and discord around, yet what is to be done? I find as much fault with it as any one, yet should be very sorry to be forc'd to live here. Everything I see and hear of the state of Ireland drives me wild; so little would set all right, and that little is so difficult. People may say what they please of its present tranquillity; the calling it quiet now is only a proof of the dreadful state it must be in when they think it unquiet. I told you, I believe, of our finding the man shot near Kilkenny; it really was talked of as so common an occurrence as to be scarce worth mentioning. Coming here, we saw fires lit on several Hills. They told us they were White Boy signals, but I need not be frightened—they would not *interrupt us*. No day passes without hearing of some outrage, yet as far as I can see, neither religion or Politicks have much to do with it. This reminds me of the story I threaten'd you with some time ago. Clergymen, finding no Parishioners, become absentees like other people, and trusting the care of the Diocese to what is call'd a Tythe messenger, generally establish the most tyrannical oppression instead of the care they should take of their ouailles. These people rate the tythes pretty much as they like, and in dread of being highly rated the people dare not oppose any thing they please. A poor man who could not pay his five shillings gave a Guinea note for the next year (an Irishman would sign away his whole estate at a year's distance for a momentary respit). The year ended, and the surveyor took a three guinea note for the next. So on till it came to five, when the Man being unable to pay, he seiz'd his cow and put it up to auction. Nobody dar'd bid against him; it went for 40 shillings. In vain the poor Man, after borrowing this Sum among his Neighbours, offer'd it in exchange for his cow; the Surveyor said he had bought it fairly at auction, and should keep it as well as his Cabin and goods, till he could pay all. The man and his whole family, utterly ruin'd by this, readily join'd the first party of White boys who offer'd to revenge him. They burnt down the Surveyor's house, and after such an outrage, not daring to return near home, he continued with them, committing daily outrages from mere despair. He was taken assisting to set fire to some houses, and will probably be hang'd, and the most distant relation or companion he ever had will unite to revenge his death, and vow hatred to the Religion that caus'd, and the Government that punishes, the crime. This is a single, and I hope an extreme, case; but something of the same nature is continually happening. That one simple change, if it could be managed, of relieving them from the tythe, would do more towards quieting Ireland than all the rest put together, and is more within the possibility of accomplishing. . . .

Lord Bessborough had an Irish estate.   White Boys] Irish agrarian society, formed in 1761 to oppose high rents and tithes; they wore shirts over their other clothes.   Ouailles] flocks.

104. To Granville Leveson Gower, 13 September 1811

There has been a sad affray at Holland House between little Lewis (he was living there), and Ly. H. He is par trop tiresome and provoking, but, to use a Vulgar phrase, she gave him his own. It came to such high words that he told her common decency should prevent her using such language to Ld. Holland's guests (he was staying at H. H. by Ld. H.'s invitation). She replied that when people forc'd themselves into a House against the will of its owners, they must take the consequence. He said he would remain no longer: she, the sooner he went the better (it was after supper about one). He walk'd out of the room. After scoldings and soothings by turn from Ld. Holland, Sydney Smith, and Mr Allen, Ly. Holland own'd she had been too violent, especially in her own house, and dispatch'd a peace Messenger to his room. The little man had pack'd up his night things and trudg'd to London. Many were the notes that pass'd backwards and forwards. Ly. Holland absolutely condescended to ask forgiveness, and at last the little Monk yielded, and was brought back in triumph to Holland House to dinner yesterday, and will probably be driven off again before the week is out. I was at the play last night, d'Infantado, Syd^y Smith and Ld. John Russell with me. Ld. and Ly. Holland, little Lewis, Ld. B., and a tall Spaniard were in the next box. Mr Allen gone to Dulwich. S. Smith says the road he and his buggy went will be disputed upon and trac'd out by future Philosophers seeking the real exact *Via Alleni*. S. Smith's flashes of *Merriment* more than wit will not bear repetition, but he made us laugh very much—amongst other things, with comparing the various effects of ennui on different people. He insisted upon it that Mr Lewis tried people as an experiment in Natural Philosophy; that he put Ld. Donoughmore to sleep, made Ly Holland grow red and furious, me pale and cry:

> 'She never told her grief,
> But let Monk Lewis, like a worm in the leaf,
> Prey on her sinking Spirits.'

This, he said, was very beautiful, and made Ld. Holland translate the original and Parody into Spanish.

Lewis] Matthew ('Monk') Lewis (1775–1818), author of the Gothic novel *The Monk* (1796).   Allen] Dr John Allen (1771–1843), distinguished member of the Holland House set, became Warden of Dulwich College in 1811.   'She never told . . .'] parody of *Twelfth Night*, II. iv. 110–12.

JANE AUSTEN
(1775–1817)

Jane Austen was the youngest of the seven children of the rector of Steventon in Hampshire, where she lived till 1801, when the family moved to Bath. From 1809 she lived at Chawton, not far from Steventon. She never married.

105. To Cassandra Austen, 20 November 1800

Cassandra (1773–1845) was Jane Austen's only sister.

My dear Cassandra,

Your letter took me quite by surprise this morning; you are very welcome however, & I am very much obliged to you.—I beleive I drank too much wine last night at Hurstbourne; I know not how else to account for the shaking of my hand today;—You will kindly make allowance therefore for any indistinctness of writing by attributing it to this venial Error.— Naughty Charles did not come on tuesday; but good Charles came yesterday morning. About two o'clock he walked in on a Gosport Hack.—His feeling equal to such a fatigue is a good sign, & his finding no fatigue in it a still better.—We walked down to Deane to dinner, he danced the whole Evening, & today is no more tired than a gentleman ought to be.—Your desiring to hear from me on Sunday will perhaps bring in you a more particular account of the Ball than you may care for, because one is prone to think much more of such things the morning after they happen, than when time has entirely driven them out of one's recollection.—It was a pleasant Evening, Charles found it remarkably so, but I cannot tell why, unless the absence of Miss Terry—towards whom his conscience reproaches him with now being perfect indifferent—was a releif to him.—There were only twelve dances, of which I danced nine, & was merely prevented from dancing the rest by the want of a partner.—We began at 10, supped at 1, & were at Deane before 5.—There were but 50 people in the room; very few families indeed from our side of the Country, & not many more from the other.—My partners were the two St Johns, Hooper Holder—and very prodigious—Mr Mathew, with whom I called the last, & whom I liked the best of my little stock.—There were very few Beauties, & such as there were, were not very handsome. Miss Iremonger did not look well, & Mrs Blount was the only one much admired. She appeared exactly as she did in September, with the same broad face, diamond bandeau, white shoes, pink husband, & fat neck.—The two Miss Coxes were there; I traced in one the remains of the vulgar, broad featured girl who danced at Enham eight years ago;—the other is refined into a nice, composed looking girl like Catherine Bigg.—I looked at Sir Thomas Champneys & thought of poor Rosalie; I looked at his daughter & thought her a queer animal with a white neck.— Mrs Warren, I was constrained to think a very fine young woman, which I much regret. She has got rid of some part of her child, & danced away with great activity, looking by no means very large.—Her husband is ugly enough; uglier even than his cousin John; but he does not look so *very* old.—The Miss Maitlands are both prettyish; very like Anne; with brown skins, large dark eyes, & a good deal of nose.—The General has got the Gout, and Mrs Maitland the Jaundice.—Miss Debary, Susan & Sally all in black, but without any Statues, made their appearance, & I was as civil to them as their bad breath would allow me. They told me nothing new of Martha.—I mean to go to her on Thursday, unless Charles should determine on coming over again with his friend Shipley for the Basingstoke ball, in which case I shall not go till friday.—I shall write to you again however before I set off, & I shall hope to hear from you in the mean time. If I do not stay for the Ball, I would not on any account do so uncivil a thing by the Neighbourhood as to set off at that very time for another place, & shall therefore make a point of not being later than Thursday *morning*.—Mary said that I looked very well last night; I wore my aunt's gown & handkercheif, & my hair was at least tidy, which was all my ambition.—I will now have done with the Ball; & I will moreover go and dress for dinner.—*Thursday Even*. Charles leaves us on saturday, unless Henry should take us in his way to the Island, of which we have some hopes, & then they will probably go together on sunday.—The young lady whom it is suspected that Sir Thomas is to marry, is Miss Emma Wabshaw;—she lives somewhere between Southampton and Winchester, is handsome, accomplished, amiable, & everything but rich.—He is certainly finishing his house in a great hurry.—Perhaps the report of his being to marry a Miss Fanshawe might originate in his attentions to this very lady; the names are not unlike.— Miss Summers has made my gown very well indeed, & I grow more and more pleased with it.—Charles does not like it, but my father and Mary do; my Mother is very much rec[oncile]d to it, & as for James, he gives it the preference over everything of the kind he ever saw; in proof of which I am desired to say that if you like to sell yours, Mary will buy it.—We had a very pleasant day on monday at Ashe; we sat down 14 to dinner in the study, the dining room being not habitable from the Storm's having blown down it's chimney.—Mrs Bramston talked a good deal of nonsense, which Mr Bramston & Mr Clerk seemed almost equally to enjoy.—There was a whist & a casino table, & six outsiders.—Rice & Lucy made love, Mat: Robinson fell asleep, James & Mrs Augusta alternately read Dr Jenner's pamphlet on the cow pox, & I bestowed my company by turns on all. On enquiring of Mrs Clerk, I find that Mrs Heathcote made a great blunder in her news of the Crooks & Morleys; it is young Mr Crooke who is to marry the second Miss Morley—& it is the Miss Morleys instead of the second Miss Crooke, who were the beauties at the Music meeting.—This seems a more likely tale, a better devised Impostor.—The three Digweeds all came on tuesday, & we played a pool at Commerce.—James Digweed left Hampshire today. I think he must be in love with you, from his anxiety to have you go to the Faversham Balls, & likewise from his supposing, that the two Elms fell from their greif at your absence. Was not it a galant idea?—It never occurred to me before, but I dare say it was so.—Hacker has been here today, putting in the fruit trees.—A new plan has been suggested concerning the plantation of the new inclosure on the right hand side of the Elm Walk—the doubt is whether it would be better to make a little orchard of it, by planting apples, pears & cherries, or whether it should be larch, Mountain-ash & acacia.—What is your opinion?—I say nothing, & am ready to agree with anybody.—You & George walking to Eggerton!—

What a droll party!—Do the Ashford people still come to Godmersham Church every Sunday in a cart?—It is *you* that always disliked Mr N. Toke so much, not *I*.—I do not like his wife, & I do not like Mr Brett, but as for Mr Toke, there are few people whom I like better.—Miss Harwood & her friend have taken a house 15 miles from Bath; she writes very kind letters, but sends no other particulars of the situation.—Perhaps it is one of the first houses in Bristol.—Farewell. Charles sends you his best love & Edward his worst.—If you think the distinction improper, you may take the worst yourself.—He will write to you when he gets back to his Ship—& in the meantime desires that you will consider me as

Your affec: sister
J. A.

Charles likes my gown now.

Friday.—I have determined to go on Thursday, but of course not before the post comes in.—Charles is in very good looks indeed. I had the comfort of finding out the other evening who all the fat girls with short noses were that disturbed me at the 1st H. ball. They all prove to be Miss Atkinsons of En. . . .

I rejoice to say that we have just had another letter from our dear Frank.—It is to you, very short, written from Larnica in Cyprus & so lately as the 2^d of October.—He came from Alexandria & was to return there in 3 or 4 days, knew nothing of his promotion, & does not write above twenty lines, from a doubt of the letter's ever reaching you & an idea of all letters being open'd at Vienna.—He wrote a few days before to you from Alexandria by the Mercury, sent with dispatches to Lord Keith.—Another letter must be oweing to us besides this,—*one* if not *two*—because none of these are to me.—Henry comes tomorrow, for one night only.—

My mother has heard from Mrs E. Leigh. Lady S & S—— and her daughter are going to remove to Bath.—Mrs Estwick is married again to a Mr Sloane, a young Man under age—without the knowledge of either family.—He bears a good character however.—

Charles] of the brothers mentioned here, Charles and Francis were in the Navy; Francis eventually became an Admiral of the Fleet.   Jenner] Edward Jenner's historic pamphlet was published in 1798; his Complete Statement on the subject in 1800.

106. To Fanny Knight, 18 November 1814

Fanny Austen Knight (1793–1882) was Jane Austen's favourite niece, 'almost another sister'. She married (1820) Sir Edward Knatchbull, not the suitor discussed in this letter.

I feel quite as doubtful as you could be my dearest Fanny as to *when* my Letter may be finished, for I can command very little quiet time at present, but yet I must begin, for I know you will be glad to hear as soon as possible,

& I really am impatient myself to be writing something on so very interesting a subject, though I have no hope of writing anything to the purpose. I shall do very little more I dare say than say over again, what you have said before.—I was certainly a good deal surprised *at first*—as I had no suspicion of any change in your feelings, and I have no scruple in saying that you cannot be in Love. My dear Fanny, I am ready to laugh at the idea— and yet it is no laughing matter to have had you so mistaken as to your own feelings—And with all my heart I wish I had cautioned you on that point when first you spoke to me;—but tho' I did not think you then so *much* in love as you thought yourself, I did consider you as being attached in a degree—quite sufficiently for happiness, as I had no doubt it would increase with opportunity.—And from the time of our being in London together, I thought you really very much in love—But you certainly are not at all—there is no concealing it.—What strange creatures we are!—It seems as if your being secure of him (as you say yourself) had made you Indifferent.—There was a little disgust I suspect, at the Races—& I do not wonder at it. His expressions there would not do for one who had rather more Acuteness, Penetration & Taste, than Love, which was your case. And yet, after all, I *am* surprised that the change in your feelings should be so great.—He is, just what he ever was, only more evidently & uniformly devoted to *you*. This is all the difference.—How shall we account for it?— My dearest Fanny, I am writing what will not be of the smallest use to you. I am feeling differently every moment, & shall not be able to suggest a single thing that can assist your Mind.—I could lament in one sentence & laugh in the next, but as to Opinion or Counsel I am sure none will [be] extracted worth having from this Letter.—I read yours through the very even^g I received it—getting away by myself—I could not bear to leave off, when I had once begun.—I was full of curiosity & concern. Luckily your Aunt C. dined at the other house, therefore I had not to manœuvre away from *her*;—& as to anybody else, I do not care.—Poor dear Mr J. P.!—Oh! dear Fanny, your mistake has been one that thousands of women fall into. He was the *first* young Man who attached himself to you. That was the charm, & most powerful it is.—Among the multitudes however that make the same mistake with yourself, there can be few indeed who have so little reason to regret it;—*his* Character and *his* attachment leave you nothing to be ashamed of.—Upon the whole, what is to be done? You certainly *have* encouraged him to such a point as to make him feel almost secure of you— you have no inclination for any other person—His situation in life, family, friends, & above all his character—his uncommonly amiable mind, strict principles, just notions, good habits—*all* that *you* know so well how to value, *All* that really is of the first importance—everything of this nature pleads his cause most strongly.—You have no doubt of his having superior

Abilities—he has proved it at the University—he is I dare say such a scholar as your agreable, idle Brothers would ill bear a comparison with.— Oh! my dear Fanny, the more I write about him, the warmer my feelings become, the more strongly I feel the sterling worth of such a young Man & the desirableness of your growing in love with him again. I recommend this most thoroughly.—There *are* such beings in the World perhaps, one in a Thousand, as the Creature You and I should think perfection, Where Grace & Spirit are united to Worth, where the Manners are equal to the Heart & Understanding, but such a person may not come in your way, or if he does, he may not be the eldest son of a Man of Fortune, the Brother of your particular friend, & belonging to your own County.—Think of all this Fanny. Mr J. P.—has advantages which do not often meet in one person. His only fault indeed seems Modesty. If he were less modest, he would be more agreable, speak louder & look Impudenter;—and is not it a fine Character of which Modesty is the only defect?—I have no doubt that he will get more lively & more like yourselves as he is more with you;—he will catch your ways if he belongs to you. And as to there being any objection from his *Goodness*, from the danger of his becoming even Evangelical, I cannot admit *that*. I am by no means convinced that we ought not all to be Evangelicals, & am at least persuaded that they who are so from Reason and Feeling, must be happiest & safest.—Do not be frightened from the connection by your Brothers having most wit. Wisdom is better than Wit, & in the long run will certainly have the laugh on her side; & don't be frightened by the idea of his acting more strictly up to the precepts of the New Testament than others.—And now, my dear Fanny, having written so much on one side of the question, I shall turn round & entreat you not to commit yourself farther, & not to think of accepting him unless you really do like him. Anything is to be preferred or endured rather than marrying without Affection; and if his deficiencies of Manner &c &c strike you more than all his good qualities, if you continue to think strongly of them, give him up at once.—Things are now in such a state, that you must resolve upon one or the other, either to allow him to go on as he has done, or whenever you are together behave with a coldness which may convince him that he has been deceiving himself.—I have no doubt of his suffering a good deal for a time, a great deal, when he feels that he must give you up;—but it is no creed of mine, as you must be well aware, that such sort of Disappointments kill anybody.—Your sending the Music was an admirable Device, it made everything easy, & I do not know how I could have accounted for the parcel otherwise; for tho' your dear Papa most conscientiously hunted about till he found me alone in the Din^g-parlour, your Aunt C. had seen that he *had* a parcel to deliver.—As it was however, I do not think anything was suspected.—We have heard nothing fresh from Anna. I trust she is very comfortable in her new home. Her Letters have been very sensible & satisfactory, with no *parade* of happiness, which I liked them the better for.—I have often known young married Women write in a way I did not like, in that respect.

You will be glad to hear that the first Edit: of M. P. is all sold.—Your Uncle Henry is rather wanting me to come to Town, to settle about a 2^d Edit:—but as I could not very conveniently leave home now, I have written him my Will and pleasure, & unless he still urges it, shall not go.—I am very greedy & want to make the most of it;—but as you are much above caring about money, I shall not plague you with any particulars.—The pleasures of Vanity are more within your comprehension, & you will enter into mine, at receiving the *praise* which every now & then comes to me, through some channel or other.—

Saturday.—Mr Palmer spent yesterday with us, & is gone off with Cassy this morn^g. We have been expecting Miss Lloyd the last two days, & feel sure of her today.—Mr Knight and Mr Edw: Knight are to dine with us.— And on Monday they are to dine with us again, accompanied by their respectable Host & Hostess.—*Sunday.* Your Papa had given me messages to you, but they are unnecessary, as he writes by this post to Aunt Louisa. We had a pleasant party yesterday, at least *we* found it so.—It is delightful to see him so chearful & confident.—Aunt Cass: & I dine at the G^t House today. We shall be a snug half dozen.—Miss Lloyd came, as we expected, yesterday, & desires her Love.—She is very happy to hear of your learning the Harp.—I do not mean to send you what I owe Miss Hare, because I think you would rather not be paid beforehand.—

Yours very affec^ly

J. Austen

Your trying to excite your own feelings by a visit to his room amused me excessively.—The dirty Shaving Rag was exquisite!—Such a circumstance ought to be in print. Much too good to be lost.—Remember me particularly to Fanny C.—I thought you w^d like to hear from me, while you were with her.

Aunt C.] Cassandra Austen.   M. P.] *Mansfield Park* (1814).

LORD NELSON
(1758–1805)

Horatio, Lord Nelson met Sir William (1730–1803) and Lady Hamilton (1761–1815) in 1793 at Naples, where Hamilton was British ambassador, but the intimacy between Nelson and Lady Hamilton seems to have begun on another visit in 1798. It was conducted under a pretence of Platonic attachment that deceived few, though they seem to have included Sir William ('I well know the purity of Lord Nelson's friendship for Emma and me') and Nelson's family.

107. *To Lady Hamilton, 17 February 1801*

I am so agitated that I can write nothing. I knew it would be so, and you can't help it. Why did you not tell Sir William? Your character will be gone. Good God! he will be next you, and telling you soft things. If he does, tell it out at table, and turn him out of the house. Do not sit long. If you sing a song, I know you cannot help it, do not let him set next you, but at dinner he will hob glasses with you. I cannot write to Sir Wm, but he ought to go to the Prince and not suffer your character to be ruined by him. O, God, that I was dead! But I do not, my dearest Emma, blame you, nor do I fear your inconstancy. I tremble, and God knows how I write. Can nothing be thought of? I am gone almost mad, but you cannot help it. It will be in all the newspapers with hints. Recollect what the villain said to Mr Nisbet, *how you hit his fancy.* I am mad, almost dead, but ever for ever yours to the last moment, your, only your, &c.

I could not write another line if I was to be made King. If I was in town nothing should make me dine with you that damned day, but, my dear Emma, I do not blame you, only remember your poor miserable friend, that you must be singing and appear gay. I shall that day have no one to dinner; it shall be a fast day to me. He will put his foot near you. I pity you from my soul, as I feel confident you wish him in hell. Have plenty of people and do not say a word you can help to him. He wishes, I dare say, to have you alone. Don't let him touch, nor yet sit next you; if he comes, get up. God strike him blind if he looks at you—this is high treason, and you may get me hanged by revealing it. Oh, God! that I were. I have read your letter, your resolution never to go where the fellow is, but you must have him at home. Oh, God! but you cannot, I suppose, help it, and you cannot turn him out of your own house. He will stay and sup and sit up till 4 in the morning, and the fewer that stay the better. Oh, God! why do I live? But I do not blame you; it is my misfortune. I feel nobody uses me ill. I am only fit to be second, or third, or 4, or to black shoes. I want no better part than I have. I see your determination to be on your guard, and am as fixed as fate. If you'll believe me, don't scold me; I am more dead than alive, to the last breath yours. If you cannot get rid of this I hope you will tell Sir William never to bring the fellow again.

I send a note for Mrs T.

February 19th, 1801

Forgive my letter wrote and sent last night, perhaps my head was a little affected. No wonder, it was such an unexpected, such a knockdown blow, such a death. But I will not go on, for I shall get out of my senses again.

Will you sing for the fellow, *The Prince, unable to Conceal His Pain*, &c? No, you will not. I will say no more for fear of my head. It was so good of you to send to thank Mr Nisbet for his not asking you to meet the fellow, as he knew his vile intent, and yet, the same morning to let him come and dine with you en famille!—but I know it was not my Emma; Sir William always asks all partys to dinner. I forgive you. Forgive, I beseech, your old and dear friend! Tell me all, every word, that passes. He will propose if you—no, you will not try; he is Sir Wm's guest.

Thursday.—I have just got your letter and I live again. DO NOT let the lyar come. I never saw him but once, the 4th day after I came to London, and he never mentioned your name. May God blast him! Be firm! Go and dine with Mrs Denis on Sunday. Do not, I beseech you, risk being at home. Does Sir William want you to be a whore to the rascal? Forgive all my letter; you will see what I feel, and have felt. I have eat not a morsel, except a little rice, since yesterday morning, and till I know how this matter is gone off. But I feel confident of your resolution, and thank you 1,000,000 of times. I write you a letter, which may be said as coming from me if you like, I will endeavour to word it properly. Did you sit alone with the villain for a moment? No, I will not believe it! O, God! keep my sences. Do not let the rascal in. Tell the Duke that you will never go to his house. Mr G. must be a scoundrel; he treated you once ill enough, and cannot love you, or he would sooner die. Ever for ever, aye for ever, your, &c.

I have this moment got my orders to put myself under Sir Hyde Parker's orders, and suppose I shall be ordered to Portsmouth tomorrow or next day, & then I will try & get to London for 3 days. May Heaven bless us! but do not let that fellow dine with you. Don't write here after you receive this, I shall be gone. You can, in Sir Wm's name, write a note to Sir H. Parker, asking if the *St George* is ordered to Spithead. If so, write to Portsmouth desiring my letters to be left at the Post Office till the ship's arrival.

Forgive every cross word, I now live.

He will be next to you] i.e. the Prince of Wales.   *The Prince, unable . . .*] Dryden, 'Alexander's Feast', which was set to music by Handel.   Mr G.] Charles Greville, an earlier lover of Lady Hamilton.   Sir Hyde Parker] (1739–1807), admiral and for a time Nelson's commanding officer.

108. To Lady Hamilton, 1 March 1801

Now, my dear wife, for such you are in my eyes and in the face of heaven, I can give full scope to my feelings, for I daresay Oliver will faithfully deliver this letter. You know, my dearest Emma, that there is nothing in this world that I would not do for us to live together, and to have our dear little child with us. I firmly believe that this campaign will give us peace, and then we will sett off for Bronte. In twelve hours we shall be across the water and freed from all the nonsence of his friends, or rather pretended ones. Nothing but an event happening to him could prevent my going, and I am sure you will think so, for unless all matters accord it would bring 100 of tongues and slanderous reports if I separated from her (which I would do with pleasure the moment we can be united; I want to see her no more), therefore we must manage till we can quit this country or your uncle dies. I love, I never did love any one else. I never had a dear pledge of love till you gave me one, and you, thank my God, never gave one to any body else. I think before March is out you will either see us back, or so victorious that we shall insure a glorious issue to our toils. Think what my Emma will feel at seeing return safe, perhaps with a little more fame, her own dear loving Nelson. Never, if I can help it, will I dine out of my ship, or go on shore, except duty calls me. Let Sir Hyde have any glory he can catch—I envy him not. You, my beloved Emma, and my country, are the two dearest objects of my fond heart—a heart susceptible and true. Only place confidence in me and you never shall be disappointed. I burn all your dear letters, because it is right for your sake, and I wish you would burn all mine—they can do no good, and will do us both harm if any seizure of them, or the dropping even one of them, would fill the mouths of the world sooner than we intend. My longing for you, both person and conversation, you may readily imagine. What must be my sensations at the idea of sleeping with you! it setts me on fire, even the thoughts, much more would the reality. I am sure my love & desires are all to you, and if any woman naked were to come to me, even as I am this moment from thinking of you, I hope it might rot off if I would touch her even with my hand. No, my heart, person, and mind is in perfect union of love towards my own dear, beloved Emma—the real bosom friend of her, all hers, all Emma's, &c.

Oliver is gone to sleep, he is grown half foolish. I shall give him £10 in the morning, and I have wrote a letter recommending a friend of his to the Chairman of the East India Company, which he said you would be glad I should do for him. I have nothing to send my Emma, it makes me sorry you & Sir Wm could not come to Yarmouth, that would be pleasant, but we shall not be there more than a week at farthest. I had a letter this day from the Rev. Mr Holden, who we met on the Continent; he desired his kind compliments to you and Sir William: he sent me letters of my name, and recommended it as my motto—Honor est a Nilo—HORATIO NELSON. May the Heavens bless you. (My love, my darling angel, my heaven-given wife, the dearest only true wife of her own till death, &c. I know you will never let that fellow or any one come near you.)

Monday Morning.—Oliver is just going on shore; the time will ere long arrive when Nelson will land to fly to his Emma, to be for ever with her. Let that hope keep us up under our present difficulties. Kiss and bless *our* dear Horatia—think of that.

'Little child'] a daughter, Horatia.   Bronte] Nelson's Irish estate.   Separated from her] Nelson and his wife did not meet again.   Your uncle] Sir William.   Honor est a Nilo] the anagram of his name means 'honour is from the Nile' (remembering Nelson's victory there in 1798).

109. Sir William Hamilton to Lady Hamilton, 1802

I have passed the last 40 years of my life in the hurry & bustle that must necessarily be attendant on a publick character. I am arrived at the age when some repose is really necessary, & I promised myself a quiet home, & altho' I was sensible, & said so when I married, that I shou'd be super-annuated when my wife wou'd be in her full beauty and vigour of youth. That time is arrived, and we must make the best of it for the comfort of both parties. Unfortunately our tastes as to the manner of living are very different. I by no means wish to live in solitary retreat, but to have seldom less than 12 or 14 at table, & those varying continually, is coming back to what was become so irksome to me in Italy during the latter years of my residence in that country. I have no connections out of my own family. I have no complaint to make, but I feel that the whole attention of my wife is given to Ld N. and his interest at Merton. I well know the purity of Ld N's friendship for Emma and me, and I know how very uncomfortable it wou'd make his Lp, our best friend, if a separation shou'd take place, & am therefore determined to do all in my power to prevent such an extremity, which wou'd be *essentially detrimental* to all parties, but wou'd be more sensibly felt by our dear friend than by us. Provided that our expences in housekeeping do not encrease beyond measure (of which I must own I see some danger), I am willing to go on upon our present footing; but as I cannot expect to live many years, every moment to me is precious, & I hope I may be allow'd sometimes to be my own master, & pass my time accord-ing to my own inclination, either by going my fishing parties on the Thames or by going to London to attend the Museum, R. Society, the Tuesday Club, & Auctions of pictures. I mean to have a light chariot or post chaise by the month, that I may make use of it in London and run backwards and forwards to Merton or to Shepperton, &c. This is my plan, & we might go on very well, but I am fully determined not to have more of the very silly altercations that happen between us but too often and embitter the present moments exceedingly. If realy one cannot live comfortably together, a wise and well concerted separation is preferable; but I think, considering the probability of my not troubling any party long in this world, the best for us all wou'd be to bear those ills we have rather than flie to those we know not of. I have fairly stated what I have on my mind. There is not time for nonsense or trifling. I know and admire your talents & many excellent qualities, but I am not blind to your defects, & confess having many myself; therefore let us bear and forbear for God's sake.

Bear those ills . . .] *Hamlet*, III. i. 80–1.

WILLIAM WORDSWORTH
(1770–1850)

110. To Sara Hutchinson, 14 June 1802

> Sara was the sister of Mary Hutchinson, who married Wordsworth later in 1802. The poem is 'Resolution and Independence', a work of such power and originality that the author himself struggles to explain it. 'The Thorn' and 'The Idiot Boy' appeared in *Lyrical Ballads* (1798). This letter was contained in a longer one from Wordsworth and his sister Dorothy to the Hutchinson sisters.

My dear Sara,

I am exceedingly sorry that the latter part of the Leech-gatherer has displeased you, the more so because I cannot take to myself (that being the case) much pleasure or satisfaction in having pleased you in the former part. I will explain to you in prose my feeling in writing that Poem, and then you will be better able to judge whether the fault be mine or yours or partly both. I describe myself as having been exalted to the highest pitch of delight by the joyousness and beauty of Nature and then as depressed, even in the midst of those beautiful objects, to the lowest dejection and despair. A young Poet in the midst of the happiness of Nature is described as overwhelmed by the thought of the miserable reverses which have befallen the happiest of all men, viz Poets—I think of this till I am so deeply impressed by it, that I consider the manner in which I was rescued from my dejection and despair almost as an interposition of Providence. 'Now whether it was by peculiar grace A leading from above'. A person reading this Poem with feelings like mine will have been awed and controuled, expecting almost something spiritual or supernatural—What is brought forward? 'A lonely place, a Pond' 'by which an old man *was*, far from all house or home'—not stood, not sat, but '*was*'—the figure presented in the most naked simplicity possible. This feeling of spirituality or supernatural-ness is again referred to as being strong in my mind in this passage—'*How came he here* thought I or what can he be doing?' I then describe him, whether ill or well is not for me to judge with perfect confidence, but this I can *confidently* affirm, that, though I believe God has given me a strong imagination, I cannot conceive a figure more impressive than that of an old Man like this, the survivor of a Wife and ten children, travelling alone among the mountains and all lonely places, carrying with him his own fortitude, and the necessities which an unjust state of society has entailed upon him. You say and Mary (that is you can say no more than that) the Poem is *very well* after the introduction of the old man; this is not true, if it is not more than very well it is very bad, there is no intermediate state. You speak of his speech as tedious: everything is tedious when one does not read with the feelings of the Author—'*The Thorn*' is tedious to hundreds; and so is the *Idiot Boy* to hundreds. It is in the character of the old man to tell his story in a manner which an *impatient* reader must necessarily feel as tedious. But Good God! Such a figure, in such a place, a pious self-respecting, miserably infirm, and [?] Old Man telling such a tale!

My dear Sara, it is not a matter of indifference whether you are pleased with this figure and his employment; it may be comparatively so, whether you are pleased or not with *this Poem*; but it is of the utmost importance that you should have had pleasure from contemplating the fortitude, independence, persevering spirit, and the general moral dignity of this old man's character. Your feelings upon the Mother, and the Boys with the Butterfly, were not indifferent: it was an affair of whole continents of moral sympathy. I will talk more with you on this when we meet—at present, farewell and Heaven for ever bless you!

W. W.

111. To Thomas De Quincey, 29 July 1803

When the 18-year-old De Quincey (see below, Letter 146) wrote out of the blue to Wordsworth he was living near Liverpool while waiting to matriculate at Oxford.

Dear Sir,

Your Letter dated May 31 (owing I presume to the remissness of Messeurs Longman and Rees in forwarding it) I did not receive till the day before yesterday. I am much concerned at this as though I am sure you would not suppose me capable of neglecting such a Letter, yet still my silence must needs have caused you some uneasiness.

It is impossible not to be pleased when one is told that one has given so much pleasure: and It is to me a still higher gratification to find that my poems have impressed a stranger with such favorable ideas of my character as a man. Having said this which is easily said I find some difficulty in replying more particularly to your Letter.

It is needless to say that it would be out of nature were I not to have kind feelings towards one who expresses sentiments of such profound esteem and admiration of my writings as you have done. You can have no doubt but that these sentiments however conveyed to me must have been acceptable; and I assure you that they are still more welcome coming from yourself. You will then perceive that the main end which you proposed to yourself in writing to me is answered, viz. that I am already kindly disposed towards you. My friendship it is not in my power to give: this is a gift which no man can make, it is not in our own power: a sound and healthy friendship is the growth of time and circumstance, it will spring up and thrive like a wildflower when these favour, and when they do not, it is in vain to look for it.

I do not suppose that I am saying any thing which you do not know as well as myself. I am simply reminding you of a common place truth which your high admiration of me may have robbed perhaps of that weight which it ought to have with you. And this leads me to what gave me great concern, I mean the very unreasonable value which you set upon my writings, compared with those of others. You are young and ingenuous and I wrote with a hope of pleasing the young the ingenuous and the unworldly above all others, but sorry indeed should I be to stand in the way of the proper influence of other writers. You will know that I allude to the great names of past times, and above all to those of our own Country. I have taken the liberty of saying this much to hasten on the time, when you will value my poems not less, but those of others, more. That time I know would come of itself; and may come sooner for what I have said, which at all events I am sure you cannot take ill.

How many things are there in a mans character of which his writings however miscellaneous or voluminous will give no idea. How many thousand things which go to making up the value of a frank and moral man concerning not one of which any conclusion can be drawn from what he says of himself or of others in the Worlds Ear. You probably would never guess from any thing you know of me, that I am the most lazy and impatient Letter writer in the world. You will perhaps have observed that the first two or three Lines of this sheet are in a tolerably fair, legible hand, and, now every Letter, from A to Z, is in complete route, one upon the heals of the other. Indeed so difficult Do I find it to master this ill habit of idleness and impatience, that I have long ceased to write any Letters but upon business. In justice to myself and you I have found myself obliged to mention this, lest you should think me unkind if you find me a slovenly and sluggish Correspondent.

I am going with my friend Coleridge and my Sister upon a tour into Scotland for six weeks or two months. This will prevent me hearing from you as soon as I could wish, as most likely we shall set off in a few days. If however you write immediately I may have the pleasure of receiving your Letter before our departure; if we are gone, I shall order it to be sent after me. I need not add that it will give me great pleasure to see you at Grasmere if you should ever come this way. I am dear sir with great sincerity and esteem

Yours sincerely,
W. Wordsworth

P.S. I have just looked my letter over, and find that towards the conclusion I have been in a most unwarrantable hurry, especially in what I have said on seeing you here. I seem to have expressed myself absolutely with coldness. This is not in my feelings I assure you. I shall indeed be very happy to see you at Grasmere; if you ever find it convenient to visit this delightful country. You speak of yourself as being very young; and therefore may have many engagements of great importance with respect to your wor[l]dly concerns and future happiness in life. Do not neglect these on any account; but if consistent with these and your other duties, you could find time to visit this country which is no great distance from your present residence I should, I repeat it, be very happy to see you.

W. W.

LADY HESTER STANHOPE
(1776–1839)

Granddaughter of Pitt the Elder and niece of Pitt the Younger, Lady Hester had a youthful career as a political hostess, but left England in 1810. From 1814 she lived in oriental splendour in the Lebanon. She entered Damascus unveiled and on horseback, and was the first European woman to enter Palmyra. Her imperiousness and eccentricity were celebrated by A. W. Kinglake in his travel book *Eothen* (1844). 'Though always complaining of neglect, she had upwards of thirty personal attendants' (*The Dictionary of National Biography*), as well as innumerable cats and horses. She died a pauper in 1839. Her remains were discovered, and reburied by the British ambassador to Lebanon, in 1989.

112. To Patrick Craufurd Bruce, c.27 June 1810

Bruce (1748–1820) was the father of Michael Bruce, who was living with Lady Hester in Malta. Michael wrote at the same time saying his father should be flattered to receive such a letter as Lady Hester's. The father in reply expressed his pleasure that his son had the benefit of her company. The correspondence was discovered by Ian Bruce, a descendant of Michael's, and published in 1951.

Private

Sir,

If your character inspired me with less respect, I should not give you the opportunity of perhaps accusing me of impertinence, in presuming to address you upon a subject which requires all my courage to touch upon, & great liberality on your part, to do justice to those motives which induce me to expaciate upon it. You may have heard that I have become acquainted with your Son, his elevated and Statesmanlike mind, his brilliant talents to say nothing of his beautiful person, cannot be contemplated by any feeling mind with indifference; to know him is to love & admire him, & I *do both*! Should you hear this in any irregular way, it might give you uneasiness, & you might not only mistake the nature of the sentiments I feel towards him, but my *views* altogether, & imagine that he had fallen into the hands of an artful woman who wd. take him in, as far as it lay in her power. Sir, you need not be under any of these apprehensions, the affection I feel for him wd. only prompt me the more to consider his advantage in every point of view, & at this very moment (while loving him to destraction) I look forward to the period when I must resign him to some thrice happy woman really worthy of him. While seeking knowledge & considering plans of future ambition, few persons are perhaps better calculated for his companion than I am, but when he has once taken his line, & become a public character, I shall then like a dethroned Empress, resign to virtue the possession of that perfection which she alone has a right to, & see whether a sacrifice demanded by principle & true feeling, cannot be made with as good a grace as one dictated by policy and interest. Sir, if you knew me, I flatter myself that it wd. be unnecessary to give you any further assurance of the sincerity of my intentions, but as you do not, there is no *promise however solemn* I am not willing to make upon this subject. After what I have said I trust that no feeling of anxiety will remain as far as relates to your Son's welfare. It wd. be a satisfaction to me to learn (tho' I do not wish you to write to me) that this candid confession of my sentiments, has not displeased you; do not however Sir *mistake* the tone of humility I have adopted thro' this letter, which proceeds in fact from my being one of the proudest women in the world, so proud, as to despise the opinion of the world altogether, *as far* as relates *to myself*, but when I am addressing the parent of a man I so tenderly love; (& for whom he has so great an affection) a sacred sort of reverence steals upon my mind, which I hope has communicated itself to my expressions, as I have intended they should convey the confidence & respect with which Sir I have the honour to remain.

Yours &c &c
Hester Lucy Stanhope

113. To Mr Murray, 2 January 1812

Dear Sir,

Before this letter reaches you, you will have heard, in all probability, an account of my shipwreck from Mr Coutts. That I am here to relate it is rather extraordinary, for I escaped not only a sinking ship, but put to sea in a boat when one could hardly have supposed it could have lived five minutes—the storm was so great. Unable to make the land, I got ashore, not on an island, but a bare rock which stuck up in the sea, and remained thirty hours without food or water. It becoming calmer the second night, I once more put to sea, and fortunately landed upon the island of Rhodes, but above three days' journey from the town, travelling at the rate of eight hours a day over mountains and dreadful rocks. Could the fashionables I once associated with believe that I could have sufficient composure of mind to have given my orders as distinctly and as positively as if I had been sitting in the midst of them, and that I slept for many hours very sound on the bare rock, covered with a pelisse, and was in a sweet sleep the second night, when I was awoke by the men, who seemed to dread that, as it was becoming calmer, and the wind changing (which would bring the sea in another direction), that we might be washed off the rock before morning. So away I went, putting my faith in that God who has never quite forsaken me in all my various misfortunes. The next place I slept in was a mill, upon sacks of corn; after that, in a hut, where I turned out a poor ass to make more room, and congratulated myself on having a bed of straw. When I arrived (after a day of tremendous fatigue) at a tolerable village, I found myself too ill to proceed the next day, and was fortunate enough to make the acquaintance of a kind-hearted, hospitable Greek gentleman, whom misfortune had sent into obscurity, and he insisted upon keeping me in his house till I was recovered. At the end of a few days I continued my journey, and arrived here, having suffered less than any other woman would have done whose health was as precarious as mine has been for so long a time. Everything I possessed I have lost; had I attempted to have saved anything, others would have done the same, and the boat would have been sunk. To collect clothes in this part of the world to dress as an Englishwoman would be next to impossible; at least, it would cost me two years' income. To dress as a Turkish woman would not do, because I must not be seen to speak to a man; therefore I have nothing left for it but to dress as a Turk—not like the Turks you are in the habit of seeing in England, but as an Asiatic Turk in a travelling dress—just a sort of silk and cotton shirt; next a striped silk and cotton waistcoat; over that another with sleeves, and over that a cloth short jacket without sleeves or half-sleeves, beautifully worked in coloured twist, a large pair of breeches, and Turkish boots, a sash into which goes a brace of pistols, a knife, and a sort of short sword, a belt for powder and shot made of variegated leather, which goes over the shoulder, the pouches the same, and a turban of several colours, put on in a particular way with a large bunch of natural flowers on one side. This is the dress of the common Asiatic; the great men are covered with gold and embroidery, and nothing can be more splendid and becoming than their dress. At this moment I am a wretched figure—half a Greek, half a Turk, but most of all like a blackguard (Gallongi), a Turkish sailor. As there is nothing interesting in the town of Rhodes, and the Bey being the only disagreeable Turk I ever met with, once a slave, and now a tyrant, but not of my sort—ignorant, sordid, and vulgar—I have left him and his city for a little habitation on the sea coast, about three miles distant from the town. The situation of this summer residence is enchanting, even at this season of the year. Let those who envied me in my greatness alike envy me in rags; let them envy that contented and contemplative mind which rises superior to all worldly misfortunes which are independent of the affections of the heart. Tell them I can feel happier in wandering over wilds, observing and admiring the beauties of Nature, than ever I did when surrounded by pomp, flatterers, and fools. . . . All my curiosities, all my discoveries, are gone to the bottom, and many valuable ones I have made with *so much trouble*. If I want a Turk, it is the Ramazan, it is the feast of the Bairam; he is either at prayers, asleep, or in the bath. If I want a Greek, his shop is shut—it is a saint's day. If I want an Armenian, it is the same thing. The Jews are less provoking; but, between them all and their different languages, it requires not a little patience and exertion to get through with anything out of the common way. I have never yet received one letter from you. . . . I cannot hardly suppose that you have never written to me, but I think you cannot have forwarded my letters through the channel I have so repeatedly directed. To be ignorant about poor dear Grandmama, and not to know what is become of poor Nash, and if I have the means to assist her, is really very painful to me. William Hillier and Mr Norman have alike disobeyed my orders. I desired they would be sure to write to me about Nash, and never have I had one line from any one of them. This is gratitude; but such has been my fate—to be forgotten the moment I am no longer useful. I am never low, but when I think of England and the monsters it contains—when I put them out of my mind I am happy, for I have great reason to be so; but who do I owe my comforts to?—to strangers!

Murray] her solicitor.   Coutts] apparently she had already written to Coutts, her banker.   Ramazan] Turkish form of 'Ramadan'.   Bairam] a Muslim feast.   Nash] her childhood nurse.

HARRIET, COUNTESS GRANVILLE

Harriet Cavendish, daughter of the 5th Duke of Devonshire, married Leveson Gower Granville in 1809 (see above, Letters 101–4).

114. To Lady Georgiana Morpeth, 28 August 1810

Lady Granville's sister, Georgiana Cavendish, married Viscount Morpeth, son of the Earl of Carlisle.

I am delighted with this place, and I do not think its faults great enough to prevent one's thinking it beautiful. We arrived here yesterday in time to drive over the park and the beautiful wood. The house is comfortable, with two fine rooms.

We fared sumptuously at the rich man's table. Our reception has really been ridiculous, but you shall judge. The dinner for us two was soup, fish, fricassee of chicken, cutlets, venison, veal, hare, vegetables of all kinds, tart, melon, pineapple, grapes, peaches, nectarines, with wine in proportion. Six servants to wait upon us, whom we did not dare dispense with, a gentleman-in-waiting and a fat old housekeeper hovering round the door to listen, I suppose, if we should chance to express a wish. Before this sumptuous repast was well digested, about four hours later, the doors opened, and in was pushed a supper in the same proportion, in itself enough to have fed me for a week. I did not know whether to laugh or cry. Either would have been better than what I did, which was to begin again, with the prospect of a pill to-night, and redoubled abstemiousness for a week to come.

The house is full of portraits, which amuse me more than all the rest. Two of Lord Stafford, positive and important, three of her, one by Phillips, very fierce and foreign. Three of Lady Carlisle, all very handsome, but less so than I have always heard she was. Poor dear Lady Louisa Macdonald, very pretty and sentimental, leaning upon an anchor; and last, not least, Granville, between three and four, dancing with all his might with his sisters, and a drawing of him, by Downman, when he was seven and a half, in a sky-blue coat, making eyes, and perfectly angelic and beautiful. There are a few of Anne, which do not justify the Archbishop in my eyes; one of the late Lady Stafford, and several of her husband, who must have been a magnificent old man. God bless you. I am summoned to an immense cold collation. We breakfasted two hours ago.

This place] Trentham, the great Staffordshire house of Lady Granville's extraordinarily rich kinsman George Granville Leveson Gower, 1st Duke of Sutherland.   Macdonald] Lady Louisa Macdonald and Anne Vernon, wife of the archbishop of York, were sisters to Lord Granville; Lady Stafford was his mother.   Downman] John Downman, a fashionable portrait painter.

FANNY BURNEY

(1752–1840)

The daughter of Dr Charles Burney, the musical historian and friend of Dr Johnson, Frances (Fanny) Burney was author of the novels *Evelina* (1778), *Cecilia* (1782), and *Camilla* (1796). Her diaries and letters are important for their accounts of life at court and in France, where she lived with her husband General Alexandre d'Arblay from 1802 till 1812. In 1811 she was diagnosed as having cancer of the right breast, and suffered the mastectomy described in this letter to her elder sister Esther. The letter, written over four months, is extremely long as well as painfully interesting, and we have accordingly printed only a part of it.

115. To Esther Burney, March–June 1812

. . . The good M. Larrey, when he came to me next after the last of these trials, was quite thrown into a consternation, so changed he found all for the worse —'Et qu'est il donc arrive?' he cried, & presently, sadly announced his hope of dissolving the hardness were nearly extinguished. M. Ribe was now again called in—but he only corroborated the terrible judgement: yet they allowed to my pleadings some further essays, & the more easily as the weather was not propitious to any operation. My Exercise, at this time, though always useful & chearing, occasioned me great suffering in its conclusion, from mounting up three pair of stairs: my tenderest Partner, therefore, removed me to La Rue de Mirmenil, where I began my Paris residence nearly 10 Years ago!—*quite* 10 next month! Here we are *au premier*—but alas—to no effect! once only have I yet descended the short flight of steps from which I had entertained new hopes. A Physician was now called in, Dr Moreau, to hear if he could suggest any new means: but Dr Larrey had left him no resources untried. A formal consultation now was held, of Larrey, Ribe, & Moreau—&, in fine, I was formally condemned to an operation by all Three. I was as much astonished as disappointed—for the poor breast was no where discoloured, & not much larger than its healthy neighbour. Yet I felt the evil to be deep, so deep, that I often thought if it could not be dissolved, it could only with life be extirpated. I called up, however, all the reason I possessed, or could assume, & told them—that if they saw no other alternative, I would not resist their opinion & experience:—the good Dr Larrey, who, during his long attendance had conceived for me the warmest friendship, had now tears in his Eyes; from my dread he had expected resistance. He proposed again calling in M. Dubois. No, I told him, if I could not by himself be saved, I had no sort of hope elsewhere, &, if it must be, what I wanted in courage should be supplied by Confidence. The good man was now dissatisfied with himself, and declared I ought to have the First & most eminent advice his Country could afford; 'Vous êtes si considerée, Madame, said he, ici, que le public même sera mecontent si vous n'avez pas tout le secours que nous avons à vous offrir.—' Yet this modest man is premier chirugien de la Garde Imperiale, & had been lately created a Baron for his eminent services!—M. Dubois, he added, from his super-skill & experience, might yet, perhaps, suggest some cure. This conquered me quickly, ah—Send for him! Send for him! I cried—& Dr Moreau received the commission to consult with him.—What an interval was this! Yet my poor M. d'A was more to be pitied than myself, though he knew not the terrible idea I had internally annexed to the trial—but Oh what he suffered!—& with what exquisite tenderness he solaced all I had to bear! My poor Alex I kept as much as possible, and as long, ignorant of my situation.—M. Dubois behaved extremely well, no pique intervened with the interest he had professed in my well-doing, & his conduct was manly & generous. It was difficult still to see him, but he appointed the earliest day in his power for a general & final consultation. I was informed of it only on the Same day, to avoid useless agitation. He met here Drs Larrey, Ribe, & Moreau. The case, I saw, offered uncommon difficulties, or presented eminent danger, but, the examination over, they desired to consult together. I left them— what an half hour I passed alone!—M. d'A. was at his office. Dr Larrey then came to summon me. He did not speak, but looked very like my dear Brother James, to whom he has a personal resemblance that has struck M. d'A. as well as myself. I came back, & took my seat, with what calmness I was able. All were silent, & Dr Larrey, I saw, hid himself nearly behind my Sofa. My heart beat fast: I saw all hope was over. I called upon them to speak. M. Dubois then, after a long & unintelligible harangue, from his own disturbance, pronounced my doom. I now saw it was inevitable, and abstained from any further effort. They received my formal consent, & retired to fix a day.

All hope of escaping this evil being now at an end, I could only console or employ my mind in considering how to render it less dreadful to M. d'A. M. Dubois had pronounced 'il faut s'attendre à souffrir, Je ne veux pas vous trompez—Vous Souffrirez—vous souffrirez *beaucoup*!—' M. Ribe had *charged* me to cry! to withhold or restrain myself might have seriously bad consequences, he said. M. Moreau, in ecchoing this injunction, enquired whether I had cried or screamed at the birth of Alexander—Alas, I told him, it had not been possible to do otherwise; Oh then, he answered, there is no fear!—What terrible inferences were here to be drawn! I desired, therefore, that M. d'A. might be kept in ignorance of the day till the operation should be over. To this they agreed, except M. Larrey, with high approbation: M. Larrey looked dissentient, but was silent. M. Dubois protested he would not undertake to act, after what he had seen of the agitated spirits of M. d'A. if he were present: nor would he suffer me to know the time myself over night; I obtained with difficulty a promise of 4 hours warning, which were essential to me for sundry regulations.

From this time, I assumed the best spirits in my power, *to meet the coming blow*;—& support my too sympathising Partner. They would let me make no preparations, refusing to inform me what would be necessary; I have known, since, that Mad^e de Tessé, an admirable old friend of M. d'A, now mine, equally, & one of the first of her sex, in any country, for uncommon abilities, & nearly universal knowledge, had insisted upon sending all that might be necessary, & of keeping me in ignorance. M. d'A filled a Closet with Charpie, compresses, & bandages—All that to *me* was owned, as wanting, was an arm Chair & some Towels.—Many things, however, joined to the depth of my pains, assured me the business was not without danger. I therefore made my Will—unknown, to this moment, to M. d'A, & entrusted it privately to M. La Tour Maubourg, without even letting my friend his Sister, Mad^e de Maisonneuve, share the secret. M. de M^g conveyed it for me to Maria's excellent M. Gillet, from whom M. de M^g brought me directions. As soon as I am able to go out I shall reveal this clandestine affair to M. d'A.—till then, it might still affect him. Mad^e de Maisonneuve desired to be present at the operation;—but I would not inflict such pain. Me de Chastel belle sœur to Mad^e de Boinville, would also have sustained the shock; but I secured two Guards, one of whom is known to my two dear Charlottes, Mad^e Soubiren, portière to l'Hotel Marengo: a very good Creature, who often amuses me by repeating '*ver. vell, Mawm*;' which she tells me she learnt of Charlotte the younger, whom she never names but with rapture, The other is a workwoman whom I have often employed. The kindnesses I received at this period would have made me for-ever love France, had I hitherto been hard enough of heart to hate it— but Mad^e d'Henin—the tenderness she shewed me surpasses all description. Twice she came to Paris from the Country, to see, watch & sit with me; there is nothing that can be suggested of use or comfort that she omitted. She loves me not only from her kind heart, but also from her love of Mrs Lock, often, often exclaiming 'Ah! si votre angelique amie étoit ici!—' But I must force myself from these episodes, though my dearest Esther will not think them *de trop*.

After sentence thus passed, I was in hourly expectation of a summons to execution; judge, then, my surprise to be suffered to go on full 3 Weeks in the same state! M. Larrey from time to time visited me, but pronounced nothing, & was always melancholy. At length, M. d'A. was told that he waited himself for a Summons! & that, a formal one, & in writing! *I* could

not give one, a *consent* was my utmost effort. But poor M. d'A. wrote a
desire that the operation, if necessary, might take place without further
delay. In my own mind, I had all this time been persuaded there were
hopes of a cure: why else, I thought, let me know my doom thus long? But
here I must account for this apparently useless, & therefore cruel measure,
though I only learnt it myself 2 months afterwards. M. Dubois had given
his opinion that the evil was too far advanced for any remedy; that the
cancer was already internally declared; that I was inevitably destined to that
most frightful of deaths, & that an operation would but accellerate my
dissolution. Poor M. Larrey was so deeply affected by this sentence, that—
as he has lately told me,—he regretted to his Soul ever having known me,
& was upon the point of demanding a commission to the furthest end of
France in order to force me into other hands. I had said, however, he
remembered, once, that I would far rather suffer a quick end without, than
a lingering life with this dreadfullest of maladies: he finally, therefore,
considered it might be possible to save me by the trial, but that without it
my case was desperate, & resolved to make the attempt. Nevertheless, the
responsibility was too great to rest upon his own head entirely; & therefore
he waited the formal summons.—In fine, One morning—the last of September, 1811, while I was still in Bed, & M. d'A. was arranging some
papers for his office, I received a Letter written by M. de Lally to a
Journalist, in vindication of the honoured memory of his Father against the
assertions of Mad^e du Deffand. I read it aloud to My Alexanders, with tears
of admiration & sympathy, & then sent it by Alex: to its excellent Author,
as I had promised the preceding evening. I then dressed, aided, as usual for
many months, by my maid, my right arm being condemned to total inac-
tion; but not yet was the grand business over, when another Letter was
delivered to me—another, indeed!—'twas from M. Larrey, to acquaint
me that at 10 o'clock he should be with me, properly accompanied, & to
exhort me to rely as much upon his sensibility & his prudence, as upon his
dexterity & his experience; he charged to secure the absence of M. d'A: &
told me that the young Physician who would deliver me this *announce*,
would prepare for the operation, in which he must lend his aid: & also that
it had been the decision of the consultation to allow me but two hours
notice.—Judge, my Esther, if I read this unmoved!—yet I had to disguise
my sensations & intentions from M. d'A!—Dr Aumont, the Messenger &
terrible Herald, was in waiting; M. d'A stood by my bed side; I affected to
be long reading the Note, to gain time for forming some plan, & such was
my terror of involving M. d'A. in the unavailing wretchedness of witnessing what I must go through, that it conquered every other, & gave me the
force to act as if I were directing some third person. The detail would be
too *Wordy*, as James says, but the *wholesale* is—I called Alex. to my Bed

side, & sent him to inform M. Barbier Neuville, chef du division du Bureau de M. d'A. that *the moment was come*, & I entreated him to write a summons upon urgent business for M. d'A. & to detain him till all should be over. Speechless & appalled, off went Alex, &, as I have since heard, was forced to sit down & sob in executing his commission. I then, by the maid, sent word to the young Dr Aumont that I could not be ready till one o'clock: & I finished my breakfast, &—not with much appetite, you will believe! forced down a crust of bread, & hurried off, under various pretences, M. d'A. He was scarcely gone, when M. Du Bois arrived: I renewed my request for one o'clock: the rest came; all were fain to consent to the delay, for I had an apartment to prepare for my banished Mate. This arrangement, & those for myself, occupied me completely. Two engaged nurses were out of the way—I had a bed, Curtains, & heaven knows what to prepare—but business was good for my nerves. I was obliged to quit my room to have it put in order:—Dr Aumont would not leave the house; he remained in the Sallon, folding linen!—He had demanded 4 or 5 old & fine left off under Garments—I glided to our Book Cabinet: sundry necessary works & orders filled up my time entirely till One O'clock, When all was ready——but Dr Moreau then arrived, with news that M. Dubois could not attend till three. Dr Aumont went away—& the Coast was clear. This, indeed, was a dreadful interval. I had no longer any thing to do—I had only to think—TWO HOURS thus spent seemed never-ending. I would fain have written to my dearest Father—to You, my Esther—to Charlotte James—Charles—Amelia Lock—but my arm prohibited me: I strolled to the Sallon—I saw it fitted with preparations, & I recoiled—But I soon returned; to what effect disguise from myself what I must so soon know?—yet the sight of the immense quantity of bandages, compresses, spunges, Lint——made me a little sick:—I walked backwards & forwards till I quieted all emotion, & became, by degrees, nearly stupid—torpid, without sentiment or consciousness;—& thus I remained till the Clock struck three. A sudden spirit of exertion then returned,—I defied my poor arm, no longer worth sparing, & took my long banished pen to write a few words to M. d'A—& a few more for Alex, in case of a fatal result. These short billets I could only deposit safely, when the Cabriolets—one—two—three—four—succeeded rapidly to each other in stopping at the door. Dr Moreau instantly entered my room, to see if I were alive. He gave me a wine cordial, & went to the Sallon. I rang for my Maid & Nurses,—but before I could speak to them, my room, without previous message, was entered by 7 Men in black, Dr Larry, M. Dubois, Dr Moreau, Dr Aumont, Dr Ribe, & a pupil of Dr Larry, & another of M. Dubois. I was now awakened from my stupor—& by a sort of indignation—Why so many? & without leave?—But I could not utter a syllable. M. Dubois acted as

Commander in Chief. Dr Larry kept out of sight; M. Dubois ordered a
Bed stead into the middle of the room. Astonished, I turned to Dr Larry,
who had promised that an Arm Chair would suffice; but he hung his head,
& would not look at me. Two *old mattrasses* M. Dubois then demanded, &
an old Sheet. I now began to tremble violently, more with distaste &
horrour of the preparations even than of the pain. These arranged to his
liking, he desired me to mount the Bed stead. I stood suspended, for a
moment, whether I should not abruptly escape—I looked at the door, the
windows—I felt desperate—but it was only for a moment, my reason then
took the command, & my fears & feelings struggled vainly against it. I
called to my maid—she was crying, & the two Nurses stood, transfixed, at
the door. Let those women all go! cried M. Dubois. This order recovered
me my Voice—No, I cried, let them stay! *qu'elles restent*! This occasioned
a little dispute, that re-animated me—The maid, however, & one of the
nurses ran off—I charged the other to approach, & she obeyed. M. Dubois
now tried to issue his commands *en militaire*, but I resisted all that were
resistable—I was compelled, however, to submit to taking off my long robe
de Chambre, which I had meant to retain—Ah, then, how did I think of
my Sisters!—not one, at so dreadful an instant, at hand, to protect—
adjust—guard me—I regretted that I had refused M^c de Maisonneuve—
Mc Chastel—no one upon whom I could rely—my departed Angel!—how
did I think of her!—how did I long—long for my Esther—my Charlotte!—My distress was, I suppose, apparent, though not my Wishes, for
M. Dubois himself now softened, & spoke soothingly. Can *You*, I cried,
feel for an operation that, to *You*, must seem so trivial?—Trivial? he
repeated—taking up a bit of paper, which he tore, unconsciously, into a
million of pieces, *oui—c'est peu de chose—mais—*' he stammered, & could
not go on. No one else attempted to speak, but I was softened myself, when
I saw even M. Dubois grow agitated, while Dr Larry kept always aloof, yet
a glance shewed me he was pale as ashes. I knew not, positively, then, the
immediate danger, but every thing convinced me danger was hovering
about me, & that this experiment could alone save me from its jaws. I
mounted, therefore, unbidden, the Bed stead—& M. Dubois placed me
upon the mattress, & spread a cambric handkerchief upon my face. It was
transparent, however, & I saw, through it, that the Bed stead was instantly
surrounded by the 7 men & my nurse. I refused to be held; but when,
Bright through the cambric, I saw the glitter of polished Steel—I closed
my Eyes. I would not trust to convulsive fear the sight of the terrible
incision. A silence the most profound ensued, which lasted for some minutes, during which, I imagine, they took their orders by signs, & made their
examination—Oh what a horrible suspension!—I did not breathe—& M.
Dubois tried vainly to find any pulse. This pause, at length, was broken by

Dr Larry, who, in a voice of solemn melancholy, said 'Qui me tiendra ce sein?—'

No one answered; at least not verbally; but this aroused me from my passively submissive state, for I feared they imagined the whole breast infected—feared it too justly,—for, again through the Cambric, I saw the hand of M. Dubois held up, while his fore finger first described a straight line from top to bottom of the breast, secondly a Cross, & thirdly a Circle; intimating that the WHOLE was to be taken off. Excited by this idea, I started up, threw off my veil, &, in answer to the demand 'Qui me tiendra ce sein?', cried 'C'est moi, Monsieur!' & I held my hand under it, & explained the nature of my sufferings, which all sprang from one point, though they darted into every part. I was heard attentively, but in utter silence, & M. Dubois then re-placed me as before, &, as before, spread my veil over my face. How vain, alas, my representation! immediately again I saw the fatal finger describe the Cross—& the circle—Hopeless, then, desperate, & self-given up, I closed once more my Eyes, relinquishing all watching, all resistance, all interference, & sadly resolute to be wholly resigned.

My dearest Esther,—& all my dears to whom she communicates this doleful ditty, will rejoice to hear that this resolution once taken, was firmly adhered to, in defiance of a terror that surpasses all description, & the most torturing pain. Yet—when the dreadful steel was plunged into the breast—cutting through veins—arteries—flesh—nerves—I needed no injunctions not to restrain my cries. I began a scream that lasted unintermittingly during the whole time of the incision—& I almost marvel that it rings not in my Ears still! so excruciating was the agony. When the wound was made, & the instrument was withdrawn, the pain seemed undiminished, for the air that suddenly rushed into those delicate parts felt like a mass of minute but sharp & forked poniards, that were tearing the edges of the wound—but when again I felt the instrument—describing a curve—cutting against the grain, if I may so say, while the flesh resisted in a manner so forcible as to oppose & tire the hand of the operator, who was forced to change from the right to the left—then, indeed, I thought I must have expired. I attempted no more to open my Eyes,—they felt as if hermettically shut, & so firmly closed, that the Eyelids seemed indented into the Cheeks. The instrument this second time withdrawn, I concluded the operation over—Oh no! presently the terrible cutting was renewed—& worse than ever, to separate the bottom, the foundation of this dreadful gland from the parts to which it adhered—Again all description would be baffled—yet again all was not over,—Dr Larry rested but his own hand, &—Oh Heaven!—I then felt the Knife [rack]ling against the breast bone—scraping it!—This performed, while I yet remained in utterly speechless torture, I heard the

Voice of Mr Larry,—(all others guarded a dead silence) in a tone nearly tragic, desire every one present to pronounce if any thing more remained to be done; The general voice was Yes,—but the finger of Mr Dubois— which I literally *felt* elevated over the wound, though I saw nothing, & though he touched nothing, so indescribably sensitive was the spot—pointed to some further requistion—& again began the scraping!—and, after this, Dr Moreau thought he discerned a peccant attom—and still, & still, M. Dubois demanded attom after attom—My dearest Esther, not for days, not for Weeks, but for Months I could not speak of this terrible business without nearly again going through it! I could not *think* of it with impunity! I was sick, I was disordered by a single question—even now, 9 months after it is over, I have a head ache from going on with the account! & this miserable account, which I began 3 Months ago, at least, I dare not revise, nor read, the recollection is still so painful.

To conclude, the evil was so profound, the case so delicate, & the pre-cautions necessary for preventing a return so numerous, that the operation, including the treatment & the dressing, lasted 20 minutes! a time, for sufferings so acute, that was hardly supportable—However, I bore it with all the courage I could exert, & never moved, nor stopt them, nor resisted, nor remonstrated, nor spoke—except once or twice, during the dressings, to say 'Ah Messieurs! que je vous plains!—' for indeed I was sensible to the feeling concern with which they all saw what I endured, though my speech was principally—*very* principally meant for Dr Larry. Except this, I ut-tered not a syllable, save, when so often they re-commenced, calling out 'Avertissez moi, Messieurs! avertissez moi!—' Twice, I believe, I fainted; at least, I have two total chasms in my memory of this transaction, that impede my tying together what passed. When all was done, & they lifted me up that I might be put to bed, my strength was so totally annihilated, that I was obliged to be carried, & could not even sustain my hands & arms, which hung as if I had been lifeless; while my face, as the Nurse has told me, was utterly colourless. This removal made me open my Eyes—& I then saw my good Dr Larry, pale nearly as myself, his face streaked with blood, & its expression depicting grief, apprehension, & almost horrour.

When I was in bed,—my poor M. d'Arblay—who ought to write you himself his own history of this Morning—was called to me—& afterwards our Alex.—

[Alexandre d'Arblay added these words]

No! No my dearest & ever more dear friends, I shall not make a fruitless attempt. No language could convey what I felt in the deadly course of these seven hours. Nevertheless, every one *of you, my dearest dearest friends*, can guess, must even know it. Alexandre had no less feeling, but showed more fortitude. He, perhaps, will be more able to describe to you, nearly at least, the torturing state of my poor heart & soul. Besides, I must own, to you, that these details which were, till just now, quite unknown to me, have almost killed me, & I am only able to thank God that this more than half Angel has had the sublime courage to deny herself the comfort I might have offered her, to spare me, not the sharing of her excruciating pains, that was impossible, but the witnessing so terrific a scene, & perhaps the remorse to have rendered it more tragic, for I don't flatter myself I could have got through it—I must confess it.

Thank Heaven! She is now surprisingly well, & in good spirits, & we hope to have many many still happy days. May that of peace soon arrive, and enable me to embrace better than with my pen my beloved & ever ever more dear friends of the town & country. Amen. Amen!

Larrey] (or Larry) her surgeon. There had been hopes of avoiding surgery; news that they were false had coincided with bad news of friends at home.   Ribe] an anatomist who provided a second opinion.   Alex] her son Alexander, born 1794.   Charpie] linen torn in strips for surgical dressings.   Madᶜ de Maisonneuve] a divorced aristocrat, friend of Burney through d'Arblay's close friendship with her brother, Victor de Latour-Maubourg.   Two . . . Charlottes] a younger sister and her daughter, later Burney's editor.   My Alexanders] her husband and son.

MARIA EDGEWORTH
(1768–1849)

Maria Edgeworth's father was an Irish landowner, four times married and with twenty-two children; he had scientific interests, was an inventor and a friend of Erasmus Darwin, and had a powerful influence on his daughter's writing. Her novels, especially *Castle Rackrent* (1800), were greatly admired by, among others, Scott, Jane Austen, Thackeray, and Turgenev, and she achieved great popularity in London. Her first book, *Letters to Literary Ladies* (1795), was a defence of female education.

116. To Mrs Edgeworth, October 1812

Maria Edgeworth became a close friend of her father's fourth wife, née Honora Sneyd. James Sadler made his first flight in 1785. On 1 Oct. 1812 he ascended, as here described, from the grounds of Belvedere House, Dublin, in an attempt to fly across the Irish Sea, but he came down in the sea and was rescued by a fishing boat. George III was interested in his exploits. His son (b. 1796) flew from Dublin to Holyhead in 1817, but was killed in a ballooning accident in 1824. We do not know where Erasmus Darwin described a balloon.

After a most delightful journey with Mr and Mrs Henry Hamilton, laughing, singing, and talking, we dined with them. Dear old Mr Sackville

Hamilton dined with us, fresh from London: intellectual and corporeal dainties in abundance. The first morning was spent in cursing Mr Sadler for not going up, and in seeing the Dublin Society House. A charming picture of Mr Foster, by Beachy, with plans in his hand, looking full of thought and starting into life and action. Spent an hour looking over the books of prints in the library. Fanny particularly pleased with a Houbracken: Harriet with Daniel's Indian Antiquities: my father with Sir Christopher Wren's and Inigo Jones's designs. After dinner Richard Ruxton came in, and said my aunt and uncle had thoughts of coming up to see the balloon. In the evening at Astley's. The second day to see the elephant: how I pitied this noble animal, cooped up under the command of a scarcely human creature, who had not half as much reason as himself. Went on to see the Panorama of Edinburgh: I never saw a sight that pleased me more; Edinburgh was before me—Princes Street and George Street—the Castle—the bridge over dry land where the woman met us and said, 'Poor little things they be.' At first a mistiness, like what there is in nature over a city before the sun breaks out; then the sun shining on the buildings, trees, and mountains.

Thursday morning, to our inexpressible joy, was fine, and the flag, the signal that Sadler would ascend, was, to the joy of thousands, flying from the top of Nelson's Pillar. Dressed quickly—breakfasted I don't know how—job coach punctual: crowds in motion even at nine o'clock in the streets: tide flowing all one way to Belvidere Gardens, lent by the proprietor for the occasion: called at Sneyd's lodgings in Anne Street: he and William gone: drove on, when we came near Belvidere such strings of carriages, such crowds of people on the road and on the raised footpath, there was no stirring: troops lined the road at each side: guard with officers at each entrance to prevent mischief; but unfortunately there were only two entrances, not nearly enough for such a confluence of people. Most imprudently we and several others got out of our carriages upon the raised footpath, in hopes of getting immediately at the garden door, which was within two yards of us, but nothing I ever felt was equal to the pressure of the crowd: they closed over our little heads, I thought we must have been flattened, and the breath squeezed out of our bodies. My father held Harriet fast, I behind him held Fanny with such a grasp! and dragged her on with a force I did not know I possessed. I really thought your children would never see you again with all their bones whole, and I cannot tell you what I suffered for ten minutes. My father, quite pale, calling with a stentor voice to the sentinels. A fat woman nearly separated me from Fanny. My father fairly kicked off the terrace a man who was intent upon nothing but an odious bag of cakes which he held close to his breast, swearing and pushing. Before us Mrs Smyley and Mr Smyley, with a lady he was protecting, and unable to protect anybody, looked more frightened than if he had lost a hundred causes: the lady continually saying, 'Let me back! let me back! if I could once get to my carriage!'

The tide carried us on to the door. An admirable Scotch officer, who was mounting guard with a drawn sword, his face dropping perspiration, exclaimed at the sight of Harriet, 'Oh the child! take care of that child! she will be crushed to death!' He made a soldier put his musket across the doorway, so as to force a place for her to creep under: quick as lightning in she darted, and Fanny and I and my father after her. All serene, uncrowded, and fresh within the park.

Instantly met Sneyd and William, and the two Mr Foxes. Music and the most festive scene in the gardens: the balloon, the beautiful many-coloured balloon, chiefly maroon colour, with painted eagles, and garlands, and arms of Ireland, hung under the trees, and filling fast from pipes and an apparatus which I leave for William's scientific description: terrace before Belvidere House—well-dressed groups parading on it: groups all over the gardens, mantles, scarves, and feathers floating: all the commonalty outside in fields at half price. We soon espied Mr and Mrs Hamilton, and joined company, and were extremely happy, and wished for you and dear Honora. Sun shining, no wind. Presently we met the Solicitor-General: he started back, and made me such a bow as made me feel my own littleness; then shook my hands most cordially, and in a few moments told me more than most men could tell in an hour: just returned from Edinburgh—Mrs Bushe and daughters too much fatigued to come and see the balloon.

The Duke and Duchess of Richmond, and Sir Charles Vernon, and Sir Charles Saxton. The Miss Gunns seated themselves in a happily conspicuous place, with some gentlemen, on the roof of Belvidere House, where, with veils flying and telescopes and opera glasses continually veering about, they attracted sufficient attention.

Walking on, Sneyd exclaimed, 'My Uncle Ruxton!' I darted to him: 'Is my aunt here?' 'Yes, and Sophy, and Margaret, but I have lost them; I'm looking for them.' 'Oh, come with me, and we'll find them.' Soon we made our way behind the heels of the troopers' horses, who guarded a sacred circle round the balloon: found my aunt, and Sophy, and Mag—surprise and joy on both sides: got seats on the pedestal of some old statue, and talked and enjoyed ourselves: the balloon filling gradually. Now it was that my uncle proposed our returning by Black Castle.

The drum beats! the flag flies! balloon full! It is moved from under the trees over the heads of the crowd: the car very light and slight—Mr Sadler's son, a young lad, in the car. How the horses stood the motion of this vast body close to them I can't imagine, but they did. The boy got out. Mr Sadler, quite composed, this being his twenty-sixth aërial ascent, got into his car: a lady, the Duchess of Richmond, I believe, presented to him a pretty flag: the balloon gave two majestic nods from side to side as the cords were cut. Whether the music continued at this moment to play or not, nobody can tell. No one spoke while the balloon successfully rose, rapidly cleared the trees, and floated above our heads: loud shouts and huzzas, one man close to us exclaiming, as he clasped his hands, 'Ah, musha, musha, God bless you! God be wid you!' Mr Sadler, waving his flag and his hat, and bowing to the world below, soon pierced a white cloud, and disappeared, then emerging, the balloon looked like a moon, black on one side, silver on the other; then like a dark bubble; then less and less, and now only a speck is seen; and now the fleeting rack obscures it. Never did I feel the full merit of Darwin's description till then . . .

117. To Mrs Edgeworth, 30 April 1831

My dear mother . . . You must have been shocked by the death of the Duchess of Wellington which the newspapers must have told you but your shock cannot have equalled mine. Monday last—Fanny lying down to rest I drove to Apsley House by myself without the slightest suspicion that she was worse than when I had last seen her. When I saw the gate only just opened enough to let out the porters head and saw Smith parleying with him, nothing occurred to me but that the man doubted whether I was a person that ought to be admitted—So I put out my card—and Smith returning said 'Ma'am The Duchess of Wellington died on Saturday morning.'

The good natured porter seeing that I was really as he said a friend went into the house at my request to ask if I could see her maid. And after some minutes the gates opened softly and I went into that melancholy house— that great silent hall—window shutters closed—not a creature to be seen or heard. One man servant appeared at last and as I moved towards that side of the house where I had formerly been 'Not that way Ma'am walk in here if you please' and then came in black that maid of whose attachment the Duchess the last time I saw her had spoken highly and *truly* as I now saw— by the first look and words 'Too true Ma'am. *She* is gone from us! Her Grace died on Saturday.' 'Was the Duke in Town?' 'Yes Ma'am—beside her.' Not a word more on that subject but I was glad to know that certain. Lord Charles arrived in time—not Lord Douro. The Duchess had re- mained nearly as I saw her on the sofa for a fortnight—then had been worse and had been confined to her bed some days but afterwards seemed much better—had been up again and in that room and on the sofa as well apparently as when we heard her conversing so calmly so charmingly. They had no apprehension of her danger nor had she herself as the maid told me till friday morning when she was seized with violent pain! (Cancer I believe it was)—and she continued in torture till she died on Saturday morning 'calm and resigned'. The poor maid could hardly speak. She went in and brought me a lock of her mistress's hair—silver grey—all but a few light brown that just recalled the beautiful Kitty Pakenham's formerly! So ended that sweet innocent—shall we say happy or unhappy life of hers! *Happy* I think—*through all*—in her good feelings and good conscience and warm affections—still loving on! Happy in her faith—her hope and her charity— Yes happier I am sure than those who injured her can ever have been or ever be. (Just as I had written so far before breakfast I asked Fanny whether she had told you of the Duchess of Wellington's death and when I found she had I was going to tear this but Fanny held my hand and insisted on my sending it.)

I drove away and then came back all the bustle of this living world which goes on let who will die or who will feel—and it must be so. I went to Whitehall place to return Mrs Stanleys visit and there saw the Secretary for Ireland the youngest looking statesman I ever saw and he was in the midst of bustle of election thoughts and preparation for going to Ireland. 'We shall get into the Phoenix at last' said he. Phoenix! At first—my head not being very clear did not understand *Phoenix park* but thought of Phoenix insurance office.

What a dreadful fire that in Harley Street! Lord Walsingham—Wretched man! All the newspapers said about his going to bed intoxicated was true and he had the habit of reading in bed and trying to do so in this state it is supposed set fire to the curtains. The butterman with whom Fanny deals told her cook that he had been much shocked by Lord Walsingham's death because he had seen him the very day before a few hours before in such a brutal passion. Lord Walsingham had sent for a cream cheese—there was not one to be had. When his servant told him so he doubting that the servant had told him truth went down to the shop himself and finding it was truth and that he could not have the *cheese* scolded and stormed and that was the last seen of him—till they heard next morning of his horrid death.

His Lordships body was not found for some days and then in such a state—the head and feet burned off. Lady Walsingham a poor nervous lady was so terrified when her servant opened her door (she did not sleep in Lord Walsingham's room) and told her the house was on fire that she immediately threw up the sash and jumped out of the window into the back yard. Why the servant did not hold her back by force I cannot concieve. She was dreadfully smashed. They lifted her up and put her into the coachman's bed and she died in a few hours.

I have not written to you this week past because all my leisure moments have been taken up in writing 2 folio sheets of Chinese light paper to dear

Francis who had taken it into his wise head that I had taken something ill
of him because I had not written these 2 months. If he knew how many notes
about nothing I have to answer. And here are three authoress's books lying
unread on the table before me and letters of thanks that must be penned—
Mrs S. C. Hall superb silk and morocco copy of Old and new Irish sketches
the 2d volume dedicated to Miss E with warmest sentiments &c Next a
novel in 3 volumes Abroad & at Home (which by the by was the title of the
first sketch of Belinda). This Abroad & at Home is by Mrs Eaton née
Waldy v Rome in the 19th Cent—and there is a preface with much about
Miss E in it which neither Miss E nor anybody else in this house has yet
had time to read—But answered she must be—by and by. Then there is
Geraldine Desmond—time of Elizabeth—3 volumes and long preface and
Miss E in it—and very learned notes which tho uncut I can see are long
and learned—and it is a book of great pretension by Miss Crumpe who
sent it me with a note and a card and it was impossible not to return her
visit—which accordingly I did yesterday (after having breakfasted with
Rogers). Luckily as I thought she was not at home and I felt clear off but
at night found on the table in hall another note from Miss Crumpe—'could
not leave to chance opportunity of seeing Miss E—regrets disappointment—will wait upon her at one on saturday'. So I must finish this letter
to be ready for her.

The breakfast at Rogers's was very agreeable—only that he had not
asked Fanny with me. His sister as young and old as ever and as goodnatured
presided. Lord Normanby grown within the last month into Lord
Mulgrave—Mr Luttrell and Tommy Moore. Mr Luttrell was in very good
humor and very witty and pleasant. Mrs Lockhart saw him in a very
different pin one morning at breakfast at Rogers he came in late and
snapped at every creature living and dead. Lord Mulgrave is a very handsome gentlemanlike fashionable person—black hair well curled and very
like a picture—I think his own—which I have seen somewhere—or in a
dream. He conversed well and told many anecdotes Foreign and domestic—especially of *Landor*—whose poems (new) lay on the table (N B—His
shaking a Florence judge by the ends of his cravat—in a fury—His fancying a Florence beauty in love with him—offering to be her Cicisbeo—and
how received).

Friday
Fanny had a dinner at home yesterday and a very pleasant evening
party and all went off delightfully—Dinner—Mrs and Miss Holland—
Mrs and Mr Horsley Palmer and eldest son—contemporary of Francis at
Charterhouse—Mr Whishaw—Mr Chantrey and Sneyd and Pakenham
and selves. Sneyd had arrived in the morning and was delighted to dine

here. Chantrey and Horsley Palmer you might not guess had aught in common but they had—about the coinage—alloy of metals—in which I should never have guessed Chantrey was skilled. But he has been consulted much about the designs for coins and medals and learned all about the alloys of metals for himself. 5 different dies were made and broke for the last coinage before they got one that would stand. But I'm only telling you that the dinner was excellent and well attended by a professional Butler *added* to Smith and John—My aunt Mary's icepails much admired by Sneyd. Chantrey and Pakenham suited well and talked charmingly across Fanny at dinner. Chantrey is a fine jolly hearted being and he told me he sat for *Sancho* once to a painter who could not hit off a Sancho.

In the evening besides the diners came Mrs Hofland and son—Mr Willing (an American from Mr Ralston—very agreeable and gentleman-like)—Mr Drummond—Mr and Mrs Guillemard—Miss Gilbert nice girl Mrs Somerville and Mrs Chantrey—Mrs Horner and her daughter and William Carr. These people spreading through the two drawing rooms stood and sat well and were not the least crowded and there was a great variety of conversation and all seemed happy . . .

Oh it is impossible to give you an idea of the talking and hurry-flurry about elections at this moment. You know quite as much as either party here I am sure how the elections will turn out. I forgot to tell you that I dined at Lansdowne house on tuesday—Mr and *Mrs Osman Ricardo*—just the same charming amiable person—Mr Milne just he same—dry and opiniated and clever and wearisome—Mr Lubbock Junr.—silent man—clever I'm assured—Mr Corbin—American very agreeable—Mr Murray *not* the bookseller but from Scotland—and I found out tell Harriet that he can be very entertaining—sat beside him at Dinner.

The result of all I heard at Lansdowne house convinced me that *that* party are in great doubt how the elections will turn out but as far as I can *guess* it will be favorably for the *Bill* and the present Ministry. Even if the majority should be against them and Peel and Duke of Wellington should come in it is thought by all and said *now* by the Tory party that they must and would grant some kind of reform for instance members for Manchester and Birmingham. 'But save my Boroughs Heaven' would be their first and last. And if a few rotten ones were left to drop off, I am not sure whether it might not be best to let the rest alone.

I enclose 'a leaf from future history of England' which was given to me by Lord Mahon and is written by him not published. It was written for the end of the Article in new Quarterly on reform. Lockhart as Murray the bookseller told me thought it too jocular for the present *serious* moment and had the pages taken out persuading Lord Mahon that in consequence of the Dissolution of Parliament it was necessary to make a new ending to the

article. I think the rejected leaf very good except the hit which is a miss at
Sydney Smith—and how foolish to make an enemy for *nothing* of such a
man. Rogers at his breakfast settled that he and the company at breakfast
would have done the same thing better—I doubt it . . .

'Talking of coincidencies' as Mr Ward would say—The other day we
went down to Gravesend you know to see the Minerva and Pakenham's
birth. Mrs Probyn after doing the first honors of our reception on deck
came to me and said 'Here is a lady who says you met her mother and sister
at Slough and begs to be made known to you.' Mrs Lowther a sister of Mrs
Gwatkin Sir Joshua Reynolds niece—Very well—that was something of a
coincidence that she and a young niece should be going out to join her
husband in India in the Minerva with my brother at this time. But go on—
after sitting beside me some time—she mentioned that her husband lives
at *Meerut*—Collector. At the word *Meerut* Pakenham said to me 'That is
the place where Harry Bohle is.' 'Mr Bohle! Oh I know him very well'
cried this sister of Sir Joshua Reynolds niece. 'Mr Bohle I see often he is
our factotum.' He lives about 40 miles from their country house. She says
he is a very clever fellow—that everybody knows him.

She went down to the cabin soon afterwards to write a letter and she
petitioned me to give her my autograph—a few lines a few sentences in her
album. You know how I detest the Album and autograph nonsense but as
she can be good to Pak I complied and she was so well pleased that she
promised to send me a little sketch done by the hand of Sir Joshua Reynolds.
If she remembers it how much I shall be obliged to her but I don't expect
it—too much! too much! I shall be quite content if she is goodnatured to
Pakenham on the voyage and after.

Fanny has told you about his 7 Haileybury companions and his birth and
chum. I liked his chum Maltby very much and his cabin as well as I can like
any cabin in ship. Fanny thinks she did not mention to you a Mr Martin
a wondrous rich East Indian who is going out in the Minerva to see his
mother. He has a superb cabin fitted up with a gilt backed nice collection
of books and luxurious low sofas all round &c &c and they say that Mr
Martin will make this cabin very agreeable during the voyage to his select
parties. It chanced that I was looking over the library I said to somebody
that I thought I could have added some entertaining books to his collection
and I mentioned Captain Halls *new* book. Some days afterwards came a
note from Mrs Skinner that most goodnatured of female Pidcocks who is
the kindest of lion hunters and lion shewwomen. Mr Martin had been told
she heard by somebody who had heard Miss E say that she could have
recommended some books to Mr Martin. In short she advised me to send
him a list in my own handwriting (invaluable) and she was sure he would
do I don't know how much for Pakenham on sea and land. So this morning

at 7 I made a list and my note and I hope P may be the better of it—Little worth it was.

But here comes Mr South—Mr South I have never seen—Enter and stay he did!! and talk he did! Oh how much but much more agreeably than I expected! And a great deal of heart he has I'm sure—for Robinson especially—*and* remarkably civil to me and I pushed Pakenham and his going to India forward and his wish to see everything worth seeing &c. So Mr South has asked him to breakfast and see all things and we are to go there after P is gone—Oh melancholy words—next Sunday—luncheon.

Scarcely had I settled here at my little table in library window to pen and ink work again when *'Miss Crumpe Ma'am'* announced by Smith in his most aggravating tone. *'She is in the drawing room Ma'am.'* So out I went— a very handsome too magnificently dressed lady!—about 30—and a squeezed up poke bonnetted old mother that looks and speaks as if she never had been used to sit at good mens or womens tables. I recollected at sight that these were the people that Lockhart had described to me as having met at an odd dinner given by Campbell to which he had entrapped the Countess de Salis. Lockhart said that Campbell was over head in love with the young lady and that she drank too much Champagne and that the mother was 'like a body from the streets—Regent Street now!' But this was satirical exaggeration. Still there was something too like it. Miss Crumpe talked and talked—on admiration—of me and of herself—and a nervous fever she had had pending the fate and reviews of her novel and then all the 16 reviews there had been of it and how she could feel or remember much about them I could not from any nature or experience of my own concieve.

Then the mother asked me about a horrid trial of Luke Dillon of which I had never heard and she was wonderful surprised. Both ladies are from Limerick or neighborhood and Cats I should guess. Be that as may they both began at once to tell me the whole story—'not seduction Miss Edgeworth' said the young lady 'but much worse'. And all the worse and all that could be told they a l'envie l'une de l'autre told with all details and in a way which you could not have told it to me alone or I to you they retold it. Fanny came in and sat and could not look. 'And the man is to be hung I hear.' 'But why did the young lady go into a house with him by the way to eat and drink?' 'She was a Catholic and from Tipperary or Roscommon so it was no way strange to her.' All I can say is that Miss Crumpe may have every virtue and accomplishment but she wants the natural feeling of modesty and yet all she said was quite moral and high-sentimental—very strange mixture. And at last they went away and then it was luncheon time and now having finished *that* I must make up this packet because the carriage will be at the door in 2 minutes.

Fanny is much better and was not killed off by her two dinners. Lestock was pleased and as far as I could judge pleased. I am sure his wines did—Champagne and Sauterne and Hock—and Claret & co and Constantia and Noyau &c &c. And pray remember that I dont forget to tell you about a *chicken and maccaroni pye*—Savoury pye or by whatever name—Much approved by Conoscenti.

I forgot to tell you that our windows escaped unbroken the night of the illuminations. Lestock had ordered that if the mob came half a dozen candles should be stuck up in drawing room windows. There they were prepared stuck in wine bottles. A *poor* but numerous mob came from Grosvenor Square pouring about 12 oclock and as they rushed I shouted Huzzas and Lights. The candles were lighted but none were put up in F's bedchamber nor in mine nor in my dressing room and the mob after poking sticks in at the windows of next door kitchen passed on shouting—Many women in straw bonnets and children running and shouting as they ran—an odious noise and I saw and heard no more after they died away at the end of the street. I went to bed and fast asleep—and heard next day—*all* you have seen in the papers. It is true that they began to break windows at Apsley House and were fired at by servants and stopped when policemen told them that the Duchess's corpse lay in the house. Crockford's—£60 worth of thick plate glass broke. *Can* no more

yr ever

M E

Duchess of Wellington] née Catherine Pakenham, the daughter of Lord Longford, to whom Edgeworth's father was related by marriage.   Apsley House] Wellington's London residence, but the couple had long been apart.   *Phoenix park*] the official residence of the Lord-Lieutenant of Ireland.   Mrs S. C. Hall . . . Mrs Eaton] novelists.   Geraldine Desmond] a novel with an Irish setting by Miss Crumpe.   Rogers] Samuel Rogers, a banker poet, famous for his breakfasts.   Luttrell] Henry Luttrell, a wit and a poet.   Moore] Thomas Moore, author of *Irish Melodies*, friend of Byron.   Landor] W. S. Landor's *Gebir* had just appeared.   Cicisbeo] licensed lover of a married Italian lady.

SIR WALTER SCOTT
(1771–1832)

118. To Joanna Baillie, April 1816

Joanna Baillie (1762–1851), dramatist and poet, called by Scott 'the immortal Joanna', had written to tell him of Byron's disgraceful treatment of his wife, and ask him to entreat Byron to allow her a generous settlement on their separation (the terms of the marriage settlement awarded practically all her money to her husband). Scott declined to intervene directly. Baillie wrote again to say Byron had left the country ('and will I hope return no more') after a settlement more satisfactory to his wife.

My dear friend,

I am glad you are satisfied with my reasons for declining a direct interference with Lord B[yron]. I have not however been quite idle and as an old seaman have tried to go by a side wind when I had not the means of going before it and this will be so far plain to you when I say that I have every reason to believe the good intelligence is true that a separation is signed between Lord and Lady Byron. If I am not so angry as you have good reason to expect every thinking and feeling man to be it is from deep sorrow and regret that a man possessed of such noble talents should so utterly and irretrieveably lose himself. In short I believe the thing to be as you state it and therefore Lord Byron is the object of anything rather than indignation. It is a cruel pity that such high talents should have been joined to a mind so wayward and incapable of seeking content where alone it is to be found in the quiet discharge of domestic duties and filling up in peace and affection his station in society. The idea of his ultimately resisting that which should be fair and honourable to Lady B. did not come within my view of his character at least of his natural character but I hear that as you intimated he has had execrable advisers. I hardly know a more painful object of consideration than a man of genius in such a situation those of lower minds do not feel the degradation and become like pigs familiarized with the filthy elements in which they grovel but it is impossible that a man of Lord Byrons genius should not often feel the want of that which he has forfeited the fair esteem of those by whom genius most naturally desires to be admired and cherished.—I am much obliged to Mrs Baillie for excluding me in her general censure of authors but I should have hoped for a more general spirit of toleration from my good friend who had in her own family and under her own eye such an exception to her general censure— unless indeed (which may not be far from the truth) she supposes that female genius is more gentle and tractable though as high in tone and spirit as that of the masculine sex. But the truth is I believe we will find a great equality when the different habits of the sexes and the temptations they are exposed to are taken into consideration. Men early flatterd and coaxd and told they are fitted for the higher regions of genius and unfit for anything else, that they are a superior kind of automaton and ought to move by different impulses than others indulging their friends and the public with freaks and caprioles like those of that worthy knight of La Mancha in Sierra Morena. And then, if our man of genius escapes this temptation how is he to parry the opposition of the blockheads who join all their hard head and horns together to but him out of the ordinary pasture send him back to Parnassus and 'bid him on the barren mountain starve'—It is amazing how far this goes if a man will let it go in turning him out of the ordinary course of life and into the stream of odd-bodies so that authors come to be regarded as tumblers who are expected to go to church in a summerset because they sometimes throw a Catherine-wheel for the amusement of the public. A man once told me at an Election thinking I believe he was saying a severe thing that I was a *poet* and therefore that the subject we were discussing lay out of my way. I answerd as quietly as I could that I did not apprehend my having written poetry renderd me incapable of speaking common sense in prose and that I requested the audience to judge of me not by the nonsense I might have [written for] their amusement but by the sober sense I was endeavouring to speak for their information and only expected them in case I had ever happend to give any of them pleasure in a way which was supposed to require some information and talent they would not for that sole reason suppose me incapable of understanding or explaining a point of the profession to which I had been educated. So I got a patient and very favourable hearing. But certainly these joint exertions of friends and enemies have forced many a poor fellow out of the common path of life and obliged him to make a trade of what can only be gracefully executed as an occasional avocation. When such a man is encouraged in all his freaks and frolics the bit is taken out of his mouth and as he is turnd out upon the common he is very apt to deem himself exempt from all the rules incumbent on those who keep the kings highway—And so they play fantastic tricks before high heaven—The lady authors are not exempt from these vagaries being exposed to the same temptations and all I can allow Mrs Baillie in favour of the fair sex is that since the days of the Afra's and Orinda's of Charles IId's time the authoresses have been chiefly ridiculous only while the authors have too often been both absurd and vicious. As to our feal friend Tom Campbell I have heard stories of his morbid sensibility chiefly from the Minto family with whom he lived for some time and I think they all turnd on little foolish points of capricious affectation which perhaps had no better foundation than in an ill-imagined mode of exhibiting his independence. But whatever I saw of him myself and we were often together and sometimes for several days was open quiet composed and manly. Indeed I never worried him to make him get on his hind legs and spout poetry when he did not like it. He deserves independence well and if the day which now awakes him merely to the recollection his possessing it happened formerly to disturb the short sleep that drownd the recollection of the want of so great a blessing there is good reason for enduring the disturbance with more patience than before.

But surely admitting all our temptations and all our irregularities there are men of genius enough living to redeem the mere possession of talent from the charge of disqualifying the owner for the ordinary occupations and duties of life. There never were better men and especially better husbands and fathers and real patriots than Southey and Wordsworth they might even be pitchd upon as most exemplary characters. I myself if I may rank myself in the list am as Hamlet says indifferent honest and at least not worse than an infidel in loving those of my own house. And I think generally speaking that authors like actors being rather less commonly believed to be eccentric than was the faith fifty years since do conduct themselves as amenable to the ordinary rules of society.

This tirade was begun a long time since but is destined to be finishd at Abbotsford. Your bower is all planted with its evergreens but must for some years retain its original aspect of a gravel pit. But my things are on the whole mending in spite of the barest and most unkindly spring I ever witnessed. Positively things looked more forward in february than in the midst of April and I think if the weather does not soon become steady we shall be cured of our national grievance of plenty of cheap meal.

I have added a most romantic inmate to my family a large bloodhound allowd to be the finest dog of the kind in Scotland perfectly gentle affectionate and good-natured and the darling of all the children. I had him in a present from Glengarry who has refused the breed to people of the very first rank. He is between the deer greyhound and mastiff with a shaggy mane like a lion and always sits beside me at dinner—his head as high as the back of my chair. Yet it will gratify you to know that a favorite cat keeps him in the greatest possible order insists upon all rights of precedence and scratches with impunity the nose of an animal who would make no bones of a wolf and pulls down a red-deer without fear or difficulty. I heard my friend set up some most piteous howls and I assure you the noise was no joke—all occasioned by his fear of passing puss who had stationed himself on the stairs.

I am very glad to hear Terry's play is like to do him good service. He speaks highly of the setting of your beautiful song 'The chough and crow' and if the music answers the words he cannot say too much for it. He is a very deserving man and a modest member of rather a forward and self sufficient profession. I am truly sorry at their using Sotheby so ill. But in fact the present management of the London theatres ought to disgust as it has done almost without exception any person of taste or genius to write for them.

Charlotte & I are here alone the weather very ungenial. We join in kindest love to Miss Agnes Baillie to the Dr and Mrs Baillie and I need not say how much I wish to live in your memory As your sincere and affectionate friend

Walter Scott

Mrs Baillie] Joanna's mother. Bid him . . . starve] *1 Henry IV*, I. iii. 89 ('. . . on the barren mountains let him starve'). Summerset] somersault. Fantastic tricks . . . heaven] *Measure for Measure*, II. ii. 121. Feal] loyal. Tom Campbell] Thomas Campbell

(1777–1844), Scottish poet.   Indifferent honest] *Hamlet*, III. i. 121.   Terry] Daniel
Terry, actor and playwright, who made several adaptations of Scott for the stage, including a
musical based on *Guy Mannering*.   Sotheby] William Sotheby, a small poet; his plays
(despite Byron's support) failed.

119. To Abel Moysey, 15 June 1819

Moysey wrote *Forman: A Tale* in 3 vols. (1819).

Mr Walter Scott is at a loss whether to address his anonymous correspondent as serious or in jest. Many of his compliments are to be considered as
a little hyperbolical and what is much worse his congratulations upon
Mr Scott's restoration to health are unhappily premature. He is however
recovering from a painful disease under a severe and unpleasing medical
treatment. So that at no time could he be more grateful for the present of
a good novel & such he ventures to pronounce Forman. The supernatural
part is very well managed & much more satisfactory that there is no
attempt to explain it away by natural causes. A tale of witchcraft was once
to be received with as little doubt as a passage of scripture and therefore is
a species of machinery of which the author of a work of fiction is entitled
by all the rules of composition to avail himself. But these lame explanations
are more improbable than the existence of the black art itself and always
disgust the reader. Mr S. is not sure that the comic passages are managed
with the same [*illegible*]. Jas. vi (your Jas. i) is represented as a drunken
driveller. The 'wisest fool in Christendom' ought to have had a more
marked character. I have sometimes thought his wit, his shrewdness, his
pedantry, his self-importance & vanity, his greed & his prodigality, his love
of minions & his pretensions to wisdom made him one of the richest
characters for comedy who ever existed in real history. The author will
pardon Mr S. the frankness of his criticism and judge by it of the sincerity
of his praise. He is not able to write more at present the use of the pen
having been in great measure prohibited.

LORD BYRON
(1788–1824)

In 1816 George Gordon, Lord Byron left England for ever, having, in the previous
five years, had affairs with his half-sister Augusta Leigh and with Lady Caroline
Lamb. He had also, in 1815, married Annabella Milbanke, who soon left him.

120. To Thomas Moore, 28 January 1817

Moore (1779–1852), author of *Irish Melodies*, was at first an enemy, then a favourite
of Byron's, whose *Letters and Journals* he edited (1830).

Your letter of the 8th is before me. The remedy for your plethora is
simple—abstinence. I was obliged to have recourse to the like some years
ago, I mean in point of *diet*, and, with the exception of some convivial
weeks and days, (it might be months, now and then), have kept to Pythago-
ras ever since. For all this, let me hear that you are better. You must not
indulge in 'filty beer,' nor in porter, nor eat *suppers*—the last are the devil
to those who swallow dinner *

I am truly sorry to hear of your father's misfortune—cruel at any time,
but doubly cruel in advanced life. However, you will, at least, have the
satisfaction of doing your part by him, and, depend upon it, it will not be
in vain. Fortune, to be sure, is a female, but not such a b * * as the rest
(always excepting your wife and my sister from such sweeping terms); for
she generally has some justice in the long run. I have no spite against her,
though between her and Nemesis I have had some sore gauntlets to run—
but then I have done my best to deserve no better. But to *you*, she is a good
deal in arrear, and she will come round—mind if she don't: you have the
vigour of life, of independence, of talent, spirit, and character all with you.
What you can do for yourself, you have done and will do; and surely there
are some others in the world who would not be sorry to be of use, if you
would allow them to be useful, or at least attempt it.

I think of being in England in the spring. If there is a row, by the sceptre
of King Ludd, but I'll be one; and if there is none, and only a continuance
of 'this meek, piping time of peace,' I will take a cottage a hundred yards
to the south of your abode, and become your neighbour; and we will
compose such canticles, and hold such dialogues, as shall be the terror of
the *Times* (including the newspaper of that name), and the wonder, and
honour, and praise, of the Morning Chronicle and posterity.

I rejoice to hear of your forthcoming in February—though I tremble for
the 'magnificence,' which you attribute to the new Childe Harold. I am
glad you like it; it is a fine indistinct piece of poetical desolation, and my
favourite. I was half mad during the time of its composition, between
metaphysics, mountains, lakes, love unextinguishable, thoughts unutterable, and the nightmare of my own delinquencies. I should, many a good
day, have blown my brains out, but for the recollection that it would have
given pleasure to my mother-in-law; and, even *then*, if I could have been
certain to haunt her—but I won't dwell upon these trifling family matters.

Venice is in the *estro* of her carnival, and I have been up these last two
nights at the ridotto and the opera, and all that kind of thing. Now for

an adventure. A few days ago a gondolier brought me a billet without a subscription, intimating a wish on the part of the writer to meet me either in gondola or at the island of San Lazaro, or at a third rendezvous, indicated in the note. 'I know the country's disposition well'—in Venice 'they do let Heaven see those tricks they dare not show,' &c. &c.; so, for all response, I said that neither of the three places suited me; but that I would either be at home at ten at night *alone*, or at the ridotto at midnight, where the writer might meet me masked. At ten o'clock I was at home and alone (Marianna was gone with her husband to a conversazione), when the door of my apartment opened, and in walked a well-looking and (for an Italian) *bionda* girl of about nineteen, who informed me that she was married to the brother of my *amorosa*, and wished to have some conversation with me. I made a decent reply, and we had some talk in Italian and Romaic (her mother being a Greek of Corfu), when lo! in a very few minutes, in marches, to my very great astonishment, Marianna S[egati], *in propria persona*, and after making polite courtesy to her sister-in-law and to me, without a single word seizes her said sister-in-law by the hair, and bestows upon her some sixteen slaps, which would have made your ear ache only to hear their echo. I need not describe the screaming which ensued. The luckless visitor took flight. I seized Marianna, who, after several vain efforts to get away in pursuit of the enemy, fairly went into fits in my arms; and, in spite of reasoning, eau de Cologne, vinegar, half a pint of water, and God knows what other waters beside, continued so till past midnight.

After damning my servants for letting people in without apprizing me, I found that Marianna in the morning had seen her sister-in-law's gondolier on the stairs, and, suspecting that his apparition boded her no good, had either returned of her own accord, or been followed by her maids or some other spy of her people to the conversazione, from whence she returned to perpetrate this piece of pugilism. I had seen fits before, and also some small scenery of the same genus in and out of our island: but this was not all. After about an hour, in comes—who? why, Signor S[egati], her lord and husband, and finds me with his wife fainting upon the sofa, and all the apparatus of confusion, dishevelled hair, hats, handkerchiefs, salts, smelling-bottles—and the lady as pale as ashes without sense or motion. His first question was, 'What is all this?' The lady could not reply—so I did. I told him the explanation was the easiest thing in the world; but in the mean time it would be as well to recover his wife—at least, her senses. This came about in due time of suspiration and respiration.

You need not be alarmed—jealousy is not the order of the day in Venice, and daggers are out of fashion; while duels, on love matters, are unknown—at least, with the husbands. But, for all this, it was an awkward affair; and though he must have known that I made love to Marianna, yet

I believe he was not, till that evening, aware of the extent to which it had gone. It is very well known that almost all the married women have a lover; but it is usual to keep up the forms, as in other nations. I did not, therefore, know what the devil to say. I could not out with the truth, out of regard to her, and I did not choose to lie for my sake;—besides, the thing told itself. I thought the best way would be to let her explain it as she chose (a woman being never at a loss—the devil always sticks by them)—only determining to protect and carry her off, in case of any ferocity on the part of the Signor. I saw that he was quite calm. She went to bed, and next day—how they settled it, I know not, but settle it they did. Well—then I had to explain to Marianna about this never to be sufficiently confounded sister-in-law; which I did by swearing innocence, eternal constancy, &c. &c. * * * But the sister-in-law, very much discomposed with being treated in such wise, has (not having her own shame before her eyes) told the affair to half Venice, and the servants (who were summoned by the fight and the fainting) to the other half. But, here, nobody minds such trifles, except to be amused by them. I don't know whether you will be so, but I have scrawled a long letter out of these follies.

Believe me ever. &c.

Kept to Pythagoras] been a vegetarian.   Misfortune] Moore's father, a Dublin barrack-master, had lost his job.   This meek . . . peace] *Richard III*, I. i. 24 ('this weak . . . peace'). Forthcoming] Moore's *Lalla Rookh* (1817).   *Estro*] height of animation.   I know . . . show] *Othello*, III. iii. 201–3 ('our country disposition . . . the pranks . . .').   Marianna] Segati was at this time Byron's landlady and mistress.   The asterisks signify cuts made by Moore when he published the letter, of which no other version survives.

121. To John Murray, 1 August 1819

With his publisher Murray (1779–1817) Byron had a relationship alternately stormy and cordial.

Dear Sir,

Don't be alarmed.—You will see me defend myself gaily—that is—if I happen to be in Spirits—and by *Spirits* I don't mean your meaning of the word—but the spirit of a bull-dog when pinched—or a bull when pinned— it is then that they make best sport—and as my Sensations under an attack are probably a happy compound of the united energies of those amiable animals—you may perhaps see what Marrall calls 'rare sport'—and some good tossing and goring in the course of the controversy.—But I must be in the right cue first—and I doubt I am almost too far off to be in a sufficient fury for the purpose—and then I have effeminated and enervated myself with love and the summer in these last two months.—I wrote to Mr Hobhouse the other day—and foretold that Juan would either fall entirely or succeed completely—there will be no medium—appearances are not favourable—but as you write the day after publication—it can hardly be decided what opinion will predominate.—You seem in a fright—and doubtless with cause.—Come what may—I never will flatter the Million's canting in any shape—circumstances may or may not have placed me at times in a situation to lead the public opinion—but the public opinion— never led nor ever shall lead me.—I will not sit on 'a degraded throne' so pray put Messrs Southey—or Sotheby—or Tom Moore—or Horace Twiss upon it—they will all of them be transported with their coronation.—— You have bought Harlow's drawings of Margarita and me rather dear methinks—but since you desire the story of Margarita Cogni—you shall be told it—though it may be lengthy.——Her face is of the fine Venetian cast of the old Time—and her figure though perhaps too tall not less fine— taken altogether in the national dress.——In the summer of 1817, Hobhouse and myself were sauntering on horseback along the Brenta one evening— when amongst a group of peasants we remarked two girls as the prettiest we had seen for some time.—About this period there had been great distress in the country—and I had a little relieved some of the people.— Generosity makes a great figure at very little cost in Venetian livres—and mine had probably been exaggerated—as an Englishman's——Whether they remarked us looking at them or no—I know not—but one of them called out to me in Venetian—'Why do not you who relieve others—think of us also?'—I turned round and answered her—'Cara—tu sei troppo bella e giovane per aver' bisogno del' soccorso mio'—she answered—[']if you saw my hut and my food—you would not say so[']—All this passed half jestingly—and I saw no more of her for some days—A few evenings af- ter—we met with these two girls again—and they addressed us more seriously—assuring us of the truth of their statement.—They were cous- ins—Margarita married—the other single.—As I doubted still of the cir- cumstances—I took the business up in a different light—and made an appointment with them for the next evening.—Hobhouse had taken a fancy to the single lady—who was much shorter—in stature—but a very pretty girl also.——They came attended by a third woman—who was cursedly in the way—and Hobhouse's charmer took fright (I don't mean at Hobhouse but at not being married—for here no woman will do anything under adultery), and flew off—and mine made some bother—at the propo- sitions—and wished to consider of them.—I told her 'if you really are in want I will relieve you without any conditions whatever—and you may make love with me or no just as you please—*that* shall make no differ- ence—but if you are not in absolute necessity—this is naturally a rendez- vous—and I presumed that you understood this—when you made the appointment'.——She said that she had no objection to make love with me—as she was married—and all married women did it—but that her

husband (a baker) was somewhat ferocious—and would do her a mischief.—In short—in a few evenings we arranged our affairs—and for two
years—in the course of which I had [almost two] more women than I can
count or recount—she was the only one who preserved over me an ascendancy—which was often disputed & never impaired.—As she herself used
to say publicly—'It don't matter—he may have five hundred—but he will
always come back to me'.——The reasons of this were firstly—her person—very dark—tall—the Venetian face—very fine black eyes—and certain other qualities which need not be mentioned.—She was two & twenty
years old—and never having had children—had not spoilt her figure—nor
anything else—which is I assure you—a great desideration in a hot climate
where they grow relaxed and doughy and *flumpity* in a short time after
breeding.——She was besides a thorough Venetian in her dialect—in her
thoughts—in her countenance—in every thing—with all their naïveté and
Pantaloon humour.—Besides she could neither read nor write—and could
not plague me with letters—except twice that she paid sixpence to a public
scribe under the piazza—to make a letter for her—upon some occasion
when I was ill and could not see her.——In other respects she was somewhat fierce and 'prepotente' that is—overbearing—and used to walk in
whenever it suited her—with no very great regard to time, place, nor
persons—and if she found any women in her way she knocked them
down.—When I first knew her I was in 'relazione' (liaison) with la Signora
Segati—who was silly enough one evening at Dolo—accompanied by
some of her female friends—to threaten her—for the Gossips of the
Villeggiatura—had already found out by the neighing of my horse one
evening—that I used to 'ride late in the night' to meet the Fornarina.——
Margarita threw back her veil (fazziolo) and replied in very explicit
Venetian—'*You* are *not* his *wife*: *I* am *not* his *wife*—*you* are his Donna—
and *I* am his *donna*—*your* husband is a cuckold—and mine is another;—for
the rest, what *right* have you to reproach me?—if he prefers what is mine—
to what is yours—is it my fault? if you wish to secure him—tie him to your
petticoat-string—but do not think to speak to me without a reply because
you happen to be richer than I am.'——Having delivered this pretty piece
of eloquence (which I translate as it was related to me by a byestander) she
went on her way—leaving a numerous audience with Madame Segati—to
ponder at her leisure on the dialogue between them.—When I came to
Venice for the Winter she followed:—I never had any regular *liaison* with
her—but whenever she came I never allowed any other connection to
interfere with her—and as she found herself out to be a favourite she came
pretty often.—But She had inordinate Self-love—and was not tolerant of
other women—except of the Segati—who was as she said my regular
'Amica'—so that I being at that time somewhat promiscuous—there was

great confusion—and demolition of head dresses and handkerchiefs—
and sometimes my servants in 'redding the fray' between her and other
feminine persons—received more knocks than acknowledgements for their
peaceful endeavours.——At the 'Cavalchina' the masqued ball on the last
night of the Carnival—where all the World goes—she snatched off the
mask of Madame Contarini—a lady noble by birth—and decent in conduct—for no other reason but because she happened to be leaning on my
arm.—You may suppose what a cursed noise this made—but this is only
one of her pranks.—At last she quarrelled with her husband—and one
evening ran away to my house.—I told her this would not do—she said she
would lie in the street but not go back to him—that he beat her (the gentle
tigress) spent her money—and scandalously neglected his Oven. As it was
Midnight—I let her stay—and next day there was no moving her at all.—
—Her husband came roaring & crying—& entreating her to come back, *not*
She!—He then applied to the Police—and they applied to me—I told
them and her husband to *take* her—I did not want her—she had come and
I could not fling her out of the window—but they might conduct her
through that or the door if they chose it——She went before the Commis-
sary—but was obliged to return with that 'becco Ettico' (consumptive
cuckold), as she called the *poor* man who had a Ptisick.—In a few days she
ran away again.—After a precious piece of work she fixed herself in my
house—really & truly without my consent—but owing to my indolence—
and not being able to keep my countenance—for if I began in a rage she
always finished by making me laugh with some Venetian pantaloonery or
other—and the Gipsy knew this well enough—as well as her other powers
of persuasion—and exerted them with the usual tact and success of all She-
things—high and low—they are all alike for that.—Madame Benzone also
took her under her protection—and then her head turned.—She was always in extremes either crying or laughing—and so fierce when angered
that she was the terror of men women and children—for she had the
strength of an Amazon with the temper of Medea. She was a fine animal—
but quite untameable. *I* was the only person that could at all keep her in
any order—and when she saw me really angry—(which they tell me is
rather a savage sight), she subsided.—But she had a thousand fooleries—
in her fazziolo—the dress of the lower orders—she looked beautiful—but
alas! she longed for a hat and feathers and all I could say or do (and I said
much) could not prevent this travestie.—I put the first into the fire—but
I got tired of burning them before she did of buying them—so that she
made herself a figure—for they did not at all become her.—Then she
would have her gowns with a *tail*—like a lady forsooth—nothing would
serve her—but 'l'abito colla *coua*', or *cua*, (that is the Venetian for 'la *Coda*'
the tail or train) and as her cursed pronunciation of the word made me

laugh—there was an end of all controversy—and she dragged this diabolical tail after her every where.——In the mean time she beat the women—and stopped my letters.—I found her one day pondering over one—she used to try to find out by their shape whether they were feminine or no—and she used to lament her ignorance—and actually studied her Alphabet—on purpose (as she declared) to open all letters addressed to me and read their contents.——I must not omit to do justice to her housekeeping qualities—after she came into my house as 'donna di governo' the expences were reduced to less than half—and every body did their duty better—the apartments were kept in order—and every thing and every body else except herself.——That she had a sufficient regard for me in her wild way I had many reasons to believe—I will mention one.——In the autumn one day going to the Lido with my Gondoliers—we were overtaken by a heavy Squall and the Gondola put in peril—hats blown away—boat filling—oar lost—tumbling sea—thunder—rain in torrents—night coming—& wind increasing.—On our return—after a tight struggle: I found her on the open steps of the Mocenigo palace on the Grand Canal—with her great black eyes flashing though her tears and the long dark hair which was streaming drenched with rain over her brows & breast;—she was perfectly exposed to the storm—and the wind blowing her hair & dress about her tall thin figure—and the lightning flashing round her—with the waves rolling at her feet—made her look like Medea alighted from her chariot—or the Sibyl of the tempest that was rolling around her—the only living thing within hail at that moment except ourselves.—On seeing me safe—she did not wait to greet me as might be expected—but calling out to me—'Ah! Can' della Madonna xe esto il tempo per andar' al' Lido?' (ah! Dog of the Virgin!—is this a time to go to Lido?) ran into the house—and solaced herself with scolding the boatmen for not foreseeing the 'temporale'.—I was told by the servants that she had only been prevented from coming in a boat to look after me—by the refusal of all the Gondoliers of the Canal to put out into the harbour in such a moment and that then she sate down on the steps in all the thickest of the Squall—and would neither be removed nor comforted. Her joy at seeing me again—was moderately mixed with ferocity—and gave me the idea of a tigress over her recovered Cubs.——But her reign drew near a close.—She became quite ungovernable some months after—and a concurrence of complaints some true and many false—'a favourite has no friend'—determined me to part with her.—I told her quietly that she must return home—(she had acquired a sufficient provision for herself and mother, &c. in my service,) and She refused to quit the house.—I was firm—and she went—threatening knives and revenge.—I told her—that I had seen knives drawn before her time—and that if she chose to begin—there was a knife—and fork also at her service on the table

and that intimidation would not do.—The next day while I was at dinner—she walked in, (having broke open a glass door that led from the hall
below to the staircase by way of prologue) and advancing strait up to the
table snatched the knife from my hand—cutting me slightly in the thumb
in the operation.—Whether she meant to use this against herself or me I
know not—probably against neither—but Fletcher seized her by the arms—
and disarmed her.—I then called my boatmen—and desired them to get
the Gondola ready and conduct her to her own house again—seeing carefully that she did herself no mischief by the way.—She seemed quite quiet
and walked down stairs.—I resumed my dinner.—We heard a great noise—
I went out—and met them on the staircase—carrying her up stairs.—She
had thrown herself into the Canal.—That she intended to destroy herself
I do not believe—but when we consider the fear women and men who can't
swim have of deep or even of shallow water—(and the Venetians in particular though they live on the waves) and that it was also night—and
dark—& very cold—it shows that she had a devilish spirit of some sort
within her.—They had got her out without much difficulty or damage
except the salt water she had swallowed and the wetting she had undergone.—I foresaw her intention to refix herself, and sent for a Surgeon—
enquiring how many hours it would require to restore her from her agitation,
and he named the time.—I then said—'I give you that time—and more if
you require it—but at the expiration of the prescribed period—if *She* does
not leave the house—*I* will'.——All my people were consternated—they
had always been frightened at her—and were now paralyzed—they wanted
me to apply to the police—to guard myself—&c. &c.—like a pack of
sniveling servile boobies as they were——I did nothing of the kind—
thinking that I might as well end that way as another—besides—I had been
used to savage women and knew their ways.—I had her sent home quietly
after her recovery—and never saw her since except twice at the opera—at
a distance amongst the audience.—She made many attempts to return—
but no more violent ones.—And this is the story of Margharita Cogni—as
far as it belongs to me.—I forgot to mention that she was very devout—and
would cross herself if she heard the prayer-time strike—sometimes—when
that ceremony did not appear to be much in unison with what she was then
about.—She was quick in reply—as for instance;—one day when she had
made me very angry with beating somebody or other—I called her a *Cow*
(*Cow* in Italian is a sad affront and tantamount to the feminine of dog in
English) I called her 'Vacca' she turned round—curtsied—and answered
'Vacca *tua*—'Celenza' (i.e. Eccelenza) *your* Cow—please your Excellency.—
In short—she was—as I said before—a very fine Animal—of considerable
beauty and energy—with many good & several amusing qualities—but
wild as a witch—and fierce as a demon.—She used to boast publicly of her

ascendancy over me—contrasting it with that of other women—and assigning for it sundry reasons physical and moral which did more credit to her person than her modesty.——True it was that they all tried to get her away—and no one succeeded—till her own absurdity helped them.—Whenever there was a competition, and sometimes—one would be shut in one room and one in another—to prevent battle—she had generally the preference.——

yrs. very truly and affectly

B

P.S.—The Countess G[uiccioli] is much better than she was.—I sent you before leaving Venice—a letter containing the real original sketch—which gave rise to the 'Vampire' &c. did you get it?—

Rare sport] Massinger, *A New Way to Pay Old Debts*, v. i. ('brave sport').   Southey] Robert Southey (1774–1843), Poet Laureate from 1813, much despised by Byron.   Sotheby] William Sotheby (1757–1833), a lesser poet, also despised.   Horace Twiss] later biographer of Lord Eldon.   Harlow] George Henry Harlow (1787–1819) painted Byron's portrait in London and sketched him in Venice.   Cara . . . mio] My dear, you're too young and beautiful to need my help.   Redding the fray] from Scott's *Waverley*.   Benzone] Countess Benzoni kept a salon, at which Byron met Teresa Guiccioli, with whom he formed a lasting relationship.   Donna di governo] housekeeper.   Temporale] thunderstorm.   'A favourite has no friend'] Thomas Gray, 'Ode on the Death of a Favourite Cat'.   Fletcher] Byron's sometimes reluctant and often teased valet.

BENJAMIN ROBERT HAYDON
(1786–1846)

Haydon, despite poor eyesight, was a painter of such epic subjects as *Christ's Entry into Jerusalem*, which is famous for containing portraits of Wordsworth, Keats, and others. He met Keats at Leigh Hunt's in Oct. 1816. They admired each other greatly—see Keats's sonnet 'Great spirits on the earth are sojourning'—but their friendship cooled because of a loan Haydon did not repay. He died by suicide.

122. To John Keats, March 1817

My dear Keats,

Consider this letter a sacred secret—Often have I sat by my fire after a day's effort, as the dusk approached, and a gauzey veil seemed dimming all things—and mused on what I had done and with a burning glow on what I would do till filled with fury I have seen the faces of the mighty dead crowd into my room, and I have sunk down & prayed the great Spirit that I might be worthy to accompany these immortal beings in their immortal glories, and then I have seen each smile as it passed over me, and each shake [his] hand in awful encouragement—My dear Keats, the Friends

who surrounded me, were sensible to what talent I had,—but no one reflected my enthusiasm with that burning ripeness of soul, my heart yearned
for sympathy,—believe me from my Soul in you I have found one,—you
add fire, when I am exhausted, & excite fury afresh—I offer my heart &
intellect & experience—at first I feared your ardor might lead you to disregard the accumulated wisdom of ages in moral points—but the feelings
put forth lately—have delighted my soul—always consider principle of
more value than genius—and you are safe—[but] because on the score of
genius, you can never be vehement enough—I have read your Sleep &
Poetry—it is a flash of lightening that will sound men from their occupations, and keep them trembling for the crash of thunder that *will* follow—
    God bless you let our hearts be buried in each other
                B R Haydon

Ill be at Reynolds to night but latish
 March 1817—
I confide these feelings to your honor—

Reynolds] J. H. Reynolds, poet and intimate friend of Keats.

SYDNEY SMITH
(1771–1845)

Acknowledged the wittiest man of his age, Smith as a young curate in Edinburgh
helped to found the *Edinburgh Review*, to which he was a frequent contributor. Later
he became an intimate at Holland House, the social centre of the Whigs. Relative
poverty compelled him to accept livings in Yorkshire and Somerset (at Combe
Florey) but in 1831 he became a canon of St Paul's and renewed his social life in
London.

123. To the Farmer's Magazine, *August 1819*

Sir,
 It has been my lot to have passed the greater part of my life in cities—
About six or seven years ago, I was placed in the country, in a situation
where I was under the necessity of becoming a farmer; and amongst the
many expensive blunders I have made, I warn those who may find themselves in similar situations, against *Scotch Sheep* and *Oxen for ploughing*. I
had heard a great deal of the fine flavour of Scotch mutton, and it was one
of the great luxuries I promised myself in farming. A luxury certainly it is;
but the price paid for it is such, that I would rather give up the use of
animal food altogether, than obtain it by such a system of cares and anxieties. Ten times a day my men were called off from their work to hunt the

Scotch sheep out of my own or my neighbour's wheat. They crawled through hedges where I should have thought a rabbit could hardly have found admission; and, where crawling would not do, they had recourse to leaping. Five or six times they all assembled, and set out on their return to the North. My bailiff took a place in the mail, pursued, and overtook them half way to Newcastle. Then it was quite impossible to get them fat. They consumed my turnips in winter, and my clover in the summer, without any apparent addition to their weight; 10 or 12 per cent. always died of the rot; and more would have perished in the same manner, if they had not been prematurely eaten out of the way.

My ploughing oxen were an equal subject of vexation. They had a constant purging upon them, which it was impossible to stop. They ate more than twice as much as the same number of horses. They did half as much work as the same number of horses. They could not bear hot weather, nor wet weather, nor go well down hill. It took five men to shoe an ox. They ran against my gate-posts, lay down in the cart whenever they were tired, and ran away at the sight of a stranger.

I have now got into a good breed of English sheep, and useful cart-horses, and am doing very well. I make this statement to guard young gentlemen farmers against listening to the pernicious nonsense of brother gentlemen, for whose advice I am at least poorer by 300l, or 400l.

Yours etc.

Z

124. To Lady Georgiana Morpeth, 16 February 1820

Dear Lady Georgiana,

   . . . Nobody has suffered more from low spirits than I have done—so I feel for you. 1st. Live as well as you dare. 2nd. Go into the shower-bath with a small quantity of water at a temperature low enough to give you a slight sensation of cold, 75° or 80°. 3rd. Amusing books. 4th. Short views of human life—not further than dinner or tea. 5th. Be as busy as you can. 6th. See as much as you can of those friends who respect and like you. 7th. And of those acquaintances who amuse you. 8th. Make no secret of low spirits to your friends, but talk of them freely—they are always worse for dignified concealment. 9th. Attend to the effects tea and coffee produce upon you. 10th. Compare your lot with that of other people. 11th. Don't expect too much from human life—a sorry business at the best. 12th. Avoid poetry, dramatic representations (except comedy), music, serious novels, melancholy sentimental people, and everything likely to excite feeling or emotion not ending in active benevolence. 13th. *Do good*, and endeavour to please everybody of every degree. 14th. Be as much as you can in the open air without fatigue. 15th. Make the room where you commonly sit, gay and pleasant. 16th. Struggle by little and little against idleness. 17th. Don't be too severe upon yourself, or underrate yourself, but do yourself justice. 18th. Keep good blazing fires. 19th. Be firm and constant in the exercise of rational religion. 20th. Believe me, dear Lady Georgiana,

Very truly yours,
Sydney Smith

Lady Georgiana] see above, Letter 114. She was the wife of George Howard, Viscount Morpeth. Smith had become an intimate at Castle Howard when rector of Foston in Yorkshire. She was pregnant and in low spirits.

125. To John Allen, 9 November 1826

Allen (1771–1843), a physician and historian, and according to Macaulay 'a man of vast information and great conversational powers', was a prominent member of the Holland House set.

Dear Allen,

Pray tell me something about Lord and Lady Holland as it is several centuries since I have seen them. I heard of Lady Holland on a sofa. I thought she had done with sofas. How are you—are you quite well? I was in the same house in Cheshire with Vane but he was too ill to see me; extreme depression of spirits seems to be his complaint, an evil of which I have a full comprehension. Mrs Taylor appears to be really alarmed about him.

Have you finished your squabbles with Lingard? The Catholics are outrageous with you, and I have heard some of the most violent express a doubt whether you are quite an orthodox member of the Church of England.

You will be amused with John Murray's marriage. It was concocted at Mr Philips under the auspices of Mrs Sydney and myself. The lady has £60,000, is a considerable Greek Scholar, a Senior Wrangler in Mathematics and the most perfect Instrumental Musician I ever heard. Ten days finished the matter; indeed she has no time to lose since she is 39. I never saw two longer fatter Lovers, for she is as big as Murray. They looked enormous as they were making love in the plantations. She is so fond of Murray that she pretends to love porridge, cold weather and metaphysics. Seriously speaking it is a very good marriage, and acting under the direction of medical men, with perseverance and the use of stimulating diet there may be an heir to the house of Henderland.

I never saw Lord Carlisle looking so well; is not happiness good for the gout? I think that remedy is at work upon him. I cannot say how agreeable their neighborhood is to me.

I am very glad to find that Mcintosh is really at work upon his History;

it will immortalize him and make Ampthill classical from recollections.

I think of going to Edinburgh in the spring with my family on a visit to Jeffrey who was with us this summer Bag and Baggage. Health and respect my dear Allen, prosperity to the Church, and power to the Clergy.

ever yrs
Sydney Smith

We have seen a good deal of old Whishaw this summer; he is as pleasant as he is wise and honest; he has character enough to make him well received if he was dull and wit enough to make him popular if he was a rogue.

Lingard] Allen had adversely reviewed a *History of England* by the Catholic John Lingard in the *Edinburgh Review*.   John Murray] a Scottish judge, and a contributor to the *Review*. He married Mary Rigby, well known for her musical proficiency.   Lord Carlisle] until 1825 Lord Morpeth.   Mcintosh] Sir James Mackintosh, friend of Lord Holland and author of a *History of the Revolution in England in 1688* (1834).   Ampthill] one of Holland's houses.   Jeffrey] Francis Jeffery, a Scottish judge, co-founder of *the Edinburgh Review* in 1802 and editor till 1829.   Whishaw] James Whishaw, a member of the Holland House circle.

126. To Dr Henry Holland, 8 June 1835

Holland (1788–1873) married Smith's daughter Saba and later became personal physician to Queen Victoria.

My dear Holland,

We shall have the greatest pleasure in receiving you and yours—and if you were twice as numerous it would be so much the better. The Hibberts are arrived well and safe—they had a prosperous journey. Illness must be peculiarly disagreeable to the Duchess of Sutherland, as I take it all Duchesses descend when they die, and there are some peculiar circumstances in the life of that Lady that will certainly not occasion any exemption in her favor. The defunct Duke must by this time be well informed of her infidelities and their first meeting in Tartarus will not therefore be of the most agreeable description.

What do you think of this last piece of Legislation for Boroughs? It was necessary to do a good deal; the question is one of degree. I shall be in town on Tuesday 23rd, and be at Hibbert's house in Weymouth Street—I hope under better auspices than last year. I have followed your directions and therefore deserve a better fortune than fell to my lot on that occasion. Sr Henry Halford is the Mahomet of rhubarb and magnesia—the greatest medical impostor I know.—if once ill he will soon go.

I am suffering from my old complaint, the Hay-fever (as it is calld). My fear is of perishing by deliquescence.—I melt away in Nasal and Lachrymal profluvia. My remedies are warm Pediluvium, Cathartics, topical application of a watery solution of Opium to eyes ears, and the interior of the nostrils. The membrane is so irritable, that light, dust, contradiction, an absurd remark, the sight of a dissenter,—anything, sets me a sneezing and if I begin sneezing at 12, I don't leave off till two o'clock—and am heard distinctly in Taunton when the wind sets that way at a distance of 6 miles. Turn your mind to this little curse. If Consumption is too powerful for Physicians at least they should not suffer themselves to be outwitted by such little upstart disorders as the Hay-fever.

I am very glad you married my daughter, for I am sure you are both very happy, and I assure you I am proud of my son-in-law.

I have ordered a Brass Knocker against you come and we have a case of Chronic Bronchitis next door—some advanced cases of Dyspepsia not far off—and a considerable promise of acute Rheumatism at no great distance—a neighboring Squire has water forming on the chest so that I hope things will be comfortable and your visit not unpleasant.

I did not think that Copplestone with all his nonsense could have got down to Tar-water. I have as much belief in it as I have in Holy water.— it is the water has done the business, not the tar. They could not induce the sensual prelate to drink water but by mixing it up with nonsense and disguising the simplicity of the receipt. You must have a pitch battle with him about his tar-water, and teach him what he has never learnt—the rudiments of common sense. Kindest love to dear Saba.

Ever your affectionate father

Sydney Smith

The Duchess of Sutherland] see above, Letter 114. She was Countess of Sutherland in her own right, and married George Granville Leveson Gower, who in 1833 became Duke of Sutherland and died.   Boroughs] a bill to institute the reform of municipal government necessitated by the 1832 Reform Act was introduced in June and passed in Sept.   Sir Henry Halford] described by Smith in a letter of 1819 as 'a base little fellow but a very considerable physician', he was physician to George IV, William IV, and Victoria. Despite the prediction that his self-treatment would kill him he lived till 1844.   Pediluvium] feet-washing.   Brass Knocker] for patients summoning the doctor.   Copplestone] Smith had a long-standing quarrel with Edward Coplestone, bishop of Llandaff and dean of St Paul's.   Tar-water] a nostrum strongly advocated by Bishop Berkeley (*Siris*, 1744).

127. To Miss Lucie Austin, 22 July 1835

Lucie Austin (1821–69) was the only child of John and Sarah Austin (see next letter).

Lucy, Lucy, my dear child, don't tear your frock: tearing frocks is not of itself a proof of genius; but write as your mother writes, act as your mother acts; be frank, loyal, affectionate, simple, honest; and then integrity or laceration of frock is of little import.

And Lucy, dear child, mind your arithmetic. You know, in the first sum of yours I ever saw, there was a mistake. You had carried two (as a cab is licensed to do), and you ought, dear Lucy, to have carried but one. Is this a trifle? What would life be without arithmetic, but a scene of horrors?

You are going to Boulogne, the city of debts, peopled by men who never understood arithmetic; by the time you return, I shall probably have received my first paralytic stroke, and shall have lost all recollection of you; therefore I now give you my parting advice. Don't marry anybody who has not a tolerable understanding and a thousand a year; and God bless you, dear child.

Sydney Smith

128. To Mrs Austin, 13 October 1842

Sarah Taylor Austin (1793–1867) was a close friend and later first editor of Smith's correspondence. The Austins lived much abroad.

My dear Mrs Austin,

You lie heavy upon my conscience, unaccustomed to bear any weight at all. What can a country parson say to a travelled and travelling lady, who neither knows nor cares anything for wheat, oats, and barley? It is this reflection which keeps me silent. Still she has a fine heart, and likes to be cared for, even by me.

Mrs Sydney and I are in tolerable health,—both better than we were when you lived in England; but there is much more of us, so that you will find you were only half acquainted with us! I wish I could add that the intellectual faculties had expanded in proportion to the augmentation of flesh and blood.

Have you any chance of coming home? or rather, I should say, have we any chance of seeing you at home? I have been living for three months quite alone here. I am nearly seventy-two, and I confess myself afraid of the very disagreeable methods by which we leave this world; the long death of palsy, or the degraded spectacle of aged idiotism. As for the *pleasures* of the world,—it is a very ordinary, middling sort of place. Pray be my tombstone, and say a good word for me when I am dead! I shall think of my beautiful monument when I am going; but I wish I could see it before I die. God bless you!

Sydney Smith

129. To Lady Carlisle, 1 October 1844

Lady Carlisle was formerly Lady Morpeth (see above, Letters 114 and 124).

My dear Lady Carlisle,

From your ancient goodness to me, I am sure you will be glad to receive a bulletin from myself, informing you that I am making a good progress; in fact, I am in a regular train of promotion: from gruel, vermicelli, and sago, I was promoted to panada, from thence to minced meat, and (such is the effect of good conduct) I was elevated to a mutton-chop. My breathlessness and giddiness are gone—chased away by the gout. If you hear of sixteen or eighteen pounds of human flesh, they belong to me. I look as if a curate had been taken out of me. I am delighted to hear such improved accounts of my fellow-sufferer at Castle Howard. Lady Holland is severe in her medical questions; but I detail the most horrible symptoms, at which she takes flight.

Accept, my dear Lady Carlisle, my best wishes for Lord Carlisle and all the family—
Sydney Smith

Panada] a sort of bread-pudding.

JOHN KEATS
(1795–1821)

In 1818 Keats began to suffer from the tuberculosis that had killed his mother and brother; despite this handicap, and concurrent financial difficulties, he wrote the bulk of his best poetry in 1818 and 1819. He also met and fell in love with Fanny Brawne.

130. To Percy Bysshe Shelley, 16 August 1820

Shelley had written to invite Keats to spend the winter with him at Pisa, making some comments on Keats's *Endymion* and asking if he had received a copy of his play *The Cenci* (1819). Keats went to Rome, not Pisa, fearing that he would not be a 'free agent' in Shelley's circle. A copy of Keats's last volume was found in Shelley's pocket when his drowned body was recovered.

My dear Shelley,

I am very much gratified that you, in a foreign country, and with a mind almost over occupied, should write to me in the strain of the Letter beside me. If I do not take advantage of your invitation it will be prevented by a circumstance I have very much at heart to prophesy—There is no doubt that an english winter would put an end to me, and do so in a lingering hateful manner, therefore I must either voyage or journey to Italy as a soldier marches up to a battery. My nerves at present are the worst part of me, yet they feel soothed when I think that come what extreme may, I shall not be destined to remain in one spot long enough to take a hatred of any four particular bed-posts. I am glad you take any pleasure in my poor

Poem;—which I would willingly take the trouble to unwrite, if possible, did I care so much as I have done about Reputation. I received a copy of the Cenci, as from yourself from Hunt. There is only one part of it I am judge of; the Poetry, and dramatic effect, which by many spirits now a days is considered the mammon. A modern work it is said must have a purpose, which may be the God—*an artist* must serve Mammon—he must have 'self concentration' selfishness perhaps. You I am sure will forgive me for sincerely remarking that you might curb your magnanimity and be more of an artist, and 'load every rift' of your subject with ore. The thought of such discipline must fall like cold chains upon you, who perhaps never sat with your wings furl'd for six Months together. And is not this extraordina[r]y talk for the writer of Endymion? whose mind was like a pack of scattered cards—I am pick'd up and sorted to a pip. My Imagination is a Monastry and I am its Monk—you must explain my metaphysics to yourself. I am in expectation of Prometheus every day. Could I have my own wish for its interest effected you would have it still in manuscript—or be but now putting an end to the second act. I remember you advising me not to publish my first-blights, on Hampstead heath—I am returning advice upon your hands. Most of the Poems in the volume I send you have been written above two years, and would never have been publish'd but from a hope of gain; so you see I am inclined enough to take your advice now. I must exp[r]ess once more my deep sense of your kindness, adding my sincere thanks and respects for Mrs Shelley. In the hope of soon seeing you [I] remain

most sincerely yours,
John Keats—

Load every rift] an allusion to Spenser, *The Faerie Queene*, II. vii. 28, 5.

131. To Fanny Brawne, August? 1820

I do not write this till the last, that no eye may catch it.
My dearest Girl,

I wish you could invent some means to make me at all happy without you. Every hour I am more and more concentrated in you; every thing else tastes like chaff in my Mouth. I feel it almost impossible to go to Italy—the fact is I cannot leave you, and shall never taste one minute's content until it pleases chance to let me live with you for good. But I will not go on at this rate. A person in health as you are can have no conception of the horrors that nerves and a temper like mine go through. What Island do your friends propose retiring to? I should be happy to go with you there alone, but in company I should object to it; the backbitings and jealousies of new colonists who have nothing else to amuse them selves, is unbearable.

Mr Dilke came to see me yesterday, and gave me a very great deal more pain than pleasure. I shall never be able any more to endure the society of any of those who used to meet at Elm Cottage and Wentworth Place. The last two years taste like brass upon my Palate. If I cannot live with you I will live alone. I do not think my health will improve much while I am separated from you. For all this I am averse to seeing you—I cannot bear flashes of light and return into my glooms again. I am not so unhappy now as I should be if I had seen you yesterday. To be happy with you seems such an impossibility! it requires a luckier Star than mine! it will never be. I enclose a passage from one of your Letters which I want you to alter a little—I want (if you will have it so) the matter express'd less coldly to me. If my health would bear it, I could write a Poem which I have in my head, which would be a consolation for people in such a situation as mine. I would show some one in Love as I am, with a person living in such Liberty as you do. Shakspeare always sums up matters in the most sovereign manner. Hamlet's heart was full of such Misery as mine is when he said to Ophelia 'Go to a Nunnery, go, go!' Indeed I should like to give up the matter at once—I should like to die. I am sickened at the brute world which you are smiling with. I hate men and women more. I see nothing but thorns for the future—wherever I may be next winter in Italy or nowhere Brown will be living near you with his indecencies—I see no prospect of any rest. Suppose me in Rome—well, I should there see you as in a magic glass going to and from town at all hours,——I wish you could infuse a little confidence in human nature into my heart. I cannot muster any—the world is too brutal for me—I am glad there is such a thing as the grave— I am sure I shall never have any rest till I get there At any rate I will indulge myself by never seeing any more Dilke or Brown or any of their Friends. I wish I was either in your a[r]ms full of faith or that a Thunder bolt would strike me.

God bless you—
J. K—

I do not write this] the salutation 'My dearest girl'.   Go to a Nunnery] *Hamlet*, III. i. 120.

132. *To Charles Brown, 1 November 1820*

Charles Armitage Brown (1787–1842) was the friend, biographer, and landlord of the poet (the present Keats House in Hampstead was Brown's property).

My dear Brown,

Yesterday we were let out of Quarantine, during which my health suffered more from bad air and a stifled cabin than it had done the whole voyage. The fresh air revived me a little, and I hope I am well enough this morning to write to you a short calm letter;—if that can be called one, in which I am afraid to speak of what I would the fainest dwell upon. As I have gone thus far into it, I must go on a little;—perhaps it may relieve the load of WRETCHEDNESS which presses upon me. The persuasion that I shall see her no more will kill me. I cannot q——*(Note) My dear Brown, I should have had her when I was in health, and I should have remained well. I can bear to die—I cannot bear to leave her. Oh, God! God! God! Every thing I have in my trunks that reminds me of her goes through me like a spear. The silk lining she put in my travelling cap scalds my head. My imagination is horribly vivid about her—I see her—I hear her. There is nothing in the world of sufficient interest to divert me from her a moment. This was the case when I was in England; I cannot recollect, without shuddering, the time that I was prisoner at Hunt's, and used to keep my eyes fixed on Hampstead all day. Then there was a good hope of seeing her again—Now!—O that I could be buried near where she lives! I am afraid to write to her—to receive a letter from her—to see her hand writing would break my heart—even to hear of her any how, to see her name written would be more than I can bear. My dear Brown, what am I to do? Where can I look for consolation or ease? If I had any chance of recovery, this passion would kill me. Indeed through the whole of my illness, both at your house and at Kentish Town, this fever has never ceased wearing me out. When you write to me, which you will do immediately, write to Rome (poste restante)—if she is well and happy, put a mark thus +,—if—Remember me to all. I will endeavour to bear my miseries patiently. A person in my state of health should not have such miseries to bear. Write a short note to my sister, saying you have heard from me. Severn is very well. If I were in better health I should urge your coming to Rome. I fear there is no one can give me any comfort. Is there any news of George? O, that something fortunate had ever happened to me or my brothers!—then I might hope,—but despair is forced upon me as a habit. My dear Brown, for my sake, be her advocate for ever. I cannot say a word about Naples; I do not feel at all concerned in the thousand novelties around me. I am afraid to write to her. I should like her to know that I do not forget her. Oh, Brown, I have coals of fire in my breast. It surprised me that the human heart is capable of containing and bearing so much misery. Was I born for this end? God bless her, and her mother, and my sister, and George, and his wife, and you, and all!

Your ever affectionate friend,
John Keats

Thursday. I was a day too early for the courier. He sets out now. I have

---

* (Note) He could not go on with this sentence, nor even write the word 'quit',—as I suppose. The word WRETCHEDNESS above he himself wrote in large characters. [C.A.B.]

been more calm to-day, though in a half dread of not continuing so. I said nothing of my health; I know nothing of it; you will hear Severn's account from Haslam. I must leave off. You bring my thoughts too near to——

God bless you!

I cannot q——] Brown's note seems a poor guess; Elizabeth Cook in her Oxford Authors *John Keats* (1990) prefers 'quiff', meaning 'fuck', and has the support of *OED* as well as the context.   Severn] Joseph Severn (1793–1879), a painter, accompanied Keats to Rome, nursed him in his last illness, and was long afterwards buried beside him.   Haslam] William Haslam, a friend from schooldays, being unable to travel himself, arranged for Severn to go with Keats.

ANNA FRANCIS

Mrs Francis reports on her experience as an emigrant to South Africa. This, together with a letter to her sister, was published in the *Manchester Guardian*, 5 May 1821, the first number of the newspaper.

133. To Mrs Galabin, 22 January 1821

The letter was written from 'Assagya Bush' (Assegaibosch) on the Nossar River near Grahamstown, and directed to Mrs Galabin, 12 Old Jewry, London. The settlers in this part of South Africa met with opposition and suffered hardships they had not been led to expect.

My dear Fanny,

I expected long before this I should have had the pleasure of receiving a line from you; but that, as well as every other consolation is denied me. I have received but two letters from England, both from my dear sister, the last dated the 9th August. I wrote to my sister a short time since, and explained to her my uncomfortable situation in this miserable solitude. I thought my situation bad enough then, although I told her that I wanted for nothing, being provided by the government for twelve months, or more if required. All the parties that came off with us were upon the same terms, as some remuneration for the very great expense and loss of time we had incurred. For this we had the governor's verbal promise, as well as a circular letter. We have now received a communication that all rations are to be stopped, unless paid for, or unless undeniable security be given for payment hereafter. This is a blow which, if persisted in, must break up the whole enterprise, as it is impossible to procure corn at any price, the whole of the crops having failed in every part of the colony. As for me, you would hardly think I was the same creature. When I arrived at the Cape, I had grown fat and strong—the sea voyage had entirely restored my long lost health, and I fondly looked forward to happiness. But alas! my dear friend, this is the last place in the world where I could expect to find it; for the country, from every part we have seen of it, is the most barren and desolate you can imagine, except some spots near Cape Town, which have been long made, at a vast expense, and are occupied by the Dutch merchants, and the few monied people, for almost every estate in the country is deeply mortgaged. As a proof of the poverty of the soil, vegetables are sold in the capital at the most extravagant prices. You must give half-a-crown for a cabbage, and 3s.6d. for a cauliflower; 6s. a pound for fresh better [butter], and everything else in proportion. And it was the some [same] at Simon's Bay, but I had very good friends there, who were mostly English.

And is this the place in which I am to live out the remainder of my wretched existence? Forbid it Heaven! I find I cannot live on such terms. To be buried like a dog in a place surrounded by wild beasts—to me who have been used to every comfort! Think of my sensations when I hear the wolves howling round our dismal dwelling. You can have no idea of the dismal yell they make, as loud as a cow bellowing; add to this, the barking of the jackals, and the blowing of the porcupines. The ground swarms with insects and reptile[s.] I have had a snake a yard long coiled up by my bedside, and a mouse, as large as a small rat, in my bed, when I was lying very ill. We cannot set a single article of provisions out of the way, but it is covered with millions of ants, some of them an inch long. The state of my mind is such, that I cannot work for half an hour. I do nothing but cry, and read over and over again the books and old newspapers, I have read a hundred times before.—Poor David blames himself continually for bringing me out, and has promised, that if I am no more reconciled in a year, he will send me to England; but I shall never live that time. And if the government do not assist us, it will be impossible that any one can stay.

If I was near you, I could be happy to sit and work from morning to night. David has written a long letter to Colonel Strutt, explaining his situation. I envy this paper, because it is going to England; and I declare, rather than stay here, I would leave the country in an open boat.

Anna Francis

LEIGH HUNT
(1784–1859)

Hunt was a poet and journalist, and a friend of Shelley and Keats, some of whose poems he published in his journal, the *Examiner*.

134. To Joseph Severn, 8 March 1821

Dear Severn,

You have concluded, of course, that I have sent no letters to Rome, because I was aware of the effect they would have on Keats's mind; and this is the principal cause; for, besides what I have been told about letters in Italy, I remember his telling me upon one occasion that, in his sick moments, he never wished to receive another letter, or ever to see another face, however friendly. But still I should have written to you, had I not been almost at death's door myself. You will imagine how ill I have been, when you hear that I have but just begun writing again for the *Examiner* and *Indicator*, after an interval of several months, during which my flesh wasted from me with sickness and melancholy. Judge how often I thought of Keats, and with what feelings. Mr Brown tells me he is comparatively calm now, or rather quite so. If he can bear to hear of us, pray tell him; but he knows it already, and can put it in better language than any man. I hear that he does not like to be told that he may get better; nor is it to be wondered at, considering his firm persuasion that he shall not survive. He can only regard it as a puerile thing, and an insinuation that he shall die. But if his persuasion should happen to be no longer so strong, or if he can now put up with attempts to console him, of what I have said a thousand times, and what I still (upon my honour) think always, that I have seen too many instances of recovery from apparently desperate cases of consumption not to be in hope to the very last. If he still cannot bear this, tell him— tell that great poet and noble-hearted man—that we shall all bear his memory in the most precious part of our hearts, and that the world shall bow their heads to it, as our loves do. Or if this, again, will trouble his spirit, tell him that we shall never cease to remember and love him; and that, Christian or infidel, the most sceptical of us has faith enough in the high things that nature puts into our heads, to think all who are of one accord in mind or heart are journeying to one and the same place, and shall unite somewhere or other again, face to face, mutually conscious, mutually delighted. Tell him he is only before us on the road, as he is in everything else; or, whether you tell him the latter or no, tell him the former, and add that we shall never forget that he was so, and that we are coming after him. The tears are again in my eyes, and I must not afford to shed them. The next letter I write shall be more to yourself, and more refreshing to your spirits, which we are very sensible must have been greatly taxed. But whether your friend dies or not, it will not be among the least lofty of your recollections by-and-by that you helped to smooth the sick-bed of so fine a being. God bless you, dear Severn.

Your sincere friend,
Leigh Hunt

MARY WOLLSTONECRAFT SHELLEY

(1797–1851)

Daughter of William Godwin and Mary Wollstonecraft, Mary married Shelley in 1816 and then wrote her first novel, *Frankenstein*. In April 1822 they moved to Lerici, where Mary had a miscarriage. Shelley was drowned on 8 July 1822. Mary returned to England in 1823.

135. To Maria Gisborne, 15 August 1822

Maria Gisborne (1770–1836), a close friend, addressee of a verse letter from Shelley.

I said in a letter to Peacock, my dear Mrs Gisborne, that I would send you some account of the last miserable months of my disastrous life. From day to day I have put this off, but I will now endeavour to fulfill my design. The scene of my existence is closed & though there be no pleasure in retracing the scenes that have preceded the event which has crushed my hopes yet there seems to be a necessity in doing so, and I obey the impulse that urges me. I wrote to you either at the end of May or the beginning of June. I described to you the place we were living in:—Our desolate house, the beauty yet strangeness of the scenery and the delight Shelley took in all this—he never was in better health or spirits than during this time. I was not well in body or mind. My nerves were wound up to the utmost irritation, and the sense of misfortune hung over my spirits. No words can tell you how I hated our house & the country about it. Shelley reproached me for this—his health was good & the place was quite after his own heart—What could I answer—that the people were wild & hateful, that though the country was beautiful yet I liked a more *countryfied* place, that there was great difficulty in living—that all our Tuscans would leave us, & that the very jargon of these *Genovese* was disgusting—This was all I had to say but no words could describe my feelings—the beauty of the woods made me weep & shudder—so vehement was my feeling of dislike that I used to rejoice when the winds & waves permitted me to go out in the boat so that I was not obliged to take my usual walk among tree shaded paths, allies of vine festooned trees—all that before I doated on—& that now weighed on me. My only moments of peace were on board that unhappy boat, when lying down with my head on his knee I shut my eyes & felt the wind & our swift motion alone. My ill health might account for much of this—bathing in the sea somewhat relieved me—but on the 8th of June (I think it was) I was threatened with a miscarriage, & after a week of great ill health on sunday the 16th this took place at eight in the morning. I was so ill that for seven hours I lay nearly lifeless—kept from fainting by brandy, vinegar eau de Cologne &c—at length ice was brought to our solitude—it came before the doctor so Claire & Jane were afraid of using it but Shelley overuled them & by an unsparing application of it I was restored. They all thought & so did I at one time that I was about to die— I hardly wish that I had, my own Shelley could never have lived without me, the sense of eternal misfortune would have pressed to heavily upon him, & what would have become of my poor babe? My convalescence was slow and during it a strange occurence happened to retard it. But first I must describe our house to you. The floor on which we lived was thus

 1 is a terrace that went the whole length of our house & was precipitous to the sea. 2 the large dining hall— 3, a private staircase. 4 my bedroom 5 M^{rs} [Williams's] bedroom, 6 Shelleys & 7 the entrance from the great staircase. Now to return. As I said Shelley was at first in perfect health but having over fatigued himself one day, & then the fright my illness gave him caused a return of nervous sensations & visions as bad as in his worst times. I think it was the saturday after my illness while yet unable to walk I was confined to my bed—in the middle of the night I was awoke by hearing him scream & come rushing into my room; I was sure that he was asleep & tried to waken him by calling on him, but he continued to scream which inspired me with such a panic that I jumped out of bed & ran across the hall to M^{rs} W's room where I fell through weakness, though I was so frightened that I got up again immediately—she let me in & Williams went to S. who had been wakened by my getting out of bed—he said that he had not been asleep & that it was a vision that he saw that had frightened him— But as he declared that he had not screamed it was certainly a dream & no waking vision—What had frightened him was this—He dreamt that lying as he did in bed Edward & Jane came into him, they were in the most horrible condition, their bodies lacerated—their bones starting through their skin, the faces pale yet stained with blood, they could hardly walk, but Edward was the weakest & Jane was supporting him—Edward said—'Get up, Shelley, the sea is flooding the house & it is all coming down.' S. got up, he thought, & went to his window that looked on the terrace & the sea & thought he saw the sea rushing in. Suddenly his vision changed & he saw the figure of himself strangling me, that had made him rush into my room, yet fearful of frightening me he dared not approch the bed, when my jumping out awoke him, or as he phrased it caused his vision to vanish. All this was frightful enough, & talking it over the next morning he told me that he had had many visions lately—he had seen the figure of himself which met him as he walked on the terrace & said to him—'How long do you mean to be content'—No very terrific words & certainly not prophetic of what has occurred. But Shelley had often seen these figures when ill; but

the strangest thing is that Mrs W. saw him. Now Jane though a woman of sensibility, has not much imagination & is not in the slightest degree nervous—neither in dreams or otherwise. She was standing one day, the day before I was taken ill, at a window that looked on the Terrace with Trelawny—it was day—she saw as she thought Shelley pass by the window, as he often was then, without a coat or jacket—he passed again—now as he passed both times the same way—and as from the side towards which he went each time there was no way to get back except past the window again (except over a wall twenty feet from the ground) she was struck at seeing him pass twice thus & looked out & seeing him no more she cried—'Good God can Shelley have leapt from the wall? Where can he be gone?' Shelley, said Trelawny—'No Shelley has past—What do you mean?' Trelawny says that she trembled exceedingly when she heard this & it proved indeed that Shelley had never been on the terrace & was far off at the time she saw him. Well we thought [no] more of these things & I slowly got better. Having heard from Hunt that he had sailed from Genoa, on Monday July 1st S., Edward & Captain Roberts (the Gent. who built our boat) departed in our boat for Leghorn to receive him—I was then just better, had begun to crawl from my bedroom to the terrace; but bad spirits succeded to ill health, and this departure of Shelley's seemed to add insuferably to my misery. I could not endure that he should go—I called him back two or three times, & told him that if I did not see him soon I would go to Pisa with the child—I cried bitterly when he went away. They went & Jane, Claire & I remained alone with the children—I could not walk out, & though I gradually gathered strength it was slowly & my ill spirits encreased; in my letters to him I entreated him to return—'the feeling that some misfortune would happen,' I said, 'haunted me': I feared for the child, for the idea of danger connected with him never struck me— When Jane & Claire took their evening walk I used to patrole the terrace, oppressed with wretchedness, yet gazing on the most beautiful scene in the world. This Gulph of Spezia is subdivided into many small bays of which ours was far the most beautiful—the two horns of the bay (so to express myself) were wood covered promontories crowned with castles—at the foot of these on the furthest was Lerici on the nearest San^t Arenzo—Lerici being above a mile by land from us & San Arenzo about a hundred or two yards—trees covered the hills that enclosed this bay & then beautiful groups were picturesquely contrasted with the rocks the castle on [and] the town—the sea lay far extended in front while to the west we saw the promontory & islands which formed one of the extreme boundarys of the Gulph—to see the sun set upon this scene, the stars shine & the moon rise was a sight of wondrous beauty, but to me it added only to my wretchedness—I repeated to myself all that another would have said to console me,

& told myself the tale of love peace & competence which I enjoyed—but I answered myself by tears—did not my William die? & did I hold my Percy by a firmer tenure?—Yet I thought when he, when my Shelley returns I shall be happy—he will comfort me, if my boy be ill he will restore him & encourage me. I had a letter or two from Shelley mentioning the difficulties he had in establishing the Hunts, & that he was unable to fix the time of his return. Thus a week past. On Monday 8th Jane had a letter from Edward, dated saturday, he said that he waited at Leghorn for S. who was at Pisa That S's return was certain, 'but' he continued, 'if he should not come by monday I will come in a felucca, & you may expect me tuesday evening at furthest.' This was monday, the fatal monday, but with us it was stormy all day & we did not at all suppose that they could put to sea. At twelve at night we had a thunderstorm; Tuesday it rained all day & was calm—the sky wept on their graves—on Wednesday—the wind was fair from Leghorn & in the evening several felucca's arrived thence—one brought word that they had sailed monday, but we did not believe them—thursday was another day of fair wind & when twelve at night came & we did not see the tall sails of the little boat double the promontory before us we began to fear not the truth, but some illness—some disagreable news for their detention. Jane got so uneasy that she determined to proceed the next day to Leghorn in a boat to see what was the matter—friday came & with it a heavy sea & bad wind—Jane however resolved to be rowed to Leghorn (since no boat could sail) and busied herself in preparations—I wished her to wait for letters, since friday was letter day—she would not—but the sea detained her, the swell rose so that no boat would venture out—At 12 at noon our letters came—there was one from Hunt to Shelley, it said—'pray write to tell us how you got home, for they say that you had bad weather after you sailed monday & we are anxious'—the paper fell from me—I trembled all over—Jane read it—'Then it is all over!' she said. 'No, my dear Jane,' I cried, 'it is not all over, but this suspense is dreadful—come with me, we will go to Leghorn, we will post to be swift & learn our fate.' We crossed to Lerici, despair in our hearts; they raised our spirits there by telling us that no accident had been heard of & that it must have been known &c— but still our fear was great—& without resting we posted to Pisa. It must have been fearful to see us—two poor, wild, aghast creatures—driving (like Matilda) towards the *sea* to learn if we were to be for ever doomed to misery. I knew that Hunt was at Pisa at Lord Byrons' house but I thought that L.B. was at Leghorn. I settled that we should drive to Casa Lanfranchi that I should get out & ask the fearful question of Hunt, 'do you know any thing of Shelley?' On entering Pisa the idea of seeing Hunt for the first time for four years under such circumstances, & asking him such a question was so terrific to me that it was with difficulty that I prevented myself from going into convulsions—my struggles were dreadful—they knocked at the door & some one called out 'Chi è?' it was the Guiccioli's maid L.B. was in Pisa—Hunt was in bed, so I was to see LB. instead of him—This was a great relief to me; I staggered up stairs—the Guiccioli came to meet me smiling while I could hardly say—'Where is he—Sapete alcuna cosa di Shelley'—They knew nothing—he had left Pisa on sunday—on Monday he had sailed—there had been bad weather monday afternoon—more they knew not. Both LB & the lady have told me since—that on that terrific evening I looked more like a ghost than a woman—light seemed to emanate from my features, my face was very white   I looked like marble—Alas. I had risen almost from a bed of sickness for this journey—I had travelled all day—it was now 12 at night—& we, refusing to rest, proceeded to Leghorn—not in despair—no, for then we must have died; but with suf-ficient hope to keep up the agitation of the spirits which was all my life. It was past two in the morning when we arrived—They took us to the wrong inn—neither Trelawny or Capⁿ Roberts were there nor did we exactly know where they were so we were obliged to wait until daylight. We threw ourselves drest on our beds & slept a little but at 6 o'clock we went to one or two inns to ask for one or the other of these gentlemen. We found Roberts at the Globe. He came down to us with a face which seemed to tell us that the worst was true, and here we learned all that had occurred during the week they had been absent from us, & under what circumstances they had departed on their return.——Shelley had past most of the time a[t] Pisa—arranging the affairs of the Hunts—& skrewing LB's mind to the sticking place about the journal. He had found this a difficult task at first but at length he had succeeded to his heart's content with both points. Mʳˢ Mason said that she saw him in better health and spirits than she had ever known him, when he took leave of her sunday July 7ᵗʰ His face burnt by the sun, & his heart light that he had succeeded in rendering the Hunts' tolerably comfortable. Edward had remained at Leghorn. On Monday July 8ᵗʰ during the morning they were employed in buying many things— eatables &c for our solitude. There had been a thunderstorm early but about noon the weather was fine & the wind right fair for Lerici—They were impatient to be gone. Roberts said, 'Stay until tomorrow to see if the weather is settled'; & S. might have staid but Edward was in so great an anxiety to reach home—saying they would get there in seven hours with that wind—that they sailed! S. being in one of those extravagant fits of good spirits in which you have sometimes seen him. Roberts went out to the end of the mole & watched them out of sight—they sailed at one & went off at the rate of about 7 knots—About three—Roberts, who was still on the mole—saw wind coming from the Gulph—or rather what the Italians call a temporale, anxious to know how the boat wᵈ weather the storm, he got leave to go up the tower & with the glass discovered them about ten miles out at sea, off Via Reggio, they were taking in their top-sails—'The haze of the storm,' he said, 'hid them from me & I saw them no more—when the storm cleared I looked again fancying that I should see them on their return to us—but there was no boat on the sea.'—This then was all we knew, yet we did not despair—they might have been driven over to Corsica & not knowing the coast & Gone god knows where. Reports favoured this belief.—it was even said that they had been seen in the Gulph—We resolved to return with all possible speed—We sent a courier to go from tower to tower along the coast to know if any thing had been seen or found, & at 9 AM. we quitted Leghorn—stopped but one moment at Pisa & proceeded towards Lerici. When at 2 miles from Via Reggio we rode down to that town to know if they knew any thing—here our calamity first began to break on us—a little boat & a water cask had been found five miles off—they had manufactured a *piccolissima lancia* of thin planks stitched by a shoemaker just to let them run on shore without wetting themselves as our boat drew 4 feet water.—the description of that found tallied with this—but then this boat was very cumbersome & in bad weather they might have been easily led to throw it overboard—the cask frightened me most—but the same reason might in some sort be given for that. I must tell you that Jane & I were not now alone—Trelawny accompanied us back to our home. We journied on & reached the Magra about ½ past ten P.M. I cannot describe to you what I felt in the first moment when, fording this river, I felt the water splash about our wheels—I was suffocated—I gasped for breath—I thought I should have gone into convulsions, & I struggled violently that Jane might not perceive it—looking down the river I saw the two great lights burning at the *foce*—A voice from within me seemed to cry aloud that is his grave. After passing the river I gradually recovered. Arriving at Lerici we [were] obliged to cross our little bay in a boat—San Arenzo was illuminated for a festa—what a scene—the roaring sea—the scirocco wind—the lights of the town towards which we rowed—& our own desolate hearts—that coloured all with a shroud—we landed; nothing had been heard of them. This was saturday July 13. & thus we waited until Thursday July 25th thrown about by hope & fear. We sent messengers along the coast towards Genoa & to Via Reggio—nothing had been found more than the *lancetta*; reports were brought us—we hoped—& yet to tell you all the agony we endured during those 12 days would be to make you conceive a universe of pain—each moment intolerable & giving place to one still worse. The people of the country too added to one's discomfort—they are like wild savages—on festa's the men & women & children in different bands—the sexes always separate—pass the whole night in dancing on the sands close to our door running into the sea then back again & screaming all the time one perpetuel air—the most detestable in the world—then the scirocco perpetually blew & the sea for ever moaned their dirge. On thursday 25th Trelawny left us to go to Leghorn to see what was doing or what could be done. On friday I was very ill but as evening came on I said to Jane—'If any thing had been found on the coast Trelawny would have returned to let us know. He has not returned so I hope.' About 7 o'clock P.M. he did return—all was over—all was quiet now, they had been found washed on shore—Well all this was to be endured.

Well what more have I to say? The next day we returned to Pisa And here we are still—days pass away—one after another—& we live thus. We are all together—we shall quit Italy together. Jane must proceed to London—if letters do not alter my views I shall remain in Paris.—Thus we live—Seeing the Hunts now & then. Poor Hunt has suffered terribly as you may guess. Lord Byron is very kind to me & comes with the Guiccioli to see me often.

Today—this day—the sun shining in the sky—they are gone to the desolate sea coast to perform the last offices to their earthly remains. Hunt, LB. & Trelawny. The quarantine laws would not permit us to remove them sooner—& now only on condition that we burn them to ashes. That I do not dislike—His rest shall be at Rome beside my child—where one day I also shall join them—Adonais is not Keats's it is his own elegy—he bids you there go to Rome.—I have seen the spot where he now lies—the sticks that mark the spot where the sands cover him—he shall not be there it is too nea[r] Via Reggio—They are now about this fearful office—& I live!

One more circumstance I will mention. As I said he took leave of Mrs Mason in high spirits on sunday—'Never,' said she, 'did I see him look happier than the last glance I had of his countenance.' On Monday he was lost—on monday night she dreamt—that she was somewhere—she knew not where & he came looking very pale & fearfully melancholy—she said to him—'You look ill, you are tired, sit down & eat.' 'No,' he replied, 'I shall never eat more; I have not a *soldo* left in the world.'—'Nonsense,' said she, 'this is no inn—you need not pay—'—'Perhaps,' he answered, 'it is the worse for that.' Then she awoke & going to sleep again she dreamt that my Percy was dead & she awoke crying bitterly ⟨—so bitterly th⟩ & felt so miserable—that she said to herself—'why if the little boy should die I should not feel it in this manner.' She [was] so struck with these dreams that she mentioned them to her servant the next day—saying she hoped all was well with us.

Well here is my story—the last story I shall have to tell—all that might have been bright in my life is now despoiled—I shall live to improve myself, to take care of my child, & render myself worthy to join him. soon

my weary pilgrimage will begin—I rest now—but soon I must leave Italy—
& then—there is an end of all despair. Adieu I hope you are well & happy.
I have an idea that while he was at Pisa that he received a letter from you
that I have never seen—so not knowing where to direct I shall send this
letter to Peacock—I shall send it open—he may be glad to read it—

Your's ever truly,
Mary WS

I shall probably write to you soon again.

I have left out a material circumstance—A Fishing boat saw them go
down—It was about 4 in the afternoon—they saw the boy at mast head,
when baffling winds struck the sails, they had looked away a moment &
looking again the boat was gone—This is their story but there is little down
[*doubt*] that these men might have saved them, at least Edward who could
swim. They c^d not they said get near her—but 3 quarters of an hour after
passed over the spot where they had seen her—they protested no wreck of
her was visible, but Roberts going on board their boat found several spars
belonging to her.—perhaps they let them perish to obtain these. Trelawny
thinks he can get her up, since another fisherman thinks that he has found
the spot where she lies, having drifted near shore. T. does this to know
perhaps the cause of her wreck—but I care little about it.

Peacock] Thomas Love Peacock (1785–1866), poet and novelist; a friend of Shelley's who satirized him, along with Coleridge and Byron, in *Nightmare Abbey* (1818).   Claire] Claire
Clairmont (1798–1879), Mary's stepsister, who accompanied her on her elopement with Shelley.
She had a daughter, Allegra (b. 1817), by Byron, who placed the child in a convent in Ravenna,
where she died in 1822.   Jane] Edward and Jane Williams joined Shelley's circle in Pisa in
1821. Jane played the guitar, sang, and practised 'animal magnetism'. Her husband was drowned
with Shelley.   Trelawny] Edward John Trelawny (1792–1881), a writer and friend, who
plucked Shelley's heart from the pyre at Viareggio.   My William] a son.   Percy] a
son who survived.   Hunts] Leigh Hunt and family; he was a friend of Keats and
Shelley.   Matilda] the eponymous heroine of a novella by Mary Shelley.   Casa
Lanfranchi] Byron's house in Pisa.   The Guiccioli] Countess Guiccioli, Byron's mistress.
Sapete alcuna cosa di Shelley] have you any news of Shelley?   skrewing . . . place] *Macbeth*,
I. vii. 60.   Temporale] thunderstorm.   *Piccolissima lancia*] small launch or lifeboat.
foce] harbourmouth   'Adonais'] Shelley's elegy for Keats.

THE CHEVALIER DE SANTA ROSA

Santa Rosa was a political exile who, with other Italian refugees, was befriended in
England by Sarah Austin (see below, Letter 158).

136. To Sarah Austin, 26 December 1822

Dear Madam,

I like you because you are good, and because your gentle, beautiful face
express faithfully your goodness. I could not easily close the list of

because . . . but I won't omit this. I like you because you are most affectionate in the world to your fireside. Let, let foolish people open a large
yawning when they must remain at home one whole day. I pity them,
almost I despise. I know a country-man of mine, gentle and pretty creature,
who one day tell so to his friend: 'Alas! I give handsome present to people
who will be able to learn me to use the twenty-four hours of every day.'
Shocking! twenty-four hours in every day. This gentleman, however, is
presently a outlaw. Who would guess it!

I am a little tired of the dinner I was present to yesterday, yet that
meeting was much pleasing to me. I was sitting near to Ugoni, and at the
left side sweet Arrivabene stood with much calmness. The first don't forget
to talk of your *radicalism*. The second increased very much in my favour.
Il entre de plus en plus en grâce auprès de moi, telling scripturally, and for
useful interpretation, of my bad English.

I received yesterday a very dear letter from one my friend, whom I like
heartily, from where we were yet at nineteenth year of life. He is a physician, very fond of his profession, humane, disinterested towards his sicks;
perseverant, prudent friend; he likes children of mine as well as they should
be proper things of him. His letter gives me a diligent account of those
unfortunate children—diligent and favourable, much favourable; you know
I wish only two things in the world. My country's deliverance; and obscure, private life amongst my wife, my tender wife, and my children. A
glory; I think it vaporous dream. Affections enjoyed in peace; dreams,
perhaps, but clear and delicious dreams.

I hope to see you to-morrow at two hours afternoon. Let you remember
that I will be very much angry with you if you shall wait for me only one
minute.

Let forgive my outlandish English, and believe me,

Your faithful friend,
Santa Rosa

THOMAS CARLYLE (1795–1881) AND
JANE BAILLIE WELSH (1801–1866)

At the time of these first two letters Carlyle, still far from famous, was, as he remarks,
translating Goethe. Jane Welsh, who was a remarkably talented and beautiful young
woman, and of superior social rank, had recently ended an 'understanding' with
another man; Carlyle knew nothing of that. Their marriage (Oct. 1826) was a noto-
riously difficult union. They eventually moved to Cheyne Walk in London and
became jointly and severally famous.

137. Jane Baillie Welsh to Thomas Carlyle, 16 September 1823

My dear Friend,

Your letter only reached me this morning, having sojourned at Templand more than ten days, 'expecting an opportunity'—Charming as it is, I could almost wish it had not cast up at all; for it has troubled me more than I can tell—I feel there is need I should answer it without delay—And what can I say to you? it is so hard to explain one's self in such a situation! but I must! and in plain terms; for any reserve at present were criminal and might be very fatal in its consequences to both—

You misunderstand me—you regard me no longer as a friend, a sister; but as one who at some future period may be more to you than both—is it not so? is it not true that you believe me, like the bulk of my silly sex, incapable of entertaining a strong affection for a man of my own age without having for it's ultimate object our union for life? 'Useless and dangerous to love you'! 'my happiness wrecked by you'!—I cannot have misinterpreted your meaning! And my God what have I said or done to mislead you into an error so destructive to the confidence that subsist[s] betwixt us, so dangerous to the peace of us both? In my treatment of you I have indeed disregarded all maxims of womanly prudence, have shaken myself free from the shackles of etiquette—I have loved and admired you for your noble qualities, and for the extraordinary affection you have shewn me: and I have told you so without reserve or disguise—but *not* till our repeated quarrels had produced an explanation betwixt us, which I foolishly believed would gauruntee [*sic*] my future conduct from all possibility of misconstruction—I have been to blame—I might have foreseen that such implicite confidence might mislead you as to the nature of my sentiments, and should have expressed my friendship for you with a more prudent reserve—but it is of no use talking of what I might or should have done in the time past—I have only to repair the mischief in as far as I can, now that my eyes are opened to it now that I am startled to find our relation actually assuming the aspect of an engagement for life—

My Friend I love you—I repeat it tho' I find the e[x]pression a rash one—all the best feelings of my nature are concerned in loving you—But were you my Brother I would love you the same, were I married to another I would love you the same—and is this sentiment so calm, so delightful— but so unimpassioned enough to recompense the freedom of my heart, enough to reconcile me to the existence of a married woman the hopes and wishes and ambitions of which are all different from mine, the cares and occupations of which are my disgust— Oh no! Your Friend I will be, your truest most devoted friend, while I breath[e] the breath of life; but your wife! never never! Not though you were as rich as Croesus, as honoured and renowned as you yet shall be—

You may think I am viewing the matter by much too seriously—taking fright where there is noth[ing] to fear—It is well if it be so! But, suffering as I am at this very moment from the horrid pain of seeing a true and affectionate heart near breaking for my sake, it is not to be wondered at tho' I be overanxious for your peace on which my own depends in a still greater degree—Write to me and reassure me—for God's sake reassure me if you can! Your Friendship at this time is almost necessary to my existence. Yet I will resign it cost what it may—will, will resign it if it can only be enjoyed at the risk of your future peace—

I had many things to say to you—about Musæus and all that. but I must wait till another opportunity—At present I scarcely know what I am about—

Ever Affectionately Yours

Jane B Welsh

138. Thomas Carlyle to Jane Baillie Welsh, 18 September 1823

My dear Jane,

If I were not a fool of some standing, I should not have vexed you on this occasion, or given you this fresh opportunity of testifying how true is the affection which you bear me. Your letter has set me a-thinking about matters which, with my accustomed heedlessness, I was letting take their course without accurate investigation, tho' conscious that a right under-standing of them was of vital consequence to both of us. I honour your wisdom and decision: you have put our concerns *on the very footing where I wished them to stand*. So be of good cheer, for no harm is done.

When I placed the management of our intercourse and whatever mutual interests we had or might have entirely at your own disposal, making you sole queen and arbitress of the 'commonweal', I stipulated for myself as much freedom of speech as you could conveniently grant, leaving to you an unbounded power of acting, then and in all time coming. It is to the terms of this *compact* that I still adhere in their widest acceptation. I know very well you will never be my wife. Never! Never!—I never believed it above five minutes at a time all my days. 'Tis all one as I should love a bright particular star, and think to wed it.' My fancy can form scenes, indeed, which with you to share them were worthy of a place in the heaven above; but there are items wanting, without which all these blessings were a curse, and which not your consent (if that were ever to be dreamed of) nor any influence of man can assure me of realizing. Such illusions do in truth haunt me, nor am I very sedulous to banish them. The harsh hand of Time will do it speedily enough without help of mine, and leave no truth behind that will ever give me half the pleasure. I grant it is absurd, and might be more than absurd, to utter them so freely: but what then? They give a momentary pleasure to myself, and do harm to no one. Strip life of all its baseless hopes and beautiful chimeras; it seems to me there would be little left worth having.

Thus then it stands. You love me as a sister, and will not wed: I love you in all possible senses of the word, and will not wed, any more than you. Does this reassure you? If so, let us return to our old position: let me continue writing what comes into my head, and do you continue acting now or forever after just as you judge best. I seek no engagement, I will make none. By God's blessing, I will love you with all my heart and all my soul, while the blood continues warm within me; I will reverence you as the fairest living emblem of all that is most exalted and engaging in my conceptions of human nature; I will help you according to my slender power, and stand by you closer than a brother: but these feelings are entertained for myself alone; let them be their own reward, or go unrewarded—that is *my* concern. So long as you have charity to hear me talk about affections that must end in nothingness, and plans which seem destined to be all abortive, I will speak and listen; when you tire of this, when you marry, or cast me off in any of the thousand ways that fortune is ever offering, I shall of course cease to correspond with you, I shall cease to love Mrs——, but not Jane Welsh; the image she will have left in my mind I shall always love, for even this tho' the original is gone forever, will still have more reality than mere fantasies that would replace it. In all this I see no blame; and if there were, I cannot help it. Had it pleased Providence to plant some other standard of excellence in me, or make you different from what you are, then I should have felt and acted otherwise: but as it is, I am no free agent. For the rest, do not fear the consequence so far as I am concerned. My heart is too old by almost half a score of years, and made of sterner stuff than to break in junctures of that kind. Had it not been harder than the nether millstone it must have shivered into fragments very long ago. I have no idea of dying in the Arcadian shepherd style, for the disappointment of hopes which I never seriously entertained, or had no right to entertain seriously.

Now, in the name of the ever blessed Trinity, have I done with these preliminaries? Ass that I was in forcing you to ask them! I confess it grieves me to address you in this cold formal style, as if writing to my Taylor for a suit of clothes, and directing him where to cut and where to spare; not to my own best Jane, the friend of my soul, from whom I have no secrets or separate interests, and whom I love because she has no secrets from me. Let us forget it altogether, and be as we were! If you *will* part with me, do it; but not for *my* sake! For my sake, I call God to witness, you never shall. Again I say, let us forget it utterly, forever and ever!

These woful explanations I judged it right to send without a moment's delay: your comfort seemed to be concerned in their being given you instantly. You must not count this as *any letter* or your last as any: but write to me again in your own careless style, *about Musäus and all that*, just as if this thing had never happened. I long to be again introduced to your home at Haddington, to share in all your tasks and difficulties, to cherish your fainting hopes, and tell you a thousand times without stint or fear of reproof that you are dearer to me than aught in life, and that united we will conquer every difficulty, and be two glorious characters—if it so please the Fates.

This last proviso seems a needful one for me at present, tho' in your case I esteem it little. I appear to be fast going to the devil here; my health is getting worse every week; I sleep at the easy rate of three or four hours per night, and feel throughout the day in the most beatific humour! If it had not been that the people are kind to me as if I were their son, I had been gone ere now. They design staying here all winter: I will try it another month; and if without improvement, I mount the horse Bardolph, and turn my face back again to the plain country. I was looking out, while there, in the valley of Milk, for some cottage among trees, beside the still waters; some bright little place, with a stable behind it, a garden and a rood of green,— where I might fairly commence housekeeping, and the writing of books! They laughed at me, and said it was a joke. Well! I swear it is a lovely world this, after all. What a pity that we had not *five* score years and ten of it!

Meanwhile I go on with Goethe's Wilhelm Meister; a book which I love not, which I am sure will never sell, but which I am determined to print and finish. There are touches of the very highest most etherial genius in it; but diluted with floods of insipidity, which even *I* would not have written for the world. I sit down to it every night at six, with the ferocity of a hyaena; and in spite of all obstructions my keep-lesson is more than half thro' the first volume, and travelling over poetry and prose, slowly but surely to the end. Some of the poetry is very bad, some of it rather good. The following is mediocre—the worst kind.

> Who never ate his bread in sorrow,
> Who never spent the darksome hours
> Weeping, and watching for the morrow,
> He knows you not, ye gloomy Powers.

> To Earth, this weary Earth, ye bring us,
> To guilt ye let us heedless go,
> Then leave repentance fierce to wring us:
> A moment's guilt, an age of woe!

And now my own best Jane, before leaving you, what more have I to ask? That you would love me forever, in any way, on any terms you please; that you continue while we both live to make me the confidant of all your sorrows and enjoyments great and small; and above all that you would find me means of doing you some essential service—something that might make our intercourse and affection more than a pleasing dream, when God shall see meet to put an end to it forever. Shew me, O! shew me how I may benefit you. I declare I shall not be able to die contented or sleep in my grave if I have done you no good. Write to me *instantly*, to 'reassure *me*'. Tell me *all* things that concern you—, *all things*. God bless you my dearest! Do with me as you like, I am ever yours with all my soul!

T. Carlyle

This will be at Hadd*n* on Sunday morning: I know you will not keep me waiting. Write as of old *de omnibus rebus et quibusdam aliis* [about everything and then some more]. Have you actually begun *The Tales?* How do you like them? Will they do? Have you arranged any hours for your studies? Do the gossips interfere with you? Are you happy? *Are you?* Tell me *every thing*: I am your B[r]other, and more than fifty brothers, to the end of time. Farewel[l]! Be good and diligent and fear not.

Bright particular star] *All's Well that Ends Well* I. i. 86.   Goethe] Carlyle's translation of *Wilhelm Meister* (1795–6) was published in 1812.

139. Carlyle to Ralph Waldo Emerson, 27 January 1867

Jane Welsh Carlyle died in 1866. Carlyle's biography of Frederick the Great, many years in the making, appeared in six vols. between 1858 and 1865. He wrote little thereafter. Emerson (see below, Letter 172) first met Carlyle on a visit to England in 1833, and remained a friend and correspondent for life. His *English Traits* was published in 1865.

My dear Emerson,

It is a long time since I last wrote to you; and a long distance in space and in fortune,—from the shores of the Solway in summer 1865, to this niche of the Alps and Mediterranean to-day, after what has befallen me in the interim. A longer interval, I think, and surely by far a sadder, than ever occurred between us before, since we first met in the Scotch moors, some five and thirty years ago. You have written me various Notes, too, and Letters, all good and cheering to me,—almost the only truly *human* speech I have heard from anybody living;—and still my stony silence could not be broken; not till now, though often looking forward to it, could I resolve on such a thing. You will think me far gone, and much bankrupt in hope and heart;—and indeed I am; as good as without hope and without fear; a gloomily serious, silent, and sad old man; gazing into the final chasm of things, in mute dialogue with 'Death, Judgment, and Eternity' (dialogue *mute* on *both* sides!), not caring to discourse with poor articulate-speaking fellow-creatures on *their* sorts of topics. It is right of me; and yet also it is not right. I often feel that I had better be dead than thus indifferent, contemptuous, disgusted with the world and its roaring nonsense, which I have no thought farther of lifting a finger to help, and only try to keep out of the way of, and shut my door against. But the truth is, I was nearly killed by that hideous Book on Friedrich,—twelve years in continuous wrestle with the nightmares and the subterranean hydras;—nearly *killed*, and had often thought I should be altogether, and must die leaving the monster not so much as finished! This is one truth, not so evident to any friend or onlooker as it is to myself: and then there is another, known to myself alone, as it were; and of which I am best not to speak to others, or to speak to them no farther. By the calamity of April last, I lost my little all in this world; and have no soul left who can make any corner of this world into a *home* for me any more. Bright, heroic, tender, true and noble was that lost treasure of my heart, who faithfully accompanied me in all the rocky ways and climbings; and I am forever poor without her. She was snatched from me in a moment,—as by a death from the gods. Very beautiful her death was; radiantly beautiful (to those who understand it) had all her life been: *quid plura?* I should be among the dullest and stupidest, if I were not among the saddest of all men. But not a word more on all this.

All summer last, my one solacement in the form of work was writing, and sorting of old documents and recollections; summoning out again into clearness old scenes that had now closed on me without return. Sad, and in a sense sacred; it was like a kind of *worship*; the only *devout* time I had had for a great while past. These things I have half or wholly the intention to burn out of the way before I myself die:—but such continues still mainly my employment,—so many hours every forenoon; what I call the 'work' of my day;—to me, if to no other, it is useful; to reduce matters to writing means that you shall know them, see them in their origins and sequences, in their essential lineaments, considerably better than you ever did before. To set about writing my own *Life* would be no less than horrible to me; and shall of a certainty never be done. The common impious vulgar of this earth, what has it to do with my life or me? Let dignified oblivion, silence, and the vacant azure of Eternity swallow *me*; for my share of it, that, verily, is the handsomest, or one handsome way, of settling my poor account with the *canaille* of mankind extant and to come. 'Immortal glory', is not that a beautiful thing, in the Shakespeare Clubs and Literary Gazettes of our improved Epoch?—I did not leave London, except for fourteen days in August, to a fine and high old Lady-friend's in Kent; where riding about the woods and by the sea-beaches and chalk cliffs, in utter silence, I felt sadder than ever, though a little less *miserably* so, than in the intrusive babblements of London, which I could not quite lock out of doors. We read, at first, Tennyson's *Idyls*, with profound recognition of the finely elaborated execution, and also of the inward perfection of *vacancy*,—and, to say truth, with considerable impatience at being treated so very like infants, though the lollipops were so superlative. We gladly changed for one Emerson's *English Traits*; and read that, with increasing and ever increasing satisfaction every evening; blessing Heaven that there were still Books for grown-up people too! That truly is a Book all full of thoughts like winged arrows (thanks to the Bowyer from us both):—my Lady-friend's name is Miss Davenport Bromley; it was at Wooton, in her Grand-father's House, in Staffordshire, that Rousseau took shelter in 1760; and one hundred and six years later she was reading Emerson to me with a recognition that would have pleased the man, had he seen it.

About that same time my health and humors being evidently so, the Dowager Lady Ashburton (*not* the high Lady you saw, but a Successor of Mackenzie-Highland type), who wanders mostly about the Continent since her widowhood, for the sake of a child's health, began pressing and inviting me to spend the blade months of Winter here in her Villa with her;—all friends warmly seconding and urging; by one of whom I was at last snatched off, as if by the hair of the head, (in spite of my violent No, no!) on the eve of Christmas last, and have been here ever since,—really with improved omens. The place is beautiful as a very picture, the climate superlative (to-day a sun and sky like very June); the *hospitality* of usage beyond example. It is likely I shall be here another six weeks, or longer. If you please to write me, the address is on the margin; and I will answer.

Adieu.
T. Carlyle

Quid plura] what more need I say?

BENJAMIN DISRAELI
(1804–1881)

The author of several novels, notably *Coningsby* (1844) and *Sybil* (1845), Disraeli (later 1st Earl of Beaconsfield) was Tory Prime Minister in 1868 and 1874–80.

140. To John Murray, 29 July 1824

Disraeli had his first story published at 17 and his novel *Vivian Grey* (1826) was a great success. In May 1824 he sent another, a satire called *Aylmer Papillon*, to the publisher Murray, who turned it down. (Two chapters survive.)

My dear Sir,
Until I received your note this morning, I had flattered myself, that my indiscretion had been forgotten.

It is to me a matter of great regret, that, as appears by your letter, any more trouble should be given respecting this unfortunate MS., which will, most probably, be considered too crude a production for the public, and which if it is even imagined to possess any interest, is certainly too late for this Season, and will be obsolete in the next.

I think therefore that the sooner it be put behind the fire, the better, and as you have some small experience in burning MSS., you will be perhaps so kind as to consign it to the flames.

Once more apologising for all the trouble I have given you

I remain | ever my dear Sir, | Yours very faithfully
B. Disraeli

Burning MSS.] in May 1824 Murray had burned Byron's 'Memoirs'.

141. To Henry Colburn, 14 February 1830

Colburn was a publisher. The enclosed letter was to be forwarded to Catherine Gore, a novelist on his list.

PRIVATE

Dear Sir,

Forward the enclosed and don't look pale about the postage, which I will religiously discharge when we meet. I have not forgotten you, tho' the preparations for my departure and another cause have prevented me lately sending you a contribution. In a word, being declared to be in a decline, which is all stuff, but really with positive Exile, probable Death, and possible Damnation hanging over me, I have been fool enough to be intent upon a novel—But such a novel! It will astound you, draw tears from Princesses, and grins from Printers devils: it will atone for all the stupid books you have been lately publishing, and allow me to die in a blaze. In a word to give you an idea of it. It is exactly the kind of work which you wo[ul]d write yourself, if you had time, and delightfully adapted to the most corrupt taste. This immortal work which will set all Europe afire and not be forgotten till at least 3 months has only one fault—it is not written.

Seriously however *a volume and ½* are finished, but as I must go off before the end of March, I am afraid it is impossible to let you have it, but perhaps I can finish it at Rome before I go off to Greece, and then you can have it for next Season. A pity because it is exactly suited to the present. Write if you wish me to hatch this Phoenix—but any rate be SECRET AS THE GRAVE.

in haste
B. Disraeli

P.S. I have not yet read Mrs C[atherine] G[ore]'s novel, which howr. I have. You are publishing a good deal of dull stuff. *Imitations of imitations.*

142. To Sarah Disraeli, 12 November 1831

Disraeli's sister Sarah was his regular correspondent.

My dearest Sister,

I write you tho' I have of course but little to tell you, and I am afraid our beloved Sire will justly grumble at the postage, but I hope some day to be a privileged correspondt. when I may even send you a billet doux by the Royal Mail.

I shall not sacrifice the pipes as indeed there is no need. Had I fifty thousand a year, I should sell them, as really now I have quitted the land of splendor, they strike me as too magnificent for any Frank. I have not yet finally arranged about them, as I do not choose to appear in a hurry, but I have no doubt I shall satisfactorily.

I hope that Jem will not be in despair when I tell you, that I have resolved to bring down neither horse nor groom at present. The fact is I am already touched by another cold, and I foresee, that I must be a very wary wanderer in the fields during this winter. I shall therefore postpone till the spring, the establishment of my stud. In coming to this resolution, I must however observe, that I have been influenced by the consideration, that my father always had two saddlehorses at my command, and at this time of the year, when William is so little employed by you, even a groom. Jem's *fiasco* howr is a blow to this arrangement., but I hope we may recover, and put ourselves in our old, or a similar, position.

I hope to be with you on Tuesday, and sho[ul]d perhaps on Monday, but the most extraordinary thing has happened. My friend Henry Stanley, who came over very much involved, and to whom I gave very good advice etc. lost his good genius when I left London, and instead of having the courage to go to his father, is playing hide and seek and can nowhere be heard of. His family are in a state of frenzy. His father has opened one of my letters addressed to Knowsley Park, and writes up to me full of heartrend[in]g apologies at the liberty and paternal exclamations to save his son. It was fortunately a letter of very good advice. Ld Stanley looks entirely to me for succour, and I am surrounded by Stanleys, all day long, full of despair, making researches and following clues. My colleague in all this is Col. Long of the G[uar]ds. We have made some very extraordinary discoveries, and you cannot imagine what curious characters I am obliged to see. Under these circumstances, I cannot leave London until I receive Lord Stanleys answer to my letter of this evening, which will be Tuesday. I shall come down on that day, provided I am not anxiously requested to remain. I think you will agree with me that it will be neither kind nor judicious to desert them. Is not this an adventure? Ralph thinks an establishment may be procured at Sharpes in the Haymarket which will suit us. I dined with Ward yesterday alone at Austens. He is quite himself again both in health and intellect, and was more than kind, but so deaf, that to me he is a dead man. Conversation is impossible. Love to all. How I long to be with you— and a thousand, thousand loves to my dearest Sa, from her devoted brother—

BD

Postage] at this date the recipient paid the postage, unless the letter was franked; members of Parliament could send up to ten letters a day with franks. 'Before franking was abolished in 1840, up to one-ninth of all letters passing through the Post Office were franked' (the editors of the current edn. of the *Correspondence*). Any Frank] any European; Disraeli had collected the pipes in the Levant. Jem] a servant, reputed to have bad judgement in horseflesh. Henry Stanley] son of Baron Stanley, later Earl of Derby.

143. To Sarah Disraeli, 9 May 1835

Before he was elected to Parliament for Maidstone in 1837 Disraeli had failed in 1832 and 1835 at High Wycombe and Taunton. At Taunton he attacked the Irish politician Daniel O'Connell (1775–1847), who in reply described Disraeli as 'the impenitent thief'. O'Connell had killed a man in a duel and thereafter would not fight, so Disraeli addressed his challenge to the politician's second son Morgan (1804–85), assuring him of the utter contempt in which he held his father. Morgan had actually fought a duel on 4 May, and also declined Disraeli's challenge. Duelling had been made illegal in 1808, but the practice continued.

Dearest,

This morning as I was lying in bed, thankful that I had kicked all the O'Connells and that I was at length to have a quiet morning, Mr Collard the Police Officer of Marybone, rushed into my chamber and took me into custody. In about an hour and a half being dressed (having previously sent to Sykes) we all went in a hackney coach to the Office and where I found that the articles were presented by a Mr Bennett residing in some street in Westminster and an acquaintance of the O'Connells. We were soon dismissed, but I am now bound to keep the peace in £500 2 sureties in £250 each. As far as the present affair is concerned 'twas a most unnecessary precaution, as if all the O'Connells were to challenge me, I cd. not think of meeting them *now*. I consider, and everyone else, that they are kicked[.] They are in a kennel, and there I shall le[*ave*] them. I have not seen Ralph to day to communicate this intelligence. It is my intention to come down on Monday, but I am very alarmed lest Sykes shd. accompany me. He threatens terribly.

Love to all

D

Ralph] a brother of Disraeli's.

144. To Sarah Disraeli, 22 June 1838

Dearest,

We had a very agreeable party indeed at D'Orsay's yesterday. Zichy, who has cut out even Esterhazy, having two jackets, one of diamonds more brilliant than E's, and another, which he wore at the Drawing Room yesterday, of *turquoises*. This makes the greatest sensation of the two. He speaks English perfectly, is a great traveller, been to Nubia, all over Asia and to Canada and the U.S. Then there was the Duke of Ossuna, a young man, but a Grandee of the highest grade. He is neither Carlist nor Christino and does not mean to return to Spain, until they have settled everything. Therefore they have confiscated his estates, but he has a large property in Italy and also in Belgium. He is a great dandy, and looks like Philip the 2nd—but tho' the only living descendant of the Borgia's he has the reputation of being very amiable. When he was last at Paris, he attended a repres[entati]on of V[ictor] Hugo's Lucrece Borgia. She says in one of the scenes

'Great crimes are in our blood.'

All his friends looked at him with an expression of fear 'but the blood has degenerated' he sd 'for I have committed only weaknesses.['] Then there was the real Prince Poniatowsky, also young, and with a most brilliant star. Then came Kissiloffs and Stroganoffs 'and other offs and ons' and De Belancour, a very agreeable person, Lyndhurst, Gardner, Bulwer and myself completed the party—which was a fine banquet.

I must give up going to the Coron[ati]on, as we go in state, and all the MPs *must be* in Court Dresses or uniforms. As I have withstood making a costume of this kind for other purposes, I will not make one now, and console myself by the conviction that to get up very early (8 o'ck:) to sit dressed like a flunky in the Abbey for seven or eight hours and to listen to a sermon by the Bp of London can be no great enjoyment.

I called on the Austens (not at home); I have heard no more of my legal friends. I paired off on the Vixen. It was useless attending the Cop[y] Right. Lyndhurst made a very successful speech the other night on Spain. Foreign Pol[itic]s are coming into fashion.

Love

D'Orsay] The Count d'Orsay (1801–52), Lady Blessington's lover, and with her responsible for a celebrated London salon; he was a painter, sculptor, and leader of fashionable society. Disraeli sketched him as Count Mirabel in *Henrietta Temple*. The other guests were mostly ambassadors and grandees of other sorts.   Drawing Room] formal royal reception.   Carlist . . . Christino] the two sides in the current Spanish civil war.   The Copy Right] a bill to amend the law of copyright was postponed till the following session.

145. To Lady Bradford, 25 November 1875

Disraeli began his second term as Prime Minister in 1874. The Suez Canal was opened in 1869, changing the sea route to India. The Khedive, in financial difficulties, sold his shares in the Canal Company. Disraeli bought them through the Rothschilds and got the consent of Parliament later. The Faery was Queen Victoria,

who loved Disraeli. In the following year he persuaded her to become Empress of
India.

As you complain sometimes, though I think unjustly, that I tell you nothing, I will now tell you a great State secret, though it may not be one in 4
and 20 hours (still, you will like to know it 4 and 20 hours sooner than the
newspapers can tell you)—a State secret, certainly the most important of
this year, and not one of the least events of our generation. After a fortnight
of the most unceasing labor and anxiety, I (for, between ourselves, and
ourselves only, I may be egotistical in this matter)—I have purchased for
England, the Khedive of Egypt's interest in the Suez Canal.

We have had all the gamblers, capitalists, financiers of the world, organised and platooned in bands of plunderers, arrayed against us, and secret
emissaries in every corner, and have baffled them all, and have never been
suspected.

The day before yesterday, Lesseps, whose Company has the remaining
shares, backed by the French Government, whose agent he was, made a
great offer. Had it succeeded, the whole of the Suez Canal would have
belonged to France, and they might have shut it up!

We have given the Khedive 4 millions sterling for his interest, and run
the chance of Parliament supporting us. We could not call them together
for the matter, for that would have blown everything to the skies, or to
Hades.

The Faery is in ecstacies about 'this great and important event'—wants
'to know all about it when Mr D. comes down to-day.'

I have rarely been though a week like the last—and am to-day in a state
of prostration—coma—sorry I have to go down to Windsor—still more
sorry not to have had a line to-day, which would have soothed.

Your affectionate
D

P.S.—Though secret here, the telegraph will send the news from Egypt, I
doubt not, to-day.

THOMAS DE QUINCEY
(1785–1859)

The critic and essayist De Quincey is especially noted for his *Confessions of an English
Opium Eater* (1821). His admiration for Wordsworth led him to settle in the Lake
District, where, in 1817, he married Margaret Simpson, a farmer's daughter. He was
much in London, earning a living as a writer, but often desperate for money and
plagued by his opium habit.

146. To Dorothy Wordsworth, 16 July 1825

My dear Madam,

I am at this time in great agitation of mind, and I solicit your assistance in a way where you can give it effectually.—Call, I beg and pray you, my dear Miss Wordsworth, on my poor wife—who suffers greatly from a particular case of embarrassment affecting me just now. What this is, and how it arose, I began to explain in a very long letter: but repeated interruptions from the Press have not allowed me to finish it. Suffice it however here to say—that in a few weeks I shall be free from all distresses of the kind which have so long weighed upon me. Meantime, she writes me the most moving and heart-rending letters—not complaining, but simply giving utterance to her grief. In her very last letter she concludes by begging me 'not to take her grief amiss': and in fact she disturbs my fortitude so much, that I cannot do half what I else could. For my fear is—that being thrown entirely upon herself, with no soul (unless her eldest sister) to speak a word of comfort to her—she will suffer her grief to grow upon her, and in her present uncomfortable situation will fret herself to illness. If that should happen, I know what I must look for next: and I shall never have any peace of mind, or a happy hour, again. Assure her that all will be well in a very few weeks; and the greater part in a fortnight. What a sad thing then that she should give way to a momentary pressure, just at the time when I have first a prospect of for ever getting over any pressure of that kind.—Oh! Miss Wordsworth,—I sympathised with you—how deeply and fervently—in your trials 13 years ago:—now, when I am prostrate for a moment—and the hand of a friend would enable me to rise before I am crushed, do not refuse me this service. But I need not conjure you in this way: for you are full of compassion and goodness to those whose hearts are overburthened with long affliction.—What I wish is—that you would give my wife the relief of talking over her distress with one whom she can feel to be sympathising with her.—To do this with the less constraint, perhaps you will be so good as to go over and drink tea with her. And let me know, if you please, how she is in health:—Direct to me—To the care of Chas. Knight Esqr., Pall Mall East,—London.

Say whatever you can think of to raise and support her spirits: beg her not to lie down too much, as she is apt to do in states of dejection, but to walk in the fields when it is cool; and to take some *solid* food, which she is very apt to neglect.—She is amused by newspapers: perhaps you could lend her a few just for the present, until I am able to send one down.

Having written so much of my longer letter, I shall finish and send it on Monday or Tuesday. I must beg you to excuse my putting you to the expense of 2 letters: which, in any other circumstances, I would not have done.

If I had any chearful news from home,—I am *now* in a condition to extricate myself in 28 days.

God bless you, my dear Miss Wordsworth,—stand my friend at this moment.

Trials] probably the deaths of William Wordsworth's children Thomas and Catharine in 1812.

EMILY EDEN
(1797–1869)

Emily Eden was a novelist (*The Semi-detached House*, 1859, and *The Semi-attached Couple*, 1860). She accompanied her brother George to India when he was Governor-General (1835–42) and wrote informatively about Indian life.

147. To Theresa Villiers, 1825

My dear Miss Villiers,

What a shame it is that I should have been so long writing to you, particularly after Mrs Villiers had made the discovery that my letters amused her. My sister Louisa [Colvile] and four of her children passed a fortnight here at the end of last month, and our whole time was spent in 'exploring in the barouche landau,' as Mrs Elton observes.

By the time I have had nine or ten more of my sisters here, and thirty or forty of their children, I shall be tired of my own enthusiasm in the great picturesque cause; but at present all other employments are sacrificed to it. However, it may amuse you.

I shall continue to think a visit to Chatsworth a very great trouble. You are probably right in thinking the Duke takes pleasure in making people do what they don't like, and that accounts for his asking me so often. We have now made a rule to accept one invitation out of two. We go there with the best dispositions, wishing to be amused, liking the people we meet there, loyal and well affected to the King of the Peak himself, supported by the knowledge that in the eyes of the neighborhood we are covering ourselves with glory by frequenting the *great house*; but with all these helps we have never been able to stay above two days there without finding change of air absolutely necessary,—never could turn the corner of the third day,—at the end of the second the great depths of *bore* were broken up and carried all before them: we were obliged to pretend that some christening, or a grand funeral, or some pressing case of wedding (in this country it is sometimes expedient to hurry the performance of the marriage ceremony) required Robert's immediate return home, and so we departed yawning. It is odd it should be so dull. The G. Lambs are both pleasant, and so is Mr Foster and Mrs Cavendish and a great many of the habitués of Chatsworth; and though I have not yet attained the real Derbyshire feeling which would bring tears of admiration into my eyes whenever the Duke observed that it was a fine day, yet I think him pleasant, and like him very much, and can make him hear without any difficulty, and he is very hospitable and wishes us to bring all our friends and relations there, if that would do us any good. But we happen to be *pleasanter* at home. However private vices may contribute to public benefit, I do not see how private bore can contribute to public happiness, do you?

Pray give my love to your mother, and believe me,

your affectionate

E.E.

Exploring . . . landau] in Jane Austen's *Emma*.   The Duke] 6th Duke of Devonshire, whose seat is at Chatsworth, Derbyshire.   G. Lambs] George Lamb was a son of Lord Melbourne. Private vices . . . public benefit] alluding to Bernard de Mandeville's famous satire *The Fable of the Bees* (1723).

148. To Theresa Villiers, 15 December 1826

My dear Theresa,

I wish to apprise you not to go in search of me in Grosvenor Street, because I am not there. 'I am very bed with the ague,' as people must be in the habit of saying in these fenny districts. I '*ticed* my poor dear George out of town into this horrid place, and here he is with nobody to play with and nothing to do, and missing his Woburn shooting. . . . Still the idea of another's bore is a heavy weight on my mind.

You will be happy to hear that Mr Robinson is very well. George says he never saw him better, and he makes a point of telling him so three times a day at least. The poor man is starving, as Sarah will not allow him to dine except in her dressing-room at two o'clock, because, as she does not dine down with the family, she says she cannot trust to his promises not to eat more than is right, as she is not there. He happens to have an immensely good appetite since his headache, and frets like a child about this; but has not courage to dine like a man on the most unwholesome things he can find. I would live on mushrooms and walnuts and fried plum-pudding if I were him.

This conversation passed verbatim yesterday, but do not for your life mention it again. He wanted to go to the stables when he was out walking, but said Sarah had told him not. However, he went boldly to her window and knocked at it. 'Sarah, I wish I might go to the stables?'—'No, dearest, I told you before not to go.'—'Yes; but I want to see my horses. Mayn't I go?'—'No, darling, you said you would not ask it if I let you go out.'— 'Yes; but one of my horses is sick, and I want to see it.'—'Well, then, if

Mama will go with you, you may.' So Sister actually had to go with him to take care of him. She told me this, and did not know whether he was ashamed of it; but I saw him in the evening and he repeated it, evidently rather pleased that he was made so much of. He is a poor creature after all, Theresa, though you are so fond of him.

Your most affectionate
E.E.

Anne and Mary went on Wednesday. I did not see them the last two days, but Mr Auckland still does not admire them. I wish Anne would be as pleasant in society as she is alone with one. I think she is nervous.

Robinson] F. R. Robinson, Viscount Goderich (1782–1859) Prime Minister for four months in 1827. He married Sarah, daughter of the Earl of Buckingham, who lived at Nocton, Lincolnshire.

149. To Theresa Villiers, 1 September 1827

My dearest Theresa,

I ought to have written sooner, but I have been so languid and sick. Mary's lying-in was the most charming amusement in the world. I believe that is one of the points on which we have argued with all the extra-pertinacity that our complete ignorance naturally gave us, and for once I think you were right. It is *not* the awful business I thought it had been. She was ill a very short time, had no nurse (because hers did not hurry herself to arrive so much as the child did), has recovered without a check, and I left her on Wednesday nursing Mary the 2nd with great satisfaction to herself and child.

George has been as usual all kindness—willing to give up all his shoot-ing, and go with me to the sea, or even *to* sea, which did me good when I was formerly declining; and to-day is the 1st of September, and he is sitting here with me nursing and coaxing me up, and the partridges are all flying about the world, and he not shooting them. I think I shall be able to go on Wednesday, and the worst come to the worst, we can but come back again, and I shall not feel so *guilty* towards him and Fanny.

As usual there are plenty of people in London, and I had as many visitors yesterday as in the middle of June. Lady Lansdowne was here most part of the morning, Mrs G. Lamb, Mr Foster, Mr C. Greville, who heard I was sick, and came to ask if his carriage could not take me out airing every day at any time. There is nothing like those wicked *roués* at heart; they are so good-natured! But what touched me yesterday was poor Lady Grantham's coming here for an hour and being just as much interested about my foolish ailments as if she had not her favourite child dying at home. Amabel was as ill as possible on Thursday but a shade better yesterday, I never saw a more touching sight than Lady Grantham, I have thought of nothing else since. She is so calm and quiet and so perfectly miserable; she looked like a statue yesterday, there was such an immovability in her countenance and such a wan white look about her, even her lips looked quite white and still; she still has a little hope but seems to give herself as much as possible to preparing Amabel for *her* great change and herself departing with her. What would one give to save that child for her!

Sarah is, you will be happy to hear, behaving with the most perfect consistency. She fancied she was in labour three days ago, and had all the workmen sent off from the buildings in Downing Street—just as if they could not all be in labour together. If it is true (and of course it is as Shakespeare says it) that the fantastic tricks of men dressed in a little brief authority (and the Goderich authority seems likely to be brief enough) do make the Angels weep, what a deplorable time the Angels have had of it lately with Sarah! They must nearly have cried their eyes out. She has adopted a new form of tyranny with Sister; would not let her be at Eastcombe, but makes her stay in Downing Street; and then will not see her, but desires she may never leave the house. . . .

I cannot tell you the stories of his [Lord Goderich's] *ineptie* and which those who do not know him thoroughly might well take for unfair dealing; but that he is not capable of. I fancy there never was a more wretched man—so worried he cannot eat. Sister said she should hardly know him at home. He rattles in company.

Your most affect.

E.E.

Greville] Charles Greville (1794–1865), political diarist, was Clerk to the Privy Council.   Lady Grantham] Robinson's sister-in-law.   Fantastic . . . authority] *Measure for Measure*, II. ii. 117–22.

THOMAS BABINGTON MACAULAY
(1800–1859)

Macaulay was an essayist and historian, already by the time of the first letter below well known for his essay on Milton. He was called to the Bar in 1826 and joined the northern circuit. He was a Whig MP from 1830; in 1834 he became member of the Supreme Council of India, where he exerted great influence on legal and educational matters. He returned and began his *History of England* in 1838 (published 1849, 1855). Made rich by his writings, he was ennobled in 1857.

150. *To Zachary Macaulay, 21 July 1826*

This letter was written while on circuit. Zachary (1768–1838), his father, was a philanthropist who fought for the abolition of slavery.

My dear Father,

I have received your letter and its inclosure. Many thanks for both. I shall soon, I hope by what I hear from the Temple, repay you.

I shall be at Skipton by nine on Monday Night, at Bradford on Wednesday evening, at Leeds on the following Monday morning by eleven. I am not quite certain when I shall reach Rotherham. But you shall know in time. There will be an interval of three or four days between the close of the Sessions for the West Riding and the Commencement of the Assizes at Lancaster. Perhaps I may go to Manchester, which lies almost in the way, and see George Phillipps.

Àpropos of visits, the other day as I was changing my neckcloth which my wig had disfigured, my good land lady knocked at the door of my bed room, and told me that Mr Smith wished to see me and was in my room below. Of all names by which men are called there is none which conveys a less determinate idea to the mind than that of Smith. Was he on the circuit? For I do not know half the names of my companions. Was he a special messenger from London? Was he a York attorney coming to be preyed upon, or a beggar coming to prey upon me; a barber to solicit the dressing of my wig, or a collector for the Jews' Society? Down I went, and to my utter amazement beheld the Smith of Smiths, Sidney Smith, alias Peter Plymely. I had forgotten his very existence till I discerned the queer contrast between his black coat and his snow-white head, and the equally curious contrast between the clerical amplitude of his person and the most unclerical wit, whim, and petulance of his eye. I shook hands with him very heartily; and on the Catholic question we immediately fell, regretted Evans, triumphed over Lord George Beresford, and abused the Bishops. He then very kindly urged me to spend the time between the close of the assizes and the Commencement of the Sessions at his house; and was so hospitably pressing that I at last agreed to go thither on Saturday afternoon. He is to drive me over again into York on Monday Morning. I am very well pleased at having this opportunity of becoming better acquainted with a man who, in spite of innumerable affectations and eccentricities, is certainly one of the wittiest and most original write[rs of] our times. I shall see him indeed in [those?] situations in which he displays his [best and?] his worst peculiarities most strongly, at the head of his table and in his pulpit. How strange an instance of self-love it is that the man who possesses perhaps the finest sense of the ridiculous of any person now living, should not perceive the exquisite absurdity of his own style of preaching.

Believe me ever Yours affectionately

T B M

Phillipps] a former Whig MP.   Jews' Society] the 'Evangelical London Society for Promoting Christianity amongst the Jews'.   Sidney Smith] see above, Letters 123–9; this was

during his time in the Yorkshire living.   Lord George Beresford] (1773–1862), an opponent of Catholic emancipation.

151. To Thomas Flower Ellis, 30 March 1831

Ellis (1796–1861) became a close friend of Macaulay when they were both barristers
on the northern circuit.

Dear Ellis,

I have little news for you, except what you will learn from the papers as
well as from me. It is clear that the Reform Bill must pass, either in this or
in another Parliament. The majority of one does not appear to me, as it
does to you, by any means inauspicious. We should perhaps have had a
better plea for a dissolution if the majority had been the other way. But
surely a dissolution under such circumstances would have been a most
alarming thing. If there should be a dissolution now there will not be that
ferocity in the public mind which there would have been if the House of
Commons had refused to entertain the Bill at all.—I confess that, till we
had a majority, I was half inclined to tremble at the storm which we had
raised. At present I think that we are absolutely certain of victory, and of
victory without commotion.

Such a scene as the division of last Tuesday I never saw, and never
expect to see again. If I should live fifty years the impression of it will be
as fresh and sharp in my mind as if it had just taken place. It was like seeing
Cæsar stabbed in the Senate House, or seeing Oliver taking the mace from
the table, a sight to be seen only once and never to be forgotten. The crowd
overflowed the House in every part. When the strangers were cleared out
and the doors locked we had six hundred and eight members present, more
by fifty five than ever were at a division before. The Ayes and Noes were
like two vollies of cannon from opposite sides of a field of battle. When the
opposition went out into the lobby,—an operation by the bye which took
up twenty minutes or more,—we spread ourselves over the benches on
both sides of the House. For there were many of us who had not been able
to find a seat during the evening. When the doors were shut we began to
speculate on our numbers. Every body was desponding. 'We have lost it.
We are only two hundred and eighty at most. I do not think we are two
hundred and fifty. They are three hundred. Alderman Thompson has
counted them. He says they are two hundred and ninety nine.' This was
the talk on our benches. I wonder that men who have been long in parliament do not acquire a better coup d'œil for numbers. The House when
only the Ayes were in it looked to me a very fair house,—much fuller than
it generally is even on debates of considerable interest. I had no hope
however of three hundred. As the tellers passed along our lowest row on

the left hand side the interest was insupportable,—two hundred and ninety one:—two hundred and ninety two:—we were all standing up and stretching forward, telling with the tellers. At three hundred there was a short cry of joy, at three hundred and two another—suppressed however in a moment. For we did not yet know what the hostile force might be. We knew however that we could not be severely beaten. The doors were thrown open and in they came. Each of them as he entered brought some different report of their numbers. It must have been impossible, as you may conceive, in the lobby, crowded as they must have been, to form any exact estimate. First we heard that they were three hundred and three—then the number rose to three hundred and ten, then went down to three hundred and seven. Alexander Baring told me that he had counted and that they were three hundred and four. We were all breathless with anxiety, when Charles Wood who stood near the door jumped on a bench and cried out, 'They are only three hundred and one.' We set up a shout that you might have heard to Charing Cross—waving our hats—stamping against the floor and clapping our hands. The tellers scarcely got through the crowd:—for the house was thronged up to the table, and all the floor was fluctuating with heads like the pit of a theatre. But you might have heard a pin drop as Duncannon read the numbers. Then again the shouts broke out—and many of us shed tears—I could scarcely refrain. And the jaw of Peel fell; and the face of Twiss was as the face of a damned soul; and Herries looked like Judas taking his neck-cloth off for the last operation. We shook hands and clapped each other on the back, and went out laughing, crying, and huzzaing into the lobby. And no sooner were the outer doors opened than another shout answered that within the house. All the passages and the stairs into the waiting rooms were thronged by people who had waited till four in the morning to know the issue. We passed through a narrow lane between two thick masses of them; and all the way down they were shouting and waving their hats; till we got into the open air. I called a cabriolet—and the first thing the driver asked was, 'Is the Bill carried?'—'Yes, by one.' 'Thank God for it, Sir.' And away I rode to Grey's Inn—and so ended a scene which will probably never be equalled till the reformed Parliament wants reforming; and that I hope will not be till the days of our grandchildren—till that truly orthodox and apostolical person Dr Francis Ellis is an archbishop of eighty.

What are your movements? Mine are not absolutely determined. Have you had many briefs? At any rate you have, I suppose, been employed against the coiners. However the weightier matters of the law may fare, the tithe of mint, I hope, goes on.

As for me, I am for the present a sort of lion. My speech has set me in the front rank, if I can keep there; and it has not been my luck hitherto to lose ground when I have once got it. Shiel and I are on very civil terms. He talks largely concerning Demosthenes and Burke. He made, I must say, an excellent speech—too florid and queer; but decidedly successful.

Why did not the great Samuel Grove Price speak? He often came to the front rows, and sate making notes. Every body expected him to rise, and prepared night-caps accordingly. But he always sneaked away. On my soul, I believe that he is a craven with all his bluster. Indeed if he is afraid, it is the best thing that I ever knew of him. For a more terrible audience there is not in the world. I wish that Praed had known to whom he was speaking. But with all his talent, he has no tact, no perception of the character of his audience; and he has fared accordingly. Tierney used to say that he never rose in the House without feeling his knees tremble under him: and I am sure that no man who has not some of that feeling will ever succeed there.

Ever yours

T B Macaulay

The Reform Bill] it had a majority of one on its second reading (22 Mar.).   Oliver] Cromwell.   Alexander Baring] a banker, opposed to the bill.   Charles Wood] later Viscount Halifax (1800–85); he was later to serve as Chancellor of the Exchequer and Secretary of State for India.   Peel] Sir Robert Peel (1788–1850) opposed the Reform and had made a notable speech on 3 Mar.   Twiss] Horace Twiss, another Tory, also opposed the bill. Herries] J. C. Herries, a Tory, was later very briefly Chancellor in Goderich's administration. Francis Ellis] the 6-year-old son of Ellis.   Shiel] an Irish barrister and a new MP. Price] a known opponent of the bill.   Praed] Winthrop Mackworth Praed (1802–39), best known as a poet, was a friend of Macaulay's but as an MP opposed the bill. His speech in the debate was, as Macaulay suggests, a failure.   Tierney] George Tierney, a leading Whig.

152. To Hannah Macaulay, 1 June 1831

My dearest Sister,

My last letter was a dull one. I mean this to be very amusing. My last was about Basinghall Street, attorneys and bankrupts. But for this—take it dramatically in the German style.

Time morning. Scene the great entrance of Holland House. Enter Macaulay and two Footmen in livery.

First Footman.
  Sir may I venture to demand your name?
Macaulay.
  Macaulay, and thereto I add M.P.
  And that addition even in these proud halls
  May well insure the bearer some respect.
Second Footman.
  And art thou come to breakfast with our Lord?

Macaulay.

    I am: for so his hospitable will

    And hers—the peerless dame ye serve—hath bade.

First Footman.

    Ascend the stair, and thou above shalt find,

    On snow-white linen spread, the luscious meal.

    (Exit Macaulay up stairs.)

In plain English prose—I went this morning to breakfast at Holland House. The day was fine, and I arrived at twenty minutes after ten. After I had lounged a short time in the dining-room, I heard a gruff good-natured voice asking, 'Where is Mr Macaulay. Where have you put him;' and in his arm-chair Lord Holland was wheeled in. He took me round the apartments, he riding and I walking. He gave me the history of the most remarkable portraits in the library—where there is by the bye, one of the few bad pieces of Lawrence that I have seen—a head of Charles James Fox,—an ignominious failure: Lord Holland said that it was the worst ever painted of so eminent a man by so eminent an artist. There is a very fine head of Machiavelli—another of Earl Grey, a very different sort of man. I observed a portrait of Lady Holland painted some thirty years ago. I could have cried to see the change. She must have been a most beautiful woman. She is now, I suppose, very near sixty, very large, and with a double chin. She still looks however as if she had been handsome;—and shews in one respect great taste and sense. She does not rouge at all; or at least not in any manner which I could detect; and her costume is not youthful, so that she looks as well in the morning as in the evening.

We came back to the dining room. Our breakfast party consisted of My Lord and Lady—myself—Lord Russell,—Luttrell—and another person whose name I could not catch. You must have heard of Luttrell. I met him once at Rogers's; and I have seen him, I think, in other places. He is a famous wit—the most popular, I think, of all the professed wits,—a man who has lived in the highest circles,—a scholar, and no contemptible poet. He wrote a little volume of verse entitled 'Advice to Julia,'—not first-rate, but neat, lively, piquant, and shewing the most consummate knowledge of fashionable life.

Well, we breakfasted on very good coffee and very good tea and very good eggs,—butter kept in the midst of ice and hot rolls. Lady Holland told us her dreams; how she had dreamed that a mad dog bit her foot, and how she set off to Brodie, and lost her way in St Martin's lane and could not find him;—she hoped, she said, the dream would not come true. I said that I had had a dream which admitted of no such hope. For I had dreamed that I heard Pollock speak in the House of Commons, that the speech was very long, and that he was coughed down. This dream of mine diverted them much, and we talked of Pollock, of law and lawyers, of the art of decyphering, and of the art of acoustics. Lord Holland told us that there was formerly something in the structure of his library which conveyed the voice from one recess to another at a great distance. He had opened a bow window between them and this had removed the evil. An evil it was indeed by his account. 'Why, Sir,' said he, 'a friend of mine asked another friend of mine in one of those recesses whether he should propose to a girl—and the adviser dissuaded him most strongly. The lady was in the other recess, and heard every word.'—A pretty business indeed!

After breakfast Lady Holland offered to conduct me to her own drawing-room;—or rather commanded my attendance. A very beautiful room it is, opening on a terrace, and wainscotted with miniature paintings interesting from their merit, and interesting from their history. Among them I remarked a great many, thirty I should think, which even I, who am no great connoisseur, saw at once could come from no hand but Stothard's. They were all on subjects from Lord Byron's poems. 'Yes,' said she; 'poor Lord Byron sent them to me a short time before the separation. I sent them back, and told him that if he gave them away, he ought to give them to Lady Byron. But he said that he would not—and that, if I did not take them, the bailiffs would, and that they would be lost in the wreck.' Her ladyship then honoured me so far as to conduct me through her dressing room into the great family-bedchamber to shew me a very fine picture by Reynolds of Fox when a boy bird's-nesting. I had seen it at the British Gallery. She then consigned me to Luttrell, asking him to shew me the grounds.

Through the grounds we went and very pretty I thought them. Much more, however, might be done at little cost. But Lady Holland, has not, I find, paid much attention to gardening. In the Dutch garden—a very appropriate and pretty appendage to such an antique building as the house,— there is an interesting object—a very fine bronze bust of Napoleon, which Lord Holland put up in 1817, while Napoleon was a prisoner at St Helena. The inscription was selected by his Lordship, and is remarkably happy. It is from Homer's Odyssey. I will translate it as well as I can extempore into a measure which gives a better idea of Homer's manner than Pope's sing-song couplet.

> 'For not, be sure, within the grave
> Is hid that prince, the wise, the brave,—
> But in an islet's narrow bound,
> With the great Ocean roaring round,
> The captive of a foeman base,
> He pineth for his native place.'—

There is a seat near the spot which is called Rogers's seat. The poet loves, it seems, to sit there. A very elegant inscription by Lord Holland is placed over it.

> 'Here Rogers sate; and here forever dwell
> With me those pleasures which he sang so well.'

Very neat and condensed, I think. Another inscription by Luttrell hangs there. Luttrell adjured me with mock pathos to spare his blushes; but I am author enough to know what the blushes of authors mean. So I read the lines; and very pretty and polished they were—but too many to be remembered from one reading.

Having gone round the grounds I took my leave, very much pleased with the place. Lord Holland is extremely kind. But that is of course; for he is kindness itself. Her Ladyship too, which is by no means of course, is all graciousness and civility. But, for all this, I would much rather be quietly walking with you, my darling. And the great use of going to these fine places is to learn how happy it is possible to be without them. Indeed I care so little for them that I certainly should not have gone to day, but that I thought that I should be able to find materials for a letter which you might like. Farewell—my sweet sister. Give my love to Selina and Fanny. I am delighted to hear that Selina has placed herself under Dr Jephson with good hopes. I believe that the hope, in her case, is half the cure. Love to my father.

Ever yours, dearest,
T B M

Lawrence] Sir Thomas Lawrence (1769–1830), portrait painter.   Lord Russell] (1792–1878), Whig and friend of the Hollands, moved the first reading of the Reform Bill; he was Prime Minister 1846–50.   Luttrell] Henry Luttrell was famous for dining out.   Rogers] Samuel Rogers (1763–1855) was a banker and a poet, famous for *The Pleasures of Memory* (1792). Brodie] Sir Benjamin Brodie, a surgeon.   Pollock] a Tory, who had not yet spoken in the House.   Stothard] Thomas Stothard, painter and illustrator of Byron.   Fox] C. J. Fox, the great Whig.   Rogers's seat] it may still be seen in Holland Park.   Dr Jephson] Henry Jephson established a strict dictary regime for his patients at Leamington Spa.

153. To Margaret Macaulay, 26 November 1832

My dearest Margaret,

When you receive this letter, I shall be on the road to Leeds; and I shall not see you again till the separation of which I cannot think without losing all my firmness shall have taken place. I have not taken leave of you. For I wished to spare you the pain of witnessing distress which you would, I know, feel acutely, but which you would not be able to relieve. I purpose to bear my affliction, as I have borne it hitherto, that is to say, alone. Mine is no case for sympathy or consolation. The heart knows its own bitterness.

My sufferings, like the sufferings of most other men, are the natural consequences of my own weakness. The attachment between brothers and sisters, blameless, amiable, and delightful as it is, is so liable to be superseded by other attachments that no wise man ought to suffer it to become indispensable to his happiness. Very few, even of those who are called good brothers, do suffer it to become indispensable. But to me it has been in the place of a first love. During the years when the imagination is most vivid and the heart most susceptible, my affection for my sisters has prevented me from forming any serious attachment. But for them I should be quite alone in the world. I have nothing else to love. Yet I knew, or ought to have known, that what was every day becoming more and more necessary to me might be withdrawn in a moment. That women shall leave the home of their birth and contract ties dearer than those of consanguinity is a law as ancient as the first records of the history of our race, and as unchangeable as the constitution of the human body and mind. To repine against the nature of things,—against the great fundamental law of all society, because, in consequence of my own want of foresight, it happens to bear heavily on me, would be the basest and most absurd selfishness. And I do not repine. You can bear me witness that I have suffered with fortitude; and, if I now break silence for the first and last time, it is only that you may not attribute my sudden departure to any want of affection for you.

I have still one more stake to lose. There remains one event for which, when it arrives, I shall, I hope, be prepared. I have another sister, no less dear to me than my Margaret, from whom I may be separated in the same manner. From that moment, with a heart formed, if ever any man's heart was formed for domestic happiness, I shall have nothing left in this world but ambition.

There is no wound, however, which time and necessity do not render endurable. And, after all, what am I more than my fathers,—than the millions and tens of millions who have been weak enough to pay double price for some favourite number in the lottery of life, and who have suffered double disappointment when their ticket came up a blank? All life is a system of compensations. My reason tells me that, but for the strong attachment which is at this moment a cause of pain to me, I might, like my friend Charles Grant, have been crossed in love, or, what is much worse, might, like his brother, have married a fool. I am glad too, in the midst of my sorrow, that I shall not be at the wedding, that I shall pass the next fortnight in a constant storm, that I shall have no time to be sad, and that, at the worst, I shall be able to wreak all the bitterness of my heart on Michael Sadler.

When we meet I shall, I hope, be reconciled to what is inevitable. But I cannot think, without a flood of tears, of that meeting. Once so much to each other—and henceforth to be so little.

Farewell, dearest. From my soul I thank you for the many happy days which I have owed to you, and for the innumerable proofs which I have received of your affection. May he to whom you are about to entrust the care of your happiness love you as much as you deserve,—as much as I have loved you. And, at this parting,—for it is a parting scarcely less solemn than that of a death bed,—forgive me, my own Margaret, if I have ever neglected you, if I have ever, from thoughtlessness or in a moment of irritation, wounded your feelings. God knows that it must have been by inadvertence, and that I never in my life did or said anything intended to give you pain.

Lastly, shew this letter to no person,—not even to my dear Nancy. I do not wish her to know how deeply this separation has affected me, lest, on some future occasion, she should take my feelings into the account in forming a decision which she ought to form with a view to her own happiness alone.

Again and again, dearest, farewell.

T B Macaulay

Michael Sadler] an opponent of Reform, who was engaged with Macaulay in a controversy arising out of Macaulay's hostile review of a work in which Sadler tried to refute the views of Malthus.

ROBERT SOUTHEY
(1774–1843)

Southey was a poet, historian, and biographer. As a young man he settled in the Lake District and was closely associated with Wordsworth and Coleridge. Later, like them, he renounced his revolutionary opinions. He was made Poet Laureate in 1813.

154. To Charlotte Brontë, March 1837

Charlotte Brontë had asked Southey's advice about her prospects as a writer. She wrote on the cover of this letter, 'Southey's advice to be kept for ever. My twenty-first birthday . . .' Southey mentioned to another correspondent that, at the same time Charlotte wrote to him, her brother Branwell was writing to Wordsworth, praising him and disparaging Southey.

Madam,

You will probably, ere this, have given up all expectation of receiving an answer to your letter of December 29. I was on the borders of Cornwall when the letter was written; it found me a fortnight afterwards in Hampshire. During my subsequent movements in different parts of the country, and a tarriance of three busy weeks in London, I had no leisure for replying to it; and now that I am once more at home, and am clearing off the arrears of business which have accumulated during a long absence, it has lain unanswered till the last of a numerous file, not from disrespect or indifference to its contents, but because, in truth, it is not an easy task to answer it, nor a pleasant one to cast a damp over the high spirits and the generous desires of youth. What you are I can only infer from your letter, which appears to be written in sincerity, though I may suspect that you have used a fictitious signature. Be that as it may, the letter and the verses bear the same stamp; and I can well understand the state of mind they indicate. What I am you might have learnt by such of my publications as have come into your hands; and had you happened to be acquainted with me, a little personal knowledge would have tempered your enthusiasm. You might have had your ardour in some degree abated by seeing a poet in the decline of life, and witnessing the effect which age produces upon our hopes and aspirations; yet I am neither a disappointed man nor a discontented one, and you would never have heard from me any chilling sermons upon the text 'All is vanity.'

It is not my advice that you have asked as to the direction of your talents, but my opinion of them; and yet the opinion may be worth little, and the advice much. You evidently possess, and in no inconsiderable degree, what Wordsworth calls the 'faculty of verse.' I am not depreciating it when I say that in these times it is not rare. Many volumes of poems are now published every year without attracting public attention, any one of which, if it had appeared half a century ago, would have obtained a high reputation for its author. Whoever, therefore, is ambitious of distinction in this way ought to be prepared for disappointment.

But it is not with a view to distinction that you should cultivate this talent, if you consult your own happiness. I, who have made literature my profession, and devoted my life to it, and have never for a moment repented of the deliberate choice, think myself, nevertheless, bound in duty to caution every young man who applies as an aspirant to me for encouragement and advice against taking so perilous a course. You will say that a woman has no need of such a caution; there can be no peril in it for her. In a certain sense this is true; but there is a danger of which I would, with all kindness and all earnestness, warn you. The day dreams in which you habitually indulge are likely to induce a distempered state of mind; and, in proportion as all the ordinary uses of the world seem to you flat and unprofitable, you will be unfitted for them without becoming fitted for anything else. Literature cannot be the business of a woman's life, and it ought not to be. The more she is engaged in her proper duties, the less leisure will she have for it, even as an accomplishment and a recreation. To those duties you have not yet been called, and when you are you will be less eager for celebrity. You will not seek in imagination for excitement, of which the vicissitudes of this life, and the anxieties from which you must not hope to be exempted, be your state what it may, will bring with them but too much.

But do not suppose that I disparage the gift which you possess, nor that I would discourage you from exercising it. I only exhort you so to think of it, and so to use it, as to render it conducive to your own permanent good. Write poetry for its own sake; not in a spirit of emulation, and not with a view to celebrity; the less you aim at that the more likely you will be to deserve and finally to obtain it. So written, it is wholesome both for the heart and soul; it may be made the surest means, next to religion, of soothing the mind, and elevating it. You may embody in it your best thoughts and your wisest feelings, and in so doing discipline and strengthen them.

Farewell, madam. It is not because I have forgotten that I was once young myself, that I write to you in this strain; but because I remember it. You will neither doubt my sincerity, nor my goodwill; and, however ill what has here been said may accord with your present views and temper, the longer you live the more reasonable it will appear to you. Though I may be an ungracious adviser, you will allow me, therefore, to subscribe myself, with the best wishes for your happiness here and hereafter, your true friend,

Robert Southey

CHARLOTTE BRONTË
(1816–1855)

Charlotte Brontë was the author of *Jane Eyre* (1847) and *Villette* (1853).

155. To Robert Southey, 16 March 1837

See Southey's letter above, to which this is a reply.

Sir,

I cannot rest till I have answered your letter, even though by addressing you a second time I should appear a little intrusive; but I must thank you for the kind and wise advice you have condescended to give me. I had not ventured to hope for such a reply; so considerate in its tone, so noble in its spirit. I must suppress what I feel, or you will think me foolishly enthusiastic.

At the first perusal of your letter I felt only shame and regret that I had ever ventured to trouble you with my crude rhapsody; I felt a painful heat rise to my face when I thought of the quires of paper I had covered with what once gave me so much delight, but which now was only a source of confusion; but after I had thought a little, and read it again and again, the prospect seemed to clear. You do not forbid me to write; you do not say that what I write is utterly destitute of merit. You only warn me against the folly of neglecting real duties for the sake of imaginative pleasures; of writing for the love of fame; for the selfish excitement of emulation. You kindly allow me to write poetry for its own sake, provided I leave undone nothing which I ought to do, in order to pursue that single, absorbing, exquisite gratification. I am afraid, sir, you think me very foolish. I know the first letter I wrote to you was all senseless trash from beginning to end; but I am not altogether the idle, dreaming being it would seem to denote.

My father is a clergyman of limited though competent income, and I am the eldest of his children. He expended quite as much in my education as he could afford in justice to the rest. I thought it therefore my duty, when I left school, to become a governess. In that capacity I find enough to occupy my thoughts all day long, and my head and hands too, without having a moment's time for one dream of the imagination. In the evenings, I confess, I do think, but I never trouble any one else with my thoughts. I carefully avoid any appearance of preoccupation and eccentricity, which might lead those I live amongst to suspect the nature of my pursuits. Following my father's advice—who from my childhood has counselled me, just in the wise and friendly tone of your letter—I have endeavoured not only attentively to observe all the duties a woman ought to fulfil, but to feel deeply interested in them. I don't always succeed, for sometimes when I'm teaching or sewing I would rather be reading or writing; but I try to deny myself; and my father's approbation amply rewarded me for the privation. Once more allow me to thank you with sincere gratitude. I trust I shall never more feel ambitious to see my name in print; if the wish should rise, I'll look at Southey's letter, and suppress it. It is honour enough for me that I have written to him, and received an answer. That letter is consecrated; no one shall ever see it but papa and my brother and sisters. Again I thank you. This incident, I suppose, will be renewed no more; if I live to be an old woman, I shall remember it thirty years hence as a bright dream. The signature which you suspected of being fictitious is my real name. Again, therefore, I must sign myself

C. Brontë

P.S.—Pray, sir, excuse me for writing to you a second time; I could not help writing, partly to tell you how thankful I am for your kindness, and partly to let you know that your advice shall not be wasted, however sorrowfully and reluctantly it may at first be followed.

C. B.

156. To Emily J. Brontë, 8 June 1839

Emily Brontë (1818–48) was the author of *Wuthering Heights* (1847). At the time of this letter, Charlotte was in her first job as governess to the Sidgwick family near Skipton. Their sister Anne Brontë (1820–49) was also employed as a governess.

Dearest Lavinia,

I am most exceedingly obliged to you for the trouble you have taken in seeking up my things and sending them all right. The box and its contents were most acceptable. I only wish I had asked you to send me some letter-paper. This is my last sheet but two. When you can send the other articles of raiment now manufacturing, I shall be right down glad of them.

I have striven hard to be pleased with my new situation. The country, the house, and the grounds are, as I have said, divine. But, alack-a-day! there is such a thing as seeing all beautiful around you—pleasant woods, winding white paths, green lawns, and blue sunshiny sky—and not having a free moment or a free thought left to enjoy them in. The children are constantly with me, and more riotous, perverse, unmanageable cubs never grew. As for correcting them, I soon quickly found that was entirely out of the question: they are to do as they like. A complaint to Mrs Sidgwick brings only black looks upon oneself, and unjust, partial excuses to screen the children. I have tried that plan once. It succeeded so notably that I shall try it no more. I said in my last letter that Mrs Sidgwick did not know me. I now begin to find that she does not intend to know me, that she cares nothing in the world about me except to contrive how the greatest possible quantity of labour may be squeezed out of me, and to that end she over-whelms me with oceans of needlework, yards of cambric to hem, muslin nightcaps to make, and, above all things, dolls to dress. I do not think she likes me at all, because I can't help being shy in such an entirely novel scene, surrounded as I have hitherto been by strange and constantly chang-ing faces. I used to think I should like to be in the stir of grand folks' society but I have had enough of it—it is dreary work to look on and listen. I see now more clearly than I have ever done before that a private governess has no existence, is not considered as a living and rational being except as connected with the wearisome duties she has to fulfil. While she is teaching the children, working for them, amusing them, it is all right. If she steals a moment for herself she is a nuisance. Nevertheless, Mrs Sidgwick is universally considered an amiable woman. Her manners are fussily affable. She talks a great deal, but as it seems to me not much to the purpose. Perhaps I may like her better after a while. At present I have no call to her. Mr Sidgwick is in my opinion a hundred times better—less profession, less bustling condescension, but a far kinder heart. It is very seldom that he speaks to me, but when he does I always feel happier and more settled for some minutes after. He never asks me to wipe the children's smutty noses or tie their shoes or fetch their pinafores or set them a chair. One of the pleasantest afternoons I have spent here—indeed, the only one at all pleasant—was when Mr Sidgwick walked out with his children, and I had orders to follow a little behind. As he strolled on through his fields with his magnificent Newfoundland dog at his side, he looked very like what a frank, wealthy, Conservative gentleman ought to be. He spoke freely and unaffectedly to the people he met, and though he indulged his children and allowed them to tease himself far too much, he would not suffer them grossly to insult others.

I am getting quite to have a regard for the Carter family. At home I should not care for them, but here they are friends. Mr Carter was at Mirfield yesterday and saw Anne. He says she was looking uncommonly well. Poor girl, *she* must indeed wish to be at home. As to Mrs Collins' report that Mrs Sidgwick intended to keep me permanently, I do not think that such was ever her design. Moreover, I would not stay without some alterations. For instance, this burden of sewing would have to be removed. It is too bad for anything. I never in my whole life had my time so fully taken up. Next week we are going to Swarcliffe, Mr Greenwood's place near Harrogate, to stay three weeks or a month. After that time I hope Miss Hoby will return. Don't show this letter to papa or aunt, only to Branwell. They will think I am never satisfied, wherever I am. I complain to you because it is a relief, and really I have had some unexpected mortifications to put up with. However, things may mend, but Mrs Sidgwick expects me to do things that I cannot do—to love her children and be entirely devoted to them. I am really very well. I am so sleepy that I can write no more. I must leave off. Love to all.—Good-bye.

Direct your next despatch—J. Greenwood, Esq., Swarcliffe, near Harrogate.

C. Brontë

157. To Ellen Nussey, 2 June 1851

Ellen Nussey was a schoolfellow of Charlotte Brontë's at Miss Wooler's school at Roehead, Yorkshire, 1831–2, and remained a friend and correspondent.

Dear Nell,

I came here on Wednesday—being summoned a day sooner than I expected in order to be in time for Thackeray's second lecture which was delivered on Thursday afternoon. This—as you may suppose—was a genuine treat to me and I was glad not to miss it. It was given in Willis's rooms where the Almacks Balls are held—a great painted and gilded saloon with long sofas for benches—The audience was said to be of the cream of

London Society and it looked so. I did not at all expect that the great Lecturer would know me or notice me under these circumstances—with admiring Duchesses and Countesses seated in rows before him—but he met me as I entered—shook hands—took me to his Mother whom I had not before seen and introduced me—She is a fine—handsome—young-looking old lady—was very gracious and called with one of her grand-daughters the next day—Thackeray called too separately—I had a long talk with him and I think he knows me now a little better than he did—but of this I cannot yet be sure—he is a great and strange man—There is quite a furor for his Lectures—they are a sort of essays characterized by his own peculiar originality and power—and delivered with a finished taste and ease which is felt but cannot well be described. Just before the Lecture began—somebody came behind me—leaned over and said 'Permit me—as a Yorkshireman to introduce myself'—I turned round—saw a strange not handsome face which puzzled me for half a minute and then I said—'You are Lord Carlisle.' He nodded and smiled—he talked a few minutes very pleasantly and courteously—Afterwards came another man with the same plea that he was a Yorkshireman—and this turned out to be Mr Monckton Milnes—Then came Dr Forbes whom I was sincerely glad to see. On Friday I went to the Crystal Palace—it is a marvellous, stirring, bewilder-ing sight—a mixture of a Genii Palace and a mighty Bazaar—but it is not much in my way—I liked the Lecture better. On Saturday I saw the Exhibition at Somerset House—about half a dozen of the pictures are good and interesting—the rest of little worth. Sunday—yesterday—was a day to be marked with a white stone—through most of the day I was very happy without being tired or over-excited—in the afternoon I went to hear D'Aubigny—the great Protestant French Preacher—it was pleasant—half sweet—half sad—and strangely suggestive to hear the French language once more. For health—I have so far got on very fairly considering that I came here far from well. Mr Taylor is gone some weeks since—I hear more open complaints now about his temper than I did so long as he was in London—I am told it is unfortunately irritable. Of Mr Williams' society I have enjoyed one evening's allowance and liked it and him as usual—on such occasions his good qualities of ease, kindliness and intelligence are seen and his little faults and foibles hidden. Mr S. is somewhat changed in appearance—he looks a little older, darker and more careworn—his ordi-nary manner is graver—but in the evening his spirits flow back to him—Things and circumstances seem here to be as usual—but I fancy there has been some crisis in which his energy and filial affection have sustained them all—this I judge from seeing that Mother and sisters are more pecu-liarly bound to him than ever and that his slightest wish is an unquestioned law.

Your visitors will soon be with you—if they are not at Brookroyd already—I trust their sojourn will pass as you could wish—and bring you all pleasure. Remember me to all—especially your mother. Write soon and believe me—

faithfully yours,
C. Brontë

Monckton Milnes] later Lord Houghton (1809–85), a friend of Tennyson's and the biographer of Keats.   The Crystal Palace] built in Hyde Park by Joseph Paxton for the Great Exhibition of 1851.   French language] she had spent much time in Brussels.   Taylor] probably John Taylor (1781–1864), publisher of Keats and other poets.   Williams] perhaps Isaac Williams (1802–65), poet and Oxford Movement theologian.

SARAH AUSTIN
(1793–1867)

In 1820 Sarah married John Austin, jurist and friend of James and John Stuart Mill and Jeremy Bentham. He was one of the founders of University College, London. She was a writer and translator, mostly from German, though she also knew Italian. She wrote advocating reform of the nation's educational provision. Their only child was Lucie (b.1821), later Lady Duff Gordon, addressed by Sydney Smith in his letter of 22 July 1835 (above, Letter 127).

158. To Susan Reeve, 9 August 1837

Susan Reeve was Mrs Austin's sister. John Austin had been sent to report on the operation of the judicial system in Malta. Cholera reached Europe from the East in 1831; after a devastating epidemic it retreated eastward about this time.

Dear Susan,

Heat interruptions, but above all a shock that really unfitted me for anything, have kept me from writing. I must tell you this tragical history. One of the persons whom I know the best and like the best here is a Mrs Sammut, wife of a Dr Sammut, whom I never saw, he having, for the sake of securing a small pension, gone on board an English man-of-war as surgeon two years ago. They had just lost a beautiful little girl when we came, and Mrs Sammut only began to recover enough to go out. She had eight children. The two eldest daughters, both married, had been the most admired girls in Malta; the grown-up single daughter was an excellent and charming girl. From the first appearance of cholera, poor Mrs Sammut was overwhelmed with terror; her daughter, Mrs Dedminno, and she came together to see me one evening, looking like spectres, and I said then, 'If

they are attacked, they will die.' The daughter was attacked, struggled a
week, and died, leaving a baby. Last Monday, what was my horror (knowing the mother) at hearing that Carmela was attacked and dying. On Wednesday morning she died. But imagine that on Tuesday, the father—the most
doting of fathers—returned, after his two years' exile from his family! I had
sent on Tuesday to ask Mrs Sammut to send me her two little children,
and I cannot describe to you how affecting it was to hear them talk of the
presents papa had brought from England for mamma and Carmela. Poor
Carmela said on Tuesday, 'As soon as I am up again, I shall take papa to
see Mrs Austin.' From the first, I have endeavoured to make my large
house and fine situation useful to convalescents, and thus I have had two
young men who had just escaped, and several poor girls, who had been
passing the last two months under the combined influence of rigorous
confinement to the house, insufficient food, and incessant fear and gloom.
This feeble, abject terror, this inability to look death in the face, was always
despicable to me; it is now odious. Under its influence I have seen mothers
refuse to go near their children, husbands their wives. I have seen one of
eight brothers (in the upper classes), not *one* of whom would approach their
father's death-bed. In short, every variety of atrocious selfishness. These
are the people who die. For myself I never feared; I am not very solicitous
to live, nor do I think myself very obnoxious to this sort of complaint. As
to cure, it is anything, everything, nothing. Nobody knows. Everything
succeeds—everything fails. I have kept on my course, eating the same,
riding in the much-dreaded *sereno* every evening, bathing in the sea (prohibited most emphatically, I cannot guess why) every day—in short, altering nothing; and but for the dreadful heart I should be perfectly well.
To-day is terrific. You have not the faintest idea what *sun* means. The
rocks in my little bay where I bathe, if only a hand's-breadth is out of the
water, are so hot you cannot touch them. Yet it is seldom stifling as in
London. You sit still, and the perspiration runs off in a continued stream.
Then the sea-breeze comes, rustling the leaves and rippling the sea, and
you are refreshed. The trying days are those of the *scirocco* or the *libeccio*;
and once in a few years they are reminded that Malta is in Africa by a blast
of the simoom.

August 15.

I add a word to say that we are all alive. We have lost about four thousand
people off our little rock; you may think how thankful I am Lucie is not
here—God help her! I trust she is gone, or going, to Coed Dhu. The
thought of the wood and the river makes me *thirsty*. But I must not forget
our oranges, figs, melons, water-melons, peaches, nectarines, grapes, all so
fine, so plentiful—and our boats on the blue sea. If made the most of,

Malta might have many attractions. This is a sad letter; pray send me something cheerful.

Obnoxious to] subject to.   *Sereno*] evening wind (?)   *Scirocco*] hot moist wind.
Libeccio] south-west wind.

ABRAHAM LINCOLN
(1809–1865)

Lincoln was the 16th President of the USA (1861–5); in 1838 he was practising as a lawyer.

159. To Mrs O. H. Browning, 1 April 1838

Mrs Browning was the wife of a friend. The date is probably significant.

Dear Madam,

Without apologizing for being egotistical, I shall make the history of so much of my life as has elapsed since I saw you the subject of this letter. And, by the way, I now discover that in order to give a full and intelligible account of the things I have done and suffered since I saw you, I shall necessarily have to relate some that happened before.

It was, then, in the autumn of 1836 that a married lady of my acquaintance, and who was a great friend of mine, being about to pay a visit to her father and other relatives residing in Kentucky, proposed to me that on her return she would bring a sister of hers with her on condition that I would engage to become her brother-in-law with all convenient despatch. I, of course, accepted the proposal, for you know I could not have done otherwise had I really been averse to it; but privately, between you and me, I was most confoundedly well pleased with the project. I had seen the said sister some three years before, thought her intelligent and agreeable, and saw no good objection to plodding life through hand in hand with her. Time passed on, the lady took her journey and in due time returned, sister in company, sure enough. This astonished me a little, for it appeared to me that her coming so readily showed that she was a trifle too willing, but on reflection it occurred to me that she might have been prevailed on by her married sister to come, without anything concerning me ever having been mentioned to her, and so I concluded that if no other objection presented itself, I would consent to waive this. All this occurred to me on hearing of her arrival in the neighborhood—for, be it remembered, I had not yet seen her, except about three years previous, as above mentioned. In a few days we had an interview, and, although I had seen her before, she did not look as my imagination had pictured her. I knew she was over-size, but she now appeared a fair match for Falstaff. I knew she was called an 'old maid,' and I felt no doubt of the truth of at least half of the appellation, but now, when I beheld her, I could not for my life avoid thinking of my mother; and this, not from withered features—for her skin was too full of fat to permit of its contracting into wrinkles—but from her want of teeth, weatherbeaten appearance in general, and from a kind of notion that ran in my head that nothing could have commenced at the size of infancy and reached her present bulk in less than thirty-five or forty years; and, in short, I was not at all pleased with her. But what could I do! I had told her sister that I would take her for better or for worse, and I made a point of honor and conscience in all things to stick to my word, especially if others had been induced to act on it, which in this case I had no doubt they had, for I was now fairly convinced that no other man on earth would have her, and hence the conclusion that they were bent on holding me to my bargain. 'Well,' thought I, 'I have said it, and, be the consequences what they may, it shall not be my fault if I fail to do it.' At once I determined to consider her my wife, and this done, all my powers of discovery were put to work in search of perfections in her which might be fairly set off against her defects. I tried to imagine her handsome, which, but for her unfortunate corpulency, was actually true. Exclusive of this, no woman that I have ever seen has a finer face. I also tried to convince myself that the mind was much more to be valued than the person, and in this she was not inferior, as I could discover, to any with whom I had been acquainted.

Shortly after this, without attempting to come to any positive understanding with her, I set out for Vandalia, when and where you first saw me. During my stay there I had letters from her which did not change my opinion of either her intellect or intention, but, on the contrary, confirmed it in both.

All this while, although I was fixed 'firm as the surge-repelling rock' in my resolution, I found I was continually repenting the rashness which had led me to make it. Through life I have been in no bondage, either real or imaginary, from the thraldom of which I so much desired to be free. After my return home I saw nothing to change my opinion of her in any particular. She was the same, and so was I. I now spent my time in planning how I might get along in life after my contemplated change of circumstances should have taken place, and how I might procrastinate the evil day for a time, which I really dreaded as much, perhaps more, than an Irishman does the halter.

After all my sufferings upon this deeply interesting subject, here I am, wholly, unexpectedly, completely out of the 'scrape,' and I now want to know if you can guess how I got out of it—out, clear, in every sense of the term—no violation of word, honor, or conscience. I don't believe you can guess, and so I might as well tell you at once. As the lawyer says, it was done in the manner following, to wit: After I had delayed the matter as long as I thought I could in honor do (which, by the way, had brought me round into the last fall), I concluded I might as well bring it to a consummation without further delay, and so I mustered my resolution and made the proposal to her direct; but, shocking to relate, she answered, No. At first I supposed she did it through an affectation of modesty, which I thought but ill became her under the peculiar circumstances of her case, but on my renewal of the charge I found she repelled it with greater firmness than before. I tried it again and again, but with the same success, or rather with the same want of success.

I finally was forced to give it up, at which I very unexpectedly found myself mortified almost beyond endurance. I was mortified, it seemed to me, in a hundred different ways. My vanity was deeply wounded by the reflection that I had so long been too stupid to discover her intentions, and at the same time never doubting that I understood them perfectly; and also that she, whom I had taught myself to believe nobody else would have, had actually rejected me with all my fancied greatness. And, to cap the whole, I then for the first time began to suspect that I was really a little in love with her. But let it all go! I'll try and outlive it. Others have been made fools of by the girls, but this can never with truth be said of me. I most emphatically, in this instance, made a fool of myself. I have now come to the conclusion never again to think of marrying, and for this reason—I can never be satisfied with any one who would be blockhead enough to have me.

When you receive this, write me a long yarn about something to amuse me. Give my respects to Mr Browning.

Your sincere friend,
A. Lincoln

160. To Major-General Joseph Hooker, 26 January 1863

Hooker, known as 'Fighting Joe', succeeded General Ambrosa Burnside as commander-in-chief of the Army of the Potomac. He was relieved of his command in June.

General,

I have placed you at the head of the Army of the Potomac. Of course I have done this upon what appear to me to be sufficient reasons. And yet I think it best for you to know that there are some things in regard to which, I am not quite satisfied with you. I believe you to be a brave and a skilful soldier, which, of course, I like. I also believe you do not mix politics with your profession, in which you are right. You have confidence in yourself, which is a valuable, if not an indispensable quality. You are ambitious, which, within reasonable bounds, does good rather than harm. But I think that during Gen. Burnside's command of the Army, you have taken counsel of your ambition, and thwarted him as much as you could, in which you did a great wrong to the country, and to a most meritorious and honorable brother officer. I have heard, in such way as to believe it, of your recently saying that both the Army and the Government needed a Dictator. Of course it was not *for* this, but in spite of it, that I have given you the command. Only those generals who gain successes, can set up dictators. What I now ask of you is military success, and I will risk the dictatorship. The government will support you to the utmost of it's ability, which is neither more nor less than it has done and will do for all commanders. I much fear that the spirit which you have aided to infuse into the Army, of criticising their Commander, and withholding confidence from him, will now turn upon you. I shall assist you as far as I can, to put it down. Neither you, nor Napoleon, if he were alive again, could get any good out of an army, while such a spirit prevails in it.

And now, beware of rashness. Beware of rashness, but with energy, and sleepless vigilance, go forward, and give us victories.

Yours very truly
A. Lincoln

RICHARD BOWLER

Richard Bowler, of Brill, Buckinghamshire, was transported to Vandiemens Land (his crime not known) in 1821 when he was 16 or 17 years old. He was assigned to a farmer for whom he worked seven years and ten months; he then worked for the government till eligible for a ticket-of-leave (after eight years and being of good conduct). He did not write home until 1835; the last of his six surviving letters is dated 24 Apr. 1843. Granted conditional pardon in 1836, a free pardon in the Colony in 1840, he still had not received his absolute pardon from England in Apr. 1843.

161. To his brother, John Bowler, clockmaker, of Brill, 15 April 1838

Dear Mother Brother Sisters and all your children,

I write to you with my kind love hoping to find you all in good health as it leaves me at present and I thank God for it   Dear friends I am very happy to inform you that her gracious Majesty queen Victoria has granted my immancipati which gives me the pleasure to say I am a free man in this Country   I did explain to you in a letter the meaning of this liberty I now hold   Dear Brother I think it very strange I have not received any letter from you this eighteen months which I have sent you two since that time But never recd any answer and I am certain the came to england for letters

I wrote for other people that was sent in the same ship as mine the have got their answers which I think their must be some Negligence in some way or other   Dear Brother I was very sorry to hear that your wife suffered with such illness and I was more surprised to hear you are so corpolent   give my love to your children and all my sisters children & I still live in hopes to see you all once more if God spares my life   you told me that Gibbins & Stevens was very poor   the cannot expect to be otherways for Stevens would swear the legs off a iron pot & Gibbins allways gloried at any persons downfall   I hope Brother you will write to me and tell me all particulars about Brill and give my love to my sister Ann Newton and tell her when I come home we will sing all bass & burn the bellows

> At Brill I was born the truth you well know
> I being wild and rakeish which proved my overthrow
> I being young and foolish my parents advice forsook
> so to Vandiemens Land was sent   they thought to make me droop
> But through seventeen years good conduct my liberty I gained
> and in the course of a few years to Brill I'll be again
> How happy will they moments be my friends for to embrace
> and my poor old tender Mother once more to see her face
> The last time that I saw her she was in grief and woe
> To think I was a going some where but where she did not know
> Dear Brother you was like her your heart being filled with grief
> And I so far in bondage I could not you releive
> But now the day his different I am happy for to say
> Once more I am out of bondage   I am happy far away
> I may for twelve months longer and then my free pardon gain
> and thus success unto our Queen and long may she reign

Brother give my best respects to my Uncle & Aunts & Cousins & their familys if the are married   Likewise to your father & mother in law and all their family   tell them I shall call at Islip and see them when I return   so no more at present from your affectionate son & Brother

Richard Bowler

At Brill I was born . . .] in a letter of 1841 there is another doggerel poem or ballad describing the voyage to Tasmania: 'our irons being light, our usage being kind . . .'

SAMUEL PALMER
(1805–1881)

Palmer was a painter of 'visionary landscape' and follower of William Blake. He was introduced to Blake by the painter John Linnell (1792–1882), whose daughter Hannah (Anny) Palmer married.

162. To the Linnells, 9 October 1838

My dear Mr and Mrs Linnell—

We came this afternoon to Pausillippo (Putioli) where St Paul landed and I managed with my morsel of Italian to get food and lodging at ¾ per day for both of us. We are on the shore of Baiæ and I ascertained from Sig^r. Vianelli's sketches that there are two first rate views of Baiæ from the hill above us. We are in a wild kind of inn—with a large room about 16 feet high looking rather dreary—but Anny is now a good traveller—pulls out her knitting and makes herself at home in a moment. I have endeavoured in what I have been doing to get all that is essentially Italian on the spot and having those two great desiderata—effect and foreground arranged—look forward with delight to completing my drawings or making others from them in Grove St—and when I am at a loss—(as I now wish to have studies from nature for everything) to running out into the Regent's Park or Kensington Gardens for a study of a group of leaves or a bit of ground whenever I want it, and I hope we shall bring home a stock of subjects which will last us a long time and which the material that lies ever close about London will render thoroughly effective. The pain in my right fist which I attributed at Corpo de Cava to clenching my brushes still continues in a small degree and I feel a slight pain and stiffness in it when I wake in the morning—so that I am inclined to think it arises from something which the world would think much more dignified than art—namely a touch of the gout!! My fingers have a little redness and swelling in the mòrning sometimes I think—will you tell me what is good to do if it be incipient gout? You will tell me not to stuff any more ducks—would I had ducks to stuff! and the great king of birds—on which I could not help wasting one tender thought on the twenty ninth of Septr. cackles and struts on no green commons here—and green tea and toast and the hissing urn and the capacious sofa littered with ancient books and the piano and Gregorian chants are absent—but Anny is here and those delights partaken with her in London—with two or three commissions to start with would make me too happy. I do not mean the delights of goose for that should be used only occasionally, to grease the wheels of life a little when they begin to creak with study, but those cheap and blessed intellectuals which a hundred a year will buy though ten thousand often fail to purchase them. I must now go to bed that I may begin the siege of Baiæ with daylight. Thursday—We tried yesterday to climb an almost inaccessible mountain which baffled all our attempts (but having set my teeth at it I hope to try again on a donkey tomorrow morning and if I fail then I will be pulled up by ropes)—however I got a beautiful long subject from Monte Nuovo—with a foreground made up—but not by me but Nature: for a volcanic explosion threw up the whole hill in 36 hours. Anny is pleased beyond measure with anything volcanic and has the heart of a lion the moment she begins to slip about on cinders and ashes. Today I tried to draw in the streets in spite of insolence and annoyance which made it almost impossible even to me who have drawn in the streets of Rome during carnival—— finding no other means would answer, I did as our government have probably (for I see no papers) done with O'Connell—I hired the ring leader of the mob for a trifle, to keep off the rest; which he did with all authority and I finished my study in sweet peace. You cannot stir a step here undogged with cicerones boatmen etc.—but our inflexibility has nearly tired them out. The incessant struggle with imposition and the snares everywhere set to catch our cash sometimes really sicken me—but after a night's rest and a breakfast of coffee, milk, butter, four eggs, beef steaks, pears and grapes we turn out again to the combat panoplied in slow and sallow obstinacy. We had a great storm hurled after us yesterday because I civilly declined the offer of a boy to carry my sketching apparatus which was very heavy and nearly rubbed the skin off my hip bone. I wonder what aspect I was born under—other people slide on without all this bother—but I—though far from courting difficulties and trying to follow American Jeffries' advice to his nephew always to 'take hold of things by their smooth handle'—am a sort of little Esau with every one's hand against me—tho' my hand or heart are I am sure not against any one—not even against the Devil—for though I hate his ways and his works I wish him well, most sincerely—and would not carry an additional faggot to burn him on any account unless the same fire would burn up all his mischiefs—and yet I am called Papist and persecutor by one—infidel by another, madman by a third—one calls me extravagant, another miserly—one says I starve myself—another that I love goose—if a tailor makes me a coat in the fashion there is not room for a pocket handkerchief—if I contrive a coat for use I am hooted—I am buffetted cheated pelted, belied, abused, trodden on, tripped up and spitted on—and what do I care? only if possible to get a little money and keep out of debt—and then I could stand as steadfast as one of the pyramids if all the world 'laughed at me in chorus' I try to rank myself as neat and passable as may be—have begun with Falstaff to 'purge and live cleanly like a gentleman'—perk up in a neat stock and a clean collar—and yet when I come alongside any regular dandy look like a coal barge by a royal yacht. Having so many times found your advice to be based upon good reasons I took it and came to these shores of Baiæ and though I think people generally overrate scenery very much—and that though many places afford wonderful scraps, yet there are very few perfect *views*—must confess that Baiæ is an epitome of all that is beautiful. Every point I have seen affords the finest lines of capes—reaches—and islands—and a months stay would furnish distances for life—after having, however, secured the grand scene from the mountain that withstands me, and got one subject of Avernus we must return to Naples or poor Tivoli with all its waterfalls will be lost— and I want to get as many cascades as possible that with my Welsh ones I may have a good stock. If Lord Holland would pension all his poorer kinsmen—or give me a nice little whig sinecure I would go to Rome by the upper road which is now too expensive, and spend next spring in Turner's favorite place Aosta, under the Alps but as at present I am likely to get more kicks than halfpence—I must make my halfpence last and try to turn a penny as soon as possible in London. I long to be there, and have a great curiosity to see what will become of me—*I think*, as has always hitherto been the case, Providence will provide in time of need—but having had such good living in Italy—it will be hard to feed on pulse and I must turn rat-catcher if things are at an ebb—that I may get plenty of animal food. Tho' the rabble of cicerone boat men etc. have sneezed at us yet the clever and good people have done differently. Messrs Gibson Williams and Ackland have treated us with marked attention and respect—and we go back to Rome as to a house of old friends. Saturday night. I have been putting pen to paper and find that we shall be able to stand our ground well, IF Grove St lodgers do but cover the rates and taxes and IF Robert Foreman pays his rent. I had forgotten at what quarters his rent was due but find by referring to your letters that it is at Lady day and Mms—therefore on that great goose day £15.0.0 were due and I should esteem it a great favor if on your next visit to the city he has not paid—you would have the goodness to jog his memory by a letter. If he does but pay and the house cover taxes (and I think it ought to do much more) we are sure of standing our ground for our year and a half in Italy and of having something to begin upon when we come back—I have in my calculation set down that the odd money my cousins received before the Lady Day payment was £10.0.0—perhaps when you see them you would ask if that were the sum. We have now in hand £64.6.8 and with the exception of the great loan I owe not a penny to anybody; moreover this day I think I have ascertained that I have found out the art of imitation at last—and thro' obliging myself to arrange all my things from my first coming to Rome as if they were finished pictures, that I now get with very little comparative time and labour in every subject the essentials for a finished work—this may be true or may be a self delusion but I think I have not indulged in a too flattering view of things thro' any part of this adventure. Anny too is now able to make really consistent, beautiful, and I think saleable drawings from nature—and though I never dreamed of throwing upon her half the onus of getting a living, yet it is very pleasing just at a critical time to see her labours becoming so thor- oughly available as by helping to start us it may enable me afterwards to get her many comforts and enjoyments. I should like to fight up into fame and get her a Greek and Latin master from Oxford—Novello for music lessons—I see her quite a Lady Callcott—tho' I hope she will be much more—namely a fine original Artist—which I take to be more than a whole hogshead of other accomplishments. If I during my former sojourn at Naples was a little anxious about the future I can say with truth that Anny has never been so in the least—but as hopeful and cheerful as if I had had the fortune of my Clapham cousins—but I think if I had twenty thousand pounds and the expectation of much more I should not be so happy as I am now—for next to the best of all happiness is that of the semper agendi— and I am afraid I should be cramming a great house full of pictures and books and harps and organs and never know how to make the best use of them. What I want now is just a little dawn of prosperity and the little Grove St House blackguardly as the situation may be, a model of cleanliness neatness and order within—with all the implements and tackle of art—in polished preservation and readiness. When I saw a blessed man of war for the first time—I saw what a painters house ought to be. If I once begin to be neat, I will be neat with a vengeance. I now regard my drawing boards, rulers, T squares—syringes, pannels etc. as dear children, and shall always carry about a duster in my pocket, as my Father does, to polish up their pretty shining faces. After all—self knowledge and self government are the great points and if a man can but accomplish them—the rest will be easy—if we could but see ourselves with the eyes of an indifferent spectator with all that is good and all that is disgusting about us, we should know at once what to cultivate and what to tear out by the roots—but how difficult is this to come at! With respect to the insurance of my houses at Shoreham and Grove St I think I can now afford to renew it and should be very much obliged if you would do it next time you renew your own as I believe we both insure at the same office—the Sun. I think Grove St is insured for £500.0.0 and Shoreham for 400.—This extempore letter writing without revisions and erasures or even a rough copy—tumbles out a strange hotch potch—but as carelessness and slang are the fashion of the day I suppose it may be very gentlemanly and shew more breeding than one of Cicero's epistles. When I consider the distance we have travelled and the things we have seen—I think the amount we have spent was never better laid out or brought more for money—and I hope and believe it will turn out a good bargain in the end. Being in haste I can write no more but that I am Dear Mr and Mrs Linnell

ever yours affectionately
Sam.[1] Palmer

Twenty ninth of Sept[r]] Michaelmas, when it was traditional to eat goose.   O'Connell] Daniel O'Connell (see above, Letter 143) had been in difficulties after a public reprimand by the Speaker of the House.   Jeffries] Thomas Jefferson (1743–1826), who advised 'Take things

always by their smooth handle.'   Falstaff] *1 Henry IV*, v. iv. 164.   Lady day] 25 Mar.
Mms] Michaelmas.   The great loan] from his friend, the successful painter George Rich-
mond.   Novello] Vincent Novello, musician.   Lady Callcott] traveller and author.
Semper agendi] continual activity.

163. To Polly Linnell, 13 November 1838

Polly was Hannah Palmer's younger sister.

My dear Miss Polly,

Write once more to your old friend. Your letter to me was very nicely
written and if you take pains you will soon be able to write better than me,
whose old knuckles are grown stiff with squeezing paint-brushes. Tell me
what poem you have been learning to recite—and how you made your
Papa's great room echo with the sound. Open your jaws wide, and let the
words and syllables come forth as clear as the ringing of bells. Lord Chatham
used to put his little boys upon the table and make them repeat Milton as
if they were great men, which they afterwards became. There is nothing in
common talking which even birds can not do. Parrots can talk a great
deal—and jays and magpies, but they can not with a sweet clear voice as
pleasant as music—repeat Cowper's poems—which I hope you begin to do
beautifully by this time. Anny says you may use her Cowper which is in the
drawer Mamma lent her. Pray practise your pieces very SLOWLY at first and
do not grunt or snuffle the words through your nose or choak them in your
throat or bite them with your teeth—but throw them out boldly till they
resound again and you will soon find the poems you repeat seem much
more beautiful than they did at first. King George the fourth when Prince
Regent said to John Kemble the great actor 'Will you *obleege* me with a
pinch of snuff'—Mr Kemble answer'd 'Open your royal jaws a little wider
and say *oblige*' Open *your* jaws so wide my dear Polly that it may rejoice my
old heart to hear you when I come back and believe me

your affectionate friend
S. Palmer.

John Kemble] John Philip Kemble (1757–1823), actor.

164. To Thomas More Palmer, 6 October 1844

Thomas More was his son, who died aged 19 in 1862.

My dear Thomas More,

You are not able to read writing yet—but whenever you have been quite
a good boy and your kind Mamma has time—I dare say she will read you
some of this letter. I wanted to write you another letter but did not know
whether you had been quite a good boy minding all your Mamma said to

you AT THE MOMENT—for I should not wish to write a letter to a boy who did not mind what was said to him—but a letter came yesterday from your Mamma who tells me that you mind all she says. You cannot think how glad I was to hear it.—I longed to take you up upon my knee and kiss you a great many times—and I wished that your Mamma and you and Sarah and little sister could take a walk with me upon these high hills—and see all these villages farms and woods—with oxen ploughing and farm yards full of sheep—Your Mamma will explain my words which you do not understand. St Catherine's Hill near Guildford is a pretty place with the ruins of a church upon it [*Two sketches*] Well! on the round hill where the church stands, there was a FAIR the other day—they built tents there with large poles [*Sketch*] The day before the Fair. The Dancing Bear. They built tents there with long poles which they then covered with cloth called canvas (your Mamma will show you a bit)—with canvas to keep out the winds and the rain. Then they put into these tents all the curious people and curious beasts and curious things they had to show. There were little men not so high as the table—and standing by them you would see a great giant almost as tall as the grand pianoforte in my study—and men without arms that could hold a pen between their toes and write anybody's name—and a learned pig that knew his letters—and had some laid upon the ground (like those in your box of letters) and then if you asked him which was H for Hog or P for pig or g for grunter—he would point to the right letter with his nose. And among these great tents there were numbers of smaller tents called booths filled with all manner of curious things for good boys who had learned their book well and minded what was said to them at the moment—there were playthings without number—Drums and tamborines and penny trumpets and poppet shows a half-penny each—kites to fly and boats to swim in a basin——song books and picture books and—O! the cakes! Pies made in the shape of little pigs and filled with sweetmeats—with a currant for each eye and a curly tail which bit crisp in the mouth—and ginger bread nuts and gingerbread and *gilded* gingerbread made into the shape of crows and crowing cocks and stars.

And all the while there was *such* a noise—There were crowds of people and hundreds of little children there all dancing and shouting and laughing but you could hardly hear them while the drums were beating and the trumpets sounding—and the men at the wild beast shows were banging the great GONGS and halooing though great speaking trumpets. Walk in! Walk in ladies and Gentlemen! *Here's* no mistake—only just walk in and see the Lion of the desert—and the famous Dog Billy and the Mermaid of the Ocean half fish and half woman—and the wild man of the woods and the fiery lynx off the burning mountains! And there were tumblers and rope dancers and harlequins and merry Andrews. Now I did not go to the fair but I know what was there because I saw some fairs when I was a boy— If *you* had been with me I would have taken you to see it all—you should have sat upon my shoulders as you do when you see the soldiers—and you should have gone in to see the wild beasts and should have had a penny trumpet and a poppet show to take home with you. When night came on and it got dark they lighted up great lamps and let off fireworks and all the hill was in a blaze—and they made more noise than ever and they beat the drums so hard and so fast that you would have thought they must have been broken in pieces—I had been drawing all day a good way off and at night coming home—as I came out at the end of a dark lane covered with trees—suddenly I saw before me the great hill with its top all glittering with lights—and torches—and such a ringing of drums as if the men were mad who beat them—This put me in mind of the story of Pentheus and the wakes of Bacchus among the mountains—which you will read about when you are a great boy—if you live and do well.—People come from all parts to see the fair at St Catherines—from villages 15 miles off——But I think that is silly—because it takes up so much of their time. I think we should spend our time in doing things that are useful—in learning to *make* things—being careful not to break them—and we should try to be very good and very wise. I hope you will soon learn to make things—When you can draw and write a little you will be able to make books. Your Mamma makes things—she has made a great many pictures—and she makes clothes for you and little Mary—and if you take notice when you are with your Mamma you will see that whenever she is not nursing the baby she is always making something or other.—And now my dearest Thomas More when you do your reading with your Mamma—try to do it as well as you possibly can—do not play with your fingers or look about the room but LOOK AT YOUR BOOK and say the letters quickly when you spell the words— for you know all your letters—You must not teaze Mamma to read you this letter when she is busy—but if you are still a very good boy and do what Mamma tells you AT THE MOMENT I dare say she will read you a bit now and then. The way to become good is to pray to the Good and Blessed God to make you good—and then to try yourself how good you can possibly be— Good boys do what they are told to do whether they like it or not. If they are told to do what they do *not* like to do—they do it *directly*—and then they feel very happy—and when their Papas come home again they love them very much indeed—I am much obliged to you for the letter you sent me—and I take care of it—and suppose that you also will take care of my letters—for when you grow up to be a young man—I shall die and my body will be put into a hole and you will never see me again while you live in this world—and perhaps then you will like to look at some of the letters I have written to you. But if we love the Blessed God—and do what He has told us to do—we shall *come to life again*—much better and happier than we are now—and Papa and Mamma and Thomas More and little Sister will live together and make each other happy—and never do any thing that is wrong—and never die nor go away from each other any more. I am delighted to hear that you have been such a good boy—and shall soon I hope—come home and give you a great many kisses—Ask your Mamma to give you a few kisses

from | Your affectionate FATHER

SAMUEL PALMER

P.S. Your Mamma has seen one of the greatest fairs in the world—the carnival of Rome—perhaps she will tell you about it—they throw sugar plums at each other and go about in masks.

Sarah] probably his nurse.   Pentheus] torn to pieces by his mother and sisters in Dionysus' revenge for his having resisted the introduction of the latter's worship into Thebes.

165. To Miss Julia Richmond, September 1866

Julia Richmond was a daughter of George Richmond the portrait painter, with whom the Palmers had gone to Italy after their marriage.

My dear Julia,

I would do anything I could to please you, but a LETTER is really quite out of my power. Letters should be so artless you know, so negligently elegant; they want a natty native-grace-Gainsborough-kind-of-a-touch:— at least so the critics say—and I really don't think we want any more of them: letters I mean;—or either; we have Pope's and Cowper's and Gray's. Cowper's name is with me the synonym of elegance, and some say that Pope's smell of the lamp, but I like oil, and would recommend you to breakfast upon Betts's cocoa with oleaginous globosities bobbing about as you stir it like porpoises of the deep.

And if this is 'too rich', for gross it is *not*, then a slice of roast beef and a pint of home-brewed.—Perhaps we grow, both in mind and body, to be somewhat like our diet, therefore, though it should never be gross, it need not be nervous, vapoury, fantastical, like strong green tea: much less, narcotic; (by the bye, they are now making 'cigarettes' for the ladies) like that detestable tobacco—the substitute for food, which they cannot afford to buy, with our half starved field labourers. I am told that the target practice is in every case impossible until cigars are relinquished—London-season-ladies go to opium at once. The labourer's pipe smells comfortable in a country lane on a chilly autumn evening, as he is plodding home from the furrows—and we have no reason to complain of Milton's single pipe and glass of water before going to bed for he rose early and soar'd without roaming,—but all these things have their mental analogies. There is a kind of green-tea-poetry and smoky philosophy of which we may have too much. Shelley, if I remember, in his ode to the lark, assures that bird that after all he is no lark at all but a spirit! a spirit! 'I say—none of that!' the bird might have replied, as the Tower Warder to dear Mr Finch when he saw him sketching the armour.

Poetry may be *too* transcendent, and so may music may it not? Are paradox muddle and bombast the 'three graces' of literature? 'What have ladies to do with literature?' Who said that? O you brute! Tell me barbarian, are there not ladies, *many* ladies in England who have made Cowper a pocket companion? And who can read Cowper without being the better morally and mentally? 'He's flat,' is he? What, because he doesn't bother you about the 'mystery of Being', and that kind of thing. Flat, I suppose as fine music is flat after the barbaric crash of unprepared German discords.

I beg pardon dear Julia, I was rebuking that demon who whispered something about ladies not reading. O, *don't* they read? Did not they rush to hear Carlyle lecture against all sorts of vanities, with rings on their fingers, a French novel in the carriage and a poodle looking out of the window? Besides they read Milton—O yes! once—*quite through*, as a pious duty—and think the battle of the angels 'awfully sublime'—as it is. Upon the whole I think women, (when not rebellious,) better creatures than men:—less irreligious less selfish and self indulgent, but their views of the sublime are peculiar. I remember that John Varley whose lady pupils were legion (*angelic* legions you will understand) was dreadfully 'put out' by this peculiarity. 'Why, they think Salvator Rosa more sublime than Claude!' he used to say—and rub his face, and look as cross as he *could* look for he was the soul of good nature.

And now, as I am *not* writing a letter, (I mean what I say) but scribbling over a piece of paper because you tell me to do it—and lest you should think I can ever be cross with *you*: —this being the case, I will digress to the Babbacombe rocks near Torquay and to those about that coast—much of which I have not seen—to mention that Mr Horsley long ago described them as most various and gorgeous in colour. You could not get a long ride I fear through Newton up to Hay Tor rocks over Ilsington—'wild country that' to adopt the modern construction—Chudleigh too is at some distance, but worth seeing, if you don't stop short, as the tourists do, on the wrong side of the chasm, gaping at the opposite cliff—while the real spectacle is what they are standing upon.—I found it all strewed with Pic Nic bottles and broken plates.

As 'ladies *read*' let me recommend you Fairfax's Tasso even though you may have read the original He was born with music on his tongue, and moreover was Queen Elizabeth's Godson!!!!!!!!!!!!!!!!!!! There's a climax! perhaps he kept a gig!

To sit in shoes wet with salt water *will* give you cold—I caught a violent cold sketching 3 or 4 hundred feet above the sea after sunset in Cornwall. Anecdotes I have none, except that I think a distinguished person was married at Reigate the other day but I know it only by report. Now dear Julia write me as many letters as ever you like—they always give me pleasure—(Oyez! you'll write me *such* Devon descriptions that I shall seem to be sweetly smothered in cream.) Do tell me all about that dear country but I really *can't* write anything rational—so you see, unanswer'd letters of yours will be a virtuous iteration of returning good for evil.

Many happy returns of your coming birth day with all my heart

Yours affectionately

S.P.

Mr Finch] probably Francis Oliver Finch, water-colourist (1802–62).   John Varley] (1778– 1842), painter, famous for the number of his fashionable pupils (and his casting of horoscopes). Horsley] John Callcott Horsley (1817–1903), painter.   Fairfax] Edward Fairfax's transla- tion of the *Gerusalemme liberata* appeared in 1660. He was not Queen Elizabeth's godson.

166. To Mrs Julia Robinson, 9 December 1872

The same addressee as the previous letter; her daughter Iona was born in 1870.

My dear Mrs Robinson,

Your 'Iona' passage gives me more pleasure than Dr Johnson's, though it is one of his finest. 'To abstract the mind etc.':—read it in his 'Tour'. I should not be inclined to encourage the young lady's walking efforts, but should prefer crawling and kicking, which are, with the strongest children, the first natural movements, and, in the stronger sex, an important element of advancement in after life.

What is statesmanship but successful crawling and kicking? With a view to this, at our public schools, the fag crawls to be kicked, and, in his turn, kicks the fag who crawls to him; and the ruling powers are far too cunning to abolish a system which so perfectly represents and so admirably prepares for the requirements of public life.

Politics however often reverse the process. Pulteney kicked long and lustily before he crawled into the Earldom of Bath; and this is found to be very successful in detail: you kick and squabble a little with the givers of good things, just to make moral capital by it, but always let your stubborn honesty be convinced by their arguments.

Illness apart, parental anxieties begin when a child begins to walk; for beginning to walk is beginning to tumble. It is a defiance of gravitation, and

Newton is sometimes avenged. By 'natural selection' they come down upon sharp corners, edges of fenders or coal-scuttles; or, if precocious ambition prompt them to rise by crawling, a little head is seen near the top of a steep stone staircase, while the 'square of the distance' is growling for its prey at the bottom.

Fastened into my little chair, screwed into its stool, I can just remember the whole coming down with a crash; my Mother screaming—Riga Balsam applied; (sovereign for cuts;) and here I am alas! writing nonsense in my old age, no chair of discipline it would seem having been screwed into the 'stool of repentance'.

But seriously:—Margate is a noble place for air, is it not? I heard all about Iona's weighings and her daily increase of gravity, which had reached its ackme when I sought and found her on the cliffs. She was entirely polite, and more in sorrow than in anger seemed to say 'Your manners are plausible,—your principles inadmissible'. Her fair junior, *whom you maligned*, seemed rather interested in the 'singular old gentleman.'

He, in turn is really pleased and *more* than pleased that you should sympathise with the simple details of his pilgrimage. Sorrow, in its saddest phase of bereavement, has followed him; yet perhaps without sorrow there is little sympathy for others; by sympathy I do not mean any amount of good nature, but fellowship in suffering.

Without free street-fellowship, open air all day, and gambols by the kennel-side with negation of brain-work, London is a sorry place to bring up children in. 'Alexandrina, you little muck, come out of the gutter,' a mother exclaimed. It would have been to little purpose, had she set the little muck to grind Decimals, which are said to be so cultivated in one of our Reigate schools, as to leave the poor girls scarce any time for plain needlework. Can there be folly more infatuated than that which would leave the children of the poor ignorant of household management and practical duties? Muriatic acid, is it not? which now so pervades the London atmosphere as to render building impossible without speedy corrosion of the stone. Before the East end of Westminster Palace was finished, the West end had begun to rot; and what will peel a stone wall is not likely to put flesh upon a baby. Then there is the filthy GAS. Muses of Phlegethon assist the mortal who would set forth half its loathsomeness!—destroying vegetation;—the noble suburban elms which Milton celebrates; rotting to pieces ancient muniments and toughest parchment; and yet, forsooth, through blind subserviency to custom admitted into our dwelling houses; and, incredible as such wicked carelessness may seem, even into our nurseries! Such, with the visible typhus, steaming up through the drain-vents in the street, is the atmosphere in which we strive to rear the tenderest infancy. No horse breeder or dog trainer would consent to rear his whelps or fillies in such a medium. But in everything which does not relate to dogs and horses, our national idols, we follow each other like sheep to the slaughter house. Life itself we hold cheaply if it may not be preserved by precedent. 'I would rather die' said a lady 'under Sir Henry Halford, than be cured by any one else'.

Often and often I bless my Father's memory for making me repeat almost daily 'Custom is the plague of wise men and the idol of fools.'

Evil drainage however is by no means peculiar to London. It has proved fatal in Brighten, and is very bad in several parts of Margate. Yours was the choicest spot and I trust that your dear Iona, will there drink in currents of vigorous and established health. What evidence has Iona borne to the importance of the atmosphere we inspire! At Margate she respired and eat: in London she respired and could *not* eat. Ought not children to eat first rate (not heavy) home made bread?—But then, is the flour pure? Or are we so accustomed to poisons that they have become an essential part of our idiosyncracy?

I never write notes if I can help it, because there are no news to tell. Things go evenly if perilously. Herbert travels, for the Brompton Schools, about fifty miles daily Saturday and Sunday excepted, is Sidesman to his Revd Friend and one of his Church Council! I am very fond of the brothers, and have some delightful talks with Howard in the vacations, albeit I have once had the misfortune to make him red with rage. How *could* it happen? I dislike reverting to myself, but will just remark that in the article you read there is a mistake of 10 years as to the date of my first exhibited picture, as in 1809 I had not very long emerged from long clothes—not long enough at least to approximate the hope of pockets and inexpressibles. The first exhibition I saw, in 1819 is fixed in memory by the first Turner 'The orange merchant on the bar'—and being by nature a lover of smudginess, I have revelled in him from that day to this. May not half the Art be learned from the gradations in coffee-grouts? My Wife desires to be [remembered] most affectionately to you, and it is very kind to have borne Herbert so long in memory. He well remembers you at Kensington. Pray give my kindest regards to Mr Robinson whose sketches with yours I should so much like to see—and believe me.

Ever affectionately yours
S. Palmer

Dr Johnson's . . . 'Tour'] *A Journey to the Western Islands of Scotland* (1775).   Pulteney] William Pulteney, Earl of Bath (1684–1764), statesman.   Fair junior] a younger child, Hilda.   Muriatic] hydrochloric.   Phlegethon] a burning river in Hades.   Elms] these may be from 'L'Allegro', 1. 58.   Sir Henry Halford] (1766–1844), a distinguished doctor.   Turner] the picture is in the Tate Gallery.   Inexpressibles] presumably long trousers.

CHARLES DICKENS
(1812–1870)

167. To Daniel Maclise, 22 July 1840

Maclise (1806–70) was a portrait painter (his portrait of his close friend Dickens is in the National Portrait Gallery).

My Dear Maclise,

Kate has a girl stopping here, for whom I have conceived a horrible aversion, and whom I *must* fly. Shall we dine together today in some sequestered pothouse, and go to some theatre afterwards? (My Examiner promise in the latter respect, lies heavy on my mind.) If yea, will you be here at 4, *or as soon as you like.* If nay, whither can I turn from this fearful female! She is the Ancient Mariner of young ladies. She 'holds me with her glittering eye', and I cannot turn away. The basilisk is now in the dining room and I am in the study, but I *feel* her through the wall. She is of a prim and icy aspect, her breast tight and smooth like a sugar loaf,—she converseth with fluency, and hath deep mental lore—her name is Martha Ball—she breakfasted in the dining room this morning, and I took my solitary food, tight locked-up in the study. I went out last night and in my desolation, had my hair cut—merely to avoid her. Evins, this is dreadful!

Your wretched friend
Charles Dickens

P.S. Is Davis of an excitable and ardent nature—I mean the enthusiastic sculptor? Do you think if I asked him here, he might be got to run away with this tremendous being? She is remarkable for a lack of development everywhere, and might be useful as a model of a griffin or other fabulous monster.

P.P.S Or would he make her bust, and 'aggrawate' it. That would be some revenge.

Kate] Catherine Hogarth, Dickens's wife.   Examiner promise] of a theatrical review which appeared four days later.   Davis] Edward Davis (1813–78) did a bust of Maclise.

168. To Daniel Maclise, 12 March 1841

My Dear Maclise,

You will be greatly shocked and grieved to hear that the Raven is no more.

He expired to-day at a few minutes after Twelve o'Clock at noon. He had been ailing (as I told you t'other night) for a few days, but we anticipated no serious result, conjecturing that a portion of the white paint he swallowed last summer might be lingering about his vitals without having any serious effect upon his constitution. Yesterday afternoon he was taken so much worse that I sent an express for the medical gentleman (Mr Herring) who promptly attended, and administered a powerful dose of castor oil. Under the influence of this medicine, he recovered so far as to be able at 8 o'Clock p.m. to bite Topping. His night was peaceful. This morning at daybreak he appeared better; received (agreeably to the doctor's directions) another dose of castor oil; and partook plentifully of some warm gruel, the flavor of which he appeared to relish. Towards eleven o'Clock he was so much worse that it was found necessary to muffle the stable knocker. At half past, or thereabouts, he was heard talking to himself about the horse and Topping's family, and to add some incoherent expressions which are supposed to have been either a foreboding of his approaching dissolution, or some wishes relative to the disposal of his little property—consisting chiefly of halfpence which he had buried in different parts of the garden. On the clock striking twelve he appeared slightly agitated, but he soon recovered, walked twice or thrice along the coach-house, stopped to bark, staggered, exclaimed 'Halloa old girl!' (his favorite expression) and died.

He behaved throughout with a decent fortitude, equanimity, and self-possession, which cannot be too much admired. I deeply regret that being in ignorance of his danger I did not attend to receive his last instructions. Something remarkable about his eyes occasioned Topping to run for the doctor at Twelve. When they returned together our friend was gone. It was the medical gentleman who informed me of his decease. He did it with great caution and delicacy, preparing me by the remark that 'a jolly queer start had taken place', but the shock was very great notwithstanding.

I am not wholly free from suspicions of poison—a malicious butcher has been heard to say that he would 'do' for him—his plea was, that he would not be molested in taking orders down the Mews, by any bird that wore a tail—other persons have also been heard to threaten—among others, Charles Knight who has just started a weekly publication, price fourpence; Barnaby being, as you know, Threepence. I have directed a post mortem examination, and the body has been removed to Mr Herring's school of Anatomy for that purpose.

I could wish, if you can take the trouble, that you would inclose this to Forster when you have read it. I cannot discharge the painful task of communication more than once. Were they Ravens who took Manna to somebody in the wilderness? At times I hope they were, and at others I fear they were not, or they would certainly have stolen it by the way.

In profound sorrow, I am ever Your bereaved friend.

CD

Kate is as well as can be expected, but terribly low as you may suppose.

The children seem rather glad of it. He bit their ancles. But that was play——

The Raven] he appeared as Grip in *Barnaby Rudge*. He had eaten white lead left by painters in the stable.   Mr Herring] he dealt in birds and animals.   Topping] the coachman. Charles Knight] (1791–1873), publisher and Shakespearian; his *London* appeared in weekly parts from 6 Mar.   Forster] John Forster (1812–76), Dickens's close friend and biographer.

169. To Albany Fonblanque, from Washington D.C., 12 March 1842

Fonblanque (1793–1872) was editor of the *Examiner*.

My Dear Fonblanque,

I have reserved my fire upon you until I came to this place, thinking you would best like to know something about the political oddities of this land. No doubt you have heard the leading points in my adventures—as how we had a bad passage out, of 18 days—how I have been dined, and balled (there were 3000 people at the ball) and feted in all directions—and how I can't stir, without a great crowd at my heels—and am by no means in my element, in consequence. I shall therefore spare you these experiences, whereof Forster is a living chronicle; and carry you straightway to the President's house.

It's a good house to look at, but—to follow out the common saying—an uncommon bad 'un to go; at least I should think so. I arrived here on Wednesday night; and on Thursday morning was taken there by the Secretary to the Senate: a namesake of mine, whom 'John Tyler' had despatched to carry me to him for a private interview which is considered a greater compliment than the public audience. We entered a large hall, and rang a large bell—if I may judge from the size of the handle. Nobody answering the bell, we walked about on our own account, as divers other gentlemen (mostly with their hats on, and their hands in their pockets) were doing, very leisurely. Some of them had ladies with them to whom they were shewing the premises; others were lounging on the chairs and sofas; others, yawning and picking their teeth. The greater part of this assemblage were rather asserting their supremacy than doing anything else; as they had no particular business there, that anybody knew of. A few were eyeing the moveables as if to make quite sure that the President (who is not popular) hadn't made away with any of the furniture, or sold the fixtures for his private benefit.

After glancing at these loungers who were scattered over a pretty drawing room, furnished with blue and silver, opening upon a terrace with a beautiful prospect of the Potomac River and adjacent country—and a larger state room, not unlike the dining room at the Athenæum—we went up stairs into another chamber, where were the more favored visitors who were waiting for audiences. At sight of my conductor, a black in plain clothes and yellow slippers, who was moving noiselessly about, and whispering messages in the ears of the more impatient, made a sign of recognition and glided off to announce us.

There were some twenty men in the room. One, a tall, wiry, muscular old man from the West, sunburnt and swarthy,—with a brown white hat and a giant umbrella, who sat bolt upright in his chair, frowning steadily at the carpet, as if he had made up his mind that he was going to 'fix' the President in what he had to say, and wouldn't bate him a grain. Another, a Kentucky farmer nearly seven feet high, with his hat on, and his hands under his coat tails, who leaned against the wall, and kicked the floor with his heel, as though he had Time's head under his shoe, and were literally 'killing' him. A third, a short, round-faced man with sleek black hair cropped close, and whiskers and beard shaved down into blue dots, who sucked the head of a big stick, and from time to time took it out of his mouth to see how it was getting on. A fourth did nothing but whistle. The rest balanced themselves, now on one leg, and now on the other, and chewed mighty quids of tobacco—such mighty quids, that they all looked as if their faces were swoln with erisypelas. They all constantly squirted forth upon the carpet, a yellow saliva which quite altered its pattern; and even the few who did not indulge in this recreation, expectorated abundantly.

In five minutes time, the black in yellow slippers came back, and led us into an upper room—a kind of office—where, by the side of a hot stove, though it was a very hot day, sat the President—all alone; and close to him a great spit box, which is an indispensable article of furniture here. In the private sitting room in which I am writing this, there are two; one on each side of the fire place. They are made of brass, to match the fender and fire irons; and are as bright as decanter stands.—But I am wandering from the President. Well! The President got up, and said, 'Is *this* Mr Dickens?'—'Sir', returned Mr Dickens—'it is'. 'I am astonished to see so young a man Sir', said the President. Mr Dickens smiled, and thought of returning the compliment—but he didn't; for the President looked too worn and tired, to justify it. 'I am happy to join with my fellow citizens in welcoming you, warmly, to this country', said the President. Mr Dickens thanked him, and shook hands. Then the other Mr Dickens, the secretary, asked the President to come to his house that night, which the President said he should be glad to do, but for the pressure of business, and measles. Then the President And the two Mr Dickenses sat and looked at each other, until Mr Dickens of London observed that no doubt the President's time was fully occupied, and he and the other Mr Dickens had better go. Upon that they all rose up; and the President invited Mr Dickens (of London) to come again, which he said he would. And that was the end of the conference.

From the President's house, I went up to the Capitol, and visited both the Senate, and the House of Representatives, which, as I dare say you know are under one roof. Both are of the amphitheatre form, and very tastefully fitted up; with large galleries for ladies, and for the public generally. In the Senate, which is much the smaller of the two, I made the acquaintance of everybody in the first quarter of an hour—among the rest of Clay, who is one of the most agreeable and fascinating men I ever saw. He is tall and slim, with long, limp, gray hair—a good head—refined features—a bright eye—a good voice—and a manner more frank and captivating than I ever saw in any man, at all advanced in life. I was perfectly charmed with him. In the other house, John Quincey Adams interested me very much. He is something like Rogers, but not so infirm; is very accomplished; and perfectly 'game'. The rest were in appearance a good deal like our own members—some of them very bilious-looking, some very rough, some heartily good natured, and some very coarse. I asked which was Mr Wyse, who lives in my mind, from the circumstance of his having made a very violent speech about England t'other day, which he emphasized (with great gentlemanly feeling and good taste) by pointing, as he spoke, at Lord Morpeth who happened to be present. They pointed out a wild looking, evil-visaged man, something like Roebuck, but much more savage,with a great ball of tobacco in his left cheek. I was quite satisfied.

I didn't see the honorable member who on being called to order by another honorable member some three weeks since, said 'Damn your eyes Sir, if you presume to call *me* to order, I'll cut your damnation throat from ear to ear';—he wasn't there—but they shewed me the honorable member to whom he addressed this rather strong Parliamentary language; and I was obliged to content myself with him.

Yesterday, I went there again. A debate was in progress concerning the removal of a certain postmaster, charged with mal-practises, and with having interfered in elections. The speaking I heard, was partly what they call 'Stump Oratory'—meaning that kind of eloquence which is delivered in the West, from that natural rostrum—and partly, a dry and prosy chopping of very small logic into very small mincemeat. It was no worse than ours, and no better. One gentleman being interrupted by a laugh from the opposition, mimicked the laugh, as a child would in quarrelling with another child, and said that 'before he had done he'd make honorable members sing out, a little more on the other side of their mouths'. This was the most remarkable sentiment I heard, in the course of a couple of hours.

I said something just now, about the prevalence of spit-boxes. They are everywhere. In hospitals, prisons, watch-houses, and courts of law—on the bench, in the witness box, in the jury box, and in the gallery; in the stage coach, the steam boat, the rail road car, the hotel, the hall of a private gentleman, and the chamber of Congress; where every two men have one of these conveniences between them—and very unnecessarily, for they flood the carpet, while they talk to you. Of all things in this country, this practice is to me the most insufferable. I can bear anything but filth. I would be content even to live in an atmosphere of spit, if they would but *spit clean*; but when every man ejects from his mouth that odious, most disgusting, compound of saliva and tobacco, I vow that my stomach revolts, and I cannot endure it. The marble stairs and passages of every handsome public building are polluted with these abominable stains; they are squirted about the base of every column that supports the roof; and they make the floors brown, despite the printed entreaty that visitors will not disfigure them with 'tobacco spittle'. It is the most sickening, beastly, and abominable custom that ever civilization saw.

When an American gentleman is polished, he *is* a perfect gentleman. Coupled with all the good qualities that such an Englishman possesses, he has a warmth of heart and an earnestness, to which I render up myself hand and heart. Indeed the whole people have most affectionate and generous impulses. I have not travelled anywhere, yet, without making upon the road a pleasant acquaintance who has gone out of his way to serve and assist me. I have never met with any common man who would not have been hurt and offended if I had offered him money, for any trifling service he has been able to render me. Gallantry and deference to females are universal. No man wod. retain his seat in a public conveyance to the exclusion of a lady, or hesitate for an instant in exchanging places with her, however much to his discomfort, if the wish were but remotely hinted. They are generous, hospitable, affectionate, and kind. I have been obliged to throw open my doors at a certain hour, in every place I have visited, and receive from 300 to 7 or 800 people; but I have never once been asked a rude or impertinent question, except by an Englishman—and when an Englishman has been settled here for ten or twelve years, he is worse than the Devil.

For all this, I would not live here two years—no, not for any gift they could bestow upon me. Apart from my natural desire to be among my friends and to be at home again, I have a yearning after our English Customs and english manners, such as you cannot conceive. It would be impossible to say, in this compass, in what respects America differs from my preconceived opinion of it, but between you and me—privately and confidentially—I shall be truly glad to leave it, though I have formed a perfect attachment to many people here, and have a public progress through the Land, such as it never saw, except in the case of Lafayette. I am going away, now, into the Far West. A public entertainment has been arranged in every town I have visited; but I found it absolutely necessary to decline them—with one reservation.—I am going now, to meet a whole people of my readers in the Far West—two thousand miles from N. York—on the borders of the Indian Territory!

Since I wrote the inclosed sheet, I have had an Invitation from the President to dinner. I couldn't go: being obliged to leave Washington before the day he named. But Mrs Dickens and I went to the public drawing room where pretty nearly all the natives go, who choose. It was most remarkable and most striking to see the perfect order observed— without one soldier, sailor, constable, or policeman in attendance, within the house or without; though the crowd was immense.

I have been as far South, as Richmond in Virginia.—I needn't say how odious the sight of Slavery is, or how frantic the holders are in their wrath against England, because of this Creole business.—If you see Forster soon, ask him how the Negroes drive in rough roads.

And if you should ever have time to scratch a few lines to a poor transported man, address them to the care of David Colden Esquire 28 Laight Street, Hudson Square, New York. He will forward them to me wherever I be. You must do on your side, what I can't do on this—pay the postage—or your letter will come back to you.

How long will the Tory Ministry last? Say six months, and receive my blessing.

Mrs Dickens unites with me in best regards to Mrs Fonblanque and her sister. And I am always, My Dear Fonblanque

Faithfully Your friend
Charles Dickens

Tyler] President W. H. Harrison had died a month after his inauguration in 1841, to be succeeded by John Tyler.   Clay] Henry Clay (1777–1852), Whig politician.   Rogers] for
the poet Samuel Rogers, see footnote, Letter 152.   Wyse] H. A. Wise was a representative
from Virginia, a friend of Tyler's and a defender of slavery. He had accused J. Q. Adams of
partiality to England and a desire to destroy the Constitution.   Lord Morpeth] (1802–64),
a Whig MP and an abolitionist.   Roebuck] J. A. Roebuck was an English Radical.
Lafayette] the Marquis de Lafayette (1757–1834) was honoured as a hero of both American and
French Revolutions.   Creole] an American ship which was taken over by slaves and put
into the British port of Nassau. The refusal of the British authorities to surrender the slaves was
greatly resented in the South. An indemnity was paid in 1853.   Tory Ministry] Peel's
ministry lasted from 1841 to 1846.

170. To Thomas Mitton, 13 June 1865

Mitton had been a fellow clerk of Dickens's in the solicitor's office where he worked
for a few weeks in 1827. The railway accident happened on 9 June; the train from
Folkestone to London was derailed on a bridge and fell into a stream. Ten people
died; Dickens was returning from Paris with Ellen Ternan and her mother; their
carriage escaped damage. The manuscript was part of *Our Mutual Friend* (1864–5).

My dear Mitton,

I should have written to you yesterday or the day before, if I had been quite up to writing.

I was in the only carriage that did not go over into the stream. It was caught upon the turn by some of the ruin of the bridge, and hung suspended and balanced in an apparently impossible manner. Two ladies were my fellow-passengers, an old one and a young one. This is exactly what passed. You may judge from it the precise length of the suspense: Suddenly we were off the rail, and beating the ground as the car of a half-emptied balloon might. The old lady cried out, 'My God!' and the young one screamed. I caught hold of them both (the old lady sat opposite and the young one on my left), and said: 'We can't help ourselves, but we can be quiet and composed. Pray don't cry out.' The old lady immediately answered: 'Thank you. Rely upon me. Upon my soul I will be quiet.' We were then all tilted down together in a corner of the carriage, and stopped. I said to them thereupon: 'You may be sure nothing worse can happen. Our danger *must* be over. Will you remain here without stirring, while I get out of the window?' They both answered quite collectedly, 'Yes,' and I got out without the least notion what had happened. Fortunately I got out with great caution and stood upon the step. Looking down I saw the bridge gone, and nothing below me but the line of rail. Some people in the two other compartments were madly trying to plunge out of window, and had no idea that there was an open swampy field fifteen feet down below them, and nothing else! The two guards (one with his face cut) were running up and down on the down side of the bridge (which was not torn up) quite wildly. I called out to them: 'Look at me. Do stop an instant and look at me, and tell me whether you don't know me.' One of them answered: 'We know you very well, Mr Dickens.' 'Then,' I said, 'my good fellow, for God's sake give me your key, and send one of those labourers here, and I'll empty this carriage.' We did it quite safely, by means of a plank or two, and when it was done I saw all the rest of the train, except the two baggage vans, down in the stream. I got into the carriage again for my brandy flask, took off my travelling hat for a basin, climbed down the brickwork, and filled my hat with water.

Suddenly I came upon a staggering man covered with blood (I think he must have been flung clean out of his carriage), with such a frightful cut across the skull that I couldn't bear to look at him. I poured some water over his face and gave him some drink, then gave him some brandy, and laid him down on the grass, and he said, 'I am gone,' and died afterwards. Then I stumbled over a lady lying on her back against a little pollard-tree, with the blood streaming over her face (which was lead colour) in a number of distinct little streams from the head. I asked her if she could swallow a little brandy and she just nodded, and I gave her some and left her for somebody else. The next time I passed her she was dead. Then a man, examined at the inquest yesterday (who evidently had not the least remembrance of what really passed) came running up to me and implored me to help him find his wife, who was afterwards found dead. No imagination can conceive the ruin of the carriages, or the extraordinary weights under which the people were lying, or the complications into which they were twisted up among iron and wood, and mud and water.

I don't want to be examined at the inquest and I don't want to write about it. I could do no good either way, and I could only seem to speak about myself, which, of course, I would rather not do. I am keeping very quiet here. I have a—I don't know what to call it—constitutional (I suppose) presence of mind, and was not in the least fluttered at the time. I instantly remembered that I had the MS. of a number with me, and clambered back into the carriage for it. But in writing these scanty words of recollection I feel the shake and am obliged to stop.

Ever faithfully.

171. To Henry Dickens, 15 October 1868

Henry Fielding Dickens (1849–1933), Dickens's sixth son, later had a distinguished legal career.

My dear Harry,

I have your letter here this morning. I enclose you another cheque for twenty-five pounds, and I write to London by this post, ordering three dozen sherry, two dozen port, six bottles of brandy, and three dozen light claret, to be sent down to you. And I enclose a cheque in favour of the Rev. F. L. Hopkins for £5:10:0.

Now, observe attentively. We must have no shadow of debt. Square up everything whatsoever that it has been necessary to buy. Let not a farthing be outstanding on any account, when we begin with your allowance. Be particular in the minutest detail.

I wish to have no secret from you in the relations we are to establish together, and I therefore send you Joe Chitty's letter bodily. Reading it, you will know exactly what I know, and will understand that I treat you with perfect confidence. It appears to me that an allowance of two hundred and fifty pounds a year will be handsome for all your wants, if I send you your wines. I mean this to include your tailor's bills as well as every other expense; and I strongly recommend you to buy nothing in Cambridge, and to take credit for nothing but the clothes with which your tailor provides you. As soon as you have got your furniture accounts in, let us wipe all those preliminary expenses clean out, and I will then send you your first quarter. We will count in it October, November, and December; and your second quarter will begin with the New Year. If you dislike, at first, taking charge of so large a sum as sixty-two pounds ten shillings, you can have your money from me half-quarterly.

You know how hard I work for what I get, and I think you know that I never had money help from any human creature after I was a child. You know that you are one of many heavy charges on me, and that I trust to your so exercising your abilities and improving the advantages of your past expensive education, as soon to diminish *this* charge. I say no more on that head.

Whatever you do, above all other things keep out of debt and confide in me. If ever you find yourself on the verge of any perplexity or difficulty, come to me. You will never find me hard with you while you are manly and truthful.

As your brothers have gone away one by one, I have written to each of them what I am now going to write to you. You know that you have never been hampered with religious forms of restraint, and that with mere unmeaning forms I have no sympathy. But I most strongly and affectionately impress upon you the priceless value of the New Testament, and the study of that book as the one unfailing guide in life. Deeply respecting it, and bowing down before the character of our Saviour, as separated from the vain constructions and inventions of men, you cannot go very wrong, and will always preserve at heart a true spirit of veneration and humility. Similarly I impress upon you the habit of saying a Christian prayer every night and morning. These things have stood by me all through my life, and remember that I tried to render the New Testament intelligible to you and lovable by you when you were a mere baby.

And so God bless you.—Ever your affectionate Father.

Hopkins] a Fellow of Trinity Hall, Harry's college.   Chitty] Sir Joseph Chitty (1828–99) was a lawyer.

RALPH WALDO EMERSON
(1803–1882)

Emerson, the essayist, lecturer, and poet, was associated with the Transcendentalist movement, centred in Concord, Mass.

172. To Margaret Fuller, 24 October 1840

Margaret Fuller (1810–50) was the editor of the *Dial*, the journal of the Transcendentalist movement, and a feminist. Married to a follower of Mazzini, she took part in the Italian revolution of 1848, but was drowned with her husband and child on the passage back to America.

My dear Margaret,

I have your frank & noble & affecting letter, and yet I think I could wish it unwritten. I ought never to have suffered you to lead me into any conversation or writing on our relation, a topic from which with all persons my Genius ever sternly warns me away. I was content & happy to meet on a human footing a woman of sense & sentiment with whom one could exchange reasonable words & go away assured that wherever she went there was light & force & honour. That is to me a solid good; it gives value to thought & the day; it redeems society from that foggy & misty aspect it wears so often seen from our retirements; it is the foundation of everlasting friendship. Touch it not—speak not of it—and this most welcome natural alliance becomes from month to month,—& the slower & with the more intervals the better,—our air & diet. A robust & total understanding grows up resembling nothing so much as the relation of brothers who are intimate & perfect friends without having ever spoken of the fact. But tell me that I am cold or unkind, and in my most flowing state I become a cake of ice. I can feel the crystals shoot & the drops solidify. It may do for others but it is not for me to bring the relation to speech. Instantly I find myself a solitary unrelated person, destitute not only of all social faculty but of all private substance. I see precisely the double of my state in my little Waldo when in the midst of his dialogue with his hobby horse in the full tide of his eloquence I should ask him if he loves me?—he is mute & stupid. I too have never yet lived a moment—have never done a deed—am the youngest child of nature,—I take it for granted that everybody will show me kindness & wit, and am too happy in the observation of all the abundant particulars of the show to feel the slightest obligation resting on me to do any thing or say any thing for the company. I talk to my hobby & will join you in harnessing & driving him, & recite to you his virtues all day—but ask me what I think of you & me,—& I am put to confusion.

Up to this hour our relation has been progressive. I have never regarded you with so much kindness as now. Sometimes you appeal to sympathies I have not and sometimes you inquire into the state of this growth.—that for the moment puts me back, but you presently return to my daylight & we get on admirably.

There is a difference in our constitution. We use a different rhetoric. It seems as if we had been born & bred in different nations. You say you understand me wholly. You cannot communicate yourself to me. I hear the words sometimes but remain a stranger to your state of mind.

Yet are we all the time a little nearer. I honor you for a brave & beneficent woman and mark with gladness your steadfast good will to me. I see not how we can bear each other anything else than good will though we had sworn to the contrary.

And now what will you? Why should you interfere? See you not that I cannot spare you? that you cannot be spared? that a vast & beautiful Power to whose counsels our will was never party, has thrown us into strict neighborhood for best & happiest ends? The stars in Orion do not quarrel this night, but shine in peace in their old society. Are we not much better than they? Let us live as we have always done, only ever better, I hope, & richer. Speak to me of every thing but myself & I will endeavor to make an intelligible reply. Allow me to serve you & you will do me a kindness; come & see me & you will recommend my house to me; let me visit you and I shall be cheered as ever by the spectacle of so much genius & character as you have always the gift to draw around you.

I see very dimly in writing on this topic. It will not prosper with me. Perhaps all my words are wrong. Do not expect it of me again for a very long time.

I will go look for the letters you ask for & which should have been returned before; but I liked to keep them. And could you not send Alcott a remembrance that smacked not so much of Almacks?

You shall have whatever I can muster for the Dial—yet I do not now know what I can offer you.

Yours affectionately,
R. W. Emerson

Alcott] Bronson Alcott, an educator who belonged to the Transcendentalist movement. Almacks] a fashionable assembly room in London.

HENRY COCKBURN
(1779–1854)

Lord Cockburn was a great Scottish lawyer, historian, and politician.

173. To John Cockburn, 22 October 1841

John Cockburn, a brother, was a wine (and evidently also a spirit) merchant.

My dear John,

Have you any *perfect* whiskey? *Absolutely perfect*, for instant use? Lord Dunfermline and another person dine here on Monday, who rejoice in no other liquor, and who are super-eminently fastidious. If you have none which ought to make them ashamed of all they ever tasted, send me none. If you have such as they have no notion of, send me a gallon—or even a single bottle,—addressed to me—to Charlotte Square tomorrow.

Ever,
H. Cockburn

Put some sort of seal on it by which I may know it from some base stuff which will probably come out here along with it.

174. To John Marshall (afterwards Lord Curriehill) 22 July 1847

My dear Marshall,

Many thanks. But if I had known that your Kelly was reduced to 3 bottles, I should not have asked you for one, or expected you to give it to me. Restitution, however, is now impossible.

As to the prescription for making the delicate composition, it is very simple.

One lemon—about 10 pieces of sugar of the ordinary tea size—and one small glass of Rum—to a quart bottle of water. This is my rule. But something must be left to taste, as all lemons don't produce the same juice—nor all 10 bits of sugar the same sweetness. The chief thing is the Rum—which should be as flavourless as possible. The criterion of success is to have nothing sticking out in the browst [*i.e.* brew]. If there be a plain edge of sweetness—or of sourness—or of rumminess—quash it, and produce a vague general homogeneity—a gentle harmony—a steady, mild, well poised fusion of contrarieties, like the British Constitution. Hit that and you hit the thing.

The general composition should resemble a calm temper, a soft sunset, a quiet conscience, a well balanced complete argument, a peaceful country holiday in the Summer Session, a gentle slumber under a sermon.

And to any elements and rules must be added the exquisite tact, the delicate sensibility, the profound experience of the Finished Punchifex Maximus. A rash, rough, ignorant and conceited hand may easily throw in the ingredients—a sow may mix as a sow may drink. But it is not thus that the Poetry of Potation is to be produced. It is by a nicety of hand—fine taste—deep thought—and long reflective practice.

These—*and Ice*—effect a result which exhibit chemistry in its brightest light. Cold is essential.

Iced Punch is the final end of the West Indies. What pious eye can avoid seeing that it was for this product that islands of Rum, of Sugar, and of Lemons are scattered over the Ocean? It is the chief use of each.

'Spirits are not finely touched but to fine issues.'

So wishing you much success, and a great reputation,

Believe me, Yours faithfully,
H. Cockburn

Sermon] Karl Miller's *Cockburn's Millennium* (1975, 272) indicates that in the original letter the word 'roaracious' precedes the word 'sermon'. 'Spirits . . . issues'] from *Measure for Measure*, I. i. 35–6.

F. W. LUDWIG LEICHHART
(1813–1848)

Born in Prussia, Leichhart went to London in 1837 and to Australia by emigrant ship in 1841. A skilled geologist, biologist, and linguist, he explored much of the eastern coast of Australia, and in 1848 led an expedition to cross the continent westward. It was lost without trace. Leichhart is the model for the eponymous hero of Patrick White's novel *Voss* (1957). His letters are in German, French, Italian, and English.

175. To John Murphy, 3 December 1842

Murphy (1829–70) was the son of James Murphy, a Welshman who emigrated at the same time as Leichhart, and became his friend. He was later mayor of Sydney. J. S. Proudt was a well-known artist.

My dear John,

I received your letter of the 28th of November, which is the 3d letter I received from you. I thought I had answered the first. Yesterday I returned from a very fatiguing walking expedition to Point Stephens, which forms the South head of Port Stephens, opposite to the grant of the Australian Agricultural Company. I was four days in the bush and found only once (at Telligerry) a hut where I could restore my exhausted strength. The heat was intolerable, fresh water was scarce, the provisions were soon consumed. It is difficult to find the way in the bush, as the people in this part of the country are not careful in marking the trees, to show that the footpath leads to an inhabited place, and as many great swamps exist here, which are the favourite places for cattle, which form in filing one behind the other tracks exactly resembling to the footpaths made by man. Thus I lost my way hundred times and I had only my compass to guide me. My dear boy, you have no idea how sweet a cup of tea with brown sugar and a piece of damper tastes after such a days journey in the bush. I prefer the tea in the bush to the most excellent wine and I am convinced that no beverage agrees so well with the constitution in this climate, as the tea. You know that the tea contains 2 principles, an exciting one and an adstringent one. The people in town make only an infusion of boiling water on the tea, in order to obtain only the exciting principle, which for itself alone is injurious to health. But in the bush they leave the old leaves and boil them again and again, adding allways a small quantity of fresh tea. They obtain the adstringent part of the tea united with a certain degree of the exciting one and this I imagine, is the cause of the wholesome effect on the stomach. The brown sugar and the milk weaken also its influence. I have found that even cold tea without sugar or milk quenches the thirst most effectively.— The bush was everywhere in fire and I was exposed to great danger in crossing one part, the trees changed into columns of fire and falling every-where around me with a deafening noise. At night I lighted a fire and stretched myself under a forest oak (casuarina) and slept soundly, till the cold of the early morning made me uncomfortable and compelled me to stir my fire again and to dry the dew from my clothes. The deep silence was only interrupted by the browsing wallabis rustling through dry leaves or by the cry of the opossum. The first night I was however at the seaside and the roar of the breakers lulled me into sleep. Such a loneliness makes you feel your weakness and approaches you more to the heavenly father and to his providence than the finest sermon in a full church: it is as if he himself was before you in this awful silence, which surrounds you, which makes you almost hear the beating of your own heart.—Yesterday I was travelling along a sandy beach 20 miles long. There was not a drop of fresh water and I had eaten nothing for the last 24 hours. I found a bed of shells (Donax) of which I devoured a dozen; but they were so briny, that my thirst was considerably increased. When my strength was almost entirely exhausted, I found a cask on shore, which was perhaps thrown over board by a vessel in danger; I went up to it and to my greatest joy and wonder I found it full of fresh water; I need not tell you how thankful I was and how I did drink. I am glad to hear that you are getting on well and that Mr Proudt takes some pains with you. Make my compliments to your father and mother and to Proudts and Marshes if you see them.

> Your affectionate friend,
> L. Leichhardt

[P.S.] Next week I hope to go up to Glendon and to Patricks plains; I want sadly a good companion, who had the same interest as I have. Perhaps I may still get one. Should you have time to walk out at a Sunday gather as many seeds as you can from all the plants, which are now in seed. You know that the seed is quite as characteristic as the flower (seed and seed [vessel]).

REBECCA BUTTERWORTH

A native of Rochdale, Lancashire, daughter of a land surveyor, Rebecca Butterworth emigrated with her husband to Arkansas.

176. To her father, W. W. Barton, 5 July 1846

Charlotte Erickson, whose *Invisible Immigrants* (1972) is the source of this letter, remarks that whereas middle-class people were used to consulting doctors, working-class immigrants depended on herbal remedies, hence Butterworth's reliance on calomel (mercury).

Back Woods of America

My very dear and tender father,

I have been long in answering your and my dear sisters letters. The reason is I was taken sick a month since today. I commenced with bilious intermittant fever which nobody thought I would get over. Thomas was with me nearly all the time. He did not expect me getting over it. I was almost covered with mustard plasters, had a large blister on my back and I cannot tell you what kind of medcine. On the Thursday Thos said their was no help but [salination?]. If not he said before 24 hours it would reach the low typhoid [grian?] and then if preamature labour came on it would be certain death. Well, I had nearly 60 grains of calomel steamed bricks put to me. I had a burning head, my extreamities getting quite cold. My feet they could not get warm at times. Well, the result was the mercury had a happy effect. I had one of my cheeks cut half way through. Indeed it would have scared you to look in my mouth. On Sunday the 14th of June labour came on. I had a many came to see me expecting it almost the last time. I was insensible at times. We did not know I had labour and John and Sarah would have been alone with me on Sunday night but Thos and his wife got very uneasy about me at 9 o'clock and concluded to come and sit up that night, knowing John and Sarah were weared down which I know I attach to a kind Providence. I suppose I had a dread few hours still not knowing I was in labour beside having ben so prostrated a whole week with fever. However I suppose about 3 o'clock on Monday morning my dear baby was born. Not 5 minutes before they say I forced myself out of bed and from sister and run round the bed to a pallet on the floor. Well our little Wm Barton was born and crying like a child at full time. Thos did not like to help me as he had not studied midwifery much. I had to remain in that situation for two hours before the doctor could be got, the little dear boy crying all the time and alarmed at what would be the result. Doctor Howard come when he took the little darling and gave it to sister. In about ten minutes after he took his flight to heaven above to join my other 3 little angels. I know it is the Lords will. We are quite resigned. Both Docter Howard and Thos said I may be very thankfull I am spared myself, for if I had lived to come to my time the child was so large I could not of borne it. You would have been astonished to see. He is laid beside Polly and Rebecca. She would often tell tacky they were going to have another little broder Billy. So they have and seen him too. I felt when I heard him crying so if I could have him in my arms and put him to his breast I would be glad, but the Lords will be done and not ours.

I am now again able to sit up about a half a day at once. I have had another sever attack this past week which threw me down again owing to a dreadfull thunder storm and wind which scared me and threw the blood to my head. I have ridden on horseback to Thos once since. John had to lead the horses head and with being worse again I could not sit on a horse. Mary Ann is out, came in a buggy, so Thos brought last Fridy and took me to his house. I am so nervous that riding when able helps me. Yesterday he brought me in his carry all to Fathers. I am their now. Inded if it aint for him through the providence of God I expect I would have been in my grave now. You would hardly know me now. I am so pulled down but am out of danger now but has to be very careful. My dear Father and Sisters. . . . Be very thankful to God for shewing us so many mercies. The family have really all been very kind to me in this sickness. Father & mother shed tears when he helped me in his house. I can forgive all the past. He wished me to tell you to be kind enough to see James and tell him the have not had an answer to his letter and are very uneasy for fear it has miscarried. Mary Ann is well and going to have a baby middle of September. I have not heard of poor Ebijah which makes me feel bad for fear he is dead.

John is not satisfied here. What little corn we had the cattle as jumped the fence and eaten it so that it will not make even cattle feed. We are [dammed?] up in corner. We have not bread to last above a week and no meat, very little coffee, about ½ lb of sugar. John can milk one cow which makes us a little butter but the other wont let him. He as had to be with me a month. We try to put our trust in the Lord knowing he is able to open the way. We want to sell the horse but cannot meet with a customer. If we could we think we could get along untill spring. We are going to do our best to part with the place. If we sell soon and the Lord spares us, we will be out in fall; if not, I will write again soon and if you can help us along without hurting yourself we should be glad to get home.

We want to [go] through Philadelphia. Mr Moore got there in 2 weeks & 2 days. It will cost very little more by taking deck passage. Will you try to get to know what Captn West charges steerage passage from Phildia to England? He knows you and would perhaps favour us. Now, Father, John is in good earnest, you may depend. Please do your best and if we are spared let me meet you all again. I feel a pang, that is leaving the homes of our 3 little ones but I cannot see their faces. Docter Howard charged 5 dollars but expect to pay him with a big 2 horse plough. Thos as given me a deal of medicine beside attention twice a day. Indeed the whole family was afraid of having done. His charege is nothing but a little sewing of bridles which is nothing.

Tell my dear sisters not to feel slighted I have not written. I fully intended to do it, am not yet able. You see how my hand trembles. I have had to rest in doing this. Excuse a long letter as I am so weak. Please write immediately when you get this and advise with us for the best way. Coming that way we can see more of America and get home in 3 weeks less sea. When Mr Moore comes back we can get to know pretty near price to Philidelphia. When I get your letter I will write and say what it is. My love to all and every one as if mentioned. Tell my sisters to think of us. John would have written this letter and . . . [illegible word] Sisters to but I though[t] if I could do it any how I would, and now my dear father may our God bless us all and give us more grace to receive chastisement and trust more in him. What is this world without a hope of a better? May he at last take us all to meet with him and all our dear children and Mother. Wont that be a blessed time? Bless you all with a kiss for you sisters and not forgeting little John. Ask him what I shall bring him. I wish I had one of the children with me. Mr Massel, the post master, sent you 3 newspapers, which was very kind in him. Now I must conclude as I have had hard work to write so much from your poor weak daughter,

Rebecca Butterworth

HERMAN MELVILLE

(1819–1891)

177. To Evert A. Duyckinck, 3 March 1849

> Duyckinck was an editor at Wiley & Putnam, the firm that published Melville's novel *Typee* in 1846. A correspondence began, and turned into a friendship.

Nay, I do not oscillate in Emerson's rainbow, but prefer rather to hang myself in mine own halter than swing in any other man's swing. Yet I think Emerson is more than a brilliant fellow. Be his stuff begged, borrowed, or stolen, or of his own domestic manufacture he is an uncommon man. Swear he is a humbug—then is he no common humbug. Lay it down that had not Sir Thomas Browne lived, Emerson would not have mystified—I will answer, that had not Old Zack's father begot him, Old Zack would never have been the hero of Palo Alto. The truth is that we are all sons, grandsons, or nephews or great-nephews of those who go before us. No one is his own sire.—I was very agreeably disappointed in Mr Emerson. I had heard of him as full of transcendentalisms, myths & oracular gibberish; I had only glanced at a book of his once in Putnam's store—that was all I knew of him, till I heard him lecture.—To my surprise, I found him quite intelligible, tho' to say truth, they told me that that night he was unusually plain.—Now, there is a something about every man elevated above mediocrity, which is, for the most part, instinctuly perceptible. This I see in Mr Emerson. And, frankly, for the sake of the argument, let us call him a fool;—then had I rather be a fool than a wise man.—I love all men who *dive*. Any fish can swim near the surface, but it takes a great whale to go down stairs five miles or more; & if he dont attain the bottom, why, all the lead in Galena can't fashion the plumet that will. I'm not talking of Mr Emerson now—but of the whole corps of thought-divers, that have been diving & coming up again with bloodshot eyes since the world began.

I could readily see in Emerson, notwithstanding his merit, a gaping flaw. It was, the insinuation, that had he lived in those days when the world was made, he might have offered some valuable suggestions. These men are all cracked right across the brow. And Never will the pullers-down be able to cope with the builders-up. And this pulling down is easy enough—a keg of powder blew up Block's Monument—but the man who applied the match, could not, alone, build such a pile to save his soul from the shark-maw of the Devil. But enough of this Plato who talks thro' his nose. To one of your habits of thought, I confess that in my last, I seemed, but only *seemed* irreverent. And do not think, my boy, that because I, impulsively broke forth in jubillations [at discovering] over Shakspeare, that, therefore, I am of the number of the *snobs* who burn their tuns of rancid fat at his shrine. No, I would stand afar off & alone, & burn some pure Palm oil, the product of some overtopping trunk.

—I would to God Shakspeare had lived later, & promenaded in Broadway. Not that I might have had the pleasure of leaving my card for him at the Astor, or made merry with him over a bowl of the fine Duyckinck punch; but that the muzzle which all men wore on their souls in the Elizebethan day, might not have intercepted Shakspers full articulations. For I hold it a verity, that even Shakspeare, was not a frank man to the uttermost. And, indeed, who in this intolerant Universe is, or can be? But the Declaration of Independence makes a difference.—There, I have driven my horse so hard that I have made my inn before sundown. I was going to say something more—It was this.—You complain that Emerson tho' a denizen of the land of gingerbread, is above munching a plain cake in company of jolly fellows, & swiging off his ale like you & me. Ah, my dear sir, that's his misfortune, not his fault. His belly, sir, is in his chest, & his brains descend down into his neck, & offer an obstacle to a draught of ale or a mouthful of cake. But here I am.

Good bye—
H. M.

Emerson] see above, Letter 172.   Old Zack] Zachary Taylor, later 12th President, defeated the Mexicans at Palo Alto in 1845.   Galena] Galena, Ill., was famous for lead-mines.   A great whale] Melville was at this time writing *Moby-Dick* (1851).   Horse] the figure of the hard-driven horse means that he was nearing the end of the page and had to tighten the spacing of his letter.

178. To Nathaniel Hawthorne, 29 January? 1851

The friendship of Melville with another remarkable novelist, Nathaniel Hawthorne, began in 1850, when they were neighbours in Massachusetts. Melville was writing *Moby-Dick* and Hawthorne had just published *The Scarlet Letter* (1850) and was writing *The House of the Seven Gables* (1851). Sophia Hawthorne had sent a note postponing a planned visit.

That side-blow thro' Mrs Hawthorne will not do. I am not to be charmed out of my promised pleasure by any of that lady's syrenisims. *You*, Sir, I hold accountable, & the visit (in all its original integrity) must be made.— What! *spend the day*, only with us?—A Greenlander might as well talk of spending the day with a friend, when the day is only half an inch long.

As I said before, my best travelling chariot on runners, will be at your door, & provision made not only for the accommodation of all your family, but also for any quantity of *baggage*.

Fear not that you will cause the slightest trouble to us. Your bed is already made, & the wood marked for your fire. But a moment ago, I looked into the eyes of two fowls, whose tail feathers have been notched, as destined victims for the table. I keep the word 'Welcome' all the time in my mouth, so as to be ready on the instant when you cross the threshold.

(By the way the old Romans you know had a Salve carved in *their* thresholds)

Another thing, Mr Hawthorne—Do not think you are coming to any prim nonsensical house—that is nonsensical in the ordinary way. You must be much bored with punctilios. You may do what you please—say or say *not* what you please. And if you feel any inclination for that sort of thing— you may spend the period of your visit *in bed*, if you like—every hour of your visit.

Mark—There is some excellent Montado Sherry awaiting you & some most potent Port. We will have mulled wine with wisdom, & buttered toast with story-telling & crack jokes & bottles from morning till night.

Come—no nonsense. If you dont—I will send Constables after you.

On Wednesday then—weather & sleighing permitting I will be down for you about eleven o'clock A. M.

By the way—should Mrs Hawthorne for any reason conclude that *she*, for one, can not stay overnight with us—then *you* must—& the children, if you please.

H. Melville

CAROLINE NORTON
(1808–1877)

Caroline Norton was a poet, and a granddaughter of the dramatist Richard Brinsley Sheridan. Her unhappy marriage to the Hon. George Chapple Norton led to a *cause célèbre*, Chapple bringing an action for 'criminal conversation' between his wife and Lord Melbourne. They were acquitted. Norton's attempts to claim his wife's literary income resulted in her pamphlet 'English Laws for Women in the Nineteenth Century' (1853) and others on the Divorce Bill of 1853 and on the custody of children, where the husband also had a prior claim, as in Trollope's *He Knew He Was Right*.

179. To Sir Alexander Duff Gordon, 9 June 1849

Duff Gordon was the husband of Lucie Austin (see above, Letter 127). Their son Maurice was born in Mar. 1849. They were both 'exceedingly attached' to Caroline Norton.

Dear Semi-Hub,

I would have *delighted* in being Maurice's godmother. I thought of asking Lucie, but then I bethought me, 'Lo! 'tis a *male* child, and a hidalgo, and there will be some family grandee who will be invited to the dignity of being the fat darling's godmother,' so I desisted.

I am most glad that Lucie goes on well. How often I wish for you both, I cannot say; sometimes selfishly, for *me*, sometimes for your own sakes. Fletcher is too weak, Harry Howard too lazy and dispirited to see any of the sights of Lisbon, and Brownie (hear it, O Punch!) is *too fine* to like walking with me and my donkey, and says, 'ladies in a foreign capital' ought not to ride donkeys. Often I am reduced to converse with the faithful Childe, who, after a pause, thus renews the topics of the day: '*I beg your pardon, ma'am*, but is it true Her Majesty has been shot at?' '*I beg your pardon, ma'am*, but there is most astonishing shabby turn-outs among the noblemen's carriages in this country,'—an observation which chimes in with my own opinions, and which I therefore receive with the more cordiality.

I had a woman friend, very intelligent, but what with her constant rehearsals for private theatricals and performances of love (already some years rehearsed) with a velvet-eyed Spanish *attaché* here, I see little of her. The Pope's nuncio is a great friend, but he has bursts of absence (during which, I believe, he does penance for our interviews—to no purpose), reappearing gay, boyish, and sinful, like an otter coming up to breathe. The Portuguese society is stiff and disjointed—indeed, it ain't jointed at all; *only* stiff. Every one civil, smiling, and apparently anxious *if they knew how* to '*lier amitié*' with you, but never an inch nearer. A Portuguese gentleman told me, it was not unusual to see a lady in the winter and dance with her several nights, and never meet her again till the winter after. They hardly ever visit, or receive visits—never *men*, at least in very few Portuguese families. The women meet with apparent cordiality, kiss each other, and then sit down in a formal row, never stir afterwards the whole evening, and seldom speak even to those they have just embraced. Nobody reads or writes. They sing sometimes, and *always* look out of the window. I am sure it is good for the eyes to be ignorant, and to stare out of the window, for oh! the pretty eyes I see here among the women. The look of mingled laziness, curiosity and passion, which replaces the English intelligence and *good behaviour* of expression! I think the Infanta's daughter, Comtesse Quináres, has the most beautiful eyes that ever opened on the world, like pools among the dead brown autumn leaves on a warm summer night, with stars looking down into them.

Love to Lucie and the children.

Your affectionate
Carry

Fletcher] her eldest son (b. 1829).   Childe] her maid.

CHARLES KINGSLEY
(1819–1875)

Famous for his novels about social conditions (*Yeast*, 1848; *Alton Locke*, 1850) and for his polemics against Tractarianism and celibacy, Kingsley was a parson and a writer of varied talent and great energy.

180. To his wife, 24 October 1849

I was yesterday with W. and M. over the cholera districts of Bermondsey; and, oh, God! what I saw! people having no water to drink—hundreds of them—but the water of the common sewer which stagnated full of . . . dead fish, cats and dogs, under their windows. At the time the cholera was raging, Walsh saw them throwing untold horrors into the ditch, and then dipping out the water and drinking it!! . . . And mind, these are not dirty, debauched Irish, but honest hard working artizans. It is most pathetic, as W. says, it makes him literally cry—to see the poor souls' struggle for cleanliness, to see how they scrub and polish their little scrap of pavement, and then to go through the house and see 'society' leaving at the back poisons and filth—such as would drive a lady mad, I think, with disgust in twenty-four hours. Oh, that I had the tongue of St James, to plead for those poor fellows! to tell what I saw myself, to stir up some rich men to go and rescue them from the tyranny of the small shopkeeping landlords, who get their rents out of the flesh and blood of these men. Talk of the horrors of 'the middle passage.' Oh, that one-tenth part of the money which has been spent in increasing, by mistaken benevolence, the cruelties of the slave-trade, had been spent in buying up these nests of typhus, consumption, and cholera, and rebuilding them into habitations fit—I do not say for civilized Englishmen—that would be too much, but for hogs even! . . . Twenty pounds sent to us, just to start a water-cart, and send it round at once—at once—for the people are still in these horrors, would pay itself. I can find men who will work the thing—who will go and serve out the water with their own hands, rather than let it go on. Pray, pray, stir people up, and God will reward you. Kiss my darlings for me. . . .

P.S.—Do not let them wait for committee meetings and investigations. While they will be maundering about 'vested interests,' and such like, the people are dying. I start to-morrow for Oxford to see the Bishop about these Bermondsey horrors.

Oxford.— . . . I saw the Bishop (Wilberforce). Most satisfactory interview. I am more struck with him than with any man, except Bunsen, I have seen for a long time. . . . How I long for your dear face and voice. . . .

181. To Thomas Hughes, 1851

Thomas Hughes (1822–96) was the author of *Tom Brown's Schooldays* (1857) and advocate, with Kingsley, of 'muscular Christianity', including a passion for sports, as inculcated at Rugby.

. . . And if I had £100,000, I'd have, and should have, staked and lost it all in 1848–50. I should, Tom, for my heart was and is in it, and you'll see it will beat yet. Still, some somedever, it's in the fates, that Association is the pure caseine, and must be eaten by the human race if it would save its soul alive. . . . I have had a sorter kinder sample day. Up at five to see a dying man; ought to have been up at two, but Ben King, the rat-catcher, who came to call me, was taken nervous!!! and didn't make row enough; from 5.30 to 6.30 was with the most dreadful case of agony—insensible to me, but not to his pain. Came home, go a wash and a pipe, and again to him at eight. Found him insensible to his own pain, with dilated pupils, dying of pressure of the brain—going any moment. Prayed the commendatory prayers over him, and started for the river with W. Fished all the morning in a roaring N.E. gale, with the dreadful agonised face between me and the river, pondering on *The* mystery. Killed eight on 'March brown,' and 'governor,' by drowning the flies, and taking 'em out gently to see if aught was there, which is the only dodge in a north-easter. 'Cause why? The water is warmer than the air—*ergo*, fishes don't like to put their noses out o' doors, and feeds at home down stairs. It is the only wrinkle, Tom. The Captain fished a-top, and caught but three all day. They weren't going to catch a cold in their heads to please him or any man. Clouds burn up at 1 P.M. I put on a minnow, and kill three more; I should have had lots, but for the image of the dirty hickory stick, which would 'walk the waters like a thing of life,' just ahead of my minnow. Mem. never fish with the sun in your back; it's bad enough with a fly, but with a minnow its strychnine and prussic acid. My eleven weighed together four and a-half pounds, three to the pound; not good, considering I had passed many a two-pound fish, I know. Corollary.—Brass minnow don't suit the water. Where is your wonderful minnow? Send me one down, or else a horn one, which I believes in desperate. One pounder I caught to-day on the 'March brown,' womited his wittles, which was rude, but instructive; and among worms was a gudgeon three inches long and more. Blow minnows—gudgeon is the thing. Came off the water at three. Found my man alive, and, thank God, quiet. Sat with him, and thought him going once or twice. What a mystery that long, insensible death-struggle is! . . . Then had to go to Hartley Row for an Archdeacon's Sunday-school meeting—three hours speechifying. Got back at 10.30, and sit writing to you. So goes one's day. All manner of incongruous things to do, and the very incongruity keeps one beany and jolly. Your letter was delightful. I read part of it to W., who says you are the best fellow on earth, to which I agree. So no more from your sleepy and tired

C. Kingsley

JOHN CLARE
(1793–1864)

Clare was a labourer-poet whose works include *The Shepherd's Calendar* (1827); from 1841 he spent his life in Northampton General Asylum.

182. To Mary Collingwood, 1850

M Drst Mr Cllngwd

    M nrl wrn t & wnt t hr frm Nbd wll wn M r hv m t n prc & wht hv dn D knw wht r n m Dbt—kss's fr tn yrs & lngr stll & lngr thn tht whn ppl mk sch mstks s t cll m Gds bstrd & whrs p m b shttng m p frm Gds ppl t f th w f cmmn snse & thn tk m hd ff bcs th cnt fnd m t t hrds hrd

    Drst Mr r fthfll r d thnk f m knw wht w sd tgthr—dd vst m n hll sm tm bck bt dnt cm hr gn fr t s ntrs bd plc wrs nd wrs nd w r ll trnd Frnchmn flsh ppl tll m hv gt n hm n ths wrld nd s dnt believe n th thr nrt t mk mslf hvn wth m drst Mr nd sbscrb mslf rs fr vr & vr

Jhn Clr

For the code, see, if necessary, Eric Robinson and Geoffrey Summerfield, 'John Clare: An Interpretation of Certain Asylum Letters', *Review of English Studies*, NS 13 (1962), 135–46.

183. To James Hipkins, 8 March 1860

Hipkins had written to an asylum doctor asking about Clare; in his reply the doctor explained that the poet was in good bodily health but mentally enfeebled. 'I endeavoured to induce him to write a few lines to you . . . but I could get nothing from him but the few words I enclose.'

Dear Sir,
I am in a Madhouse & quite forget your Name or who you are you must excuse me for I have nothing to commu[n]icate or tell of & why I am shut up I dont know I have nothing to say so I conclude

yours respectfully
John Clare

HARRIET BEECHER STOWE
(1811–1896)

The novelist Harriet Beecher Stowe is most famous for her first book, *Uncle Tom's Cabin* (1852). Her later works include *My Wife and I* (1871), arguing that women had the right to a career.

184. To Mrs George Beecher, December 1850

Mrs Beecher was her sister-in-law. Mrs Stowe's husband Calvin Ellis Stowe was at this time a theological professor in Cincinnati; he soon moved to Bowdoin College in Brunswick, Maine.

My dear Sister,
Is it really true that snow is on the ground and Christmas coming, and I have not written unto thee, most dear sister? No, I don't believe it! I haven't been so naughty—it's all a mistake—yes, written I must have— and written I have, too—in the night-watches as I lay on my bed—such beautiful letters—I wish you had only received them; but by day it has been hurry, hurry, hurry, and drive, drive, drive! or else the calm of a sick-room, ever since last spring.

I put off writing when your letter first came, because I meant to write you a long letter,—a full and complete one; and so days slid by,—and became weeks,—and my little Charley came . . . etc. and etc.!!! Sarah, when I look back, I wonder at myself, not that I forget any one thing that I should remember, but that I have remembered anything. From the time that I left Cincinnati with my children to come forth to a country that I knew not of almost to the present time, it has seemed as if I could scarcely breathe, I was so pressed with care. My head dizzy with the whirl of railroads and steamboats; then ten days' sojourn in Boston, and a constant toil and hurry in buying my furniture and equipments; and then landing in Brunswick in the midst of a drizzly, inexorable north-east storm, and beginning the work of getting in order a deserted, dreary, damp old house. All day long running from one thing to another, as, for example, thus:—

'Mrs Stowe, how shall I make this lounge, and what shall I cover the back with first?'

Mrs Stowe. 'With the coarse cotton in the closet.'

Woman. 'Mrs Stowe, there isn't any more soap to clean the windows.'

Mrs Stowe. 'Where shall I get soap?'

'Here, H., run up to the store and get two bars.'

'There is a man below wants to see Mrs Stowe about the cistern. Before you go down, Mrs Stowe, just show me how to cover this round end of the lounge.'

'There's a man up from the depot, and he says that a box has come for Mrs Stowe, and it's coming up to the house; will you come down and see about it?'

'Mrs Stowe, don't go till you have shown the man how to nail that carpet in the corner. He's nailed it all crooked; what shall he do? The black thread is all used up, and what shall I do about putting gimp on the back of that sofa? Mrs Stowe, there is a man come with a lot of pails and tinware from Furbish; will you settle the bill now?'

'Mrs Stowe, here is a letter just come from Boston inclosing that bill of lading; the man wants to know what he shall do with the goods. If you will tell me what to say, I will answer the letter for you.'

'Mrs Stowe, the meat-man is at the door. Hadn't we better get a little beefsteak, or something, for dinner?'

'Shall Hatty go to Boardman's for some more black thread?'

'Mrs Stowe, this cushion is an inch too wide for the frame. What shall we do now?'

'Mrs Stowe, where are the screws of the black walnut bedstead?'

'Here's a man has brought in these bills for freight. Will you settle them now?'

'Mrs Stowe, I don't understand using this great needle. I can't make it go through the cushion; it sticks in the cotton.'

Then comes a letter from my husband, saying he is sick abed, and all but dead; don't ever expect to see his family again; wants to know how I shall manage, in case I am left a widow; knows we shall get in debt and never get out; wonders at my courage; thinks I am very sanguine; warns me to be prudent, as there won't be much to live on in case of his death, etc., etc., etc. I read the letter and poke it into the stove, and proceed. . . .

Some of my adventures were quite funny; as for example: I had in my kitchen-elect no sink, cistern, or any other water privileges, so I bought at the cotton factory two of the great hogsheads they bring oil in, which here in Brunswick are often used for cisterns, and had them brought up in triumph to my yard, and was congratulating myself on my energy, when lo and behold! it was discovered that there was no cellar door except one in the kitchen, which was truly a strait and narrow way, down a long pair of stairs. Hereupon, as saith John Bunyan, I fell into a muse,—how to get my cisterns into my cellar. In days of chivalry I might have got a knight to make me a breach through the foundation walls, but that was not to be thought of now, and my oil hogsheads, standing disconsolately in the yard, seemed to reflect no great credit on my foresight. In this strait I fell upon a real honest Yankee cooper, whom I besought, for the reputation of his craft and mine, to take my hogsheads to pieces, carry them down in staves, and set them up again, which the worthy man actually accomplished one fair summer forenoon, to the great astonishment of 'us Yankees.' When my man came to put up the pump, he stared very hard to see my hogsheads thus translated and standing as innocent and quiet as could be in the cellar, and then I told him, in a very mild, quiet way, that I got 'em taken to pieces and put together,—just as if I had been always in the habit of doing such things. Professor Smith came down and looked very hard at them and then said, 'Well, nothing can beat a willful woman.' Then followed divers negotiations with a very clever, but (with reverence) somewhat lazy gentleman of jobs, who occupieth a carpenter's shop opposite to mine. This same John Titcomb, my very good friend, is a character peculiar to Yankeedom. He is part owner and landlord of the house I rent, and connected by birth with all the best families in town; a man of real intelligence, and good education, a great reader, and quite a thinker. Being of an ingenious turn, he does painting, gilding, staining, upholstery jobs, varnishing; all in addition to his primary trade of carpentry. But he is a man studious of ease, and fully possessed with the idea that man wants but little here below; so he boards himself in his workshop on crackers and herring, washed down with cold water, and spends his time working, musing, reading new publications, and taking his comfort. In his shop you shall see a joiner's bench, hammers, planes, saws, gimlets, varnish, paint, picture frames, fence posts, rare old china, one or two fine portraits of his ancestry, a bookcase full of books, the tooth of a whale, an old spinning-wheel and spindle, a lady's parasol frame, a church lamp to be mended, in short, Henry says Mr Titcomb's shop is like the ocean; there is no end to the curiosities in it.

In all my moving and fussing Mr Titcomb has been my right-hand man. Whenever a screw was loose, a nail to be driven, a lock mended, a pane of glass set,—and these cases were manifold,—he was always on hand. But my sink was no fancy job, and I believe nothing but a very particular friendship would have moved him to undertake it. So this same sink lingered in a precarious state for some weeks, and when I had *nothing else to do*, I used to call and do what I could in the way of enlisting the good man's sympathies in its behalf.

How many times I have been in and seated myself in one of the old rocking-chairs, and talked first of the news of the day, the railroad, the last proceedings in Congress, the probabilities about the millennium, and thus brought the conversation by little and little round to my sink! . . . because, till the sink was done, the pump could not be put up, and we couldn't have any rain-water. Sometimes my courage would quite fail me to introduce the subject, and I would talk of everything else, turn and get out of the shop, and then turn back as if a thought had just struck my mind, and say:—

'Oh, Mr Titcomb! about that sink?'

'Yes, ma'am, I was thinking about going down street this afternoon to look out stuff for it.'

'Yes, sir, if you would be good enough to get it done as soon as possible; we are in great need of it.'

'I think there's no hurry. I believe we are going to have a dry time now, so that you could not catch any water, and you won't need a pump at present.'

These negotiations extended from the first of June to the first of July, and at last my sink was completed, and so also was a new house spout, concerning which I had had divers communings with Deacon Dunning of the Baptist church. Also during this time good Mrs Mitchell and myself made two sofas, or lounges, a barrel chair, divers bedspreads, pillow cases, pillows, bolsters, mattresses; we painted rooms; we revarnished furniture; we—what *didn't* we do?

Then came on Mr Stowe; and then came the eighth of July and my little Charley. I was really glad for an excuse to lie in bed, for I was full tired, I can assure you. Well, I was what folks call very comfortable for two weeks when my nurse had to leave me. . . .

During this time I have employed my leisure hours in making up my engagements with newspaper editors. I have written more than anybody, or

I myself, would have thought. I have taught an hour a day in our school, and I have read two hours every evening to the children. The children study English history in school, and I am reading Scott's historic novels in their order. To-night I finish the 'Abbot;' shall begin 'Kenilworth' next week; yet I am constantly pursued and haunted by the idea that I don't do anything. Since I began this note I have been called off at least a dozen times; once for the fish-man, to buy a codfish; once to see a man who had brought me some barrels of apples; once to see a book-man; then to Mrs Upham, to see about a drawing I promised to make for her; then to nurse the baby; then into the kitchen to make a chowder for dinner; and now I am at it again, for nothing but deadly determination enables me ever to write; it is rowing against wind and tide.

I suppose you think now I have begun, I am never going to stop, and, in truth, it looks like it; but the spirit moves now and I must obey.

Christmas is coming, and our little household is all alive with preparations; every one collecting their little gifts with wonderful mystery and secrecy. . . .

To tell the truth, dear, I am getting tired; my neck and back ache, and I must come to a close.

Your ready kindness to me in the spring I felt very much; and *why* I did not have the sense to have sent you one line just by way of acknowledgment, I'm sure I don't know; I felt just as if I had, till I awoke, and behold! I had not. But, my dear, if my wits are somewhat wool-gathering and unsettled, my heart is as true as a star. I love you, and have thought of you often.

This fall I have felt often *sad*, lonesome, both very unusual feelings with me in these busy days; but the breaking away from my old home, and leaving father and mother, and coming to a strange place affected me naturally. In those sad hours my thoughts have often turned to George; I have thought with encouragement of his blessed state, and hoped that I should soon be there, too. I have many warm and kind friends here, and have been treated with great attention and kindness. Brunswick is a delightful residence, and if you come East next summer, you must come to my new home. George would delight to go a-fishing with the children, and see the ships, and sail in the sailboats, and all that.

Give Aunt Harriet's love to him, and tell him when he gets to be a painter to send me a picture.

Affectionately yours,
H. Stowe

Mrs Upham] the wife of a Bowdoin professor.   George] her dead brother; the second
George, his son.

JOHN RUSKIN
(1819–1900)

In 1851–2 Ruskin was in Venice, working on *The Stones of Venice* and married to Euphemia Gray. In 1854 she divorced him on the ground of impotence. In 1858 he met and became obsessed with an 11-year-old Irish girl, Rose La Touche. In 1866 his proposal of marriage was frustrated. Rose died insane in 1875. From 1878 he himself was intermittently demented. The first two of these letters were written during the Venetian years, the second two are from a later period when he tended to write more excitedly and obscurely.

185. To John James Ruskin, 3 October 1851

My dearest Father,

I never have had time to tell you anything about the emperor's visit to us; in fact I was rather upset by it; for I am getting into such quiet ways that sitting up till two that night made me feel very sleepy the next day— and then we had Roberts to dinner—which tired me the evening after— so that I did not get quite right again till yesterday. For the Emperor announced himself for 10 o'clock at night—only about 10 o'clock on the previous morning—and there was little enough time to get ready for him— Everybody on the Grand canal was requested by the municipality to illuminate their houses *inside*: and the Rialto was done at the public expense. They spent altogether—in Bengal lights and other lamps about 300 pounds— a large sum for Venice in these days—but I never saw the Rialto look so lovely: There were no devices or letters or nonsense on it—only the lines of its *architecture* traced in chains of fire—and two lines of bright ruby lamps set along its arch underneath—so as to light the vault of it; all streaming down in bright reflection on the canal—We went out a little before 10—and rowed down under it to the part of the grand canal nearest the railroad station—there are two churches there, one the Scalzi, the other a small Palladian one—I forget its name opposite each other, and a great breadth of canal between them: which was literally as full of boats as it could hold—They were jammed against each other as tight as they could be—leaving just room for each boatman to get his oar down into the water at the side—and so we waited for some half-hour. It was a strange sight in the darkness, the crowd fixed, yet with a kind of undulation in it which it could not have had upon land, every gondolier at his stern, balanced, ready for the slightest movement of the boats at his side—lest they should oust him out of his place—and the figures standing up on the lower level, in the open part of the boats—from one side of the canal to the other—one could not see on what they stood—only here and there the flashing of the tide beneath, as it flowed fiercely in the torchlight—and beside and among the figures the innumerable beaks of the Gondolas, reared up with their strange curving crests like a whole field full of dragons—the black glittering bodies just traceable close beside one—one would have thought Cadmus had been sowing the wrong teeth—and grown dragons instead of men: There was a boat close beside us with some singers—beggarly fellows enough— but with brown faces and good voices—and another with a band in it farther on—and presently after there was some report of the emperor's coming, and they began burning Bengal lights among the boats, which showed all the fronts of the palaces far down the canal against the night— And presently the emperor *did* come—in his grey coat and travelling cap— and they pushed him down the steps into his boat—and then the whole mass of floating figures and dragons' heads began to glide after him—He had expressly invited everybody who had a gondola to come and meet him, and there were no measures taken to keep them off so it was who should get the closest to him. And one could not see the water—but the dashing of the oars was like the rushing of a great waterfall—and there—standing on the black gliding field, were all the gondoliers writhing and struggling, one could not see what for—but all in violent and various effort—pushing their utmost to keep their boats in their places and hold others back—and a great roar of angry voices besides—We had held on for ten minutes or so to the singers who had been ordered to precede the emperor up the canal— but we got pushed away from them, and fell back a few yards into the thick of the press—and presently came crash up against the bow of the emper- or's own boat—and so stuck fast. There was no moving for a minute or two—Effie and I were standing—I of course with my hat off and I made signs to my boatman to keep off the emperor if he could—There was no stirring however for half a minute—when we managed to push back the gondola on the other side of us—and slip clear of the emperor—who passed ahead—giving us a touch of his cap. We fell astern of him—but the next moment were pushed forward on the other side—until our first boat- man was exactly abreast of him—This time it was not a gondola on our other side, but a barge full of very ill looking fellows, who I thought might just as well have me between them and the emperor as not—so I let Beppo keep his place, which for the rest he was anxious enough to do—and so rowing and fighting with all his might—and ably seconded by the stern boatsman, he kept guard on the emperor's flank for a quarter of an hour: the worst of it was that we were continually forced up against his boat— and so shook him and splashed him not a little—until at last another gondola forced its beak in between us, and I was glad enough to give way— It took us something like an hour to get along the whole course of the

canal—so impossible was it for the gondolas to move in the choked breadth
of it—and as the emperor did not arrive till eleven, and after we got to St
Mark's place there was music and showing himself at windows, &c. it was
near one before we could get away towards home—and we left him still at
his window. I lay in bed till eight—but the emperor reviewed the troops at
seven in the morning. He went away for Trieste at 4 afternoon.

I hope you will be able to make out this very ill written letter but I am
getting sleepy and my hand is cramped with rowing.

Dearest love to my mother.

Ever my dearest Father. | Your most aff^e Son,

J Ruskin

The emperor's visit] Franz Joseph, Emperor of Austria from 1848 to 1916.   Bengal lights]
these produced a steady blue light.   Beppo] the Ruskins' gondolier.

186. To John James Ruskin, 20 February 1852

My dearest Father,

I am getting quite into the world again—I took Effie to the opera last
night as they said there would be a good many masques there. There were
none however—or only three in a side box—but St Mark's place was
worth seeing both before and after we went; it was lighted up with large
temporary circlets of gas, and full of masques—some showing a good deal
of spirit, and all making a very sufficient quantity of noise, which however
mixed itself altogether into a great murmur, not harsh nor discordant—but
soothing—lost amidst the great walls and wide sea air.

The opera was intensely disagreeable—bad singing—bad dancing and
plot at once tragic and absurd. It is difficult to express the degree of
degradation into which the operatic amusement is sinking the European
mind—First you have every possible means of excitement—music—passion—acting of the coarsest and most violent kind—glaring scenery—
everything that can excite in the highest degree—then, the people, who are
rich and idle—take this excitement every night—till it ceases to be an
excitement any [more?]. But they still go, because it is fashionable—and—
not caring to look or to listen—open their boxes as drawingrooms—and
receive their company in the theatre instead of at home. No conversation
except of the lightest kind is possible in such a place of course—but every
body talks—and nobody listens—Thus the tone of all conversation is rendered habitually frivolous—the *ear* loses its refinement from talking in the
midst of an orchestra—the actors—unable to draw attention by just or
quiet play—seek for it by rant—and only obtain it—momentarily—by
shrieking or performing miracles of pirouettes—so the entire school of
dramatic writing, music—and dancing, is degraded lower and lower—

and—one evil reacting on another, the final result of the general corruption is still unseen—and to come.

Dearest love to my mother.

Ever my dearest Father | Your most aff^e. Son

J Ruskin

187. To Lady Mount-Temple, 4 June 1869

Evelyn Ashley, Baron Mount-Temple (1836–1907), fourth son of the 7th Earl of Shaftesbury, was a politician and the biographer of Palmerston. He married Sybella Farquhar in 1866. She died in 1886. Ruskin had confided to Lady Mount-Temple his sufferings over Rose.

My dear φίλη,

This morning, as I was drawing, in the Piazza dei Signori, just in front of that building of which φίλη gave me the photograph, there came up the poet Longfellow and his daughter, a girl of 13 or 14, with a firm and nice fair face—and curly waves of flaxen hair over the forehead breaking over into little crests and spray in pure spirit of life—very pleasant to look upon in the midst of this pale—weary—and wicked people who fill the streets with their wretchedness.

They stood talking some little time by me, and I was vain enough to think that if the square of Verona could have been photographed then, with that exquisite building in the morning light, and Longfellow and his daughter standing talking to me at my easel—a great many people would have liked the photograph—on both sides of the Atlantic. I went to several of the places I like best with them—yesterday, and the lessons I got on the walk were several—also.

First. I found I was so very angry and hot—in my mind underneath—in perpetual Hades of indignation—where the worm dieth not & the fire—that I was not fit to talk to or be with, anybody else. They—Longfellow and his brother, and daughter, and an old friend travelling with them—were very nice and interested in things. But the coldness and content that all should be—(bad or good) as it is, was like a frightful glacier gulph to me, which moved beside me, and I was always falling into it with a shiver. It was no use trying to tell them what I thought about things—I should only have seemed mad to them.

Lesson the second. In these best possible examples of Americans I still felt the want of the ease—courtesy—delightfulness—of our best old English or French families—not that in Longfellow the substance of any courtesy is wanting—he is very nearly perfect—but still—that I should feel the Americanism even in these, shows the intenseness and extent of the Rude Evil of that life of Liberty.

Lesson Third.

I had ordered the carriage to meet us at such a place. The coachman and valet-de-place—instead of doing as I bid them—obsequiously haunted and spied us from street to street—giving me constant—unexpected & most troublesome runnings into the middle of horses and wheels—just when I wanted the quietest bits of my street effects. Nothing short of a fit of rabbiatura would have compelled them to do as they were bid.

Now one of the things which I want you to think of and to tell people as part of my main plan—(and a great part of it)—is the practice of an accurate and unquestioning obedience—as a most important part of Education. The great error in teaching Obedience has been the leaning on the *Submission* of it—instead of the *Accuracy* of it—as its chief virtue. It is not necessary always—or often—that it should be given in Humility. But it *is* necessary that it should be given in Perfectness.

To day—I may obey you—and tomorrow you may obey me, which of us is under the other's orders, may be a matter of chance—convenience—or momentary agreement. But whichever *is* under the other's orders must *do* them, and not think about them. Half the power of the world is lost, because people are not trained to accuracy of obedience enough to be able to act with certainty. It does not matter half so much who is captain—as that the captain—for the time—should be sure of everything's being done as he expected. And I want this to be made a daily element of discipline among children—giving first one—then another, the conduct of the play— enterprise—or study of the day; and requiring the others to give the most close—finished—absolutely unquestioning fidelity of obedience to his orders.

Of course, in other respects, the advantages to character will be great,— but the *distinctive* teaching among us will be, that one man must obey another, not that the other may crush him, but that he may *count upon* him.

I've so much to say—I must send this bit—and another tomorrow.

Ever your grateful

S^t C

φίλη] friend (f. and m.).   Longfellow] H. W. Longfellow (1807–82), the American poet.

188. To Lady Mount-Temple, 4 October 1872

Rose's mental condition began to deteriorate in 1872.

My dearest Isola,

The good that you may be sure you have done me remember, is in my having known, actually, for one whole day, the *perfect* joy of love. For I think, to be *quite* perfect, it must still have *some* doubt and pain—the pride of war and patience added to the intense actual pleasure. I don't think any *quite* accepted & beloved lover could have the Kingly and Servantly joy together, as I had it in that ferry boat of yours, when she went into it herself, and stood at the stern, and let me stop it in mid-stream and look her full in the face for a long minute, before she said 'Now go on'—The beautiful place—the entire peace—nothing but birds & squirrels near—the trust, which I had then in all things being—finally well—yet the noble fear mixed with the enchantment—her remaining still above me, not mine, and yet mine.

And this after ten years of various pain—and thirst. And this with such a creature to love—For you know, Isola, people may think her pretty or not pretty—as their taste may be, but she is a *rare* creature, and that kind of beauty happening to be *exactly* the kind I like,—and my whole life being a worship of beauty,—fancy how it intensifies the whole.

Of course, every lover, good for anything, thinks his mistress perfection—but what a difference between this instinctive, foolish—groundless preference, and my deliberate admiration of R, as I admire a thin figure in a Perugino fresco, saying 'it is the lovliest figure I know after my thirty years study of art'—Well—suppose the Perugino—better than Pygmalions statue,—holier—longer sought, *had* left the canvas—come into the garden—walked down to the riverside with me—looked happy—been happy, (—for she *was*—and said she was)—in being with me.

Was'nt it a day, to have got for me?—all your getting.

And clear gain—I am no worse now than I was,—a day or two more of torment and disappointment are as nothing in the continued darkness of my life. But that day is worth being born and living seventy years of pain for.

And I can still read my Chaucer, and write before-breakfast letters—Mad, or dead, she is still mine, now.

Ever your loving

S^t C

ARTHUR HUGH CLOUGH (1819–1861) AND JAMES RUSSELL LOWELL
(1819–1891)

Clough, a close friend of Matthew Arnold, wrote two long poems in hexameters, *The Bothie of Tober-na-Vuolich* (1848) and *Amours de voyage* (1858). Lowell, an American poet and satirist, later a distinguished professor and diplomat, wrote his invitation in hexameters, and Clough replied in kind, adding rhyme in his postscript.

189. Lowell to Clough, 23 December 1852

Dear Clough

   Hard-studying Pierce [*sic*], by this time I think you have entered
Deep enough in Geometry's lore to test it a little by practice; Suppose
You should happen to try the neat little problem that follows?
At ½ past one, on that day known to us mortals as Xmas,
(Not such a nightmare-compeller, nor fatal to beeves and to turkeys
Here 'mid us Yankees lean as with you in dear old England,)
I say at half past one, descend till you reach the sidewalk,
Then, turning short to the left and putting one foot before the other,
Ever, which foot is behind, bringing *that* in front of the other,
(A description, I think, as clear as one very like it in Dante)
You will find in the course of time (not half so tedious as Pollok's)
That you have measured the earth (or Geometrized it) to Elmwood.
There you will find, perhaps, no very great shakes of a dinner,
But very great shakes of the hand implying perennial welcome.
No *very* great shakes of a dinner, because one half of our servants,
(By which poetical term I mean a lady from Erin,)
Have leave of absence that day and go to see their relations,
Half our servants, I say, and every one of them cooks, too.
Crowe has promised to come, who, I found, would be at the Tremont,
Alone in the widowed nest, for Thackeray goes to Manhatten.—
Allow me to quote the plusquam Solomonian wisdom of Tupper:
'He who dines with a friend is better far and greater
Than he who gets his grub with a mercenary physician,'
(No disrespect is meant to be offered to Dr Johnson)
'Especially when the day on which he eats is Xmas.'
So come if you can, unless some one offers you better.
You will be, at least, in a Home and have a hearty welcome
From folks who will ever hold dear his name who wrote the Bothie
And so I remain ever yours,

the hoping-to-see-you
Lowell

Pierce] Peirce Thackeray was lecturing in the USA 1851–3.   Tupper] Martin Tupper
(1810–89) was the author of the best-selling *Proverbial Philosophy* (4 series, 1838–76).

190. Clough to Lowell, 24 December 1852

Brother Hexametrist:

   Is it not given, or am I confusing, as an axiom in Peirce
Or postulate in Euclid, that a monad in space cannot eat
Two several dinners at the same hour of the day and in two different
   houses;

He therefore, who is engaged to partake of turkey and pie
with Mr and Mrs Longfellow at Mr Appleton's table
Cannot, he grieves to infer, hope also to take them at Elmwood.
   Such is this life! In a better world where we keep Merry Xmas
We shall be able perhaps to eat simultaneous turkey
With each one of our friends in each of the many mansions;
Here,—good wishes, alas, and the compliments of the season,
Pending a happier time, are all that can on this occasion
Wait upon you and yours from
                                                                 Yours sincerely
Mrs Howe's, Friday morning
   ¼ after 11   A. H. Clough
[P.S.] Pray remember me kindly to Crowe, who I hope's in good
   feather;
At the lecture this evening we may perhaps all meet together.
Thackeray was to have been at a party to which I was taken
Last night at 10 o'clock in the house of Mrs Bacon,
But was gone to attend—on *Providence*, as I heard it.
Is he to lecture tonight? I did hear he had deferred it.
I haven't seen him—have you? I wish I had, but it's endless
Calling at an hotel upon people not wholly friendless—
There are a hundred places of course where his company's needed.
Were you at the first lecture,—I hear everywhere it succeeded—
Farewell. I've given you almost as long a lecture as he did.

Longfellow] H. W. Longfellow (1807–82), poet, was a leader of Boston intellectual society.

ROBERT E. LEE
(1807–1870)

Lee, the great Confederate general, was Superintendent of West Point, 1852–5.

191. To Anne Lee, 25 February 1853

My Precious Annie,

   I take advantage of your gracious permission to write to you, and there
is no telling how far my feelings might carry me were I not limited by the
conveyance furnished by the Mim's letter, which lies before me, and which
must, the Mim says so, go in this morning's mail. But my limited time does
not diminish my affection for you, Annie, nor prevent my thinking of you
and wishing for you. I long to see you through the dilatory nights. At dawn
when I rise, and all day, my thoughts revert to you in expressions that you

cannot hear or I repeat. I hope you will always appear to me as you are now painted on my heart, and that you will endeavour to improve and so conduct yourself as to make you happy and me joyful all our lives. Diligent and earnest attention to *all* your duties can only accomplish this. I am told you are growing very tall, and I hope very straight. I do not know what the Cadets will say if the Superintendent's *children* do not practice what he demands of them. They will naturally say he had better attend to his own before he corrects other people's children, and as he permits his to stoop it is hard he will not allow them. You and Agnes must not, therefore, bring me into discredit with my young friends, or give them reason to think that I require more of them than of my own. I presume your mother has told all about us, our neighbours and our affairs. And indeed she may have done that and not said much either, so far as I know. But we are all well and have much to be grateful for. To-morrow we anticipate the pleasure of your brother's company, which is always a source of pleasure to us. It is the only time we see him, except when the Corps come under my view at some of their exercises, when my eye is sure to distinguish him among his comrades and follow him over the plain. Give much love to your dear grandmother, grandfather, Agnes, Miss Sue, Lucretia, and all friends, including the servants. Write sometimes, and think always of your

Affectionate father,

R. E. Lee.

The Mim] his wife.   Agnes] another daughter.

ZADUCK BAMFORD

In 1854 Bamford went to the goldfields of Victoria and New South Wales to seek his fortune in the building trade, leaving his wife and children behind in Derbyshire. His first surviving letter is very optimistic—he promises to bring back 'ten hundred pounds to make us happy the remainder of our days, and bring up my ever dear little children in plenty and respectability . . . this is the place to make money the best place in the world . . . I come here a beggar but I shall return a Gentleman'. His second letter, printed here, is only slightly more tempered in its optimism; but his letters of 1855 and 1856 tell of increasing hardships. On the eve of returning to England he falls ill and has to forfeit the passage money; meanwhile he discovers that he has been robbed of the money he believed he was sending home to his wife. Later he becomes so ill that he cannot write home. During one such long silence his wife Frances writes that she was broken-hearted not to have heard, and fears that he will forsake her and the children, but promises that 'if you will but come I have got Pickle Onunes and cabage and Preserve and every think I can think of I think you would like'. Zaduck again announces his imminent return, but nine months later has to explain that he has not been able to write because he has lost the middle finger of his right hand to a bite from a centipede. However, he has established a business, which he plans to sell, and by Aug. 1856 he is hoping to return to England the following summer. Nothing more is known of the fate of Bamford and his family.

192. To Frances Bamford, 8 October 1854

Forest Creek Gold Fields
My ever dear wife and beloved children it is with the greatest delight I sit me down to write these few lines hoping by the blessing of God they will find you all well as it leaves me at present thank God for it   I have been on these gold fields but a few days yet and can scarsely speak of their richness but I hope to be able to save a few hundreds in three months And with what I have allready I hope to be able to see old England and them I love so dear   I hope my ever dear dear and loving wife you have received the money   I sent you 11£ on the 8th of August and 50£ on the 29th Sepr but a few days ago and as I stated in my last letter I shall bring the next myself   O that will be a joyful meeting for us all   and you see that I have not forgot you   no all my thoughts are upon you and my little pretty children   pray God bless you all is my ever fervent prayer of your dear husband   I do work my dear wife very hard and am very saving   it is for you and my dear little children to enjoy it with me when I come home   you may be sure they is no enjoyment on these gold fields nothing but drunkenness and debauchery not fit for human witnesses   diggers think nothink of spending 4 or 5 hundred pounds at a time and then set to work again for more   and what I used to read to you at home on an evening is but triveling to what I witness   I shall finish my work I am at on thursday next one weeks work   I took peicework and shall receive 15£ for it what think you of that   and then I am off gold digging   you would stare to see me with my jumper on and a six barrel revolver pistol in my belt by my side   you would think I am some highwayman but every body is likewise armed   I do so wish my brothers were out here and yours too   they would never repent crossing the seas   tell Matthew this is the place for money   getting a pound here is not so much as a shilling at home   in fact every body can get plenty of money if they only take the trouble to work   there are no poor here nor poor houses and rubishing vituals would not go down here   you could not get tripe out here nor sheep heads as neither cows nor sheeps heads are used they are all thrown away in this country   I hope my dear wife to be able to see you about our next birth days 21st and 23 of June   then that will be a happy day   I do so often run over my little childrens names and birthdays   it is allways a crying bout for me when any of them comes   as I do think of them so I would at this moment freely give one hundred pounds to know how you all are   O what a pleasure it would be for me   I know my dear wife you often think of me

and I sincerely think you will keep yourself as a virtuous woman ought to do if not you know what my determination would be for sooner than any disgrace should come on you I love so dear I would end both our days but in you I place my trust of happier days to come   I cannot at present give you my directions as I shall be shifting about so every few days   give my love to all my brothers and sisters and to my mother and Mr Waters and tell my dear little Frederic Albert Agnes and Alice how much father do think of them and I hope they are getting on well with their schooling as I shall want Mr Frederic to be my clark in a buisness when I return home   I think of establishing a timber yard in Derby when I return if it would be agreeable for you my dear wife   if not your will shall be mine as we can do without it with what money I shall have when I return   I shall somewhat astonish the people at home when I return with my purse and you will see I was not blind in coming out here   adieu for a short time only my ever ever loving and affectionate wife and children

I am your affectionate and loving husband & father

Z. Bamford

GEORGE ELIOT
(1819–1880)

Marian Evans (who later adopted the name George Eliot) renounced her early evangelical faith under the influence of her Coventry friends Charles Bray (1811–84), his wife Caroline (Cara), and his brother-in-law Charles Hennell (1809–50), a pioneer of the new biblical criticism in England. Hennell married Rufa, the daughter of R. H. Brabant, a doctor from Devizes who was in touch with the German biblical critics. Sarah Hennell, another learned lady, was Hennell's and Cara's sister. When George Eliot decided to live with George Henry Lewes (1817–78), who could not obtain a divorce, she wrote to tell Charles Bray and John Chapman, editor of the *Westminster Review*, but did not inform Cara and Sara, who were both shocked and angry not only about her decision but because she had trusted these men and not her women friends. Eliot wrote these letters in response to angry recriminations from them.

193. To Sara Hennell, 31 October 1854

My dear Sara,

The mode in which you and Cara have interpreted both my words and my silence makes me dread lest in writing more I should only give rise to fresh misconceptions. I am so deeply conscious of having had neither the feeling nor the want of feeling which you impute to me that I am quite unable to read into my words, quoted by you, the sense which you put upon them. When you say that I do not care about Cara's or your opinion and friendship it seems much the same to me as if you said that I didn't care to eat when I was hungry or to drink when I was thirsty. One of two things: either I am a creature without affection, on whom the memories of years have no hold, or, you, Cara and Mr Bray are the most cherished friends I have in the world. It is simply self-contradictory to say that a person can be indifferent about her dearest friends; yet this is what you substantially say, when you accuse me of 'boasting with what serenity I can give you up,' of 'speaking proudly' etc. The only reply I can give to such an accusation is an absolute denial that I have been actuated by such a spirit as you describe with regard to any one thing which I have written, done, or left undone.

You say: 'You' shew that 'you wish to have communication with Charles only.' The reason why I wrote to Mr Bray and not to you and Cara is simply this. Before I left England, I communicated, by Mr Lewes's desire, certain facts in strict confidence to Mr Bray and Mr Chapman and I did so for special reasons which would not apply to any female friend. After your kind letters came to me, we heard much painful news from London as to reports which were partly a perversion of the truth, partly pure falsehood. I cannot, even now, see that I did anything deserving so severe a reproach as you send me, in writing to Mr Bray who was already in possession of the main facts, and in intimating that my silence to you arose from no want of affection, but from what I, falsely perhaps, but still sincerely, regarded as the very reverse of *pride* and a spirit of *boasting*.

There is now no longer any secrecy to be preserved about Mr Lewes's affairs or mine, and whatever I have written to Mr Bray, I have written to you. I am under no foolish hallucinations about either the present or the future and am standing on no stilts of any kind. I wish to speak simply and to act simply but I think it can hardly be unintelligible to you that I shrink from writing elaborately about private feelings and circumstances. I have really felt it a privation that I have been unable to write to you about things not personal, in which I know you would feel a common interest, and it will brighten my thoughts very much to know that I may do so. Cara, you and my own sister are the three women who are tied to my heart by a cord which can never be broken and which really *pulls* me continually. My love for you rests on a past which no future can reverse, and offensive as the words seem to have been to you, I must repeat, that I can feel no bitterness towards you, however you may act towards me. If you remain to me what you have ever been, my life will be all the happier, and I will try not to be unworthy of your love so far as faithfulness to my own conscience can make me worthy of it.

I have written miserably ill, and I fear all the while I am writing that I may be giving rise to some mistake. But interpret my whole letter so as to make it accord with this plain statement—I love Cara and you with unchanged and unchangeable affection, and while I retain your friendship I retain the best that life has given me next to that which is the deepest and gravest joy in all human experience.

Marian Evans

194. To Mrs Charles Bray, 4 September 1855

Dear Cara,

No one has better reason than myself to know how difficult it is to produce a true impression by letters, and how likely they are to be misinterpreted even where years of friendship might seem to furnish a sufficient key. And it seems the more probable to me that I misinterpreted your letter to me at Berlin since I find that my answer to it produced totally false conclusions in your mind. Assuredly if there be any one subject on which I feel no levity it is that of marriage and the relation of the sexes—if there is any one action or relation of my life which is and always has been profoundly serious, it is my relation to Mr Lewes. If any expression or parallel in my letter bore an opposite construction it must have been, because you interpreted as of general application what I intended simply in answer to what I considered Mr Combe's petty and absurd views about the effect on his reputation of having introduced me to one or two of his friends. *Nothing* that I said in that letter was intended as a discussion of the principles of my conduct or as an answer to your opinions on the subject.

It is, however, natural enough that you should mistake me in many ways, for not only are you unacquainted with Mr Lewes's real character and the course of his actions, but also, it is several years now since you and I were much together, and it is possible that the modifications my mind has undergone may be in quite the opposite direction to what you imagine. No one can be better aware than yourself that it is possible for two people to hold different opinions on momentous subjects with equal sincerity and an equally earnest conviction that their respective opinions are alone the truly moral ones. If we differ on the subject of the marriage laws, I at least can believe of you that you cleave to what you believe to be good, and I don't know of anything in the nature of your views that should prevent you from believing the same of me. *How far* we differ I think we neither of us know; for I am ignorant of your precise views and apparently you attribute to me both feelings and opinions which are not mine. We cannot set each other quite right on this matter in letters, but one thing I can tell you in few words. Light and easily broken ties are what I neither desire theoretically nor could live for practically. Women who are satisfied with such ties do *not* act as I have done—they obtain what they desire and are still invited to dinner.

That any unworldly, unsuperstitious person who is sufficiently acquainted with the realities of life can pronounce my relation to Mr Lewes immoral I can only understand by remembering how subtle and complex are the influences that mould opinion. But I *do* remember this, and I indulge in no arrogant or uncharitable thoughts about those who condemn us, even though we might have expected a somewhat different verdict. From the majority of persons, of course, we never looked for anything but condemnation. We are leading no life of self-indulgence, except indeed, that being happy in each other, we find everything easy. We are working hard to provide for others better than we provide for ourselves, and to fulfil every responsibility that lies upon us. Levity and pride would not be a sufficient basis for that.

Pardon me, dear Cara, if in vindicating myself from some unjust conclusions, I seem too cold and self-asserting. I should not care to vindicate myself, if I did not love you and desire to relieve you of the pain which you say these conclusions have given you. Whatever I may have misinterpreted before, I do not misinterpret your letter this morning, but read in it nothing else than love and kindness towards me to which my heart fully answers yes. I should like never to write about myself again—it is not healthy to dwell on one's own feelings and conduct, but only to try and live more faithfully and lovingly every fresh day.

I think not one of the endless words and deeds of kindness and forbearance you have ever shewn me has vanished from my memory. I recall them often, and feel, as about everything else in the past, how deficient I have been in almost every relation of my life. But that deficiency is irrevocable and I can find no strength or comfort except in 'pressing forward towards the things that are before,' and trying to make the present better than the past. But if we should never be very near each other again, dear Cara, do bear this faith in your mind, that I was not insensible or ungrateful to all your goodness, and that I am one amongst the many for whom you have not lived in vain.

Those dreadful sheets and pillow cases! Pray give them away if you won't use them, for I don't want them, and can never set up housekeeping on that small stock.

I am very busy just now, and have been obliged to write hastily. Bear this in mind, and believe that no meaning is mine which contradicts my assurance that I am your affectionate and earnest friend

Marian

My love to Sara. I can't write more today but will write to her another day.

Mr Combe] a celebrated phrenologist whom Eliot met through the Brays.

195. To John Chapman, 1 February 1856

Chapman (1821–94) published R. W. Mackay's *Progress of the Intellect* (1851) and arranged for Eliot to review. This famous review strengthened her attachment to Chapman, which became amorous, though Chapman already had a wife and a mistress. When he took on the *Westminster Review* she contributed and did most of the editorial work. Later this year the Review published her article 'Silly Novels by Lady Novelists'.

Dear Friend,

I am going to speak strongly about the article you have sent me, because I feel strong speaking on the subject a duty of friendship towards you, and not because I have any wish to depreciate Miss H. of whom I know nothing except from distant report. Before I had read the article I supposed her to be a woman of talent; I *now* think her one of the numerous class of female scribblers who undertake to edify the public before they know the proper use of their own language. The *whole* of the introduction, and every passage where Miss H. launches into more than a connecting sentence or two, is feminine rant of the worst kind, which it will be simply *fatal* to the Review to admit.

You have opened the subject of Woman's position by a sober, manly article, containing real information. What can be more suicidal than to follow this up by bombastic stuff, every other sentence of which is utterly without meaning to people who know the value of language? I would not trust the most ordinary subject, still less the more delicate, to a woman who writes such trash as this—'In the attitude thus assumed we find Mrs D. consciously or unconsciously saying the law of her mind'—'She does not point a moral to every work as it leaves the press'—'Art—not the sectarian art of the painter, poet & musician, but the broad, generous art, comprehending and containing all arts, which takes humanity for its meaning [?], God for its master, and life for its expression'!!! etc., etc.

Everything she says about George Sand is undiscriminating Bosh. No omissions can do more than reduce the quantity of the Bosh. The extracts from the 'History of My Life' might make an interesting article, with many more added and some left out, but, as I said before, I would not trust that lady to do anything in the form of literature. To reject the article on Maurice & accept this, wd indeed be straining at a gnat & swallowing a camel. Better admit ten such articles as that on Maurice, than one such as this. In fact, to accept articles of this calibre would be the damnation of the Review. Pray admit nothing that touches on the Position of Women, that is not sober, well thought out, & expressed in good English.

A dull & ill-written article on the Navigation Laws may pass muster, & not positively contribute to ruin the Review, but a foolish & ill-written article about George Sand would be an invitation to all circles, except that of Miss H., to think meanly of the Westminster.

Of course you will not mention even to the most intimate friend, that I have seen the article. I assure you I have no pleasure in writing uncomplimentary things about another woman's productions. But the fortunes of the Westminster are much more important than the fortunes of Miss H's writings, & indeed the less encouragement she has to offer such trash as this to the editors the better for herself and all concerned.

Ever yours truly
Marian Evans

for its meaning [?]] the question is Eliot's interpolation.

196. To Mrs Harriet Beecher Stowe, 29 October 1876

Mrs Stowe (see above, Letter 184), author of *Uncle Tom's Cabin* (1852), wrote admiringly of *Silas Marner* in 1869. The writers began a correspondence that ended only with Eliot's death, but they never met.

Dear Friend,

'Evermore thanks' for your last letter, full of a generous sympathy that can afford to be frank. The lovely photograph of the grandson will be carefully preserved. It has the sort of beauty which seems to be peculiarly abundant in America—at once rounded and delicate in form.

I do hope you will be able to carry out your wish to visit your son at Bonn, notwithstanding that heavy crown of years that your dear Rabbi has to carry. If the sea-voyage could be borne without much disturbance, the land-journey might be made easy by taking it in short stages—the plan we always pursue in travelling. You see, I have an interested motive in wishing you to come to Europe again, since I can't go to America. But I enter thoroughly into the disinclination to move when there are studies that make each day too short. If we were neighbours, I should be in danger of getting troublesome to the revered Orientalist, with all kinds of questions.

As to the Jewish element in 'Deronda', I expected from first to last in writing it, that it would create much stronger resistance and even repulsion than it has actually met with. But precisely because I felt that the usual attitude of Christians towards Jews is— —I hardly know whether to say more impious or more stupid when viewed in the light of their professed principles, I therefore felt urged to treat Jews with such sympathy and understanding as my nature and knowledge could attain to. Moreover, not only towards the Jews, but towards all oriental peoples with whom we English come in contact, a spirit of arrogance and contemptuous dictatorialness is observable which has become a national disgrace to us. There is nothing I should care more to do, if it were possible, than to rouse the imagination of men and women to a vision of human claims in those races of their fellow-men who most differ from them in customs and beliefs. But towards the Hebrews we western people who have been reared in Christianity, have a peculiar debt and, whether we acknowledge it or not, a peculiar thorough-ness of fellowship in religious and moral sentiment. Can anything be more disgusting than to hear people called 'educated' making small jokes about eating ham, and showing themselves empty of any real knowledge as to the relation of their own social and religious life to the history of the people they think themselves witty in insulting? They hardly know that Christ was a Jew. And I find men educated at Rugby supposing that Christ spoke Greek. To my feeling, this deadness to the history which has prepared half our world for us, this inability to find interest in any form of life that is not clad in the same coat-tails and flounces as our own lies very close to the worst kind of irreligion. The best that can be said of it is, that it is a sign of the intellectual narrowness—in plain English, the stupidity, which is still the average mark of our culture.

Yes, I expected more aversion than I have found. But I was happily independent in material things and felt no temptation to accommodate my writing to any standard except that of trying to do my best in what seemed to me most needful to be done, and I sum up with the writer of the Book of Maccabees—'if I have done well, and as befits the subject, it is what I desired, but if I have done ill, it is what I could attain unto.'

You are in the middle of a more glorious autumn than ours, but we too are having now and then a little sunshine on the changing woods. I hope that I am right in putting the address from which you wrote to me on the 25th September, so that my note may not linger away from you and leave you to imagine me indifferent or negligent.

Please offer my reverent regard to Mr Stowe, and believe me, dear Friend

Always your gratefully affectionate
M. E. Lewes

We spent three months in East Switzerland, and are the better for it.

Rabbi] Stowe's husband Professor Calvin Stowe, a theologian.   'Deronda'] *Daniel Deronda* (1876), Eliot's last novel.   Greek] it is not now thought quite impossible that Jesus spoke Greek.   'If I have done well . . .'] 2 Macc. 15: 38.

EDWARD LEAR

(1812–1888)

Lear was an artist, nonsense-writer, and traveller.

197. To Chichester Fortescue, 1855

Fortescue (Lord Carlingford) was a pupil of Lear's and a Liberal politician. In 1861
he became the fourth husband of the famous hostess Lady Waldegrave. She inherited
Walpole's house Strawberry Hill from her second husband.

My dear 40scue,

I came to 'leave a card' on you, as you axed me to the dinner yesterday—
so here it is—

I was disgusted at being aperiently so rude to Lady Waldegrave—but I
was not well from the East winds, & so completely uncertain whether I had
any voice or not, that I thought it better not to sing, than to go to the piano
& be obliged to quit it. I felt like a cow who has swallowed a glass bottle—
or a boiled weasel—& should probably have made a noise like a dyspeptic
mouse in a fit.

But I passed a very pleasant evening, & was delighted with Lady
Waldegrave's perfectly natural & kind manner. I should have liked to sit
next to you, but I couldn't resist moving up to my next neighbour. I came
out purposing to leave cards at Carlton Gardens—so I shall do so, though
I know the Lady is out, for I nearly ran under the veels of her Chariot just
now:—whereby she made me a bough.

I must add that I think your room looks extremely pretty—& the Pigchr is stunning as it hangs now. How nicely you have had the 'Morn broadens' done as to frame.—

Your's affly.
Edward Lear.

There was an old man who said, 'How,
shall I flee from this terrible cow?
    I will sit on this stile
    & Continue to smile—
wh: may soften the heart of that cow.

Whats the difference between the Czar & the Times paper?—
One is the type of Despotism the other the despotism of Type.
    What is the difference between a hen & a kitchen maid?—
One is a domestic fowl, the other a foul domestic.
    Why need you not starve in the Desert? Because you might eat all the Sand which is there.
    Why *are* the sandwiches there? Because there the family of *Ham* was *bread & mustard*.

198. To Chichester Fortescue, 9 July 1860

Dear F.
Washing my rosecoloured flesh and brushing | my beard with a hairbrush,—
—Breakfast of tea, bread & butter, at nine | o'clock in the morning,
Sending my carpetbag onward I reached the | Twickenham station,
(Thanks to the civil domestics of good Lady | Wald.'grave's establishment.)
Just as the big buzzing brown booming | bottlegreen bumblebizz boiler
Stood on the point of departing for | Richmond & England's metropolis.

I say—(and if I ever said anything to the | contrary I hereby retract it)—

I say—I took away altogether unconsciously | your borrowed white fillagree
    handkerchief;
After the lapse of a week I will | surely return it,
And then you may either devour it or keep it, or burn it,—
Just as you please. But remember | I have not forgotten,
After the 26th. day of the month of | the present July—,
That is the time I am booked for | a visit to Nuneham.

Certain ideas have arisen & flourished | within me,
As to a possible visit to Ireland— | but nobody,
Comes to a positive certainty all in a hurry:
If you are free & in London, next | week shall we dine at the *Blue*
    Posts?

Both Mrs Clive & her husband have | written most kindly
Saying the picture delights them | (the Dead Sea) extremely,—

Bother all painting! I wish I'd 200 per annum!
—Wouldn't I sell all my colours and | brushes and damnable messes!
Over the world I should rove, North South | East & *West*, I would—
Marrying a black girl at last, & | slowly preparing to walk into Paradise!

A week or a month hence, I will | find time to make a queer Alphabet,
All with the letters beversed & | be-aided with pictures,
Which I shall give—(but don't tell | him just yet,) to Charles Braham's
    little one.
Just only look at the Times of today | for accounts of the Lebanon.
Now I must stop this jaw | & write myself quite simultaneous,
Yours with al ([. . . .]) affection— | the globular foolish Topographer.

                                          E.L.

Twickenham] Strawberry Hill is near Twickenham.   Nuneham] Nuneham Park, the
Oxfordshire home of Lady Waldegrave's husband.   Charles Braham] Lady Waldegrave's
brother.

ROBERT BROWNING (1812–1889) AND ELIZABETH BARRETT BROWNING (1806–1861)

The Brownings, who married in 1846, differed on the question of spiritualism. Daniel Dunglas Home (1833–86) was a celebrated medium. In August 1855 he gave the Brownings, who lived in Florence and were on a brief visit to London, a spiritualist demonstration which satisfied the wife but not the husband. He decided that Home was a fraud. Among the contemporaries who were on the side of Home were Ruskin, Harriet Beecher Stowe, and the Czar of Russia. Browning maintained his animus but withheld publication of his long poem 'Mr Sludge, the Medium', attacking Home, until after his wife's death.

199. To Miss M. A. de Gaudrion, 30 August 1855

Elizabeth Barrett Browning's letter enclosed the third-person remarks of her husband.

Dear Madam,

I hope you will pardon my delay in replying to your letter, and attribute it to the right cause; my time being much occupied during our brief visit to London. You address me in a name which could not do otherwise than move me to an answer, even if the tone of your application had not made me willing to be open with you on your account.

I went with my husband to witness the so-called spiritual manifestations at Ealing. I enclose to you in his handwriting an account of the impression he received. Mine, I must frankly say, were entirely different.

The class of phenomena in question appears to me too numerous not to be recognized as facts. I believe them to occur often under circumstances which exclude the possibility of imposture. That there is sometimes impostures is natural and necessary—for wherever there is a truth there will be a counterfeit of truth. But if you ask me (as you do) whether I would rank the phenomena witnessed at Ealing among the counterfeits, I sincerely answer that I may be much mistaken of course, but for my own part and in my own conscience I find no reason for considering the Medium in question responsible for anything seen or heard on that occasion.

Having said so much, I am anxious to guard myself against misunderstanding. I consider that the idea of looking for theological teaching or any other sort of teaching to these supposed spirits would be absolutely disastrous. Also that the seeking for intercourse with any particular spirit would be apt to end in either disappointment or delusion. In the present undeveloped state of the subject, with the tendency to personation on the part of the (so-called) spirits and the difficulties on ours as well as theirs, the manifestations are apt to be so slow and our apprehensions so unsteady, that we could hope to see our faces as well in a shivered looking-glass, as catch a clear view of a desired truth or lost friend by these means. What we do see, is a shadow on the window: the sign of something moving without—the proof of a beginning of access from a spiritual world—of which we shall presently learn more perhaps and I, for one, believe we shall.

You may be unaware that many persons who are called 'believers' in these things, believe simply in the physical facts, attribute them to physical causes, and dismiss the spiritual theory as neither necessary nor tenable.

This is not my view, however. I enclose back to you, the letter of my dear friend, knowing well the value of such a memorial. And with a most thankful sense for the sympathy which you have given to myself personally,

I remain, very faithfully yours,
Elizabeth Barrett Browning

Mr Browning presents his compliments to Miss de Gaudrion, and feels it his duty to say a word for himself in reply to her note—though he has overcome a real repugnance at recurring to the subject of it.

Mr Browning did, in company with his wife, witness Mr Home's performances at Ealing on the night Miss de Gaudrion alludes to—and he is hardly able to account for the fact that there can be another opinion than his own on the matter—that being that the whole display of 'hands', 'spirit-utterances', etc. were a cheat and imposture. Mr Browning believes in the sincerity and good faith of the Rymer family, and regrets proportionately that benevolent and worthy people should be subjected to the consequences of those admirable qualities of benevolence and worth when unaccompanied by a grain of worldly wisdom—or indeed divine wisdom, either of which would dispose of all this melancholy stuff in a minute. Mr Browning has, however, abundant experience that the best and rarest of natures may begin by the proper mistrust of the more ordinary results of reasoning when employed in such investigations as these; go on to an abnegation of the regular tests of truth and rationality in favour of these particular experiments, and end in a voluntary frustration of the whole intelligence before what is assumed to transcend all intelligence. Once arrived at this point, no trick is too gross; absurdities are referred to 'low spirits', falsehoods to 'personating spirits', and the one, terribly apparent spirit—Father of Lies—has it all his own way. Mr Browning had some difficulty in keeping from an offensive expression of his feelings at Mr Rymer's—he has since seen Mr Hume and relieved himself. Mr Browning recommends leaving this business to its natural termination, and will console himself for any pain to the dupes by supposing that their eventual profit in improved intelligence would be no otherwise procurable.

Spiritual manifestations] the séance in question was given at the house of J. S. Rymer in Ealing. Miss de Gaudrion, who had also attended a Home séance, had written to Mrs Browning asking her view.

H. D. THOREAU

(1817–1862)

200. *To H. G. O. Blake, 6 December 1856*

Thoreau, the author of *Walden* (1854), conducted, from 1848, a serious correspondence with H. G. O. Blake, once a Unitarian minister and later attached to the
Transcendentalists.

Mr Blake,

What is wanting above is merely an engraving of Eagleswood, which I
have used. I trust that you got a note from me at Eagleswood about a
fortnight ago. I passed thru' Worcester on the morning of the 25th of
November, and spent several hours (from 3.30 to 6.20) in the travellers'
room at the Depot, as in a dream, it now seems. As the first Harlem train
unexpectedly connected with the first from Fitchburg, I did not spend the
forenoon with you, as I had anticipated, on account of baggage &c—If it
had been a seasonable hour I should have seen you, i.e. if you had not been
gone to a horse-race. But think of making a call at half past three in the
morning! (Would it not have implied a 3 o clock in the morning courage in
both you & me?) As it were ignoring the fact that mankind are really not
at home—are not out, but so deeply in that they cannot be seen—nearly
half their hours at this season of the year. I walked up & down the Main
Street at half past 5 in the dark, and paused long in front of Brown's store
trying to distinguish its features; considering whether I might safely leave
his 'Putnam' in the door handle, but concluded not to risk it. Meanwhile
a watchman (?) seemed to be watching me, & I moved off. Took another
turn around there, a little later, and had the very earliest offer of the
Transcript from an urchin behind, whom I actually could not see, it was so
dark. So I withdrew, wondering if you & B. would know that I had been
there. You little dream who is occupying Worcester when you are all
asleep. Several things occurred there that night, which I will venture to say
were not put into the Transcript. A cat caught a mouse at the depot, & gave
it to her kitten to play with. So that world famous tragedy goes on by night
as well as by day, & nature is *emphatically* wrong. Also I saw a young
Irishman kneel before his mother, as if in prayer, while she wiped a cinder
out of his eye with her tongue; and I found that it was never too late (or
early?) to learn something.—These things transpired while you and B.
were, to all practical purposes, no where, & good for nothing—not even
for society,—not for horse-races,—nor the taking back of a Putnam's
Magazine. It is true I might have recalled you to life, but it would have
been a cruel act, considering the kind of life you would have come back to.

However, I would fain write to you now by broad daylight, and report to you some of my life, such as it is, and recall you to your life, which is not always lived by you, even by day light.

Blake! Blake! Are you awake? Are you aware what an ever-glorious morning this is? What long expected never to be repeated opportunity is now offered to get life & knowledge?

For my part I am trying to wake up,—to wring slumber out of my pores;—For, generally, I take events as unconcernedly as a fence post,—absorb wet & cold like it, and am pleasantly tickled with lichens slowly spreading over me. Could I not be content then to be a cedar post, which lasts 25 years? Would I not rather be that than the farmer that set it? or he that preaches to that farmer?—& go to the heaven of posts at last? I think I should like that as well as any would like it. But I should not care if I sprouted into a living tree, put forth leaves & flowers, & have fruit.

I am grateful for what I am & have. My thanksgiving is perpetual. It is surprising how contented one can be with nothing definite—only a sense of existance. Well anything for variety. I am ready to try this for the next 1000 years, & exhaust it. How sweet to think of! My extremities well charred, and my intellectual part too, so that there is no danger of worm or rot for a long while. My breath is sweet to me. O how I laugh when I think of my vague indefinite riches. No run on my bank can drain it—for my wealth is not possession but enjoyment.

What are all these years made for? and now another winter comes, so much like the last? Cant we satisfy the beggars once for all? Have you got in your wood for this winter? What else have you got in? Of what use a great fire on the hearth & a confounded little fire in the heart? Are you prepared to make a decisive campaign—to pay for your costly tuition—to pay for the suns of past summers—for happiness & unhappiness lavished upon you?

Does not Time go by swifter than the swiftest equine trotter or racker?

Stir up Brown—Remind him of his duties, which outrun the date & span of Worcester's years past & to come. Tell him to be sure that he is on the Main Street, however narrow it may be—& to have a lit sign, visible by night as well as by day.

Are they not patient waiters—They who wait for us? But even they shall not be losers.

Dec. 7

That Walt Whitman, of whom I wrote to you, is the most interesting fact to me at present. I have just read his 2nd edition (which he gave me) and it has done me more good than any reading for a long time. Perhaps I remember best the poem of Walt Whitman an American & the Sun Down Poem. There are 2 or 3 pieces in the book which are disagreeable to say the least, simply sensual. He does not celebrate love at all. It is as if the beasts spoke. I think that men have not been ashamed of themselves without reason. No doubt, there have always been dens where such deeds were unblushingly recited, and it is no merit to compete with their inhabitants. But even on this side, he has spoken more truth than any American or modern that I know. I have found his poem exhilirating encouraging. As for its sensuality,—& it may turn out to be less sensual than it appeared— I do not so much wish that those parts were not written, as that men & women were so pure that they could read them without harm, that is, without understanding them. One woman told me that no woman could read it as if a man could read what a woman could not. Of course Walt Whitman can communicate to us no experience, and if we are shocked, whose experience is it that we are reminded of?

On the whole it sounds to me very brave & American after whatever deductions. I do not believe that all the sermons so called that have been preached in this land put together are equal to it for preaching—

We ought to rejoice greatly in him. He occasionally suggests something a little more than human. You cant confound him with the other inhabitants of Brooklyn or New York. How they must shudder when they read him! He is awefully good.

To be sure I sometimes feel a little imposed on. By his heartiness & broad generalities he puts me into a liberal frame of mind prepared to see wonders—as it were sets me upon a hill or in the midst of a plain—stirs me well up, and then—throws in a thousand of brick. Though rude & sometimes ineffectual, it is a great primitive poem,—an alarum or trumpet-note ringing through the American camp. Wonderfully like the Orientals, too, considering that when I asked him if he had read them, he answered 'No: tell me about them.'

I did not get far in conversation with him,—two more being present,— and among the few things which I chanced to say, I remember that one was, in answer to him as representing America, that I did not think much of America or of politics, and so on, which may have been somewhat of a damper to him.

Since I have seen him, I find that I am not disturbed by any brag or egoism in his book. He may turn out the least of a braggart of all, having a better right to be confident.

He is a great fellow.

Eagleswood] Thoreau's house in Concord.   Putnam] *Putnam's Magazine.*   Transcript] the *Boston Evening Transcript.*   Walt Whitman] (1819–92); the 2nd edition of *Leaves of Grass* (1856) contained 21 poems not in the 1st edition of 1855. The two poems which Thoreau remembers best became known, in subsequent editions, as 'Poem of Myself' and 'Crossing Brooklyn Ferry'.

BARBARA LEIGH SMITH BODICHON
(1827–1891)

Barbara Leigh Smith was a friend of George Eliot; they had both been mistresses of John Chapman, the editor of the *Westminster Review*. She is said to have been the model for Romola. Ruskin admired her paintings. She was active in all manner of agitation for the rights of women, and her *Brief Summary, in Plain Language, of the Most Important Laws Concerning Women* was published in 1854, advocating reforms that did not come to pass till the Married Women's Property Act of 1882. She took the lead in the foundation of Girton College, Cambridge. In July 1857 she married Dr Eugène Bodichon, a Frenchman from Algiers—eccentric, physician, republican, abolitionist, and, like her, feminist—and they went off on a wedding tour of North America. Her American diary is in the form of letters to her father, also a feminist and a free spirit (he never married).

201. *To Benjamin Smith, 7–11 December 1857*

Monday, 7 December. Yesterday I was going on to write of a man who makes the voyage very unpleasant, but as I sat writing he passed me very often and looked over me [so] I was afraid. He is mad, but a man of great intellect and wonderful beauty and strength, nearly seven feet high. He has been a Representative, a general in Texas, is a good poet and has an amount of learning quite extraordinary for an American. I know him very well, for ever since we came on board last Friday he has talked, read letters or his own poetry aloud often, to me particularly. He was almost too violent to be agreeable and I got out of his way as much as possible. I was afraid of him after yesterday afternoon. When I was quietly reading Olmsted's book on the South States he comes, flings himself close to by me on the sofa, seizes the book and begins a violent attack on it and the Northerners, then breaks off and says he means to have my jacket, then breaks off and says, 'Your husband is one of those French republicans—hates Louis Napoleon— quite wrong, etc.—there will be a destruction of this boat, your husband will be killed and I shall marry you—whether you like or no.' I was frightened by his violence, but got away quietly and locked myself up in my room and did not go out except with the Doctor.

In the evening Doctor and I were sitting together in the ladies' cabin, where no one has a right to come but the gentlemen belonging to ladies (I forgot to say that this general drinks in the evening and is always worse, but that everyone lets him have his way, and he had been throwing himself on the necks of two or three men, once round the Doctor, which he bore very quietly)—but while we were reading, up rushes the man, mad or drunk, and smashes his hat with great violence on the Dr's head who starts up and says he will not be touched by anyone, and if it is attempted again he will defend himself with pistols or cane, and he took the hat and flung it at the General. The General seemed quite cowed and begged the Doctor's pardon, but everyone round interfered and took the General's part and all thought the Doctor's behaviour *very wrong*. I think he was too violent and so in the wrong, but certainly all the rest were in the wrong to take the General's part, and it was entirely because he was an American.

The Captain came and said if pistols were mentioned before ladies he should put the Doctor on shore directly, and—yet his ideas of liberty—allowed a mad man to talk in the most indecent manner before women and risk the lives of all on board, for he might set fire to the boat in an instant. Last week a vessel was set fire to by one person out of spite to some one other on board and *seventy-five people* were burnt or drowned.

This General has been in an asylum but has been sent out *cured* and is alone; it is very likely he was well enough in the House where he could not get rum or whiskey. This is a specimen on a Southern steamboat company. There are other disorderly characters on board. I wish you could have heard the account of an elopement which one of the assistant actors in it gave. He and the lover got into a boarding school and ran off with a young girl into another state, and they were married by a clergyman who asked no questions but charged $100!!!

Tuesday, 8 December. Since I wrote to you I have read in the Louisville paper an account of General Haskell. He seems to be a great genius driven mad with excitements—politics and wine. He seems to be *the man* of Tennessee. They are as proud of him as possible.

We are on the MISSISSIPPI now, it is a magnificent river and the everlasting woods on either side are very striking. We stop very often at little places like this very ugly and queer. The mistletoe here grows in the trees in immense quantities. I could not think what plant it could be.

The mist often lies on the water in a very beautiful and curious manner but is too like a fever spirit altogether to please me.

We have seen six or seven families in their houses floating down on rafts. It is one of the most curious sights I ever saw in my life. They have an immensely long rudder, no oars, no sails. They just live quietly with their animals doing their household work every day, and at last finding themselves at their destination without any trouble but that of keeping away from banks and snags.

We pass plots of ground which the Captain says he knows have grown from 60 to 75 bushels of wheat for 57 years, and he knows a man here at Kickman City (which I have drawn) who grew 125 barrels of potatoes on one acre and sold them on the land for one dollar and a half a barrel. He put them into barrels on the land; barrels cost him one quarter of a dollar each.

The banks of the river do really look as if their riches were inexhaustible and yet the beginning of civilization—a log hut, a field of maize with black stumps standing up all over it is very desolate. The monotony of forest at the edge of the water is very fine with certain effects of sky.

Now for the end of General H. He came up to me two nights ago and said in the most eloquent way how sorry he was he had offended the Dr, and would the Dr shake hands, and would I go and ask him. So I went and the Dr came up and there was a grand scene. Dr said, 'I bear no rancour —' 'No, no, let us be friends,' and after they talked and I danced two everlasting cotillions with the General, negroes playing for us. It was great fun, for the music seemed to have the best effect on the General, soothing his mind. It was quite dramatic, that reconciliation. The people round clapped their hands! very unlike the Northerners.

Friday, 11 December.
Baltic Steamer, Mississippi.

Last night I sat finishing up my sketches at the public table. *Company*: the pretty little Mrs H. and her fair Scotch-looking husband, Mr C. the intellectual-looking Californian gentleman and Mrs B. who has a very beautiful expression and is the most refined woman on the boat. Mr C. is reading a paper and read out loud the announcement of the marriage of a mulatto and a white girl; it excites from all expressions of the utmost disgust and horror. I say, 'It is very uncommon?' Mr C.: 'Yes! thank God. Only permitted in Massachusetts and a few states.' 'There seems to be nothing disgusting in it. My brothers went to school with a mulatto and I with a mulatto girl, and I have seen mulattoes in England who were not unlikely to marry with white.' *All*: 'At school! At school with niggers!' 'Yes.' *All*: 'Horrid idea, how could you?' *BLS*: 'Why, your little children all feel it possible to come in close contact with negroes, and they seem to like it; there is no natural antipathy.' *Some*: 'Yes, there is an inborn disgust *which prevents amalgamation.*' (Mark this: only one-half the negroes in the United States are full-blooded Africans—the rest [the] produce of white men and black women.) *Some*: 'No, it is only the effect of education.' *Mr C.*: 'There is no school or college in the U.S. where negroes could be educated with whites.' *BLS*: 'You are wrong, Sir. At Oberlin men, women and negroes are educated together.' *Mrs B.*: 'Yes, I know that, because Lucy Stone was educated there with people of colour.' *Mr C.*: 'Lucy Stone—she is a Woman's Rights woman, and an atheist. All those people are. Have you heard her speak?' *Mrs B.*: 'Yes, she speaks wonderfully well. She is an elegant orator. I was carried away by her at first.—She said women had a right to vote and all that sort of nonsense.' *Mr C.*: 'Nonsense indeed! Why, women, if that they have not certain rights are exempt from certain duties.' *Mrs B.*: 'Oh, yes, certainly Woman's Rights are great rubbish.' There is evidently a feeling that Abolition and Woman's Rights are supported by the same people and same arguments, and that both are allied to atheism—and all these slave owners are very religious people. I wanted the conversation to stick to slavery so I did not answer this argument with the other side which settles that objection. Women perform as great service to the state in bringing citizens into it as men do in preserving their lives. This is women's duty to the state which counterbalances the services men do the state a thousand times. Mr C. might have said, 'But this very duty incapacitates them for the right of voting and taking part in the governmental concerns of the state.' The answer is, so does the duty of men to fight, to go to sea, to go to distant parts to defend the state. When it does incapacitate them, let it incapacitate them, all men and women. When it does not, *let it not.* To a candid mind it is evident the duties they fulfil to the state are more onerous than those which men fulfil. They make and educate for ten years all the citizens in the state, and they receive no rights for these services!

But to return, I said instantly, 'Do not you think it right to give any education to the negro race?' *Mrs B.*: 'Oh, yes. Every child should be taught to read the Bible.' *Mrs H.*: 'I do not think they ought to be taught to read. It makes them unhappy, and all the negroes who run away, you will find, are those who have learnt how to read. I would not teach them to read.' *BLS*: 'But have they not souls and should not they read the Bible.' *Some*: 'Oh, yes, they have souls, but oral instruction is best for them.' *Mrs B.*: 'No, I do think everyone should be able to read the Bible.' *Mrs H.*: 'If you teach them to read they *will* run away.' *Mrs B.* (who lives in Louisville and is evidently very kind to her slaves): 'Well, I say if they will run away, let them.' *Mr and Mrs H.* (who, by the bye are bringing south *a woman who leaves a husband and five children behind in Kentucky*): 'Let them run away if they will! Why, every negro would run away if they could—people don't like to lose their servants.' Some said it makes the negroes unhappy to know how to read—what is the use of it to them? They are inferior to the whites and must be so always. *BLS*: 'But you say they improve and are better off every year, and that there is a wonderful difference between the African as he comes from Africa and the African after two or three generations in America. How can you tell where that improvement will stop?' *Mr C.*: 'Yes, they improve, but that is no reason for giving them *much* instruction and us making them discontented—for they *never will be emancipated. We cannot consent to lose our property.'*

Mrs B. after some general observations, says, 'Have you read *Uncle*

Tom?' I say, 'Yes.' Mrs B. says, 'If there is a creature living I *hate it is that Mrs Beecher.*' This was said with an expression of bitter feeling which distorted her good face, and every vestige of humanity disappeared, under the influence of this feeling. She might equal Brooks' 'glorious manifestation against Sumer.' I do not know how other people feel, but I cannot come amongst these people without the perception that every standard of right and wrong is lost,—that they are perverted and degraded by this one falsehood. To live in the belief of a vital falsehood poisons all the springs of life. I feel in England how incapable men and women are of judging rightly on any point when they hold false opinions concerning the rights of one half of the human race.

Some great questions there are which are ever before us. Every hour of the day brings up occasion of action involving these questions, and we have to consider how we shall act and we see what is the result of our action. To hold false ideas on these great questions which are woven in with every-day life perverts, embitters, poisons the souls more than to hold the most monstrously absurd doctrines of religious faith. It is bad enough to believe all will be damned but yourself and a few friends, but to believe a man has a right to hold fellow-men as slaves, to breed slaves—to sell his own children,—this doctrine perverts a man infinitely more, because when a man daily acts a faith it is a very different thing from thinking you believe. Of all who cry 'God condemns you to *eternal* punishment unless you believe certain dogmas,' would thrust you and himself into the fire he believes the good Lord prepares for you. To believe in transubstantiation or the divinity of the Virgin is not so perverting to the mind as to believe that women have no rights to full development of all their faculties and exercise of all their powers, to believe that men have rights over women, and as fathers to exercise those pretended rights over daughters, as husbands exercising those rights over wives. Every day men acting on this false belief destroy their perception of justice, blunt their moral nature, so injure their consciences that they lose the power to perceive the highest and purest attributes of God. Slavery is a greater injustice, but it is allied to the injustice to women so closely that I cannot see one without thinking of the other and feeling how soon slavery would be destroyed if right opinions were entertained upon the other question.

We passed Vicksburg, a prettily situated town on one of the rare hills along this vast Mississippi plain. On a hill close to the town about twenty years ago, ten gamblers were hung by the inhabitants of the place. A gang of gamblers had made the town quite unsafe for honest folk. They corrupted the young, fleeced them and sometimes murdered them, it was supposed. The inhabitants could bear it no longer so they met together and said, 'Leave the town in three days or we hang you.' The gang did not leave, so the townsmen took ten and hung them on that hill (see sketch).

On the opposite side of the river (in Louisiana) is the fighting ground. The laws are severe in Mississippi against duelling, so when a duel is to be fought they go over to Louisiana. I asked the Captain how many duels a year—about one a month, and two or three fatal ones a year. Sometimes they begin with double-barrelled guns loaded with shot, at 100 yards, then go nearer and take pistols, then quite close and pull out their bowie knives.

Very often fathers will go over with their sons—quite boys—to see them fight. 'Why do they fight so much in the South,' I asked, 'as you think the Southerners are so much better than the Northerners?' 'Well I don't know as there is any reason for it—they *are* much better than Northerners. Why, if a beggar asks alms a Northerner will give some cents, and a Southerner will give a quarter of a dollar at least.'

There is a recklessness and carelessness about these Southerners which I did not think the Anglo-Saxon race could attain under any circumstances.

Olmsted's book] F. L. Olmsted, *Journey in the Seaboard Slave States*, 1856.   The House] a lunatic asylum, not the House of Representatives.   Oberlin] the first college to admit blacks (1835) and the first to award degrees to women (1844).   Lucy Stone] (1818–93) paid her way through Oberlin by teaching and manual labour. She became a campaigner for abolition, and for women's rights.   Uncle Tom] Harriet Beecher Stowe's *Uncle Tom's Cabin* appeared in 1852.   Sumner] after Charles Sumner, a senator from Massachusetts, made a speech against slavery he was physically assaulted by Preston Brooks, a representative from South Carolina, and seriously injured.   Sketch] no sketch of the hill survives.

202. To Benjamin Smith, 13–14 February 1858

Saturday, 13 February. Mrs P. (the wife of a sugar planter) came to call on me. She is creole but her parents are *of the North*. I have seen no one here towards whom I have felt so much sympathy and esteem as towards her. She looks like one of the old Puritan stock. Today for the first time we had a little confidential talk about 'the institution'. She told me that one of her relations who owned a plantation wished to free all his negroes gradually— would have freed them at once if he had thought it right, but she said, 'Freed negroes cannot live in Louisiana—the Northern states will not receive them—and sending them to Liberia is cruel. Mr —— whom we know has received letters from his negroes there, and many are absolutely starving—that plan is a failure.

My relation hoped to prepare the way gradually for the amelioration of his people and their ultimate freedom. But it is very difficult to know what to do.'

She told me on their estate the negroes were so very happy that she did not think any would leave there except perhaps some hands lately bought.

She has a church and all the negroes are compelled to go once on Sunday; if not, there are many who would not go, she says. Some years ago they had many Congos—now only one remains and he clings to his old idolatry in spite of all she can do to cure him of it. She dare not instruct the mass of the negroes because it is contrary to law, but she teaches every one she can to read and to write who come near enough to her! She loves the plantation and tries to do all the good she can there.

Mrs P. took me to see a picture which produces a great sensation in America wherever it is exhibited: Peale's *Court of Death*, an immense allegorical picture with twenty-three figures as large as life. It is very badly painted, the figures ill-drawn and inelegant, which as the picture is on the Greek model is unpardonable. The allegory is not perfect: the *ministers* (war, famine, apoplexy, consumption, suicide, etc.) have men about to die mixed up with them. This spoils the picture, for the picture has the merit of being interesting and the monarch (stern and calm sitting in the cave heavily clothed in sable drapery, the head and shoulders almost lost in shadow) is a fine idea for the King—but badly done. There is very little knowledge of art in America, very little love of any art, but scarcely any for landscape art or small treasures like old Hunts.

Some people like my drawings because they see they are like their woods but only one person has *enjoyed* them here, and that was a poor Italian image boy who came two or three times and looked at me painting for a long time through the window and enjoyed the colours, he said. When he went away the last time he begged of me to accept a bas relief of some horses, young and old together, which he said I might paint into a field with trees round them.

As all my paintings are finished and my easel packed up I seem to have unlimited hours in the day, so I went to a Slave Auction. I went alone (a quarter of an hour before the time) and asked the auctioneer to allow me to see everything. He was very smiling and polite, took me upstairs, showed me all the articles for sale—about thirty women and twenty men, twelve or fourteen babies. He took me round and told me what they could do: 'She can cook and iron, has worked also in the field,' etc., 'This one a No. 1 cook and ironer—,' etc. He introduced me to the owner who wanted to sell them (being in debt) and he did not tell the owner what I had told him (that I was English and only came from curiosity), so the owner took a great deal of pains to make me admire a dull-looking mulatress and said she was an excellent servant and could just suit me. At twelve we all descended into a dirty hall adjoining the street big enough to hold a thousand people. There were three sales going on at the same time, and the room was crowded with rough-looking men, smoking and spitting, bad-looking set—a mêlée of all nations. I pitied the slaves, for these were slave buyers.

The polite auctioneer had a steamboat to sell, so I went to listen to another who was selling a lot of women and children. A girl with two little children was on the block: 'Likely girl, Amy and her two children, good cook, healthy girl, Amy—what! only seven hundred dollars for the three? that is giving 'em away! 720! 730! 735!—740! why, gentlemen, they are worth a thousand dollars—healthy family, good washer, house servant, etc. $750.' Just at this time the polite gentleman began in the same way: 'Finigal Sara, twenty-two years old, has had three children, healthy gal, fully guaranteed—sold for no fault, etc. and six hundred dollars? Why, gentlemen, I can't give you this likely gal,' etc. etc. Then a girl with a little baby got up and the same sort of harangue went on until eight hundred dollars, I think, was bid and a blackguard-looking gentleman came up, opened her mouth, examined her teeth, felt her all over and said she was dear or something to that effect.

I noticed one mulatto girl who looked very sad and embarrassed. She was going to have a child and seemed frightened and wretched. I was very sorry I could not get near to her to speak to her. The others were not sad at all. Perhaps were glad of a change. Some looked round anxiously at the different bearded faces below them, but there was no great emotion visible.

I changed my place and went round to the corner where the women were standing before they had to mount the auction stage. There were two or three young women with babies, laughing and talking with the gentlemen who were round, in a quiet sad sort of way, not merrily. The negroes laugh very often when they are not merry. Quite in the corner was a little delicate negro woman with a boy as tall as herself. They were called on together, and the polite gentleman said that they were mother and son and their master would not let them be separated on any account. Bids not being good they came on down and I went up to them. The girl said she thought she was twenty-five and her son ten. She came from South Carolina. She had always lived in one family and her boy had been a pet in her master's house. He sold them for debt. He was sorry but he could not help it, and her young missises cried very much when they parted with her boy. She was religious and always went to church. She was much comforted to hear there were good black churches in this strange country. While we talked two or three men came up and questioned her particularly about her health; she confessed it was not strong. They spoke kindly to her but went about their examination exactly as a farmer would examine a cow. It is evident (as Mrs P. said this morning) planters in general only consider the slaves as a means of gaining money. There is not that consideration for them which they pretend in drawing-room conversations. The slave-owners talk of them as the Patriarchs might have spoken of their families and call it a patriarchal institution always, but it is not so—they do not consider their feelings except in rare instances. They tell you in drawing rooms that marriage is encouraged.—It is a farce to say so, if the father is not considered as a part of the family in sales. Of course there are exceptions and my experience is very limited. I came away very sick with the noise and the sickening moral and physical atmosphere.

Before I went the young man in our house had said, 'Well, I don't think there is anything to see—they sell them just like so many rocking chairs. There's no difference.' And that is the truest word that can be said about the affair. When I see how Miss Murray speaks of sales and separations as regretted by the owners and as disagreeable (that is her tone if not her words), I feel inclined to condemn her to attend all the sales held in New Orleans in two months. How many that would be you may guess, as three were going on the morning I went down.

Sunday, 14 February.
New Orleans.

I went down to my Baptist friends at half past ten and finding only one old negress there sitting under the veranda I was afraid there would be no church but she assured me there would be in time, that she came early, that church would begin at twelve o'clock. So I sat down and there came straggling in other old ladies and gay young ladies and fine gentlemen in spotless shirts and broadcloth of various complexions from pale yellow or olive to jet black or rather *deep chocolate with blue lights on it*, which is the blackest complexion I have seen here.

We all shook hands and sat and talked in the most friendly manner. They were very cheerful and pleasant. One old lady, nearly white, said she was very ill yesterday and thought her time was come, whereupon her friend said, 'Ah yes, what children we are. We fix ourselves all ready to go but God don't want us—we must abide his time and *he will tackle us up pretty quick*. He knows when it is right to fix us. Why, I remember being very ill and feeling sure I should die, so I gets out of bed and puts on a clean shift, washes my face, and unlocks my door and I lies down all decent and ready.' The old lady said she had been very ill and had administered the sacrament to herself, blessing the wine and bread, and after that she lay down and exclaimed, 'Lord, come. I am ready fixed, oh Lord.'

The handsomest dressed woman (and the woman whose face expressed the greatest intelligence) told me she was free. She had bought herself. She had a book in her hand and a Sunday School newspaper. She told me she attended the Sunday School of Christ Church, that there white ladies taught free coloured people. She was near fifty and was learning to read. She told me she was a washer and ironer and gained a good living, but that many free coloured women were not respectable. I wish I could give you every word of the conversation but I cannot do it. I have so much to write.

Presently came a mean-looking white man who wished to preach. He said he was sent by some other minister. The negroes were nervous but told him the Revnd. Benjamin was going to preach, when the polite old bully the police officer came up and said to the small white man (who was very like the Revnd. Kenrick, Pater's particular friend), '*Sir!* no preaching here by anyone I don't know, Sir! Where do you come from? What is your name, Sir? I know nothing about you. You can't come here. The coloured folks have their own preacher.'

The little gentleman was frightened and went off. 'How do I know he is not one of your Northern men, one of your sneaking abolitionists, etc.' and he asked me if I knew him. Then there came another white man who was allowed to preach there, so I would not stay. I know so well how they preach.

I went on to the Methodist and seeing a black man in the pulpit I went in and took my old place. He was in the midst of the history of the woman of Samaria and the congregation in a state of great enjoyment. 'Now Christ was going to Jerusalem and the city of Samaria was right in the road so he thought he could go there on his way, and my brothers you see he had a very little time to do anything so he wished to convince them he was a prophet as quick as possible, so he devises this plan.' (A good description of the difference between Jew and Samaritan came in here and moral charity). 'I like a well. I like a seat by a well. It is a pleasant place and Christ knew that women like to sit down and talk, so when he comes to this well he sees a woman and he asks her for water to drink. Now, my brother, Christ was not thirsty—it was only for conversation that he said, "Give me a cup of water." Now, my brother, this woman was not of the fairest character and Christ knew that, so he said to her, "Go call thy husband," and she said "I have no husband"' (the manner of giving this was so comical that all the negroes showed their white teeth and some laughed out loud). 'Then our Lord told her she had had five husbands! Now he knew very well that women like talking and that too he knew he could not do better than speak to a woman. He knew she would run and tell it all directly, and say, "Here is a prophet", and mark, my brothers, how she exaggerated as women will. She runs to the city and calls out, "A prophet is come who has told me everything that ever I did!" Now, my brothers and sisters, Christ had only said, "*You have had five husbands, and the last is not your husband,*" and you see how she thought that was everything. Perhaps it might be, my brothers, that her conscience suddenly waked up and she felt all her sins in the presence of Christ and that she felt as if he had told her all. x x x Christ did not care for *opinion religion*. All he wanted was *heartfelt* religion—be born again, be born again in the heart!' (Here was a shout of 'yes! oh yes, blessed Lord!' and jumping up and down with their hands up in the air—one day a man jumped himself quite out of his trousers.)

He spoke about the Jews and the captivity, and I remarked as I have often done that they (the congregation) always identify themselves with that chosen people in bondage and look forward to the release. Some look to heaven, but some, I am sure, look for a better time on earth.

They sang 'I'm going home to glor*ie*. Peter, John I then shall see. I'm going home to glor*ie*. Matthew, Luke I then shall see. I'm going home to glorie, etc.' I think they put in the names of anyone they wanted to see, for they sang different names—all the time stamping time, so that as the singing *surged* along I felt carried along too and sang with them. One old lady sang so intensely that she dropped down from exhaustion. There was no occasion to say to her (as all of the men called out to another old lady who was timid), 'Sing up, my sister, sing up!'

I spoke to some of my friends. They told me the prayer meeting had been 'beautiful.' How I wish I might get in, but I am a Gentile they say.

I dined with a coloured lady who was in the chapel, a planter up the river, such a shrewd, clever little old lady, rich and very hospitable. She told me that numbers of Italians, French and Irish come and ask her for a lodging. The other day a poor old Italian who looked very miserable slept at her house, and in the morning rang the bell and asked the servant to bring him a looking-glass to shave by—cool for a beggar. I like the little old lady and if I had time would go and see her plantation. Just off for Mobile.

Court of Death] Rembrandt Peale painted the allegory.   Hunts] William Henry Hunt had taught Bodichon in her youth.   Image boy] a seller of religious images.

ANTHONY TROLLOPE
(1815–1882)

Though the most prolific of novelists, Trollope was not a great letter writer.

203. To Dorothea Sankey, 24 March 1861

In 1942 Sotheby's catalogue called this 'one of the most extraordinary letters ever offered for sale'. Michael Sadleir (*Trollope: A Commentary*, 1927, 3rd edn. 1961) is almost certainly right in calling it a joke. Dorothea Sankey may have been an acquaintance of the Trollopes when they lived in Ireland.

My dearest Miss Dorothea Sankey

My affectionate & most excellent wife is as you are aware still living—and I am proud to say her health is good. Nevertheless it is always well to take time by the forelock and be prepared for all events. Should anything happen to her, will you supply her place,—as soon as the proper period for decent mourning is over.

Till then I am your devoted Servant

Anthony Trollope

EMILY DICKINSON
(1830–1886)

Emily Dickinson lived a recluse in Amherst, Mass., writing over a thousand poems, only six of which were published in her lifetime.

204. To T. W. Higginson, 7 June 1862

Thomas Wentworth Higginson worked for *Atlantic Monthly*. Dickinson asked his opinion of some poems, and began a correspondence in which she says more than once that Higginson 'saved her life'. After her death he was co-editor of her work.

Dear friend,

Your letter gave no Drunkenness, because I tasted Rum before—Domingo comes but once—yet I have had few pleasures so deep as your opinion, and if I tried to thank you, my tears would block my tongue—

My dying Tutor told me that he would like to live till I had been a poet, but Death was much of Mob as I could master—then—And when far afterward—a sudden light on Orchards, or a new fashion in the wind troubled my attention—I felt a palsy, here—the Verses just relieve—

Your second letter surprised me, and for a moment, swung—I had not supposed it. Your first—gave no dishonor, because the True—are not ashamed—I thanked you for your justice—but could not drop the Bells whose jingling cooled my Tramp—Perhaps the Balm, seemed better, because you bled me, first.

I smile when you suggest that I delay 'to publish'—that being foreign to my thought, as Firmament to Fin—

If fame belonged to me, I could not escape her—if she did not, the longest day would pass me on the chase—and the approbation of my Dog, would forsake me—then—My Barefoot-Rank is better—

You think my gait 'spasmodic'—I am in danger—Sir—

You think me 'uncontrolled'—I have no Tribunal.

Would you have time to be the 'friend' you should think I need? I have a little shape—it would not crowd your Desk—nor make much Racket as the Mouse, that dents your Galleries—

If I might bring you what I do—not so frequent to trouble you—and ask you if I told it clear—'twould be control, to me—

The Sailor cannot see the North—but knows the Needle can—

The 'hand you stretch me in the Dark,' I put mine in, and turn away—I have no Saxon, now—

> As if I asked a common Alms,
> And in my wondering hand
> A Stranger pressed a Kingdom,
> And I, bewildered, stand—
> As if I asked the Orient
> Had it for me a Morn—
> And it should lift it's purple Dikes,
> And shatter me with Dawn!

But, will you be my Preceptor, Mr Higginson?

Your friend
E Dickinson—

'Dying Tutor'] Benjamin F. Newton, a law student in her father's office, who had encouraged her poetry.   I have no Saxon] 'words fail me'.

205. To Mrs J. G. Holland, early October 1870

Elizabeth Holland and her husband Dr Josiah Gilbert Holland were among Dickinson's closest friends; she wrote to Mrs Holland over many years. Holland was in New York editing a new monthly journal. The Franco-Prussian war was in progress.

I guess I wont send that note now, for the mind is such a new place, last night feels obsolete.

Perhaps you thought dear Sister, I wanted to elope with you and feared a vicious Father.

It was not quite that.

The Papers thought the Doctor was mostly in New York. Who then would read for you? Mr Chapman, doubtless, or Mr Buckingham! The Doctor's sweet reply makes me infamous.

Life is the finest secret.

So long as that remains, we must all whisper.

With that sublime exception I had no clandestineness.

It was lovely to see you and I hope it may happen again. These beloved accidents must become more frequent.

We are by September and yet my flowers are bold as June. Amherst has gone to Eden.

To shut our eyes is Travel.
The Seasons understand this.
How lonesome to be an Article! I mean—to have no soul.
An Apple fell in the night and a Wagon stopped.
I suppose the Wagon ate the Apple and resumed it's way.
How fine it is to talk.
What Miracles the News is!
Not Bismark but ourselves.

> The Life we have is very great.
> The Life that we shall see
> Surpasses it, we know, because
> It is Infinity.
> But when all Space has been beheld
> And all Dominion shown
> The smallest Human Heart's extent
> Reduces it to none.

Love for the Doctor, and the Girls.
Ted might not acknowledge me.

Emily

206. To Louise and Frances Norcross, early July 1879

Louise (Loo) and Frances were Dickinson's 'little cousins', the orphaned daughters of her aunt Lavinia. The fire that began in the early hours of 4 July 1879 destroyed the business centre of Amherst.

Dear Cousins,

Did you know there had been a fire here, and that but for a whim of the wind Austin and Vinnie and Emily would have all been homeless? But perhaps you saw *The Republican*.

We were waked by the ticking of the bells,—the bells tick in Amherst for a fire, to tell the firemen.

I sprang to the window, and each side of the curtain saw that awful sun. The moon was shining high at the time, and the birds singing like trumpets.

Vinnie came soft as a moccasin, 'Don't be afraid, Emily, it is only the fourth of July.'

I did not tell that I saw it, for I thought if she felt it best to deceive, it must be that it was.

She took hold of my hand and led me into mother's room. Mother had not waked, and Maggie was sitting by her. Vinnie left us a moment, and I whispered to Maggie, and asked her what it was.

'Only Stebbins's barn, Emily;' but I knew that the right and left of the village was on the arm of Stebbins's barn. I could hear buildings falling, and oil exploding, and people walking and talking gayly, and cannon soft as velvet from parishes that did not know that we were burning up.

And so much lighter than day was it, that I saw a caterpillar measure a leaf far down in the orchard; and Vinnie kept saying bravely, 'It's only the fourth of July.'

It seemed like a theatre, or a night in London, or perhaps like chaos. The innocent dew falling 'as if it thought no evil', . . . and sweet frogs prattling in the pools as if there were no earth.

At seven people came to tell us that the fire was stopped, stopped by throwing sound houses in as one fills a well.

Mother never waked, and we were all grateful; we knew she would never buy needle and thread at Mr Cutler's store, and if it were Pompeii nobody could tell her.

The post-office is in the old meeting-house where Loo and I went early to avoid the crowd, and—fell asleep with the bumble-bees and the Lord God of Elijah.

Vinnie's 'only the fourth of July' I shall always remember. I think she will tell us so when we die, to keep us from being afraid.

Footlights cannot improve the grave, only immortality.

Forgive me the personality; but I knew, I thought, our peril was yours. Love for you each.

Emily

207. To Susan Gilbert Dickinson, early October 1883

> Susan was Dickinson's sister-in-law. Her son Gilbert had died of typhoid fever, at the age of 8.

Dear Sue—

The Vision of Immortal Life has been fulfilled—

How simply at the last the Fathom comes! The Passenger and not the Sea, we find surprises us—

Gilbert rejoiced in Secrets—

His Life was panting with them—With what menace of Light he cried 'Dont tell, Aunt Emily'! Now my ascended Playmate must instruct *me*. Show us, prattling Preceptor, but the way to thee!

He knew no niggard moment—His Life was full of Boon—The Playthings of the Dervish were not so wild as his—

No crescent was this Creature—He traveled from the Full—

Such soar, but never set—

I see him in the Star, and meet his sweet velocity in everything that flies—His Life was like the Bugle, which winds itself away, his Elegy an echo—his Requiem ecstasy—

Dawn and Meridian in one.

Wherefore would he wait, wronged only of Night, which he left for us—
Without a speculation, our little Ajax spans the whole—

> Pass to thy Rendezvous of Light,
> Pangless except for us—
> Who slowly ford the Mystery
> Which thou hast leaped across!

Emily

JOHN HENRY NEWMAN
(1801–1890)

Newman, poet, preacher and theologian, had joined the Church of Rome in 1845. His *Apologia pro Vita Sua* (1864) was his masterpiece. He was made a cardinal in 1897.

208. To R. W. Church, 11 July 1865

Church (1815–90) was dean of St Paul's; he met Newman when a Fellow of Oriel College, Oxford and joined the Oxford Movement.

My dear Church,

I have delayed thanking you for your great kindness in uniting with Rogers in giving me a fiddle, till I could report upon the fiddle itself. The Warehouse sent me three to choose out of —and I chose with trepidation, as fearing I was hardly up to choosing well. And then my fingers have been in such a state, as being cut by the strings, that up to Saturday last I had sticking plaster upon their ends—and therefore was in no condition to bring out a good tune from the strings and so to return good for evil. But on Saturday I had a good bout at Beethoven's Quartetts—which I used to play with poor Blanco White—and thought them more exquisite than ever—so that I was obliged to lay down the instrument and literally cry out with delight. However, what is more to the point, I was able to ascertain that I had got a very beautiful fiddle—such as I never had before. Think of my not having a good one till I was between sixty and seventy—and beginning to learn it when I was ten! However, I really think it will add to my power of working, and the length of my life. I never wrote more than when I played the fiddle. I always sleep better after music. There must be some electric current passing from the strings through the fingers into the brain and down the spinal marrow. Perhaps thought is music.

I hope to send you the 'Phormio' almost at once.

Ever yrs affly,
John H Newman

Rogers] J. E. T. Rogers (1825–90); economist and one-time Tractarian.   White] Joseph
Blanco White (1775–1841), who had been a priest in both Roman Catholic and Anglican orders,
was an early friend of Newman.   'Phormio'] Newman published a school edition of Terence's
Phormio in 1864.

JOHN ADDINGTON SYMONDS
(1840–1893)

Symonds was the son of a well-known doctor, and author of *The Renaissance in Italy*
(1875–86) and of *A Problem in Modern Ethics* (1891) which dealt with the question of
homosexuality.

209. To Charlotte Symonds (and other readers), 8 December 1865

Charlotte (1842–1929) was Symonds's sister.

My father came to us this afternoon. He is going to dine with [Thomas]
Woolner, to meet Tennyson, Gladstone & Holman Hunt. I am to go in the
evening at 9.30.

When I arrived at Woolner's the maid said she supposed I was 'for the
gentlemen'. On my replying 'yes', she showed me into the dining room,
where they were finishing dessert. Woolner sat of course at the bottom of
the table, Tennyson on his left, my father on his right hand. Gladstone
sat next Tennyson & Hunt next my father. I relapsed into an armchair
between Woolner & my father.

The conversation continued. They were talking about the Jamaica business—Gladstone bearing hard on Eyre, Tennyson excusing any cruelty in
the case of putting down a savage mob. Gladstone had been reading official
papers on the business all the morning, & said with an expression of intense
gravity just after I had entered—'& that evidence wrung from a poor black
boy with a revolver at his head!' He said this in an orator's tone, pity
mingled with indignation, the pressure of the lips, the inclination of the
head, the lifting of the eyes to heaven, all marking man's moral earnestness.
He has a face like a lion's; his head is small above it, though the forehead
is broad & massive, something like Trajan's in its proportion to the features. Character, far more than intellect, strikes me in his physiognomy, &
there is a remarkable duplicity of expression—iron vicelike resolution combined with a subtle mobile ingeniousness.

Tennyson did not argue. He kept asserting various prejudices & convictions. 'We are too tender to savages, we are more tender to a black than to ourselves.' 'Niggers are tigers, niggers are tigers,' in *obbligato, sotto voce*, to Gladstone's declamation. 'But the Englishman is a cruel man—he is a strong man,' put in Gladstone. My father illustrated this by the stories of the Indian Mutiny. 'That's not like Oriental cruelty,' said Tennyson: 'But I would not kill a cat, not the tame cat who scratches & miaus over his disgusting amours & keeps me awake'—thrown in with an undefinable impatience & rasping hatred. Gladstone looked glum & iron at this speech, thinking probably of Eyre. Then they turned to the insufficiency of evidence as yet in Eyre's case & to other instances of his hasty butchery—the woman he hung, though recommended by Court Martial, because women had shown savageness in mutilating a corpse 'because *women*, not *the woman*—& that too after being recommended to mercy *by Court Martial*, & he holding the Queen's Commission!' said Gladstone with the same hostile emphasis. The question of his personal courage came up—that, said Gladstone, did not prove his capability of remaining cool under & dealing with such special circumstances. Anecdotes about sudden panics were related. Tennyson said to my father: 'As far as I know my own temperament, I could stand any sudden thing, but give me an hour to reflect, & I should go here & go there & all would be confused. If the fiery gulf of Curtius opened in the city, I would leap at once into it on horseback. But if I had to reflect on it, no—especially the thought of death—nothing can be weighed against that. It is the moral question, the fear, wh would perplex me. I have not got the English courage. I could not wait 6 hours in a Square expecting a battery's fire.' Then stories of martial severity were told. My father repeated the anecdote of Bosquet in the Malakoff. Gladstone said Cialdini had shot a soldier for being without his regimental jacket. Tennyson put in sotto voce 'If they shot paupers perhaps they wouldnt tear up their clothes,' & laughed very grimly.

Frank Palgrave here came in, a little man in morning dress, with short beard & moustache, well cut features & a slight cast in his eye, an impatient dissatisfied look & some selfassertion in his manner. He diverted the conversation to the subject of newspapers. Tennyson all the while kept drinking glasses of port, & glowering round the room through his spectacles. His moustache hides the play of his mouth, but as far as I cd see that feature is as grim as the rest. He has cheek bones carved out of iron. His head is domed, quite the reverse of Gladstone's, like an Elizabethan head, strong in the coronal, narrow in the frontal regions, but very finely moulded. It is like what Conington's head seems trying to be.*

---

* This is not uncommon, with heads. They seem verging to some type wh one attains better than another, various minute differences coming in to modulate the assimilation. Arthur's face seems striving after the National Gallery portrait of Masaccio.

Something brought up the franchise. Tennyson said 'That's what we're coming to—when we get your Reform Bill Mr Gladstone, not that I know anything about it.' 'No more does any man in England' said Gladstone taking him up quickly with a twinkling laugh, then adding 'But I'm sorry to see you getting nervous.' 'Oh! I think a state in wh every man wd have a vote is the ideal. I always thought it might be realized in England if anywhere with our Constitutional history. But how to do it.' This was the mere reflector. The man of practise said nothing.

Soon after came coffee. Tennyson grew impatient, moved his great gaunt body about, & finally was left to smoke a pipe.—It is hard to fix the difference between the two men, both with their strong provincial accent, Gladstone with his rich flexible voice, Tennyson with his deep drawl rising into an impatient falsetto when put out, Gladstone arguing, Tennyson putting in a prejudice, Gladstone asserting rashly, Tennyson denying with a bold negative, Gladstone full of facts, Tennyson relying on impressions, both of them humorous, but the one polished & delicate in repartee, the other broad & coarse & grotesque. Gladstone's hands are white & not remarkable. Tennyson's are huge, unwieldy, fit for moulding clay or dough. Gladstone is in some sort a man of the world, Tennyson a child & treated by him like a child. Woolner played the host well—with great simplicity. His manner was agreeably subdued. He burst into no unseasonable fits of laughing, no selfassertive anecdotes. He became a gentleman, yet by his manliness animated the whole. Palgrave rasped a little. Hunt was silent. My father made a good third to the two great people. I was like a man hearing a concerto, Gladstone first violin, Tennyson violincello, Woolner Bass viol, Palgrave viola, & perhaps Hunt a second but very subordinate viola.

When we left the diningroom we found Mrs Woolner & her sister Miss Waugh (engaged to Holman Hunt) in the drawing room. Both of these ladies are graceful. They affect the simplicity of Preraphaelite nature, & dress without crinoline very elegantly. Miss Waugh, though called 'the goddess', is nowise unapproachable. She talked of Japanese fans like a common mortal. Mrs Woolner is a pretty little maidenly creature who seems to have walked out of a missal margin.

Woolner gave Gladstone a Ms Book containing translations of the Iliad by Tennyson to read. Gladstone read it by himself till Tennyson appeared. Then Woolner went to him & said 'You will read your translation won't you?' And Palgrave 'Come you! A shout in the trench!' 'No, I shant' said Tennyson standing in the room with a pettish voice & jerking his arms & body from the hips. 'No, I shant read it: it's only a little thing—must be judged by comparison with the Greek—can only be appreciated by the difficulties overcome'—then seeing the Ms in Gladstone's hand—'This isn't fair—no, this isnt fair'—he took it away & nothing would pacify him. 'I meant to read it to Mr Gladstone & Dr Symonds.' My father urged him

to no purpose, told him he would be φωνοῦντα ουνετοῖσιν ; but he cried—
'Yes, you & Gladstone—but the rest don't understand it' 'Here's my son
an Oxford first class man' 'Oh! I should be afraid of him.' Then my father
talked soothingly in an admirable low voice to him, such as those who have
to deal with fractious people wd do well to acquire. He talked to him of his
poems—Mariana in the moated grange. This took them to the Lincolnshire flats—as impressive in their extent of plain as mountain heights. My
father tried to analyse the physical conditions of ideas of size. But Tennyson
preferred fixing his mind on the ideas themselves. 'I do not know whether
to think the Universe great or little. When I think about it, it seems now
one & now the other. What makes its greatness? Not one Sun or one set of
Suns, or is it the whole together?' Then to illustrate his sense of size he
pictured a journey through space like Jean Paul Richter's leaving first one
galaxy a spot of light behind him, then another, & so on through infinity.
Then about matter. Its incognizability puzzled him. 'I cannot form the
least notion of a brick. I don't know what it is. It's no use talking about
atoms, extension, colour, weight. I cannot penetrate the brick. But I have
far more distinct ideas of God—of Love & such emotions. I can sympathize with God in my poor way. The human Soul seems to be always in
some way, how we do not know, identical with God. That's the value of
prayer. Prayer is like opening a sluice between the great ocean & our little
channels.' Then of Eternity & Creation 'Huxley says we may have come
from monkeys. That makes no difference to me. If it is God's way of
creation, he sees the whole past, present, & future as one' (entering as an
elaborate statement of Eternity à la Sir Th. Browne). Then of morality: 'I
cannot but think morality is the crown of man. But what is it without
immortality? Let us eat & drink for tomorrow we die. If I knew the world
were coming to an end in 6 hours, sd I give my money to a starving beggar?
No. If I did not believe myself immortal. I have sometimes thought men of
sin might destroy their immortality. The eternity of punishment is quite
incredible. Xt's words were parables to suit the sense of the times.' Further
of morality: 'There are some young men who try to do away with morality.
They say, we won't be moral. Comte, I believe, & perhaps Mr Grote too
deny that Immortality has anything to do with being moral.' Then from
material to moral difficulties: 'Why do mosquitoes exist? I believe that after
God had made his world the devil began & added something.' (Cat &
Mouse. Leopards) (My father raised moral evil. Morbid art.) The conversation turned on Swinburne for the moment & then dropped.

In all this metaphysical vagueness about Matter, Morals, the existence of
Evil, & the evidences of God there was something almost childish. Such
points pass with most men for settled as insoluble, after a time. But Tennyson
has a perfect simplicity about him, wh recognizes the real greatness of such

questions & regards them as always worthy of consideration. He treats them with profound moral earnestness. His *In Memoriam* & *Two Voices* illustrate this habit. There is nothing original or startling, on the contrary a general commonplaceness, about his metaphysics, yet so far as they go, they express real agitating questions, express in a poet's language what most men feel & think about.

A move was made into the diningroom. Tennyson had consented to read his translations to Gladstone & my father. I followed them & sat unperceived behind them. He began by reading in a deep bass growl the passage of Achilles shouting in the trench. Gladstone continually interrupted him with small points about words. He has a combative House of Commons mannerism, wh gives him the appearance of thinking too much about himself. It was always to air some theory of his own that he broke Tennyson's recital; & he seemed listening only in order to catch something up. Tennyson invited criticism.

Tennyson was sorely puzzled about the variations in Homeric readings & interpretations. 'They change year after year. What we used to think right in my days, I am now told is all wrong. What is a poor translator to do?' But he piqued himself very much on his exact renderings: 'These lines are word for word. You could not have a closer translation: one poet could not express another better. There, those are good lines.' Gladstone wd object; 'but you will say Jove & Greeks: can't we have Zeus & Achaeans?' 'But the sound of Jove! Jove is much softer than Zeus—Zeus—Zeus.' 'Well, Mr Worsley gives us Achaeans.' 'Mr Worsley—has chosen a convenient long metre, he can give you Achaeans, & a great deal else.' Much was said about the proper means of getting a certain pause, how to give equivalent suggestive sounds & so on.

Woolner] Thomas Woolner (1825–92), sculptor. Holman Hunt] (1827–1910), painter, member of the Pre-Raphaelite Brotherhood.   The Jamaica business] the controversy, which divided the intelligentsia, over Governor Eyre's harsh repression of a revolt in Jamaica. Eyre was dismissed and tried for murder, but acquitted.   Trajan] Roman emperor 51–117.   Curtius] Marcus Curtius rode his horse into a gulf that opened up in the Forum.   Bosquet] Pierre Bosquet, marshal of France, was distinguished for bravery at the storming of Malakoff in the Crimean War. Enrico Cialdini was an Italian general in that war.   Palgrave] F. T. Palgrave (1824–97), friend of Tennyson and editor of *The Golden Treasury* (1861).   Conington] John Conington, a classicist, who taught Symonds at Oxford.   Arthur] Sidgwick, a classical scholar and friend of Symonds   Masaccio] the 'portrait of a young man' is now attributed to Botticelli.   φωνοῦντα ουνετοῖσιν] speaking to an understanding audience.   Mariana in the moated grange] a poem by Tennyson based on *Measure for Measure*.   Jean Paul Richter] 'Jean Paul' (1763–1825), German novelist; the planetary flight referred to is in his *Life of Quintus Fixlein*.   Huxley] T. H. Huxley (1825–95), exponent of Darwin's evolutionism. Brown] Sir Thomas Browne (1605–82), author of *Religio Medici* (1635).   Comte] Auguste Comte (1798–1857), founder of Positivism, very influential at the time.   Grote] George Grote (1794–1871), historian and philosopher.   Worsley] P. S. Worsley translated Homer into Spenserian stanzas.   This letter ends with technical discussion of Greek words for colours etc.

Joseph Upher

On 28 Apr. 1863, at the age of 15, Upher signed on as an apprentice seaman for three years, at a premium of £50. He sailed on 30 Apr. from Plymouth. On 15 Oct. 1864 he wrote to his parents to say he had run from his ship, having been bullied by a big fellow who was to be third mate on the return journey. He went to work in the Australian interior, and later went to the gold diggings. A letter home in 1874 is the last heard of him.

210. To his parents, 1 February 1868

My dear Father and Mother,

I hope you will forgive me for not writing since last Sept, but I have not been in any settled spot lately. I suppose you will be surprised to hear I am in Queensland now, but the wages are so low in the Sydney side, that one could never save much money there. I started from the Lachlan R. in Sept & came right over to Queensland about 1200 mls, in 6 wks. There are not many horses at home, that could do that on grass. At present I'm shepherding, at £1 wk. The blacks are not to be trusted here, although they are not what you can call bad, but 200 or 300 mls higher up to the north they will devour you alive. The government has a whole lot of black troopers stationed about the country, with a white sergeant over them, & as soon as the blacks begin to kill whites, the troopers scour the country & shoot them down in droves, women and children too, so they manage to keep them pretty well frightened. Prince Alfred has arrived & is visiting the different colonies, he is now in Sydney, & the people are making a great deal of him. I read in the paper the other day, that Captain Philips who had the Young Australia died on board the John Duthie a week before she arrived in Sydney. Some new diggings are going ahead first rate at Maryborough, Queensland, about 300 mls from where I am, there are above 20,000 diggers working on them & some are making small fortunes. I am sorry I cant go to them, for I am booked for 6 months, but if there are any good accounts from them bye & bye, I think I shall try my luck as I've tried almost every thing except digging. A great many of the squatters are trying to save money by importing South Sea Islanders, they can get them for 6£ a year for 7 yrs. It begins to look very like slavery for there are reports getting about that they are beginning to flood [flog?] them. At the next station to where I'm at, they have got 40 of them, they are trying to make shepherds of them 6 men to a flock of 2000 sheep, but they are a regular failure, they'd lose all the sheep in the country. They eat 3 times as much as a white man and that is no joke when you have sometimes to pay 2s a pound for flour. It is terrible hot up here from Dec to March about a week ago it was 116 deg. in the shade & that I'm sure is too hot for any European to stand comfortably. I am rather troubled at present with sore eyes, the flies are a regular pest to everyone, you are obliged to wear a veil constantly. All the grass is dried up and a match will set the whole country in a blaze, but it is not here as in Victoria, for the grass is not thought so much of as there is no water so it is no good to a great many squatters. I suppose you are still living at Bedford & are in good health. Hoping you will write the first mail & tell me all the home news & send an old newspaper, then I will hear from you before I leave this place for the diggings.

With kind love to all of you at home & hoping you will all send me a letter each

I remain | Your affectionate Son
Joseph

WILLIAM JAMES
(1842–1910)

The distinguished psychologist and 'Pragmatist' philosopher, whose works include *The Principles of Psychology* (1890) and *The Varieties of Religious Experience* (1902), James was the son of an extraordinary father, and elder brother of two more people of genius, Henry (1843–1916) and Alice (1848–92).

211. To Alice James, 4 June 1868

James had interrupted his medical studies for health reasons and spent eighteen months in Germany learning the language. He returned in the autumn of 1868.

Beloved Sisterkin,—

I take my pen in hand to waft you my love across the jumping waves of the Atlantic, and to express a hope that you are better. . . . Ever since I have been here I have been the object of motherly attentions from all classes of the population, which I might have sought during a long life in the U.S. and never found away from my own hearth. They are a queer race in the abundance and homeliness of their kindness. . . . We at home value people for what they have of productive and positive about them,—and try at most to enjoy them by *abstracting* our attention from their personal defects and unpleasantness. The Germans, 'enthused' by the perception of some scrap of a good quality, proceed to stir the whole personality of its possessor up with it, making a kind of indistinguishable broth in which they take a sort of unnatural delight, half-ridiculous, half-offensive, to one

of our more fastidious race. The gum-boil or the deficient teeth of a hero
are thought of with the same romantic affection as his more strictly heroic
'points'. This want of what we call 'fastidiousness' which leads to refinement of various kinds, spreads all through the German character. . . .

(I was interrupted at this point by dinner, and am just back.) . . . To
return to the previous subject, here is an example of the German con-
founding of everything in a broth of sentiment, though it may seem to you
at first sight to belong to a different order of facts. When we got our
strawberries I proceeded to eat them in the usual manner—when I was
startled by a sudden cry from [Fräulein von] Bose: 'Ach! schmecken die
Erdbeeren so *wun*derschön!' I looked at her,—her eyes were closed, and
she seemed to be in a sort of mystic rapture. She had been smashing her
strawberries with her spoon so that they made a sort of pulp on her plate
with the cream. I replied: 'Ja, wunderschön'; but was rebuked by Mme.
Spangenberg for leaving the berries whole on my plate, for when crushed,
'Sie schmecken *so* viel schöner!' The *attendrissement* of the expression with
which the words were pronounced was the *peculiarly* German part of the
occurrence, and that I can't convey to you in writing. It implied a sort of
religious melting of the whole emotional nature in this one small experience of the sense of taste. The washing out of all boundary lines is implied
in the application of the word *wunderschön* to such an experience. It is
employed continually to describe articles of diet and always with an into-
nation that denotes that the speaker is swimming in sentiment: 'Der
Kalbsbraten ist aber *wun*derschön!!! Ach!!!' And up go the eyes to heaven.
And in the same way when the Germans do what they call *Partie-machen*
(that is go out on holidays in the country, and sit for hours over beer and
coffee at little tables, in leafy places if possible) they remain speechless and
apparently vacant-minded most of the time, but at intervals say with enthusiasm: 'Ach! ist es doch hier *wun*derschön zu sitzen!!!' . . . The sluices
of a German's wonder and affection are ever trembling to be unlocked. The
slightest touch sets the flood in motion and when it is once going, the
creature abandons himself to the sentiment and cares very little about its
original exciting cause.

They lack the sense of form throughout. Take, for instance, the word
Kunst or Art. It has a magic effect on Germans which we are quite incapable of conceiving. They write poems about it, couple it with religion and
virtue as one of the sacred things in human life,—lose, in short, their
critical power when thinking of it, just as we do when thinking of morality,
for instance. But (except, perhaps, in music) they produce no works of art
good for anything, nor do I believe that as a rule those who are most struck
by the divinity of *Kunst* in the abstract, have the power of discriminative
appreciation thereof in the concrete. The tender emotion carries their

sagacity and judgment off its legs. They believe that the mission of art is to represent or create in anticipation a regenerate world, and over every so-called work of art, however contemptible, they are apt to cast the halo which belongs to the generic idea, and to accept it without criticizing. . . .

Heaven forbid that I should seriously find fault with a characteristic so amiable and beneficent as this soft-heartedness of the Germans. Only I am born elsewhere, and whereas they would find us Americans cold, thin, dry, and often prudish and hypocritical, I find in them a sloppiness of temper which suggests a surfeit to me before I have fairly begun to taste the sweets of their companionship. I have been the object of more advice and curiosity and sympathy about my health since I've been here, from my different landladies, servant girls, and lady acquaintances, than would found several hospitals at home; and strange to say, instead of placating me, it rouses my scorn both for my dorsal infirmity and for the poor deluded beings who can see anything touching and 'interesting' in it. How much more pleasing to *this* heart is a good insolent American girl (like yourself), who by her unconcealed repugnance of everything unhealthy about you, and ill-feigned contempt of your person generally, goads you and spurs you to desperate exertions of manliness to keep your head above water at all and in the air of her mere courtesy. . . . Ever your affectionate brother

W. J.

Ach . . . wunderschön] ah, the strawberries are so delicious.   Sie . . . schöner] they taste so much better.   Der kalbsbraten . . . wunderschön] the roast veal is superb.   Ach . . . sitzen] it's wonderful to be sitting here.

212. *To Henry James, Sr., 14 December 1882*

> James was in Paris attending Charcot's famous clinics at the Salpétrière mental hospital, when news of his father's illness decided him to stay at Henry's London home, while Henry took ship for New York. His father died on 19 Dec. This letter arrived on the 30th, and on the 31st Henry read it aloud before his father's grave.

Darling old Father,

Two letters, one from my Alice last night, and one from Aunt Kate to Harry just now, have somewhat dispelled the mystery in which the tele-grams left your condition; and although their news is several days earlier than the telegrams, I am free to suppose that the latter report only an aggravation of the symptoms the letters describe. It is far more agreeable to think of this than of some dreadful unknown and sudden malady.

We have been so long accustomed to the hypothesis of your being taken away from us, especially during the past ten months, that the thought that this may be your last illness conveys no very sudden shock. You are old enough, you've given your message to the world in many ways and will not be forgotten; you are here left alone, and on the other side, let us hope and pray, dear, dear old Mother is waiting for you to join her. If you go, it will not be an inharmonious thing. Only, if you are still in possession of your normal consciousness, I should like to see you once again before we part. I stayed here only in obedience to the last telegram, and am waiting now for Harry—who knows, the exact state of my mind, and who will know yours— to telegraph again what I shall do. Meanwhile, my blessed old Father, I scribble this line (which may reach you though I should come too late), just to tell you how full of the tenderest memories and feelings about you my heart has for the last few days been filled. In that mysterious gulf of the past into which the present soon will fall and go back and back, yours is still for me the central figure. All my intellectual life I derive from you; and though we have often seemed at odds in the expression thereof, I'm sure there's a harmony somewhere, and that our strivings will combine. What my debt to you is goes beyond all my power of estimating,—so early, so penetrating and so constant has been the influence. You need be in no anxiety about your literary remains. I will see them well taken care of, and that your words shall not suffer for being concealed. At Paris I heard that Milsand, whose name you may remember in the 'Revue des Deux Mondes' and elsewhere, was an admirer of the 'Secret of Swedenborg', and Hodgson told me your last book had deeply impressed him. So will it be; especially, I think, if a collection of *extracts* from your various writings were pub- lished, after the manner of the extracts from Carlyle, Ruskin, & Co. I have long thought such a volume would be the best monument to you.—As for us; we shall live on each in his way,—feeling somewhat unprotected, old as we are, for the absence of the parental bosoms as a refuge, but holding fast together in that common sacred memory. We will stand by each other and by Alice, try to transmit the torch in our offspring as you did in us, and when the time comes for being gathered in, I pray we may, if not all, some at least, be as ripe as you. As for myself, I know what trouble I've given you at various times through my peculiarities; and as my own boys grow up, I shall learn more and more of the kind of trial you had to overcome in superintending the development of a creature different from yourself, for whom you felt responsible. I say this merely to show how my *sympathy* with you is likely to grow much livelier, rather than to fade—and not for the sake of regrets.—As for the other side, and Mother, and our all possibly meeting, I *can't* say anything. More than ever at this moment do I feel that if that *were* true, all would be solved and justified. And it comes strangely over me in bidding you good-bye how a life is but a day and expresses mainly but a single note. It is so much like the act of bidding an ordinary good-night. Good-night, my sacred old Father! If I don't see you again— Farewell! a blessed farewell!

Your
William

213. To Alice James, 6 July 1891

Alice James, an inveterate invalid, was relieved when her breast cancer was diagnosed.

Dearest Alice,

. . . Of course if the tumor should turn out to be cancerous that means, as all men know, a finite length of days; and then, good-bye to neurasthenia and neuralgia and headache, and weariness and palpitation and disgust all at one stroke—I should think you would be reconciled to the prospect with all its pluses and minuses! I know you've never cared for life, and to me, now at the age of nearly fifty, life and death seem singularly close together in all of us—and life a mere farce of frustration in all, so far as the realization of the innermost ideals go to which we are made respectively capable of feeling an affinity and responding. Your frustrations are only rather more flagrant than the rule; and you've been saved many forms of self-dissatisfaction and misery which appertain to such a multiplication of responsible relations to different people as I, for instance, have got into. Your fortitude, good spirits and unsentimentality have been simply unexampled in the midst of your physical woes; and when you're relieved from your post, just *that* bright note will remain behind, together with the inscrutable and mysterious character of the doom of nervous weakness which has chained you down for all these years. As for that, there's more in it than has ever been told to so-called science. These inhibitions, these split-up selves, all these new facts that are gradually coming to light about our organization, these enlargements of the self in trance, etc., are bringing me to turn for light in the direction of all sorts of despised spiritualistic and unscientific ideas. Father would find in me today a much more receptive listener—all *that* philosophy has got to be brought in. And what a queer contradiction comes to the ordinary scientific argument against immortality (based on body being mind's condition and mind going *out* when body is gone), when one must believe (as now, in these neurotic cases) that some infernality in the body *prevents* really existing parts of the mind from coming to their effective rights at all, suppresses them, and blots them out from participation in this world's experiences, although they are *there* all the time. When that which is *you* passes out of the body, I am sure there will be an explosion of liberated force and life till then eclipsed and kept down. I can hardly imagine *your* transition without a great oscillation of both 'worlds' as they regain their new equilibrium after the change! Everyone will feel the shock, but you yourself will be more surprised than anybody else.

It may seem odd for me to talk to you in this cool way about your end; but, my dear little sister, if one has things present to one's mind, and I know they are present enough to *your* mind, why not speak them out? I am sure you appreciate that best. How many times I have thought, in the past year, when my days were so full of strong and varied impression and activities, of the long unchanging hours in bed which those days stood for with you, and wondered how you bore the slow-paced monotony at all, as you did! You can't tell how I've pitied you. But you *shall* come to your rights erelong. Meanwhile take things gently. Look for the little good in each day as if life were to last a hundred years. Above all things, save yourself from bodily pain, if it can be done. You've had too much of that. Take all the morphia (or other forms of opium if that disagrees) you want, and don't be afraid of becoming an opium-drunkard. What was opium created for except for such times as this? Beg the good Katharine (to whom *our* debt can never be extinguished) to write me a line every week, just to keep the currents flowing, and so farewell until I write again.

Your ever loving,
WJ

214. Alice James to William James, 30 July 1891

Dictated to her devoted friend Katharine Loring. On 5 Mar. 1892 Alice cabled William to announce her imminent death; she died on the following day.

My dearest William,

A thousand thanks for your beautiful & fraternal letter, which came, I know not when, owing to Katharine's iron despotism. Of course I could have wanted nothing else and should have felt, notwithstanding my 'unsentimentality' very much wounded & incomprise, had you walked round & not up to my demise.

It is the most supremely interesting moment in life, the only one in fact, when living seems life, and I count it as the greatest good fortune to have these few months so full of interest & instruction in the knowledge of my approaching death. It is as simple in one's own person as any fact of nature, the fall of a leaf or the blooming of a rose, & I have a delicious consciousness, ever present, of wide spaces close at hand, & whisperings of release in the air.

Your philosophy of the transition is entirely mine & at this remoteness I will venture upon the impertinence of congratulating you upon having arrived 'at nearly fifty' at the point at which I started at fifteen!—'Twas always thus of old, but in time, you usually, as now, caught up.

But you must believe that you greatly exaggerate the tragic element in my commonplace little journey; & so far from ever having thought that 'my frustrations were more flagrant than the rule', I have always simmered complacently in my complete immunity therefrom. As from early days the elusive nature of concrete hopes shone forth, I always rejoiced that my temperament had set for my task the attainment of the simplest rudimentary ideal, which I could carry about in my pocket & work away upon equally in shower as in sunshine, in complete security from the grotesque obstructions supposed to be *life*, which have indeed, only strengthened the sinews to whatever imperfect accomplishment I may have attained.

You must also remember that a woman, by nature, needs much less to feed upon than a man, a few emotions & she is satisfied: so when I am gone, pray don't think of me simply as a creature who might have been something else had neurotic science been born; notwithstanding the poverty of my outside experience I have always had a significance for myself, & every chance to stumble along my straight & narrow little path, & to worship at the feet of my Deity, & what more can a human soul ask for?

This year has been one of the happiest I have ever known, surrounded by such affection & devotion, but I won't enter into details, as I see the blush mantle the elderly cheek of my scribe, already—We are smothered in flowers from kind friends: Annie Richards has been perfect in her constant & considerate friendship, that you must remember in the years to come, her atrophied cousin of Basset is *incroyable*!

You can't imagine the inspiring effect of Baldwin, from amid your surroundings.

Ansonia, Conn., *pur sang*! emitting a theory about you from every pore, grasping you as a whole, instead of as a stomach or a dislocated elbow, after the fashion of the comatose creature sicklied o'er with bed-side manner, manufactured by the wholesale here. The soothing nature of his imaginative manipulations after the succession of bruises administered by the anchylosed joints to which I have been exposed of late years, has been most restorative.

Give much love to Alice & to all the household, great & small.

Be sure, please, to give my love to Henrietta Child & to thank her for her sweet & pretty letter, & my love to Mrs Child, too.

Your always loving & grateful sister
Alice James

P.S. I have many excellent & kind letters, but the universal tendency 'to be reconciled' to my passing to the summer land, might cause confusion in the mind of the uninitiated!

Atrophied cousin of Basset] Sara Sedgwick Darwin.   Baldwin] W. W. Baldwin, a physician.

215. To Alexander James, 28 August 1898

James sends to his small son Alexander a photograph of a boy and girl standing on a rock above the Yosemite Valley.

Darling old Cherubini,

See how brave this girl and boy are in the Yosemite Valley! I saw a moving sight the other morning before breakfast in a little hotel where I slept in the dusty fields. The young man of the house had shot a little wolf

called a coyote in the early morning. The heroic little animal lay on the
ground, with his big furry ears, and his clean white teeth, and his jolly
cheerful little body, but his brave little life was gone. It made me think how
brave all these living things are. Here little coyote was, without any clothes
or house or books or anything, with nothing but his own naked self to pay
his way with, and risking his life so cheerfully—and losing it—just to see
if he could pick up a meal near the hotel. He was doing his coyote-business
like a hero, and you must do your boy-business, and I my man-business
bravely too, or else we won't be worth as much as that little coyote. Your
mother can find a picture of him in those green books of animals, and I
want you to copy it.

Your loving
Dad

216. To Henry James and William James, Jr., 9 May 1906

William was James's eldest son. Earthquake and fire devastated San Francisco
18–20 Apr. 1906.

Dearest Brother and Son,

Your cablegram of response was duly received, and we have been also
'joyous' in the thought of your being together. I knew, of course, Henry,
that you would be solicitous about us in the earthquake, but did n't reckon
at all on the extremity of your anguish as evinced by your frequent cable-
grams home, and finally by the letter to Harry which arrived a couple of
days ago and told how you were unable to settle down to any other occupation, the thought of our mangled forms, hollow eyes, starving bodies,
minds insane with fear, haunting you so. We never reckoned on this extremity of anxiety on your part, I say, and so never thought of cabling you
direct, as we might well have done from Oakland on the day we left,
namely April 27th. I much regret this callousness on our part. For *all* the
anguish was yours; and in general this experience only rubs in what I have
always known, that in battles, sieges and other great calamities, the pathos
and agony is in general solely felt by those at a distance; and although
physical pain is suffered most by its immediate victims, those at the *scene
of action* have no *sentimental* suffering whatever. Everyone at San Francisco
seemed in a good hearty frame of mind; there was work for every moment
of the day and a kind of uplift in the sense of a 'common lot' that took away
the sense of loneliness that (I imagine) gives the sharpest edge to the more
usual kind of misfortune that may befall a man. But it was a queer sight, on
our journey through the City on the 26th (eight days after the disaster), to
see the inmates of the houses of the quarter left standing, all cooking their
dinners at little brick camp-fires in the middle of the streets, the chimneys

being condemned. If such a disaster had to happen, somehow it could n't have chosen a better place than San Francisco (where everyone knew about camping, and was familiar with the creation of civilizations out of the bare ground), and at five-thirty in the morning, when few fires were lighted and everyone, after a good sleep, was in bed. Later, there would have been great loss of life in the streets, and the more numerous foci of conflagration would have burned the city in one day instead of four, and made things vastly worse.

In general you may be sure that when any disaster befalls our country it will be *you* only who are wringing of hands, and we who are smiling with 'interest or laughing with gleeful excitement'. I did n't hear one pathetic word uttered at the scene of disaster, though of course the crop of 'nervous wrecks' is very likely to come in a month or so.

Although we have been home six days, such has been the stream of broken occupations, people to see, and small urgent jobs to attend to, that I have written no letter till now. Today, one sees more clearly and begins to rest. 'Home' looks extraordinarily pleasant, and though damp and chilly, it is the divine budding moment of the year. Not, however, the lustrous light and sky of Stanford University. . . .

I have just read your paper on Boston in the 'North American Review'. I am glad you threw away the scabbard and made your critical remarks so straight. What you say about 'pay' here being the easily won 'salve' for privations, in view of which we cease to 'mind' them, is as true as it is strikingly pat. *Les intellectuels*, wedged between the millionaires and the handworkers, are the really pinched class here. They feel the frustrations and they can't get the salve. *My* attainment of so much pay in the past few years brings home to me what an all-benumbing salve it is. That whole article is of your best. We long to hear from W., Jr. No word yet.

Your ever loving,
W. J.

CHARLES ELIOT NORTON
(1827–1906)

Norton, a distinguished American professor, met Ruskin (see above, Letters 185–8) in 1855, when he went to see the Turners in Ruskin's collection at Denmark Hill. Despite some vicissitudes, caused by Ruskin's cool attitude to the Northern cause in the Civil War, the friendship was very close, and survived Ruskin's difficult final decade.

217. To John Ruskin, 15 June 1870

My dearest Ruskin,

It was a great comfort to me to get your letter last night, with its fairly good news of you. It came to me at the end of the day that had been saddened by the news of Dickens's death. What a loss to mankind,—the man who has done most in his time to make the hearts of men cheerful & kindly, and to draw them together in sympathy & goodwill,—the passionate lover and devoted servant of men with such powers of service as no other had! His death takes more from the world than any other death could take. Never has a man been mourned with such wide spread affection,—& never has a man better deserved the affection of his fellows. Happy to die so loved, in the fulness of power, by a sudden stroke! But what a loss to us all!

But the pang which comes with the news is not so much of personal sorrow as of grief for the household which his death renders desolate. We have known them so well, & love them so truly that their grief is a grief to us.

Just at this time England can ill spare such a leader in the uncertain battle in which you & all other humane & thoughtful & patriotic men are engaged. The prospect of the field, dark enough before, grows visibly darker, with the loss of one who so long had been among the foremost in the struggle. Dickens took the most serious view of the conditions of society in England. The last long talk I had with him was very striking from the display of his clear, strong, masculine sense as to the nature of the evils that are imperilling the foundations of the state, and as to the remedies for them,—combined with an almost tragic intensity of feeling, & prophetic vigor of expression. We were waiting for a train, and as we walked up & down the platform, he seemed so strong & likely to live long, that I thought of him as almost certain to come to the fore in case of any sudden terrible overflow of the ignorance, misery & recklessness which the selfishness of the upper classes has fostered, & which now, as Dickens believed, are far more threatening to those classes than they seem to have the power of conceiving. 'If the storm once sets in it will be nothing short of a tornado, & will sweep down old fences'.

He would have read your Inaugural with the deepest interest.

Thank you for sending it to me, & for the other sheets. I have been reading it this morning, & my imagination is not vigorous enough to see how you could have done anything much better. It is a very noble & a very full introduction to the teaching of the Fine Arts in the University. With what seems to me a too narrow patriotism I should quarrel. I believe it better, a higher ideal, to endeavour to make one's nation only *prima inter pares*, & not to encourage that spirit of jealous superiority which has been, as I read history, the curse of Greece & England alike. Make England beautiful & strong, but believe that she can be neither beautiful nor strong, unless side by side with her the other civilized powers & countries grow beautiful & strong also. England cannot be selfishly saved.—But what a perverse spirit I am to find fault, where mainly I admired with no stinted admiration, and learned, as I read, to be humble. Your scheme of instruction, and your generous execution of it, ought to be of the utmost service not only to the students who may attend your lectures, but in raising the level of general instruction at Oxford, and stimulating all good culture. I rejoice for you, and I am glad for Oxford that you are filling this post.

And now for plans. I want you very much to come here, not only because I want to see you, but because I think you would like to see this landscape that surrounds us, & because there is much in Siena which would be serviceable to you as illustration & example in your Oxford courses. The remains of Italian gothic building both public & domestic are more numerous than in any city south of Verona; and the use of brick in the Renaissance buildings (especially by Peruzzi) is instructive & often delightful in the highest degree. There are brick dwelling houses here which are charming both in proportion & adornment, and which are as cheap as charming. They could be built cheaply in England or America today, & would be both suitable to our needs & beautiful in themselves. There is much else to see. The air here is dry & clear, of a delicate quality, and cool. The beauty of this part of Italy in summer is marvellous. There are neither mosquitoes nor Americans except ourselves. We are in a great big rectangular Villa, beautifully situated, about a mile & a half from the city. You shall have a quiet study. There is a room for Crawley if you like to bring him,—and if Miss Joan would come with you we should be truly delighted to see her.—Come soon, before it becomes too hot to travel with comfort. Perhaps I might meet you at Florence, and we could see the lately uncovered Giottos, & some few other pictures together.

I want very much to see you. There are many things I want to say to you.

Ever Your loving
C. E. N.

Yes, you long ago taught me that 'there *is* none like him,—none', and since then I learned it from himself.

The Sodomas here are worth seeing. There are Luinesque touches in them; one figure is among the most beautiful the school produced.—The Geology too is interesting. Don't say *no* to my request to you to come. This is one of the very few years that we shall be in the same hemisphere,—let us not lose their offered good. I would not urge you merely for pleasure's sake, but for love's I will.

Dickens] died 9 June. Norton had met him in 1855.   Inaugural] Ruskin was appointed
Slade Professor of Fine Art at Oxford in 1870.   Peruzzi] Baldassare Peruzzi (1481–1536),
a Sienese painter and architect.   Crawley] Ruskin's manservant.   Miss Joan] Joan
Severn, a cousin who looked after Ruskin.   Giottos] frescoes found under whitewash in the
church of Santa Croce and recovered by 1863.   Sodomas] Sodoma was Giovanni Antonio
Bazzi (1477–1549) of the Sienese school.

James Thomson

(1834–1882)

Thomson was a Scottish poet, the author (as 'B.V.') of *The City of Dreadful Night*
(1880). A drunkard, insomniac, and pessimist, he had moments of cheerfulness, as
here. He was a friend of Charles Bradlaugh, the propagandist of atheism, who was
responsible for the publication of *The City of Dreadful Night*, and of his daughter
Hypatia, who later wrote her father's biography.

218. To Hypatia Bradlaugh, 5 July 1871

My dear Hypatia,

This is exactly how the case stood, to the best of my recollection. Yourself, Alice, and I, with two or three more who were very vague people and
apt to change into other persons, had been roaming about for a long day in
a country place something like Jersey. We had dinner at an inn, and were
very jolly. Roaming farther, I found myself upon the top of a sandy sort of
a cliff looking down upon a sandy beach, and you girls just pulling to land
in a boat. You were nearly touching land among a group of boatmen when
your boat settled quietly down by the stern, and I saw your heads go
quietly under water. I cried out, 'The girls are in the water!'; but saw the
boatman pulling you out. I wanted to get to you, but couldn't attempt to
run down the cliff. Presently, however, a tall guardsman stepped lightly
down on business of his own, and his example gave me courage. I found it
as easy to run down a concave slope as a fly finds it to walk on the ceiling.
When I reached the shore, you and Alice and another girl were all nestled
rosy and cosy in a kind of caboose or bathing machine, muffled or sunk up
to your necks in a heap of boatman's guernseys or some such garments.
You said that you were none the worse for your ducking save a few bruises.
I said that you must have something to restore you. You all agreed to this;
and one proposed dinner with ale (although we had just had a dinner
before), another tea. It was resolved that you should have a meat tea, and
I went off to be your waiter. I went up by an easy path to the inn, and
entered a room. I found a pale tall old-fashioned semi-genteel lady there,
dressed and with her bonnet on, and I said: 'Can you serve—'. She cut me

short in a very mild and cutting manner, saying: 'If you want to be served, the servant is in the next room. *I* am a teetotaller, Sir, and don't serve'. Here she opened the door, and said to the girl in the next room: 'Serve this gentleman, and give him a copy of the *Independent*' (which I understood to be a teetotal publication). 'Well,' said I, 'ma'am, it seems funny to me that you should boast of your teetotalism and yet keep a public-house'; for I was rather nettled by her ways. The girl nudged my elbow from behind as a hint to go on with my scolding; the mistress spit fire at the girl for liking to see her insulted. I then told Mary that I only wanted to be served with tea, a good meat tea for three or four, when I heard a knock at the door and a voice crying out cruelly: 'It is quite eight o'clock, Sir; eight o'clock. Are you sure you are awake?' So I had to leave you there in the caboose or bathing-machine, buried in guernseys waiting for your dinner-tea; and had to be awake and get up myself. Was it not a sad case? I hope you won't starve. I hope all the people at home won't suffer too much from anxiety.

This remarkable adventure of ours this morning put me in mind that I have not written to you for an age. So I resolved to write this very day.

How are you enjoying this delightful summer? Are your chilblains very bad? Do you often slide on the pond? Or is the country all one pond, and do you go to school by boat? I had to get up this morning and throw coats on my bed, being awakened by the cold. It is raining this moment as hard as it can, and has been raining for I don't know how many days. June chilled us to the bone, July is drowning us.

When Mr Grant last wrote me, he had been foolish enough to get up early to work in his garden, and had just managed to lose his purse with more than £2 in it. That was a nice fat worm for some other early bird. Moral: Never get up early if you can help it, and never have two pounds in your purse.

As I am sure to be interrupted again in a few minutes (for I am really writing this at the office, in spite of the humbugging heading), I may as well finish it up while I can.

I hope you will let me hear from you soon, if only to tell me whether you suffered much from your dip, what sort of a tea you were served with, and how you got out of the caboose and home.

Love to all and best wishes.

Yours affectionately,
James Thomson

MARK TWAIN (1835–1910) AND
WILLIAM DEAN HOWELLS (1837–1920)

Samuel Langhorne Clemens adopted the pseudonym Mark Twain when, in 1862, he launched his writing career, initially as a journalistic humorist. His friendship with Howells—novelist, critic, editor, traveller—was lifelong.

219. Mark Twain to W. D. Howells, 15 June 1872

Friend Howells—

Could you tell me how I could get a copy of your portrait as published in Hearth & Home? I hear so much talk about it as being among the finest works of art which have yet appeared in that journal, that I feel a strong desire to see it. Is it suitable for framing? I have written the publishers of H & H time & again, but they say that the demand for the portrait immediately exhausted the edition & now a copy cannot be had, even for the European demand, which has now begun. Bret Harte has been here, & says his family would not be without that portrait for any consideration. He says his children get up in the night & yell for it. I would give anything for a copy of that portrait to put up in my parlor. I have Oliver Wendell Holmes's & Bret Harte's, as published in Every Saturday, & of all the swarms that come every day to gaze upon them none go away that are not softened & humbled & made more resigned to the will of God. If I had yours to put up alongside of them, I believe the combination would bring more souls to earnest reflection & ultimate conviction of their lost condition, than any other kind of warning would. Where in the nation *can* I get that portrait? Here are heaps of people that want it,—that *need* it. There is my uncle. *He* wants a copy. He is lying at the point of death. He has *been* lying at the point of death for two years. He wants a copy—& I want him to *have* a copy. And I want you to send a copy to the man that shot my dog. I want to see if he is dead to Every human instinct.

Now you send me that portrait. I am sending you mine, in this letter; & am glad to do it, for it has been greatly admired. People who are judges of art, find in the execution a grandeur which has not been equalled in this country, & an expression which has not been approached in *any*.

Ys Truly

S. L. Clemens

P.S.—62,000 copies of Roughing It sold & delivered in 4 months.

Portrait] the 30 Mar. issue of *Hearth and Home* included an article on Howells, and bore a crude portrait of him on the cover.   Bret Harte] (1836–1902), author of *The Luck of Roaring Camp* (1870) and at this time a friendly rival of Mark Twain's.   Holmes] (1809–94), author of *The Autocrat of the Breakfast-Table* (1860) and other books.   In this letter] Twain included a bad picture of himself clipped from the Salt Lake City *Tribune.*

220. *Mark Twain to W. D. Howells, 18 May 1880*

My Dear Howells—

I know you hate Clubs—at least they are an unpleasant suggestion to you, & doubtless they are borous to you—still I have been urged to ask you to consent to join a Club—the easiest way to disburden myself of the matter is to unload it onto you & leave you to consent or refuse, as shall seem best. I wish to hold myself purely neutral & say nothing to influence you one way or the other. The Club would be proud to have your name; that goes without saying; the membership is consonant with yourself, for it is refined, cultured, more than ordinarily talented, & of exceptionally high character. These facts are in its favor; but I think I ought not to conceal a fact of another sort—one which I must ask you to treat as confidential: the intent of the Club is, by superior weight, character & influence to impair & eventually destroy the influence of [illegible]—not from any base feeling, but from a belief that this is a thing required in the interest of the public good. The name of the new organization is peculiar—The Modest Club— & the first & main qualification for membership is modesty. At present, I am the only member; & as the modesty required must be of a quite aggravated type, the enterprize did seem for a time doomed to stop dead still with myself, for lack of further material; but upon reflection I have come to the conclusion that you are eligible.—Therefore I have held a meeting & voted to offer you the distinction of membership. I do not know that we can find any others, though I have had some thought of Hay, Warner, Twichell, Aldrich, Osgood, Fields, Higginson, & a few more— together with Mrs Howells, Mrs Clemens, & certain others of the sex.

But I will append the 'Laws,' & you just drop me a line & say whether you & Mrs Howells would care to belong—& John Hay. I have long felt that there ought to be an organized gang *of our kind.*

Yrs Ever
Mark

LAWS

The organization shall sue & be sued, persecute & be persecuted, & eat, drink, & be merry, under the name & style, of THE MODEST CLUB of the United States of America.

OVER.

The object of the Club shall be, to eat & talk.

over again.

Qualification for membership shall be, aggravated modesty, unobtrusive-ness, native humility; learning, talent, intelligence; and unassailable character.

Both sexes admitted.

Two adverse votes shall destroy the applicant.

Any member may call a meeting, when & where he or she may choose.

Two members shall constitute a quorum; & a meeting thus inaugurated shall be competent to eat & talk.

There shall be no fees or dues. There shall be no regular place of meeting.

There Shall be no [permanent] officers, except a President; & any member who has anything to eat & talk about, may constitute himself President for the time being, & call in any member or members he pleases, to help him devour & expatiate.

At all Club gatherings the membership shall wear the official symbol of the order, a single violet.

Any brother or sister of the order finding a brother or sister in imminent deadly peril, shall forsake his own concerns, no matter at what cost, & call the police.

Any member knowing anything scandalous about himself, shall immediately inform the Club, so that they may call a meeting & have the first chance to talk about it.

Any member who shall

[Illegible]] the editors say that the 'illegible' word was 'Bret Harte', and that the cancellation was probably made by Howells. The letter is unfinished.

221. W. D. Howells to Mark Twain, 23 May 1880

My dear Clemens,

The only reason I have for not joining the Modest Club is that I am too modest: that is, I am afraid that I am not modest enough. If I could ever get over this difficulty, I should like to join, for I approve highly of the Club and its objects: it is calculated to do a great deal of good, and it ought to be given an annual dinner at the public expense. If *you* think I am not too modest, you may put my name down, and I will try to think the same of you. Mrs Howells applauded the notion of the Club from the very first. She said she knew *one* thing: that *she* was modest enough, *any* way. Her manner of saying it implied that the other persons you had named were not, and created a painful impression in my mind.—I have sent your letter and the rules to Hay. But I doubt his modesty; he will think he has a *right* to belong as much as you or I; whereas other people ought only to be admitted on sufferance.—We had a magnificent time in Washington, and were six days at the White House. I wish you could have come on, as you intended, but as your friend advised, I suppose it would have been useless as far as copy right is concerned. I spoke about international copyright treaty to the President, one day, and he said that the administration would be willing to act if the authors and publishers would agree among themselves on some basis. Now, could they not agree on this basis: Englishmen to have copyright if they have an American publisher, and Americans, vice versa. Our publishers would never agree to anything else, and this would secure us our rights. If some such house as Harpers would send this proposition to all the authors and decent publishers for signature, I believe that it would be universally signed, and that if presented as a memorial to the State Department, it would before this administration goes out, become a treaty. I am going to write to the Harpers about it.

With regards to all from all

Yours ever,
W. D. Howells

Hay] John Hay had been a private secretary to Lincoln and was, at this time, Assistant Secretary of State.　　　Harpers] the publishers Harper & Bros, had submitted a draft of a copyright treaty between the United States and Britain.

222. Mark Twain to W. D. Howells, 21 July 1885

My Dear Howells—

You are really my only author; I am restricted to you; I wouldn't give a damn for the rest. I bored through Middlemarch during the past week, with its labored & tedious analyses of feelings & motives, its paltry & tiresome people, its unexciting & uninteresting story, & its frequent blinding flashes of single-sentence poetry, philosophy, wit, & what-not, & nearly died from the over-work. I wouldn't read another of those books for a farm. I did try to read one other—Daniel Deronda. I dragged through three chapters, losing flesh all the time, & then was honest enough to quit, & confess to myself that I haven't *any* romance-literature appetite, as far as I can see, except for your books.

But what I started to say, was, that I have just read Part II of Indian Summer, & to my mind there isn't a waste-line in it, or one that could be improved. I read it yesterday, ending with that opinion; & read it again to-day, ending with the same opinion emphasized. I haven't read Part I yet, because that number must have reached Hartford after we left; but we are going to send down town for a copy, & when it comes I am to read both parts aloud to the family. It is a beautiful story, & makes a body laugh all the time, & cry inside, & feel so old & so forlorn; & gives him gracious glimpses of his lost youth that fill him with a measureless regret, & build up in him a cloudy sense of his having been a prince, once, in some enchanted far-off land, & of being in exile now, & desolate—& lord, no chance to ever get back there again! That is the thing that hurts. Well, you have done it with marvelous facility—& you make all the motives & feelings perfectly clear without analyzing the guts out of them, the way George

Eliot does. I can't stand George Eliot, & Hawthorne & those people; I see what they are at, a hundred years before they get to it, & they just tire me to death. And as for the Bostonians, I would rather be damned to John Bunyan's heaven than read that.

Yrs Ever
Mark

Indian Summer] this novel by Howells had appeared in instalments, as did Henry James's *The Bostonians* (1886). Howells was a great admirer of George Eliot, Hawthorne, and James.

223. W. D. Howells to Mark Twain, 12 February 1903

This letter is a joke or recounts a dream. Twain wrote on the envelope 'Bet Howells is drunk yet'.

My dear Clemens,

I know you are harassed by a great many things, and I hate to add to your worries, but I must really complain to you of the behavior of your man Sam. I called last night at your place with our old friend Stoddard, and found that to reach the house, I had to climb a plowed field, at the top of which Sam was planting potatoes. A number of people were waiting at the bottom of the field, and hesitating whether to go up, but I explained that we were old acquaintances, and we were going to see you at once. We pushed on, and when we came in easy hail of Sam, he called very rudely to us, and asked us what we wanted. I said we wanted to see you, and he said, 'Well, you can't do it,' and no persuasion that I could use had the least effect with him. He said that nobody could see you, and when I gave him my card, and promised him that he would not have a pleasant time with you, when you found out whom he had turned away, he sneered and said he would not give you the card. To avoid mortifying inquiries from the people we had left at the foot of the hill, we came down another way, and though I momently expected a recall from your house, none followed us, and we made our way home the best we could. This happened, as nearly as I can make out, at about three o'clock in the morning. I have only too much reason to believe that Sam really withheld my card, and I wish you would ask him for it, and make him account in some way for our extraordinary treatment. I cannot remember that Stoddard said anything, but I felt he was as much annoyed as myself.

Yours ever,
W. D. Howells

224. Mark Twain to W. D. Howells, 13 February 1903

Dear Howells—

I am infinitely sorry. I was lying awake at the time, & felt sure I heard voices; so sure, that I put on a dressing-gown & went down to inquire into the matter, but you were already gone. I encountered Sam coming up as I turned the lower corner of the house, & he said it was a stranger, who insisted on seeing me—'a stumpy little gray man with furtive ways & an evil face.'

'What did he say his name was?'

'He didn't say. He offered his card, but I didn't take it.'

'That was stupid. Describe him again—& more in detail.'

He did it.

'I can't seem to locate him—I wish you had taken the card. Why didn't you?'

'I didn't like his manners.'

'Why? What did he do?'

'He called me a quadrilateral astronomical incandescent son of a bitch.'

'Oh, that was Howells. Is *that* what annoyed you! What is the matter with it? Is that a thing to distort into an offence, when you couldn't possibly know but that he meant it as a compliment? And it *is* a compliment, too.'

'I don't think so, it only just sounds so. I am not finding any fault with the main phrase, which is hallowed to me by memories of childhood's happy days, now vanished never to return, on account of it's being my sainted mother's diminutive for me, but I did not like those adverbs. I have an aversion for adverbs. I will not take adverbs from a stranger.'

'Very well,' I said, coldly, 'such being your theology, you can get your money after breakfast, & seek another place. I know you are honest, I know you are competent, & I am sorry to part with you; you are the best gardener I have ever had, but in matters of grammar ⟨I think⟩ you are morbid, & this makes you over-sensitive & altogether too God dam particular.'

I am sorry & ashamed, Howells, & so is Clara, who is helping write this letter, with expressions she got of her mother, but the like will not happen again on this place, I can assure you.

Ys Ever
Mark

P.S. This page had to be re-written & made parlor-mentory, because I found Mrs Clemens had given orders that the letter be brought under her blue pencil before mailing. But I knew 2 of the pages would pass.

MT

'Very well,' I said, coldly, 'such being your theology, you can get your money after breakfast, & seek another place. I know you are honest, I know you are competent, & I am sorry to part with you; you are the best gardener I have ever had, but in matters of grammar you are morbid, & this makes you over sensitive & altogether too amsterdam particular.'

I am sorry & ashamed, Howells, & so are Clara & Mrs Clemens, who blame me for allowing it to happen, but the like will not happen again on this place, I can assure you.

Ys Ever
Mark

The paragraph beginning 'Very well' is struck through; the postscript explains why.   Clara]
Twain's second daughter.

225. Mark Twain to W. D. Howells, 12 June 1904

Dear Howells,

We have to sit & hold our hands & wait—in the silence & solitude of this prodigious house; wait until June 25, then we go to Naples & sail in the Prince Oscar the 28th. There is a ship 12 days earlier (but we came in that one.) I see Clara twice a day—morning- & evening-greeting—nothing more is allowed. She keeps her bed, & says nothing. She has not cried yet. I wish she could cry. Our old Katy stays near by, in the days, and Miss Lyon (secretary) sleeps in the room with her, nights. It would break Livy's heart to see Clara. We excuse ourselves from all the friends that call— though of course only intimates come. Intimates—but they are not the old old friends, the friends of the old old times when we laughed. Shall we ever laugh again? If I could only see a dog that I knew in the old times! & could put my arms around his neck & tell him all, everything, & ease my heart.

Think—in 3 hours it will be a week!—& soon a month; & by & by a year. How fast our dead fly from us.

She loved you so, & was always as pleased as a child with any notice you took of her.

Soon your wife will be with you, oh fortunate man! And John, whom mine was so fond of. The sight of him was such a delight to her. Lord, the old friends, how dear they are.

It was too pitiful, these late weeks, to see the haunting fear in her eyes, fixed wistfully upon mine, & hear her say, as pleading for denial & heartening, 'You don't think I am going to die, do you? oh, I don't want to die.' For she loved her life, & so wanted to keep it.

SLC

Solitude] Olivia Clemens had died in Florence.   John] Howells's son.

WILKIE COLLINS
(1824–1889)

Collins was the author of *The Woman in White* (1860) and *The Moonstone* (1868). He suffered from gout and opium addiction.

226. To Holman Hunt, 11 March 1873

Hunt (1827–1910) was a co-founder of the Pre-Raphaelite Brotherhood in 1848.

My dear Holman,

I was very sorry to miss you the other night, and I am vexed at not having been able to propose an evening before this for your visit with Mr Ferguson. But a recent decision in a Court of Law has declared that anybody may dramatise any of my novels or of any man's novels, without the leave of the author. Two plays on 'Man and Wife' are all ready to compete with *my* play in the country theatres—and I am obliged to make arrangements with the Bancrofts to meet this competition *instantly*—or I shall get nothing by 'Man and Wife' *as performed in the country theatres.*

Add to this that I am obliged to dramatise the novel I am now writing, *against time*—and bring it out forthwith in London—or the theatre will take *that* from me also. The result is that I must ask your indulgence and the Fergusons'—for I really don't know when I have an hour to myself in this whirl of work and worry. I only sustain it by going to bed—when I *am* at home—at nine o'clock to rest my brains.

Yours affly
W. C.

You shall hear the moment I am at leisure.

Plays] Collins's novels lent themselves to adaptation for the stage; hence these copyright problems.   Man and Wife] this novel (1870) attacked excessive athleticism and the state of the marriage laws.   The Bancrofts] Sir Squire Bancroft and his wife, successful theatrical producers.   The novel I am now writing] *The New Magdalen*; both this and *Man and Wife* were successful as plays.

227. To Holman Hunt, 8 October 1885

My dear Hunt,

There is but one reason why I don't answer your letter in person—I am rowing in the same boat with you, and my Doctor's orders send me away to Ramsgate to be patched up. *My* nerves make sketches with red hot needles under the skin of my chest—and some kind friends are reporting that my death from Angina Pectoris may be shortly expected! I too have been stethoscoped and reported weak in the heart—but no organic disease.

It is really and truly a grief to me to hear such melancholy news of you— I had hoped that you were happy healthy and idle. We have both worked too hard—And I should like to know who *doesn't* work too hard, excepting always the contemptible impostors in your Art and mine.

The three rules of life that I find the right ones, by experience, in the matter of health, are:

1. as much fresh air as possible (*I* don't get as much as I ought).

2. live well—eat light *and* nourishing food, eggs, birds, fish, sweetbreads—no heavy chops or joints. *And* find out the wine that agrees with you, and don't be afraid of it (Here, I set an excellent example!)

3. Empty your mind of your work before you go to bed—and don't let the work get in again until after breakfast the next morning (This is a serious struggle—many defeats must be encountered—but the victory may be won at last, as I can personally certify.)

One last word—and I have done preaching. If you don't find that you make better progress, under your present medical guidance, try my old friend, *F. Carr Beard, 44 Welbeck Street, Cavendish Square.* He kept Dickens alive, he kept Fechter alive, he is keeping me alive. The most capable, and the most honest, doctor I have ever known.

My best thanks (and the best thanks of my girls) for your kindness in sending the cards. They will go either today—or tomorrow, if the light gets worse today—and will see the finest work of sacred Art that modern times have produced. I shut my eyes—and see that wonderful face of the Virgin as plain as I saw it in your studio.

always affectionately yours
Wilkie Collins

I am going to Ramsgate—to what address, I am not yet sure—but all letters will be forwarded.

Fechter] Charles Albert Fechter (1824–79), French actor, playwright, and sculptor.

RANDOLPH CALDECOTT
(1846–1886)

Caldecott was a water-colour painter and illustrator, especially of children's books.

228. To William ——, 29 March 1873

My dear Will,

I never saw the University Boat Race before, and I very nearly never saw it again, as you shall hear.

So many reports of the race are written—a whole steamboat load of reporters following the race—that I may be allowed to let off a few remarks on the subject. Personal impressions literally.

The morning was very foggy in town, the sun looking like a pink wafer. I got on board a steamboat, went about a hundred yards, when the vessel moored itself to a pier to wait for the departure of the fog. So then I took train, and the train took me up the riverside. Lovely day outside town. Miles of people and carriages. Lots of good-looking girls. Scores of 'nigger' minstrels, troubadours, coco-nut and stick-throwing proprietors. Popping of champagne corks from the carriages. Hundreds of adventurous people in small boats and on river barges. Charming garden parties on pleasant lawns. Fat ladies on horseback. Swells in four-in-hand drags. Cads in cabs. Beer served through the windows of the inns. Hardy pleasureseekers seated on broken-glass-bottle-topped walls. Nimble youths swarming trees, securing places of advantage at the ends of boughs, and then falling down on to the heads of the pleased multitude. A few hand to hand contests. Much shoving. Bawling of police. Treading on toes. Upsetting of stands commanding fine views of the race. Hats off! Cheers. Here they come! There they go! Cambridge winning. Tide flows over osier beds. Happy payers of 5/- each up to their knees in water. Wash of the steamers undermines respectable elderly gentlemen taking care of their plump partners. They struggle. They slip. Down they go. Damp just below the back of the waistcoat. Strong men carry timid people on their backs through the water. Foot in a hole. All roll over together. Jeers of the populace. A rush. Several benches and forms with rows of British ratepayers slide about in the mud. Clutching of neighbours. Lurch. Splash. Over they go. Swearing. All safe to land. Plenty for the money. Not only good view of the race; but wet legs and damp clothes—some wet and muddy all over.

So much for other people. I—after the race—walked along the river bank and was soon in the closest crush and squeezingest mob in which I was ever a party—and I have been in a few. Between the water and a high

wall were a carriage road and footpath. There was a close row of unhorsed
vehicles of every description; and a swaying, surging crowd of all classes of
folks moving each way. And in addition, horsed carriages and people on
horseback trying to get along. Then did ladies scream and infants cry.
Then did protruding elbow find soft concealement in yielding waistcoat,
and tender faces unwillingly repose on manly bosoms. Corns were ground.
Bonnets said farewell to chignons. Chests had no room to sigh, lips that
seldom swore spake grunted oaths, and unknown forms were welded together and blended in sardine-like harmony. Then slid the purse and fled
the watch. (A gentleman near me lost seventy pounds.)

I found myself one while jammed up against a pony carriage driven by
a fair-haired damsel. I clutched the rail, the crowd pressed, my toes were
near the wheels, and my noble form doubled up on the wing. The vehicle
turned part round, the pony objected, and eventually the persevering crowd
made me lift the carriage off two of its wheels. The girls screamed and
raised their hands in supplication (I believe they thought that I desired to
overturn them). I managed to get away, and spying a nook under the stern
of a drag and the splashboard of a cab, I crept therein, and was joined by
others. Into this temporary haven we dragged a fair young girl from amongst
the swaying crowd and kicking horses. She shed a few tears on one man's
shoulder, and her bosom heaved so much that I dropped one or two tears
in sympathy, which refreshed me and comforted her. After some time,
when there was a little more room, she went west to look for her lost
friends, and I went east and saw her no more.

The police told me that the crush and crowd were greater than heretofore.

I enjoyed the sight of the many thousands of people; it was good fun to
watch the manner of passing away the time before the race. This was about
the best.

I noticed one young creature busily engaged in sketching the people. I mentally sketched her. Here she is—and this is the man she was sketching.

So you will observe that there is very much to be seen besides the boat race. As for that, you only see the fine fellows glide easily and beautifully past for a moment—unless you have a good place by paying for it at an extortionate rate, or by doing the civil to people whom you know that have a house on the river side.

Most people were adorned in some way with dark or light blue ribbons to shew their partizanship. Many glorious ladies were attired in blue from head to foot. I observed that the light blue predominated—not so much for the sake of good wishes to Cambridge, but because the fair creatures considered that the lighter tint suited them better. Mark the deception! Moral—it is not prudent to give persons credit for the best motives without careful and due consideration.

We—that is Wales, Albert Victor, and myself—all got home as soon as possible and felt *better after a good dinner.*

I have retired from the turf: but *Disturbance* was the only horse I fancied all along. I've seen him going. Goes very like a house.

Thank Mrs Etches and Amy for kind enquiries about my cold. My voice is now more harmonious and winning than ever. A dying swan would be ridiculous in comparison. I am all right again, thank you, and hope that Mrs Etches' cold is gone.

Say unto Amy that a magnificent portrait of me is in preparation and will be forwarded shortly, together with some remarks on the application of the language of flowers.

I hope you are all well, and with kind regards to each, remain, my dear William,

Yours faithfully,
Randolph Caldecott

P.S. 31st inst. On a review of the preceding I feel somewhat timid about sending such an effusion, although it is all true; but trust that you will make every allowance for the probably variegated state of my mind and body on Saturday evening. R. C.

Vale!

HENRY JAMES
(1843–1916)

229. To William James, 29 May 1878

James had a close but uneasy relationship with his brother, the philosopher and psychologist William James (see above, Letters 211–16). He had at the time of this letter been resident for years in London, a diner-out and a member of such clubs as the Reform.

Dear William,

You have my blessing indeed, & Miss Gibbens also; or rather Miss Gibbens particularly, as she will need it most. (I wish to pay her a compliment at your expense & to intimate that she gives more than she receives; yet I wish not to sacrifice you too much.) Your letter came to me yesterday, giving me great joy, but less surprise than you might think. In fact, I was not surprised at all, for I had been expecting to get some such news as this from you. And yet of Miss Gibbens & your attentions I had heard almost nothing—a slight mention a year ago, in a letter of mother's, which had never been repeated. The wish, perhaps, was father to the thought. I had long wished to see you married; I believe almost as much in matrimony for most other people as I believe in it little for myself—which is saying a good deal. What you say of Miss Gibbens (even after I have made due allowance for natural partiality) inflames my imagination & crowns my wishes. I have great faith in the wisdom of your choice & am prepared to believe everything good & delightful of its object. I am sure she has neither flaw nor failing. Give her then my cordial—my already fraternal—benediction. I look forward to knowing her as to one of the consolations of the future. Very soon I will write to her—in a few days. Her photograph is indispensable to me—please remember this; & also that a sketch of her from another hand than your's—father's, mother's & Alice's—would be eminently satisfactory.

This must be a very pleasant moment to you—& I envy you your ac-
tualities & futurities. May they all minister to your prosperity & nourish
your genius! I don't believe you capable of making a marriage of which one
must expect less than this. Farewell, dear brother, I will write before long
again, & meanwhile I shall welcome all contributions to an image of Miss
Gibbens.

Always yours

H. J. jr

Miss Gibbens] William became engaged to Alice Gibbens on 10 May.

230. *To William James, 1 January 1883*

> Henry James had returned to Cambridge, Mass., because of his father's illness. He
> arrived just too late for the funeral. William was on sabbatical from Harvard and
> living, not very happily, in Henry's apartments in London, where his brother wished
> him to remain. William saw the announcement of his father's death in the London
> papers. He had already written his father the moving farewell letter to which Henry
> refers (above, Letter 212).

Dear William,

I receive this a.m. your note of the 20*th*, written after you had seen the
news of Father's death in the *Standard*. I can imagine how sadly it must
have presented itself, as you sit alone in those dark, far-away rooms of
mine. But it would have been sadder still if you also had arrived only to
hear that after those miserable eight days at sea he was lost forever &
forever to our eyes. Thank God we haven't another parent to lose; though
all Aunt Kate's sweetness & devotion makes me feel, in advance, that it will
be scarcely less a pang when *she* goes! Such is the consequence of cherish-
ing our 'natural ties!' After a little, Father's departure will begin to seem a
simple & natural fact however, as it has begun to appear to us here. I went
out yesterday (Sunday) morning, to the Cambridge cemetery (I had not
been able to start early enough on Saturday afternoon, as I wrote you I
meant to do)—& stood beside his grave a long time & read him your letter
of farewell—which I am sure he heard somewhere out of the depths of the
still, bright winter air. He lies extraordinarily close to Mother & as I stood
there and looked at this last expression of so many years of mortal union,
it was difficult not to believe that they were not united again in some
consciousness of my belief. On my way back I stopped to see Alice & sat
with her for an hour & admired the lovely babe, who is a most loving little
mortal. Then I went to see F. J. Child, because I had been told that he has
been beyond every one full of kindness & sympathy since the first of
father's illness, & had appeared to feel his death more than any one outside
the family. Every one, however, has been full of kindness—absolutely
tender does this good old Boston appear to have shown itself. Among others

Wendell Holmes (who is now a Judge of the Supreme Court) has shone—
perhaps a little unexpectedly, in this respect. Alice has been ill this last 24
hours—but not with any nervousness; only from nausea produced apparently from the doses of salvic soda that Beach has been giving her. She is
at present much better. Your letter makes me nervous in regard to your
dispositions of coming home. *Don't for the world think of this, I beseech
you*—it would be a very idle step. There is *nothing* here for you to do, not
a place even for you to live, & there is every reason why you should remain
abroad till the summer. Your wishing to come is a mere vague, uneasy
sentiment, not unnatural under the circumstances, but corresponding to
no real fitness. Let it subside as soon as possible, we all beg you. I wrote
you two days ago everything that there is to be told you as yet as regards
Father's will. Wait quietly till you hear more from me. I am going as soon
as I can get away, to Milwaukee, & I will write you more as soon as I have
been there. A. K. is still here. Make the most of London.

Ever yours
H. James jr

I receive your enclosures.

Stopped to see Alice] i.e. William's wife.   F. J. Child] (1825–96) the great collector of
ballads, professor at Harvard.   Alice . . . ill] i.e. their sister.   Holmes] Oliver Wendell
Holmes (1841–1935) served as a justice on the Supreme Court of Massachusetts, and later on the
United States Supreme Court.   Beach] the James's physician.   A. K.] Aunt Kate,
Katherine Walsh.

231. To W. M. Fullerton, 26 November 1907

> For Fullerton see below, Letter 250. James was extremely fond of him, finding him
> 'tenderly, magically *tactile*'. Fullerton had confided to James that he was being black-
> mailed by an ex-mistress, Henriette Mirecourt, who had rifled his desk and removed
> evidence of his homosexual interests. James and Edith Wharton contrived by means
> of a complicated little plot involving a publisher's advance to provide Fullerton with
> money to pay her off.

Dearest Morton,

I returned but last night (to find your letter here) from a four days'
ordeal—lugubrious and funereal—of 'going to meet' an old American
Friend (Lawrence Godkin) at Liverpool and seeing him through the dreary
and complicated business of effecting the interment of a near relation (the
mortal *dépouille* brought over)—who was a still older friend of mine—in a
terribly out of the way and inaccessible part of the Midlands—a *pays perdu*
of Northamptonshire twelve miles from a station—and such bleak and
dreary and dreadful and death-dealing miles. But it's over—only my letters
have been piling up here *en attendant*—and yours is the first, *bien entendu*,
that I (oh so tenderly and responsively, my dear Morton, my hideously

tormented friend) deal with. Sickened as I am by what *you* have to deal with, and with no pang of your ordeal muffled or dim or faint, to me, I yet find myself very robustly conscious of two things. (1) That you are *hypnotized* by nearness and contact and converse—hypnotized by the utterly wrong fact of being—of remaining—under the same roof with the atrocious creature into a belief in her possible *effect* on any one she may so indecently and insanely approach that has no relation to any potential reality. She can possibly appear to no one but as a mad, vindictive and obscene old woman (with whom, credibly, you may well, in Paris, have lived younger, but who is now only wreaking the fury [of] an *idée fixe* of resentment on you for not having perpetrated the marriage with her that it was—or would be—inconceivable you *should* perpetrate). She can only denounce and describe and exhibit *herself*, in the character of a dangerous blackmailer, and thereby render very dangerous and absolutely compromising *any* commerce held with her. If you were not breathing the poisoned air of her proximity and her access you would *see* this and feel it—and the whole truth and reality and proportion and measure of things. The woman can *do* nothing but get (in literal truth) 'chucked out,' with refusal to touch or look at her calumnious wares—her overtures to your people at home, e.g. simply burned on the spot, unlooked at, as soon as *smelt*. And so throughout, she can absolutely in the very nature of the case and on the very face of it—but inspire a *terror* not only of intercourse, credence or reciprocity—but of the act or appearance *of attention* itself—for she will reek with every sign of vindictive and demented calumny. No one will *touch*, or listen to, e.g., anything with the name of the Ranee in it—it will serve only to scare them. As for R[onald] G[ower], he is very ancient history and, I think, has all the appearance today of a regularized member of society, with his books and writings everywhere, his big movement (not so bad) to Shakespeare, one of the principal features of Stratford on Avon. However, I didn't mean to go into any detail—if you [have] known him you've known him (R.G.); and it is absolutely your own affair, for you to take your own robust and frank and perfectly manly stand on. Many persons, as I say, moreover, knowing him at this end of Time (it is my impression); the point is what I especially insist on as regards your falsified perspective and nervously aggravated fancy. I have a horror-stricken apprehension of your *weakening*, morbidly to her: the one and only thing that could lose you. You have but one course—to say: You most demented and perverted and unfortunate creature, *Do* your damnedest—you *m'en donnerez des nouvelles*. If after this you make any pact or compromise with her in the interest of an insane (for it would be *that* in you), compassion, *then*, dearest Morton, it would be difficult to advise or inspire you. It is detestable that you should still be under the same roof with her—but if you should remain so after she had lifted a finger to attempt to *colporter* her calumnies—you would simply commit the folly of your life. My own belief is that if you really *break* with her—utterly and absolutely—you will find yourself *free*—and leave her merely beating the air with grotesque *gestes* and absolutely 'getting' nowhere. If any echo of her deportment should come back to you send anyone to *me*—they will find *à qui parler*. But for God's sake after any *act* (though her dealings with you are indeed now all acts) don't again in any degree however small or indirect, temporize an inch further, but take your stand on your honour, your manhood, your courage, your decency, your intelligence and on the robust affection of your old, old, and faithful, faithful friend

Henry James

The Ranee] Margaret Brooke, an earlier mistress.

232. *To Max Beerbohm, 19 December 1908*

Beerbohm (1872–1956), who had often caricatured James, had written a letter prais-ing the story 'The Jolly Corner', just published.

My dear Max Beerbohm,

I won't say in acknowledgment of your beautiful letter that it's exactly the sort of letter I like best to receive, because that would sound as if I had *data* for generalizing—which I haven't; and therefore I can only go so far as to say that if it belonged to a class, or weren't a mere remarkable individual, I *should* rank it with the type supremely gratifying. On its mere lonely independent merits it appeals to me intimately and exquisitely, and I can only gather myself in and up, arching and presenting my not incon-siderable back—a back, as who should say, offered for any further stray scratching and patting of that delightful kind. I can bear wounds and fell smitings (so far as I have been ever honoured with such—and indeed life smites us on the whole enough, taking one thing with another) better than expressive gentleness of touch; so you must imagine me for a little while quite prostrate and overcome with the force of your good words. But I shall recover, when they have really sunk in—and then be not only the 'better,' but the more nimble and artful and alert by what they will have done for me. You had, and you obeyed, a very generous and humane inspiration; it charms me to think—or rather so authentically to know, that my (I confess) ambitious Muse does work upon you; it really helps me to believe in her the more myself—by which I am very gratefully yours

Henry James

233. To Rhoda Broughton, 10 August 1914

Rhoda Broughton (1840–1920), a good friend of James, had just published a new
novel, *Concerning a Vow*. James was deeply distressed by the outbreak of war.

Dearest Rhoda!

It is not a figure of speech but an absolute truth that even if I had not
received your very welcome and sympathetic script I should be writing to
you this day. I have been on the very edge of it for the last week—so had
my desire to make you a sign of remembrance and participation come to a
head; and verily I must—or may—almost claim that this all but 'crosses'
with your own. The only blot on our unanimity is that it's such an unanimity of woe. Black and hideous to me is the tragedy that gathers, and I'm sick
beyond cure to have lived on to see it. You and I, the ornaments of our
generation, should have been spared this wreck of our belief that through
the long years we had seen civilization grow and the worst become impossible. The tide that bore us along was then all the while moving to *this* as
its grand Niagara—yet what a blessing we didn't know it. It seems to me
to *undo* everything, everything that was ours, in the most horrible retro-
active way—but I avert my face from the monstrous scene!—you can hate
it and blush for it without my help; we can each do enough of that by
ourselves. The country and the season here are of a beauty of peace, and
loveliness of light, and summer grace, that make it inconceivable that just
across the Channel, blue as *paint* today, the fields of France and Belgium
are being, or about to be, given up to unthinkable massacre and misery.
One is ashamed to admire, to enjoy, to take any of the normal pleasure, and
the huge shining indifference of Nature strikes a chill to the heart and
makes me wonder of what abysmal mystery, or villainy indeed, such a cruel
smile is the expression. In the midst of it all at any rate we walked, this
strange Sunday afternoon (9th), my niece Peggy, her youngest brother and
I, about a mile out, across the blessed grass mostly, to see and have tea with
a genial and garrulous old Irish friend (Lady Mathew, who has a house
here for the summer), and came away an hour later bearing with us a
substantial green volume, by an admirable eminent hand, which our hostess had just read with such a glow of satisfaction that she overflowed into
easy lending. I congratulate you on having securely put it forth before this
great distraction was upon us—for I am utterly pulled up in the midst of
a rival effort by finding that my job won't at all consent to be done in the
face of it. The picture of little private adventures simply fades away before
the great public. I take great comfort in the presence of my two young
companions, and above all in having caught my nephew by the coat-tail
only *just* as he was blandly starting for the continent on August 1st. Poor
Margaret Payson is trapped somewhere in France—she *having* then started,

though not for Germany, blessedly; and we remain wholly without news of her. Peggy and Aleck have four or five near maternal relatives lost in Germany—though as Americans they may fare a little less dreadfully there than if they were English. And I have numerous friends—we all have, haven't we?—inaccessible and unimaginable there; it's becoming an anguish to think of them. Nevertheless I do believe that we shall be again gathered into a blessed little Chelsea drawing-room—it will be like the reopening of the salons, so irrepressibly, after the French revolution. So only sit tight, and invoke your heroic soul, dear Rhoda, and believe me more than ever all-faithfully yours,

Henry James

234. To H. H. Asquith, 28 June 1915

Asquith, the Prime Minister, sponsored James's application, which is said to have been processed in record time.

My dear Prime Minister and Illustrious Friend,

I am venturing to trouble you with the mention of a fact of my personal situation, but I shall do so as briefly and considerately as possible. I desire to offer myself for naturalization in this country, that is, to change my status from that of American citizen to that of British subject. I have assiduously and happily spent here all but forty years, the best years of my life, and I find my wish to testify at this crisis to the force of my attachment and devotion to England, and to the cause for which she is fighting, finally and completely irresistible. It brooks at least no inward denial whatever. I can only testify by laying at her feet my explicit, my material and spiritual allegiance, and throwing into the scale of her fortune my all but imponderable moral weight—'a poor thing but mine own.' Hence this respectful appeal. It is necessary (as you may know) that for the purpose I speak of four honorable householders should bear witness to their kind acquaintance with me, to my apparent respectability, and to my speaking and writing English with an approach of propriety. What I presume to ask of you is whether you will do me the honour to be the pre-eminent one of that gently guaranteeing group? Edmund Gosse has benevolently consented to join it. The matter will entail on your part, as I understand, no expenditure of attention at all beyond your letting my solicitor wait upon you with a paper for your signature—the affair of a single moment; and the 'going through' of my application will doubtless be proportionately expedited. You will thereby consecrate my choice and deeply touch and gratify yours all faithfully,

Henry James

235. To H. G. Wells, 10 July 1915

Wells (1866–1946) was much admired by James, but in his satirical book *Boon*, just published, Wells wrote a cruel parody of the older man's manner, and sent James a copy. Having read the comparison of his typical novel to an empty church with 'on the altar, very reverently placed, intensely there, . . . a dead kitten, an egg-shell, a piece of string', James protested. Wells wrote to excuse himself, saying the book was written to relieve tension caused by the war and was nothing but a wastepaper basket. This reply of James ended their correspondence.

My dear Wells,

I am bound to tell you that I don't think your letter makes out any sort of case for the bad manners of *Boon*, so far as your indulgence in them at the expense of your poor old H.J. is concerned—I say 'your' simply because he has *been* yours, in the most liberal, continual, sacrificial, the most admiring and abounding critical way, ever since he began to know your writings: as to which you have had copious testimony. Your comparison of the book to a waste-basket strikes me as the reverse of felicitous, for what one throws into that receptacle is exactly what one *doesn't* commit to publicity and make the affirmation of one's estimate of one's contemporaries by. I should liken it much rather to the preservative portfolio or drawer in which what is withheld from the basket is savingly laid away. Nor do I feel it anywhere evident that my 'view of life and literature,' or what you impute to me as such, is carrying everything before it and becoming a public menace—so unaware do I seem, on the contrary, that my products constitute an example in any measurable degree followed or a cause in any degree successfully pleaded: I can't but think that if this were the case I should find it somewhat attested in their circulation—which, alas, I have reached a very advanced age in the entirely defeated hope of. But I *have* no view of life and literature, I maintain, other than that our form of the latter in especial is admirable exactly by its range and variety, its plasticity and liberality, its fairly living on the sincere and shifting experience of the individual practitioner. That is why I have always so admired your so free and strong application of it, the particular rich receptacle of intelligences and impressions emptied out with an energy of its own, that your genius constitutes; and *that* is in particular why, in my letter of two or three days since, I pronounced it curious and interesting that you should find the case I constitute myself only ridiculous and vacuous to the extent of your having to proclaim your sense of it. The curiosity and the interest, however, in this latter connection are of course for my mind those of the break of perception (perception of the vivacity of *my* variety) on the part of a talent so generally inquiring and apprehensive as yours. Of course for myself I live, live intensely and am fed by life, and my value, whatever it be, is in my own kind of expression of that. Therefore I am pulled up to wonder by the fact that for you my kind (my sort of sense of expression and sort of sense of life alike) doesn't exist; and that wonder is, I admit, a disconcerting comment on my idea of the various appreciability of our addiction to the novel and of all the personal and intellectual history, sympathy and curiosity, behind the given example of it. It is when that history and curiosity have been determined in the way most different from my own that I myself want to get at them—precisely *for* the extension of life, which is the novel's best gift. But that is another matter. Meanwhile I absolutely dissent from the claim that there are any differences whatever in the amenability to art of forms of literature aesthetically determined, and hold your distinction between a form that is (like) painting and a form that is (like) architecture for wholly null and void. There is no sense in which architecture is aesthetically 'for use' that doesn't leave any other art whatever exactly as much so; and so far from that of literature being irrelevant to the literary report upon life, and to its being made as interesting as possible, I regard it as relevant in a degree that leaves everything else behind. It is art that *makes* life, makes interest, makes importance, for our consideration and application of these things, and I know of no substitute whatever for the force and beauty of its process. If I were Boon I should say that any pretence of such a substitute is helpless and hopeless humbug; but I wouldn't be Boon for the world, and am only yours faithfully

Henry James

Edward, Prince of Wales, later King Edward VII
(1841–1910)

236. To Admiral Sir Henry F. Stephenson, 17 October 1880

My dear Harry,

Many thanks for your letter fr. Plymouth, and I am delighted to hear that you have had such a satisfactory trial of your ship, and that you are perfectly satisfied with her and the ship's company. You will now look forward to your cruize with all the more pleasure. It had come to my knowledge that 'Carysfort' was likely to be detached fr. the Squadron on reaching the Pacific but I think I have taken steps to prevent it. This is only for your private ear, so don't mention it to *anyone* please.

Here we are once again in dingy London, and we have been favoured by the densest yellow fog to greet us on our arrival here this morning.

The day after you left Abergeldie Jim Farquharson's deer drive at Invercauld turned out a great success, and we killed 13 stags. I was fortunate enough to get 6! We had another Ghillies' Ball—at Balmoral—which went off admirably, and another at Aboyne—given by Huntly. He gave me also a charming day's shooting, and we killed roe deer, grouse, pheasants, partridges, woodcocks, woodpigeons, black game, hares and rabbits amounting to 345 head, making an uncommonly pretty day's shooting as you will allow—and over lovely ground.

I suppose you heard that the Gosfords started for Lisbon in their yacht a week ago. I wonder if you will meet, but I fear not. Now goodbye, and God bless you, my dear Harry, and write as often as you can. I hope this will still reach you at Vigo. With the Princess' kindest remembrances and best wishes, and Miss Charlotte's and Francis' love.

I am, | Yrs. most sincerely
A.E.

Huntly] Charles, 11th Marquis (1847–1937). Gosfords] Archibald Gosford and his wife
were courtiers.   The Princess] Alexandra.   Charlotte . . . Francis] Knollys.

RUDYARD KIPLING
(1865–1936)

From 1882 for seven years Kipling worked as a journalist in India.

237. To Edith Macdonald, 4 February 1884

Dearest Auntie,

Verily India is a strange land, and its people are still stranger. Yesterday morning I got an invitation to come to an old Afghan's house somewhere in the city. You must know that we have more than one of the Afghan Sirdars who fought against us in the war, as prisoners at Lahore. They are under no sort of surveillance but they *have* to stay here and keep quiet. When I got the note—couched in flowery English and flowerier Persian— I rode off into the City, wondering what on earth the old sinner could want with me. He was a Kizil Bash if that conveys any meaning to you.

In the end, I was shown his house and rode into the square courtyard with the Sirdar's mounted follower at my heels. Then we went up stairs— *such* filthy stairs—to Kizil bash's room a dirty place but stuffed full of embroideries, gold cloth, old armour and inlaid tables. The old boy, who was sitting at one end of the room, rose to meet me and made me sit down

after enquiring how I did. We conversed in Urdu, to the following extraordinary effect:—

(K.B.).   Your honour's health and prosperity are they well assured?

(I).   By your favour, Khan, they are so.

(K.B.).   I have heard of the fame of your honour, so far north as Peshawar—
            that you have the ear of the Lat-Sahib (our Lieutenant Governor)
            and that he fears your *Khubber-Ke-Kargus* (newspaper) more than
            God or the Sheitans. Therefore, (this with the air of a King) I
            have *sent* for you, Sahib.

Here I began to feel rather uneasy and answered 'The Khan honours me
too greatly. Who am I that I should know the heart of the Lat-Sahib or that
the Lat-Sahib should fear me. It is true (here I couldn't help advertising
the CMG.) that my Khubber-Ke-Kargus, is heard from Karachi and Scinde
to Benares, and from Peshawur to Delhi—but it is a little thing O Khan.
How should *I* help you?' Then the old boy began in a low tone about the
iniquity of his being a prisoner in Lahore. 'My wives and my women are
at Cabul, but I am here. Write in your Khubber Ke Kargus Sahib that I
will do anything they ask me, write that it is cruel and unjust to keep me
here.' Write (and so he went on for about twenty minutes like a madman
and finally wound up by throwing me a bundle of currency notes and asked
me to count them. I did so and I found them about Rs 16,000—that is to
say about £1300). These I was told would be the price of merely recommending him to be released, a thing I might have done in ten lines on the
front page any day if I had only known of his case. Of course it wasn't
possible to do anything after an insult like that, but I daren't give him a
piece of my mind in his own house for fear of accidents—fatal ones may
be—so I threw back the notes and told him that the years had impaired his
eyesight and I wasn't a Bunnoochi or a Baluchi (two races the most covetous on earth) but an English Sahib. Then he pulled up and thought for a
few moments. Finally he blurted out that we English were 'fools' and
didn't know the value of money but that '*all* sahibs knew how to value
women and horses'. Whereupon he sent a small boy into an inner chamber
and, to my intense amusement, there came out a Cashmiri girl that Moore
might have raved over. She was very handsome and beautifully dressed,
but I didn't quite see how she was to be introduced into an English
household like ours. I rather lost my temper and abused the Khan pretty
freely for this last piece of impudence and told him to go to a half caste
native newspaper walla for what he wanted (all the same I'm afraid I kissed
the damsel when the Khan's broad back was turned). At the end of my
harangue I found that I couldn't make a dignified exit as I had intended,
'cos the door was shut and bolted. Then I pulled up and told the old
gentleman to open the door. It was a funny scene to think over afterwards

because, all the time I was talking to the Khan [he] was shrugging his shoulders and waving his hands in protest, and I could hear the devil's own noise in the courtyard—sounds of horses and men. Never having been in a position like this I, naturally, began to sweat big drops, and cursed the Khan's female relatives in a manner which made the Cashmiri titter. It seemed that the man only wanted to get his horses out to show me and when that was done he went down to the yard—I followed—and saw about seven of the most beautiful beasts it has ever been my lot to look on. There were two bay Arabs, one Kathiawar mare, and four perfect little Hagara country breds. Then I'm afraid my resolution began to waver, 'specially when he said I might pick any three I liked—they were such beauties and had such perfect manners. However I explained very gravely that I wasn't going to help him a bit and he ought to have known better than to 'blacken an Englishman's face' in the way he had done and if I had had my own way I'd keep him in Lahore till he died. When I come to think of the way in which I slanged him, I'm rather astonished to think he didn't stick me then and there. No one would have been any the wiser and there would have been one unbeliever less. However he kept his temper very fairly and told me to come upstairs again and have a smoke and some coffee. If I refused I knew he would think I was afraid of poison, and if I accepted I was afraid I should get some *dhatura* with the coffee. However I accepted the offer and we went up stairs again and here began the cleverest part of the old man's policy. I saw when I came in that he meant no bodily harm, for the money was out on the table, from my couch in the window I could see the horses being marched to and fro in the yard and the Kashmiri was superintending the coffee and getting my pipe ready. The Khan took his seat out of sight of me and left me there to sip and smoke, and watch, if I chose the money, the horses, and the girl. This went on for nearly half an hour, and I was so thoroughly indignant with the old beast that I resolved to inflict myself upon him for a time till I sobered down. When I had smoked out one pipe, drunk my coffee and talked Oriental platonics with the Kashmiri I rose up to go and my host didn't attempt to hinder me. He had lost about three cups of coffee, one smoke, and a couple of hours of his time (but that didn't count) and had heard some plain truths about his ancestry. Of course I couldn't do anything for him—tho' his case is a hard one I admit—but I can mention the subject to Wheeler, and he can, if he likes, take notice of it, so that I shan't be concerned in the affair. When I mounted my old Waler (he *did* look such a scarecrow) I found that beneath the gullet plate of the saddle had been pushed a little bag of uncut sapphires and big greasy emeralds. This was his last try I presume and it might have seriously injured my brute's back if I hadn't removed it. I took it out and sent it through one of the windows of the upper story where it will be a good find for somebody. Then I rode out of the city and came to our peaceful civil station just as the people were pouring out of church—it seems so queer an adventure that I went and set it down and am sending you the story thereof. I haven't told anyone here of the bribery business because, if I did, some unscrupulous beggar might tell the Khan that *he* would help him and so lay hold of the money, the lady or, worse still, the horses. Besides I may be able to help the old boy respectably and without any considerations.

Wasn't it a rummy adventure for a Sunday morning.

Your
Ruddy

The war] the Second Afghan War, 1879–90.   Kizil Bash] member of the Persian Shi'ite community.   CMG] *Civil and Military Gazette*.   Moore] Tom Moore, Irish poet, author of *Lalla Rookh*, an oriental narrative poem.   *Dhatura*] thorn apple, an intoxicant. Waler] horse imported from New South Wales.

ROBERT LOUIS STEVENSON
(1850–1894)

Stevenson's movements were dictated by his constant search for relief from disease, and he spent time at Davos (where he met Symonds and finished *Treasure Island*, 1883) and Hyères and in California before he began his travels and residences in the South Pacific. He was at Bournemouth with his wife Fanny for three years from 1884, leading the life of an invalid. Their house was called Skerryvore after a famous lighthouse designed by Stevenson's uncle.

238. To J. A. Symonds, Spring 1886

For Symonds, see above, Letter 209.

My Dear Symonds,

If we have lost touch, it is (I think) only in a material sense; a question of letters, not hearts. You will find a warm welcome at Skerryvore from both the lightkeepers; and, indeed, we never tell ourselves one of our financial fairy tales, but a run to Davos is a prime feature. I am not changeable in friendship; and I think I can promise you you have a pair of trusty well-wishers and friends in Bournemouth: whether they write or not is but a small thing; the flag may not be waved, but it is there.

Jekyll is a dreadful thing, I own; but the only thing I feel dreadful about is that damned old business of the war in the members. This time it came out; I hope it will stay in, in future.

Raskolnikoff is easily the greatest book I have read in ten years; I am glad you took to it. Many find it dull: Henry James could not finish it: all I can say is, it nearly finished me. It was like having an illness. James did not care for it because the character of Raskolnikoff was not objective; and at that I divined a great gulf between us, and, on further reflection, the existence of a certain impotence in many minds of to-day, which prevents them from living *in* a book or a character, and keeps them standing afar off, spectators of a puppet show. To such I suppose the book may seem empty in the centre; to the others it is a room, a house of life, into which they themselves enter, and are tortured and purified. The Juge d'Instruction I thought a wonderful, weird, touching, ingenious creation: the drunken father, and Sonia, and the student friend, and the uncircumscribed, protoplasmic humanity of Raskolnikoff, all upon a level that filled me with wonder: the execution also, superb in places. Another has been translated—*Humiliés et Offensés*. It is even more incoherent than *Le Crime et le Châtiment*, but breathes much of the same lovely goodness, and has passages of power. Dostoieffsky is a devil of a swell, to be sure. Have you heard that he became a stout, imperialist conservative? It is interesting to know. To something of that side, the balance leans with me also in view of the incoherency and incapacity of all. The old boyish idea of the march on Paradise being now out of season, and all plans and ideas that I hear debated being built on a superb indifference to the first principles of human character, a helpless desire to acquiesce in anything of which I know the worst assails me. Fundamental errors in human nature of two sorts stand on the skyline of all this modern world of aspirations. First, that it is happiness that men want; and second, that happiness consists of anything but an internal harmony. Men do not want, and I do not think they would accept, happiness; what they live for is rivalry, effort, success—the elements our friends wish to eliminate. And, on the other hand, happiness is a question of morality—or of immorality, there is no difference—and conviction. Gordon was happy in Khartoum, in his worst hours of danger and fatigue; Marat was happy, I suppose, in his ugliest frenzy; Marcus Aurelius was happy in the detested camp; Pepys was pretty happy, and I am pretty happy on the whole, because we both somewhat crowingly accepted a *via media*, both liked to attend to our affairs, and both had some success in managing the same. It is quite an open question whether Pepys and I ought to be happy; on the other hand, there is no doubt that Marat had better be unhappy. He was right (if he said it) that he was *la misère humaine*, cureless misery— unless perhaps by the gallows. Death is a great and gentle solvent; it has never had justice done it, no, not by Whitman. As for those crockery chimney-piece ornaments, the bourgeois (*quorum pars*), and their cowardly dislike of dying and killing, it is merely one symptom of a thousand how utterly they have got out of touch of life. Their dislike of capital punishment and their treatment of their domestic servants are for me the two flaunting emblems of their hollowness.

God knows where I am driving to. But here comes my lunch.

Which interruption, happily for you, seems to have stayed the issue. I have now nothing to say, that had formerly such a pressure of twaddle. Pray don't fail to come this summer. It will be a great disappointment, now it has been spoken of, if you do.

Yours ever,
Robert Louis Stevenson

Jekyll] *The Strange Case of Dr Jekyll and Mr Hyde* was published in 1886.   Raskolnikoff] *Crime and Punishment* (1866), which influenced *Dr Jekyll*, was translated into English (from the French translation) in 1886; Raskolnikov is the principal character.   *Humiliés et Offensés*] *The Insulted and the Injured.*   *Quorum pars*] part of whom I am.

239. Mrs R. L. Stevenson to Mrs Sitwell, March 1889

In 1880 Stevenson married Fanny Osbourne. In 1888 they set out for the South Seas, finally settling at Vailima in Samoa, where Stevenson died. This letter announces an extension of their stay in the South Seas and includes a translation of a letter Stevenson had received from his ceremonial brother Ori a Ori. 'Rui' was Ori's name for Louis, here ceremonially applied to Ori. In a letter to Henry James in the same month Stevenson said, 'I think the receipt of such a letter might humble, shall I say even—? and for me, I would rather have received it than have written *Redgauntlet* or the sixth *Aeneid*. All told, if my books have enabled or helped me to make this voyage, to know Rui, and to have received such a letter, they have (in the old prefatorial expression) not been writ in vain.'

My Dear Friend,

Louis has improved so wonderfully in the delicious islands of the South Seas, that we think of trying yet one more voyage. We are a little uncertain as to how we shall go, whether in a missionary ship, or by hiring schooners from point to point, but the 'unregenerate' islands we must see. I suppose we shall be off some time in June, which will fetch us back to England in another year's time. You could hardly believe it if you could see Louis now. He looks as well as he ever did in his life, and has had no sign of cough or hemorrhage (begging pardon of Nemesis) for many months. It seems a pity to return to England until his health is firmly re-established, and also a pity not to see all that we can see quite easily starting from this place: and which will be our only opportunity in life. Of course there is the usual risk from hostile natives, and the horrible sea, but a positive risk is so much more wholesome than a negative one, and it is all such joy to Louis and Lloyd. As for me, I hate the sea, and am afraid of it (though no one will believe that because in time of danger I do not make an outcry—nevertheless I *am* afraid of it, and it is not kind to me), but I love the tropic weather, and the wild people, and to see my two boys so happy. Mrs Stevenson is going back to Scotland in May, as she does not like to be longer away from her old sister, who has been very ill. And besides, we do not feel justified in taking her to the sort of places we intend to visit. As for me, I can get comfort out of very rough surroundings for my people, I can work hard and enjoy it; I can even shoot pretty well, and though I 'don't want to fight, by jingo if I must,' why I can. I don't suppose there will be any occasion for that sort of thing—only in case.

I am not quite sure of the names, but I *think* our new cruise includes the Gilberts, the Fijis, and the Solomons. A letter might go from the Fijis; Louis will write the particulars, of which I am not sure. As for myself, I have had more cares than I was really fit for. To keep house on a yacht is no easy thing. When Louis and I broke loose from the ship and lived alone amongst the natives I got on very well. It was when I was deathly sea-sick, and the question was put to me by the cook, 'What shall we have for the cabin dinner, what for tomorrow's breakfast, what for lunch? and what about the sailors' food? Please come and look at the biscuits, for the weevils have got into them, and show me how to make yeast that will rise of itself, and smell the pork which seems pretty high, and give me directions about making a pudding with molasses—and what is to be done about the bugs?'—etc. etc. In the midst of heavy dangerous weather, when I was lying on the floor clutching a basin, down comes the mate with a cracked head, and I must needs cut off the hair matted with blood, wash and dress the wound, and administer restoratives. I do not like being 'the lady of the yacht,' but ashore! O, then I felt I was repaid for all. I wonder did any of my letters from beautiful Tautira ever come to hand, with the descriptions of our life with Louis's adopted brother Ori a Ori? Ori wrote to us, if no one else did, and I mean to give you a translation of his letter. It begins with our native names.

Tautira, 26 Dec. 1888

To Teriitera (Louis) and Tapina Tutu (myself) and Aromaiterai (Lloyd) and Teiriha (Mrs Stevenson) Salutation in the true Jesus.

I make you to know my great affection. At the hour when you left us, I was filled with tears; my wife, Rui Tehini, also, and all of my household. When you embarked I felt a great sorrow. It is for this that I went upon the road, and you looked from that ship, and I looked at you on the ship with great grief until you had raised the anchor and hoisted the sails. When the ship started, I ran along the beach to see you still; and when you were on the open sea I cried out to you, 'farewell Louis': and when I was coming back to my house I seemed to hear your voice crying 'Rui farewell.' Afterwards I watched the ship as long as I could until the night fell; and when it was dark I said to myself, 'if I had wings I should fly to the ship to meet you, and to sleep amongst you, so that I might be able to come back to shore and to tell Rui Tehini, "I have slept upon the ship of Teriitera."' After that we passed that night in the impatience of grief. Towards eight o'clock I seemed to hear your voice, 'Teriitera—Rui—here is the hour for putter and tiro' (cheese and syrup). I did not sleep that night, thinking continually of you, my very dear friend, until the morning: being then awake I went to see Tapina Tutu on her bed, and alas, she was not there. Afterwards I looked into your rooms; they did not please me as they used to do. I did not hear your voice crying, 'hail Rui.' I thought then that you had gone, and that you had left me. Rising up I went to the beach to see your ship, and I could not see it. I wept, then, till the night, telling myself continually, 'Teriitera returns into his own country and leaves his dear Rui in grief, so that I suffer for him, and weep for him.' I will not forget you in my memory. Here is the thought: I desire to meet you again. It is my dear Teriitera makes the only riches I desire in this world. It is your eyes that I desire to see again. It must be that your body and my body shall eat together at our table: there is what would make my heart content. But now we are separated. May God be with you all. May His word and His mercy go with you, so that you may be well and we also, according to the words of Paul.

Ori a Ori; that is to say, Rui

After reading this to me Louis has left in tears saying that he is not worthy that such a letter should be written to him. We hope to so manage that we shall stop at Tahiti and see Rui once more. I tell myself that pleasant story when I wake in the night.

I find my head swimming so that I cannot write any more. I wish some rich Catholic would send a parlour organ to Père Bruno of Tautira. I am going to try and save money to do it myself, but he may die before I have enough. I feel ashamed to be sitting here when I think of that old man who cannot draw because of scrivener's paralysis, who has no one year in and year out to speak to but natives (our Rui is a Protestant not bigoted like the rest of them—but still a Protestant) and the only pastime he has is playing on an old broken parlour organ whose keys are mostly dumb. I know no more pathetic figure. Have you no rich Catholic friends who would send him an organ that he could play upon? Of course I am talking nonsense, and yet I know somewhere that person exists if only I knew the place.

Our dearest love to you all.

Fanny

ERNEST CLARK

(?–1893)

240. To the editor of the Daily Chronicle, *14 August 1893*

This letter appeared in the newspaper on 16 Aug., under the heading 'Tired of Life'.

Sir,

When you receive this I shall have put an end to my existence by the aid of a bullet. This act is thoroughly premeditated, being planned six months ago. My best and most serious thoughts have been given to it, and my sanity, if ever man was sane, can be acknowledged by the friends I have spent the last fortnight with.

I resolved long ago that life is a sequence of shams. That men have had to create utopias and heavens to make it bearable; and that all the wisest men have been disgusted with life as it is. Carlyle and Voltaire advise hard work, but only as an anaesthetic. The good Socialists look forward to society with brains and love, but there will always be the animal, in and out of us, to fight with. The apostles of sensuousness have always had an interest for me, but when seen from a distance their lives, from Rousseau to the great Frenchmen of today, are despicable. The religions give each man an entity after this life, but why not all other animals, insects etc? which even they will say is absurd. Only the transcendental and aesthetic in life are worth our thought. Only a life following beauty and creating it approaches any degree of joyousness, but the ugliness and vile monotony in my life have crowded beauty out . . .

Three weeks ago I bought a revolver. On going to spend my holiday in Cambridgeshire I left it at the cloak-room, Liverpool-street, until this evening. The last two weeks, the happiest days in my life, were spent with my only friend. We had George Meredith and Théophile Gautier for companions. We lived in the fields, sketching, reading to each other, with strolls and days on the Cam. My greatest agony all these months is the idea of causing grief to my darling, whose friendship is the most sacred thing life has given me. But rather this blow than render her life wretched with my gloom.

I consider this explanation due to my fellows, to those who care. I was not consulted when I became a sentient being. Having reached maturity I object to life. Will not have it. Hate and despise it. That there should be no doubt in my own mind have been at least three months with the certainty of my end before my eyes.

This is the only writing concerning my death.

August 14th, 8.5 p.m., Liverpool-street Waiting Room.
Ernest Clark

A. E. HOUSMAN

(1859–1936)

Housman became professor of Latin at University College London in 1892. *A Shropshire Lad* was published in 1896. He moved to the Cambridge Chair of Latin in 1911.

241. To the Editor of the Standard, *12 March 1894*

Sir,

In August 1886 Highgate Wood became the property of the Mayor and Commonalty and Citizens of the City of London. It was then in a very sad state. So thickly was it overgrown with brushwood, that if you stood in the centre you could not see the linen of the inhabitants of Archway Road hanging to dry in their back gardens. Nor could you see the advertisement of Juggins's stout and porter which surmounts the front of the public house at the south corner of the wood. Therefore the Mayor and Commonalty and Citizens cut down the intervening brushwood, and now when we stand in the centre we can divide our attention between Juggins's porter and our neighbours' washing. Scarlet flannel petticoats are much worn in Archway Road, and if anyone desires to feast his eyes on these very bright and picturesque objects, so seldom seen in the streets, let him repair to the centre of Highgate Wood.

Still we were not happy. The wood is bounded on the north by the railway to Muswell Hill; and it was a common subject of complaint in Highgate that we could not see the railway from the wood without going quite to the edge. At length, however, the Mayor and Commonalty and Citizens have begun to fell the trees on the north, so that people in the centre of the wood will soon be able to look at the railway when they are tired of the porter and the petticoats. But there are a number of new red-brick houses on the east side of the wood, and I regret to say that I observe no clearing of timber in that direction. Surely, Sir, a man who stands in the centre of the wood, and knows that there are new red-brick houses to the east of him, will not be happy unless he sees them.

Sir, it is spring: birds are pairing, and the County Council has begun to carve the mud-pie which it made last year at the bottom of Waterlow Park. I do not know how to address the Mayor and Commonalty; but the Citizens of the City of London all read the *Standard*, and surely they will respond to my appeal and will not continue to screen from my yearning gaze any one of those objects of interest which one naturally desires to see when one goes to the centre of a wood.

I am, Sir your obedient servant

A. E. H.

242. To Laurence Housman, 12 May 1897

> Laurence (1865–1959), Housman's brother, was a poet, playwright, and autobiographer.

My dear Laurence,

. . . There is a notice of *Gods and their Makers* in last week's *Athenaeum*: I don't know if it is depreciatory enough to suit your taste.

George Darley was the writer of the excellent sham 17th century song 'It is not beauty I demand' which Palgrave printed as genuine in the second part of the *Golden Treasury*. Because it was so good I read another thing of his, a sort of fairy drama whose name I forget, and was disappointed with it and read no more. But the piece you quote about the sea is capital. He was also the chief praiser of Beddoes' first play, and a great detester of Byron's versification when it was all the vogue.

The sea is a subject by no means exhausted. I have somewhere a poem which directs attention to one of its most striking characteristics, which hardly any of the poets seem to have observed. They call it salt and blue and deep and dark and so on; but they never make such profoundly true reflexions as the following:

> O billows bounding far,
> How wet, how wet ye are!
>
> When first my gaze ye met
> I said 'Those waves are wet'.
>
> I said it, and am quite
> Convinced that I was right.
>
> Who saith that ye are dry?
> I give that man the lie.
>
> Thy wetness, O thou sea,
> Is wonderful to me.
>
> It agitates my heart,
> To think how wet thou art.
>
> No object I have met
> Is more profoundly wet.
>
> Methinks, 'twere vain to try,
> O sea, to wipe thee dry.
>
> I therefore will refrain.
> Farewell, thou humid main.

Farewell thou irreligious writer . . .

                                        Your affectionate brother
                                        A. E. Housman

Gods and their Makers] a novel of Laurence Housman's (1897).   George Darley] (1795–
1846), Irish poet.   *Golden Treasury*] Francis Palgrave's influential poetry anthology, first
published 1861.   Fairy drama] *Sylvia* (1827). The piece about the sea may be from *Nepenthe*
(1836).   Beddoes] Thomas Love Beddoes (1803–49), best known for *Death's Jest-Book*
(1850); his first play was *The Bride's Tragedy* (1822).

243. To Alice Rothenstein, 28 May 1909

Alice Rothenstein was an actress before her marriage in 1899 to William Rothenstein,
painter and principal of the Royal College of Art.

Dear Mrs Rothenstein,

I hope that my conversation through the telephone yesterday did not
sound brusque. I am very little accustomed to using that instrument. I was
very sorry not to be able to come to the theatre with you, but I had an
engagement out of town for the evening, and I was just leaving the college
to catch my train when the beadle told me that someone had been enquiring for me.

Please tell Rothenstein that all my Jewish students are absenting themselves from my lectures from Wednesday to Friday this week on the plea
that these are Jewish holidays. I have been looking up the Old Testament,
but I can find no mention there of either the Derby or the Oaks.

Yours sincerely
A. E. Housman

Jewish holidays] in 1909 the Jewish Feast of Weeks (seven weeks and a day after Passover) fell
on 26 and 27 May; the Derby and the Oaks were run on 26 and 28 May.

244. To Lily Thicknesse, 11 August 1909

Mrs Thicknesse had sent Housman a copy of her husband's pamphlet *The Rights and
Wrongs of Women*.

Dear Mrs Thicknesse,

... My blood boils. This is not due to the recent commencement of
summer, but to the Wrongs of Woman, with which I have been making
myself acquainted. 'She cannot serve on any Jury'; and yet she bravely lives
on. 'She cannot serve in the army or navy'—oh cruel, cruel!—'except'—
this adds insult to injury—'as a nurse'. They do not even employ a Running Woman instead of a Running Man for practising marksmanship. I
have been making marginal additions. 'She cannot be ordained a Priest or
Deacon': add *nor become a Freemason*. 'She cannot be a member of the
Royal Society': add *nor of the Amateur Boxing Association*. In short your
unhappy sex seem to have nothing to look forward to, except contracting a
valid marriage as soon as they are 12 years old; and that must soon pall.

Thanks for the picture card. I did not know, or had forgotten, that you were at Woodbridge. If you can find an old hat of Edward FitzGerald's they will let you write three columns about it in the *Athenaeum*. But some literary people are so proud that they despise these avenues to fame . . .

Yours sincerely
A. E. Housman

Edward FitzGerald] FitzGerald (1809–83), translator of Omar Khayyam, lived at Woodbridge, Suffolk.

A. T. HARRIS

245. To the Superintendent, Atlantic City Railroad, New Jersey, September 1896

Dear Sir,

On the 15th yore trane that was going to Atlanta ran over mi bull at 30 mile post

He was in my Pastur
You orter see him

Yore ruddy trane took a peece of hyde outer his belly between his nable and his poker at least fute square and took his bag most off and he lost his seeds I don't believe he is going to be any more use as a bull.

I wish you would tell the President he is ded, for he is as good as ded ever since he was hit by yore trane.

Yours respectfully
A. T. Harris

P.S.—Be sure and report him as ded as he has nothing left but his poker. He was a red bull but he stand around in these days looking dam blue.

OSCAR WILDE
(1856–1900)

In May 1895 Wilde was sentenced to two years' imprisonment with 'hard labour for homosexual offences'. After his release in May 1897 he lived in France under the name of Sebastian Melmoth. This letter of thanks to the governor of Reading Gaol, where Wilde had served most of his sentence, was written little more than a week after his release.

246. To Major James Ormond Nelson, 28 May 1897

Dear Major Nelson,

I had of course intended to write to you as soon as I had safely reached French soil, to express, however inadequately, my real feelings of what you must let me term, not merely sincere, but *affectionate* gratitude to you for your kindness and gentleness to me in prison, and for the real care that you took of me at the end, when I was mentally upset and in a state of very terrible nervous excitement. You must not mind my using the word 'gratitude.' I used to think gratitude a burden to carry. Now I know that it is something that makes the heart lighter. The ungrateful man is one who walks slowly with feet and heart of lead. But when one knows the strange joy of gratitude to God and man the earth becomes lovelier to one, and it is a pleasure to count up, not one's wealth but one's debts, not the little that one possesses, but the much that one owes.

I abstained from writing, however, because I was haunted by the memory of the little children, & the wretched half witted lad who was flogged by the Doctor's orders. I could not have kept them out of my letter, and to have mentioned them to you might have put *you* in a difficult position. In your reply you *might* have expressed sympathy with my views—I think you would have—and then on the appearance of my public letter you might have felt as if I had, in some almost ungenerous or thoughtless way, procured your private opinion on official things, for use as corroboration.

I longed to speak to you about these things on the evening of my departure, but I felt that in my position as a prisoner it would have been wrong of me to do so, and that it would, or might have put you in a difficult position afterwards, as well as at the time. I only hear of my letter being published by a telegram from Mr Ross, but I hope they have printed it in full, as I tried to express in it my appreciation and admiration of your own humane spirit and affectionate interest in *all* the prisoners under your charge. I did not wish people to think that any exception had been specially made for me. Such exceptional treatment as I received was by order of the Commissioners. You gave me the same kindness as you gave to everyone. Of course I made more demands, but then I think I had really more needs than others—and I lacked often their cheerful acquiescence—

Of course I side with the prisoners—I was one, and I belong to their class now—I am not a scrap ashamed of having been in prison. I am horribly ashamed of the materialism of the life that brought me there. It was quite unworthy of an artist.

Of Martin, and the subjects of my letter I of course say nothing at all, except that the man who could change the system—if any one man can do so—is yourself. At present I write to ask you to allow me to sign myself, once at any rate in life,

your sincere and grateful friend
Oscar Wilde.

'BERT'

247. To Oscar Browning, 1 July 1897

Oscar Browning (1837–1923) was a Fellow of King's College, Cambridge, from 1859 till his death and a master at Eton from 1860 till 1875, when he was dismissed for alleged over-familiarity with some of the boys. He returned to King's and was its most considerable figure, a great organizer and patron. He 'made himself acquainted with a number of boys in the town and the neighbouring villages, and started them in their careers' (*The Dictionary of National Biography*). Subsequently some of these protégés kept in touch with him, and he preserved their letters, now in the modern archive at King's.

Dear Mr Browning,

Just a few lines to you hoping to find you well and to thank you very much indeed for your kindness in sending those beautiful books, its really very good of you to think so much of me, and me only a common Flat Foot my ship mates were simply amazed or to put it more in my Lingo fairly knocked in the old Kent Road, we have been having rather a rough time of it lately, we were forced to leave Galatz just after the Queen's Birthday as the river overflowed and we had no place to lay, about 200 people got drowned farther up the River, and 20 thousand are at the present time homeless, the poor devils were knocking about in these small canoes with their bed and a few pots and pans etc all they possessed in the wide world, there was a large house just 'longside where we lay, and one day just as they piped dinner down it came with an oosh, but no one was hurt; we left on the 23rd oh by the way, we had rather a good turn out at the Gardina Chiriac a nice little private garden messrs Watson and Yowell and a few more got it up, it was a social gathering of English subjects about 30 were there besides 35 members of H. M. S. Cocky, who played old Harry I'm sorry to say as soon as they had got a few dead marines in front of them, a dead marine you know is of course an empty bottle, they were singing, and fighting and goodness knows what; the Ladies liked the songs but when they got sousing each other they thought it a bit off, we left next morning about 4 o'c got under weigh and proceeded down the River called at Soulina and took in coal, while we were there we had an accident a large Steam Ship name Helvio [?] got her anchor foul of ours, and of course delayed us taking 2 days to clear it, as some of our men were ashore casting off hawsers, wires, etc one of them a tall fellow called Lofty Ford went to heave a grass hawser from the land to the ship, and he gave it such a tremendous heave, and overbalanced and fell striking his head against an iron pontoon alongside the bank I was at work on the shipside ready to get our bearing off spar in, I knew he couldn't swim, so I dived after him the current was running 7 knots an hour at the time, when I was in he hadn't made his appearance, and the Captain was beginning to get anxious but all of a sudden he came bobbing to the surface, and the Captain on the Bridge sung out to me in an excited tone, 'there he is, pick him up, pick him up', as soon as I saw him I was on him like a Bromley kite on a dead Malay, I just managed to mitten him as he was going down for the second time, I fisted hold of his hair, he weighs 12 st. 2, but I managed him all sublime and kept him up & was taking him in shore when a steamer picked him up, or rather took him from me and left me floating away in the current, but I soon reached shore and a couple of Greeks came running up with a rope they thought I was the chap who was drowning, when I got aboard the chap had come round a bit, but the Captain never said a word to either of us, but Lofty when he came on deck, and they were all smoking round the Mast, said there goes the chap I'm holden to for my life, and he came up afterwards and said, 'here old chap I've got you to thank for my life', I said thats all right Lofty Boy, I would only be too glad to risk my life for any of my shipmates in danger like that: We are doing a little surveying business now, so we are having a rare lot of work building beacons etc, well dear mr B. I think I shall leave the Navy in 99 when we pay off if I can get a good place. I'm sorry Ive no more paper so I must knock off this yarn. with my very best and sincerest Respects to you.

yr affectionate debtor
Bert

W. T. STEAD

(1849–1912)

William Thomas Stead, a journalist, fearless social reformer, and exposer of injustice, was drowned in the *Titanic*. These letters are part of his plan to importune the Pope to support a proposal of the Czar for a conference on armament reduction. Characteristically, he travelled to Rome for the purpose, but without enough time or influence to ensure success; no papal audience was granted.

248. To the Cardinal Secretary of State, the Vatican, 20 November 1898

Your Eminence,

Of Rome it has been well said *Patiens quia Aeterna*. But I am but an ephemeral creature of time and my patience necessarily limited. Last Monday I submitted to the Holy Father a request for an audience which your Eminence was good enough to promise to support.

I have now waited a week for an answer. I cannot wait another. The very business on which I came to the Vatican demands my return to London. If the Holy Father is unable or unwilling to comply with my request and your Eminence will permit me, I propose to call upon you on Monday evening to take my leave, present my thanks and express my profound regret that the effort you were so kind as to encourage, should have failed.

I have the honour to be | Your Eminence's obedient servant,

W. T. Stead

Patiens quia Aeterna] long-suffering because eternal.

249. To the Cardinal Secretary of State, 21 November 1898

Your Eminence,

I am afraid I have failed in conveying to the mind of your Eminence and of the Holy Father, the importance of the matter before you and its bearing upon the question as to whether or not the Holy See will be represented at the Peace Conference?

I have heard much since I came to Rome that has occasioned me much misgiving as to whether the presence of the representative of the Holy Father would conduce to the success of the Conference. If I have no opportunity of hearing from your Eminence and the Holy Father how to answer these difficulties and objections, I am afraid that the result will be that the conference will assemble without the presence of any representative of the Pope. This has not hitherto been manifest to your Eminence and I would therefore as a last resource earnestly appeal to you not to allow me to leave Rome without an opportunity of hearing authoritatively the truth concerning the attitude of the Holy See in relation to this matter.

I have the honour to be | Your Eminence's obedient servant,

W. T. Stead

W. M. FULLERTON

(1865–1952)

Morton Fullerton (see also Letters 231 and 259) was an American journalist who in 1890 joined the staff of the London *Times* and lived in Paris. Among his many female

lovers were the Ranee of Sarawak and Edith Wharton, to whom Henry James introduced him. He was also a member of Wilde's 'gay' circle, and the lover of Lord
Ronald Gower, the sculptor responsible for the Shakespeare memorial at Stratford.

250. To Oscar Wilde, 23 June 1899

Wilde, in disgrace, and calling himself Sebastian Melmoth, was reduced to writing
begging letters to his friends. Fullerton's response is presumably the nastiest letter in
this collection.

My dear Melmoth,

I am distressed to have left your touching appeal unanswered for so long.
But I have been on congé in the *patrie* of Stendhal, and had cognizance of
your *gêne* only yesterday.

You do me too much honour in asking me to come to the rescue of an
artist such as you. And if I could have known of the situation 3 weeks ago
when I had money in my pocket I should not have hesitated for a moment,
especially as I had just received your play [*Earnest*] and was in the state of
mind of one who says of a thing without thinking: 'it is worth its weight in
gold.' But at present, after an expensive journey, I am unable, with the best
good-will in the world, to seize the event and to accept the *rôle* in this
particular comedy—I use the word in its Hellenic and Gallic sense, *bien
entendu*, in the sole sense in which it exists for the admirers of *Lady
Windermere's Fan* and of *The Importance of Being Earnest*. The maker of
those masterpieces has too much delicacy and *esprit* not to sympathize
sincerely with the regret of a man obliged to reply thus to an appeal which
certainly he could not have expected and for which it was impossible for
him to prepare, but which is none the less precious for that. I grope at the
hope that meanwhile the stress has passed, and that you will not have
occasion to put, *malgré vous*, either me or any one else again into such a
position of positive literal chagrin.

Yours sincerely
W. M. Fullerton

SIR EDWARD ELGAR
(1857–1934)

251. To Sir Edward Elgar, 28 September 1900

Elgar had given tickets for the rehearsal of his new work *The Dream of Gerontius*
(1900) to three teachers, one English, one French, and one German, at a Birmingham
school. Their letter of thanks he sent on to the editor of the *Musical Times*, who
printed it (1 Nov. 1900). See also Letter 274.

My cher Herr!

We sommes so full de Dankbarkeit and débordante Entzücken and sentons so weak et demütig that la Kraft of une Sprache seems insuffisante auszudrücken our sentiments. Deshalb we unissons unsere powers et versuchen to express en Englisch, French, and Allemand das for que wir feel n'importe quelle Sprache to be insuffisante. Wie can nous beschreiben our accablante Freude and surprise! Wir do pas wissen which nous schätzen most: notre Vergnügen to-morrow, ou die fact, que von all gens Sie thought à uns.

We sommes alle three fières und happy, et danken you de ganz our cœur.

AUGUSTUS JOHN
(1878–1961)

John was famous as a portrait painter. See also Letter 283.

252. To Alexandra Schepeler, September 1907

Alexandra Schepeler, addressed by Yeats as 'Seraphita' (alluding to his favourite Balzac story), was painted by John.

Dear Alick,

Many thanks for your letter, so friendly as it was. I will get Robert to sit and if they like the drawing they can have it. This is a much better plan than a definite commission which generally puts me quite off. Robert sat to me for a sketch in oils which came off quite successfully. Lady Gregory, much as I love and admire her, has her eye still clouded a little by the visual enthousiasms of her youth and cannot be expected to *see* the merits of my point of view, tho' her intelligence assures her of their existence.

Painting Yeats is becoming quite a habit. He has a natural and sentimental prejudice in favour of the W. B. Yeats he & other people have been accustomed to see & imagine for so many years. He is now 44 and a robust virile and humourous personality (while still the poet of course). I cannot see in him any definite resemblance to the youthful Shelley in a lace collar. To my mind he is far more interesting as he is, as maturity is more interesting than immaturity. But my unprejudiced vision must seem brutal and unsympathetic to those in whom direct vision is supplanted by a vague and sentimental memory.

It is difficult also to assure people that my point of view is not that of a particularly ill-natured Camera—but on the contrary that of a profoundly sympathetic and clairvoyant intelligence. Another thing is I never paint without admiring.

This country is very beautiful. I generally go for a row on the lakes in the evenings. Yeats and I sit up late talking. He is very delightful, nobody seems to know him but me—unless it is the Gregorys, but that is my conceit no doubt.

I hope to see your charming rooms before long, also your charming self.

John

Coole Park] the house of Lady Gregory (1852–1932), playwright and patron.　　Robert] (1881–1918), her son, whose death in the Great War prompted Yeats's great elegy 'In Memory of Major Robert Gregory'.　　Yeats] actually 42 at the time.

LEONARD WOOLF
(1880–1969)

After Trinity College, Cambridge, where he came to know Strachey, Woolf entered the colonial service and from 1904 to 1911 was a district officer in Ceylon. In 1912 he married Virginia Stephen.

253. To Lytton Strachey, 29 September 1907

Strachey (1880–1932) was a biographer and a central Bloomsbury figure.

. . . I read *Madame Bovary* again as I went up to Hatton in the train last week to look after cattle disease. As I read it again, it seemed to me the saddest & most beautiful book I had ever read. Surely it is the beginning & end of realism. Was it he who discovered what no one seems to have noticed before the 19th Century, the futility & sordidness of actual existence? They never really saw it before, even *Candide,* for they always believed in some absurd fetish of the nobility of man. One can't believe in anything except beauty after reading Flaubert. Read the paragraph beginning 'Dans l'après midi, quelquefois, une tête d'homme apparaissait derrière les vitres de la salle. . . .' (page 70 in my copy); but the astonishing thing is that one really ought to have read straight through from the beginning to get the full effect of it. I had in this case & as paragraph succeeded paragraph & the inevitable sentences rolled out, it was overwhelming. One day I shall sit down & read straight on to the end: I don't think one would ever reach the end, I think one might die with Emma at

> Il souffla bien fort ce jour-là
> Et le jupon court s'envola.

I saw a most appalling spectacle the other day. I had to go (as Fiscal) to see four men hanged one morning. They were hanged two by two. I have a strong stomach but at best it is a horrible performance. I go to the cells & read over the warrant of execution & ask them whether they have anything to say. They nearly always say no. Then they are led out clothed in white, with curious white hats on their heads which at the last moment are drawn down to hide their faces. They are led up on to the scaffold & the ropes are placed round their necks. I have (in Kandy) to stand on a sort of verandah where I can actually see the man hanged. The signal has to be given by me. The first two were hanged all right but they gave one of the second too big a drop or something went wrong. The man's head was practically torn from his body & there was a great jet of blood which went up about 3 or 4 feet high, covering the gallows & priest who stands praying on the steps. The curious thing was that this man as he went to the gallows seemed to feel the rope round his neck: he kept twitching his head over into the exact position they hang in after death. Usually they are quite unmoved. One man kept on repeating two words of a Sinhalese prayer (I think) over & over again all the way to the gallows & even as he stood with the rope round his neck waiting for the drop.

I don't know why I have written all this to you except that whenever I stand waiting for the moment to give the signal, you & Turner & the room at Trinity come to my mind & the discussion in which Turner enraged us so by saying that he would not turn his head if anyone said there was a heap of corpses in the corner by the gyproom [college servants' pantry]. I don't think I should any more.

Yr

L.

Il souffla] Emma Bovary poisons herself at the end of Gustave Flaubert's *Madame Bovary* (1857). The verses quoted were her last words.   Fiscal] Procurator Fiscal, Woolf's role in the Colonial Service.

W. B. YEATS
(1865–1939)

254. *To John Quinn, 4 October 1907*

Quinn (1870–1924), an Irish American collector and patron, was a benefactor to Pound and Joyce as well as the Yeatses.

My dear Quinn,
Very many thanks for your long letter which I was very glad indeed to get. I have just come up from Coole for the production of a new play called *The Country Dressmaker*. It is by a new writer called Fitzmaurice. A harsh, strong, ugly comedy. It really gives a much worse view of the people than

The Playboy. Even I rather dislike it, though I admire its sincerity, and yet it was received with enthusiasm. The truth is that the objection to Synge is not mainly that he makes the country people unpleasant or immoral, but that he has got a standard of morals and intellect. They never minded Boyle, whose people are a sordid lot, because they knew what he was at. They understood his obvious moral, and they don't mind Fitzmaurice because they don't think he is at anything, but they shrink from Synge's harsh, independent, heroical, clean, wind-swept view of things. They want their clerical conservatory where the air is warm and damp. Of course, we may not get through to-morrow night, but the row won't be very bad. Nothing is ever persecuted but the intellect, though it is never persecuted under its own name. I don't think it would be wise for me to write a reply to that absurd article by McManus. As I never now write about politics people would think I was paying him off or his party off for *The Playboy.* I argued that question at the meeting not because I thought I would convince anybody but because the one thing that seemed possible was that all should show, players and playwrights, that we weren't afraid. The result has been that we have doubled the enthusiasm of our own following. The principal actors are now applauded at their entrances with a heartiness unknown before, and both Lady Gregory and myself received several times last spring what newspaper writers call 'an ovation.' We have lost a great many but the minority know that we are in earnest, and if only our finances hold out we will get the rest . . .

We have had another performance of *The Country Dressmaker* since I wrote, and the success was greater than before. The dear *Freeman*, or rather its evening issue which is called by another name, has congratulated us on having got a play at last 'to which nobody can take the slightest exception' or some such words, and yet Fitzmaurice, who wrote it, wrote it with the special object of showing up the sordid side of country life. He thinks himself a follower of Synge, which he is not. I have now no doubt that there will be enthusiasm to-night, and that the author, who has been thirsting for the crown of martyrdom, will be called before the curtain for the third night running. We are putting the play on again next week owing to its success.

Synge has just had an operation on his throat and has come through it all right. I am to see him to-day for the first time. When he woke out of the ether sleep his first words, to the great delight of the doctor, who knows his plays, were: 'May God damn the English, they can't even swear without vulgarity.' This tale delights the Company, who shudder at the bad language they have to speak in his plays. I don't think he has done much this summer owing to bad health but he will probably set to work now . . .

Augustus John has been staying at Coole. He came there to do an etching of me for the collected edition. Shannon was busy when I was in

London and the collected edition was being pushed on so quickly that I found I couldn't wait for him. I don't know what John will make of me. He made a lot of sketches with the brush and the pencil to work the etching from when he went home. I felt rather a martyr going to him. The students consider him the greatest living draughtsman, the only modern who can draw like an old master . . . He exaggerates every little hill and hollow of the face till one looks like a gypsy, grown old in wickedness and hardship. If one looked like any of his pictures the country women would take the clean clothes off the hedges when one passed, as they do at the sight of a tinker. He is himself a delight, the most innocent-wicked man I have ever met. He wears earrings, his hair down over his shoulders, a green velvet collar . . . He climbed to the top of the highest tree in Coole garden and carved a symbol there. Nobody else has been able to get up there to know what it is; even Robert stuck half way. He is a magnificent looking person, and looks the wild creature he is. His best work is etching. He is certainly a great etcher, with a savage imagination.

Yours ever
W B Yeats

FitzMaurice] George Fitzmaurice had several plays put on at the Abbey Theatre.   Synge] J. M. Synge's *The Playboy of the Western World* caused a great disturbance at the Abbey in 1907, with repercussions here alluded to.   Boyle] William Boyle, playwright, author of several Abbey plays, withdrew them as a protest against the production of *The Playboy*.   Augustus John] see above, Letter 252.   Shannon] C. H. Shannon (1863–1937), friend of Charles Ricketts; painter and editor.   Robert] Gregory; see above, Letter 252.

255. To John Quinn, 30 October 1920

My dear Quinn,

When your letter arrived some weeks ago it awaited us at breakfast. Before I opened it George told me of a dream she had had that morning. I had two spots in my throat and she and I were disputing whether I should have them taken out in Dublin or in London. She thought I would be better cared for in Dublin but I was for London. When I read your letter I saw that her dream expressed it in allegory. This dream proves (like much else) that people explain by telepathy what telepathy has nothing to do with. No telepathy could have told George that your letter was about to arrive.

Some time afterwards I went to London, having made an appointment with a surgeon there. But when I rang at his door the servant maid, who was in a wild hurry, explained that he was no longer there. She gave me a new address and when I went to it he wasn't there either; she had given me a wrong address. I went to the telephone book, but couldn't find it, through a muddle of my own. He had a hyphenated name and I looked him up under the second half. I went back to Oxford and, being a superstitious

man, began to think the finger of providence was in it. George consulted
the stars and they said quite plainly that if I went to the London operator
I would die, probably of hemorrhage. Then later we did another figure to
know should I go to the Dublin operator. Then the stars were as favourable
as possible—Venus, with all her ribbons floating, poised upon the mid-
heaven! We went to Dublin. Gogarty, with his usual exuberant gaiety,
removed my tonsils. As long as I retained consciousness he discussed
literature, and continued the discussion when I awoke. He would probably
have continued it most of the afternoon (he came 6 times) but I had a
hemorrhage and was preoccupied with my possible end. I was looking,
secretly, of course, for a dying speech. I rejected Christian resignation as
too easy, seeing that I no longer cared whether I lived or died. I looked
about for a good model (I have always contended that a model is necessary
to style), but could think of nothing save a certain old statesman who,
hearing a duck quack, murmured 'Those young ducks must be ready for
the table,' and added to that 'Ruling passion strong in death.' Then I
wondered if I could give the nurses a shock by plucking at the bedclothes.

The day after I came out of the home we went on shipboard to be ready
for the morning start and returned to Oxford, taking three days upon the
road. We had to hurry because a railway strike was supposed inevitable and
it might have lasted weeks. I am now almost well again. But it is too soon
to say how much I have benefitted. My rheumatism seems already better.
There is no fear that the operation has not been done thoroughly, for as
Gogarty looked at me over the end of the bed as I was meditating on the
ducks he said, 'I have been *too* thorough.' I am bored by convalescence, not
having yet my full powers of work. And when I am dressing in the morning
I look out of the window at Anne strapped into her perambulator in the
garden. I watch her twisting about trying to get into the bottom of the
perambulator, with her heels up, and I say to myself, 'Which is the greater
bore, convalescence or infancy?'

I have been arranging the portraits in my study. Swift wrote to Stella
once, 'I am bringing back with me portraits of all my friends;' meaning by
that, doubtless, mezzotints. I have lithographs, photogravures, pencil drawings, photographs from pictures. There is only one absent—John Quinn.
Will you send me a photograph of Augustus John's drawing of you? My
sister has one, but I don't like to beg it of her . . .

Yours ever

W B Yeats

I don't write about politics, for obvious reasons. Censorship is exceedingly
severe, if capricious.

George] Mrs Yeats.   Gogarty] Oliver St John Gogarty (1878–1957), surgeon, poet, wit; the
Buck Mulligan of Joyce's *Ulysses*.   Anne] the Yeats's daughter.   Capricious] the
capriciousness of the censorship must have been due to the civil war then in progress.

256. To Olivia Shakespear, 1 June 1930

Olivia Shakespear (1863–1938) had been Yeats's mistress and remained a close friend.

My dear Olivia,

The children are here and are—now that Dorothy and Ezra are gone—our only event. Anne has achieved her first act of independence. At lunch she was not to be found and Michael said, with a voice full of disgust, 'Anne has run away.' Meanwhile a friend of George's and mine had met her on a country road 'talking to herself and trying to walk like a queen in a faery tale' and asked her to lunch. Anne accepted but insisted on eating her own food and unpacked a knapsack. She brought out (wrapped up in separate pieces of newspaper), biscuits, a bottle of lemonade, a looking-glass, a comb, a brush, and a piece of soap. She said she would go home 'after dark' but was persuaded to do so at the end of lunch by the suggestion that George and Michael were probably making ices. Anne and Michael have been given their first chess-board and taught the moves. An hour later there came yells and bangs from the nursery. All the chairs were upset, and Michael had his two hands in Anne's hair, and Anne was pounding Michael. The point was—had Michael check-mated Anne? What a lot Dorothy is missing by leaving Omar in London!

If nothing happens to change our plans we shall stay here till well on in July. Gogarty says John wants 'to paint a serious portrait' of me, and should this turn out true we may have to leave rather sooner. I hope not for I am writing verse again, and pleased with what I am doing. I enjoy my life when it is not interrupted by too many days of fatigue, but those days come more seldom. I am trying to avoid them by working three days and then resting three days. We sit in the sun—George and the children on the sea-shore after a bathe—I on my balcony, as naked as usage permits—and then oil ourselves. We colour like old meerschaum pipes.

I read Swift constantly and George reads out Morris's *Well at the World's End*. I read to the children at six every evening. O how intolerable *The Lay of the Last Minstrel* is, and yet the magic book in Melrose made them put their faces up side by side at the edge of my bed. I generally go to bed before dinner for a while. I have read them *The Ancient Mariner, The Lays of Ancient Rome, How the Good News* and *The Pied Piper.*

Yours affectionately
W B Yeats

Dorothy] Olivia Shakespear's daughter Dorothy was married to Ezra Pound, and their son was Omar.   Michael] the Yeats's son.

257. To Olivia Shakespear, 27 December 1934

Written shortly after Yeats's Steinach operation, intended to restore sexual potency. He was having an affair of sorts with the novelist Ethel Mannin.

My dear Olivia,

Are you back? Wonderful things have happened. This is Bagdad. This is not London.

Yours
W B Yeats

258. To Lady Elizabeth Pelham, 4 January 1939

Lady Elizabeth Pelham was one of a group, to which Yeats belonged, which cultivated Shri Purohit Swami, an exponent of Indian mysticism, who arrived in London in 1931. Yeats died on 28 Jan. The letter exists only as a fragment.

. . . I know for certain that my time will not be long. I have put away everything that can be put away that I may speak what I have to speak, and I find 'expression' is a part of 'study.' In two or three weeks—I am now idle that I may rest after writing much verse—I will begin to write my most fundamental thoughts and the arrangement of thought which I am convinced will complete my studies. I am happy, and I think full of an energy, of an energy I had despaired of. It seems to me that I have found what I wanted. When I try to put all into a phrase I say, 'Man can embody truth but he cannot know it.' I must embody it in the completion of my life. The abstract is not life and everywhere draws out its contradictions. You can refute Hegel but not the Saint or the Song of Sixpence . . .

EDITH WHARTON

(1862–1937)

The American novelist Edith Wharton lived in France from 1907, and was active in relief work from the start of the war of 1914–18.

259. To Morton Fullerton, March 1908

For Fullerton, Wharton's lover, see above, Letters 231 and 250.

Dear,

Remember, please, how impatient & anxious I shall be to know the sequel of the Bell letter . . .

——Do you know what I was thinking last night, when you asked me, & I couldn't tell you?—Only that the way you've spent your emotional life, while I've—bien malgré moi—hoarded mine, is what puts the great gulf between us, & sets us not only on opposite shores, but at hopelessly distant points of our respective shores . . . Do you see what I mean?

And I'm so afraid that the treasures I long to unpack for you, that have come to me in magic ships from enchanted islands, are only, to you, the old familiar red calico & beads of the clever trader, who has had dealings in every latitude, & knows just what to carry in the hold to please the simple native—I'm so afraid of this, that often & often I stuff my shining treasures back into their box, lest I should see you smiling at them!

Well! And if you do? It's *your* loss, after all! And if you can't come into the room without my feeling all over me a ripple of flame, & if, wherever you touch me, a heart beats under your touch, & if, when you hold me, & I don't speak, it's because all the words in me seem to have become throbbing pulses, & all my thoughts are a great golden blur—why should I be afraid of your smiling at me, when I can turn the beads & calico back into such beauty—?

The Bell letter] a letter to the *Observer* newspaper relative to a dispute concerning the control of *The Times*.

260. To Henry James, 28 February 1915

James was Wharton's professional inspiration and close friend.

Dearest Cher Maître,

After nearly six months at the same job I felt a yearning to get away for a few days, & also a great desire to find out what was really wanted in some of the hospitals near the front, from which such lamentable tales have reached us.

It took a good deal of démarching & counter marching to get a laissez-passer, for it has always been a great deal more difficult to go East than North, & especially so, these last weeks, on account of the 'spies & espions' (as White calls them), & also of the movements of troops, more recently. However, thanks to Paul & to Mr Cambon (the Berlin one) I did, a day or two ago, get a splendid permesso, & immediately loaded up the motor with clothes & medicaments & dashed off from Paris with Walter yesterday morning. We went first to Châlons s/ Marne, & it was extraordinary, not more than 4 hours from Paris, to find ourselves to all appearance completely in the war-zone. It is the big base of the Eastern army, & the streets swarm with soldiers & with military motors & ambulances. We went to see a hospital with 900 cases of typhoid, where *everything* was lacking—a depressing beginning, for even if I had emptied my motor-load into their laps it would have been a goutte d'eau in a desert. But I promised to report, & try to come back with more supplies next week.

This morning we left Châlons & headed for Verdun. At Ste Menehould we had to get permission to go farther, as the Grand Quartier Général can't give it unless the local staff consents. First they said it was impossible—but the Captain had read one of my books, so he told the Colonel it was all right, & the Colonel said: 'Very well—mais filez vite, for there is big fighting going on nearby, & this afternoon the wounded are to be evacuated from the front, & we want no motors on the road.'

About 15 kms farther we came to Clermont-en-Argonne, of which you have read—one of the most utterly ravaged places in this region. It looks exactly like Pompeii—I felt as if I must be going to lunch at the Hotel Diomède!

Instead we ate filet & fried potatoes in the kitchen of the Hospice where Sœur Rosnet, the wonderful sister who stuck to her wounded when the Germans came, gave us a welcome proportioned to the things she needed for the new batch of wounded that she is expecting tonight.—Suddenly we heard the cannon roaring close by, & a woman rushed in to say that we could see the fighting from the back of a house across the street. We tore over, & there, from a garden we looked across the valley to a height about 5 miles away, where white puffs & scarlet flashes kept springing up all over the dark hillside. It was the hill above Vauquois, where there has been desperate fighting for two days. The Germans were firing from the top at the French trenches below (hidden from us by an intervening rise of the ground); & the French were assaulting, & *their* puffs & flashes were half way up the hill. And so we saw the reason why there are to be so many wounded at Clermont tonight!

We went to Verdun after lunch, stopping at Blercourt to see a touching little ambulance where the sick & the nervously shattered are sent till they can be moved. Most of them are in the village church, four rows of beds down the nave, & when we went in the curé was just ringing the bell for vespers. Then he went & put on his vestments, & reappeared at the lighted altar with his acolyte, & incense began to float over the pale heads on the pillows, & the villagers came into the church, &, standing between the beds, sang a strange wailing thing that repeats at the end of every verse:

'*Sauvez, sauvez la France,*
Ne l'abandonnez pas!'—It was poignant.

To complete our sensations—I forgot to put the incident in its right place—we saw a column of soldiers marching along the road this morning, coming toward us, between a handful of cavalry. Walter said: 'Look at their coats! They're covered with mud.' And when they came nearer, we saw the coats were pale grey, & they were a hundred or so German prisoners, fresh picked from that dark wood where we were to see the red flashes later in the day.

We got here about 4, & presented ourselves at the Citadel, where the officer who took our papers had read me too—wasn't it funny?—& turned out to be Henri de Jouvenel, the husband of Colette Willy!!!—He was very nice, but much amazed at my having succeeded in getting here. He said: 'Vous êtes la première femme qui soit venue à Verdun'—& at the Hospital they told me the same thing. The town is dead—nearly all the civil population evacuated, & the garrison, I suppose, in the trenches. The cannon booms continuously about 10 miles away.—Tomorrow we go to Bar le Duc & then back to Châlons & home. I shall come again in a few days with lots of things, now that I know what is needed.

This reads like one of Mme Waddington's letters to Henrietta, but I'm so awed by all I've seen that I can only prattle.

I shall have to take this to Paris to post—it takes 8 days for letters to go from here.

I thought my sensations de guerre might interest you even in this artless shape.

Your devoted Edith

9 p.m. & the cannon still booming.

Paul] Bourget (1852–1935), French critic and novelist.　　Cambon] Jules Cambon (1845–1935) was Secretary-General in the Ministry of Foreign Affairs; until 1914 he had been French Ambassador in Berlin.　　Henri de Jouvenel] journalist and the second husband of the novelist Colette, still known as Colette Willy from books written by her but published as by her first husband, whose pen-name was 'Willy'.　　Waddington] Mary King Waddington wrote *Italian Letters of a Diplomat's Wife* (1905).

D. H. LAWRENCE
(1885–1930)

261. To Rachel Annand Taylor, 3 December 1910

Rachel Taylor (1876–1960) met Lawrence through Ford Madox Ford (Hueffer), editor of the *English Review*, in which Lawrence was first published. She was a poet and a biographer of considerable fame at this time; Lawrence gave his talk about her to the Croydon branch of the English Association in Nov. 1910.

Dear Mrs Taylor,

I did not know where you were. I am glad you wrote to me.

I have been at home now ten days. My mother is very near the end. Today I have been to Leicester. I did not get home till half past nine. Then I ran upstairs. Oh she was very bad. The pains had been again.

'Oh my dear' I said, 'is it the pains?'

'Not pain now—Oh the weariness' she moaned, so that I could hardly hear her. I wish she could die tonight.

My sister and I do all the nursing. My sister is only 22. I sit upstairs hours and hours, till I wonder if ever it were true that I was at London. I seem to have died since, and that is an old life, dreamy.

I will tell you. My mother was a clever, ironical delicately moulded woman, of good, old burgher descent. She married below her. My father was dark, ruddy, with a fine laugh. He is a coal miner. He was one of the sanguine temperament, warm and hearty, but unstable: he lacked principle, as my mother would have said. He deceived her and lied to her. She despised him—he drank.

Their marriage life has been one carnal, bloody fight. I was born hating my father: as early as ever I can remember, I shivered with horror when he touched me. He was very bad before I was born.

This has been a kind of bond between me and my mother. We have loved each other, almost with a husband and wife love, as well as filial and maternal. We knew each other by instinct. She said to my aunt—about me:

'But it has been different with him. He has seemed to be part of me.'— and that is the real case. We have been like one, so sensitive to each other that we never needed words. It has been rather terrible, and has made me, in some respects, abnormal.

I think this peculiar fusion of soul (don't think me high-falutin) never comes twice in a life-time—it doesn't seem natural. When it comes it seems to distribute one's consciousness far abroad from oneself, and one 'understands'. I think no one has got 'Understanding' except through love. Now my mother is nearly dead, and I don't quite know how I am.

I have been to Leicester today, I have met a girl who has always been warm for me—like a sunny happy day—and I've gone and asked her to marry me: in the train, quite unpremeditated, between Rothley and Quorn— she lives at Quorn. When I think of her I feel happy with a sort of warm radiation—she is big and dark and handsome. There were five other people in the carriage. Then when I think of my mother:—if you've ever put your hand round the bowl of a champagne glass and squeezed it and wondered how near it is to crushing-in and the wine all going through your fingers— that's how my heart feels—like the champagne glass. There is no hostility between the warm happiness and the crush of misery: but one is concentrated in my chest, and one is diffuse—a suffusion, vague.

Muriel is the girl I have broken with. She loves me to madness, and demands the soul of me. I have been cruel to her, and wronged her, but I did not know.

Nobody can have the soul of me. My mother has had it, and nobody can have it again. Nobody can come into my very self again, and breathe me like an atmosphere. Don't say I am hasty this time—I know. Louie— whom I wish I could marry the day after the funeral—she would never demand to drink me up and have me. She loves me—but it is a fine, warm, healthy, natural love—not like Jane Eyre, who is Muriel, but like—say Rhoda Fleming or a commoner Anna Karénin. She will never plunge her hands through my blood and feel for my soul, and make me set my teeth and shiver and fight away. Ugh—I have done well—and cruelly—tonight.

I look at my father—he is like a cinder. It is very terrible, mis marriage.

They sent me yesterday one copy of the *Peacock* for my mother. She just looked at it. It will not be out till spring.

I will tell you next time about that meeting when I gave a paper on you. It was *most* exciting. I worked my audience up to red heat—and I laughed.

Are you any better?—you don't say so. Tell me you are getting strong, and then you and I will not re-act so alarmingly—at least, you on me.

Goodnight
D. H. Lawrence

A girl] Louise Burrows (1888–1962); Lawrence was engaged to her for over a year.   *Muriel*] Jessie Chambers (1887–1944), the Miriam of *Sons and Lovers*, called 'Muriel' in 'A Modern Lover' and other early stories.   Rhoda Fleming] the heroine of George Meredith's novel of that name (1865).   *Peacock*] *The White Peacock*, Lawrence's first novel, was published in Jan. 1911.

262. *To Henry Savage, 31 October 1913*

Savage (1881–?) had given *The White Peacock* an enthusiastic review in the *Academy*. His friend Richard Middleton (1882–1911), poet and short-story writer, had previously done so in *Vanity Fair*. Savage had sent Middleton's *Monologues* (1913).

Dear Savage,

We were glad to get your letter and the book. The latter interests me— the things are nice and slight. Frieda thinks they are stupid—Middleton's essays—particularly about women. I think myself he was stupid about women. It seems to me silly to rage against woman—as Sphinx, or Sphinx without a secret, or cunning artist in living—or in herself. It seems to me that the chief thing about a woman—who is much of a woman—is that in the long run she is not to be had. A man may bring her his laurel wreaths and songs and what not, but if that man doesn't satisfy her, in some undeniable physical fashion—then in one way or other she takes him in her mouth and shakes him like a cat a mouse, and throws him away. She is not to be caught by any of the catch-words, love, beauty, honor, duty, worth, work, salvation—none of them—not in the long run. In the long run she only says 'Am I satisfied, or is there some beastly unsatisfaction gnawing and gnawing inside me.' And if there is some unsatisfaction, it is physical at least as much as psychic, sex as much as soul. So she goes for man, or men, after her own fashion, and so is called a Sphinx, and her riddle is that the man wasn't able to satisfy her—riddle enough for him: And an artist— a poet—is like a woman in that he too must have this satisfaction. There is that much life in him, more than in other people, which will not let him be. He must get his bodily and spiritual want satisfied in one and the same draught. So he must endlessly go for women, and for love. And I reckon an artist is only an ordinary man with a greater potentiality—same stuff, same make up, only more force. And the strong driving force usually finds his weak spot, and he goes cranked, or goes under. Middleton seems to me to have been wrongly directed. I think if you could have made him simply voluptuous, that would have been his salvation. He hated his flesh and blood. His life went on apart from his own flesh and blood—something like a monk who mortifies the flesh. It is a curious thing how poets tend to become ascetics, in the last sense of the word. Even a debauch for them is a self-flagellation. They go on the loose in cruelty against themselves, admitting that they are pandering to, and despising, the lower self. The lower self is the flesh, and the physical sensation, which they hate even when they praise it. For it is so much more difficult to live with one's body than with one's soul. One's body is so much more exacting: what it won't have it won't have, and nothing can make bitter into sweet. And this inexorable stubbornness of his body, that doesn't really care about little mistresses even when they are flung to it, that *isn't* satisfied even with debauch, makes a poet hate his body. He should submit to it, but he wants to be master of it. So Middleton was an ascetic who bitterly disbelieved in asceticism. But that, by training, was the only way he could work—by denying he'd got a body. He despised his own flesh and stamped it out of life, before he died. We are all alike.—You should watch the free Italians, then you'd know what we've done. We've denied the life of our bodies, so they, our bodies, deny life unto us. Curious, dried people we've become, always submitting ourselves to some damned rigid purpose, some idea, instead of fructifying in the sun while it shines.

Which is a beautifully long tirade, that you needn't read. Frieda says I'm always stupid when I'm didactic. I suppose I am—it doesn't bother me— I don't believe it—I'm only clumsy.

I retract what I say against Dickens characters—I am jealous of them. But there is something fundamental about *him* that I dislike. He is mid-Victorian, he is so governessy towards life, as if it were a naughty child. His God is a Sunday-School Superintendent, on the prize-giving day, and he is the mistress of the top class. Curse him.

It is really wonderfully beautiful here—wonderful. Sometimes the thought of the English autumn comes strangely to me, here where the sunshine is so fine, and evenings such magnificent coloured things. It makes me feel as if autumn and gossamer were only painted on the air, at England, and that you might look through like through a window, to things out here, into space and sunshine. And I seem to be able to look far down the brightness here, and see little, blue-grey, wistful-tender England.

But we've both had rotten bad colds, and have lazed about. I wish I'd got some money, and needn't work. I am feeling afraid of idling any more.

Send me a book now and then, will you—any rubbishy thing—it is so grateful. I can read Philpotts or Gissing—though I've read most of him—or anybody.

I hope your wife will go on all right. I don't agree with you about our separation from women. The only thing that is very separate—our bodies—is the via media for union again, if we would have it so. Nous pauvres Anglais—we've puritanised ourselves almost out of physical existence. It is so wrong.

I shall send you a copy of my play, when at length it comes out.

Our regards to you and to your wife. Come and see us then, after Christmas. All joy to the child.

D. H. Lawrence

Tolstoi—*Kreutzer Sonata* 4^1/$_2$d.

[*Frieda Weekley begins*]
Dear Mr Savage,

I wish I could help you but I am not good at expressing myself—But I can just say one or two things—I get so *cross* with Middleton when he hates his body, God made it and even if it was'nt Apollo like it *must* have been a lovable one—What this really means is that no woman ever loved it, if a woman had, he would not have killed himself and he would have been a very great man—It was really sex—unsatisfied sex—that killed him.—In a big soul man like Middleton *every*thing is strong, so of course the sex, that's why you say he was like a madman when in love—On the other hand he despised and hated women, quite right from his point of view, because he had so much to give to a woman and the fools had'nt the wit to take him—Perhaps they took him physically, that does'nt matter but Middleton the *whole* of him they did not take of that I am certain, a woman could have *made* him live, I loathe my sex sometimes for being cowards and fools—He is right in his article on the new sex, I think women should be satisfied to *be* and let the men *do*. We can *do* so much more *that* way—I hate the women for not having enough *pride* to be themselves just their own natural selves, they must wrap themselves in false morals, do tricks in which all the time they believe in more or less—When M. talks of women and art he is'nt quite fair, if a woman looks on herself as a work of art why belittle it? Is'nt that a form of aspiration, of perfecting herself, she may be stupid about it, but anyway she *tries*. But then, poor devil, he cant have met a girl, that was equal to him—I wish I had the poems here—I think he was eminently a lyric, and I believe for those comes a critical time when the first youth is over and the man's period should begin, o dear, it makes one so damned miserable that the best always seem to snap the chord so easily—

He fought so bravely for his ideals, he helped so much but he had suffered of the sins of his contemporaries himself—He accuses Shaw and Galsworthy for sacrificing beauty to morals and yet he had such an abstract conception of beauty himself—It makes me cross 'beauty, beauty', it's become so cheap, what does it mean—Hunting beauty, Murillo I think made a fine picture of a boy hunting a flea (there are so many here!) He was never quite able to shake off Midvictorian middle class—There I have jawed and very likely been no use! But it's gorgeous here, lazy and serene, L. does'nt want to work, it seems like wasting one's time to work, and intellectual stuff seems the Devil himself—It is so much more satisfactory to watch the waves lap at the stones, the big rocks—sometimes high and sometimes low, we are so happy with our little house and all this loveliness round us—You ought to come—I suppose the infant has arrived—I hope it will make you happy, it *ought*—I envy your wife for it—I have just revelled in J. J. Rousseau's *Confessions* which I adore, he is so awfully lovable, I really think genius consists in a great lovableness, but then, that is the woman's point of view—My regards to your wife, I felt so flattered, when you told me 'my wife would like you', it also showed me that you think more of her than you know, so there—

    L. sends love, I do hope your 'Cruise' will be successful both in print and in person—

Your with very kind regards

Frieda—at present I have not other name I believe—

Beautiful here] in Lerici, where Lawrence was living after his elopement with Frieda Weekley, the wife of a Nottingham professor.   Philpotts] Eden Phillpotts (1862–1960), novelist. Gissing] George Gissing (1857–1903), novelist.

263. To Middleton Murry, 27 November 1913

John Middleton Murry (1889–1957), critic and journalist, married the short-story writer Katherine Mansfield (1888–1923) in 1918. Murry had been offered a lektorship in a German university. He and Mansfield founded a little magazine, *Rhythm*.

Dear Murry,

    I am going to answer you immediately, and frankly.

    When you say you won't take Katherine's money, it means you don't trust her love for you: When you say she needs little luxuries, and you couldn't bear to deprive her of them, it means you don't respect either yourself or her sufficiently to do it.

    It looks to me as if you two, far from growing nearer, are snapping the bonds that hold you together, one after another. I suppose you must both of you consult your own hearts, honestly. She must see if she really *wants* you, wants to keep you and to have no other man all her life. It means forfeiting something. But the only principle I can see in this life, is that one *must* forfeit the less for the greater. Only one must be thoroughly honest about it.

She must say 'Could I live in a little place in Italy with Jack, and be lonely, have rather a bare life, but be happy'. If she could, then take her money. If she doesn't want to, don't try. But don't beat about the bush. In the way you go on, you are inevitably coming apart. She is perhaps beginning to be unsatisfied with you. And you won't make her more satisfied, by being unselfish. You must say, 'how can I make myself most healthy, strong, and satisfactory to myself and to her'? If by being lazy for six months, then be lazy, and take her money. It doesn't matter if she misses her luxuries: she won't die of it. What luxuries do you mean?

If she doesn't want to stake her whole life and being on you, then go to your University abroad for a while, alone. I warn you, it'll be hellish barren.

Or else you can gradually come apart in London, and then flounder till you get your feet again, severally. But be clear about it. It lies between you and Katherine, nowhere else.

Of course you can't dream of living long without work. Couldn't you get the *Westminster* to give you *two* columns a week, abroad? You must *try*. You must stick to criticism. You ought also to plan a book, either on some literary point or some man. I should like to write a book on English heroines. You ought to do something of that sort, but not so cheap. Don't try a novel—try Essays—like Walter Pater or somebody of that style. But you *can* do something *good* in that line: something concerning *literature* rather than life. And you must rest, and you and Katherine must heal, and come together, before you do *any serious* work of any sort. It is the split in the love that drains you. You see, while she doesn't really love you, and is not satisfied, *you* show to such frightful disadvantage. But it would be a pity not to let your mind flower—it might, under decent circumstances, produce beautiful delicate things, in perception and appreciation. And *she* has a right to provide the conditions. But not if you don't trust yourself nor her nor anybody, but go on slopping, and pandering to her smaller side. If you work yourself sterile to get her chocolates, she will most justly detest you—she is *perfectly* right. If you tell her, pandering to her uncertainty in you, that in time of great stress, you could let her go to a man like a prostitute, for money, you are a fool. You *couldn't* do it, without some violation to your soul, some rupture that would cripple you for ever. Then why don't you say 'no'. She wants to be sure that she is worth it to you, and you, instead of saying yes, sort of sacrifice yourself to her. She doesn't want you to sacrifice yourself to her, you fool. Be more natural, and positive, and stick to your own guts. You spread them on a tray for her to throw to the cats.

If you want things to come right—if you are ill, and exhausted, then take her money to the last penny, and let her do her own house-work. Then she'll know you love her. You can't blame her if she's not satisfied with you. If I haven't had enough dinner, you can't blame *me*. You've got it in you to be enough for her. But you fool, you squander yourself, not for *her*, but to provide her with petty luxuries she doesn't really want. You insult her. A woman unsatisfied must have luxuries. But a woman who loves a man would sleep on a board.

It strikes me you've got off your lines, somewhere. You've not been man enough: you've felt it rested with your honor to give her a place to be proud of. It rested with your honor to give her a man to be satisfied with—and satisfaction is never accomplished even physically without the man is strongly and surely himself, and doesn't depend on anything but his own *being* to make a woman love him. You've tried to satisfy Katherine with what you could earn for her, give her: and she will only be satisfied with what you *are*.

And you don't know what you are. You've never come to it. You've always been dodging round, getting *Rhythms* and flats and doing criticism for money. You are a fool to work so hard for Katherine—she hates you for it—and quite right. You want to be strong in the possession of your own soul. Perhaps you will only come to that when this affair of you and her has gone crash. I should be sorry to think that—I don't believe it. You must save yourself, and your self-respect, by making it complete between Katherine and you—if you devour her money till she walks in rags, if you are both outcast. Make her certain—don't pander to her—stick to *your-self*—do what you *want* to do—don't *consider* her—she hates and loathes being considered. You insult her in saying you wouldn't take her money.

The University idea is a bad one. It would further disintegrate you.

If you are disintegrated, then *get integrated* again. Don't be a coward. If you are disintegrated your first duty is to yourself, and you may use Katherine—her money and everything—to get right again. You're not well, man. Then have the courage to get well. If you are strong again, and a bit complete, *she'll* be satisfied with you. She'll love you hard enough. But don't you see, at this rate, you distrain on her day by day and month by month. I've done it myself.

Take your rest—do *nothing* if you like for a while—though I'd do a *bit*. Get better, first and foremost—use *anybody's* money, to do so. Get better—and do things you like. Get yourself into condition—it drains and wearies Katherine to have you like this. What a fool you are, what a fool. Don't bother about her—what she wants or feels. Say 'I am a man at the end of the tether, therefore I become a man blind to everything but my own need'. But keep a heart for the long run.

Look. We pay 60 Lire a month for this house: 25 Lire for the servant: and food is *very* cheap. You could live on 185 Lire a month, in plenty—and be greeted as the 'Signoria' when you went out together—it is the same as 'Guten Tag, Herrschaften'. That would be luxury enough for Katherine.

Get up, lad, and be a man for yourself. It's the man who dares to take, who is independent, not he who gives.

I think Oxford did you harm.

It is beautiful, wonderful, here. A ten pound note is 253 Lire. We could get you, I believe, a jolly nice apartment in a big garden, in a house alone for 80 Lire a month. Don't waste yourself—don't be silly and floppy. You know what you *could* do—you *could* write—then prepare yourself: and first make Katherine at rest in her love for you. Say 'this I will certainly do'— it would be a relief for her to hear you. Don't be a child—don't keep that rather childish charm. Throw everything away, and say 'Now I act for my own good, at last'.

We are getting gradually nearer again, Frieda and I. It is very beautiful here.

We are awfully sorry Katherine is so seedy. She ought to write to us. Our love to her and you.

D. H. Lawrence

If you've got an odd book or so you don't want to read, would you send it us. There is nothing for Frieda to read—and we like anything and everything.

264. To Lady Cynthia Asquith, 3 June 1918

Lady Cynthia (1887–1960) was a writer and friend of many writers, and private secretary to J. M. Barrie. Lawrence is writing from a cottage in Derbyshire.

I dreamed of you so hard a few days ago, so must write, though there is no news to send. We are here with my sister, and two children—a very delightful boy of three, and a girl of seven. I am surprised how children are like barometers to their parents' feelings. There is some sort of queer, magnetic psychic connection—something a bit fatal, I believe. I feel I am all the time rescuing my nephew and my niece from their respective mothers, my two sisters: who have jaguars of wrath in their souls, however they purr to their offspring. The phenomenon of motherhood, in these days, is a strange and rather frightening phenomenon.

I dreamed also such a funny dream. When I had been to some big, crowded fair somewhere—where things were to sell, on booths and on the floor—as I was coming back down an open road, I heard such a strange crying overhead, in front, and looking up, I saw, not very high in the air above me, but higher than I could throw, two pale spotted dogs, crouching in the air, and mauling a bird that was crying loudly. I ran fast forwards and clapped my hands and the dogs started back. The bird came falling to earth. It was a young peacock, blue all over like a peacock's neck, very lovely. It still kept crying. But it was not much hurt. A woman came running out of a cottage not far off, and took the bird, saying it would be all right. So I went my way.—That dream in some oblique way or other is connected with your 'aura'—but I can't interpret it.

Would you really like to come here—it's a nice place, really—you'd like it.—But I feel as if I were on a sort of ledge half way down a precipice, and didn't know how to get up or down: and it is a queer kind of place to ask visitors to see you, such a ledge.

I signed the agreement for the poems. When proofs come I'll send them and you can tell me at once if there's anything you'd like different. But they're all right.

Poor Whibley, he is so good trying to get that money for me. Will it come off? I hope so—but if not, never bother.

Mr Billing is the last word in canaille.

DHL

Whibley] Charles Whibley (1859–1930), scholar, critic, publisher's reader.   Billing] Noel Pemberton Billing (1880–1948), MP and demagogue, notorious for his campaign against the dancer Maud Allen and for his 'Black Book' listing 47,000 German sympathizers, including the Asquith family (Lady Cynthia's father-in-law had been Prime Minister till 1916).

265. To Katherine Mansfield, 9 February 1919

My dear Katherine—

I send you *I Promessi Sposi* and *Peru*. I thought you would like the other two. I am very fond of George Sand—have read only *François le Champi* and *Maître Sonneurs* and *Villemer*—I liked *Maître Sonneurs* immensely. Have you any George Sand? and Mary Mann is quite good, I think.—It is marvellous weather—brilliant sunshine on the snow, clear as summer, slightly golden sun, distance lit up. But it is immensely cold—everything frozen solid—milk, mustard everything. Yesterday I went out for a real walk—I've had a cold and been in bed. I climbed with my niece to the bare top of the hills. Wonderful is to see the footmarks on the snow—beautiful ropes of rabbit prints, trailing away over the brows; heavy hare marks; a fox so sharp and dainty, going over the wall; birds with two feet that hop; very splendid straight advance of a pheasant; wood-pigeons that are clumsy and move in flocks; splendid little leaping marks of weasels, coming along like a necklace chain of berries; odd little filigree of the field-mice; the trail of a mole—it is astounding what a world of wild creatures one feels round one, on the hills in the snow. From the height it is very beautiful. The upland is naked, white like silver, and moving far into the distance, strange and muscular, with gleams like skin. Only the wind surprises one, invisibly cold; the sun lies bright on a field, like the movement of a sleeper. It is strange how insignificant, in all this, life seems. Two men, tiny as dots, move from a farm on a snow-slope, carrying hay to the beast. Every moment, they seem to melt like insignificant spots of dust. The sheer, living, muscular white of the uplands absorbs everything. Only there is a tiny clump of trees bare on the hill-top—small beeches—writhing like iron in the blue sky.—I wish one could cease to be a human being, and be a demon.—Allzu Menschlich.

My sister Emily is here, with her little girl—whose birthday it is to-day—Emily is cooking treacle rolly and cakes, Frieda is making Peggy a pale grey dress, I am advising and interfering—Pamela is lamenting because the eggs in the pantry have all frozen and burst—I have spent half an hour hacking ice out of the water tub—now I am going out. Peggy, with her marvellous red-gold hair in dangling curl-rags, is darting about sorting the coloured wools and cottons—scène de famille.—It is beautiful to cross the field to the well for drinking water—such pure sun, and Slaley, the tiny village away across, sunny as Italy in its snow.—I expect Willie Hopkin will come today.

Well—life itself is life—even the magnificent frost-foliage on the window. While we live, let us live—

DHL

Emily's nickname was Pamela, or *Virtue Rewarded.*

I Promessi Sposi] *The Betrothed*, novel of 1827 by Alessandro Manzoni.   *Peru*] W. H. Prescott, *History of the Conquest of Peru* (1847).   Sand] George Sand (1804–76) wrote *François le Champi* (1856), *Les Maîtres sonneurs* (1852), and *Le Marquis de Villemer* (1860).   Mary Mann] (d. 1929), a prolific popular writer.   Allzu Menschlich] all too human.   Willie Hopkin] (1862–1951), local politician and journalist, who had had considerable influence on the youthful Lawrence.   Pamela] Samuel Richardson wrote *Pamela; or, Virtue Rewarded* (1740).

George Bernard Shaw
(1856–1950)

Shaw wrote an enormous number of letters; the rather small proportion that have been published establish him as one of the greatest of all letter writers. They are addressed to an amazing variety of correspondents, famous and obscure.

266. To Gilbert Murray, 14 March 1911

Murray (1866–1957), Regius Professor of Greek at Oxford, had just translated *Oedipus Rex*. Thanking Shaw for this letter he remarked that it was 'difficult to read without tears'.

My dear Murray,

They tell me you have translated Edipus. I havnt seen your original; but the matter as between us is important. I beg your attention for a moment.

You once said you would like to write modern Medeas, Electras &c.

I once said I wished you would commit some disgraceful offence, and be extruded ignominiously from Oxford, like Shelley.

These two birds can be killed with one stone; and that stone is Edipus. Let me lead up to this gradually.

If you have recently translated Edipus, you will agree with me that Sophocles was the sort of man the English like, just as Euripides was the sort of man they loathe. That is, he had the brains of a ram, the theatrical technique of an agricultural laborer, the reverence for tradition of a bee, and, as assets, what the English call 'immense character,' and (probably) brute artistic faculty for word music galore. The Sophoclean irony I take to have been a stupidity too dense to be credible as such: at all events, I never could discover it. Possibly I am prejudiced because I got into trouble at an early age by using his name as an appropriate rhyme to cockles. Roebuck Ramsden & John Tanner in Man & Superman are Sophocles & Euripides.

From Edipus you can learn the difference between spiritual construction and mechanical stage craft. The spiritual development—the gradual loading of a man's conscience bale by bale until his back breaks—is nearly as good as a bullfight, with its provocations and tortures ending with the matador. The stage craft is, as I said, crude to rusticity. Here it is in skeleton, as I remember it.

Edipus discovered with crowd (Chorus)

Crowd—We are unwell. What is the matter with us?

Edipus—I have sent to ask the oracle. My messenger ought to be back by this: he has been away a year. Ah! Here he is. (Enter Oracle Man).

Oracle Man—Somebody murdered old King Laius; and Apollo wont stand it.

Edipus—Damn his eyes—the somebody's, not Apollo's. Who is he?

Oracle Man—I dont know. I should ask the gentle hermit of the dale, who knows everything. Ha! Here he is. How opportune! (Enter Hermit).

Edipus—Who killed the king?

Hermit—You did.

Edipus—Liar! Still, I certainly did kill somebody at a cross roads once. My wife Jocasta would know.

Hermit—(enigmatically) Your wife! Ha! ha! Here she is, by the way. (Enter Jocasta).

Edipus—Look here, Jocasta. Do you think that man I killed could have been your first husband, the old king?

Jocasta—Nonsense. A most respectable farmer saw the whole affair. Send for him and ask him.

Edipus—Why can't he turn up without being sent for, as the others do? (To the Call Boy) Go fetch him. (Exit Call Boy).

[—Enter a Corinthian Shepherd—]

C.S.—I seek Edipus, your king.

Edipus—By a happy coincidence, I am he.

C.S.—Allow me to congratulate you. Your father is dead.

Edipus—A corker for the oracle that said I should kill him! Hooray!

Jocasta—I told you so.

Edipus—If only my mother were dead, my happiness would be complete. Unfortunately, I gather that she survives. They said I should end by marrying her. I shall never feel safe until she also is buried.

C.S.—Let me be frank with you. She is not your mother. The truth is, I got you when you were a baby from a most respectable farmer, and handed you over to your reputed parents.

Jocasta—What next? Edipus, I shouldnt go on with this. Excuse me. (Exit).

Edipus—The respectable farmer must clear up this. Where can he be?

Leader of The Chorus—By one of those fortunate accidents which seldom occur more than six times even in a play by Sophocles, I recognize that most respectable man—whom I have not seen for forty years—in the gentleman who will now enter. (The Theban Shepherd does so).

Edipus—Who was the child you gave some years ago to this Corinthian?

The Theban—If I were you, I wouldnt ask.

Edipus—Scourge him until he confesses.

The Theban—Oh well, if you *will* have it, it was the child of Jocasta and Laius.

The Corinthian—The party he killed at the crossroads, probably.

The Theban—That is so.

Edipus—Then—then—I—I —Oh Lord! (Exit)

Chorus—   Ah me, no chappy
                 Call I happy
                 Until—

The noise in the auditorium makes it impossible to hear anything more. The hitherto empty benches are filling up rapidly. A slave slides an ivory goad along the front bench and prods the Archon, who wakes up with a shriek, but collects himself with such majesty that nobody dares to laugh. Greetings of acquaintances, searchings for numbered seats, sales of programs & hirings of glasses & sunshades on all hands. At last the audience settles down; and the chorus is once more heard.

Chorus—   The life of Man
                               Is but a span—

Derisive Voice from the Gods—Ten minutes for refreshments. (Ribald laughter).

Voices—Messengerrrr. Messeng-e-e-e-rrrr. Cut the cackle. Dry up. Messengerrr.

The Archon—Men of Athens: behave yourselves. Remember Marathon. Remember—

Voices—The fifth of November. Messenger. Messenger. Messengerrrrrr. (Tumult).

Enter Star Actor, as Messenger. Thunders of applause.

Voices—Brayoo Icks! Give it mouth. Pile it on. Silence for the messenger. Silennnnce!

Chorus—'He who in quest of silence, Silennnnce hoots

Semichorus—Is apt to make the hubbub he imputes.'

The Messenger proceeds to wallow at great length in the blood of Jocasta, who has butchered herself in a most sanguinary manner. The audience hangs on every drop. When he adds, in minute detail, how Edipus plucked his eyes out, the whole house is one ecstasy.

Edipus—(rushing in and scattering rose pink from his eyes all over the orchestra) Woe, woe! Pain! Ah me! Ai! ai! ai! Me miserable!

Stupendous applause. The Messenger & Edipus take six calls, and finally reappear with Sophocles between them. Immense enthusiasm.

Chorus—   Talk of bliss
                               After this!—

The house empties as if a hose had been turned on it. Nothing can be heard through the noise of the scramble for the doors.

Chorister (to the Leader) Keep it up, old man. The second lot will be in for the satyr play before you are through. (In the hope of which the Leader slows down to 20 words a minute).

—And So Forth—

Give this apparently frivolous précis to your students, and they will at once understand what Euripides had to put up with, and what a curse this blood & thunder convention of the messenger was to the Athenian stage. Also what the stage craft of Sophocles came to, and the exact depth of his choruses.

The serious mischief of the convention was that it made it impossible for an Athenian to write a play. A drama was only a driving of somebody to death. For instance, here is a fascinating dramatic problem. Given a man who discovers himself to be the murderer of his father and the husband of his mother, how will he feel and what will he do? In Athens this was not a problem at all: it was only an excuse for a particularly sanguinary description by the inevitable messenger. Sophocles saw it that way too: he was too conventional even to wish to see anything more in it. He therefore left you what you desired: a Greek theme for a modern drama. This is your chance.

Let us consider the spiritual scenario. The modern play—yours—will not end by the completed disclosure: it will begin with it. How will Edipus feel about it?

Jocasta, if I recollect aright, says that men have often dreamt thus of their mothers (how did she know, by the way?); and she implies that they were none the worse for it. Plutarch tells us that Cæsar dreamt it, and was so encouraged that he crossed the Rubicon next day. Evidently it did not shock *him*.

Let us get a little nearer home. I very seldom dream of my mother; but when I do, she is my wife as well as my mother. When this first occurred to me (well on in my life), what surprised me when I awoke was that the notion of incest had not entered into the dream: I had taken it as a matter of course that the maternal function included the wifely one; and so did she. What is more, the sexual relation acquired all the innocence of the filial one, and the filial one all the completeness of the sexual one. This surprised me the more, because my theory, as you may have noticed in my books here and there, is that blood relationship tends to create repugnance, and that family affection is factitious (I am now rather inclined to think that it is rather familiarity—that is, close domestic association—that creates sexual repugnance).

Suppose, now, I were to discover suddenly that my mother was not related to me at all, and that Charlotte was my mother. I have not the slightest doubt of what the effect would be. It would be that of the dream. My affection for Charlotte would be not only intensified but elevated. There would be the addition of the filial feeling and the redemption of the sexual feeling from 'sin' and strain. Although in my waking senses I could not possibly work up the slightest sexual feeling for my mother or filial feeling for Charlotte, yet if circumstances tricked me into marrying my mother before I knew she was my mother, I should be fonder of her than I could ever be of a mother who was not my wife, or a wife who was not my mother.

I now want to meet a woman who has dreamt she was her son's wife, so as to get Jocasta documented.

You see your drama. When Creon says to Edipus, 'Unhappy man: here are my razors. Give one of them to your wretched mother; and despatch,' Edipus replies 'Scandalous as it seems, I dont feel like that at all.' And a conflict with public opinion follows.

The messenger's speech would describe your expulsion from Oxford after the publication of your New Edipus.

I am not very appreciative of the psychiatrists; but there may be something in their theory that repressed instincts, though subconscious, play a considerable part in our lives, and that the first child's jealousy of the second, and even of its father, is the jealousy of Othello in a primitive stage of passion, before the specialization of a part of it takes place for reproductive purposes. The completeness with which that specialization is suppressed does not eradicate the passion; and in my case the suppression apparently vanishes in sleep, though it is perfectly effective when I wake. Dr Ernest Jones contends that Hamlet's inability to kill the king is produced by his subconsciousness that he was jealous of his father and would have done the same thing himself to get possession of his mother.

Has your interest in Edipus ever led you to collect any evidence on this subject?

Anyhow, even if you should conclude that the subject is too dangerous to be stirred up, especially in days when women remain attractive until they are past fifty, you may possibly see that there is a great poetic and psychological drama in it.

I mark this letter Private lest it should horrify your secretary, if you have one.

Is your translation of Sophocles published?

yrs ever
G.B.S.

PS. I have said nothing about the parricide part of the problem, because, though I can perfectly understand Dr Johnson in the rain to expiate his unkindness to his father, I am quite unable to understand any man regretting having killed his father to deliver himself from tyranny. Despotism must be tempered by assassination.

Man & Superman] Shaw's play, published 1903, acted 1905.   Dr Johnson] had worked in his father's Lichfield bookshop as a youth, and performed this penance to expiate his disobedience.

267. To Mrs Patrick Campbell, 22 February 1913

With the actress Stella Campbell (1865–1940) Shaw was long in love. Her mother was Italian. Shaw's mother died 19 Feb.

What a day! I must write to you about it, because there is no one else who didnt hate her mother, and even who doesnt hate her children. Whether you are an Italian peasant or a Superwoman I cannot yet find out; but anyhow your mother was not the Enemy.

Why does a funeral always sharpen one's sense of humor and rouse one's spirits? This one was a complete success. No burial horrors. No mourners in black, snivelling and wallowing in induced grief. Nobody knew except myself, Barker & the undertaker. Since I could not have a splendid procession with lovely colors and flashing life and triumphant music, it was best with us three. I particularly mention the undertaker because the humor of the occasion began with him. I went down in the tube to Golders Green with Barker, and walked to the crematorium; and there came also the undertaker presently with his hearse, which had walked (the horse did) conscientiously at a funeral pace through the cold; though my mother would have preferred an invigorating trot. The undertaker approached me in the character of a man shattered with grief; and I, hard as nails and in loyally high spirits (rejoicing irrepressibly in my mother's memory), tried to convey to him that this professional chicanery, as I took it to be, was quite unnecessary. And lo! it wasnt professional chicanery at all. He had done all sorts of work for her for years, and was actually and really in a state about losing her, not merely as a customer, but as a person he liked and was accustomed to. And the coffin was covered with violet cloth—no black.

I must rewrite that burial service; for there are things in it that are deader than anyone it has ever been read over; but I had it read not only because the parson must live by his fees, but because with all its drawbacks it is the most beautiful thing that can be read as yet. And the parson did not gabble and hurry in the horrible manner common on such occasions. With Barker & myself for his congregation (and Mamma) he did it with his utmost feeling and sincerity. We could have made him perfect technically in two rehearsals; but he was excellent as it was; and I shook his hand with unaffected gratitude in my best manner.

At the passage 'earth to earth, ashes to ashes, dust to dust,' there was a little alteration of the words to suit the process. A door opened in the wall; and the violet coffin mysteriously passed out through it and vanished as it closed. People think that door the door of the furnace; but it isnt. I went behind the scenes at the end of the service and saw the real thing. People are afraid to see it; but it is wonderful. I found there the violet coffin opposite another door, a real unmistakeable furnace door. When it lifted there was a plain little chamber of cement and firebrick. No heat. No noise. No roaring draught. No flame. No fuel. It looked cool, clean, sunny, though no sun could get there. You would have walked in or put your hand in without misgiving. Then the violet coffin moved again and went in, feet first. And behold! The feet burst miraculously into streaming ribbons of garnet colored lovely flame, smokeless and eager, like pentecostal tongues, and as the whole coffin passed in it sprang into flame all over; and my mother became that beautiful fire.

The door fell; and they said that if we wanted to see it all through, we should come back in an hour and a half. I remembered the wasted little figure with the wonderful face, and said 'Too long' to myself; but we went off and looked at the Hampstead Garden Suburb (in which I have shares), and telephoned messages to the theatre, and bought books, and enjoyed ourselves generally.

By the way I forgot one incident. Hayden Coffin suddenly appeared in the chapel. *His* mother also.

The end was wildly funny: she would have enjoyed it enormously. When we returned we looked down through an opening in the floor to a lower floor close below. There we saw a roomy kitchen, with a big cement table and two cooks busy at it. They had little tongs in their hands, and they were deftly and busily picking nails and scraps of coffin handles out of Mamma's dainty little heap of ashes and samples of bone. Mamma herself being at that moment leaning over beside me, shaking with laughter. Then they swept her up into a sieve, and shook her out; so that there was a heap of dust and a heap of calcined bone scraps. And Mamma said in my ear, 'Which of the two heaps is me, I wonder!'

And that merry episode was the end, except for making dust of the bone scraps and scattering them on a flower bed.

O grave, where is thy victory?

In the afternoon I drove down to Oxford, where I write this. The car was in a merry mood, and in Notting Hill Gate accomplished a most amazing skid, swivelling right round across the road one way and then back the other, but fortunately not hitting anything. . . .

And so goodnight, friend who understands about one's mother, and other things.

GBS

Barker] Harley Granville-Barker (1877–1946), theatre director, whose Shaw productions were famous.   Hayden Coffin] (1862–1935), a singer.

268. To Lillah McCarthy, 30 July 1916

Lillah McCarthy (1875–1960), an actress, married H. Granville-Barker in 1906. They were divorced in 1918.

My dear Lillah,

A new accusation! I did not answer your long letter. It was just long enough to tell me that boxes for your war matinée were 20 guineas. As if I had 20 guineas to waste on such follies! I call it cheek.

I had hardly sent off my inquiry to you—my last one—when the subject of it turned up in person, very worried and impatient, and rapidly coming to your conclusion that it is all my fault, except that you blame me because he wants a divorce and he blames me because he hasnt got it. The situation is very unsatisfactory. Unless he goes back to America to deliver a series of lectures he cannot meet his financial obligations to the settlement trustees and others, and must file a petition in bankruptcy. But as he is liable for military service, and has been passed by the doctor after three minutes' examination as sound in wind and limb, and is actually walking on as a super in the Royal Horse Artillery next Wednesday (he is at present spending the week-end in Devon with the Galsworthies) the chances of his receiving a three months furlough to go to America at the end of the year, when his training will be complete, are pretty doubtful. However, if there is a winter lull at the front, it is possible that the Adjutant General, whom he knows personally, may be induced to exercise his powers of granting furlough for the purpose of averting bankruptcy, in which case the lectures may be delivered, and before the same emergency recurs a year later the war may be over. But this seems the best that can happen.

He was not bound to return, as he was not on the register and had not been habitually resident here since the date in the Act; so he can claim to be a volunteer. He chose the artillery on the advice of some military friend of Masefield who pointed out that the artillery has some use for intelligence, and that it is possible to become a cadet gunner and get a commission if you can do leading business.

On Thursday I was at the Opera [Mozart's *Il Seraglio*, conducted by Beecham], and found myself between the acts in a very animated discussion of your and his affairs in Lady Cunard's box. It seems that Lady C. is an old friend of his idol. This was the first time I heard the matter talked about with any knowledge of who she is. Lady C. is evidently attached to her rather affectionately, so, if you meet her, be generous if anything is said about her.

We managed to restore Harley's tone to some extent here—he stayed mostly with us—but the strain of the situation has not been doing him any good; and how you stand it I dont know. He has been all these months alone in Williamstown, a little university town in New Hampshire, with all communications cut off, waiting for that divorce. Finally it got on his nerves, and he could not work, and came back to this soldiering slavery. You, meanwhile, have been working off your anguish in public appearances which have been, by all accounts, unusually glorious. But you cant have been much happier than he. Why not make an end of it and set him free before you both suffer so long that the hatred this sort of relation engenders becomes a permanent condition? Any adept yogi will tell you that if you once concentrate on a particular state of the soul completely for ninety minutes it will become part of your consciousness for the rest of your life. Well, do you want your whole life to be a repetition of the last six months? If he were bound, and you free, there might at least be vengeance in it.

But your slavery is worse than his, because he can stand loneliness much better.

It is frightful to meet you flitting round the Terrace in the moonlight like a beautiful ghost, answering in unreal far-away whispers when you are spoken to, until finally one runs away from you in terror, partly terror of the ghost, partly terror of being provoked into laying violent hands on you and convincing you that you are flesh and blood still until you are black and blue.

People will presently get tired of the affair and avoid you and Harley like the plague; and serve you right! Is any man, or any woman, worth making such a fuss about? What has become of our nobility? I shall end by feeling like a dog barking at three cats on the roof. This, too, is the best years of your life. However, I know it is no use *my* talking. Go on tormenting one another, just as the rest are killing one another in France: it is the nature of the human animal. I will go on with my play and leave you all to your devilments.

G.B.S.

Commission] Barker was commisioned as an intelligence officer.   Lady Cunard] wife of a shipping magnate, and a patron of the arts.   His idol] Helen Huntington (née Gates), a writer and the wife of a rich New York theatrical backer, whom he married in 1918.   Appearances] McCarthy had been appearing in J. M. Barrie's *The Admirable Crichton*.   The Terrace] Adelphi Terrace, where McCarthy and Shaw were neighbours.   My play] the play he was working on became *Heartbreak House*.

269. To Mrs Patrick Campbell, 7 January 1918

Stella Campbell's son was killed in France on 30 Dec. 1917. (She had lost her husband in the Boer War.)

Never saw it or heard about it until your letter came. It is no use: I cant be sympathetic: these things simply make me furious. I want to swear. I *do* swear. Killed just because people are blasted fools. A chaplain, too, to say nice things about it. It is not his business to say nice things about it, but to shout that 'the voice of thy son's blood crieth unto God from the ground.'

To hell with your chaplain and his tragic gentleness! The next shell will perhaps blow *him* to bits; and some other chaplain will write such a nice letter to *his* mother. Such nice letters! Such nice little notices in papers!

Gratifying, isnt it. Consoling. It only needs a letter from the king to make me feel that the shell was a blessing in disguise.

No: dont show me the letter. But I should very much like to have a nice talk with that dear chaplain, that sweet sky pilot, that—

No use going on like this, Stella. Wait for a week; and then I shall be very clever and broadminded again, and have forgotten all about him. I shall be quite as nice as the chaplain.

Oh damn, damn, damn, damn, damn, damn, damn, damn, DAMN

DAMN!

And oh, dear, dear, dear, dear, dear, dearest!

G.B.S.

Chaplain] she had wanted to send Shaw the letter from the company chaplain, saying it was 'full of tragic gentleness'.   'The voice . . .'] 'the voice of thy brother's blood crieth unto me from the ground' (Gen. 4: 10).

270. *To St John Ervine, 22 May 1918*

Ervine (1883–1971), a playwright, had a leg amputated after being hit by shell splinters. Shaw's foot trouble arose when, in Apr., he laced a shoe too tightly. One unusual consequence of his disablement was his marriage in June 1898.

Dear St John Ervine,

I did not believe that any mortal man could waken my sense of humor in communicating the news of the loss of your leg. But your chaplain has achieved that feat. His comment is that, the leg being off, you will 'get along all right now.'

The truth is I am not so much horrified as I should be if I had never been in the same predicament. In 1898 an operation was performed on my foot for necrosis following an abscess produced by a tight shoe; and as the discharging sinus which ensued was most carefully treated on the most approved antiseptic principles, I was unable to put my foot to the ground for eighteen months, at the end of which an ignorant but eminent old surgeon who knew not Lister stopped the antiseptic treatment and ordered a bit of oiled silk to keep my stocking off the sinus. Under this barbarous treatment I got well in a fortnight.

However, the point is that for a year and a half of my life I had worse than no left leg at all, as I had to drag a useless limb about and have it dressed every day. All that time I was on crutches; and in my first attempts to come down stairs on them I shot myself out into empty space and did a spinning nose dive right down to the hall, breaking my arm as I landed.

Now do those eighteen months stand out in my memory as a period of disablement and wretchedness? Not in the least: on the contrary they match in so perfectly with the rest of my life that I recollect the crutches and the being tethered to a radius of half a mile or so on foot as purely external facts, nothing like so unpleasant to recall as the tethering to Dublin and to an office or to school of the first twenty years of my career. I found that I could do without my leg just as easily as without eyes in the back of my head, or without any of the specific talents which I see other men possess and which I lack. I got on without the leg just as well as my wife got on without being able to write plays. During the eighteen months I wrote Caesar and Cleopatra and The Perfect Wagnerite; and I have no reason to believe that they would have been a bit better if they had been written on two legs instead of one.

You will be in a stronger position. I had to feed and nurse the useless leg. You will have all the energy you have hitherto spent on it to invest in the rest of your frame. For a man of your profession two legs are an extravagance: the Huns were nearer the mark when they attempted (as I gather from your wife) to knock off your head. Instead of lingering in a hospital for a year, and then being sent back like a lamb to the slaughter you will be down at Beer in a month, quit of the army for life, and with a wound pension which in your case should logically be a reduction of the ordinary pension. The more the case is gone into the more it appears that you are an exceptionally happy and fortunate man, relieved of a limb to which you owed none of your fame, and which indeed was the cause of your conscription; for without it you would not have been accepted for service.

I am interrupted by the maid calling for the letters for post; and I have still to send a word to your Leonora, who has kept me supplied with bulletins. So I will defer some remarks about the play and other matters to another day, and conclude hastily

ever

G. Bernard Shaw

PS Remember me to Sir Almroth Wright, if he should happen to pause by your bed.

Sir Almroth Wright] (1861–1947), a famous pathologist, whose theories Shaw opposed fiercely but amicably. Wright was partly the inspiration of The Doctor's Dilemma (1911).

271. To Ada Tyrrell, 28 January 1928

Ada Tyrrell (née Shaw) (1854–1955) was the daughter of a Fellow of Trinity College, Dublin, and unrelated to Shaw, though the families were acquainted.

My dear Ada,

I hope I have not delayed answering too long. I have so much writing to do that I never have time to write.

Quite a lot of people have been writing to me lately from America, claiming relationship with your father and assuming that I am his son. In one or two cases where they seemed to want harmless information I have referred them to you, giving your address as 53 Waterloo Road.

Your mother was certainly a remarkable woman, who would have filled a larger place in a larger world than that into which she was dropped. Her scale of values was not that of Harrington Street. Also she was a siren, and, as such, could not be confined within the ordinary circle of home interests. Apparently your father could not reconcile himself to being only one among many men whom she interested and in whom she was interested; and so the household went to pieces, leaving her in a freedom which was rather barren because she had not duties enough to balance her privileges. But why bother about her? Children never know anything about their parents; and I dont think their occasional attempts to reconstruct them after their death are ever quite successful.

I do not remember any character in my books and plays modelled consciously on your mother. I always had a vision of her as the mother of Cashel Byron in an early novel of mine called Cashel Byron's Profession (he was a prizefighter); but it was a visual impression mostly. Still, now you mention it, I daresay the visual impression led to a touch of caricature from the living model here and there.

You, I should say, are your father's daughter in so far as you are anybody but yourself. He deserves your sympathy more than she did; for he was literally what Shakespear called 'A Fellow [of Trinity College, Dublin] almost damned in a fair wife.'

Yes: I remember the Dowlings. I had a curious sort of romantic friendship with their brother who was drowned. My earliest efforts in fiction were monstrous exploits which I attributed to him: in fact I made him a character in an endless tale of impossible adventures which I used to tell to a boy named Bellhouse, who had an inappeasable appetite for Dowling stories.

But do not remind them of me: they can have no very pleasant recollections of me; and I shudder to think that they might begin to invent an imaginary past. Besides, it is rather awful to think of those two girls pulling the devil by the tail all these years. No doubt they are as happy as most people; but it would have suited me so badly that the thought of it makes me feel suicidal. Except in my secret self I was not happy in Dublin; and when ghosts rise up from that period I want to lay them again with the poker. You, however, are not one of these unwelcome ones.

My life has rushed through very quickly: I have seen very little of anyone who has not worked with me. Except with my wife I have no companionships: only occasional contacts, intense but brief. I spring to intimacy in a moment, and forget in half an hour. An empty life is peopled with the absent and the imagined: a full one has to be cleared out everyday by the housemaid of forgetfulness or the air would become unbreathable. Those who see me now are those who shove and insist and will not take no for an answer, with, of course, the great people who must be seen because they have earned a right of entry everywhere.

I wonder whether you will get this. I see by your letter that your travelling address holds good only until the end of the month; so it looks as if I should be just a day after the fair. Perhaps I had better send a card to Waterloo Road to warn you. I should not like you to suppose that your letter had not elicited an answer.

yours, dear Ada, ever
G.B.S.

Almost damned] *Othello* I. i. 21.

272. *To Helen Harris, 26 August 1931*

Frank Harris (1856–1931) was a biographer, autobiographer, editor, adventurer, and old friend of Shaw. He died as he had mostly lived, broke; Shaw sent with this letter a cheque for £50.

Dear Mrs Harris,

They have just telephoned me that you have finished the strange adventure of being married to Frank.

Death does not always select the convenient moment when there is plenty of ready money in the house to meet its expenses. Hence the enclosure. You can repay it out of the profits of the biography.

Now you can begin another life with the wisdom garnered from your first experiment; so run up the half-masted flag to the top of the staff, and away with melancholy.

ever
G.B.S.

PS I am working on the proofs and getting the facts straight. Will you leave it to me to see it through the press?

The biography] of Shaw (1931)—written with much help from Shaw himself.

273. *To Esmé Percy, 20 April 1932*

Percy played in and directed many Shavian plays, including an uncut *Man and Superman*.

Dear Esme Percy,

NEVER give a postdated cheque. Break fifty promises to pay if you are weak-minded enough to make them and you may be forgiven; but a dishonored cheque is unpardonable and irretrievable. Never do it.

You *may* have £60 in the bank on the 16th July. You *may* win the Calcutta Sweep or the next Irish lottery. You *may* get an engagement from B.I.P. for 5 years at £500 a week.

I shall not gamble on these possibilities. I shall not lend you a farthing.

But as you demonstrated the practicability of 'the entirety' of Man and Superman on the stage, and I never had the decency to say Thank You for that service I'll make you a present of £100 and leave you to await the 16th July with an easy conscience.

faithfully

G. Bernard Shaw

PS On your life, don't tell anybody.

274. To Edward Elgar, 30 May 1933

Sir Edward Elgar (1857–1934) was to fly next day to Paris to conduct his Violin Concerto with the young Yehudi Menuhin as soloist.

My dear Elgar,

Why Paris? I recommend Peiping (çi-devant Peking) where you must go to the Lama temple and discover how the Chinese produce harmony. Instead of your laborious expedient of composing a lot of different parts to be sung simultaneously, they sing in unison all the time, mostly without changing the note; but they produce their voices in some magical way that brings out all the harmonics with extraordinary richness, like big bells. I have never had my ears so supersatisfied. The basses are stupendous. The conductor keeps them to the pitch by tinkling a tiny bell occasionally. They sit in rows round a golden Buddha fifty feet high, whose beneficent majesty and intimate interest in them is beyond description. In art we do everything the wrong way and the Chinese do it the right way.

At Tientsin they had a Chinese band for me. It consisted of a most lovely toned gong, a few flageolets (I don't know what else to call them) which specialised in pitch without tone, and a magnificent row of straight brass instruments reaching to the ground, with mouthpieces like the ones I saw in the Arsenal in Venice many years ago: brass saucers quite flat, with a small hole in the middle. They all played the same note, and played it all the time, like the E flat in the Rheingold prelude; but it was rich in harmonics, like the note of the basses in the temple. At the first pause I demanded that they should play some other notes to display all the possibilities of the instrument. This atheistic proposal stunned them. They pleaded that they had never played any other note; that their fathers, grandfathers, and forbears right back to the Chinese Tubal Cain had played that note and no other note, and that to assert that there was more than one note was to imply that there is more than one god. But the man with the gong rose to the occasion and proved that in China as in Europe the drummer is always the most intelligent person in the band. He snatched one of the trumpets, waved it in the air like a mail coach guard with a posthorn, and filled the air with flourishes and fanfares and Nothung motifs. We must make the B.B.C. import a dozen of these trumpets to reinforce our piffling basses.

Then there is the Japanese theatre orchestra. I daresay you fancy your-self as a master of orchestration; but you should just hear what can be done in the way of producing atmosphere with one banjo string pizzicato and a bicycle bell. But the Chinese will reveal to you the whole secret of opera, which is, not to set a libretto to music, but to stimulate actors to act and declaim. When there is a speech to be delivered, the first (and only) fiddler fiddles at the speaker as if he were lifting a horse over the Grand National jumps; an ear splitting gong clangs at him; a maddening castanet clacks at him; and finally the audience joins in and incites the fiddler to redouble his efforts. You at once perceive that this is the true function of the orchestra in the theatre and that the Wagnerian score is only gas and gaiters.

At this point of writing I learn from the papers that you are flying to Paris to conduct for that amazing young violinist. He is worth it.

I have nothing on at Malvern this time; but we will go down to hear the old plays and cheer up Barry, who has just had to go to bed again, having racketed about too soon. We have also taken out our stewardships for the Hereford Festival; so we shall meet on or near your native heath.

How does the symphony get on? Dont you think you could get two into the time? Remember, you have to catch up on Beethoven.

always
G. Bernard Shaw

Barry] Barry Jackson directed the Birmingham Repertory Theatre. Shaw met him in 1923 when he was directing *Back to Methuselah*.

275. To H. G. Wells, 12 September 1943

Wells (1866–1946) was an old friend and opponent of Shaw. Shaw had been very tactless in his dealings with Wells when, in 1927, Jane Wells was dying of cancer. Charlotte was Shaw's wife.

Charlotte died this morning at 2.30. You saw what she had become when you last visited us: an old woman bowed and crippled, furrowed and wrinkled, and greatly distressed by hallucinations of crowds in the room, evil persons, and animals. Also by breathlessness, as the osteitis closed on her lungs. She got steadily worse: the prognosis was terrible, ending with double pneumonia.

But on Friday evening a miracle began. Her troubles vanished. Her visions ceased. Her furrows and wrinkles smoothed out. Forty years fell off her like a garment. She had thirty hours of happiness and heaven. Even after her last breath she shed another twenty years, and now lies young and incredibly beautiful. I have to go in and look at her and talk affectionately to her. I did not know I could be so moved.

Do not tell a soul until Thursday when all will be over. I could not stand flowers and letters and a crowd at Golders Green.

G.B.S.

ROBERT FROST
(1874–1963)

Frost was farming in New England, shortly before spending three years in England, where his first volume of poems, *A Boy's Will*, was published in 1913.

276. *To Susan Hayes Ward, 10 February 1912*

Ward, literary editor of the New York *Independent*, was a benefactor of Frost.

Dear Miss Ward:—

You should receive almost simultaneously with this your long-lost Sweet Singer. I ought to say that I don't think I laughed at her as much as I should have if I had been a hearty normal person, and not something of a sweet singer myself. She is only a little more self-deceived than I am. That she was not altogether self-deceived I conclude from the lines in which she declares it her delight to compose on a sentimental subject when it comes into her mind just right. There speaks something authentic anyway.

Two lonely cross-roads that themselves cross each other I have walked several times this winter without meeting or overtaking so much as a single person on foot or on runners. The practically unbroken condition of both for several days after a snow or a blow proves that neither is much travelled. Judge then how surprised I was the other evening as I came down one to see a man, who to my own unfamiliar eyes and in the dusk looked for all the world like myself, coming down the other, his approach to the point where our paths must intersect being so timed that unless one of us pulled up we must inevitably collide. I felt as if I was going to meet my own image in a slanting mirror. Or say I felt as we slowly converged on the same point with the same noiseless yet laborious strides as if we were two images about to float together with the uncrossing of someone's eyes. I verily expected to take up or absorb this other self and feel the stronger by the addition for the three-mile journey home. But I didn't go forward to the touch. I stood still in wonderment and let him pass by; and that, too, with the fatal omission of not trying to find out by a comparison of lives and immediate and remote interests what could have brought us by crossing paths to the same point in the wilderness at the same moment of nightfall. Some purpose I doubt not, if we could but have made it out. I like a coincidence almost as well as an incongruity. Enclosed is another in print. The Marion C. Smith you were talking of when I was with you I was very certain I had heard of somewhere, but I didn't know where. It must have [been] here. Heard of her? Yes it is almost as if I had met her in the pages of the [Youth's] Companion.

Nonsensically yours
Robert Frost

277. To John W. Haines, 21 July 1925

Haines was an English poet, botanist, and barrister, whom Frost had met during his sojourn in England.

Dear Jack,

Yesterday we were haying in America. We got in about two tons of Timothy not unmixed with clover. We sold to people passing in their cars some five hundred stems of sweet peas at a cent a piece. Lesley called us up on the telephone from her bookstore in Pittsfield Mass. forty miles below us in the same valley to say she was just back from a fairly successful business trip with her book caravan (a converted Ford truck) to the extremity of Cape Cod. Such might be said to be a day with us. It sounds sufficiently I hope as if we made our living as honest farmers, florists and booksellers.

A night is not very different. Last night I was awakened by the cackling of a hen in a brood coop across the road and rising set out just as I was to see what was molesting her reign. It proved to be a skunk a quiet unoffensive little varmint of the New World that operates like a chemical fire extinguisher to subdue ardors. I should have had a gun with me, but I hadn't. I hadn't even a pogamogan. All I had was a dog. There was no moon. On my way I got involved barefooted with a spring toothed harrow and fell heavily. It should have been a lesson to me, but it wasn't for I got involved with it again on my way back. We gave the skunk a good barking at. The skunk is a dignified soldier, who will walk away from anybody but run away from nobody. We should have been able to do him some damage. If there had been more light there would have been a different story. The dog and I got gassed. I had to throw away my night gown before I re-entered the house. The dog won't smell like himself for a month, especially when it rains. Our casualties were four chickens killed before the main body could be brought up. So you see what it is like.

Why I don't buy a ticket and hoist sail for England when I long to see you as much as I do! We would have to talk and walk in Leddington and Ryton if I came over. I should probably die of internal weeping. We could call on the ladies, Mrs Badney across from the Gallows who knocked at our door one dark, dark night with the news that the Germans had landed in

Portsmouth, and Ledbury was up-side-down. (This was her version of the foolish American Christmas ship bearing gifts to the Germans equally with the Belgian French and English) and Mrs Farmer next to Little Iddens who was a tree-poisoner as I've heard. She poisoned a whole apple orchard of her own husband's planting to keep it from coming into the possession of her brother when he ousted them from the farm they had rented of him. She had been punished by the Courts. The law was against her, poor lady. I can still hear her making a tremendous noise with a rattle to scare the blackbirds from the cherry trees. She was doing her best to live down her crime. I can't tell you how homesick I am. For the moment I can't seem to content myself with the characters I am in the way of meeting here. A fellow said to me the other day he supposed the trial at Dayton Tennessee would settle it once for all whether we were descended from Monkeys or the Virgin Mary. At least he knew that the same people who doubted the Biblical account of creation found it hard to believe in the immaculate conception.

All sorts of people get educated in this country. I am so deep in the educational problem that I don't write any oftener than I used to. I'm consulted on the way to handle a poem in school so as not to hurt it for the sensitive and natural. You have no idea of the authority I have become. I might do some good if good were a thing that could be done.

Our love to you all, | Faithfully thine,

Robert Frost

Lesley] a daughter of Frost.   Pogamogan] a club.   The trial at Dayton] J. T. Scopes, a high school teacher, was tried and convicted under a fundamentalist Tennessee anti-evolution statute.

J. B. YEATS

(1839–1922)

John Butler Yeats was an Irish portrait painter who lived from 1907 in New York. His son W. B. Yeats had his letters transcribed for publication by the Cuala Press, a hand-press run by the painter's daughters.

278. To W. B. Yeats, 30 August 1914

Nowadays, especially in America (who leads the world) people live so much on the surface that everywhere is an intoxicating levity. Even marriage aims at being a love passage to terminate as soon as the impulse has spent itself. Marriage used to be a setting out together of a man and woman resolved though they wait twenty years for it to find the jewel of conjugal friendship. When Dr Salmon's . . . wife died, he said to John Dowden 'When a young man's wife dies it is not much—is nothing to what it is with an old man'. Yet Dowden, who knew them well, said he never knew them to talk to each other but once, and then it was about [household matters]. They had found the jewel and could not tell you where it was hidden; nor could any happily married couple. With people who live on the surface marriage is a failure, a grotesque absurdity, and many here are now saying so— already is it come to that.

Did the contemporaries of Shakespeare live on the surface? No! for the surface though well provided with tragedies and comedies that differed little from tragedies was poorly furnished with what modern life is so rich in. With all their uproariousness and treacheries and adulteries and pro- fanities, they lived austerely, each man of them a lonely man, his nighest neighbour some threatening form of death or disease or sin, his interest not so much life itself as *what it meant*, life itself a wretched, miserable, how- ever dreadful, spectacle. The active resolute spirit might enjoy himself as in a football scrimmage. But the others—the thinker, the artist, the man aloof who watches and sees the whole of it, and yet must because of his sensitive- ness or other unfitness keep outside of it—What solace was there for him? He could not, as does the American, *admire* life—though he occasionally by good chance may have admired some of it, he recoiled from most of it. If he was to live he must escape from the surface of life, and he found his asylum in his dreams; here was his workshop where he mended life. Here also if he was a philosopher and scholar, his oracle and cave of prophecy. In modern life are no dreams, nothing but an overpowering and shining actuality and its logical processes. The dream workshop is deserted and no one visits the oracles—all are out in the crowded streets. There is another thing to be noted about Elizabethan days. Getting a living was then a comparatively easy thing; they had not that absorption to interrupt their dreams, and here again let me add, that a people who do not dream never attain to inner sincerity, for only in his dreams is a man really himself. Only for his dreams is a man responsible—his actions are what he must do. Actions are a bastard race to which a man has not given his full paternity.

People in these democratic days have learned to exult in each other and to *admire* life—yet to admire is not to love—rather does *admiration cast out love*. The recluse M. Angelo with his doctrine of the fall so vivid in his mind and Italian wickedness and its denunciation by Savonarola could not have admired life. Yet his art in which is nothing grandiose or that ex- presses admiration is full of his love and tremendous tenderness for the humanity that had fallen. M. Angelo bowed down by love and pity was sustained by his dreams of the resurrection and of Divine justice and of Paradise. Verily if we would restore its intensity to poetry and art we must rediscover the doctrine of the Fall (and may begin with the war and the Kaiser and his legions). When you express your admiration for the great

Queen it is only to accentuate the pity of her old age—as M. Angelo pondering on the fall of man would remember his nobleness. The artist who admires is a poor artist—we know that from the portrait painters.

Do you remember the statue of General Sherman which is at the entrance to the Central Park, by St Gaudens—a fine sculptor, the finest in America. Here you have art characteristic of a race living on the surface. The general and his horse vividly rendered by a man of intense observation—the Victory, just a young American girl exaggerated after the manner of Gibson, a long-legged, long-armed, bright creature, the product of the American mind in high tension—observing and admiring—the wings are a mere excrescence, quite incongruous, unless indeed one fancied them to be the latest invention of the Paris milliner, to which we have not yet become accustomed. Now we know that for the medieval artist, the Victory would have been everything—General Sherman and his horse subsidiary. How Michel Angelo would have revelled in giving her the strong shoulders to support heavy full-fledged wings, an athlete, a woman and an immortal. How Michel Angelo *loved* life is visible in his moulding and carving of the human body which palpitates with a too sentient life. The Greek sculptor had not this pity, except in the Elgin marbles, and then it was not so much pity as delight in power and force.—

Yours affectionately

J. B. Yeats

P.S. A certain Irishman, Capt. Freeman, formerly of the British Army, is in high glee foreseeing the downfall of the British Empire. He spent 18 years in the Balkans and professes to know everything. For 12 years he was foreign correspondent for the English *Standard*. He says the Ulster men are coming round to be of the same opinion. Of course I detest *all* Empires, *German* or English. [*Sketch*]

Dr Salmon] a Provost of Trinity College, Dublin, who wrote a book attacking papal infallibility.   Dowden] John Dowden (1840–1910), who became bishop of Edinburgh, was a brother of the Shakespearian scholar Edward Dowden, professor of English literature at Trinity.   Dreams] W. B. Yeats's *Responsibilities*, a collection of 1914, has an epigraph 'In dreams begin responsibility.'

HUGH MCCRAE
(1876–1958)

McCrae was an Australian poet and illustrator who took pains over his letters, adorning them with mostly whimsical drawings. He remained in the United States without learning to like New York, where, as he told Norman Lindsay in 1919, he 'lived almost as the flea of one of the lanes which sprawl to the dugs of Broadway'.

279. To his sister Helen and others, 1 October 1914

My dearest Helen,

Thank you so much for your birthday present—it just came in the nick of time. I have done a starve for three days (that is to say only buns and water) and no money. Still I have managed to get a job at the Park Theatre for £5 a week but I get no payment whatever until the 14th or 15th of November when we will be playing.

It is a very pleasant life at the theatre all the people are so young and, so far, *really and truly gentlemen*. I know what your idea of my *really and truly gentlemen* is but this time I am right.

My landlady accidentally discovered my compulsory banting, and proved herself a real trump; she has hot coffee and rolls or bread sent up to me every morning and sometimes an invitation to lunch. She never mentions rent.

Harry Burne couldn't stand the starving and went straight to the British Consul. He was passed by the doctor and shipped off to the war all in the same day.

And now I lie, coiled like a worm in a nut, thinking what a lovely place Australia is and how perfectly beautiful little Fweety was.

You wouldn't like America a bit. To die and go to Hell would be release enough for anyone who lived in New York.

Among nations, this country is the common nation. Their rotten money can't even chink, but makes a metallic clack like counters used for cardplaying. I miss the chiming sweetness of English sixpences and florins.

Of people, they are typically a dime people, with dime faces, dime minds, and dime aspirations.

And yet they are honest in a way. For instance they leave their shops and stalls nearly always quite unguarded; and it is quite a common thing, on going down a street, to see the parcels-post box at the corner heaped up all round with packets and packages too big to fit inside. The conductors in the tramcars sit in little pulpit places with a wire screen before them, a small desk for change, a perforated glass money-well to put the fares into, and a lever at their feet to open and shut the doors with. (The doors are in the middle-sides of the car, not at the ends.) To stop the tram the passenger touches a kind of buzz-press which makes a noise like a man sniffing up his nose.

The messenger-boys seen skedaddling about the streets are for the most part a one-legged race. They tear round on single skates using the spare limb (generally the left) to balance with, and for purposes of impetus.

My dearest Mother, as I haven't got many stamps and as it will be just as easy for Helen to hand this letter to you over the breakfast table I will now speak to you. After which you may kindly do the same for George's benefit when he's finished with the sausages.

I would like to take Honey and Helen Elizabeth just for one walk down Broadway at night time. A mass of fire from the edges of the footpath to far above the skyscrapers. Nothing more bewildering can be imagined, and though the novelty of it tickled me at first, I have now quite a different feeling. The flickering cats, the galloping chariots, the eagles flapping their fiery wings, the piano-banging *cabarets* and the hard dry thudding of kettle drums is enough to make any decent Australian want to run away and hang himself.

I can't for the life of me even now imagine what a blade of grass is like or remember the colour of an ordinary garden rose.

Shop women, as well as serving at the counter, scream rag-time songs through giant megaphones, and men walk about in evening dress with electric lights inside their shirtfronts to advertise Pepper's Whiskey. So is it any miracle that I have occasionally (when the times were good) bolted through huge burning glass pillars into what these lunatics call a 'gin-mill', there to drink iced beer at five cents ($2\frac{1}{2}$d) a glass? and, even then, the barman shaved the foam off the top with a little wooden stick like a paperknife.

When I first came here it was the fashion for everybody to wear straw belltoppers, and then, suddenly, on the 15th of September, the straw changed into felt; and we read in the papers of some unwise men, who, still adhering to their summer head-gear, had had them smashed over their eyes, one by one, as they emerged out of the subway down East.

When people die here, the relatives tie bunches of purple and black cloth on the front door handles; they wash and *paint* the dead faces, put gloves on their hands, dress them as for a ball, and then ring for the undertaker.

If, on the other hand, you happen to be alive, you can go to an 'Automat' and feed yourself by the simple process of pushing nickels into slots and simultaneously turning handles which open little doors with pies behind them or cups of coffee, just according to the amount you expend.

Ham with potato salad and buttered roll, fifteen cents (cents are half-pennies)

Beef Pie (hot), ten cents

Sandwiches, all kinds, ices, puddings, cakes, biscuits, etc., five cents

Coffee, tea, milk, chocolate, five cents.

Their names and the wording of their signs etc. are equally curious, as witness, Bun Jan Chop Suey House, Sausage Cake and Mashed Pie Shop, The Katzenjammer Kids Funnier than Ever, etc., etc.

And when they come to the letter Z in the alphabet they don't

pronounce it 'Zedd' but 'Zee', and explain it by saying, 'You don't say
Zed-bra. You say Ze-bra.'

Miles and miles of city side-walk are composed of rough boards similar
to those we see on our wharves at home, and where there is a proper pavement you are constantly worried by deliberate unevenesses caused by trap-
doors, coal-holes, etc., things we simply wouldn't bear with in Australia.

The houses are just square boxes made hideous by iron fire-escapes, and
every window has a man or a woman hanging out of it and often pillows are
laid on the sills for the better comfort of the watchers.

The lorry drivers crouch, or stand, under huge coloured umbrellas with
advertisements painted on them. Then there are the Italian fruit-sellers
invading the pathways with their barrels and cases of oranges, of sweet
corn, beans, cantaloupes, grapes, tomatoes, etc., and down, underneath

Dearest George——
these cases again, reached through a hole in the middle of the stall, live
other trades-people, generally Ice, Wood and Coal men, with their wives
and their children.

A sight for the gods is, I always think, the Boot-shine-Man snoring in
one of his own chairs while the Missus wheels the pram proudly up and
down close on guard beside him.

As for the American woman, she is, on the average, the plainest yellowest-
haired female under the sun. She decorates her head with a hideous jockey
cap or a black soft coffee-pot arrangement with a feather spout, while her
dress is divided into three separate overlapping folds that make her look
like a mad walking shell-fish. On her feet she wears flat rubber shoes
without any arches to them and she has eyes that turn round like snail's
horns for dollars.

Among the many other people who help to fill up the streets are the
newspaper boys who can roar louder than any Bulls of Bashan, especially
now that the war is on. And then there are two beggars I know, without any
legs, who sit on boards with wheels on them and push themselves about the
paths by their hands. Men sleep anywhere, anyhow, at any time. It's a
common sight to see a navvy, high up on a stack of bags on a cart riding
asleep in the sun. I saw one chap in the very middle of the busiest part of
the city dead to the world on a pile of earth he'd been digging in the
forenoon, another was dreaming away at a winch.

Shopmen sleep in the shops.

There are three kinds of tram-service here. The three kinds are the
Elevated (that runs on a level with everybody's bedroom window), the
Surface Car (which looks like a Dreadnought but which keeps like a normal
Melbourne tram to the roadway itself), and the Subway (which runts along

under the ground and sends up lots of steam through gridiron windows in the path).

The American boy and girl of the poorer class who cannot

Mr Hellicar's turn

afford car-fares tear through the streets in hordes on roller skates.

While I was yet new to America, the Delicatessen Shops which sell everything from an egg to a bottle of milk, were of great interest to me, but now that I have seen so much of them they have staled past any power of description. I will only say that nearly every

Mrs Hellicar please

third or fourth shop is a Delicatessen, the reason being that so many people here live in apartments instead of houses, and find it easier and quicker to get their food this way than to be troubled by preparing it for themselves.

The Moving Picture Palaces share with the Delicatessen Shops the honour of numbers.

No, I don't think we'd better let Phyllis read this

I only once went to Coney Island and then I nearly died of horror at the degradation of the people there. The Australian aboriginal is NOT the lowest type of humanity.

The confirmed Coney Islanders have him skinned a million times. They are nearly all black, and to see them naked in the utterly dirty water is to realize how awful men and women can be.

It was just as if all the villains and adventuresses of every known book had come to life on purpose to celebrate an 'Annual Rogue's Day'.

There were so many of them you couldn't pass between them; and they made love quite publicly jammed together on newspapers among the toes of little boys drying themselves.

I saw one man going into the sea with his eye-glasses stuck behind his ear while the lady of his heart sucked a yellow lollie off the end of a nicely shaved piece of pinewood. This she did with an air of so great delicacy that I wept at the sight of her.

Anatomy was never one of my strong subjects, but American anatomy, or rather the anatomy of an American flapper, has got me completely dished. It's her lower back premises that——

(Sorry, Phyllis, if you've really got to go)

puzzle me and I guess it must be the costume that's doing it. Yet judging from a casual glance in the street, she gives one the impression of a person whose sitting accommodation has dropped down to a level with her knees. She is generally fat, with big feet, and powder on her nose. And her mother is pretty sure to be wearing a little black imitation mole just over the corner of her left eye. It is very likely of course that I am prejudiced; but this I do maintain: I am not fickle.

I love Sydney, I always did love Sydney, and now I'm away I can see no good out of Sydney.

I ache to be back again.

(Charles and Dothery please)
BUT I have made my bed and so I must lie. It has not been a bed of roses so far but one made up of disappointment, of nightmares and nostalgia.

> *O land of burning gold and blue*
> *I'm crying like a child for you!*

(Cecil and Freda this way)
I will tell you a little Chinese story I read yesterday evening in the New York Library, where, as a rule, only good books are kept, no naughty ones. This is the story which must have got in somehow by a mistake, when the Librarian wasn't looking.

A woman who was entertaining a paramour during the absence of her husband, was startled by hearing the latter knock at the house-door. She hurriedly bundled the man into a rice-sack which she concealed in a corner of the room; but when her husband came in he caught sight of it and asked in a stern voice, 'What have you got in that sack?' His wife was too terrified to answer; and, after an awkward pause a voice from the sack was heard to say 'Only rice.'

(OMNES—Father and Mother and Helen. Mr and Mrs Hellicar and Phyllis. Charles and Dothery and Cecil and Freda)
I nearly got £10 a week instead of 5. You see the director at the theatre gave me two parts to study.

One *a sailor*, the other the *Captain of the Guard*.

Then, as the play is the dramatization of a fairy-tale, they thought it would be a good idea to introduce children. So they took a lot of the men's parts from them and passed them over to kids.

And thus Bang went my saxpence!

This letter seems to have stopped being a letter (if it ever even was one) so I will now wind up.

Hoping, after having made you so sleepy, it may be close to your bed-time

I remain | Your affectionate | Son, brother, brother-in-law and
neighbour,
Hugh McCrae

H. H. Asquith

(1852–1928)

Herbert Henry Asquith—1st Earl of Oxford and Asquith—was Prime Minister 1908–16. His performance as wartime leader resulted in his ousting by Lloyd George in 1916. In 1907 he began to fall in love with Venetia Stanley, a member of a powerful Liberal family, who was then 20 and a childhood friend of his elder daughter. His infatuation grew and by 1914 was obsessive; he wrote to her, sometimes twice a day, on all that was concerning him, including the most important matters of state. In 1915 she told him she was engaged to a member of his cabinet, Edwin Montagu (1879–1924).

280. To Venetia Stanley, 12 October 1914

. . . Why do you think that Raymond is one of the people who 'ought to have been rich'? I sometimes think the exact reverse. He is rarely endowed but needed a goad—or spark. . . .

I have just . . . had one of the most curious & in some ways nerve-harrowing interviews with Lady Aberdeen. I had of course no difficulty in disposing of her arguments about the terrible ruin that would be wrought to Ireland if her 'great work' (sanatoria &c &c) were now to be interrupted. I told her brutally that if her efforts & organisation were of any real value, they would go on after her disappearance from the scene: '*car il n'y a pas d'homme ni de femme nécessaire*'. Then she came to the pecuniary aspect of the affair, with a most piteous tale, and when I pointed out that the Viceroyalty was from its nature a spending & losing concern, which made a heavier drain every month that it lasted, she replied that owing to the War there would be no Dublin season, and so they would be able this next year to make large savings! This roused me, I confess: 'So you want me to continue you in an office, which in the public interest you ought to give up, in order that out of the retrenchments required by a national calamity, you may fill the gaps in your private purse'! It was most painful, as you do not need to be assured. She wept copiously, poor thing, and you know what a coward I am *au fond*: so in the end I gave them till the beginning of Feb, and he is to write a beautiful letter announcing his wish to retire now that his life-work in Ireland is done, and I am to ask the Sovereign to give him some mark of appreciation. Then *we kissed*, and she left agitated but I think appeased, and I felt for once really exhausted. This is all, I need not say, for your private eye. . . .

Raymond] Asquith (1878–1916), Asquith's eldest son, killed in action.　　　Aberdeen] Lord Aberdeen was Lord-Lieutenant of Ireland 1906–15; Lady Aberdeen was his interfering wife.

281. To Venetia Stanley, 13 October 1914

My darling

—thank you for your dear letter this morning. I can imagine that Goonie . . . was troubled what answer to give about Port Royal (I wonder what you would have said: are you well up in Pascal, and Mère Angélique, & the sacred thorn, & the controversy about Grace &c &c—perhaps! most of it now-a-days is of little more importance than the price of coals at Brentford). . . .

Oc came to London yesterday & I had a long talk with him after midnight, in the course of which he gave me a full & vivid account of the expedition to Antwerp & the retirement. Strictly between ourselves, I can't tell you what I feel of the *wicked* folly of it all. The Marines of course are splendid troops & can go anywhere & do anything: but nothing can excuse Winston (who knew all the facts) from sending in the two other Naval Brigades. I was assured that all the recruits were being left behind, and that the main body at any rate consisted of seasoned Naval Reserve men. As a matter of fact only about ¼ were Reservists, and the rest were a callow crowd of the rawest tiros, most of whom had never fired off a rifle, while none of them had ever handled an entrenching tool. Oc's battalion was commanded by George West—an ex (very-ex) Subaltern in the Guards who was incompetent & overbearing & hated impartially by both officers and men. Among its principal officers were R. Brooke (the poet) Oc himself & one Dennis Brown (a pianist), who had respectively served 1 week, 3 days, & 1 day. It was like sending sheep to the shambles. Of course when they got into the trenches they behaved most gallantly—but what could they do? The Belges ran away & had to be forced back at the point of the bayonet into the forts, while the Germans at a safe distance of 5 or 6 miles thundered away with their colossal howitzers. When at last (most unwillingly) our men obeyed the order to retire, they found the bridge across the Schelt & most of the lighters & boats in flames: they just got across on a pontoon, but Oc says that if the wind had blown the other way they cd. never have crossed & would have been left in the burning town. Then for 7 or 8 hours they marched (the one thing sailors can't do) for more than 20 miles over cobbled roads, with a ceaseless stream of Belgian refugees & soldiers blocking the way; and at last, more dead than alive, got into trains at St Gilles, wh. gradually took them to Ostend. If the Germans had had any initiative, they might with a couple of squadrons of cavalry have cut them into mincemeat at any stage of their retreat. No doubt it is a wonderful experience to look back upon, but what cruel & terrible risks! Thank God they are all now back in England, except the 1500 who, when dead beat, crossed the Dutch frontier in despair, & are now interned in Holland.

I trust that Winston will learn by experience, and now hand over to the military authorities the little circus which he is still running 'on his own' at Dunkirk—Oxfordshire Yeomen, motor-busses (more or less organised by Geoffrey) armoured cars &c &c. They have really nothing to do with the Admiralty, which ought to confine its activities to the sea & the air. . . .

We had a very rare experience at the Cabinet to-day. We had to settle the rate of pension for the widows of soldiers & sailors killed in the war. There was an elaborate report from a Committee consisting of the Assyrian Baker Macnamara & one or two others, in which they differed a good deal from one another. Finally the question emerged whether a childless widow should get per week (as now) 5/- (Montagu & Baker) or 7/6 (Macnamara) or 6/6 (proposed by Kitchener as a compromise). The argument in favour of not more than 5/- is almost overwhelming, but as the childless widows are estimated to amount to no less than one-third of the whole, & they wd. be left as they are, a 5/- rate would be generally condemned outside as mean & ungenerous. There was a long dreary desultory discussion, and in the end I said I would do what I have done (I think) only twice before in nearly 7 years—take a division in the Cabinet. The voting was very curious: (a) for 7/6 - 1 (b) for 5/- 8 (c) for 6/6 - 9. So 6/6 carried the day by a majority of one! It may amuse you to conjecture how the different people voted, and I will give you on Friday a really valuable prize if you don't make more than 5 mistakes. So send me your guesses. Some of them wanted to vote by ballot, but I said that would be cowardly & we reverted to the good old English plan of open voting. We hope that French will complete his turning movement to-morrow.

What a vast letter! My own darling—you were never more dear to me, and I hunger to see you. All *my love*. Write me a *nice* letter.

Goonie] Lady Gwendolen Churchill.   Port Royal] 17th century Jansenist convent.   Oc]
Arthur Asquith (1883–1939), Asquith's third son, a decorated and wounded soldier.
Winston] Churchill, First Lord of the Admiralty.   Geoffrey] Howard, a cousin of Venetia's.
The Assyrian] Montagu.   Baker] H. T. Baker was Financial Secretary, War Office.

282. *To Venetia Stanley, 12 May 1915*

> Asquith broke off the letter he was writing when he received Venetia's letter announcing her engagement, and wrote this one instead.

Most Loved—

As you know well, *this* breaks my heart.

I couldn't bear to come and see you.

I can only pray God to bless you—and help me.

Yours.

WYNDHAM LEWIS
(1882–1957)

Lewis was a painter, novelist, and polemicist, and editor of *BLAST*, the Vorticist magazine (1914–15).

283. To Augustus John, summer 1915

Lewis had said of John (see above, Letter 252) in the second and last issue of *BLAST* that he was a great artist but prematurely exhausted, lapsing into worn-out styles and subjects. John reacted violently, then wrote apologizing, saying that on the occasion of their meeting he 'must have been positively drunk'. This is Lewis's reply.

Dear John,

Your letter received this morning. After your clear display (in front of a lady) the other night, I looked up my article in Blast. I there found I had said that I had a mental feud with you, for 'I resented your stage-gypsies emptying their properties over your splendid painter's gift.' The fact that I open that terrible and 'unjust' attack by admitting to a 'mental feud' rather mitigates its wickedness, it seems to me.—In the same article, along with tilting at your boring Borrovian cult of the Gitane, I pay homage to the substantial talents God has endowed you with.

Had you chosen a time when neither you nor I were accompanied and overheard, I should have supplemented my remarks in the articles as follows.—I consider you had, pour commencer, as much talent as a man may comfortably possess. The time you dropped into was a rather stagnant time just after the full blast of Victorianism—surely one of the most hideous periods ever recorded. You began by shipwrecking yourself on all sorts of romantic reefs. Among other things you consumed a good deal of Verlainesque liquor. Whether a craft is still sea-worthy after such buccaneering I dont know. But lately you have not, to put it mildly, advanced in your work. That you will enter the history books, you know, of course! Blast is a history book, too. You will not be a legendary and immaculate hero, but a figure of controversy, nevertheless. What have you to grumble about? c'est mieux ainsi.—Now, to accuse me, as you did the other night, of initiating an attack on you in 'your' present state is absurd. When I think of you the work I look to is the magnificent series of paintings, drawings, etchings you led off with, and the equals of which you latterly have not exhibited. I should like only to have had those to speak of, while complaining of the manner in which your gypsy-minded contemporaries fitted you out for the pilgrimage of life, and the ridiculous properties they often slipped onto the models in your masterpieces.

As you said the other evening, I could not harm you particularly even if I would. But you may take it from me that I did not write that article with that intention: I will own to having used you as a particularly picturesque argument; and perhaps I should have remembered my early acquaintance with you and your brilliant energy at that time, and refrained, since this 'journalism', as you obviously call it, is a thing of very slight importance to me.

Now for the personal matter.—The other night I walked into the trap that you set: for had you not presented such a generous and engaging front, but allowed your true sentiments to transpire from a distance, I should have remained on my own ground.—It was natural that some years ago when I no longer agreed with you or shared your illusions you should find some abusive tag to describe my dissent. Malignant was the one you chose. A Machiavellian figure was evoked. But I may here attest that I have never found you wanting in cunning yourself, although not a good judge of it, or the absence of it, in others.—My own naiveté, when you were accusing me of 'deepness'—or darkness—was super-human.—You displayed, I think, some strategy the other night, and 'being very drunk' is an euphemism.

The thought of scrapping with you causes me a feeling of shame, referrable to our long intimacy and my position at first of a cadet.—But I do not like the names you found for me in the presence of your woman-friend. I had two reasons for not stopping you the other night.—But these reasons are local, and my more general fastidiousness [and?] fancy has limitations.

Unless you want your head broken you had better take my word for it that this is so, and not attribute my gentleness the other night to lack of spirit.—When I say, 'want your head broken' I feel I am dropping into a florid lingo, perhaps, result of infection. Let me say, that, being active and fairly strong, I will try and injure your head. Anyhow, we will not meet again in any friendly way, if you do not mind.—There are some folk I actively dislike and am disgusted by. I entertain no sentiments of that sort towards you: I never did nor ever shall, as you probably divine, despite 'quatch' about malevolence.

Yourse sincerely,
W. Lewis

'Quatch'] complaint.

CHARLES RICKETTS

(1866–1931)

Ricketts was a painter and designer, a friend of Wilde, Yeats, Shaw, and a companion of Charles Shannon (1863–1937), artist, and with him editor of the avant-garde magazine the *Dial*.

284. To Gordon Bottomley, 2 October 1916

Bottomley (1874–1938) was a poet and writer of poetic dramas.

My dear Bottomley,

Your books are packed at last and leave to-morrow. Therewith is a paper Javanese doll, as backshish for patience, and also because to-day is my fiftieth birthday and the thirty-fourth anniversary of my first meeting with Shannon at Kennington Park Road, which was bombed on Monday last. It is an Oriental custom for the birthday patient to give gifts to friends, hence paper doll. . . .

Dulac was again lucky, he saw the Zepp hit and burst into flame and slowly tilt upwards; this made his wife hysterical and affected him. He saw more than us, as he had opera-glasses.

Not a thought crossed my brain over the loss of life, that in that torch were twenty or more Germans. One part of my brain mentioned this to another, which refused to be concerned. Shannon hoped it had not fallen on a house; even this hardly impressed me, and I felt astonished, almost stunned, by my lack of excitement, as if the experience was one of those lucid dreams in which one does not believe at the time of dreaming.

To celebrate my birthday I have ordered in a pianola and spent pounds on Chopin's Preludes, Scherzos, Ballades, Schumann's *Carnaval*, Fantasia, Quintet, and *Le Coq d'Or*. Nearly all Schumann is cut; not so Wagner: of *Tristan*, for instance, there is only the 'Liebestod.' This is amazing! Yet new things, Scriabine's early works for instance, are cut, and other Russian music in course: Moussorgsky's *Pictures*, and other unexpected things. I look forward to getting drunk on sound, just as a sailor determines to get drunk on beer. Dulac has *Schéhérazade*, I shall probably get it out of him later.

Kindest greetings to Mrs Bottomley.

Yours ever,
C. Ricketts

Dulac] Edmund Dulac (1882–1953), artist and designer.   Zepp] Ricketts and Shannon had witnessed the descent of a burning Zeppelin on the night of 1 Oct.

285. To Gordon Bottomley, 14 October 1916

The pianola arrived on 6 Oct.

My dear Bottomley,

I wrote last before my actual contact with the pianola and its possibilities. These, i.e. possibilities, seem to me almost boundless, but the thing has to be learnt and played by a musician; it is also hard work, at first, or at least comparable to riding a bicycle. The first day of its arrival I played on it for some five hours, and was prostrate in the evening, in a new shirt— the former one had got wet through—and with sore insteps and back of thighs. All the same, I have found the thing comparable to an exciting holiday: I walk with a spring, sleep like a hog, and am able entirely to forget the war and the general lowering of one's vitality it has brought with it in these two tragic and tedious years. I wake up in the morning realizing that I shall go through Chopin's Ballade, Op. 52, F Minor, or the closing scene of the *Rheingold*, before work. When work clogs and cloys the brain, I can plunge into *Le Coq d'Or*, or play Debussy's *Arabesque*, things which it would take years of experience to play indifferently, and which, in a few days, I shall probably play well, or at least to my satisfaction. The pianola is a friend—a rather expensive friend, but this probably adds to friendship, affection, love!

Kindest greetings to both.

Ever sincerely yours,
C. Ricketts

P.S. I am at the present moment dripping with sweat and shaking all over with the last movement of *Schéhérazade*; its staccato chords, changes of tempo, and terrific runs form a real adventure.

286. To Lady Davis, July 1925

Mary was the wife of Sir Edmund Davis, a rich collector.

My very dear Friend,

The Sybil Thorndyke excursion was a great success. On their departure I presented them with two huge bunches of peacock feathers. The night was dark and sultry when they left; they motored, a few minutes later, straight into the thunderstorm which kept you and me wide awake all night. Bruce Winston told me blinding flashes played round the car, which bumped and throbbed under the deluge of water, on which the car seemed to float. They then drove into a dense black mist or cloud through which they could not see, the sky opened and was again torn by lightning, then they drove into a blood-red mist and had to stop.

Lewis Casson then said, 'I wonder if there is something in the peacock feathers?' 'Nonsense,' said Winston. 'It is rather awesome,' said Sybil. 'Shall I throw the feathers out?' asked Winston. 'Don't be a bloody fool,' said Casson. Violent flashes of lightning in horrid succession, thunder as never was. 'Would you like me to throw away the feathers, Sybil?' said Winston. 'No . . . Lewis thinks it's all right.' Flashes and roars. Winston hurriedly bundles the feathers out of the window, and Sybil says in a faint voice, 'Bruce, I should like you to throw away the feathers.' 'I have done so, my dear,' was the reply. More flashes and crashes. 'Didn't Ricketts put some small feathers in your hat?' asks Casson. These are promptly wrenched from Bruce's coiffure. 'Do you think there are any on the floor of the car?' and matches are lit and feathers sought for. Suddenly the storm sweeps away, the rain falls in delicious occasional blobs, and the car rolls on, lit by the occasional flashes of a distant storm.

Yours as always,
C. Ricketts

Sybil Thorndike] (1882–1976), distinguished actress who created (1924) the title-role in Shaw's *Saint Joan*; her husband Lewis Casson was also a distinguished actor.   Excursion] to Chilham Castle, built by Inigo Jones and bought by Davis, who 'sold three pictures to purchase the place', in 1918; Ricketts and Shannon were granted a cottage on the estate for life.

DORA CARRINGTON
(1893–1932)

Dora Carrington was known simply as 'Carrington'; a painter, she married Ralph Partridge (1894–1960), Leonard Woolf's secretary at the Hogarth Press. She was attached to Lytton Strachey, and committed suicide when he died.

287. *To Lytton Strachey, 29 January 1917*

Asheham as you perceive is surrounded by sunshine, and smoke surges from every chimney in dense volumes. Should you for a moment contemplate coming, do I beg you bring only the lightest of summer underclothing and some antidote for mosquitos and gnats which invest the garden in the evenings.

We arrived here after a long and dusty Journey on Saturday evening. Fortunately the old hag had some iced drinks prepared for us in the kitchen, for Saxon was nearly dropping from the heat. Um-ah-well, Thank you for a pocket handkerchief—admit my Mercy is everlasting and my goodness endureth for ever, for sparing you from the jeers of James and the scorn of servants!

Well, and how is my aged grandad. I trust he is looking after himself, and not sliding on the ponds in the Parks with the lads of the city. It often worries me that you are so careless over your health, and appetite. I should be so much happier if I could only think you were well looked after—But you were always reckless even as a boy. One day perhaps you will realise how much you have made your poor aunt suffer—We are all very happy here, and actually warm. I plastered all the windows and the bottoms of the doors up with brown paper. And we have terrific fires in all the rooms. Saxon is as I suspected a lunatic. He spent the whole of Saturday night and all Sunday breaking the ice in the cistern, and putting his arm down pipes and then drying his wet shirt *on* his arm in front of the fire. He insisted on getting up at eight o'ck and lighting the fires. It is impossible to have any control over his actions. But he seems fairly well in spite of his strange habits. Barbara is cheerful, and full of industry.

Yesterday we had a tea party. Bunny, Duncan, Adrian and Karin walked over from Charleston. They ate the most tremendous tea. Like starving stags, and brought a dog. Saxon read Swinburne to us in the evening. I loved so much the poem about the Nightingale and the man.

Did you go to the Sale or did greed overcome you at Simpsons?

It's lovely here, we walked this morning to Glynde, it was truly quite hot in the sun, and the downs exquisitely beautiful, with patches of sunlight and olive green shadows running about over them. We had a ride back in a cart, which we stopped on the road.

Every delight seems to have congregated here to rejoice us, sun in the day season and a moon by night. It is strange living here again when I remember how amazed I was with you all round the fire that evening I first came.

My love
Carrington

Saxon] Saxon Sydney-Turner (1880–1962), a Treasury official and friend of the Woolfs. Bunny . . . Karin] David Garnett, Duncan Grant, Adrian Woolf, and his wife Karin, coming from the Sussex house of Grant and Vanessa Bell.   Simpsons] a restaurant in the Strand. Glynde] a Sussex village.

288. To Lytton Strachey, 14 May 1921

My dearest Lytton,

There is a great deal to say and I feel very incompetent to write it today. Last night I composed a great many letters to you, almost till three in the morning. I then wrote an imaginary letter and bared my very soul to you. This morning I don't feel so intimate. *You* mayn't value my pent up feelings and a tearful letter. *I* rather object to them not being properly received and left about. Well there was more of a crisis than I thought when I wrote to you on Thursday. Ralph had one of his break downs and completely collapsed. He threw himself in the Woolves' arms and asked their sympathy and advice. Leonard and Virginia both said it was hopeless for him to go on as he was, that he must either marry me, or leave me completely. He came down to Reading yesterday and met me at the Coffee tea shop. He looked dreadfully ill and his mouth twitched. I'd really made my mind up some time ago that if it came to the ultimate point, I would give in. Only typically I preferred to defer it indefinitely and avoid it if possible. You see I knew there was nothing really to hope for from you— Well ever since the beginning. Then Alix told me last spring what you told James. That you were slightly terrified of my becoming dependent on you, and a permanent limpet and other things. I didn't tell you, because after all, it is no use having scenes. But you must know Ralph repeated every word you once told him in bed; that night when we were all three together. The next day we went for a walk on the Swindon downs. Perhaps you remember. I shall never forget that spot of ground, just outside Chisledon, at the foot of the downs, when he repeated every word you had said. He told me of course because he was jealous and wanted to hurt me. But it altered things, because ever after that I had a terror of being physically on your nerves and revolting you. I never came again to your bedroom. Why am I raking all this up now? Only to tell you that all these years I have known all along that my life with you was limited. I could never hope for it to become permanent. After all Lytton, you are the only person who I have ever had an all absorbing passion for. I shall never have another. I couldn't now. I had one of the most self abasing loves that a person can have. You could throw me into transports of happiness and dash me into deluges of tears and despair, all by a few words. But these aren't reproaches. For after all it's getting on for 6 years since I first met you at Asheham; and that's a long time to be happy. And I know we shall always be friends now until I die. Of course these years of Tidmarsh when we were quite alone will always be the happiest I ever spent. And I've such a store of good things which I've saved up, that I feel I could never be lonely again now. Still it's too much of a strain to be quite alone here waiting to see you or craning my nose and eyes out of the top window at 41 Gordon Square to see if you are coming down the street, when I know we'll be better friends, if you aren't haunted by the idea that I am sitting depressed in some corner of the world waiting for your footstep. It's slightly mythical of course. I can pull myself together if I want to and I am more aware than you think, the moment I am getting on your nerves and when I am not wanted. I saw the relief you felt at Ralph taking me away, so to speak, off your hands. I think he'll make me happier, than I should be entirely by myself and it certainly prevents me becoming morbid about you. And as Ralph said last night you'll never leave us. Because in spite of our dullnesses, nobody loves you nearly as much as we do. So in the café in that vile city of Reading, I said I'd marry him. And now he's written to his father and told him. After all I don't believe it will make much difference and to see him so happy is a rather definite thing. I'd probably never marry anyone else and I doubt if a kinder creature exists on this earth. Last night in bed he told me everything Virginia and Leonard had told him. Again a conversation you had with them was repeated to me. Ralph was so happy he didn't hear me gasp and as it was dark he didn't see the tears run down my cheeks. Virginia told him that you had told them you didn't intend to come to Tidmarsh much after Italy and you were nervous lest I'd feel I had a sort of claim on you if I lived with [you] for a long time, ten years and that they all wondered how you could have stood me so long and how on earth we lived together alone here, as I didn't understand a word of literature and we had nothing in common intellectually or physically. That was wrong. For nobody I think could have loved the Ballades, Donne, and Macaulay's Essays and best of all, Lytton's Essays, as much as I. Virginia then told him that she thought I was still in love with you. Ralph asked me if I was. I said I didn't think perhaps I was as much as I used to be. So now I shall never tell *you* I do care again. It goes after today somewhere deep down inside me and I'll not resurrect it to hurt either, you, or Ralph. Never again. He knows I am not in love with him. But he feels my affections are great enough to make him happy if I live with him. I cried last night Lytton, whilst he slept by my side sleeping happily. I cried to think of a savage cynical fate which had made it impossible for my love ever to be used by you. You never knew, or never will know the very big and devastating love I had for you. How I adored every hair, every curl on your beard. How I devoured you whilst you read to me at night. How I loved the smell of your face in your sponge. Then the ivory skin on your hands, your voice, and your hat when I saw it coming along the top of the garden wall from my window. Say you will remember it, that it wasn't all lost and that you'll forgive me for this out burst, and always be my friend. Just thinking of you now makes me cry so I can't see this paper, and yet so happy that the next moment I am calm. I shall be with you in Italy in two weeks, how lovely that will be. And this summer we shall all be very happy together. Please never show this letter to anyone. Ralph is such a dear, I don't feel I'll ever regret marrying him. Though I never will change my maiden name that I have kept so long—so you mayn't ever call me anything but Carrington.

I am not going to tell my mother till the day before, so she can't make a fuss, or come up to London. I think we'll probably get united by Saint Pancras next Saturday and then drift over to Paris and see Valentine. If my Fiend comes on I'll linger there for 2 days and then Italie. I've suggested Mousie and her Dan coming here for the month. And I hope I'll coerce them into it. Then we won't have to worry about the garden and the dampnesses. Nick and Barbara are still here, and this weekend Saxon, and Alan and Michael come this evening. We'll pay off all the books before we leave. Now I must leave you, and paint the other side of the grey hound.

Later.
Nick has just mown the lawn and it is now as smooth and short as a field of green plush.

All the ducks and chickens survive and Ralph spends his time lying in the sun on the lawn trying to persuade them to swim in a pan of water. I thought you had been clever to escape the thunder storms and rains, but today the heat is more wonderful than anything in your land of the Romans. Saxon is an extraordinary character!! I am telling no one what I've told you. It will remain a confession to a priest in a box in an Italian church. I saw in a London Group catalogue a picture by Walter Taylor called 'Reading Lytton Strachey's Victoria'—such is fame. I shall do a still life of a dozen Victoria's arranged in a phalanx for the next London Group. My dear I am sorry to leave you. I'll write again tomorrow. It's such a comfort having you to talk to.

My love for a dear one
Yr Carrington

3 o'ck Saturday,
PS I've just read this letter again. You mustn't think I was hurt by hearing what you said to Virginia and Leonard and *that* made me cry. For I'd faced that long ago with Alix in the first years of my love for you. You gave me a much longer life than I ever deserved or hoped for and I love you for it terribly. I only cried last night at realising I never could have my Moon, that some times I must pain you, and often bore you. You who I would have given the world to have made happier than any person could be, to give you all you wanted. But dearest, this isn't a break in our affections. I'll always care as much, only now it will never burden you and we'll never discuss it again, as there will be nothing to discuss. I see I've told you very little of what I feel. But I keep on crying, if I stop and think about you. Outside the sun is baking and they all chatter, and laugh. It's cynical, this world in its opposites. Once you said to me, that Wednesday afternoon in the sitting room, you loved me as a friend. Could you tell it to me again?

Yrs
Carrington

Alix] Strachey (1892–1973), the wife and collaborator of James Strachey (1887–1967), translator of Freud.   Sponge] she kept one of Strachey's for the purpose.   Saint Pancras] the Register Office.   Valentine] Dobrée, the wife of Bonamy Dobrée, critic and professor. Nick and Barbara] the Bagenals, members of the set.   Alan and Michael] Alan MacIver and Michael Davies.   Grey hound] Carrington was painting an inn sign for the Greyhound pub.

289. To Gerald Brenan, 5 May 1924

Brenan (1894–1987) lived mostly in Spain and was drawn into the Bloomsbury circle by Carrington, with whom he was long in love.

Amigo mio,
I doubt if I shall send you my rigmarole of Saturday after all. I have just had an absurd accident that has unhinged my, as you say my weak spot, mind. I, after breakfast, was walking over the bridge across the little duck stream, in rather a bad temper and vague mood and walked off the edge and fell with my bucket of duck's food into the stream. This for some reason drove me into such a rage that I ran into the hen's house and cried and in my rage tried to hit a hen on the head with a wooden spoon. I could blame no one. It was entirely my own fault and so I could only cry against myself. I wasn't even hurt, only rather wet, but the sudden fall has made my head feel light and empty. And fits of temper I find really make me feel ill for nearly the rest of the day. So my discourse on life, you, and your writing etc etc will not be sent till tomorrow. I sit in the sun surrounded by

dandelions with shining yellow faces, buzzing bees, and heavy trees of cherry blossom. How could one be in a bad temper on such a day! How indeed? I ran to the post very early before anyone was awake this morning with a letter for you. You ought to get it tonight. Do we write every day to each other? I forgot to ask you? I see it's important not to 'feel' life too much. Not to examine every blade of grass. It's better to take a general view of things otherwise, the moral may be, one falls into duck streams in despair. A certain laisser faire is to be cultivated je pense. I shall take some aspirins. I ought to have thought of it before. Yet how pleasant it is to have a friend to whom one can write everything. To whom I can tell my most absurd moods and all my pleasures. I shall start painting tomorrow. Because I give you such fine lectures on finishing your writing I am going to give myself a lecture. Tomorrow I shall finish two pictures although I would rather leave them alone. The Woolves come here next week end. I look forward to seeing them again. Please write me a very friendly letter. Don't reprimand me. I know I've been tiresome never finishing my proper letters, and sending you these scrawls instead. But we must, since we are no ordinary friends, forgive each other *all* our faults.

You will remember to be infinitely discreet with J.H.-J.? He is rather a gossip and I don't think has enough affection for me, not to perhaps, sometimes, throw out a word. I hope your eyes are better.

How very good it will be to see you again. Sometimes it seems impossible to write letters. Everything is too frail, and intangeable to put in paper. I confess my head aches so I *will* go indoors and take an aspirin. But you must never never worry about me dearest. Because truly I am the strongest of humans, and I am never ill. It's all a slight imitation of you, you will perceive. I see why people become naturalists, because it's the most lazy occupation. Shall I tell you in 20 minutes a dandelion on my left has been visited twice by a bee, and each time the bees stayed 58 seconds and carried away .008 grains of pollen. This is the 5 of May, 1924. One could sit here listening to birds, bees, and blue bottles and recording it all in a diary, or a letter, without using for one moment one's brain, or a monucle [?molecule] of emotion.

You see I really ought to go indoors . . . But I love the sun so much and then when this letter is over and put in its envelope, you will leave me. I can't bear to leave you just yet . . .

xxxxx Dear Sweegie. How charming you are.

Hurrzi Hurrzi Dziomal Hji!

Which is the song of the road breakers in Kairouan and at the moment my song.

My love most dear one.

Yr Cirod

J.H.-J.] John Hope-Johnstone (1883–1970), an early friend of Brenan's, later dropped.

IVOR GURNEY

(1890–1937)

Gurney was a poet and musician; he was wounded and gassed in France. From 1922 he was confined in mental institutions, still writing and composing, especially songs.

290. *To Marion Scott, June or July 1917*

Marion Scott (1877–1953) was a musician and writer, a valued correspondent of Gurney. On 19 June 1918 he sent her a suicide note; on 20 June he wrote again to say he had 'lost courage'.

My Dear Friend,

Here am I, sheltered from the sun by the parados of a trench behind a blockhouse; reading 'The Bible in Spain.' That's finished now, and 'Robinson Crusoe' need not be begun for we are being relieved tonight, and O! the relief! 'Robinson' may follow; we shall have tomorrow off anyway. What a life! What a life! My memories of this week will be,—Blockhouse; an archway there through which a sniper used his skill on us as we emerged from the rooms at the side; cold; stuffy heat; Brent Young; Smashed or stuck Tanks; A gas and smoke barrage put up by us, a glorious but terrifying sight; Fritzes shells; One sunset; two sunrises; 'Bible in Spain'; The tale of the cutting up of the KRRs in 1914; of Colonel Elkington; of the first gas attacks also; of the Brigade Orderly; and of the man who walked in his sleep to Fritz, slept well, woke, realised, and bolted; Thirst; Gas; Shrapnel; *Very* H.E.; Our liquid fire; A first sight of an aeroplane map . . . Does it sound interesting? May God forgive me if I ever come to cheat myself into thinking that it was, and lie later to younger men of the Great Days. It was damnable; and what in relation to what might have happened? Nothing at all! We have been lucky, but it is not fit for men to be here—in this tormented dry-fevered marsh, where men die and are left to rot because of snipers and the callousness that War breeds. 'It might be me tomorrow. Who cares? Yet still, hang on for a Blighty.'

Why does this war of spirit take on such dread forms of ugliness and why should a high triumph be signified by a body shattered, black, stinking; avoided by day, stumbled over by night, an offence to the hardest? No doubt there is consolation in the fact that men contemplate such things, such possible endings; and are yet undismayed, yet persistent, do not lose laughter nor the common kindliness that makes life sweet—And yet seem such boys—Yet what consolation can be given me as I look upon and endure it? Any? Sufficient? The 'End of War'? Who knows, for the thing for which so great a price is paid is yet doubtful and obscure; and our reward most sweet would seem to depend on what we make of ourselves

and give ourselves; for clearer eyes and more contented minds; more contented because of comparisons ironically to be made . . . and yet

etc (Not quite correct)

Forgive all this; and accept it as a sincere reflection; a piece of technique;
only one side of the picture; trench-weariness; thoughts of a not too cou-
rageous, not too well-balanced mind. Like Malvolio, I think nobly of man's
soul, and am distressed. God should have done better for us than this;
Could He not have found some better milder way of changing the Prussian
(whom he made) than by the breaking of such beautiful souls? Now *that* is
what one should write poetry upon. Someday I will say it in Music, after
a while . . .

Now I must go into the Blockhouse, may get a Blighty doing so . . . and
O if it were but a small hole in the leg! But I am lucky only in my friends,
and existence has gone awry for me, not by any means wholly my fault.
Maybe I am strong enough to prove the truth of 'Character is Destiny'
now. God, how I could work, how train myself in Blighty now, were it
over! Dyspepsia or no dyspepsia, I'd 'be a marvellous kid!' And yet (O the
Shakespearian insight of me!) Had I used those earlier years, still I must
have come out here for all my promise and accomplishments, and—there
you are; here.

I have made a book about Beauty because I have paid the price which
five years ago had not been paid. Someday perhaps the True, the real, the
undeniable will be shown by me, and I forgive all this.

There is a great gap in my mind, very thirsty, which shall be filled with
sunsets, trees, winds, stars, and children's faces; blossoming fairer after so
long a drought my mind shall turn freely to that which once was effort to
contemplate. I, even I, may experience Present Joy—but not yet. But were
I home, with this new ability and Passion for my work, O then perhaps . . .

It is a hard thing to accustom oneself to the resigning of life at any
moment, and to become aware and more aware of what that leaving means.
Meanwhile, while I am thus thinking and writing, our guns pour almost
incessantly a thin musical complaining watery trickle of shells; for what

purpose one may rise up and see. 'After all I might have gone to Liepsic, to Bonn, to Munich; and they might have been my friends and companions in Art.' There goes a dud, and I am glad of it.

Who will dare talk of the glory of Waterloo or Trafalgar again?

There now, I have written myself out, and feel happier. (Theirs or ours? Theirs. Bash!)

I do not forget in my preoccupations to hope you are getting stronger, and that Mr Scott is now on holiday. Nor forget the funny side of things. A few yards away are three walking cases; perhaps 'Blighty' men. To get to the Dressing Station is a slightly risky thing, but far less so than many ordinary things a soldier does. Will they risk it? In day light? Hardly! For they have that which is more precious than much fine gold.

Tea's up!

TEA!! O magic word.

Late reading with a pipe and a teapot. 5 oclock at Cranham. Willy Harvey and wonderful Mrs Harvey. Framilode. Twigworth.

O what not? All these memories have music in them. Bach and Schumann. Perhaps there are two men of that name over there:

Your sincere friend
Ivor Gurney

I wish I wasnt so lousy.

Dont trouble to sympathise. I take that for granted or would not have written comme ça.

Blighty] home; also a wound requiring a return there. 'Take me back to dear old Blighty' (popular song).

291. To Marion Scott, 4 October 1917

My Dear Friend,

Hearing a few casual catchwords flying around, it struck me that you might like to know some of them—such as I can remember. Poor bare jests, almost too familiar to remember at will.

There is one (just heard for the thousandth time) which brings a picture of a tragic roll call. A man may be shouted for who is not present, and the room answers, 'On the wire, at Loos'. A lighter answer, a mock of this last, is 'Gassed at Mons'.

A coming strafe means carrying parties, and they are greeted with 'More iron rations for Fritz'. Germans are known, affectionately, as Fritzes, Allemans or 'Johnny'. The Scots use the last name chiefly.

An intimation of a charge for crime is made by the phrase 'You're *for* it'.

Intimation of death is made as 'H—— has got it'. 'Poor old Bills snuffed it'. Or 'Shant see old George again'. To see Germans kill the wounded, is to see 'the boys done in'.

One 'goes up the line with the Boys'. Or 'over the top with the Boys'.
Practically *all* swearing ceases when one reaches Blighty, though the
language out there is frequently foul. A commentary on the life! A bad
officer, that is, a bully, is a——! A good officer, that is, a considerate, is 'a
toff'. 'I'd follow him anywhere'. 'The men's friend;' or simply, but in significant tones, a '*gent*leman'! A funk is 'windy', a bad funk, 'as windy as Hell'.

An officer always takes whisky into the line, and his being drunk on any
critical occasion is always condoned. I have never known any of our officers
really funk an order. Exact orders are always obeyed, or practically always.
A bombardment is of course 'a strafe', a bad one 'some strafe'. Men are
'glad to be out of that'. A premonition of Death is given as 'My numbers
up'. A ditto of Blighty—'I'm for Blighty' 'Blighty this journey'. A box
respirator is a 'Gaspirator'. A helmet a 'tin hat'. A rifle a 'bundoob'
(Hindustani?) A revolver 'a peashooter'.

The Germans, in anger, are referred to as 'them——bastards'. The
English soldier has an enormous reverence for Hindenburg and his strategy. An almost complete belief that man for man he is far better than Fritz.
A doubt of our air-service. A conviction that the Germans are as he is—a
sufferer under discipline, no better nor worse than he; only unluckier. A
belief that our discipline is stricter than his. A longing for home, and
English girls. A contempt for everything French, although he has learnt to
think better of the soldiers. French girls, towns (as a rule), houses, farm
implements, are all objects of scorn. He admires the .75 gun very greatly.
As for French beer, cigarettes, baccy . . . the comparison simply must not
be hinted even by dashes. For all his amorous intentions once he reaches
home, he thinks the French girls highly immoral. For all his stealing, the
French unspeakable thieves. He likes Church Parade. Loathes most of all
disciplinary parades, kit inspections and the like. Marches till he drops.
Loves to frowst, and has a marvellous ability for the making of fires,
'bivvies' etc. Fritzes splendid dugouts always move his praise.

His Guide, Philosopher, and Friend is 'John Bull', Horatio Bottomley is
recognised as a scoundrel, but, for all that, the finest man in England, the
only one to sympathise with a common soldiers woes and oppressions.
Lloyd George is also admired, and, slightly, the King. Asquith is simply
'Wait and See'. Their faith in newspapers has been sorely shaken for ever
by the comparison of accounts with realities. But chiefly by the contrast
between the phrase 'Mastery of the Air' and the reality. Parliament is a
haunt of people who talk and dont care what happens to him and his like.
Still he preserves his faith, how and in what, is obscure, but I believe it to
be his feeling that Englishmen would not condemn him to suffer longer
than was needful. But he never says so.

I may remember more, if so and it interests you, you shall have it.

ALDOUS HUXLEY

(1894–1963)

A friend of Lady Ottoline Morrell and the Bloomsbury group, Huxley was of the same circle as Lytton Strachey and Dora Carrington (see above, Letter 287).

292. To Dora Carrington, 14 July 1917

My dear Carrington,

Your nose for the scabrous is unerring. There was indeed a story buried between the lines of my postcard . . . a story from which Philip could make one of his noblest Homilies on Virgin Behaviour. The protagonists are Evan, myself and a young woman of eighteen exactly like Nell Gwynn; the scene a romantic little house in a forest discovered by a most peculiar series of chances. Immense cherry trees, laden with fruit, to right and left of the stage; Nell Gwynn, whose peculiarities are that she is partially Dutch and partially French, ascends ladders and throws cherries at the young men . . . there is a snake's-eye-view of ankles and calves, perhaps a shade thick. . . . And so it begins. In the heart of Nell Gwynn the most dangerous passion is kindled . . . not merely for one but for both simultaneously; it is the wildest desire mixed with an almost religious awe, as though for gods.

Scene two. In the forest at evening the mosquitos bite; so do the young women. Rather disquietingly it begins to occur to us that the creature is perfectly innocent.

Then the strangest scene in our bed-room. We become perfectly convinced that she is completely virginal. Without any shame she caresses both of us with all the fire of her native sensuality. We explain that we cannot take her virginity; we are simply passers by and it would be the merest robbery. She is in tears about it, begs and implores that we should. We are inexorable; Evan sitting up in bed like a young Sicilian shepherd with no clothes on orders her back to her room with his most imperious manner; he is the descendent of Welsh princes; she obeys and creeps off to a cold and solitary couch. We sink to sleep. At about three I wake up, aware that someone is passionately kissing my neck and shoulders. I hasten to add that it was not Evan. Nell Gwynn has returned. I give her the hospitality of my bed for a few minutes and send her away; it is all a little nerve-racking. The next night she goes to Evan; the fate of virginity hangs rather in the balance, but escapes intact; this time we lock the door. On Monday we depart, and there are terrible adieus. We feel that by our self control we have probably ruined a young girl's life. However, in my case the adieu is an au revoir, for making my way from Beaconsfield to Eton on Wednesday it occurs to me that it would be more amusing to spend the night with Nell Gwynn than with my tutor at Eton. I drop in and resume my study of the character of the unsophisticated virgin . . . feeling like Maurice Barrès in the process of cultivating 'son Moi'.

But the half of it can never be told; it was all so peculiar . . . like something which must have happened in the Balkans, impossible in England.

I am too unhappy about the seraphic Phyllis. I go to-day into the country, to Oxford, to stay with my antique and admirable friends the Haldanes. But if you could definitely secure Phyllis some day I might rush up . . . except that travelling is so atrociously expensive. But I expect I shall be up for a few days at the end of the month or the beginning of August and then, and then—

It was a thousand pities you couldn't come to Evan's birthday party last night. An empty place waited for you. It was a tremendous affair; at least five and twenty people and the drink flowed. Marie Beerbohm and I achieved a distinct rapprochement, positively a mutual épanchement, in our cups . . . though sober we have always been rather alarmed of one another. She is a nice creature I should say—at any rate when tight. I also established a contact with Nina Hamnett, which I had never dared to do before; at one time I even distinctly remember winding a red ribbon round her legs in the form of a Malvolio garter, but that was entirely by the way. In one corner of the room Lady Constance supported John on her bosom. A sombre group of indistinguishably vicious women—I cant remember who they were—circled about the centre of the floor, dancing. In another corner McEvoy peered out through his hair like a sheepdog with shining eyes. Then there was a curious sediment of the upper middle classes . . . two perfectly nice young men with two perfectly nasty young women . . . and they were like the people who figure in *Punch* and who enjoy that journal. They were infinitely facetious and so boring that—as by some mishap I found myself at dinner sitting in the middle of them—I had to play a little game of spillikins all by myself throughout the meal with a pile of knives and forks and spoons. But they disappeared quite soon, or at any rate one lost sight of them.

Well, au revoir my dear Carrington. Let me know what are your schemes for late July and August, what, too are the movements of the delicate, though, I take it, somewhat hyper-nubile, Phyllis. You find me at 'Cherwell, Oxford' . . . no more.

Mr Mills has asked me to go and stay with him at Pevensey, but I think it's impossible. At any rate we will see.

Devotedly,
Aldous

Give my love to Alix: I trust she recovers.

Philip] Morrell, husband of Lady Ottoline.   Evan] Morgan, a friend of Huxley's. Maurice Barrès] (1862–1923) was a novelist and diarist, known for his 'cult of the self'. Phyllis] Boyd, friend of Carrington.   The Haldanes] J. B. S. Haldane (1892–1964), biochemist; or his father R. B. Haldane (1856–1928), Liberal politician.   Marie Beerbohm] a niece of Sir Max Beerbohm.   Nina Hamnett] bohemian painter and writer.   Lady Constance] Stewart-Richardson, a modern-style dancer.   John . . . McEvoy] Augustus John and his friend Ambrose McEvoy (1878–1927), portrait painter.   Alix] Florence, later married to James Strachey, translator of Freud. Both were psychoanalysts.

WILFRED OWEN
(1893–1918)

After the Somme the poet Owen was invalided home, but returned to France in 1918 and was killed on 4 Nov., a week before the Armistice.

293. To Susan Owen, 4 October 1918

Owen wrote most of his letters to his mother. He was duly awarded the Military Cross. A letter to his friend Siegfried Sassoon repeats that his 'nerves are in perfect order'; he had suffered what was diagnosed as 'neurasthenia' and is claiming to be cured.

Strictly private   In the Field

My darling Mother,

As you must have known both by my silence and from the newspapers which mention this Division—and perhaps by other means & senses—I have been in action for some days.

I can find no word to qualify my experiences except the word SHEER. (Curiously enough I find the papers talk about sheer fighting!) It passed the limits of my Abhorrence. I lost all my earthly faculties, and fought like an angel.

If I started into detail of our engagement I should disturb the censor and my own Rest.

You will guess what has happened when I say I am now Commanding the Company, and in the line had a boy lance-corporal as my Sergeant-Major.

With this corporal who stuck to me and shadowed me like your prayers I captured a German Machine Gun and scores of prisoners.

I'll tell you exactly how another time. I only shot one man with my revolver (at about 30 yards!); The rest I took with a smile. The same thing happened with other parties all along the line we entered.

I have been recommended for the Military Cross; and have recommended every single N.C.O. who was with me!

My nerves are in perfect order.

I came out in order to help these boys—directly by leading them as well as an officer can; indirectly, by watching their sufferings that I may speak of them as well as a pleader can. I have done the first.

Of whose blood lies yet crimson on my shoulder where his head was— and where so lately yours was—I must not now write.

It is all over for a long time. We are marching steadily back.

Moreover

The War is nearing an end.

Still,

Wilfred and more than Wilfred

KATHERINE MANSFIELD
(1888–1923)

Katherine Mansfield Beauchamp, New Zealand story writer, was the wife of the critic John Middleton Murry. See also Letters 263 and 265.

294. To Princess Bibesco, 24 March 1921

Murry was having an affair with the Princess (née Asquith, 1897–1945). Mansfield did not object to the affair, only to the letters.

Dear Princess Bibesco,

I am afraid you must stop writing these little love letters to my husband while he and I live together. It is one of the things which is not done in our world.

You are very young. Won't you ask your husband to explain to you the impossibility of such a situation.

Please do not make me have to write to you again. I do not like scolding people and I simply hate having to teach them manners.

Yours sincerely,
Katherine Mansfield

EDMUND WILSON
(1895–1972)

Edmund Wilson, journalist, diarist, critic, and novelist, was the author of *Axel's Castle* (1931), *To the Finland Station* (1940), and *Patriotic Gore*.

295. To John Peale Bishop, 3 July 1921

Bishop (1892–1944), a poet and novelist, collaborated with Wilson on *The Under-taker's Garland* (1922).

Dear John,

Arriving about two weeks ago at the Gare du Nord, what was my astonishment to find myself met by a great delegation of *filles publiques* who demanded M. Bishop with eager girlish voices; I was much bewildered until a beautifully dressed old lady, of perfect dignity and manners (who was, as I afterwards found out, the doyenne of the profession), came forward and explained to me in excellent English that it had been understood in Paris that you were coming with me. When I explained that this was not the case, she could hardly conceal her emotion and from the rest of the delegation—who had been selected among much ill feeling as the most comely, the most impressive, and the most indefatigable of their craft—a great cry arose such as must go up when an ocean steamer is sinking. It seems that a new position, which I shall not attempt to explain here, had been named in your honor (*le soubresaut Bishop*). It was a heartbreaking scene. The committee decided on the spot that the whole profession should go into a period of fasting and mourning for four days—that is to say, every member should remain continent during that period—a decision which, when it was carried into effect, inflicted a veritable period of Lent upon the whole nation and will always remain a black period indeed in the memory of the *Patrie*. In fact, the government tried to prevent it, but without success.

I am enjoying myself here very much, though I haven't done much of anything yet but establish myself in a *pension*, run into a few friends, and go to the theater. I have, however, what it is the prime purpose of this letter to describe, seen Edna a couple of times. I found her in a very first-rate hotel on the Left Bank and better dressed, I suppose, than she has ever been before in her life. You were right in guessing that she was well cared for as she had never been before. She also seems to be in very good health, the phase of being run down that Crownie hated has passed. But she looks older, more mature—at least she has on the occasions when I have seen her; she assured me that perhaps the next day she would be like a little girl again. She was very serious, earnest, and sincere about herself—inspired, I suppose, by my presence; no doubt, *ça passera*—and told me that she wanted to settle down to a new life: she was tired of breaking hearts and spreading havoc. She loved, she was very happy with her present lover, a big red-haired British journalist named Slocum, the Paris correspondent of the London *Herald* (a Labor paper), who had spent three years in France and had two teeth knocked out in the war. Unfortunately, he had a wife and three children at Saint-Cloud and a very cruel situation had arisen. She did not know whether he would get a divorce or not, but, if he did, she would marry him, go to England to live, and have children. She was very happy, she said. I am sorry to say that, when I first talked to her, I was inclined, with the memory of my own scars still giving out an occasional twinge, to jeer at her seriousness and be sarcastic at the expense of the pain she expressed at having wrecked another home; but I don't think this is the thing to do, because, after all, perhaps there is something in this idea and it is probably a good thing to encourage her. I thought I discovered signs that he watched her with a jealous eye and that my presence had had to be carefully explained to him—and also that she did not want me to know this. She looks well, as I say, and has a new distinction of dress, but she can no longer intoxicate me with her beauty or throw bombs into my soul; when I looked at her it was like staring into the center of an extinct volcano. She made me sad; it made me sad, curiously enough, that I had loved her so much once and now did not love her any longer. Actually, of course, I would not love her again for anything; I can think of few more terrible calamities; but I somehow felt that, impossible and imperfect as she is, some glamour and high passion had gone out of life when my love for her died. Well, these are old Dr Wilson's last words on the chief maelstrom of his early years. Preserve them carefully, but do not publish them until all parties are dead. She asked about you and what your latest love affair was (I didn't go into it much, thinking you mightn't want the situation exposed) and wished you were there. She read me a long poem (rather good) that she had written and one or two short ones; she tells me that she has also done a short story and begun a novel (whose theme she is much disturbed to find anticipated by Cabell's 'Taboo'). She had evidently prepared the *mise en scène* very carefully when she first received me: she had put on a serious black dress and was discovered sitting before her typewriter and a pile of manuscripts. And, as a matter of fact, I think she has been working more, perhaps, lately than she had when Crownie saw her.

. . . The Fitzgeralds have recently been here and tried to get hold of me, but, to my infinite regret, couldn't. I didn't know about it until after they had gone back to London. It seems they hate Europe and are planning to go back to America almost immediately. The story is that they were put out of a hotel because Zelda insisted upon tying the elevator—one of those little half-ass affairs that you run yourself—to the floor where she was living so that she would be sure to have it on hand when she had finished dressing for dinner.

Give my best to everybody in the office and tell [Jeanne] Ballot that I shall soon send her such a postcard as she requested. Don't repeat any of this stuff about Edna, or about my own reactions to her.

Yours always,
E.W.

Edna] St Vincent Millay (1892–1950), poet and early friend of Wilson, who greatly admired her work.   Cabell's] James Branch Cabell (1879–1958), prolific novelist and poet.   Crownie] Frank Crowninshield, editor of *Vanity Fair*.   The Fitzgeralds] Scott, the novelist, and his wife Zelda.   The office] that of the *New Republic*.

296. To Louise Bogan, 19 July 1933

The poet Louise Bogan (1897–1954) was a New York friend.

Dear Louise,

. . . I have come up here for a few days to the old family place. My mother spends a couple of months here every summer, but I haven't been here for years. It gave me an awful turn at first, made me horribly gloomy the first night—everybody I ever knew here is dead, gone, or taken to drink and debt. The little town, which used to be populated by my relatives, is practically deserted. But the place here is still attractive and very interesting. My family came over here from New England in the latter part of the eighteenth century—this house was built 1800–4; I suppose it was a first Westward migration. You can get a very good idea of how people lived in America a century and a half ago. The house includes all the things usually found in antique stores, and my constant thought has been—how like an antique store! There are comb-back chairs, curly-maple chairs; bedsteads with faces like figureheads sticking out of the top of them; bed quilts in bright and faintly phallic patterns; engravings of Washington and his family and other standard historical subjects; spinning wheels, bootjacks, berry baskets; a footstool which opens into a cuspidor when you press a little wooden flap (there used to be a chair that played tunes when you sat on it, but I don't know what has become of it); a hideous bust of one of my cousins, done in Germany, and with the hair ribbon and ruffles all carefully reproduced in marble; a stuffed heron; many religious works, annals of the state legislature, and a book called *The Young Wife, or Duties of Woman in the Marriage Relation*, published in 1838 in Boston and warning against the effects of tea and coffee, which 'loosen the tongue, fire the eye, produce mirth and wit, excite the animal passions, and lead to remarks about ourselves and others that we should not have made in other circumstances, and which it were better far, for us and the world, never to have made'; perforated tin boxes to be filled with hot coals for warming the feet on sleigh rides and in church; a wooden pestle and mortar; iron cranes and other instruments for cooking things in the fireplaces; jars of dried rose leaves and colored pebbles; a decanter which says 'J. Rum'; an old wooden flute, brought over, my great-uncle told me, in an ox-team load from New England. Big rooms, well proportioned; chastely elegant fireplaces, all different; an amplitude and completeness of the large old-fashioned family (my great-grandfather had three wives and his children must have run to a dozen) whose house is a whole city in itself. Currants, gooseberries, red and white raspberry bushes, stone hitching posts; stifling attics with hoopskirts and beaver hats in old hide-covered trunks (there used to be a sealed-up place, where somebody was supposed to have been hidden). There is a gray dappled effect about the side of the house where the plaster has been dropping off the stone which resembles the light and shade in shallow rivers and recalls certain effects in your poetry. The country—hills, pastures, and forests of the first uplands of the Adirondacks—is magnificent—almost too much so: it has never been civilized, humanized, as a good deal of New England has been.

When I was a kid, I used to love coming up here with my little cousins; but when I got older, I used to be depressed and irked when my parents came back every summer. It seemed like moping around in a tomb when life was going on elsewhere. And the old gloom came down on me, as I saw, when I first arrived. Yet I find I take a certain pride in it—and satisfaction in something that stays the same through all the upheavals. Yet, though it stay the same, there is nothing alive in it any longer. The state road now runs directly in front of it, the little town is dwindling to nothing, and there will presently be nothing left but the old house confronting a hot-dog stand and gas station. Maybe I will turn the whole place into an antique shop!

What is really needed here, however, rather than a refined *Atlantic Monthly* essay like the above, is a thorough-going drinking party—such as those at which you are so much missed nowadays in New York in the role of the gracious and stimulating hostess . . . Well, love and good luck! I have greatly enjoyed hearing from you and miss you constantly.

Edmund

Old family place] the Wilson family's summer house at Talcottville, NY, is commemorated in Wilson's *Upstate* (1971); he inherited it in 1951.

297. To Alfred Kazin, December 1952

Kazin (b. 1915) is an autobiographer and literary critic.

Dear Alfred,

You flickered in and out of my consciousness the other night like a laconic interpolation by one of Stravinsky's wind instruments. I wanted to talk to you but got stuck in the crowd . . .

Christmas Greetings
and best wishes for
the New Year

בָּרוּךְ אַתָּה לַיהוָה

אֶלְמַד לְשׁוֹן יִשְׂרָאֵל

I'll bet you can't read this.

Edmund Wilson

Wellfleet] Wilson had a house in Wellfleet on Cape Cod.   In Hebrew] May you be blessed by the Lord. I will learn the language of Israel. (Wilson was learning Hebrew in preparation for his book *The Scrolls from the Dead Sea*, 1955).

298. To Mary Meigs, 26 December 1964

Mary Meigs was an important Wellfleet friend of Wilson's last years.

Dear Mary,

I missed you after you left New York and was going to write you, but as a result of walking back from Durlacher without a coat I came down with some kind of bronchitis and had to spend the next day in bed. My condition was aggravated by a strange evening I had spent the night before and in which I would have involved you if you had stayed. Arthur Schlesinger called me up rather mysteriously and invited me to a party 'to meet', as they say, Jackie Kennedy and Tennessee Williams. It turned out to be one of the rites connected with the emergence of Mrs Kennedy from mourning—in the house of a woman named vanden Heuvel, who is a big shot in the entertainment business. Lots of well-dressed ladies, very rich, and among them Saul Steinberg, John Galbraith, Truman Capote, and Arthur. I had some conversation with Steinberg, who is very much the solid, dogmatic, and serious-minded kind of Jew. He almost never allows himself to smile. On my other side was Galbraith, a very tall and equally dogmatic Canadian Scot, who smiles even more rarely than Steinberg. Mrs Kennedy spent the whole evening talking to Tennessee W., then they left together, and for some reason I never grasped, we all went on to another party in the same building, where everybody was even richer; they seemed to be a mixture of old society (Vanderbilts and Whitneys) with café society—now to some extent, I suppose, the same thing. It was evidently a kind of housewarming for a tiny little white-mouse-like couple who had just furnished a huge apartment in what Augustus John, speaking of Wilde, called 'impeccable bad taste.' When you entered, you were confronted with one of Francis Bacon's yelling Popes side by side with a Vertes drawing, and beside the piano stood two products of pop art: a girl and a boy made of wooden boxes. On the walls of a big living room were absurd abstractions. People would say, 'That's a ——, isn't it?' The host and hostess were referred to benevolently as 'these children.' I never knew why I was there or what it was all about. But you see what you missed by not staying over.

I got back to Middletown only half alive and took to my bed for two days—during which I read the Françoise Gilot book on Picasso, which is fascinating, and very illuminating when he talks about his painting. It confirmed me in my doubts about him. (You said you had read it, didn't you?) Doesn't he think too much about his public? He is so consciously preoccupied with shocking and at the same time always makes a point of putting in human or animal features in order that the ordinary person can find something he recognizes. There is something rather vulgar about him—in his art as well as his behavior.

. . . Am also enclosing an article on pop art. The author sounds very portentous and says that other people don't have the right attitude, but then doesn't seem to provide the expected illumination or to know where he stands himself. The man who teaches drawing here tells me that pop is already a thing of the past and that 'op'—optical illusions—has taken its place.

We hope you will come on again soon and succeed in seeing the Hartford gallery.

Love from all of us to everybody.
Edmund

299. To Francis Steegmuller, 27 July 1968

Steegmuller (b. 1906) is the author of books on Flaubert and Maupassant. He seems to have been collecting limericks.

Dear Mr Steegmuller,
Thank you for your card of congratulation.
Here is another Du Maurier limerick:

> Il était un gendarme à Nanteuil,
> Qui n'avait qu'une dent et qu'un œil;
> Mais cet œil solitaire
> Était plein de mystère;
> Cette dent, d'importance et d'orgueil

Sincerely,
EW

ERNEST HEMINGWAY

(1899–1961)

Hemingway's visit to Pamplona was in part responsible for scenes in *The Sun Also Rises* (1926).

300. To F. Scott Fitzgerald, 1 July 1925

Fitzgerald (1896–1940), author of *The Great Gatsby* (1925), was a friend and rival of Hemingway, especially in his Paris years. Hadley was Hemingway's wife; Zelda was Fitzgerald's.

Dear Scott,

We are going in to Pamplona tomorrow. Been trout fishing here. How are you? And how is Zelda?

I am feeling better than I've ever felt—havent drunk anything but wine since I left Paris. God it has been wonderful country. But you hate country. All right omit description of country. I wonder what your idea of heaven would be—A beautiful vacuum filled with wealthy monogamists, all powerful and members of the best families all drinking themselves to death. And hell would probably [be] an ugly vacuum full of poor polygamists unable to obtain booze or with chronic stomach disorders that they called secret sorrows.

To me heaven would be a big bull ring with me holding two barrera seats and a trout stream outside that no one else was allowed to fish in and two lovely houses in the town; one where I would have my wife and children and be monogamous and love them truly and well and the other where I would have my nine beautiful mistresses on 9 different floors and one house would be fitted up with special copies of the Dial printed on soft tissue and kept in the toilets on every floor and in the other house we would usc the American Mercury and the New Republic. Then there would be a fine church like in Pamplona where I could go and be confessed on the way from one house to the other and I would get on my horse and ride out with my son to my bull ranch named Hacienda Hadley and toss coins to all my illegitimate children that lived [along] the road. I would write out at the Hacienda and send my son in to lock the chastity belts onto my mistresses because someone had just galloped up with the news that a notorious monogamist named Fitzgerald had been seen riding toward the town at the head of a company of strolling drinkers.

Well anyway we're going into town tomorrow early in the morning. Write me at the /Hotel Quintana

Pamplona

Spain

Or dont you like to write letters. I do because it's such a swell way to keep from working and yet feel you've done something.

So long and love to Zelda from us both,

Yours,

Ernest

301. To Sara Murphy, c.27 February 1936

Sara Murphy (1883–1975) and her husband Gerald, who was rich, patronized American artists in France and had been friends of Hemingway's since the early 1920s. He writes to her from Key West, Florida.

Dearest Sara,

Just got your letter today along with a giant hangover like all the tents of Ringling. So this is letter out of the hangover into the snow [of Saranac Lake, New York]. Hangover came about through visit of my lawyer Mr [Maurice] Speiser whom I cannot see without the aid and abettment of alcohol plus seeing off in southern farewell the Judge of the Wallace Stevens evening. Remember that Judge and Mr Stevens? Nice Mr Stevens. This year he came again sort of pleasant like the cholera and first I knew of it my nice sister Ura [Ursula] was coming into the house crying because she had been at a cocktail party at which Mr Stevens had made her cry by telling her forcefully what a sap I was, no man, etc. So I said, this was a week ago, 'All right, that's the third time we've had enough of Mr Stevens'. So headed out into the rainy past twilight and met Mr Stevens who was just issuing from the door haveing just said, I learned later, 'By God I wish I had that Hemingway here now I'd knock him out with a single punch'. So who should show up but poor old Papa and Mr Stevens swung that same fabled punch but fertunatly missed and I knocked all of him down several times and gave him a good beating. Only trouble was that first three times put him down I still had my glasses on. Then took them off at the insistence of the judge who wanted to see a good clean fight without glasses in it and after I took them off Mr Stevens hit me flush on the jaw with his Sunday punch bam like that. And this is very funny. Broke his hand in two places. Didn't harm my jaw at all and so put him down again and then fixed him good so he was in his room for five days with a nurse and Dr working on him. But you mustn't tell this to anybody. Not even Ada [MacLeish]. Because he is very worried about his respectable insurance standing and I have promised not to tell anybody and the official story is that Mr Stevens fell down a stairs. I agreed to that and said it was o.k. with me if he fell down the lighthouse stairs. So please promise not to tell anybody. But Pauline who hates me to fight was delighted. Ura had never seen a fight before and couldn't sleep for fear Mr Stevens was going to die. Anyway last night Mr Stevens comes over to make up and we are made up. But on mature reflection I don't know anybody needed to be hit worse than Mr S. Was very pleased last night to see how large Mr Stevens was and am sure that if I had had a good look at him before it all started would not have felt up to hitting him. But can assure you that there is no one like Mr Stevens to go down in a spectacular fashion especially into a large puddle of water in the street in front of your old Waddel street home where all took place. So I shouldn't write you this but news being scarce your way and I know you really won't tell anybody will you really absolutely seriously. Because otherwise I am a bastard to write it. He apologised to Ura very handsomely and has gone up to Pirates Cove to rest his face for another week before going north. I think he is really one of those mirror fighters who swells his muscles and practices lethal punches in the bathroom while he hates his betters. But maybe I am wrong. Anyway I think Gertrude Stein ought to give all these people who pick fights with poor old papa at least their money back. I am getting damned tired of it but not nearly as tired of it as Mr Stevens got. It was awfully funny to have a man just declaring how he was going to annihilate you and show up just at that moment. Then have him land his awful punch on your jaw and nothing happen except his hand break. You can tell Patrick. It might amuse him. But don't tell anybody else. Tell Patrick for statistics sake Mr Stevens is 6 feet 2 weighs 225 lbs. and that when he hits the ground it is highly spectaculous. I told the Judge, the day after, to tell Mr S. I thought he was a damned fine poet but to tell him he couldn't fight. The Judge said, 'Oh, but your wrong there. He is a very good fighter. Why, I saw him hit a man once and knock him the length of this room.' And I said, 'Yes, Judge. But you didn't catch the man's name, did you?' I think it was a waiter. Nice dear good Mr Stevens. I hope he doesn't brood about this and take up archery or machine gunnery. But you promise you won't tell anybody.

Poor Sara. I'm sorry you had such a bad time. These are the bad times. It is sort of like the retreat from Moscow and Scott [Fitzgerald] is gone the first week of the retreat. But we might as well fight the best god-damned rear guard action in history and God knows you have been fighting it.

Weather has been lousy for fishing the last ten days or so. Put the boat on the ways and scraped and sanded her and repainted. Also copperpainted the bottom with a new paint called murcop that has murcury in it and is supposed to be very good. Have it looking swell. Now must write an Esquire piece, do my income tax, and then get back to my book. Hope to God the people will be gone.

Waldo [Peirce] is here with his kids like untrained hyenas and him as domesticated as a cow. Lives only for the children and with the time he puts on them they should have good manners and be well trained but instead they never obey, destroy everything, don't even answer when spoken to, and he is like an old hen with a litter of apehyenas. I doubt if he will go out in the boat while he is here. Can't leave the children. They have a nurse and a housekeeper too, but he is only really happy when trying to paint with one setting fire to his beard and the other rubbing mashed potato into his canvasses. That represents fatherhood.

[Rest of letter missing.]

Ringling] the famous circus.   Judge] Arthur Powell, a friend of Stevens'.   Wallace Stevens] the poet was 58 at the time, the novelist 36.   Insurance standing] Stevens was executive of an insurance firm in Hartford, Conn.   Pauline] Pfeiffer was Hemingway's second wife.   Gertrude Stein] (1874–1946), avant-garde novelist, resident of Paris, and an early friend of Hemingway's.

ELINOR WYLIE
(1885–1928)

The poet Elinor Wylie left her first husband Horace Wylie and in 1923 married the writer William Rose Benét.

302. *To Horace Wylie, 20 May 1927*

Dearest Horace,

A strange thing is going to happen to you, for that thing is going to come true which undoubtedly you once desired, & for which you will now not care a straw. I am going to admit to you that I wish with all my heart I had never left you. I don't want you to keep this letter, & I hope—& trust— that you will tell no one, but although the admission may afford us both a certain pain, it is founded upon such deep principles of truth & affection that I feel it should be made.

You must not tell this, because the knowledge of it would give pain to Bill, who is one of the best people who ever lived & with whom I expect to pass the remainder of my days. But you & I know that that remainder is not long, & the entire past—which is so much longer—makes me wish to tell you the truth.

I love you, Horace, with an unchanged love which is far more than friendship, & which will certainly persist until my death. It is impossible for me to tell your present sentiments towards me, but it can hardly be a matter for regret that your former devotion should have bred a devotion in me which nothing could destroy.

In Paris I was constantly reminded of you, & although even if we had been together we should have been no longer young, no longer, perhaps, lovers, nevertheless I wished we were together. In England the same thing is true—you are constantly in my thoughts, & remembered with an affection which is undoubtedly the strongest I shall ever feel.

It seems to me that our—shall we dignify it by the name of tragedy, or shall we call it failure?—our whatever it was was one of the war's cruel mishaps—as much so as my miscarriages or the loss of your money. I do not admire myself for having fallen in love with the idea of freedom, & poetry, & New York, & any individual among them: the misery of Washington, of anonymous letters, of this & that—your memory may supply the rest—spoiled what must always seem to me the happiest part of my life— my life with you. It was not your fault in any way, and mine only in my inability to stand the terrible alterations in that life which Washington made.

If we had stayed in England? You will say—impossible. If we had stayed in Bar Harbour? You will say I would have died—in some bad way. I doubt it, in both instances. But this is because I wish we had never parted.

Well, my dear, do not think I am divorcing Bill or something like that. He is the best boy imaginable. I suppose it is, in a way, devilish to write this. But I loved you first, I loved you more, I loved him afterwards, but now, that I love you both, I love you best. Surely you must, in some way, be glad to know this.

If you ever want me, I will come back to you openly. I have never cheated any one, you know. But I don't suppose you do want it, & I think it is much better as it is. Only—well, if you had been me, you would have written this letter from this little house in Chelsea. Answer it.

Your
Elinor

JAMES JOYCE
(1882–1941)

303. To Michael Healy, 1 July 1927

Healy (d. 1935), a Galway port official, was an uncle of Joyce's wife Nora.

My dear Mr Healy,

We came back here a week ago driven out of Holland by cyclones in the north and those impressive exhibitions of celestial intemperance known as thunderstorms. . . .

Otherwise we had a pleasant time in Holland. They have reduced work to a minimum there. They seem to be simple, polite and dignified folk. Well set up men and girls and women who laughed all the time, though perhaps my presence there explains their mirth. To see 600 of them in a Square eating silvery raw herrings by moonlight is a sight for Rembrandt. They put drugs from their Indies into everything—cinnamon in cauliflower, spice in spinach, curry which they call kerry—in the gravy and give you ginger and cheese (very good) as soon as they think you have your mouth open.

That dialect I spoke of, I think, is called Shelta. I fancy it is some corrupt Irish written backwards and used by gentlemen who don't pay the rent.

I hope you are keeping well. The clerk of the weather must be a student of Shelta too for seemingly he reads the word summer backwards. . . .

I get about fifty denunciations a week of my new work from all parts of the English-as-she-is-speaking world including Australia. I shall try to go away in August. I would like to go to Denmark but it's a long, long way to Copenhagen and the fare's right dear.

304. To Giorgio and Helen Joyce, 28 November 1934

George (Giorgio) Joyce (1905–76) was Joyce's son. Helen (d. 1963) was George's wife.

Dear Oigroig and Neleh,

Since everything's upside down I address you thusly. I have just spoken with Mrs E. Jolas of Neuilly s/ Seine who tells me she had such a nice long letter from you and that you have decided that she is to have the privilege of removing all the articles of furniture from the premises occupied by you in borough number given of the city of Paris. She was almost frantic with delight as she babbled over the telephone, breaking into snatches of gipsy music, yodelling, clacking her heels like Argentina and cracking her fingers. It is a perfect godsend for her. Poor Mrs E. Jolas. For months and months she has been going around asking everybody to give her some sort of light work such as snuffing candles or putting salt in the saltcellars, anything. But no one could help her. So she used to lie listlessly in a hammock all day and had begun to think there was no hope left. Now your wonderful letter has arrived and it has made her the happiest woman in all France today. She said to me 'Dearest J. Joyce, won't you give this little girl a great big hand?' and I replied 'Sure thing!'. You know I come of a most musical family and there is nothing I enjoy so much as running up and down six flights of stairs with a cottage piano on my shoulders. The Paris–Orleans line has run an extension up to your door and is placing 2 powerful locomotives and fourteen trucks at your disposal. Mrs E. J. and myself will be as gleeful as two spoiled children. She will wear a white pinafore and a big blue sash and I cricket flannels. Have we cold feet about removals? No, sir! Do we put service before self as all good and true rotarians should? You have said it. So we're off at once.

> *Goodbye, Zürich, I must leave you*
> *Though it breaks my head to [illegible]*
> *Something tells me I am needed*
> *In Paree to hump the beds.*
> *Bump! I hear the trunks a tumbling*
> *And I'm frantic for the fray.*
> *Farewell,* dolce far niente!
> *Goodbye, Zürichsee!*

Mrs E. Jolas] Eugene and Maria Jolas were friends who published Joyce in their journal *transition*.

305. From Vladimir Dixon to James Joyce, 9 February 1929

This letter, presumably of Joyce's composition, was delivered by hand to the Paris bookshop of Sylvia Beach, who published *Ulysses* (1922). The address was that of Brentano's bookshop.

Dear Mister Germ's Choice,

In gutter dispear I am taking my pen toilet you know that, being Leyde up in bad with the prewailent distemper (I opened the window and in flew Enza), I have been reeding one half ter one other the numboars of 'transition' in witch are printed the severeall instorments of your 'Work in Progress'.

You must not stink I am attempting to ridicul (de sac!) you or to be smart, but I am so disturd by my inhumility to onthorstand most of the impslocations constrained in your work that (although I am by nominals dump and in fact I consider myself not brilliantly ejewcatered but still of above Avveroëge men's tality and having maid the most of the oporto unities I kismet) I am writing you, dear mysterre Shame's Voice, to let you no how bed I feeloxerab out it all.

I am überzeugt that the labour involved in the compostition of your work must be almost supper humane and that so much travail from a man of your intellacked must ryeseult in somethink very signicophant. I would only like to know have I been so strichnine by my illnest white wresting under my warm Coverlyette that I am as they say in my neightive land 'out of the mind gone out' abd unable to combprehen that which is clear or is there really in your work some ass pecked which is Uncle Lear?

Please froggive my t'Emeritus and any inconvince that may have been caused by this litter.

Yours veri tass
Vladimir Dixon

Your 'Work in Progress'] became *Finnegans Wake* (1939).

JOHN BETJEMAN
(1906–1984)

Betjeman (Poet Laureate, 1972) worked for the *Architectural Review* from 1931. He married Penelope Chetwode, daughter of a field marshal.

306. To Lord Kinross, 13 June 1933

Patrick Balfour, Lord Kinross, an Oxford friend, became 'Mr Gossip' on the *Daily Sketch*. Philth was Betjeman's pet name for Lady Penelope. On the advice of Nancy Mitford he pursued her to France. They married, clandestinely, later in 1933.

My dear Patrick,

Thank you so much for your book which arrived today & which I have not read yet. I will try & mention it in the A.R.

I was so sorry Philth and I did not come up to yr. party the other night. Since then she has chucked me over and gone to France. I have been sick whenever I have tried to eat & wept tears all night since then. I did not think I was capable of so much emotion. Cracoley [?] caused the rift by advising her not to marry me. But perhaps it was all for the best, though I loved her so much that I now feel I haven't got an existence on this planet.

love
J.B.

JOHN STEINBECK
(1902–1968)

In 1934 Steinbeck had not yet written the novels, especially *The Grapes of Wrath* (1939), which ensured his fame.

307. To George Albee, 1934

Albee, the recipient of these unegotistical confidences, was another Californian writer and had recently moved to New York.

Dear George,

I think I am in a kind of mood to write you a letter. I got yours a little while ago. I have been writing on my new ms. which I will tell you about later, for a good many hours and I think a change will do me good.

You ask what I want? You know pretty well that I don't think of myself as an individual who wants very much. That is why I am not a good nor consecutive seducer. I have the energy and when I think of it, the desires, but I can't reduce myself to a unit from which the necessary formula emanates. I'm going to try to put this down once for all. I like good food and good clothes but faced with getting them, I can't round myself into a procuring unit. Overalls and carrots do not make me unhappy. But the thing which probably more than anything else makes me what I am is an imperviousness to ridicule. This may be simply dullness and stupidity. I notice in lots of other people that ridicule or a threat of it is a driving force which maps their line of life. And I haven't that stimulus. In fact as an organism I am so simple that I want to be comfortable and comfort consists in—a place to sleep, dry and fairly soft, lack of hunger, almost any kind of food, occasional loss of semen in intercourse when it becomes troublesome, and a good deal of work. These constitute my ends. You see it is a description of a stupid slothful animal. I am afraid that is what I am. I don't want to possess anything, nor to be anything. I have no ambition because on inspection the ends of ambition achieved seem tiresome.

Two things I really want and I can't have either of them and they are both negative. I want to forget my mother lying for a year with a frightful question in her eyes and I want to forget and lose the pain in my heart that is my father. In one year he has become a fumbling, repetitious, senile old man, unhappy almost to the point of tears. But these wants are the desire to restore the lack of ego. They are the only two things which make me conscious of myself as a unit. Except for them I spread out over landscape and people like an enormous jelly fish, having neither personality nor boundaries. That is as I wish it, complete destruction of any thing which can be called a me. The work is necessary since from it springs all the other things. A lack of work for a while and the gases concentrate and become solids and out of the solids a me comes into being and I am uncomfortable when there is a me. Having no great wants, I have neither great love nor great hate, neither sense of justice nor of cruelty. It gives me a certain displeasure to hurt or kill things. But that is all. I have no morals. You have thought I had but it was because immorality seemed foolish and often bad economy. If I objected to accounts of sexual exploits it wasn't because of the exploits but because of the cause of the accounts.

The reason we want to go away is primarily so that the two things I want may have a chance to be removed. That may be impossible. But forced and common visits to a grave yard are not conductive of such forgetfulness.

You are right when you think I am not unhappy in this new arrangement. I never come up to the surface. I just work all the time. In the matter of money, my conception doesn't extend beyond two or three hundred dollars. I love Carol but she is far more real to me than I am to myself. If I think of myself I often find it is Carol I am thinking of. If I think what I want I often have to ask her what it is. Sometimes I wish I had sharply defined desires for material things, because the struggle to get them might be very satisfying. If one should want to think of me as a person, I am under the belief that he would have to think of Carol.

I am writing many stories now. Because I should like to sell some of them, I am making my characters as nearly as I can in the likeness of men. The stream underneath and the meanings I am interested in can be ignored.

Between ourselves I don't know what Miss McIntosh means by organization of myself. If she would inspect my work with care, she would see an organization that would frighten her, the slow development of thought pattern, revolutionary to the present one. I am afraid that no advice will change me much because my drive is not one I can get at. When they get tired of my consistent financial failures, they will just have to kick me out. I'm a bum, you see, and according to my sister, a fake, and my family is ashamed of me, and it doesn't seem to make any difference at all. If I had the drive of ridicule I might make something of myself.

This is probably a terrible sounding letter. It isn't meant so. I am working so hard and so constantly that I am really quite happy. I don't take life as hard as you do. Some very bitter thing dried up in me last year.

And now I want to do one more page today before I sit down and look at the fire. The trouble is that I look at the fire and then get up and go to work again. I get around that by taking down the table and putting my manuscript book under the lower shelf of the book case where I must get a stick to get it out. Usually I am too lazy to get the stick.

I hope this letter does not depress you. It is common that anything which is not optimistic is pessimistic. I am pegged as a pessimistic writer because I do not see the millenium coming.

that's all

308. To Dorothy Rodgers, 25 July 1954

Dorothy was the wife of Richard Rodgers, who was at this time working with Oscar Hammerstein on a musical version of Steinbeck's novel *Sweet Thursday* (1954). Steinbeck took a serious interest in inventions.

Dear Dorothy,

I have an invention which I would like to submit for your consideration, while your husband is undertaking his various artistic assignments (surely a desirable practice but not a money maker as we more practical people understand it).

There should be several approaches to an invention. First, is it needed, second, can you make people believe it is needed, third, are replacements needed? I believe that my invention fulfills nearly all of these.

Many millions of women wash out their underwear and stockings every night usually in the wash basin of the bath rooms. A goodly number of them leave the clothing soaking in the basin so that a male getting up a little earlier, has to wash his razor in the bath tub. There is nothing glamourous about washing stockings, panties and bras.

One night having nothing to do, I put a couple of pairs of my own nylon socks in a fruit jar with one third water and a little detergent, replaced the cap and shook the jar about twenty times like a cocktail shaker. It worked very well. I then added four marbles to the thing and it worked doubly well because the marbles did the rubbing thing and greatly speeded up the process. This is the whole principle but a fruit jar is much too simple.

I have considered a plastic jar made like an hour glass with a screw cap on one of the ends, wide mouth for the introduction of the intimate garments. The narrow part of the hour glass to serve as a handle for the whole thing and also to cause the water and soap to cause a minor tornado when the whole is shaken. Instead of marbles the activators should be round balls of some semi-hard wood like beech wood, so smooth that they could not injure fabric and not heavy enough to crush. The lower part of the thing is filled with warm water, and on top of this a tiny envelope of detergent rather beautifully perfumed should be added. The top is then put on and the whole thing shaken say thirty times. This will completely wash ordinarily dirty things. If they are more than ordinarily dirty the clothing may be left in the container over night, in the morning a little more shaking and rinsed in the basin.

The containers should be made of a plastic in the colors to match various bath rooms, pink, yellow, blue, green or black. The packets of soap should be distinctive, (just ordinary soap or detergent but perfumed, sandalwood, lavender, etc.). The packets should not be expensive but should be exactly the proper amount so that one envelope washed one set of clothing. This is the replacement so necessary to any paying invention. The advertising should say that you keep your hands out of soap and keep your husband from blowing his brains out. The container itself should be rather handsome so that it would be one more of those bits of clutter which we love so well.

It is that simple and darn me if I don't think it would work. A little advertising magic about the gentle swirling of water, the caressing of the soap and the clean soapless hands. It should have a gay name like the socktail shaker and the indication that the thirty shakes of the thing reduced weight and built up the bust while with the other hand one washed ones teeth.

Please give my hearty regards to Richard and Oscar and all others there. And we will see you just before Christmas.

Yours in invention

John

P.S. If you don't believe my invention, put some stockings in a fruit jar and try it.

JAMES THURBER
(1894–1961)

Thurber was a humorous writer and cartoonist, associated with the *New Yorker* and its editor Harold Ross.

309. *To Herman and Dorothy Miller, August 1935*

The Millers were friends in Thurber's home town, Columbus, Oh. He was newly married to his second wife, Helen Wismer.

Dear Herman and Dorothy,

. . . Helen and I have just returned from dinner at the Elm Tree Inn in Farmington, some twenty miles from our little cot. It was such a trip as few have survived. I lost eight pounds. . . . I can't see at night and this upset all the motorists in the state tonight, for I am blinded by headlights in addition to not being able to see, anyway. It took us two hours to come back, weaving and stumbling, stopping now and then, stopping always for every car that approached, stopping other times just to rest and bow my head on my arms and ask God to witness that this should not be.

Farmington's Inn was built in 1638 and is reputed to be the oldest inn in these United States. I tonight am the oldest man. . . . A peril of the night road is that flecks of dust and streaks of bug blood on the windshield look to me often like old admirals in uniform, or crippled apple women, or the front end of barges, and I whirl out of their way, thus going into ditches and fields and up on front lawns, endangering the life of authentic admirals and apple women who may be out on the roads for a breath of air before retiring. . . .

Five or six years ago, when I was visiting my former wife at Silvermine, she had left the car for me at South Norwalk and I was to drive to her house in it, some five miles away. Dinner was to be ready for me twenty minutes after I got into the car, but night fell swiftly and there I was again. Although I had been driven over that road 75 or 100 times, I had not driven it myself, and I got off onto a long steep narrow road which seemed to be paved with old typewriters. After a half hour of climbing, during which I passed only two farm boys with lanterns, the road petered out in a high woods. From far away came the mournful woof of a farm hound. That was all. There I was, surrounded by soughing trees, where no car had ever been before. I don't know how I got out. I backed up for miles, jerking on the hand brake every time we seemed to be falling. I was two hours late for dinner.

In every other way I am fine. I am very happy, when not driving at night. And my wife is very happy too, when not being driven by me at night. We are an ideal couple and have not had a harsh word in the seven weeks of our married life. Even when I grope along, honking and weaving and stopping and being honked at by long lines of cars behind me, she is patient and gentle and kind. Of course, she knows that in the daytime, I am a fearless and skilled driver, who can hold his own with anyone. It is only after nightfall that this change comes upon me. I have a curious desire to cry while driving at night, but so far have conquered that, save for a slight consistent whimpering that I keep up—a sound which, I am sure, is not calculated to put Helen at her ease.

Looking back on my hazardous adventures of this evening I can see that whereas I was anguished and sick at heart, Helen must have felt even worse, for there were moments when, with several cars coming toward me, and two or three honking behind me, and a curved road ahead, I would take my foot off of everything and wail, 'Where the hell am I?' That, I suppose, would strike a fear to a woman's heart equaled by almost nothing else. We have decided that I will not drive any more at night. Helen can drive but she has been out of practice for some years. However, she is going to get back into it again. She can see. She doesn't care to read, in the *Winsted Evening Citizen*, some such story as this:

> Police are striving to unravel the tangle of seven cars and a truck which suddenly took place last night at 9 o'clock where Route 44 is crossed by Harmer's Lane and a wood road leading to the old Beckert estate. Although nobody seems to know exactly what happened, the automobile that the accident seemed to center about was a 1932 Ford V-8 operated by one James Thurberg. Thurberg, who was coming into Winsted at 8 miles an hour, mistook the lights of Harry Freeman's hot-dog stand, at the corner of Harmer's Lane and Route 44, for the headlight of a train. As he told the story later: he swerved out to avoid the oncoming hot-dog stand only to see an aged admiral in full dress uniform riding toward him, out of the old wood road, on a tricycle, which had no head-lights. In trying to go in between the hot-dog stand and the tricycle, Thurberg somehow or other managed to get his car crosswise of all three roads, resulting in the cracking up of six other cars and the truck. Police have so far found no trace of the aged admiral and his tricycle. The hot-dog stand came to a stop fifteen feet from Thurberg's car.

We got the Ford on Martha's Vineyard, where we spent July. Now we are at Colebrook, Conn., or rather three miles out of it at the summer cottage of Helen's parents. It is a delightful place and why don't you motor here and visit us for a while? . . . You'll like my wife and she already knows she will like you. She is as calm as ice when I am driving at night, or as cold anyway.

Love,
Jim

310. To Robert Leifert, 4 January 1958

Dear Robert,

Since a hundred schoolchildren a year write me letters like yours—some writers get a thousand—the problem of what to do about such classroom 'projects' has become a serious one for all of us. If a writer answered all of you he would get nothing else done. When I was a baby goat I had to do my own research on projects, and I enjoyed doing it. I never wrote an author for his autograph or photograph in my life. Photographs are for movie actors to send to girls. Tell your teacher I said so, and please send me her name. . . .

One of the things that discourage us writers is the fact that 90 percent of you children write wholly, or partly, illiterate letters, carelessly typed. You yourself write 'clarr' for 'class' and that's a honey, Robert, since *s* is next to *a*, and *r* is on the line above. Most schoolchildren in America would do a dedication like the following (please find the mistakes in it and write me about them):

> *To Miss Effa G. Burns*
> *Without who's help*
> *this book could never*
> *of been finished it,*
> *is dedicated with*
> *gartitude by it's*
> *arthur.*

Show that to your teacher and tell her to show it to her principal, and see if they can find the mistakes. . . .

Just yesterday a letter came in from a girl your age in South Carolina asking for biographical material and photograph. That is not the kind of education they have in Russia, we are told, because it's too much like a hobby or waste of time. What do you and your classmates want to be when you grow up—collectors? Then who is going to help keep the United States ahead of Russia in science, engineering, and the arts?

Please answer this letter. If you don't I'll write to another pupil.

Sincerely yours,
James Thurber

VIRGINIA WOOLF
(1882–1941)

311. To Vanessa Bell, 1 October 1938

Vanessa Bell (1879–1961) was Woolf's artist sister.

Monks House

Your letter has just come. I scrambled off a very hurried letter to you last Wednesday, half thinking you'd be marooned somewhere, and thus not get it. Now still in a hurry and therefore typing to save your old eyes I will continue the narrative. I daresay its an old story now; but no doubt you will excuse repetitions. Never never has there been such a time. Last week end we were at Charleston and very gloomy. Gloom increased on Monday. It was pouring. Then in the morning Kingsley Martin rang up to insist that L. must come to London at once and make a desperate attempt to unite labour and liberals—to do what was not obvious. But he seemed desperate, and so we flung a nightgown into a bag and started. In London it was hectic and gloomy and at the same time despairing and yet cynical and calm. The streets were crowded. People were everywhere talking loudly about war. There were heaps of sandbags in the streets, also men digging trenches, lorries delivering planks, loud speakers slowly driving and solemnly exhorting the citizens of Westminster Go and fit your gas masks. There was a long queue of people waiting outside the Mary Ward settlement to be fitted. L. went off at once to see K.M. I discussed matters with Mabel. We agreed that she had better go to Bristol—whether she has or not I dont yet know. Then L came back and said Kingsley was in despair; they had talked for two hours; everybody came into the N. S [*New Statesman*] office and talked; telephones rang incessantly. They all said war was certain; also that there would be no war. Kingsley came to dinner. He had smudges of black charcoal round his eyes and was more melodramatic and histrionic than ever. Hitler was going to make his speech at 8. We had no wireless, but he said he would ring up the BBC after it was over and find out the truth. Then we sat and discussed the inevitable end of civilisation. He strode up and down the room, hinting that he meant to kill himself. He said the war would last our life time; also we should very likely be beaten. Anyhow Hitler meant to bombard London, probably with no warning; the plan was to drop bombs on London with twenty minutes intervals for forty eight hours. Also he meant to destroy all roads and railways; therefore Rodmell would be about as dangerous as Bloomsbury. Then he broke off; rang up Clark, the news man at The BBC; 'Ah—so its hopeless . . .' Then to us, 'Hitler is bawling; the crowds howling like wild beasts.' More conversation of a lugubrious kind. Now I think I'll ring up Clark again . . . Ah so it couldnt be worse . . . To us. No Hitler is more mad than ever . . . Have some Whiskey Kingsley, said L. Well, it dont much matter either way, said K. At last he went: What are you going to do? I asked. Walk the streets. Its no good—I cant sleep. So we clasped hands, as I understood for the last time.

Next morning Tuesday every one was certain it was war. Everyone, except one poor little boy in a shop who had lost his head and was half crying when I asked for a packet of envelopes (and he may have been in some sort of row) was perfectly calm; and also without hope. It was quite different from 1914. Every one said Probably we shall win but it'll be just as bad if we do. I went to the London Library to look up some papers about Roger. I sat in the basement with the Times open of the year 1910. An old man was dusting. He went away; then came back and said very kindly, 'Theyre telling us to put on our gas masks, Madam' I thought the raid had begun. However, he explained that it was the loudspeaker once more addressing the citizens of Westminster. Then he asked if he could dust under my chair; and said they had laid in a supply of sand bags, but if a bomb dropped there wouldnt be many books left over. After that I walked to the National Gallery, and a voice again urged me to fit my gas mask at once. The Nat Gallery was fuller than usual; a nice old man was lecturing to an attentive crowd on Watteau. I suppose they were all having a last look.

I went home, and found that L. had arranged that the Press was to go on; but the clerks to go away into the country if they liked. Then Miss Hepworth the traveller said the shops were mostly refusing to buy at all, and were mostly going to close. So it seemed we should have to shut down. The clerks wanted to go on, as they had no place in the country; and of course no money. We arranged to pay wages as long as we could—but plans were vague. Mrs Nicholls said she should prefer to lie in the trench that was being dug in the square; Miss Perkins preferred to sit in the stock room, which she had partly prepared with mattresses etc. Then, after lunch, an American editor arrived to ask me to write an article upon Culture in the United States. We agreed however that culture was in danger. In fact she said most English authors were either in Suffolk, or starting for America. In Suffolk they were already billeting children from the East end in cottages. Then Rosinsky came; he thought he had a visa for

America and was going to try to go at once. Then Mrs Woolf rang up to say she was going to Maidenhead if she could get rooms. Then an express arrived from Victoria Ocampo who had just landed from South America, wished to see me at once, was trying to fly to America and what could she do with a sister who was ill—could we advise a safe retreat? Also Phil Baker and others rang up Leonard. With it all we were rather harassed; what should we need if we were marooned in Rodmell, without petrol, or bicycles? L. took his mackintosh and a thick coat; I Rogers letters to you, and a packet of stamped envelopes. Then we had to say good bye to the press, and I felt rather a coward, as clearly they were nervous although very sensible; and they had no garden. But the Govt; asked all who could to leave London and there was John in command. So off we went.

It was pouring terrific torrents; the roads packed; men nailing up shutters in shop windows; sandbags being piled; and a general feeling of flight and hurry. Also it was very dark; and we took about three hours to get back. At ten oclock Mr Perkins knocked and entered with a box of gas bags which he fitted on us. No sooner had he gone than Mr Jansen came with another box. He said that children were arriving from the East End next morning. Sure enough, next day,—but I wrote to you and told you how we had the news of the Prime Ministers sensational statement—we thought it meant anyhow a pause—well, after that, Mr Perkins came and said the children were coming—9,000 had to be billeted in Sussex; fifty in Rodmell; how many could we put up? We arranged to take two. By that time, the nightmare feeling was becoming more nightmarish; more and more absurd; for no one knew what was happening; and yet everyone was behaving as if the war had begun. Mr Hartman had turned his barn into a hospital and so on. Of course we thought it was ridiculous; yet still they went on broadcasting messages about leaving London; about post cards with stamps being given to refugees who would be deposited safely, but they must not ask where. At any moment the fifty children might arrive. Also the Archbishop would offer up prayers; and at one moment the Pope's voice was heard . . . But I will shorten; and skip to Sissinghurst; where we went on Thursday; and heard that the Italian King had saved the situation by threatening to abdicate. Harold had seen the PM grow visibly ten years younger as he read the message which was handed him. It was all over. And I must play bowls. Leonard sends a message to Q; in his opinion we have peace without honour for six months.

I'll write again. Maynard comes tomorrow. Plans vague; but we write here, where we shall probably stay at present. No time to read this through.

Post going,
B.

Monk's House] the Woolfs' house in Sussex.   Charleston] in Sussex, the house in which
Vanessa Bell lived with the painter Duncan Grant and the writer David Garnett; it became the
country retreat of Bloomsbury.   Gloomy] the alarms of late Sept. 1938 ended when on the
29th Britain and France, at Munich, agreed to transfer the Sudetenland to Germany in return for
a guarantee that the remaining frontiers of Czechoslovakia would be respected. Neville Chamberlain, the Prime Minister, returned with a paper signed by Hitler and made a 'sensational statement' promising peace in our time.   Kingsley Martin] 'K.M.' (1897–1969), flamboyant
editor of the left-wing weekly, *New Statesman*.   L.] Leonard Woolf.   The Mary
Ward settlement] an education centre in Bloomsbury.   Mabel] the Woolfs' maid.
Roger] Fry (1866–1934), painter, whose biography Woolf was writing.   Rosinsky] Herbert
Rosinski, author of a book about the German army, published by the Woolfs at their Hogarth
Press.   Mrs Woolf] Leonard Woolf's mother.   Phil Baker] Philip Noel-Baker (1889–
1961), Labour MP, awarded the Nobel Peace Prize for work on disarmament (1954).   John]
Lehmann (1907–87), poet, publisher, editor, at this time working at the Hogarth Press.
Sissinghurst] Sissinghurst Castle, Kent, the house and garden of Vita Sackville-West and Harold
Nicolson.   Q] Quentin Bell, Vanessa's son; painter and biographer of Woolf.   Maynard]
John Maynard Keynes (1883–1946), economist.

EVELYN WAUGH
(1903–1966)

312. To Laura Waugh, 25 February 1940

> Waugh, who married in 1937, was at this date near the beginning of an adventurous
> but on the whole disappointing military career, at first in the Royal Marines. The
> episode here described is also found, with varied embellishments, in a letter to John
> Betjeman and in Waugh's diary.

Darling Laura,
          . . . My stock is high. I gave a twenty-minute lecture on reconnaissance
patrols which was greeted with universal acclaim. On the other hand I was
overheard by Major Cornwall speaking with contempt of the head of the
Hythe School of Small Arms and was rebuked, so that may have put me
down a bit.
          Yesterday was an alarming day. The Brigadier suddenly accosted Messer-
Bennetts & me & said, 'I hear you are staying in camp for the week-end.
You will spend the day with me.' So at 12.30 he picked us up in his motor-
car and drove all over the road to his house which was the lowest type of
stockbroker's Tudor and I said in a jaggering way 'Did you build this
house, sir?' and he said 'Build it! It's 400 years old!' The Brigadier's
madam is kept very much in her place and ordered about with great shouts
'Woman, go up to my cabin and get my boots'. More peculiar, she is
subject to booby-traps. He told us with great relish how the night before
she had had to get up several times in the night to look after a daughter
who was ill and how, each time she returned, he had fixed up some new

horror to injure her—a string across the door, a jug of water on top of it etc. However she seemed to thrive on this treatment & was very healthy & bright with countless children.

So after luncheon we were taken for a walk with the Brigadier who kept saying 'Don't call me "sir".' He told us how when he had a disciplinary case he always said, 'Will you be court martialled or take it from me'. The men said, 'Take it from you, sir,' so 'I bend 'em over and give 'em ten of the best with a cane.'

When we came back from our walk he showed me a most embarrassing book of rhymes & drawings composed by himself and his madam in imitation of *Just So Stories*, for one of his daughters. I had to read them all with him breathing stertorously down my neck. Then we did the cross-word puzzle until a daughter arrived from London where she is secretary to a dentist. She told me she had been a lift girl at the Times Book Club and had lost her job because at Christmas time, she hung mistletoe in the lift. The Brigadier thought this a most unsuitable story to tell me. When he is in a rage he turns slate grey instead of red. He was in an almost continuous rage with this daughter who is by a previous, dead madam. After that she & I talked about low night clubs until I thought the Brigadiers colour so unhealthy that I ought to stop. Most of the madam's reminiscences dealt with appalling injuries to one or other member of the family through their holiday exercises. The Brigadier says that the only fault he has to find with the war is that he misses his hockey. A very complex character. A lot of majors & their madams came to dinner; oddly enough all foreign—a Russian, a German and a Swede—a fact on which the Brigadier never ceased to comment adding 'I suppose I can't really tell 'em what I think of their benighted countries.' Then he asked very loudly whether it was true that he ought not to smoke his pipe with vintage port and if so why, so I told him and he got a bit grey again.

He said, 'There's only one man in Egypt you can trust. Hassanin Bey. Luckily he's chief adviser to the King. He is a white man. I'll tell you something that'll show you the kind of chap he is. He and I were alone in a carriage going from Luxor to Suez—narrow gauge, single track line, desert on both sides, blazing heat. Ten hours with nothing to do. I thought I should go mad. Luckily I had a golf ball with me. So I made Hassanin stand one end of the corridor and we threw that ball backwards & forwards as hard as we could the whole day—threw it so that it really hurt. Not many Gyppies would stand up to that. Ever since then I've known there was at least one Gyppy we could trust.'

Your friend Bailey came very near being expelled from the Brigade owing [to] the worst possible reports from all his instructors but has been given a second chance. The Brigadier said, 'I hope I'm not giving away his identity when I tell you I meant to turn one of you out. Then he said he'd been a reporter on the *Star* in civil life and I thought that a good enough excuse'. I said, 'You have given away his identity but I can assure you he is all right.' 'Yes, he spoke up for himself very well'. I did not like to ask whether he had caned him.

Capt. Macdonell has just been in here with his madam. He says he thinks that it will be o.k. for us to live out in a week or two. Yesterday he told me the Colonel had said no one was to live out. That shows how things change from day to day.

He also said, 'I hope you aren't taking a lot of notes about us all to make fun of us in a book. There was a nasty bloke called Graves wrote a book called *Goodbye To All That*. Made fun of his brigadier. Bad show!' I thought it lucky he did not know what was in this letter.

All love
Evelyn

Graves] Robert Graves (1895–1985), poet, critic, novelist; *Goodbye to All That* (1929), his war memoir.

313. To Laura Waugh, 31 May 1942

Waugh is now in the Royal Horse Guards, restored to the company of 'Bob' (Colonel Robert Laycock).

Darling,

It was a great joy to get a letter from you. I thought you had been swallowed up in some Pixton plague.

Do you know Ellwoods address? I wrote to him care Harper—no answer.

Miss Cowles leaves tonight. Everyone except me will be sorry. I have had to arrange all her movements and it has been a great deal of trouble. She is a cheerful, unprincipled young woman. She wants to be made Colonel in chief of the commando so I have suggested Princess Margaret Rose instead. Bob eats out of my hand at the moment.

So No. 3 Cmdo were very anxious to be chums with Lord Glasgow so they offered to blow up an old tree stump for him and he was very grateful and he said dont spoil the plantation of young trees near it because that is the apple of my eye and they said no of course not we can blow a tree down so that it falls on a sixpence and Lord Glasgow said goodness you are clever and he asked them all to luncheon for the great explosion. So Col. Durnford-Slater D.S.O. said to his subaltern, have you put enough explosive in the tree. Yes, sir, 75 lbs. Is that enough? Yes sir I worked it out by mathematics it is exactly right. Well better put a bit more. Very good sir.

And when Col. D. Slater D.S.O. had had his port he sent for the subaltern and said subaltern better put a bit more explosive in that tree. I don't want to disappoint Lord Glasgow. Very good sir.

Then they all went out to see the explosion and Col. D.S.D.S.O. said you will see that tree fall flat at just that angle where it will hurt no young trees and Lord Glasgow said goodness you are clever.

So soon the[y] lit the fuse and waited for the explosion and presently the tree, instead of falling quietly sideways, rose 50 feet into the air taking with it ½ acre of soil and the whole of the young plantation.

And the subaltern said Sir I made a mistake, it should have been 7½ lbs not 75.

Lord Glasgow was so upset he walked in dead silence back to his castle and when they came to the turn of the drive in sight of his castle what should they find but that every pane of glass in the building was broken.

So Lord Glasgow gave a little cry & ran to hide his emotion in the lavatory and there when he pulled the plug the entire ceiling, loosened by the explosion, fell on his head.

This is quite true.

E

Ellwood] had been his butler.   Miss Cowles] Virginia Cowles, an American journalist.

STEPHEN SPENDER (1909–) AND T. S. ELIOT (1888–1965)

Eliot, lunching at the Spenders, admired a transparent cigarette box. Spender sent it to him, enclosing the verses below. Eliot replied appropriately.

314. Stephen Spender to T. S. Eliot, 21 August 1946

TO THE MASTER OF RUSSELL SQUARE.

When those aged eagle eyes which look
Through human flesh as through a book,
Swivel an instant from the page
To ignite the luminous image
With the match that lights his smoke—
Then let the case be transparent
And let the cigarettes, apparent
To his x-ray vision, lie
As clear as rhyme and image to his eye.

To Tom with love from Stephen

To the master] Eliot's publishing firm Faber & Faber was in Russell Square.

315. T. S. Eliot to Stephen Spender, 21 August 1946

A L ORGANISATEUR DES NATIONS UNIES
POUR L ÉDUCATION, LA SCIENCE ET LA CULTURE.

The sudden unexpected gift
   Is more precious in the eyes
   Than the ordinary prize
Of slow approach or movement swift.
While the cigarette is whiffed
   And the tapping finger plies
   Here upon the table lies
The fair transparency. I lift
      The eyelids of the aging owl
      At twenty minutes to eleven
      Wednesday evening (summer time)
      To salute the younger fowl
      With this feeble halting rhyme
      The kind, the Admirable Stephen.

To Stephen, from Tom

A l'organisateur] Eliot is referring to Spender's work for Unesco.

WALLACE STEVENS
(1879–1955)

316. To Harvey Breit, 8 August 1942

Breit, a young New York writer, had requested a comment on his new book. Stevens refused it but by way of compensation wrote Breit a series of interesting letters, largely about his views on poetry and poets. This is the last and most playful. At this stage in his life Stevens was taking a keen interest in his Pennsylvania Dutch origins.

Dear Mr Breit,

Your letter making the most of the situation (which for your sake I regret) is quite the nicest and most human thing I know about you. In return for it, let me say this:

I have been away the last day or two and, while away, visited the Dutch Church at Kingston: the Reformed Protestant Dutch Church. This is one of the most beautiful churches that I know of. It is improved by the fact that it has a pleasant janitor with a red nose: merely a red nose, not a red nose due to drink. But having a red nose subdues one.

The janitor told me that at one time there were nine judges in the congregation and that often the whole nine of them were there together at a service, sitting in their separate pews. One of them was Judge Alton Parker; another was Judge Gilbert Hasbrouck. Now, Judge Hasbrouck was as well known in Kingston as Martin Luther was in Wittenberg.

The janitor gave me a pamphlet containing an extract from studies relating to the Reformed Church. The pamphlet consists of an article by Judge Hasbrouck on this particular church. It starts out with this . . .

'Indeed when Spinoza's great logic went searching for God it found Him in a predicate of substance.'

The material thing: the predicate of substance in this case, was this church: the very building. Now, if a lawyer as eminent as Judge Hasbrouck went to church because it made it possible for him to touch, to see, etc., the very predicate of substance, do you think he was anything except a poet? He was only one of nine of them, so that, instead of nine judges, there were nine poets in the congregation, all of them struggling to get at the predicate of substance, although not all of them struggled to do so through Spinoza's great logic.

Another thing that this episode makes clear is that Spinoza's great logic was appreciated only the other day in Kingston; and, still more, that lawyers very often make use of their particular faculties to satisfy their particular desires.

Very truly yours,
Wallace Stevens

GROUCHO MARX
(1895–1977)

317. To Warner Brothers, 1948

The film company, which had had a great success with the film *Casablanca* (1943), wished to prevent the Marx Brothers from calling a film of theirs *A Night in Casablanca*. Warner Brothers replied to this letter, asking twice for information about the story of the proposed film, but abandoning the correspondence on receipt of ever more absurd replies.

Dear Warner Brothers,

Apparently there is more than one way of conquering a city and holding it as your own. For example, up to the time that we contemplated making this picture, I had no idea that the city of Casablanca belonged exclusively to Warner Brothers. However, it was only a few days after our announcement appeared that we received your long, ominous legal document warning us not to use the name Casablanca.

It seems that in 1471, Ferdinand Balboa Warner, your great-great-grandfather, while looking for a shortcut to the city of Burbank, had stumbled on the shores of Africa and, raising his alpenstock (which he later turned in for a hundred shares of the common), named it Casablanca.

I just don't understand your attitude. Even if you plan on re-releasing your picture, I am sure that the average movie fan could learn in time to distinguish between Ingrid Bergman and Harpo. I don't know whether I could, but I certainly would like to try.

You claim you own Casablanca and that no one else can use that name without your permission. What about 'Warner Brothers'? Do you own that, too? You probably have the right to use the name Warner, but what about Brothers? Professionally, we were brothers long before you were. We were touring the sticks as The Marx Brothers when Vitaphone was still a gleam in the inventor's eye, and even before us there had been other brothers—the Smith Brothers; the Brothers Karamazov; Dan Brothers, an outfielder with Detroit; and 'Brother, Can You Spare a Dime?' (This was originally 'Brothers, Can You Spare a Dime?' but this was spreading a dime pretty thin, so they threw out one brother gave all the money to the other one and whittled it down to, 'Brother, Can You Spare a Dime?')

Now Jack, how about you? Do you maintain that yours is an original name? Well, it's not. It was used long before you were born. Offhand, I can think of two Jacks—there was Jack of 'Jack and the Beanstalk,' and Jack the Ripper, who cut quite a figure in his day.

As for you, Harry, you probably sign your checks, sure in the belief that you are the first Harry of all time and that all other Harrys are imposters. I can think of two Harrys that preceded you. There was Lighthouse Harry of Revolutionary fame and a Harry Appelbaum who lived on the corner of 93rd Street and Lexington Avenue. Unfortunately, Appelbaum wasn't too well known. The last I heard of him, he was selling neckties at Weber and Heilbroner.

Now about the Burbank studio. I believe this is what you brothers call your place. Old man Burbank is gone. Perhaps you remember him. He was a great man in a garden. His wife often said Luther had ten green thumbs. What a witty woman she must have been! Burbank was the wizard who crossed all those fruits and vegetables until he had the poor plants in such a confused and jittery condition that they could never decide whether to enter the dining room on the meat platter or the dessert dish.

This is pure conjecture, of course, but who knows—perhaps Burbank's survivors aren't too happy with the fact that a plant that grinds out pictures on a quota settled in their town, appropriated Burbank's name and uses it as a front for their films. It is even possible that the Burbank family is prouder of the potato produced by the old man than they are of the fact that from your studio emerged 'Casablanca' or even 'Gold Diggers of 1931.'

This all seems to add up to a pretty bitter tirade, but I assure you it's not meant to. I love Warners. Some of my best friends are Warner Brothers. It is even possible that I am doing you an injustice and that you, yourselves, know nothing at all about this dog-in-the-Wanger attitude. It wouldn't surprise me at all to discover that the heads of your legal department are unaware of this absurd dispute, for I am acquainted with many of them and they are fine fellows with curly black hair, double-breasted suits and a love of their fellow man that out-Saroyans Saroyan.

I have a hunch that this attempt to prevent us from using the title is the brainchild of some ferret-faced shyster, serving a brief apprenticeship in your legal department. I know the type well—hot out of law school, hungry for success and too ambitious to follow the natural laws of promotion. This bar sinister probably needled your attorneys, most of whom are fine fellows with curly black hair, double-breasted suits, etc., into attempting to enjoin us. Well, he won't get away with it! We'll fight him to the highest court! No pasty-faced legal adventurer is going to cause bad blood between the Warners and the Marxes. We are all brothers under the skin and we'll remain friends till the last reel of 'A Night in Casablanca' goes tumbling over the spool.

Sincerely,
Groucho Marx

DIANA COOPER
(1896–1986)

Diana Cooper (née Manners) was the widow of Duff Cooper, 1st Viscount Norwich, politician and post-war ambassador to France.

318. To Patrick Leigh Fermor, 15 June 1953

This extract from a longer letter was transcribed by the recipient, her friend the writer Patrick Leigh Fermor.

. . . Set off alone at 7.15, glass crown on fish-net, coronet in hand, also invitation card, gloves and spectacles for all distances. Jolly Bolters Lock crowd . . . forty mins. from Albert Hall, not bad, and out at the annex.

Quite ugly but spacious, unhurried garden-party atmosphere of peers and ladies—gold sticks very unlike testy genuine court officials, all friends. I might have felt alone when the moment came to process up the nave to our places but sweet Tony Rosslyn without ever a wife gave me a smacking kiss and asked me to walk with him. Lots of talk of the age of robes—one ravishing cloak of rose-pink velvet was Charles I date, and Debo Devonshire's the only becoming one there, she claimed to be George IV (Lady Elizabeth Foster) but I bet it was Victorian.

Always one to apprehend the worst, I felt I should be badly placed, so a nice surprise was in store, for from my place I dominated the 'theatre' and was next to Ava Waverly, which doubtful pleasure for many, I had hoped for—On her other side, each in a worse position, (more dog-legged than me) was Hannah Hudson (another old friend) and on my right a sympathetic old peeress, the senior baron's wife, Lady Mowbray and [?]—more of her later. The theatre was *brilliantly* lit from nowhere—it had to be, because of TV, but it suited the stained glass, playing-card primary-colour realness, and in compensation for those who might find it blatant, not a photographer not a lens or a flash was to be seen, even Cecil B. in the rafters was invisible, (Poor Cecil, he's always treated like the vet—because he's court photographer, never asked to a party or to sit down). Before the peers and peeresses had all got to their seats, first arrivals were moving out of their places to the lu's. I made a great scoff at them to Ava and Hannah who had both made the dread expedition before 10—too extraordinary I think—the lu's were arcticly cold and sported (or spouted) no water. (I'd as soon have gone in a railway station). Ava was always agrope for something under her skirts. She fumbled away for an hour occasionally saying to me quite audibly 'Ma voisine sent si mauvaise de la bouche'. At last she produced from the hot folds of her petticoats a paper-bag that one buys full of buns for the bears at the zoo and offered me a peppermint against the 'bouche' or a glucose lozenge against fainting. All the hours passed as a moment and one's eyes and ears were transported with wonder. The bravely chosen pale but bright gold-coloured carpet, the heralds, the clergy, the notables— always the arrival of another romance—look, look the spurs, 'no they're bracelets.' The first royalties the horrid Mountbattens—choirs—school-boys, the Ld. Chancellor, the Royal dukes, their duchesses—with trains yards long deftly folded & draped onto royal arms by well-born girls. The Queen Mother belied by photographs with 6 red pages—2 little Gloucesters in kilts supporters to our open-air Duchess of G, who took faint at the crowning moment and buried her poor head between her knees at least that's what I guessed she was doing by the way her boys looked down at her disappearance behind the pew. Princess Margaret, wings clipped by the King's death, not all glorious within, rather dusky and heavy-featured. The

Ducal husband; bigger, better, newer robes than the others, padded to a
François I width by admiral's epaulettes, and all these rehearsed and gesture-
perfect as London police; nothing could hurry or change the exquisite
slow-motion law. So, all the lights but One were safely lodged in the boxes,
stands, and lesser thrones. We were given a comic relief which brought the
Abbey down—an uproar, for from nowhere appeared, with brooms, maids
such as smart American garages or hamburger/hot-dog stands present—in
hygienic white overalls and caps; at circuses, they sweep up elephants'
droppings. But what could those fairy royal feet have left; soles that hadn't
left red carpets from birth? So, all clean for the Queen. She arrived, and all
that bit you will see on the pictures and it could not have been more moving and true—and touching, because of the size and grace of the central
figure. The undressing of her necklace and all, by Rocksavage. Sacrifice,
dedication—all the words are hackneyed by now—the husband's kiss, the
Byzantine effect, the canopy to sheild her, the names of the bearers; trumpets too, I've only just remembered the high-tension quivering trumpets.

My neighbour Lady Mowbray gave a little gasp earlier on, saying, 'O
look at my son, what would you do, he promised to have his hair cut.' She
pointed at one of the oddest guardsmen I ever saw. She looked nothing
more than 50 and the strange boy with a Nelson patch, albino walrus and
Oberammergau hair. 'Just like his father', she said and indeed he was, for
as the moment of swearing allegiance came on, the poor lady got more and
more agitated about her husband's performance, and indeed it's past man's
art to walk backwards down broad steps with a long train. 'He'll never
manage' she sighed, 'He has to put on his spectacles to read the oath, and
with them he cant see the floor.' 'Could he snatch them off' I suggested in
a whisper. 'I told him to, but he's so dreadfully obstinate.' The awful
ordeal was now upon us both. He was the picture of his son, only with
2 myopic eyes and, of course, a little older. When he had got up to his
sovereign's knees and was down on his own and had read the oath I heard
myself say 'Dont look', but I suppose she did look and saw with me the
anxious gathering up of the cloak and the almost crab stampede down . . . and
so it ended and in no time at all we were all eating and drinking—badly—
in the House of Lords, everyone telling their own experience, not a criticism of anything . . . That night we met on Debo & Ld Wilton's boat on
the Thames there were 100 grownups, most of them tightish, & 50 children, toddlers, and 14 year olds. It was raining and freezing so everyone
huddled into the two holds, one full of food the other of wine and spirits;
the latter was called the drunk room by the little ones; simply, like one talks
of the pump room or cloak room. I wonder what they made of it; the noise
was dead-awakening. We cowered under a bridge shivering to watch the
dampish fireworks and rushed back to the drunk room . . .

For details of the personages named in this account of a more recent coronation ceremony (cf.
Letter 54 above) readers are recommended to use Debrett or Burke.   Boulters Lock]
Boulter's Lock, on the Thames, perhaps a gathering place for somewhat lower-class users of the
river.   Lady Mowbray and [?]] 'Stourton & Segrave—all 1 person, like the Trinity' (P.
Leigh Fermor's addition).   Cecil B.] Cecil Beaton was the official Coronation photographer.
Schoolboys] from Westminster School, there to shout 'Vivat!' at the prescribed moment in the
ceremony.

FLANNERY O'CONNOR
(1925–1964)

Southern American novelist (*Wise Blood*, 1952; *The Violent Bear it Away*, 1960) and
short story writer, who was ill for much of her life.

319. To Cecil Dawkins, 22 September 1957

Cecil Dawkins was a young writer and like O'Connor a Southern Catholic; she later
published a novel and a volume of stories.

I'm a full-time believer in writing habits, pedestrian as it all may sound.
You may be able to do without them if you have genius but most of us only
have talent and this is simply something that has to be assisted all the time
by physical and mental habits or it dries up and blows away. I see it happen
all the time. Of course you have to make your habits in this conform to
what you *can* do. I write only about two hours every day because that's all
the energy I have, but I don't let anything interfere with those two hours,
at the same time and the same place. This doesn't mean I produce much
out of the two hours. Sometimes I work for months and have to throw
everything away, but I don't think any of that was time wasted. Something
goes on that makes it easier when it does come well. And the fact is if you
don't sit there every day, the day it would come well, you won't be sitting
there.

Everybody has a different problem about finding a set time to do it, but
you should do it while you have a fresh mind anyway. After you've taught
all day, you must be too tired and what creative energy you have must have
gone to the little ladies of Stevens. If I had to teach I think I'd rather teach
the Peter Bells (what they call the unteachable ones at the local college)
which end of the sentence you put the period on rather than teach the
bright ones literature. You can't be creative in all directions at once. Freshman English would suit me fine. I'd make them diagram sentences.

Guardini has a number of things on Dostoevsky and I like the one I
enclose and here is also a thing Caroline wrote on her debt to the Greeks.
This is one of Caroline's themes which in part I take with several grains of

salt; anyway, I wrote her that I was still after mastering me English and would doubtless not be getting onto no Greek . . .

Caroline] Gordon, another Southern novelist, at this time married to Allen Tate.

320. *To Maryat Lee, 16 June 1964*

Lee was a Kentuckian and a playwright who became a close friend in 1956.

I asked [the doctor] today when I could go home. Well he says we can begin to *think* about it now. Well you begin, says I, I been thinking about it all the time. So we are beginning to think about it. He has put me on a less rigid salt-free diet. For a while it was 2 grams a day, now it's about 5. I have to go slow on proteins because that is what the kidneys do not work on properly. They don't refine the poisons out of the proteins. So I can't eat as much meat & eggs & cheeze & such as I like.

I have a anecdote you can tell the next time you give a Southern party for Wellesley girls. A drove of cattle was coming down Constitution Ave. in Washington one day and Edward Everett said in the presence of Davy Crockett, 'Those are Mr Crockett's constituents. Where are they going, Mr Crockett?' 'They're going to Massachusetts, Mr Everett,' Davy Crockett said, 'to teach school.'

I got your number down but I won't call you. I can't afford it but even if I could, I don't think I could master the technical end of it yet. That *debilitates* me to think of.

That child in that picture is you all right. I'd have knowed you right off. Very happy-looking child. It's fortunate we didn't get together at that age. We would have blown something up. I would have found the matches and let you light the fuse.

EDITH SITWELL
(1887–1964)

Dame Edith Sitwell was a poet and publicist of an eccentric modernism.

321. *To Lady Snow, 20 May 1959*

Lady Snow (Pamela Hansford Johnson, 1912–81), novelist, was the wife of Sir Charles (later Lord) Snow. 'The Poet' was their son Philip.

My dear Pamela,

Thank you so much for your letter.

I am so distressed to hear you have insomnia. It is horrible, and one really suffers greatly. When I am in London, sometimes I only sleep for two hours a night, if that.

If one could only rid one's mind, completely, of *words* during the night, one would be better.

It hasn't worked lately, because I have been too tired to sleep, anyhow, but at one moment, the following would send me to sleep—and strangely enough, Osbert had the same habit—to imagine oneself in a gondola floating through Venice and regarding, under a full moon—with no sound excepting that of an oar, and nothing near one—only the sleeping palaces, as one floated on and on.

On a more mundane note, a tumbler of *hot* beer in bed can work—or indeed, cold, if it comes to that.

Those tireless nuisances the Income Tax people have written to ask me where I was last employed, and if I gave satisfaction, and when, if at all, I left it.

So I am going to reply that I was last employed, in a menial capacity, by Miss Imregarde A. Potter, of 8 The Grove, Leamington Spa, in 1911; but that I did not give satisfaction: there was some small unpleasantness, and I was dismissed without a character. And that if they want any more details, will they write to Dan Macmillan (whose temper, as you and Charles will know, needs a little sugar adding). Oh, good gracious!

My love and admiration to you both,

Yours affectionately,
Edith

And my love to the Poet, too.

ELIZABETH BISHOP
(1911–1979)

Elizabeth Bishop was an American poet (*North and South*, 1946; *Complete Poems*, 1983).

322. To Robert Lowell, 27 July 1960

Lowell (1917–77) was generally taken to be the leading American poet of his time.

July 27 (I think), 1960
Friday, at any rate marketing day, and
the day someone is bound to arrive

Please never stop writing me letters—they always manage to make me feel like my higher self (I've been re-reading Emerson) for several days.

Lots of things have been happening here, at least lots for me. But first, I don't think I've ever really commented much on 'The Drinker.' I find it even more horrendous in *Partisan Review*—although I hate to give up that soap dish. The most awful line for me is 'even corroded metal,' and the cops at the end are beautiful, of course—with a sense of release that only the poem, or another fifth of bourbon, could produce. As a cook I feel I should tell you that soured milk is NOT junket, but the picture is all too true. (I have a poem that has a galvanized bucket in it too—it is one I started in Key West—and I think I even used the phrase 'dead metal,' oh dear—but it has nothing to do with my Drunkard one.) The sense of time is terrifying—have hours gone by, or one awful moment? How long have the cars been parked?

That Anne Sexton I think still has a bit too much romanticism and what I think of as the 'our beautiful old silver' school of female writing which is really boasting about how 'nice' *we* were. V. Woolf, E. Bowen, R. West, etc.—they are all full of it. They have to make quite sure that the reader is not going to misplace them socially, first—and that nervousness interferes constantly with what they think they'd like to say. I wrote a story at Vassar that was too much admired by Miss Rose Peebles, my teacher, who was very proud of being an old-school Southern lady—and suddenly this fact about women's writing dawned on me, and has haunted me ever since.

I have re-arranged the Trollope poem ['From Trollope's Journal'], taking your advice, and I think it is improved. The whole thing should really be in quotation marks, I suppose; the reason it doesn't sound like me is because it sounds like Trollope. It probably should be quite a bit longer. Have you ever read his *North America*? I just copied out some of the Washington chapter. Well, I don't know whether it is a virtue or not, never to sound the same way more than once or twice! It sounds too much like facility, and yet I don't feel a bit facile, God knows.

Robie Macauley wrote me that I had been made a member of the P.E.N. by John Farrar, willy-nilly, and then Lota and I were invited to the Embassy luncheon given for the U.S. group—only Lota refused to go. So I went, and met Robie & his wife, and John Brooks of *The New Yorker* and his wife, and Elmer Rice, and May Sarton, none of whom I'd ever met before. I wished so much you had been there—all else aside, I would have loved to have introduced you to our Ambassador: 'Mr Cabot, Mr Lowell.' (When I told Robie about your having read to 3,000 people on the Common, he said, 'A Lowell speaks to Boston.') I liked Robie very much and am only sorry I didn't have more of a chance to talk to him—he was very busy of course being a delegate. The next day, however, Lota and I did see more of them—we dragged the Americans, with the exception of Elmer Rice, all the way up here, by Volkswagen and bus, for dinner, and I think everyone had rather a good time. But I still didn't have much chance to talk to Robie because I was too busy being a hostess, and he is very quiet, or was here at any rate. He seems very very bookish and also, from time to time, extremely funny, and I liked him a lot . . .

I'm sure Anne Macauley would have had some wonderful things to say if she'd known me better. I remarked that I was afraid I'd had some sort of falling-out with Randall and she said 'Good!' All wives seem to feel strongly about Randall! 'Never lifts a finger,' etc. Anyway, it was all very enjoyable: the weather not too good, nor the dinner. I only went to half a P.E.N. lecture, by Mario Praz, and found it sounded much better when read at home without the distractions of Graham Greene stomping out and Moravia scowling like a small Mussolini, etc. The advantage of that P.E.N. (a Brazilian finally told me what the letters stand for) seems to be that members get sent to expensive-to-get-to places, like Japan and South America. But the disadvantage is that they don't seem to have time to see the places when they get there and just have to submit to being excruciatingly bored— but maybe I underestimate what goes on, because I didn't see much of it, after all . . .

Robie told me you are going to Copenhagen—and that should be more interesting than this affair. Also that you have swapped houses with Eric Bentley for the winter in N.Y. I wish we could get there in the spring, but I don't know. I went to see a friend off to Europe last week—she was going third-class on a new English ship and it is dirt cheap, so I went to see what it is like and I think I could stand it for 13 days—to Lisbon and back for about $300. IF the Chapelbrook [award] comes through—however, I don't feel at all sure about that.

You ask if I have ever found 'reading and writing curiously self-sufficient.' Well, both Lota and I read from 7 a.m. intermittently until 1 a.m. every day, and all sorts of things, good and bad, and once in a while I think—what if I should run out of things to read, in English, by the time I'm sixty, and have to spend my old age reading French or Portuguese or even painfully taking up a new language? And then I've always had a daydream of being a lighthouse keeper, absolutely alone, with no one to interrupt my reading or just sitting—and although such dreams are sternly dismissed at 16 or so, they always haunt one a bit, I suppose. I now see a wonderful cold rocky shore in the Falklands, or a house in Nova Scotia on the bay, *exactly* like my grandmother's—idiotic as it is, and unbearable as the reality would be. But I think everyone should go, or should have gone, through a stretch of it—like your Third Avenue stretch, maybe—a *The Notebooks of Malte Laurids Brigge* stretch—and perhaps it is a recurrent need. But let us not say, to quote Miss S., 'I've fallen in love with solitude.'

What you say about meter—well, I have loads of thoughts on the subject and I think I'll have to write again tomorrow. I have a theory now that all

the arts are growing more and more 'literary'; that it is a late stage, perhaps
a decadent stage—and that un-metrical verse is more 'literary' and necessarily self-conscious than metrical. If I were Schapiro I'd write a book
about it. (And have you read *Art & Illusion* by one Gombrich?—it is
fascinating.) I find it is time to go to market. What kind of plan do you have
for your opera, or is it an opera? Now you must teach Harriet to swim—
or have you? It is just the age to learn. I believe in swimming, flying, and
crawling, and burrowing.

'The Drinker'] Lowell's poem 'Skunk Hour' (Life Studies, 1959) in an earlier version. It is
dedicated to Bishop.   Anne Sexton] (1928–74), poet.   Robie Macauley] writer and
editor.   P. E. N.] PEN, an international association of writers founded in 1921.   Lota]
Bishop's companion.   Elmer Rice] dramatist.   Randall] Jarrell (1914–65) poet, critic,
novelist, friend of Lowell.   Mario Praz] (1896–1982), Italian scholar.   Moravia] Alberto
Moravia (1907–90), Italian novelist.   Eric Bentley] theatre critic, historian, translator.
The Notebooks of Malte Laurids Brigge] (1906) by the Austrian poet Rainer Maria Rilke.
Gombrich] E. H. Gombrich's *Art and Illusion* was published in 1962.

323. To Robert Lowell, 16 January 1975

I think I sent you a postcard from Florida, but did I really? Anyway—I had
a wonderful time there; went on a 3-day sailing trip with old friends; went
to a marvelous wildlife sanctuary; went swimming almost every day; got
very *tan*—and so on. And came back feeling much much better than when
I left bleak Boston. I just got my mail yesterday & it included a letter from
you, dated Dec. 18th—I left Dec. 27th—it's odd I didn't get it before I
left—but no, I suppose not—the Christmas mail.

Now I have just talked to Frank [Bidart], who says he talked to you and
that you may get here before you get this. Well, I'll proceed with it anyway.
Frank says that you have been having arthritis(?) in your back—between
the shoulders. I'm sorry to hear that. I have it rather badly, too, and a touch
of it in that spot, although my hands are the worst. The only thing for it
is ASPIRIN—in huge doses. I go occasionally to the Robert Brigham Hospital (nothing *but* arthritis there) but have almost stopped going because with
aspirin one does as well as one possibly can, apparently. Also—hot water,
and exercise. But all that aspirin upsets the stomach—or gives you ulcers—
so I take a coated kind, ECOTRIN, that works very, very slowly, but doesn't
produce a bellyache. (There are other brands. I take from 12 to 16 every
day & don't have much pain, actually. But after seeing most of the patients
at Robert Brigham I usually think I don't have arthritis at all.)

I am now going to be very impertinent and aggressive. Please, *please*
don't talk about old age so much, my dear old friend! You are giving me
the creeps. The thing Lota admired so much about us North Americans
was our determined youthfulness and energy, our 'never-say-die' ness—
and I think she was right! In Florida my hostess's sister had recently
married again at the age of 76, for the third time—her second marriage had

been at 67—and she and her husband, also 76, went walking miles on the beach every day, hand in hand, as happy as clams, apparently, and I loved it. (A very plump, pretty, sweet lady—as naïve as a very small child.) Of course—it's different for a writer, I know—of course I know!—nevertheless, in spite of aches & pains I really don't feel much different than I did at 35—and I certainly am a great deal happier, most of the time. (This in spite of the giant oil tankers parading across my view every day.) I just *won't* feel ancient—I wish Auden hadn't gone on about it so in his last years, and I hope you won't.

However, Cal dear, maybe your memory *is* failing! Never, never was I 'tall'—as you wrote remembering me. I was always 5 ft. 4 and ¼ inches— now shrunk to 5 ft. 4 inches. The only time I've ever felt tall was in Brazil. And I never had 'long brown hair' either! It started turning gray when I was 23 or 24—and probably was already somewhat grizzled when I first met you. I tried putting it up for a very brief period, because I like long hair—but it never got even to my shoulders and is always so intractable that I gave that up within a month or so. I think you must be seeing someone else! So please don't put me in a beautiful poem 'tall with long brown hair'! What I remember about that [first] meeting is your dishevelment, your lovely curly hair, and how we talked about a Picasso show then on in N.Y., and we agreed about the Antibes pictures of fishing, etc.—and how much I liked you, after having been almost too scared to go—and how Randall and his wife threw sofa pillows at each other. And Kitten, of course, *Kitten*. You were also rather dirty, which I rather liked, too. And your stories about the cellar room you were living in and how the neighbors drank all night and when they got too rowdy, one of them would say, 'Remember the boy,' meaning you. Well, I think I'll have to write *my* memoirs, just to set things straight.

It will be nice to see you. Caroline and I had a 'real nice visit' as they say in Florida and I'm looking forward to seeing her again. Alice is at B.U. Business School, poor dear, and will soon be coming for dinner after her class on 'Taxes'—which she insists she *loves*. So I must stop and slice some green beans—See you later, alligator, as they also do say in Florida.

SYLVIA TOWNSEND WARNER
(1893–1978)

Sylvia Townsend Warner was a novelist, story writer, and poet; her work includes *Lolly Willowes* (1926) and *Mr Fortune's Maggot* (1927).

324. To William Maxwell, 22 July 1967

Maxwell was her editor at the *New Yorker* and from 1939 a frequent correspondent. Warner wrote a biography of T. H. White (1906–64), author of *The Once and Future King* (1958) and *The Goshawk* (1951), which describes his efforts to tame a hawk by following the instructions of an ancient training manual. He lived at 3 Connaught Square, in St Anne, Alderney.

Dear William,

You say everything my heart wished you to say—and one thing which illuminates a motive I had in writing the book though I had not formulated it to myself: of course you are right. He was an animal: 'one of them.' I must have admitted this subconsciously, else why should I have felt such particular *consent* to the passage about trying on the gasmask? I can remember feeling that here, at any rate, was something I needn't reconsider.

One has a dozen motives, hasn't one? I did partly undertake it as a dare; seventy is rather an advanced age to begin an entirely different technique. Partly as a rescue operation; because his literary agent was doing all he could to persuade the trustee-executors to give the job to a very inferior flashy protégé of his and Michael Howard and John Verney & Harry Griffiths were frantic to avert this. Partly because I wanted to do something that would take a long time and involve some sort of research (a Bestiary, in fact). But from the day I went to Alderney I knew I was to do it because it was a human obligation. He had been dead less than four months. His suitcases were at the foot of the stairs, as though he had just come back. The grander furniture had gone to the sale room, but the part of the house he mainly inhabited he still inhabited. His clothes were on hangers. His sewing basket with an unfinished hawk-hood; his litter of fishing-flies, his books, his *awful* ornaments presented by his hoi polloi friends, his vulgar toys bought at the Cherbourg Fairs, his neat rows of books about flagellation—everything was there, defenceless as a corpse. And so was he; morose, suspicious, intensely watchful and determined to despair. I have never felt such an *imminent* haunt. I said I would like to stay on and poke in the books; and Pat & Michael Howard and kind Harry tactfully left me. I poked in the books—and immediately found an unposted letter to David Garnett & took charge of it. I sniffed at the coats, took one down, was almost felled by its weight and massiveness. I looked out of the windows at his views. I had been left so tactfully that no one had shown me where the light switches were. And when I left, it was dark and I had to grope my way in darkness down two flights of twisting stairs and out by a back door. It was all I could do, to lock that door, to lock up that haunt and go off swinging the iron key. I went back to the hotel and drank a brandy and told Michael I expected I'd do the book.

If this were a ghost story I could tell you that when I was there, alone, the next evening, it felt quite different. It didn't. It was unchanged. The only difference was in me. I felt more at home in it.

Even so, it was like feeling at home in hell when last summer I read through those diaries he bequeathed to Michael. Michael was tied by the bequest not to let them out of his keeping; but we compromised by a transfer to the keeping of the Dorchester Museum. They were lodged there, locked in a yellow tin trunk which in turn was locked in the Hardy Room. To the reverent delight of the Museum's janitor I used to have the Hardy Room unlocked, and unlock the yellow tin trunk, and carry off one volume at a time and sit reading it in the Museum's Library. I can't tell you how eldrich it was to sit in that calm Victorian saloon, with perhaps two or three local ladies gently gossiping in a corner or a regular visitor puffing at *The Times*, with White's raving, despairing soliloquy whispering on and on in my ear. It was that I ran into at 3 Connaught Square, and locked up in the empty house.

DAVID GARNETT (1892–1981) AND SYLVIA TOWNSEND WARNER

Garnett wrote fantastic novels (*Lady into Fox*, 1922; *A Man in the Zoo*, 1924) and a three-volume autobiography. His correspondence with Warner began in 1922 and ended with her death. They had in common, among much else, a passion for cats.

325. Sylvia Townsend Warner to David Garnett, 6 June 1973

Dearest David,

I have only just heard about Amaryllis. I grieve for her, I grieve for you. It is hard to be a stoic in one's old age.

With my love
Sylvia

Amaryllis] his daughter, who lived in a houseboat at Chelsea and was drowned in the Thames.

326. David Garnett to Sylvia Townsend Warner, 13 June 1973

Dearest Sylvia,

Thank you for your note of sympathy. What is so hard to bear is that Amaryllis might have enjoyed another fifty years of the happiness and beauty of daily life, which is what I appreciate more and more.

Can you explain how and why cats make love to us? Tiber will come, if I am reading or writing or lying on my bed and will 'tease tow' with his claws. Then, coming closer, will gaze into my face, suddenly dig his pointed muzzle under my chin once or twice, retreat, roll on his side, inviting my hand, turn his head dreamily to one side, passive and luxurious. Then he will turn on me almost fiercely with a burst of purring, and so on, and so on.

But is this, as I think, reserved for human lovers? With a female cat I think he displays no such graces but is fiercely practical. It is more like the love that was shown him by his mother when he was a kitten. And naturally it is shown most strongly before and after I have fed him. But the luxury of his furry love is very beautiful.

He fights continually with the Wood Cat—a savage beast that has run wild and supports himself in the wood by hunting, flying from man. He is more versed in battle, and Tiber is continually appearing with his scalp furrowed by the Wood Cat's claws, paws bitten through and lame, ears bleeding. He has just recovered after some days of lameness when his paw was swollen like a boxing-glove. I keep him shut up at night to save further fights, but now he can put his paw to the ground he will go off to fight again.

We had a terrible storm yesterday evening, with all the artillery of Heaven and hailstones like large lumps of sugar bouncing all over the carpet from the chimney, and today the leaves are torn and many barley fields laid flat and peasants half ruined. Every room was flooded—except the bathroom.

Very much love from

David

327. Sylvia Townsend Warner to David Garnett, 18 June 1973

Dearest David,

. . . Tiber makes love to you for the good reason that he loves you, and loves making love. Cats are passionate and voluptuous, they get satisfaction from mating but no pleasure (the females dislike it, and this is wounding to the male), no voluptuousness; *and no appreciation.* Tiber has the pleasure of being pleased and knowing he pleases in his love-making with you. I am so glad you have each other. Does he roll on his head? Does he fall asleep with an ownerly paw laid over you?

We had a dark grey cat (Norfolk bred, very Norfolk in character) called Tom. He was reserved, domineering, voluptuous—much as I imagine Tiber to be. When he was middle-aged he gave up nocturnal prowlings and slept on my bed, against my feet. One evening I was reading in bed when I became aware that Tom was staring at me. I put down my book, said nothing, watched. Slowly, with a look of intense concentration, he got up and advanced on me, like Tarquin with ravishing strides, poised himself, put out a front paw, and stroked my cheek as I used to stroke his chops. A human caress from a cat. I felt very meagre and ill-educated that I could not purr.

It had never occurred to me that their furry love develops from what was shown them as kittens. I expect you are right. The ownerly paw is certainly a nursing cat's gesture.

You should encourage Tiber to sleep with you. He might come to prefer it to midnight battling with the Wood Cat. Come winter, he certainly will. I am afraid of the Wood Cat's claws, still more of his teeth.

Were your hailstones blue? We once had such a storm here, with lightning ripping hail from the sky; and the hailstones were hard as marbles, and blue as aquamarines. And there was another storm, after a long drought, when the lightning was green. It was strange to see the bleached fields, the rusty trees, momentarily sluiced with the look of spring.

I have been spared acquaintances who might have explained to me about blue hailstones and green lightning, so I can enjoy them with simple pleasure.

> Earth, that grew with joyful ease
> Hemlock for Socrates—

The longer I live, the more my heart assents to that couplet.

With love
Sylvia

Earth] Properly, 'Earth, that bare . . .', *Poem XXX* in *Marlborough and Other Poems* (1916) by Charles Sorley (1895–1915).

PHILIP LARKIN
(1922–1985)

328. To Kingsley Amis, 21 November 1985

This is the last entry in Anthony Thwaite's edition of the poet's letters; it was dictated. Larkin died 2 Dec.

Dear Kingsley,

I hope you don't mind my dictating a letter to be typed and signed by my secretary, but this is almost the only way I can communicate these days. Of course I am delighted to hear from you, and find it marvellous that someone as busy as you should find time to write letters to seedy old friends.

I thought you were pretty charitable about old Dylan, whose letters I read with almost supernatural boredom, scrounging, apologising, promising, apologising again, fixing up appointments, apologising for not keeping them, and all that nonsensical rubbish to P.H.J. in the first half and Princess whoever she was in the second. And then the letters to Caitlin. You know, what struck me most about them was that he might never have met her before. No cat, no friendliness, nothing to suggest that they had a life they shared and enjoyed. Hardly any (if my memory serves) of 'Do you remember that girl Dilys we met at Ieuan's party, well, she's gone off with that incredible fool Teithryn'—you know the kind of thing? All snivelling and grovelling and adoring and so very impersonal.

As you gather, I have been in a poor way lately. Hospital last week, hospital twice this week, and hospital again today for the big one. These are only tests, but of course they are looking for something, and I bloody well hope they don't find it. Added to which I am subsisting largely on Complan (what they give old ladies in hospices) and you will guess that my spirits are about as low as I can remember. Don't get unduly alarmed; the doctors, as always, are cheerful and lighthearted, but I don't really trust them any more. Only Monica's reiterated 'You look all right' brings me encouragement. I may say that these tests are supposed to be nothing at all to do with the operation, though of course they *could* be. Gibber gibber. I simply cannot imagine resuming normal life again, whatever that is.

Congratulations on the novel. I can't, I am afraid, do your Dylan lines, but why don't you use that wonderful stuff from *That Uncertain Feeling*? That would be a sort of double joke. 'Crewe Junction down the sleepers of the breath'—well, if I can remember that after thirty years it must be pretty good, or pretty funny, and it's perfectly clear whose behind you are kicking.

I laughed at your House of Commons anecdote. Hilly talking to Jane must be like one of those *Imaginary Conversations* some old fool wrote. As for jazz, I have a dear friend here who brings me specially-made tapes to divert me, but just between you and me his taste is a bit early for my liking. The greatest jazz man in his judgement is Jelly Roll Morton, and while I don't mind him (in the sense I mind John Coltrane) I put him about 27th or 28th in such a ranking. But he is the kindest of men, has a whole room full of hi-fi equipment, and collects like mad. Only where my taste stops at 1945, I suspect he is never really very happy after 1930.

I must mention Sally's letter and photograph which arrived this morning. Of course they deserve a separate acknowledgement, and *may* one day get one. I am so glad to see strong resemblances in her to Hilly, who is the most beautiful woman I have ever seen without being in the least pretty (I am sure you know what I mean, and I hope she will too).

Well, the tape draws to an end; think of me packing up my pyjamas and shaving things for today's ordeal, and hope all goes well. I really feel this year has been more than I deserve; I suppose it's all come at once, instead of being spread out as with most people.

You will excuse the absence of the usual valediction,

Yours ever,
Philip

Dylan] Amis had just reviewed *The Letters of Dylan Thomas* in the *Observer*.   P.H.J.] Pamela Hansford Johnson, with whom at one time Thomas had been in love.   Princess] Princess Caetani.   Caitlin] Thomas's wife.   The novel] *The Old Devils* (1986). *That Uncertain Feeling*] this, Amis's second novel (1955), contained a parody of Dylan Thomas.   Hilly . . . Jane] Amis's first and second wives.   Sally] Amis's daughter. Usual valediction] Larkin's letters to Amis usually end with 'Bum'.

Sources and Acknowledgements

1–2. *The Lisle Letters: An Abridgement*, ed. Muriel St Clare Byrne (London: Secker & Warburg, 1983). Reprinted by permission of Reed Consumer Books and the University of Chicago Press.

3. *The Correspondence of Sir Thomas More*, ed. E. F. Rogers (Princeton, NJ: Princeton University Press, 1947). Reprinted by permission of the publisher.

4. Bror Danielsson, *John Hart's Works on English Orthography and Pronunciation* (Stockholm: Almquist & Wiksell, 1955).

5. *The Complete Works of Sir Philip Sidney*, ed. A. Feuillerat, 4 vols., vol. iii (Cambridge: Cambridge University Press, 1912–26).

6. *John Stubbs's* Gaping Gulf *with Letters and Other Relevant Documents*, ed. Lloyd E. Berry (Charlottesville, VA: University Press of Virginia, 1968).

7. *Original Letters Illustrative of English History*, ed. Henry Ellis, 3 vols. (London: Hardy, Triphook, & Lepard, 1825).

8–9. *Letters of Queen Elizabeth and James VI of Scotland*, ed. John Bruce (London: Camden Society, 1849).

10. *The Letters of Queen Elizabeth I*, ed. G. B. Harrison (London: Cassell, 1935; repr. 1968).

11. *Sir Walter Raleigh: Selections from his* Historie of the World, *his Letters, etc.*, ed. G. E. Hadow (Oxford: Clarendon Press, 1917).

12–15. *The Familiar Letters of James Howell*, ed. Joseph Jacobs (London: David Nutt, 1890).

16. *The Letters, Speeches and Proclamations of King Charles I*, ed. C. Petrie (London: Cassell, 1969).

17. *Original Letters Illustrative of English History*, ed. Henry Ellis, 3 vols. (London: Hardy, Triphook, & Lepard, 1825).

18. *The Letters of Elizabeth Queen of Bohemia*, ed. L. M. Baker (London: Bodley Head, 1953).

19–20. *Letters from New England: The Massachusetts Bay Colony, 1629–1638*, ed. E. Emerson (Amherst, MA: University of Massachusetts Press, 1976). Reprinted by permission of E. Emerson.

21. *Original Letters Illustrative of English History*, ed. Henry Ellis, 2nd series, vol. iii (London: Dawsons of Pall Mall, 1969).

22. *A Declaration of the Earl of Derby concerning his Resolution to keep the Isle of Man for his Majesties service against all force whatsoever*, as repr. in *A Letter Does not Blush*, ed. N. Parsons (London: Buchan & Enright, 1984).

23. *Letters from the Originals at Welbeck Abbey*, ed. R. W. Goulding (London: John Murray, 1909).

24. F. N. L. Poynter and W. J. Bishop, *A Seventeenth Century Doctor and his Patients: John Symcotts, 1592?–1662*, Publications of the Bedfordshire Historical Record Society 31 (Luton: 1951). Reprinted with permission.

25. *The Letters of Dorothy Osborne to William Temple*, ed. G. C. Moore Smith (Oxford: Clarendon Press, 1928).

26–7. *Diary of John Evelyn, to which are added a selection from his familiar letters*, ed. W. Bray and H. B. Wheatley, 4 vols., vol. iii (London: Bickers & Son, 1906).

28. *Original Letters of Eminent Literary Men of the Sixteenth, Seventeenth, and Eighteenth Centuries*, ed. Henry Ellis (London: Camden Society, 1843).

29. *Original Letters Illustrative of English History*, ed. Henry Ellis, 2nd series, vol. iv (London: Dawsons of Pall Mall, 1969).

30. *Diary of John Evelyn, to which are added a selection from his familiar letters*, ed. W. Bray and H. B. Wheatley, 4 vols., vol. iv (London: Bickers & Son, 1906).

31. *Correspondence of the Family of Hatton . . . 1601–1704*, ed. E. M. Thompson, 2 vols., vol. i (London: Camden Society, 1878).

32. *Cotton Mather: Selected Letters*, ed. K. Silverman (Baton Rouge, LA: Louisiana State University Press, 1971).

33. *Original Letters Illustrative of English History*, ed. Henry Ellis, 2nd series, vol. iv (London: Dawsons of Pall Mall, 1969).

34. *Letters of Sir George Etherege*, ed. Frederick Bracher (Berkeley, CA: University of California Press, 1974).

35–40. *The Complete Letters of Lady Mary Wortley Montagu*, ed. Robert Halsband, 3 vols. (Oxford: Clarendon Press, 1965).

41–8. *The Correspondence of Jonathan Swift*, ed. Harold Williams, 5 vols. (Oxford: Clarendon Press, 1963).

49–50. *The Correspondence of Alexander Pope*, ed. George Sherburn, 5 vols. (Oxford: Clarendon Press, 1956).

51–2. *Lord Hervey and his Friends, 1726–38*, ed. the Earl of Ilchester (London: John Murray, 1950). Reprinted by permission of the publisher.

53–4. *Correspondence of Thomas Gray*, ed. P. Toynbee and L. Whibley, 3 vols. (Oxford: Clarendon Press, 1935).

55–60. *Selected Letters of Horace Walpole*, ed. W. S. Lewis (New Haven, CT: Yale University Press, 1973), © 1973 Yale University Press. Reprinted by permission of the publisher.

61–3. Samuel Richardson, *Familiar Letters on Important Occasions*, ed. B. W. Downs (London: Routledge & Sons, 1928).

64–6. *Correspondence of David Garrick*, ed. D. M. Little and G. M. Kahrl, 3 vols., vol. i (Cambridge, MA: Harvard University Press, 1963).

67. *The Family Memoirs of the Rev. William Stukeley, M.D. and the Antiquarian and other Correspondence of William Stukeley, Roger & Samuel Gale, etc.*, ed. W. C. Lukis (Newcastle: Surtees Society, 1882).

68–72. *The Life and Letters of Lady Sarah Lennox, 1745–1826*, ed. the Countess of Ilchester and Lord Stavordale, 2 vols. (London: John Murray, 1901).

73–8. *The Letters of Samuel Johnson*, ed. Bruce Redford, 4 vols. (Oxford: Clarendon Press, 1992–4).

79–80. *The Letters of Boswell*, ed. C. B. Tinker, 2 vols. (Oxford: Clarendon Press, 1924).

81–3. *Letters of Sir Joshua Reynolds*, ed. F. W. Hilles (Cambridge: Cambridge University Press, 1929).

84. *The Evelyns in America: Compiled from Family Papers and other Sources, 1608–1805*, ed. G. D. Scull (Oxford: Parker & Co., 1881).

85–6. *The Book of Abigail and John: Selected Letters of the Adams Family, 1762–1784*, ed. L. H. Butterfield *et al.* (Cambridge, MA: Harvard University Press, 1976), copyright © 1975 by the Massachusetts Historical Society. Reprinted by permission of the publisher.

87. Anna Seward, *Memoir of the Life of Dr Darwin* (London, 1804).

88–9. *The Correspondence of George, Prince of Wales 1770–1812*, ed. A. Aspinall, vol. i: *1770–1789* (London: Cassell, 1963). Reprinted by permission of the publisher.

90. *The Royal Letter Book*, ed. Herbert van Thal (London: Cresset Press, 1937).

91–2. *Original Letters of Eminent Literary Men of the Sixteenth, Seventeenth, and Eighteenth Centuries*, ed. Henry Ellis (London: Camden Society, 1843).

93. *The Later Correspondence of George III*, ed. A. Aspinall, 5 vols., vol. i (Cambridge: Cambridge University Press, 1962). Reprinted by permission of the publisher.

94. *Historical Manuscripts Commission: Fifteenth Report, Appendix, Part I: The Manuscripts of the Earl of Dartmouth*, vol. iii (London: Her Majesty's Stationery Office by Eyre & Spottiswoode, 1896).

95. *The Life and Letters of Gilbert White of Selborne*, ed. R. Holt-White (London: John Murray, 1901).

96. *The Later Correspondence of George III*, ed. A. Aspinall, 5 vols., vol. i (Cambridge: Cambridge University Press, 1962). Reprinted by permission of the publisher.

97. *The Correspondence of George, Prince of Wales 1770–1812*, ed. A. Aspinall, vol. i: *1770–1789* (London: Cassell, 1963). Reprinted by permission of the publisher.

98–9. *Correspondence of Edmund Burke*, ed. T. W. Copeland *et al.*, 10 vols., vol. vi (Cambridge: Cambridge University Press, 1958—). Reprinted by permission of the publisher.

100. *The Collected Letters of Mary Wollstonecraft*, ed. Ralph M. Wardle (Ithaca, NY: Cornell University Press, 1979). Reprinted by permission of the publisher.

101–4. *Lord Granville Leveson Gower, 1st Earl Granville: Private Correspondence, 1781 to 1821*, ed. Castalia, Countess Granville, 2 vols. (London: John Murray, 1916).

105–6. *Jane Austen's Letters to her sister Cassandra and others*, ed. R. W. Chapman (Oxford: Oxford University Press, 1952).

107–9. *Letters from Lord Nelson*, ed. Geoffrey Rawson (London: Staples Press, 1949).

110–11. *Letters of William Wordsworth: A New Selection*, ed. Alan G. Hill (Oxford: Clarendon Press, 1984).

112. *The Nun of Lebanon: The Love Affair of Lady Hester Stanhope and Michael Bruce*, ed. Ian Bruce (London: Collins, 1951).

113. *The Life and Letters of Lady Hester Stanhope*, ed. the Duchess of Cleveland (London: John Murray, 1914).

114. *Letters of Harriet Countess Granville, 1810–1845*, ed. F. Leveson Gower, 2 vols. (London: Longmans, Green, & Co., 1894).

115. *The Journals and Letters of Frances Burney*, ed. Joyce Hemlow *et al.*, 12 vols., vol. vi (Oxford: Clarendon Press, 1972–84).

116. Mrs Edgeworth, *A Memoir of Maria Edgeworth, with a Selection from her Letters* (London: Joseph Masters & Son, 1867).

117. *Maria Edgeworth: Letters from England, 1813–1844*, ed. Christina Colvin (Oxford: Clarendon Press, 1971).

118–19. *The Letters of Sir Walter Scott*, ed. H. J. C. Grierson, 12 vols., vols. iv, v (London: Constable, 1932–7).

120–1. *Byron's Letters and Journals*, ed. Leslie A. Marchand, 12 vols., vols. v, vii (Cambridge, MA: Harvard University Press, 1973–82), copyright © Editorial

Leslie A. Marchand, 1973, 1974, 1975, 1976, 1977, 1978, 1979, 1980, 1981, 1982; © Byron copyright material, John Murray 1973, 1974, 1975, 1976, 1977, 1978, 1979, 1980, 1981, 1982. Reprinted by permission of the publisher.

122. *The Letters of John Keats*, ed. H. E. Rollins, 2 vols., vol. i (Cambridge, MA: Harvard University Press, 1958), copyright © 1958 by the President and Fellows of Harvard College. Reprinted by permission of the publisher.

123–9. *The Letters of Sydney Smith*, ed. Nowell C. Smith, 2 vols. (Oxford: Clarendon Press, 1953).

130–2. *The Letters of John Keats*, ed. H. E. Rollins, 2 vols. (Cambridge, MA: Harvard University Press, 1958), copyright © 1958 by the President and Fellows of Harvard College. Reprinted by permission of the publisher.

133. From a facsimile in the Cory Library, Rhodes University, Grahamstown, S. Africa, MS 2031. Reprinted by permission of the Cory Library.

134. *Shelley—Leigh Hunt: How Friendship Made History*, ed. R. Brimley Johnson (London: Ingpen & Grant, 1926).

135. *The Letters of Mary Wollstonecraft Shelley*, ed. Betty T. Bennett, 3 vols., vol. i (Baltimore, MD: Johns Hopkins University Press, 1980). Reprinted by permission of the publisher.

136. *Three Generations of English Women*, ed. Janet Ross (London: T. Fisher Unwin, 1893).

137–8. *The Collected Letters of Thomas and Jane Welsh Carlyle*, ed. C. R. Sanders *et al.*, vol. ii (Durham, NC: Duke University Press, 1970). Reprinted by permission of the publisher.

139. *The Correspondence of Thomas Carlyle and R. W. Emerson* (London: Chatto & Windus, 1883).

140–4. *Benjamin Disraeli: Letters*, ed. J. A. W. Gunn, J. Matthews, *et al.*, vols. i, ii (Toronto: Toronto University Press, 1982—). Reprinted by permission of the publisher.

145. *The Letters of Disraeli to Lady Bradford and Lady Chesterfield*, ed. the Marquis of Zetland, vol. i (London: Ernest Benn, 1929).

146. John E. Jordan, *De Quincey to Wordsworth: a Biography of a Relationship, with the Letters of Thomas De Quincey to the Wordsworth Family* (Berkeley, CA: University of California Press, 1962). Reprinted by permission of the publisher.

147–9. *Miss Eden's Letters*, ed. Violet Dickinson (London: Macmillan, 1919).

150–3. *The Letters of Thomas Babington Macaulay*, ed. Thomas Pinney, 5 vols. (Cambridge: Cambridge University Press, 1974–80). Reprinted by permission of the publisher.

154–7. *The Brontës: Their Lives, Friendships and Correspondence*, in *The Shakespeare Head Brontë*, ed. T. J. Wise and J. A. Symington, vols. i–iii (Oxford: Blackwell, 1932–8).

158. *Three Generations of English Women*, ed. Janet Ross (London: T. Fisher Unwin, 1893).

159. *The Lincoln Reader*, ed. Paul M. Angle (New Brunswick, NJ: Rutgers University Press, 1947).

160. *The Collected Works of Abraham Lincoln*, ed. R. P. Basler, 9 vols., vol. vi (New Brunswick, NJ: Rutgers University Press, 1953), © 1953 by the Abraham Lincoln Association. Reprinted by permission of Rutgers University Press.

161. MS collection 4253 (NK 6451), 'Letters from a Transportee to Tasmania', National Library of Australia, Canberra. Printed with permission.

162–6. *The Letters of Samuel Palmer*, ed. R. Lister, 2 vols. (Oxford: Clarendon Press, 1974).

167–9. *The Letters of Charles Dickens*, ed. Madeline House and Graham Storey, vols. ii, iii (Oxford: Clarendon Press, 1969—).

170–1. *Charles Dickens: Selected Letters*, ed. David Paroissen (London: Macmillan, 1985), © D. Paroissen, 1985. Reprinted by permission of the publisher.

172. *The Letters of Ralph Waldo Emerson*, ed. Ralph L. Rusk, 6 vols., vol. ii (New York: Columbia University Press, 1939).

173–4. *Some Letters of Lord Cockburn*, ed. Harry A. Cockburn (Edinburgh: Grant & Murray, 1932).

175. *The Letters of F. W. Ludwig Leichhart*, ed. M. Aurousseau (Cambridge: Cambridge University Press for the Hakluyt Society, 2nd series, vol. cxxxiv, 1968). Reprinted by permission of the publisher and the Hakluyt Society.

176. Charlotte Erickson, *Invisible Immigrants: The Adaptation of English and Scottish Immigrants in 19th Century America* (London: Weidenfeld & Nicolson, 1972). Reprinted by permission of Pinter Publishers Ltd., London. All rights reserved.

177–8. *The Letters of Herman Melville*, ed. M. R. Davis and W. H. Gilman (New Haven, CT: Yale University Press, 1960), © 1960 Yale University Press. Reprinted by permission of the publisher.

179. *Three Generations of English Women*, ed. Janet Ross (London: T. Fisher Unwin, 1893).

180–1. *Charles Kingsley: His Letters and Memories of His Life*, ed. by his wife (London: Macmillan, 1908).

182–3. *The Letters of John Clare*, ed. Mark Storey (Oxford: Clarendon Press, 1985).

184. *Life and Letters of Harriet Beecher Stowe*, ed. Annie Fields (London: Sampson Low, Marston, & Co., 1898).

185–6. *Ruskin's Letters from Venice, 1851–2*, ed. J. L. Bradley (Columbus, OH: Ohio State University Press, 1955).

187–8. *The Letters of John Ruskin to Lord and Lady Mount-Temple*, ed. J. L. Bradley (Columbus, OH: Ohio State University Press, 1964), MA 1571. Reprinted by permission of the Pierpont Morgan Library, New York.

189–90. *Correspondence of Arthur Hugh Clough*, ed. F. L. Mulhauser, 2 vols. (Oxford: Oxford University Press, 1957).

191. R. E. Lee, *Recollections and Letters of General Robert E. Lee* (London: Archibald, Constable, & Co., 1904).

192. MS collection 7203, National Library of Australia, Canberra. Printed with permission.

193–4, 196. *The George Eliot Letters*, ed. Gordon S. Haight, 6 vols. (London: Oxford University Press, 1954).

195. Huntington Library collection, HM 53335. Printed by permission of the Huntington Library, San Marino, California.

197–8. *Edward Lear: Selected Letters*, ed. Vivien Noakes (Oxford: Clarendon Press, 1988).

199. Jean Burton, *Heyday of a Wizard: Daniel Home the Medium* (London: George G. Harrap & Co., 1948). A foreword by Harry Price reprints these letters, which were in Mr Price's possession. Reprinted by permission of the publisher.

200. *The Correspondence of Henry David Thoreau*, ed. W. Harding and C. Bode (New York: New York University Press, 1958).

201–2. Barbara Leigh Smith Bodichon, *An American Diary, 1857–8*, ed. J. W. Reed, Jr. (London: Routledge & Kegan Paul, 1972), © Joseph W. Reed 1972. Reprinted with permission.

203. *The Letters of Anthony Trollope*, ed. N. John Hall, 2 vols. (Stanford, CA: Stanford University Press, 1983).

204–7. *The Letters of Emily Dickinson*, ed. Thomas H. Johnson, 3 vols. (Cambridge, MA: The Belknap Press of Harvard University Press, 1958), copyright © 1958, 1986 by the President and Fellows of Harvard College. Reprinted by permission of the publisher.

208. *A Packet of Letters: A Selection from the Correspondence of John Henry Newman*, ed. Joyce Sugg (Oxford: Clarendon Press, 1983).

209. *The Letters of John Addington Symonds*, ed. H. M. Schueller and R. L. Peters, 3 vols., vol. i (Detroit, MI: Wayne State University Press, 1967). Reprinted with permission.

210. MS 1420, Item 136, National Library of Australia, Canberra. Printed with permission.

211, 213. Ralph Barton Perry, *The Thought and Character of William James*, 2 vols., vol. i (Oxford: Oxford University Press, 1935).

212, 215–16. *The Letters of William James*, ed. Henry James, 2 vols. (London: Longmans, Green, & Co., 1926).

214. *The Death and Letters of Alice James*, ed. R. B. Yeazell (Berkeley, CA: University of California Press, 1981). Reprinted by permission of the publisher.

217. *The Correspondence of John Ruskin and Charles Eliot Norton*, ed. J. L. Bradley and I. Ousby (Cambridge: Cambridge University Press, 1987). Reprinted by permission of the publisher.

218. *Poems and Some Letters of James Thomson*, ed. Anne Ridler (London: Centaur Press, 1963). Reprinted by permission of the publisher.

219–25. *Mark Twain—Howells Letters: The Correspondence of Samuel L. Clemens and William Dean Howells, 1872–1910*, ed. Henry Nash Smith and William M. Gibson, 2 vols. (Cambridge, MA: The Belknap Press of Harvard University Press, 1962). Reprinted by permission of the publisher.

226–7. ALS in Huntington Library, HH92 and HH98. Printed by permission of the Huntington Library, San Marino, California.

228. *Yours Pictorially: Illustrated Letters of Randolph Caldecott*, ed. Michael Hutchins (London: Frederick Warne, 1976).

229–30. *The Correspondence of William James*, vol. i, *William and Henry, 1861–1884*, ed. I. K. Skrupskelis and E. M. Berkeley (Charlottesville, VA: University Press of Virginia, 1992). Reprinted by permission of the University Press of Virginia.

231–5. *Henry James: Selected Letters*, ed. L. Edel (Cambridge, MA: The Belknap Press of Harvard University Press, 1987), copyright © 1974, 1975, 1980, 1984, 1987 Leon Edel, editorial; © 1974, 1975, 1980, 1984, 1987 Alexander R. James, James copyright material. Reprinted by permission of the publisher.

236. *A Royal Correspondence: Letters of King Edward VII and King George V to Admiral Sir Henry F. Stephenson*, ed. John Stephenson (London: Macmillan, 1938).

237. *The Letters of Rudyard Kipling*, vol. i, *1872–89*, ed. Thomas Pinney (London: Macmillan, 1990), © Thomas Pinney, 1990. Reprinted by permission of the publisher.

238–9. *The Letters of R. L. Stevenson*, ed. Sidney Colvin, 4 vols. (London: Methuen & Co., n.d.). Enlargement and revision of Colvin's 2 vol. edition, 1911.

240. Reprinted in John Stokes, *In the Nineties* (Brighton: Harvester, 1989). Reprinted by permission of the publisher and the University of Chicago Press.

241–4. *The Letters of A. E. Housman*, ed. Henry Maas (Cambridge, MA: Harvard University Press, 1971). Reprinted by permission of the publisher.

245. E. M. Forster's *Commonplace Book* (London: Scolar Press, facsimile edn., 1978). The entry, probably made in 1952, gives no indication of source. Reprinted by permission of Scolar Press.

246. *People's Mail: Letters of Men and Women of Letters, selected from the Henry W. and Albert A. Berg Collection*, ed. Lola L. Szladits (New York: New York Public Library, n.d.). Reprinted by permission of the New York Public Library (Henry W. and Albert A. Berg Collection and Astor, Lenox and Tildern Foundations).

247. Modern Archive, King's College, Cambridge. Printed with permission.

248–9. Frederic Whyte, *The Life of W. T. Stead*, 2 vols. (London: Jonathan Cape, 1927).

250. *Letters of Oscar Wilde*, ed. Rupert Hart-Davis (Oxford: Oxford University Press, 1979).

251. *Elgar and his Publishers: Letters of a Creative Life*, ed. J. N. Moore, 2 vols., vol. i (Oxford: Clarendon Press, 1987).

252. ALS in Huntington Library, MS 28292. Printed by permission of the Huntington Library, San Marino, California.

253. *Letters of Leonard Woolf*, ed. Frederic Spotts (London: Weidenfeld & Nicolson, 1990), copyright © 1989 by the estate of Leonard Woolf. Reprinted by permission of the publisher and Harcourt Brace and Company.

254–6, 258. *The Letters of W. B. Yeats*, ed. Allan Wade (London: Rupert Hart-Davis, 1954).

257. Communicated by Dr John Kelly.

259–60. *The Letters of Edith Wharton*, ed. R. W. B. and Nancy Lewis (New York: Simon & Schuster, 1988).

261–5. *The Letters of D. H. Lawrence*, ed. J. T. Boulton *et al.*, 7 vols., vols. i–iii (Cambridge: Cambridge University Press, 1979–93). Reprinted by permission of Laurence Pollinger Ltd., the estate of Frieda Lawrence Ravagli and Cambridge University Press.

266–75. *George Bernard Shaw: Collected Letters*, ed. Dan H. Laurence, 4 vols., vols. iii, iv (London: Max Reinhardt, 1985, 1988). Reprinted by permission of the Society of Authors on behalf of the Bernard Shaw Estate.

276–7. *Selected Letters of Robert Frost*, ed. L. Thompson (New York: Holt, Rinehart, & Winston, 1964).

278. *J. B. Yeats: Letters to his Son W. B. Yeats and Others, 1869–1922*, ed. Joseph Hone (London: Faber, 1944).

279. *The Letters of Hugh McCrae*, ed. Robert D. FitzGerald (Sidney: Angus & Robertson, 1970). Reprinted with permission.

280–2. *H. H. Asquith: Letters to Venetia Stanley*, ed. M. and E. Park (Oxford: Oxford University Press, 1982, 1985).

283. *The Letters of Wyndham Lewis*, ed. W. K. Rose (London: Methuen, 1963), © Wyndham Lewis and the estate of the late Mrs G. A. Wyndham Lewis by kind permission of the Wyndham Lewis Memorial Trust (a registered charity).

284–6. *Self-Portrait: Taken from the Letters and Journals of Charles Ricketts, R.A.*, collected and compiled by T. Sturge Moore, ed. Cecil Lewis (London: Peter Davies, 1939).

287–9. *Carrington: Letters and Extracts from her Diaries*, ed. David Garnett (London: Jonathan Cape, 1970). Reprinted by permission of Random House UK Ltd.

290–1. *Ivor Gurney: War Letters*, ed. R. K. R. Thornton (London: Hogarth Press, 1983). Reprinted by permission of the Mid-Northumberland Arts Group.

292. *Letters of Aldous Huxley*, ed. G. Smith (London: Chatto, 1969), © 1969, 1970 by Laura Huxley. Prefatory material and notes © 1969, 1970 by Grover Smith. Reprinted by permission of Harper Collins Publishers Inc. and Random House UK.

293. *Wilfred Owen: Selected Letters*, ed. John Bell, 2nd edn. (Oxford: Oxford University Press, 1985).

294. *Katherine Mansfield: Selected Letters*, ed. V. O'Sullivan (Oxford: Oxford University Press, 1990).

295–9. *Edmund Wilson: Letters on Literature and Politics, 1912–1972*, ed. E. Wilson (New York: Farrar Straus Giroux, 1977), copyright © 1977 by Elena Wilson. Reprinted by permission of the publisher.

300–1. *Ernest Hemingway: Selected Letters, 1917–1961*, ed. Carlos Baker (London: Granada, 1961).

302. *People's Mail: Letters of Men and Women of Letters, selected from the Henry W. and Albert A. Berg Collection*, ed. Lola L. Szladits (New York: New York Public Library, n.d.). Reprinted by permission of the New York Public Library (Henry W. and Albert A. Berg Collection and Astor, Lenox and Tildern Foundations).

303–5. *Letters of James Joyce*, vol. i, ed. Stuart Gilbert, copyright © 1957, 1966 by the Viking Press, renewed © 1985 by Viking Penguin Inc.; vol. iii, ed. Richard Ellmann, copyright © 1966 by F. Lionel Munro, as Administrator of the Estate of James Joyce (London: Faber, 1957, 1966). Reprinted by permission of Viking Penguin, a division of Penguin Books USA Inc.

306. ALS in Huntington Library, Kinross Collection. Printed by permission of the Huntington Library, San Marino, California.

307–8. *Steinbeck: A Life in Letters*, ed. E. Steinbeck and R. Wallsten (New York: Viking, 1975), copyright 1952 by John Steinbeck, © 1969 by the Estate of John

Steinbeck, © 1975 by Elaine A. Steinbeck and Robert Wallsten. Used by permission of Viking Penguin, a division of Penguin Books USA Inc.

309–10. *Selected Letters of James Thurber*, ed. H. Thurber (London: Hamish Hamilton, 1981; Boston, MA: Atlantic–Little Brown), copyright © 1981 Helen Thurber. Reprinted with permission.

311. *Leave the Letters till We're Dead: The Letters of Virginia Woolf*, vol. vi, *1936–1941*, ed. Nigel Nicolson (London: Hogarth Press, 1980). Reprinted by permission of Random House UK Ltd.

312–13. *The Letters of Evelyn Waugh*, ed. Mark Amory (London: Weidenfeld & Nicolson, 1980). Reprinted by permission of the Peter Fraser and Dunlop Group Ltd.

314–15. By kind permission of Sir Stephen Spender and Mrs Valerie Eliot.

316. *Letters of Wallace Stevens*, ed. H. Stevens (London: Faber, 1966), © 1966 by Holly Stevens. Reprinted by permission of Faber and Faber Ltd., and Alfred A. Knopf Inc.

317. *The Groucho Letters: Letters from and to Groucho Marx* (London: Michael Joseph, 1967), © Groucho Marx Productions Inc., 1967. All rights reserved. Represented by the Roger Richman Agency, Inc., Beverly Hills, California. Reprinted with permission.

318. Communicated by Patrick Leigh Fermor and printed with the permission of Lord Norwich.

319–20. *Flannery O'Connor: The Habit of Being*, letters ed. Sally Fitzgerald (New York: Farrar Straus Giroux, 1979), copyright © 1979 by Regina O'Connor. Reprinted by permission of the publisher.

321. *Edith Sitwell: Selected Letters*, ed. John Lehmann and Derek Parker (London: Macmillan, 1970). Reprinted by permission of David Higham Associates Ltd.

322–3. *Elizabeth Bishop: One Art*, letters ed. Robert Giroux (New York: Farrar Straus Giroux, 1973), copyright © 1994 by Alice Helen Methfessel. Reprinted by permission of the publisher.

324. *Sylvia Townsend Warner: Letters*, ed. William Maxwell (London: Chatto & Windus, 1982). Reprinted by permission of Random House UK Ltd.

325–7. *Sylvia and David: The Townsend Warner/Garnett Letters*, ed. Richard Garnett (London: Sinclair-Stevenson, 1994). Reprinted by permission of the publisher and Reed Consumer Books Ltd.

328. *Selected Letters of Philip Larkin, 1940–1985*, ed. Anthony Thwaite (London: Faber, 1992). Reprinted by permission of the publisher.

While every effort has been made to secure permission, we may have failed in a few cases to trace the copyright holder. We apologize for any apparent negligence.

Index of Writers

INDEX OF RECIPIENTS

Index of Recipients